Emerging Research in Cloud Distributed Computing Systems

Susmit Bagchi
Gyeongsang National University, South Korea

A volume in the Advances in Systems Analysis,
Software Engineering, and High Performance
Computing (ASASEHPC) Book Series

Managing Director:	Lindsay Johnston
Managing Editor:	Austin DeMarco
Director of Intellectual Property & Contracts:	Jan Travers
Acquisitions Editor:	Kayla Wolfe
Production Editor:	Christina Henning
Development Editor:	Brandon Carbaugh
Typesetter:	Amanda Smith
Cover Design:	Jason Mull

Published in the United States of America by
Information Science Reference (an imprint of IGI Global)
701 E. Chocolate Avenue
Hershey PA, USA 17033
Tel: 717-533-8845
Fax: 717-533-8661
E-mail: cust@igi-global.com
Web site: http://www.igi-global.com

Copyright © 2015 by IGI Global. All rights reserved. No part of this publication may be reproduced, stored or distributed in any form or by any means, electronic or mechanical, including photocopying, without written permission from the publisher. Product or company names used in this set are for identification purposes only. Inclusion of the names of the products or companies does not indicate a claim of ownership by IGI Global of the trademark or registered trademark.

Library of Congress Cataloging-in-Publication Data

Library of Congress Cataloging-in-Publication Data

Emerging research in cloud distributed computing systems / Susmit Bagchi, editors.
    pages cm
 Includes bibliographical references and index.
 ISBN 978-1-4666-8213-9 (hardcover) -- ISBN 978-1-4666-8214-6 (ebook) 1. Cloud computing. 2. Computer systems--Technological innovations. I. Bagchi, Susmit, 1973-, editor.
 QA76.585.E54 2015
 004.67'82--dc23
                                    2015003294

This book is published in the IGI Global book series Advances in Systems Analysis, Software Engineering, and High Performance Computing (ASASEHPC) (ISSN: 2327-3453; eISSN: 2327-3461)

British Cataloguing in Publication Data
A Cataloguing in Publication record for this book is available from the British Library.

All work contributed to this book is new, previously-unpublished material. The views expressed in this book are those of the authors, but not necessarily of the publisher.

For electronic access to this publication, please contact: eresources@igi-global.com.

Advances in Systems Analysis, Software Engineering, and High Performance Computing (ASASEHPC) Book Series

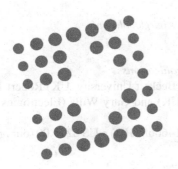

Vijayan Sugumaran
Oakland University, USA

ISSN: 2327-3453
EISSN: 2327-3461

MISSION

The theory and practice of computing applications and distributed systems has emerged as one of the key areas of research driving innovations in business, engineering, and science. The fields of software engineering, systems analysis, and high performance computing offer a wide range of applications and solutions in solving computational problems for any modern organization.

The **Advances in Systems Analysis, Software Engineering, and High Performance Computing (ASASEHPC) Book Series** brings together research in the areas of distributed computing, systems and software engineering, high performance computing, and service science. This collection of publications is useful for academics, researchers, and practitioners seeking the latest practices and knowledge in this field.

COVERAGE

- Parallel Architectures
- Performance Modelling
- Metadata and Semantic Web
- Storage Systems
- Virtual Data Systems
- Computer Graphics
- Engineering Environments
- Computer System Analysis
- Distributed Cloud Computing
- Human-Computer Interaction

IGI Global is currently accepting manuscripts for publication within this series. To submit a proposal for a volume in this series, please contact our Acquisition Editors at Acquisitions@igi-global.com or visit: http://www.igi-global.com/publish/.

The Advances in Systems Analysis, Software Engineering, and High Performance Computing (ASASEHPC) Book Series (ISSN 2327-3453) is published by IGI Global, 701 E. Chocolate Avenue, Hershey, PA 17033-1240, USA, www.igi-global.com. This series is composed of titles available for purchase individually; each title is edited to be contextually exclusive from any other title within the series. For pricing and ordering information please visit http://www.igi-global.com/book-series/advances-systems-analysis-software-engineering/73689. Postmaster: Send all address changes to above address. Copyright © 2015 IGI Global. All rights, including translation in other languages reserved by the publisher. No part of this series may be reproduced or used in any form or by any means – graphics, electronic, or mechanical, including photocopying, recording, taping, or information and retrieval systems – without written permission from the publisher, except for non commercial, educational use, including classroom teaching purposes. The views expressed in this series are those of the authors, but not necessarily of IGI Global.

Titles in this Series

For a list of additional titles in this series, please visit: www.igi-global.com

Delivery and Adoption of Cloud Computing Services in Contemporary Organizations
Victor Chang (Computing, Creative Technologies and Engineering, Leeds Beckett University, UK) Robert John Walters (Electronics and Computer Science, University of Southampton, UK) and Gary Wills (Electronics and Computer Science, University of Southampton, UK)
Information Science Reference • copyright 2015 • 519pp • H/C (ISBN: 9781466682108) • US $225.00 (our price)

Resource Management of Mobile Cloud Computing Networks and Environments
George Mastorakis (Technological Educational Institute of Crete, Greece) Constandinos X. Mavromoustakis (University of Nicosia, Cyprus) and Evangelos Pallis (Technological Educational Institute of Crete, Greece)
Information Science Reference • copyright 2015 • 432pp • H/C (ISBN: 9781466682252) • US $215.00 (our price)

Research and Applications in Global Supercomputing
Richard S. Segall (Arkansas State University, USA) Jeffrey S. Cook (Independent Researcher, USA) and Qingyu Zhang (Shenzhen University, China)
Information Science Reference • copyright 2015 • 672pp • H/C (ISBN: 9781466674615) • US $265.00 (our price)

Challenges, Opportunities, and Dimensions of Cyber-Physical Systems
P. Venkata Krishna (VIT University, India) V. Saritha (VIT University, India) and H. P. Sultana (VIT University, India)
Information Science Reference • copyright 2015 • 328pp • H/C (ISBN: 9781466673120) • US $200.00 (our price)

Human Factors in Software Development and Design
Saqib Saeed (University of Dammam, Saudi Arabia) Imran Sarwar Bajwa (The Islamia University of Bahawalpur, Pakistan) and Zaigham Mahmood (University of Derby, UK & North West University, South Africa)
Information Science Reference • copyright 2015 • 354pp • H/C (ISBN: 9781466664852) • US $195.00 (our price)

Handbook of Research on Innovations in Systems and Software Engineering
Vicente García Díaz (University of Oviedo, Spain) Juan Manuel Cueva Lovelle (University of Oviedo, Spain) and B. Cristina Pelayo García-Bustelo (University of Oviedo, Spain)
Information Science Reference • copyright 2015 • 745pp • H/C (ISBN: 9781466663596) • US $515.00 (our price)

Handbook of Research on Architectural Trends in Service-Driven Computing
Raja Ramanathan (Independent Researcher, USA) and Kirtana Raja (IBM, USA)
Information Science Reference • copyright 2014 • 759pp • H/C (ISBN: 9781466661783) • US $515.00 (our price)

DISSEMINATOR of KNOWLEDGE

www.igi-global.com

701 E. Chocolate Ave., Hershey, PA 17033
Order online at www.igi-global.com or call 717-533-8845 x100
To place a standing order for titles released in this series, contact: cust@igi-global.com
Mon-Fri 8:00 am - 5:00 pm (est) or fax 24 hours a day 717-533-8661

Editorial Advisory Board

Rajkumar Buyya, *University of Melbourne, Australia*
Vijay K. Garg, *The University of Texas – Austin, USA*
Viktor K. Prasanna, *University of Southern California, USA*
Sherali Zeadally, *University of Kentucky, USA*

List of Reviewers

Oladayo Bello, *Monash University, South Africa*
Talal Noor, *University of Adelaide, Australia*

Table of Contents

Section 1
Introduction to Systems

Chapter 1

    José C. Delgado, Universidade de Lisboa, Portugal

Section 2
Resource Management

Chapter 2

    Md Hasanul Ferdaus, Monash University, Australia
    Manzur Murshed, Federation University, Australia
    Rodrigo N. Calheiros, The University of Melbourne, Australia
    Rajkumar Buyya, The University of Melbourne, Australia

Chapter 3

    Grace A. Lewis, Carnegie Mellon Software Engineering Institute, USA
    Sebastián Echeverría, Carnegie Mellon Software Engineering Institute, USA
    Soumya Simanta, Carnegie Mellon Software Engineering Institute, USA
    James Root, Carnegie Mellon Software Engineering Institute, USA
    Ben Bradshaw, Carnegie Mellon Software Engineering Institute, USA

Chapter 4

    Nicola Cordeschi, "Sapienza" University of Rome, Italy
    Mohammad Shojafar, "Sapienza" University of Rome, Italy
    Danilo Amendola, "Sapienza" University of Rome, Italy
    Enzo Baccarelli, "Sapienza" University of Rome, Italy

Section 3
Control and Monitoring

Section 4
Concurrency and Models

Section 5
Applications

Section 6
Security

Detailed Table of Contents

Section 1
Introduction to Systems

Chapter 1
José C. Delgado, Universidade de Lisboa, Portugal

Cloud platforms constitute distributed and heterogeneous systems. Interacting applications, possibly in different clouds, face relevant interoperability challenges. This chapter details the interoperability problem and presents an interoperability framework, which provides a systematization of aspects such as coupling, compatibility, and the various levels at which interoperability must occur. After discussing the main limitations of current interoperability technologies, such as Web Services and RESTful applications, the chapter proposes an alternative technology. This entails a new distributed programming language, capable of describing both data and code in a platform-agnostic fashion. The underlying model is based on structured resources, each offering its own service. Service-oriented interfaces can be combined with the structured resources and hypermedia that characterize RESTful applications, instead of having to choose one style or the other. Coupling is reduced by checking interoperability structurally, based on the concepts of compliance and conformance. There is native support for binary data and full-duplex protocols.

Section 2
Resource Management

Chapter 2
Md Hasanul Ferdaus, Monash University, Australia
Manzur Murshed, Federation University, Australia
Rodrigo N. Calheiros, The University of Melbourne, Australia
Rajkumar Buyya, The University of Melbourne, Australia

With the pragmatic realization of computing as a utility, Cloud Computing has recently emerged as a highly successful alternative IT paradigm. Cloud providers are deploying large-scale data centers across the globe to meet the Cloud customers' compute, storage, and network resource demands. Efficiency and scalability of these data centers, as well as the performance of the hosted applications' highly depend on the allocations of the data center resources. Very recently, network-aware Virtual Machine (VM) placement and migration is developing as a very promising technique for the optimization of compute-network resource utilization, energy consumption, and network traffic minimization. This chapter presents the relevant background information and a detailed taxonomy that characterizes and classifies the various components of VM placement and migration techniques, as well as an elaborate survey and comparative analysis of the state of the art techniques. Besides highlighting the various aspects and insights of the network-aware VM placement and migration strategies and algorithms proposed by the research community, the survey further identifies the benefits and limitations of the existing techniques and discusses on the future research directions.

Chapter 3
    Grace A. Lewis, Carnegie Mellon Software Engineering Institute, USA
    Sebastián Echeverría, Carnegie Mellon Software Engineering Institute, USA
    Soumya Simanta, Carnegie Mellon Software Engineering Institute, USA
    James Root, Carnegie Mellon Software Engineering Institute, USA
    Ben Bradshaw, Carnegie Mellon Software Engineering Institute, USA

First responders and others operating in crisis environments increasingly make use of handheld devices to help with tasks such as face recognition, language translation, decision making, and mission planning. These resource-limited environments are characterized by dynamic context, limited computing resources, high levels of stress, and intermittent network connectivity. Cyber-foraging is the leverage of external resource-rich surrogates to augment the capabilities of resource-limited devices. In cloudlet-based cyber-foraging, resource-intensive computation is offloaded to cloudlets: discoverable, generic servers located in single-hop proximity of mobile devices. This chapter presents several mechanisms for cloudlet-based cyber-foraging that consider a tradeoff space beyond energy, performance, and fidelity of results. It demonstrates that cyber-foraging in resource-limited environments can greatly benefit from moving cloud computing concepts and technologies closer to the edge so that surrogates, even if disconnected from the enterprise, can provide offload capabilities that enhance the computing power of mobile devices.

Chapter 4
    Nicola Cordeschi, "Sapienza" University of Rome, Italy
    Mohammad Shojafar, "Sapienza" University of Rome, Italy
    Danilo Amendola, "Sapienza" University of Rome, Italy
    Enzo Baccarelli, "Sapienza" University of Rome, Italy

In this chapter, the authors develop the scheduler which optimizes the energy-vs.-performance trade-off in Software-as-a-Service (SaaS) Virtualized Networked Data Centers (VNetDCs) that support real-time Big Data Stream Computing (BDSC) services. The objective is to minimize the communication-plus-computing energy which is wasted by processing streams of Big Data under hard real-time constrains on the per-job computing-plus-communication delays. In order to deal with the inherently nonconvex nature of the resulting resource management optimization problem, the authors develop a solving approach that leads to the lossless decomposition of the afforded problem into the cascade of two simpler sub-problems. The resulting optimal scheduler is amenable of scalable and distributed adaptive implementation. The performance of a Xen-based prototype of the scheduler is tested under several Big Data workload traces and compared with the corresponding ones of some state-of-the-art static and sequential schedulers.

Keeping the quality of service defined by Service Level Agreements (SLAs) is a key factor to facilitate business operations of Cloud providers. SLA enforcement relies on resource and application monitoring—a topic that has been investigated by various Cloud-related projects. Application-level monitoring still represents an open research issue, especially for billing and accounting purposes. Such a monitoring is becoming fundamental, as Cloud services are multi-tenant, thus having users sharing the same resources. This chapter describes key challenges on application provisioning and SLA enforcement in Clouds, introduces a Cloud Application and SLA monitoring architecture, and proposes two methods for determining the frequency that applications needs to be monitored. The authors evaluate their architecture on a real Cloud testbed using applications that exhibit heterogeneous behaviors. The achieved results show that the architecture is low intrusive, able to monitor resources and applications, detect SLA violations, and automatically suggest effective measurement intervals for various workloads.

Science gateways, such as the Virtual Imaging Platform (VIP), enable transparent access to distributed computing and storage resources for scientific computations. However, their large scale and the number of middleware systems involved in these gateways lead to many errors and faults. This chapter addresses the autonomic management of workflow executions on science gateways in an online and non-clairvoyant environment, where the platform workload, task costs, and resource characteristics are unknown and not stationary. The chapter describes a general self-management process based on the MAPE-K loop (Monitoring, Analysis, Planning, Execution, and Knowledge) to cope with operational incidents of workflow executions. Then, this process is applied to handle late task executions, task granularities, and unfairness among workflow executions. Experimental results show how the approach achieves a fair quality of service by using control loops that constantly perform online monitoring, analysis, and execution of a set of curative actions.

Chapter 7

Georgiana Copil, Vienna University of Technology, Austria
Daniel Moldovan, Vienna University of Technology, Austria
Hung Duc Le, Vienna University of Technology, Austria
Hong-Linh Truong, Vienna University of Technology, Austria
Schahram Dustdar, Vienna University of Technology, Austria
Chrystalla Sofokleous, University of Cyprus, Cyprus
Nicholas Loulloudes, University of Cyprus, Cyprus
Demetris Trihinas, University of Cyprus, Cyprus
George Pallis, University of Cyprus, Cyprus
Marios D. Dikaiakos, University of Cyprus, Cyprus
Ioannis Giannakopoulos, National University of Athens, Greece
Nikolaos Papailiou, National University of Athens, Greece
Ioannis Konstantinou, National University of Athens, Greece
Craig Sheridan, FLEXIANT, UK
Christos K. K. Loverdos, Greek Research and Technology Network, Greece
Evangelos Floros, Greek Research and Technology Network, Greece
Kam Star, Playgen, UK
Wei Xing, CRUK Manchester Institute, UK

Today's complex cloud applications are composed of multiple components executed in multi-cloud environments. For such applications, the possibility to manage and control their cost, quality, and resource elasticity is of paramount importance. However, given that the cost of different services offered by cloud providers can vary a lot with their quality/performance, elasticity controllers must consider not only complex, multi-dimensional preferences and provisioning capabilities from stakeholders but also various runtime information regarding cloud applications and their execution environments. In this chapter, the authors present the elasticity control approach of the EU CELAR Project, which deals with multi-dimensional elasticity requirements and ensures multi-level elasticity control for fulfilling user requirements. They show the elasticity control mechanisms of the CELAR project, from application description to multi-level elasticity control. The authors highlight the usefulness of CELAR's mechanisms for users, who can use an intuitive, user-friendly interface to describe and then to follow their application elasticity behavior controlled by CELAR.

Section 4
Concurrency and Models

Chapter 8

Manjunath Gorentla Venkata, Oak Ridge National Laboratory, USA
Stephen Poole, Oak Ridge National Laboratory, USA

A parallel programming model is an abstraction of a parallel system that allows expression of both algorithms and shared data structures. To accommodate the diversity in parallel system architectures and user requirements, there are a variety of programming models including the models providing a shared memory view or a distributed memory view of the system. The programming models are implemented as libraries, language extensions, or compiler directives. This chapter provides a discussion on programming models and its implementations aimed at application developers, system software researchers, and hardware architects. The first part provides an overview of the programming models. The second part is an in-depth discussion on high-performance networking interface to implement the programming model. The last part of the chapter discusses implementation of a programming model with a case study. Each part of the chapter concludes with a discussion on current research trends and its impact on future architectures.

Section 5
Applications

Chapter 9

Cloud-Based Computing Architectures for Solving Hot Issues in Structural Bioinformatics............ 294
Dariusz Mrozek, Silesian University of Technology, Poland

Bioinformatics as a scientific domain develops tools that enable understanding the wealth of information hidden in huge volumes of biological data. However, there are several problems in bioinformatics that, although already solved or at least equipped with promising algorithms, still require huge computing power in order to be completed in a reasonable time. Cloud computing responds to these demands. This chapter shows several cloud-based computing architectures for solving hot issues in structural bioinformatics, such as protein structure similarity searching or 3D protein structure prediction. Presented architectures have been implemented in Microsoft Azure public cloud and tested in several projects developed by Cloud4Proteins research group.

Chapter 10

Cloud-Based Healthcare Systems: Emerging Technologies and Open Research Issues 315
Ahmed Shawish, Ain Shams University, Egypt
Maria Salama, British University in Egypt, Egypt

Healthcare is one of the most important sectors in all countries and significantly affects the economy. As such, the sector consumes an average of 9.5% of the gross domestic product across the most developed countries; they should invoke smart healthcare systems to efficiently utilize available resources, vastly handle spontaneous emergencies, and professionally manage the population health records. With the rise of the Cloud and Mobile Computing, a vast variety of added values have been introduced to software and IT infrastructure. This chapter provides a comprehensive review on the new Cloud-based and mobile-based applications that have been developed in the healthcare field. Cloud's availability, scalability, and storage capabilities, in addition to the Mobile's portability, wide coverage, and accessibility features, contributed to the fulfillment of healthcare requirements. The chapter shows how Cloud and Mobile opened a new environment for innovative services in the healthcare field and discusses the open research issues.

Section 6
Security

Data sharing as one of the most popular service applications in cloud computing has received wide attention, which makes the consumers achieve the shared contents whenever and wherever possible. However, the new paradigm of data sharing will also introduce some security issues while it provides much convenience. The data confidentiality, the privacy security, the user key accountability, and the efficiency are hindering its rapid expansion. An effective and secure access control mechanism is becoming one way to deal with this dilemma. In this chapter, the authors focus on presenting a detailed review on the existing access control mechanisms. Then, they explore some potential research issues for the further development of more comprehensive and secure access control schemes. Finally, the authors expect that the topic of access control in cloud computing will attract much more attention from academia and industry.

The chapter presents current security concerns in the Cloud Computing Environment. The cloud concept and operation raise many concerns for cloud users since they have no control of the arrangements made to protect the services and resources offered. Additionally, it is obvious that many of the cloud service providers will be subject to significant security attacks. Some traditional security attacks such as the Denial of Service attacks (DoS) and distributed DDoS attacks are well known, and there are several proposed solutions to mitigate their impact. However, in the cloud environment, DDoS becomes more severe and can be coupled with Economical Denial of Sustainability (EDoS) attacks. The chapter presents a general overview of cloud security, the types of vulnerabilities, and potential attacks. The chapter further presents a more detailed analysis of DDoS attacks' launch mechanisms and well-known DDoS defence mechanisms. Finally, the chapter presents a DDoS-Mitigation system and potential future research directions.

Preface

During the last couple of decades, computing platforms have evolved into the wide-array deployment of distributed computing systems. The traditional client/server computing concepts have slowly matured into cloud computing systems. However, a cloud computing platform is a geographically distributed computing platform, fundamentally. On the other hand, cloud computing and design have added additional layers of transparency to the distributed computing platforms and improved commercial viability. Undoubtedly, cloud computing platforms will continue to see widespread application, globally improving quality of life in the era of Information Technology in the 21st century.

However, the cloud computing platforms face a set of technical challenges. The technical challenges stem from the scale of cloud computing infrastructure distributed geographically and the difficulties in resource monitoring as well as provisioning of computing resources to the end-users due to the geo-distributed nature of cloud computing platforms. In the present form, the cloud computing platforms are designed as an extended platform of traditional distributed computing systems with additional layers of transparencies. Arguably, the truly large-scale cloud computing systems having continental-level distributions need fast as well as reliable networks, security, and optimal resource monitor enhancing utilizations of computing resources in the systems. These requirements bring in the issues related to large-scale distributed software engineering while designing and deploying the cloud computing software infrastructures. The heterogeneity of cloud computing platforms enhances the design and deployment challenges due to difficulties in achieving computational interoperability between heterogeneous nodes. On the contrary, it is evident that the computing systems in the future will increasingly tend to support cloud as well as distributed computing platforms by overcoming the challenges in order to avail the greater advantages of such platforms.

As a result, the area of cloud computing is brimming with innovative ideas, research issues, and applications at different dimensions to solve the existing technical challenges. This book is a timely effort to present and comprehend the technological concepts, current trends, and future directions in cloud (distributed) computing systems. The book is divided into six sections, namely "Introduction to Systems," "Resource Management," "Control and Monitoring," "Concurrency and Models," "Applications," and "Security."

The "Introduction" section of this book provides systems perspectives and design aspects of the heterogeneous cloud (distributed) systems. There is one chapter in this section dealing with the issues related to interoperability of computing nodes in the cloud computing systems. It describes the mechanisms to overcome the interoperability issues of heterogeneous cloud computing platforms.

Next, the issues of distributed resource management in the cloud computing environment are addressed in the "Resource Management" section of this book. This section contains three chapters. The first chapter of this section describes the design and deployment of network-aware Virtual Machines

(VMs) in the cloud computing infrastructures, which is an essential element of a cloud platform deployment. The second chapter of this section explains how the cloudlet technology can be designed to implement resource monitoring as well as provisioning in cloud computing infrastructures. The third chapter addresses the issues related to energy consumption and QoS in big data centres, where such big data centres are realized utilizing the cloud computing platforms.

In the next section, the computational and resource control as well as monitoring methods are described. "Control and Monitoring" contains three chapters. The first chapter of this section describes mechanisms to implement service-level agreements as well as resource-utilization monitor in the cloud computing infrastructures. The second chapter of this section deals with the design and implementation challenges of a grid computing platform supporting virtual imaging computations. This chapter explains the issues and design solutions to implement grid computing executing virtual imaging applications. The third chapter of this section explains how the elasticity of cloud computing applications can be controlled, enhancing resource utilizations.

Next, the concurrency in parallel as well as virtual-parallel computations and communication are addressed in detail in the "Concurrency and Models" section of this book. This section contains one chapter on various aspects of parallel and distributed communication mechanisms. This chapter describes the synchrony issues in network communications and the designing of message-passing interfaces.

In the next section, a set of high-end cloud computing applications are presented. "Applications" contains two chapters. The first chapter of this section describes how the cloud computing platforms can be utilized to analyze structural bioinformatics applications. The second chapter of this section illustrates the design approach of healthcare applications by using cloud computing platforms. A set of technical challenges are identified.

Finally, "Security" deals with cloud computing security. This section contains two chapters. The first chapter of this section explains the mechanisms of implementing secured user-access control to cloud computing platforms. A set of security issues and their solutions are illustrated in the second chapter of this section. This chapter explains the cloud computing security issues having broad perspectives.

This book is a useful resource to the Computer Science/Information Technology students, computer scientists, as well as practicing engineers in the domains of cloud and distributed computing systems. The audiences of this book are comprised of advanced undergraduate students and graduate students in Computer Science or Information Technology. The computer scientists will find this book an attractive reference to consult with. This book is also an attractive choice for reading to practicing engineers and computer technologists in the domain of cloud and distributed computing systems.

This book presents introductions, key definitions, design methods, applications, and open research issues in cloud (distributed) computing systems in one place, making it a very complete book on the topics having wide technical coverage.

Susmit Bagchi
Gyeongsang National University, South Korea

Introduction

SINGLE-CORE PROCESSOR TO MOBILE CLOUD COMPUTING: EVOLUTION AND FUTURE

The evolutions of computing devices, communication networks and processor-level architectures have witnessed a rapid growth during last couple of decades. The semiconductor devices are increasingly reduced in size, which have given the birth of mobile computing devices such as, smart-phones, PDAs and laptop computers. However, the mobile computing devices have an inherent limitation related to available capacity of battery power. The limitation of electrical energy source has resulted in the limitation of functionalities of mobile computing devices and their computing lifetime. However, the platforms in traditional computing domain involving computers have gone through evolution too. The single-core CPU (Central Processing Unit) architecture has grown into multi-core CPU architecture. In addition, the main memory capacity has increased enormously during last couple of decades. In the domain of data communication networks, the network architectures have evolved from LAN (Local Area Network) to WAN (Wide Area Network) and lastly the Internet, which is a geographically distributed network. The recent addition to computer networking is the mobile communication network integrated with the Internet. The integration of such heterogeneous network architectures is essential for realizations of Internet-equipped smart-phones and location-transparent mobile computing paradigm. The evolutionary trajectory of distributed computing systems involving multiple computing devices can be partitioned into several stages such as, distributed systems, cluster computing, grid computing, cloud computing and, lastly the mobile cloud computing.

Distributed Systems

The traditional distributed systems are comprised of multiple computing nodes or processors interconnected to have data communication pathways. The early model of multi-computing is categorized as a tightly-coupled system, where the address-space is single. Thus, a single system-wide primary memory is shared by multiple processors (nodes). The main limitations of this model are bus-contention and, process-wait cycles due to shared-memory at the level of system architecture. The other end of the spectrum is loosely-coupled systems, where architecture-level shared memory is replaced by distributed shared memory. In loosely-coupled multi-processor systems, the nodes have own local address-spaces and, a part of primary memory can be shared between nodes. The distributed systems are the result of integration of computer architectures and the communication networks. The architectural models of distributed systems are basically comprised of individual computing nodes connected by computer networks. Theoretically, this can be viewed as a graph of computing nodes. The main goal was to enhance speed of computation by executing relatively independent processes in virtual-parallel model. The distributed processes communicate to share data and to synchronize using communication networks. The models of traditional distributed computing systems can be classified into five broad classes [1] namely, minicomputer model, workstation model, workstation-server model, processor-pool model and, hybrid model. These models are based on multiple computers, which can be categorized as minicomputers, workstations and servers. The communication medium is reliable and high-bandwidth wired network.

Cluster Computing

In the traditional models of distributed systems, the concept of clustering of nodes to perform some dedicated computations is absent. The high-performance computations often require a dedicated set of nodes connected by very high-speed wired network to accept, distribute and schedule computational jobs (processes) with user-transparency [2]. The traditional distributed computing systems have evolved into cluster computing to achieve this goal. However, the resource management and task-assignments to nodes are the two main technical challenges of cluster computing systems. The goal is to maximize resource utilizations at each node to achieve optimal overall resource utilization globally in a cluster at any point of time. Thus, there are two issues to look at:

1. Global task-assignment to the nodes from the batch of jobs, and
2. Optimal local scheduling of tasks or processes at a node.

In general, the designing an optimal global task assignment algorithm is a computationally hard problem. A cluster comprised of heterogeneous nodes makes it difficult to design a globally optimal task assignment algorithm independent of time. The cluster computing systems often recognize the batch jobs into two such as, sequential tasks and, parallel tasks. The sequential tasks are highly data-interdependent computational processes requiring sequential computing. However, parallel tasks are comprised of data-parallel sub-tasks, where sub-tasks can execute in parallel in time at different nodes requiring data communications in intervals. This indicates, the resource management and load-balancing algorithms of cluster computing systems should consider the task categories in order to decide near optimal task assignments to nodes. However, prior determination of degree of data-dependency and data-parallelism within a large task is highly complex.

Grid Computing

The cluster computing platforms are constrained to localization of resources for speedy access. However, the advent of Internet protocol induced another change in the distributed computing paradigm. The Internet protocol allows standardized and transparent data communication between any two geographically distributed nodes. Additionally, the protocol is capable to integrate heterogeneous computing resources over the network. Thus, the grid computing paradigm is born, where the computing resources are geo-distributed and heterogeneous nodes are connected by Internet. However, the grid computing software is designed to provide user-transparency and location-transparency. The grid software architecture is designed by employing layered and component-based software architecture model [3]. Each layer of the grid software architecture implements a set of capabilities and functions based on the software layer below it. In other words, if one moves from lowest layer to highest layer of stratified layered grid software model, then one can see that capabilities and functions are getting expanded through augmentation. The lowest layer of grid software architecture represents the resource fabric of the grid. The resource discovery and sharing is implemented by specific grid communication protocol between software components. The Internet protocol provides a basic data-carrying infrastructure to be used by grid protocol for inter-component communications. The resource allocation, metering and, authentication functions are realized at different vertical layers of grid software. The inter-layer communication is implemented by standardized interface definitions and protocols. Thus, the grid computing systems provides a geo-distributed, user-transparent, location-transparent and, reliable distributed computing infrastructure comprised of large array of heterogeneous computing resources.

Cloud Computing

The grid computing paradigm is further evolved into service-oriented computing architecture. In absolute technical view, arguably cloud computing is a traditional form of distributed systems with a new commercial approach. In cloud computing paradigm, the user applications are executed on distributed systems as a service and the required system software modules provide the cloud platform [4]. In other words, a cloud platform is a cluster of distributed systems comprised of heterogeneous hardware and software offered to users for a commercial price as a service to execute user applications. If the users are general public in society needing computational facilities, then the cloud platforms providing such services for a price are called public-cloud. The other spectrum is private-cloud, where the underlying distributed systems and data centers are not accessible to common users but to specific organizations. The main technical challenge of public-cloud platforms is scalability of the systems. The employment of efficient resource virtualization mechanism is another technical area needing attention in cloud computing paradigm. However, virtual machine models are generally complex to design and, computationally expensive wasting available resources.

Hybridization I: Virtualized Cluster

The cluster computing paradigm was initially centered on homogeneity of computing software platforms in order to reduce complexity. However, the proliferations of computing applications at different domains have resulted in heterogeneous applications needing heterogeneous computing resources. The mechanism to isolate data and applications of different users residing in a cluster was not well addressed in the initial designs of cluster platforms. The users from different organizations often share a cluster computing platform, which resembles the grid computing paradigm. Thus, the need to isolate and protect data and executing applications from different users in a shared cluster becomes evident. Lastly, the performance requirements or Quality-of-Service (QoS) of different user applications are different. The requirement to maintain differential management of QoS of applications having specific QoS requirements appears to be necessary in a cluster if the respective cluster is intended to execute a wide array of heterogeneous applications concurrently.

Evidently, cluster computing platforms started to evolve another direction by hybridizing with virtualization techniques of computing resources in order to address the additional set of requirements. The employment of virtualization of computing resources in a cluster computing platform is aimed to decoupling computational services from the physical hardware devices or platforms [5]. In this hybrid model, the users have the traditional interface to cluster computing platforms; however the back-end is split into two sections. One section on back-end is comprised of virtual work-nodes connected by virtual network and, the other section on back-end is comprised of physical infrastructure. The interface between the two sections is a software layer called Distributed Virtualizer (DV). The hybrid model of cluster computing paradigm incorporating virtual machine model can support the new set of requirements arising from shared cluster platforms executing heterogeneous user applications offering QoS and data isolation.

Hybridization II: Mobile Cloud Computing

The cloud computing paradigm can be categorized into two namely, general cloud platforms and, mobile cloud platforms. In the case of general cloud platforms, the nodes (following client/server model) are static and underlying network is wired network. However, the advent of mobile computing devices has created a different environment, where the clients are resource-thin and mobile in nature. These characteristics of clients have raised two major research questions such as,

1. How to partition application and system software stacks to distributed computation between mobile clients and cloud servers, and
2. How to manage mobility of clients within the a cloud platform.

The issues related to research question (2) can be further subdivided into followings: how to manage hopping and network connectivity to multiple servers by mobile clients in a cloud, how to authenticate a mobile client in a cloud and, how to handle data migration due to mobility of clients in a cloud. One approach to address these research questions is to view the mobile cloud computing paradigm as a hybridization of general cloud computing paradigm and mobile computing paradigm [4].

Following this hybrid view, the challenges associated to mobile cloud computing paradigm are fine grained in taxonomy such as, issues related to end users, issues related to mobile cloud service providers, issues related to service-level agreements, issues related to security, authentication and protection, issues related to context of mobility of clients and, issues related to efficient data management. As mentioned earlier, the mobile clients are resource-thin having very limited computational capabilities and more importantly, mobile clients are effectively the users of services provided by cloud platforms. Often, the continuity of access to main cloud platform by a mobile user is impossible to guarantee due to involvement of heterogeneous networks comprised of back-end static wired networks and wireless/mobile communication networks on mobile user side. Thus, the concept of cloudlet is formed, where the intermediate servers are used between a mobile user (client) and a cloud platform. These intermediate compute and communication servers are called cloudlet. Hence, a mobile user (mobile client), cloudlet and a cloud platform forms a chain comprised of heterogeneous networks between different stages.

It is important to note that, offloading of computations and migration of virtual machines (computation and data) are two important research issues in general cloud as well as mobile cloud computing environments.

CONCLUSION

The traditional distributed computing systems have evolved a long way. The fundamental theoretical models and algorithmic designs of distributed computing remain unchanged. However, the evolution of user applications executing on distributed systems has resulted in a set of new requirements in designing the distributed systems. The traditional model of static-client/static-server model of distributed systems has given way to mobile-client/static-server model of distributed systems. The virtualization of computing resources becomes necessary to execute heterogeneous user applications fulfilling individual QoS requirements of different applications. However, the overall performance degradation and resource wastage due to employment of virtual machine models are major concerns.

Susmit Bagchi
Gyeongsang National University, South Korea

ADDITIONAL READING

Fernando, N., Loke, S. W., & Rahayu, W. (2013). Mobile cloud computing: A survey. *Future Generation Computer Systems Journal, 29*.

Lin, X., Mamat, A., Lu, Y., Deogun, J., & Goddard, S. (2010). Real-time scheduling of divisible loads in cluster computing environments. *Journal of Parallel and Distributed Computing, 70*.

Montero, R. S., Vozmediano, R. M., & Llorente, I. M. (2011). An elasticity model for high throughput computing clusters. *Journal of Parallel and Distributed Computing, 71*.

Sinha, P. K. (1997). *Distributed operating systems: Concepts and design*. IEEE Computer Society Press.

Yang, C. T., Cheng, K. W., & Shih, W. C. (2007). On development of an efficient parallel loop self-scheduling for grid computing environments. *Parallel Computing Journal, 33*.

Section 1
Introduction to Systems

Chapter 1
Distributed Interoperability in Heterogeneous Cloud Systems

José C. Delgado
Universidade de Lisboa, Portugal

ABSTRACT

Cloud platforms constitute distributed and heterogeneous systems. Interacting applications, possibly in different clouds, face relevant interoperability challenges. This chapter details the interoperability problem and presents an interoperability framework, which provides a systematization of aspects such as coupling, compatibility, and the various levels at which interoperability must occur. After discussing the main limitations of current interoperability technologies, such as Web Services and RESTful applications, the chapter proposes an alternative technology. This entails a new distributed programming language, capable of describing both data and code in a platform-agnostic fashion. The underlying model is based on structured resources, each offering its own service. Service-oriented interfaces can be combined with the structured resources and hypermedia that characterize RESTful applications, instead of having to choose one style or the other. Coupling is reduced by checking interoperability structurally, based on the concepts of compliance and conformance. There is native support for binary data and full-duplex protocols.

INTRODUCTION

A distributed system has modules with independent lifecycles, each able to evolve to a new version without having to change, suspend or stop the behavior or interface of the others. These modules are built and executed in an independent way. Frequently, they are programmed in different programming languages and target different formats, platforms and processors. Distribution usu-

ally involves geographical dispersion, a network and static node addresses. Nevertheless, nothing prevents two different modules from sharing the same server, physical or virtual.

Modules are usually designed to interact, cooperating towards some goal. Since they are independent and make different assumptions, an interoperability problem arises. Interoperability, as old as networking, is a word formed by the juxtaposition of a prefix (*inter*) and the agglutination

DOI: 10.4018/978-1-4666-8213-9.ch001

Copyright © 2015, IGI Global. Copying or distributing in print or electronic forms without written permission of IGI Global is prohibited.

of two other words (*operate* and *ability*), meaning literally "the ability of two or more system modules to operate together".

With virtualization pervading all aspects of information technology, the cloud delivery model provides an increased decoupling between the availability of services and the details of their implementation, in a dynamic fashion. This hides many issues but raises others, namely:

- The variability introduced by cloud service models and deployment variants (private, managed, public hybrid cloud, integration with classical applications and combinations thereof);
- The plethora of cloud providers and brokers, with a vast range of computing resources, platforms, management services and user and developer APIs (Application Programming Interfaces).

This chapter adopts a broad perspective on cloud computing, in which a cloud is viewed as an elastic set of services, implemented by a set of heterogeneous resources that are interconnected by a set of heterogeneous networks. These resources can range from high-end servers with complex, enterprise-level applications, down to very simple sensors or actuators, without application deployment capabilities. Service unreliability and resource migration are expected characteristics.

Figure 1 illustrates various scenarios, in which services deployed on general-purpose clouds need to coexist with others, provided by a set of more specific resources. These can be managed in cloud fashion, dynamically using only what is needed and paying only for what is used. Although a cloud has been represented as the centerpiece in Figure 1, any system may connect directly to any other system.

In fact, the computer-based world is a giant, distributed, and heterogeneous cloud of clouds, some more dynamic than others, but all with the same basic problems:

- How to provide enough interoperability to enable systems to cooperate without requiring exact mutual knowledge;
- How to allow them to evolve independently;
- How to introduce context information, in particular in applications and networks involving mobility.

Typical general-purpose clouds provide a management API to support non-functional features, such as deploying resources, controlling and charging resource use, monitoring performance, and so on. This chapter emphasizes the functional slant. The cloud is viewed essentially as a dynamic and distributed platform, with on-demand provisioning and deployment (including migration). The main problem is to achieve interoperability between heterogeneous systems, deployed in heterogeneous platforms and expected to migrate and sometimes fail, while minimizing the required coupling between these systems.

The main goals of this chapter are:

- To contribute to the field of cloud computing, in particular in the interoperability area, by analyzing several of the problems involved and discussing possible solutions;
- To describe a framework that explores application interoperability at various levels, to better dissect and understand what is involved and how this can help in systematizing solutions;
- To assess the potential of structural compatibility (instead of nominal compatibility) as a means to reduce coupling and increase adaptability, changeability, and reliability, while maintaining interoperability requirements;
- To cater for cloud heterogeneity, by clearly separating the aspects involved in portability, transport-level communication, message protocol, syntax, semantics, and behavior, avoiding any dependence on any network protocol (such as HTTP – HyperText Transfer Protocol) or platform;

- To introduce a new interoperability language, which considers resources and their services natively, contemplating both data and behavior, instead of building everything on top of a data description language such as XML (Extensible Markup Language);
- To propose a new architectural style that combines the best characteristics of SOA (Service Oriented Architecture) and REST (REpresentational State Transfer), endowing resources with behavioral, structural and hypermedia capabilities.

The chapter is organized as follows. The Background section describes some of the existing technologies relevant to the context

of this chapter, followed by a description of the distributed interoperability problem. An interoperability framework is outlined, including the role of coupling, the importance of structural compatibility, and a systematization of the levels at which interoperability may occur. A discussion of the limitations of current technologies leads to a proposal of an alternative solution, entailing a resource-based model and a distributed service interoperability language, with a matching protocol. The chapter ends by comparing this solution with existing technologies, outlining future directions of research, and drawing the main conclusions of this work.

Figure 1. An example of a set of heterogeneous systems

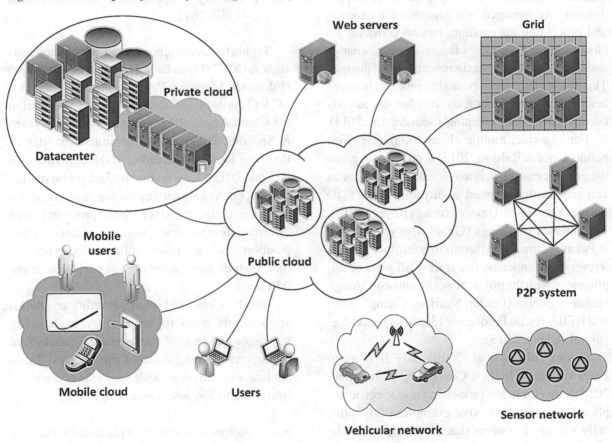

BACKGROUND

One of the most cited definitions of cloud computing, encompassing the characteristics described in the previous section, is given by Mell and Grance (2011), of the NIIST (US National Institute of Standards and Technology). This and other survey papers (Rimal, Choi & Lumb, 2009; Armbrust, 2010; Zhang, Cheng & Boutaba, 2010) discuss the most relevant issues involving cloud computing.

Big market players such as Amazon, Microsoft, and Google have their own cloud platforms. Other providers have joined the open-source movement in the cloud market (Bist, Wariya & Agarwal, 2013), with cloud management platforms such as Open-Stack (Jackson, 2012), CloudStack (Sabharwal & Shankar, 2013) and Eucalyptus (Nurmi et al., 2009).

However, the cloud concept is not limited to general-purpose clouds. Any pool of resources, dynamically managed and capable of interacting and processing information, can be considered a cloud. Figure 1 illustrates the variety of scenarios and systems that may need to coexist and to interact. This raises a huge interoperability problem between heterogeneous environments, in what has already been called 'jungle computing' (Seinstra et al., 2011).

For example, mobile cloud computing (Fernando, Loke & Rahayu, 2013) is on the rise, given the ever-increasing pervasiveness of smartphones and tablets that created a surge in the BYOD (Bring Your Own Device) trend (Keyes, 2013). The Internet of Things (Gubbi, Buyya, Marusic & Palaniswami, 2013) seems to constitute another irreversible tendency, integrating all sorts of applications with the physical world, namely through sensor networks (Potdar, Sharif & Chang, 2009) and RFID (Radio Frequency Identifier) tags (Aggarwal & Han, 2013).

Grids (Villegas et al., 2010) and P2P (Peer to Peer) systems (Hughes, Coulson & Walkerdine, 2010), used for batch processing and specific applications, constitute other examples of dynamically managed systems that are in line with the cloud computing vision.

Interoperability between different clouds is not easy. Standards have been essentially defined for the lower levels, such as:

- **Cloud Infrastructure Management Interface (CIMI):** Provides an API to provision and to manage resources typically found in clouds, such as virtual machines, storage volumes and networks (DTMF, 2013);
- **Cloud Data Management Interface (CMDI):** Provides a RESTful API to deal with storage resources (ISO/IEC, 2012);
- **Open Virtual Format (OVF):** Allows applications to be packaged and deployed to virtualized systems. It is the lowest level and the most used standard in cloud computing, constituting a means to promote portability of applications between clouds (DTMF, 2012).

Trying to cover higher-level aspects, standards such as OCCI (Open Cloud Computing Interface) (Edmonds, Metsch & Papaspyrou, 2011) and TOSCA (Topology and Orchestration Specification for Cloud Applications) (Binz, Breiter, Leyman & Spatzier, 2012), as well as initiatives such as the Intercloud (Demchenko, Makkes, Strijkers & de Laat, 2012), have no real impact yet on market players. Each cloud ends up having its own features and characteristics, since cloud providers need differentiation to attract customers. The dominant position of some players entitles them to define their own *de facto* standards, in particular at the API level.

Besides cloud API interoperability problems, applications need to interact by exchanging messages and require functional and contextual interoperability, the focus of this chapter. These applications can span a wide spectrum of domains, from high to low level, including:

- Enterprise cooperation (Jardim-Goncalves, Agostinho & Steiger-Garcao, 2012);

- E-government services (Gottschalk & Solli-Sæther, 2008);
- Military operations (Wyatt, Griendling & Mavris, 2012);
- Healthcare applications (Weber-Jahnke, Peyton & Topaloglou, 2012);
- Digital libraries (El Raheb et al., 2011);
- Sensor networks (Iyengar & Brooks, 2012);
- Vehicular networks (Hartenstein & Laberteaux, 2010).

Several frameworks have been proposed to systematize interoperability, such as Athena (Berre et al., 2007), LCIM (Wang, Tolk & Wang, 2009), the European Interoperability Framework (EIF, 2010), and the Framework for Enterprise Interoperability (Chen, 2006). The European project ENSEMBLE embodies an effort to formulate a science base for enterprise interoperability (Jardim-Goncalves et al., 2013).

Service interoperability (Athanasopoulos, Tsalgatidou & Pantazoglou, 2006) requires that interactions occur according to the assumptions and expectations of the involved applications. This involves several levels (Mykkänen & Tuomainen, 2008), such as communication protocol, message structure, data format, syntax, semantics and service composition (Khadka et al., 2011), and even non-functional and social aspects (Loutas, Peristeras & Tarabanis, 2011). Interoperability levels above interface syntax are still largely dependent on manual or semi-automated work from developers and architects, constituting an area of active research.

Regarding service interoperability, the world is divided into two main architectural styles: service-oriented, or SOA (Erl, 2008), and resource-oriented, or REST (Webber, Parastatidis & Robinson, 2010). SOA, usually implemented by Web Services, emphasizes behavior, although limited to interfaces, with state and structure hidden in the implementation. REST follows the principles defined by Fielding (2000) and emphasizes structure and state. It separates interaction and application state, which are stored in the client and server, respectively. Behavior is hidden in the dynamically changing structure and in the implementation of individual resources.

Web Services are technologically more complex, but their model is a closer match to real-world resources. REST is simpler and finer grained, but leans towards some restrictions, such as interaction statelessness, and is lower level. This implies a higher semantic gap between application concepts and REST resources, which for complex applications entails a greater effort to model, develop and maintain.

SOA and REST are not actually competitors, but rather complementary approaches, each naturally a better fit to different areas of application domains (Pautasso, Zimmermann & Leymann, 2008). What is lacking is a way to bridge them and to tune up more to one side or to the other, according to the needs of a particular application.

DISTRIBUTED INTEROPERABILITY PROBLEMS AND GOALS

This chapter defines *application* as a set of software modules with synchronized lifecycles, i.e., compiled and linked together. Applications are the unit of system distribution and their interaction is usually limited to message exchange. Applications are independent and each can evolve in ways that the others cannot predict or control.

The interaction between modules belonging to the same application can rely on names to designate concepts in the type system (types, inheritance, variables, methods, and so on). A name can have only one meaning in a given scope, which means that using a name is equivalent to using its definition. A working application usually assumes that all its modules are also working and use the same implementation language and formats, with any change notified to all modules. The application is a coherent and cohesive whole.

Figure 2. Illustration of some interoperability aspects: (a) before migration of application B; (b) after migration

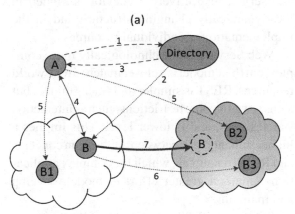 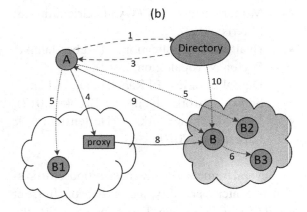

The interaction of modules belonging to different applications, however, is a completely different matter. Different applications may use the same name for different meanings, be programmed in different languages, be deployed in different platforms, use different formats and, without notifying other applications, migrate from one server to another, change its functionality or interface, and even be down for some reason, planned or not.

This raises an interoperability problem, not only in terms of correctly interpreting and understanding exchanged data but also in keeping behaviors synchronized in some choreography. The typical solutions involve a common protocol (such as HTTP), self-describing data, at the syntax and sometimes semantics levels, and many assumptions previously agreed upon. For example, XML-based interactions, including Web Services, assume a common schema. REST proponents claim decoupling between client and server (the client needs just the initial URI – Universal Resource Identifier). However, RESTful applications do require previously agreed media types (schemas) and implicit assumptions by the client on the behavior of the server when executing the protocol verbs.

It is virtually impossible for one application to know how to behave in the interaction with another application if it knows nothing about its interlocutor. Not even humans are able to achieve it. Some form of coupling (basal shared and agreed knowledge, prior to interaction) needs to exist. The goal is to reduce coupling as much as possible while ensuring the minimum level of interoperability required by the problem that motivated the interaction between applications.

Figure 2 provides an example of the sort of problems that need to be tackled in order to achieve this goal, in the context of distributed, cloud-based applications.

Figure 2 can be described as follows, with the scenario of Figure 2a until step 7:

1.   Application *A* resorts to a directory to find a suitable application, according to some specification;
2.   The directory has a reference to such an application, *B*;
3.   The directory sends that reference to *A*;
4.   Application *A* sends a message to *B*, which it must understand, react and respond according to the expectations of *A* (note the bidirectional arrow);
5.   If is unreachable, *A* can have predefined alternative applications, such as *B1* and *B2*. Resending the message to them can be done automatically or as a result from an exception;

Table 1. Interoperability problems and solutions advocated by this chapter

Topic	Problems	Solutions
Heterogeneity (types/schemas)	How can an application understand message types/ schemas from another independent application?	Self-description; Structural compatibility
Decoupling	Do applications need to share their entire interfaces or just the features that they actually use to interact?	Partial compatibility
Simplicity	How to avoid a plethora of languages to specify applications and their interfaces (APIs)? (e.g., XML, WSDL – Web Services Description Language, OWL –Web Ontology Language, BPEL – Business Process Execution Language, and so on)	One, service-based language
Reliability	If a service becomes unavailable, how can suitable alternatives be provided, in order to maintain the overall system working, as much as possible?	Foreseen alternatives, in either at the consumer or provider sides of an interaction, with automatic redirection
Migration	If an application migrates from one cloud to another (due to load-balancing, maintenance, better performance or lower cost, or some other reason), how can other applications continue to interact with it transparently?	Reverse proxy left at the original place with automatic message forwarding; Repeat search for application (updated location returned)
Heterogeneity (portability)	How can an application be deployed to different clouds, with different APIs, platforms and processors?	Portable platform (for interpreted languages); Application includes several implementations
Heterogeneity (management)	How can an application managing other applications in different clouds deal with different cloud management APIs?	Each application becomes manageable (wraps what it needs from the cloud API in its own API)

6. If *B* is reachable but somehow not functional, *B* itself (or the cloud that implements it) can forward the message to an alternative application, such as *B3*;

7. Application *B* can be migrated dynamically to another cloud, yielding the scenario of Figure 2b;

8. *B* leaves a reverse proxy as a replacement, which means that if *A* sends another message to *B* (step 4) it will be automatically forwarded to the new *B*;

9. The response, however, will be sent to the original sender, *A*, including information on the new location of *B*, which *A* will use for subsequent messages (the message protocol must support this);

10. The proxy could be garbage-collected, but this is not easy to manage in a distributed system that is unreliable by nature. Therefore, the proxy can be maintained for some time, under some policy, and destroyed afterwards. If some application still holding a reference to the old *B* sends a message to it, the protocol

should respond with a suitable error stating that *B* does not exist. *A* can then repeat steps 1 and 3, obtaining the new location of *B* from the directory.

Figure 2 raises some interesting interoperability problems, such as those mentioned in Table 1, which also hints a few solutions, some of which are further described in the following sections. Many more problems could be identified, in particular at the non-functional level, such as security and SLR (Service Level Requirements), but this chapter cannot tackle them all and concentrates on the basic interoperability issues.

A FRAMEWORK FOR DISTRIBUTED INTEROPERABILITY

To better understand the distributed interoperability problem, the following sections set up a framework that allows separating and emphasizing the most relevant aspects.

The Fundamental Interoperability Problem

In general, the distributed interoperability problem revolves around two conflicting goals:

- **Mutual Knowledge:** Applications need to interact to accomplish collaboration. This necessarily entails some form of mutual knowledge and understanding, but it also creates dependencies on other applications that may hamper evolution (a new iteration in the lifecycle) or break the collaboration due to a change in some application;
- **Decoupling:** Distributed applications need to be independent to evolve freely and dynamically. Unfortunately, completely independent applications do not understand each other and are not able to interact and collaborate.

Therefore, the fundamental interoperability problem is to provide the maximum decoupling while ensuring the minimum interoperability requirements.

In other words, the main goal is to ensure that each application knows just enough to be able to interoperate but no more than that, to avoid unnecessary dependencies and constraints. This is consistent with the principle of least knowledge (Palm, Anderson & Lieberherr, 2003).

Decoupling should be assessed between each application and those that interact with it. Applications that do not interact at all are completely decoupled, by nature. Decoupling D is defined as a number between 0 and 1 that is the complement to 1 of coupling C. The goal is to maximize decoupling, or to minimize coupling.

Coupling expresses the fraction of the modules of one application that are dependent on modules of the other applications with which it interacts. Actually, each application can perform the role of consumer, sending messages as requests, or

provider, receiving these messages and executing their requests. Therefore, two coupling metrics can be defined:

- C_F **(Forward Coupling):** Expresses how much a consumer application is dependent on its providers, defined as:

$$C_F = \frac{\sum_{i \in P} \dfrac{Up_i}{Tp_i \cdot N_i}}{|P|} \qquad (1)$$

where:

- P is the set of providers that this application uses and $|P|$ denotes the cardinality of P;
- Up_i is the number of modules that this application uses in provider i;
- Tp_i is the total number of modules that provider i has;
- N_i is the number of providers with which this application is compatible as a consumer, in all uses of modules of provider i by this application;
  - C_B **(Backward Coupling):** Expresses how much impact a provider application has on its consumers, defined as:

$$C_B = \frac{\sum_{i \in C} \dfrac{Uc_i}{Tc \cdot M}}{|C|} \qquad (2)$$

where:

- C is the set of consumers that use this application as provider and $|C|$ denotes the cardinality of C;
- Uc_i is the number of modules of this application that consumer i uses;
- Tc is the total number of modules that this application has;

Figure 3. Details of a message-based interaction between two applications

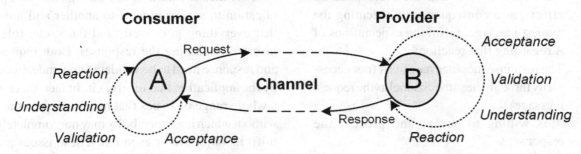

- M is the number of known applications that are compatible with this application and can replace it, as a provider.

In the same way, two metrics of decoupling can be defined:

- D_F **(Forward Decoupling):**

$$D_F = 1 - C_F \tag{3}$$

- D_B **(Backward Decoupling):**

$$D_B = 1 - C_B \tag{4}$$

The conclusion from (1) is that the existence of alternative providers to an application reduces its forward coupling C_F, thereby increasing its forward decoupling D_F (3), since more applications (with which this application is compatible, as a consumer) dilute the dependency.

Similarly, the conclusion from (2) is that the existence of alternatives to an application as a provider reduces the system dependency on it, thereby reducing the impact that application may have on its potential consumers. Backward coupling C_B decreases and backward decoupling D_B (4) increases.

The following section examines the meaning of compatibility between applications and how it can be used to reduce coupling.

Structural Compatibility

Figure 3 illustrates a message-based interaction between application A, as a consumer, and application B, as a provider. The consumer initiates the interaction with a request message and the provider executes the request and sends back a response message. A suitable channel, such as a network, is needed to support the message communication.

Intuitively, the interaction makes sense only if A is compatible with B, i.e., if B is able to understand what A is requesting, and reacts and responds accordingly to what A expects. If A and B were modules within the same application, this would be a simple task. The channel is simply a reliable pointer and module compatibility is checked by a type system that relies on shared type names and inheritance hierarchies.

In a distributed environment, however, type sharing is not guaranteed, since applications evolve independently, and messages cannot be assumed to be correct. The goal of achieving such a simple interaction can be decomposed into the following objectives:

1. The request message reaches B, through the channel;
2. B is willing to accept and process the request;
3. B validates the request, according to its requirements for requests;
4. B understands what A is requesting;

5. The reaction of *B* and the corresponding effects, as a consequence of executing the request message, fulfill the expectations of *A* regarding that reaction;

6. The response message reaches *A* (not necessarily through the same channel as the request message);

7. *A* is willing to accept and process the response;

8. *A* validates the response, according to its requirements for the response;

9. *A* understands what *B* is responding;

10. *A* reacts appropriately to the response, fulfilling the expectations of *B* for that response.

This means that it is not enough for an application to send a request to another and hope that everything goes well (and the same, roles inverted, regarding the response). Both request and response need to be validated and understood by the application that receives it. In fact, there is a whole range of issues that need to fit together, without which interoperability may not completely fulfil its objective or even fail. These issues are further discussed in the following section and systematized in Table 2. This section concentrates on understanding messages, or message level compatibility.

Table 2. Levels of interoperability

Category	Level	Main Artifact	Description
Symbiotic (purpose and intent)	Coordination	Governance	Motivations to have the interaction, with varying levels of mutual knowledge of governance, strategy and goals
	Alignment	Joint-venture	
	Collaboration	Partnership	
	Cooperation	Outsourcing	
Pragmatic (reaction and effects)	Contract	Choreography	Management of the effects of the interaction at the levels of choreography, process and service
	Workflow	Process	
	Interface	Service	
Semantic (meaning of content)	Inference	Rule base	Interpretation of a message in context, at the levels of rule, known application components and relations, and definition of concepts
	Knowledge	Knowledge base	
	Ontology	Concept	
Syntactic (notation of representation)	Structure	Schema	Representation of application components, in terms of composition, primitive components and their serialization format in messages
	Predefined type	Primitive resource	
	Serialization	Message format	
Connective (transfer protocol)	Messaging	Message protocol	Lower level formats and network protocols involved in transferring a message from the context of the sender to that of the receiver
	Routing	Gateway	
	Communication	Network protocol	
	Physics	Media protocol	
Environmental (deployment and migration)	Management	API	Cloud environment in which each application is deployed and managed and the portability problems raised
	Library (SaaS)	Utility service	
	Platform (PaaS)	Basic software	
	Computer (IaaS)	Virtual hardware	

In most cases, applications are made interoperable by design, i.e., conceived and implemented to work together. A typical solution is to resort to Web Services, in which case:

- Schemas are shared between interacting services, establishing coupling for all the possible documents satisfying each schema, even if they are not actually used;
- Searching for an interoperable service is done by schema matching with similarity algorithms (Jeong, Lee, Cho & Lee, 2008) and ontology matching and mapping (Euzenat & Shvaiko, 2007). This does not ensure interoperability and manual adaptations are usually unavoidable.

Interoperability, as defined in this chapter, introduces a different perspective, stronger than similarity but weaker than commonality (the result of sharing the same schemas and ontologies). The trick is to allow partial (instead of full) interoperability, by considering only the intersection between what the consumer needs and what the provider offers. If the latter subsumes the former, the degree of interoperability required by the consumer is feasible, regardless of whether the provider supports additional features or not. When this is true, the consumer is said to be compatible with the provider or, more precisely, that an application *A* is compatible with an application *B* regarding a consumer-provider relationship.

The main advantages of this are:

- Coupling is limited to the documents that actually contain the used features and not to all possible documents that satisfy the schema (reduced coupling);
- A consumer is more likely to find suitable providers based on a smaller set of features, rather than on a full schema;
- A provider will be able to serve a broader base of consumers, since it will impose fewer restrictions on them.

Compatibility between a consumer and a provider is designated compliance (Kokash & Arbab, 2009). The consumer must satisfy (comply with) the requirements established by the provider to accept requests sent to it, without which these cannot be validated, understood and executed.

It is important to note that any consumer that complies with a given provider can use it, independently of having been designed for interaction with it or not. The consumer and provider need not share the same schema. The consumer's schema needs only to be compliant with the provider's schema in the features that it actually uses.

Since distributed applications are independent, schema compliance must be tested structurally, feature by feature, between messages sent by the consumer and the interface offered by the provider. Hence the designation 'structural compatibility'.

Besides the usage relationship between a consumer and a provider, the replacement relationship between two providers is also of relevance. The issue is to ascertain whether a provider *B*, serving a consumer *A*, can be replaced by another provider *Y* such that the consumer-provider relationship enjoyed by *A* is not broken. In other words, the issue is whether *Y* is replacement compatible with *B*.

The reasons for replacing a provider by another may be varied, such as switching to an alternative in case of failure or lack of capacity of *B*, evolution of *B* (in which case *Y* would be the new version of *B*), or simply a management decision. The important aspect to note is that, again, *Y* does not need to support all the features of *B*, but just those that *A* actually uses (partial compatibility).

Replacement compatibility between two providers is designated 'conformance' (Kim & Shen, 2007; Adriansyah, van Dongen & van der Aalst, 2010). The provider must fulfill the expectations of the consumer regarding the effects of a request (including eventual responses), therefore being able to take the form of (to conform to) whatever the consumer expects it to be. Note that a provider may be conformant to another with

Figure 4. Application compatibility, by use (compliance, A complies with B) and replacement (conformance, Y conforms to B)

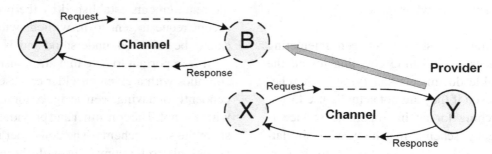

respect to one consumer but not with respect to another. It all depends on the set of features used by the consumer.

Compliance and conformance are relationship properties that are not commutative (e.g., if *A* complies with *B*, *B* does not necessarily comply with *A*) but are transitive (e.g., if *A* complies with *B* and *B* complies with *C*, then *A* complies with *C*).

Figure 4 illustrates compliance and conformance. An application *A*, in the role of consumer, has been designed to interact with an application that includes specification *B*, in the role of provider. *B* includes only the features that *A* requires and corresponds to how *A* views its provider (any other feature is irrelevant to *A*). *A* is fully compliant with *B*, in the sense that it uses only features that *B* provides, in the way that *B* expects, and *B* does not include any additional feature. At some point, *B* is replaced by an application *Y*, which has been designed to expect consumers that require no more features than those used by specification *X* (which is how *Y* views its consumers).

Can *A* use *Y* as if it were *B*? This depends on two necessary conditions:

- **Compliance:** *B* must comply with *X*. Since, by design, *A* complies with *B* and *X* complies with *Y*, transitiveness means that *A* complies with *Y* and can use *Y* as if it were *B*, as it was designed for;

- **Conformance:** *X* must conform to *B*. Since, by design, *Y* conforms to what *X* expects as a provider (and the same about *B* regarding *A*), transitiveness means that *Y* conforms to what *A* expects as a provider *B* and can replace (take the form of) *B* without *A* noticing it.

A Layered Model of Interoperability

The previous sections describes applications in terms of the set features they offer, which is an implicit reference to their interface, but the scenario is more complex and needs to be detailed. In general, and recalling the objectives depicted in Figure 3 and subsequently enumerated, meaningfully sending a message (note that request and response reverse the sender and receiver roles) entails the following aspects:

- **Transfer:** (Objectives 1 and 6).The message content needs to be successfully transferred from the context of the sender to the context of the receiver;

- **Willingness:** (Objectives 2 and 7). Usually, applications are designed to interact and therefore to accept messages, but non-functional aspects such as security and performance limitations can impose constraints;

- **Content:** (Objectives 3 and 8). This concerns the generation and interpretation of the content of a message by the sender, expressed by some representation, in such a way that the receiver is also able to interpret it, in its own context;
- **Intent:** (Objectives 4 and 9). Sending the message must have an underlying intent, inherent to the interaction to which it belongs and related to the motivation to interact and the goals to achieve. This should be aligned with the design strategy of both applications;
- **Reaction:** (Objectives 5 and 10). This concerns the reaction of the receiver upon reception of a message, which should produce effects according to the expectations of the sender.

This means that interoperability between two applications can be seen at a higher level, involving intentions (why interact and reactions sought), or at a lower level, concerning messages (what to exchange, and how). Detailing the various relevant levels leads to a systematization of interoperability such as the one described in Table 2.

Table 2 can be briefly described as follows, using the Category column as the top organizing feature:

- **Symbiotic:** Expresses the purpose and intent of two interacting applications to engage in a mutually beneficial agreement, in a tight coordination under a common governance (applications controlled by the same organization), a joint-venture agreement (applications substantially aligned), a collaboration involving a partnership agreement (some goals are shared), or a mere value chain cooperation (outsourcing contract). This is the realm of Enterprise Engineering and usually the topmost level in application interaction complexity, although the same principles apply in a more rudimentary fashion to simpler applications and their components;

- **Pragmatic:** The effect of an interaction between a consumer and a provider is the outcome of a contract, which is implemented by a choreography that coordinates processes, which in turn implement workflow behavior by orchestrating service invocations;
- **Semantic:** Interacting applications must be able to understand the meaning of the contents of the messages exchanged, both requests and responses. This implies interoperability in rules, knowledge and ontologies, so that meaning is not lost (or at least a mapping is available) when transferring a message from the context of the sender to that of the receiver;
- **Syntactic:** Deals mainly with form, rather than content. Each message has a structure, composed of data (primitive resources) according to some structural definition (its schema). Data need to be serialized as messages to be sent over the network;
- **Connective:** The main objective is to transfer a message from the context of one resource to the other's, regardless of its contents. This usually involves enclosing it in another message with control information and implementing a message protocol over a communications network, according to its own protocol, possibly involving routing gateways;
- **Environmental:** Each application also interacts with the environment in which it is deployed, anew or by migration. The cloud's API and the infrastructure level that the application requires will most likely have impact on the way applications interact, particularly if they are deployed in (or migrate between) different clouds, from different cloud vendors. Interoperability between an application and the environment in which it is deployed is usually known as *portability*.

In most cases, not all these levels are considered explicitly. Higher levels tend to be treated 'tacitly' (specified in documentation or simply assumed, but not ensured) and lower levels 'empirically' (ensured by running software, but details hidden by lower level software layers).

Syntactic is the most used category, because it the simplest and the most familiar, with interfaces that mainly deal with syntax or primitive semantics. The pragmatic category is mainly implemented by software, but without formal specification. Portability is mainly dealt with in an *ad hoc* manner and usually under some form of vendor lock-in, in particular at the API level, since cloud standards are still incipient (Lewis, 2012).

THE LIMITATIONS OF EXISTING TECHNOLOGIES

Most of the technologies in use today to solve the distributed interoperability problem are, in some form or another, an evolution of the original Web specifications, namely HTML (HyperText Markup Language) to describe data and HTTP as the protocol to exchange those data between client and server. In fact, the Web was conceived to solve an interoperability problem (Berners-Lee, 1999): how to provide seamless access to remote hypermedia documents when many platform environments are involved, both at the client and server sides.

In the beginning, text was the most important media type. Web pages were static and similar to printed documents, essentially text-based with occasional artifacts such as pictures and tables. Therefore, using text markup in HTML was a natural choice (Toshniwal & Agrawal, 2004), under influence of a document description language (SGML – Standard Generalized Markup Language) stemming from the printing world.

Today, the world and its requirements are rather different. Text is just one among other formats, with binary information (e.g., pictures, video,

voice) taking a great part of the data bandwidth. The original Web of Documents has evolved into a global Web of Services (Tolk, 2006). Services involving dynamically generated data are replacing static web pages and computer applications are filling in the web space once dominated by humans. The original client-server paradigm is now being replaced by the peer-oriented consumer-provider paradigm, with reversible roles in complex interactions.

XML evolved from HTML by adding extensibility, separating data from formatting and adding self-description capability. But the basic approach of text markup, the document paradigm and the lack of native support to binary data and behavioral description remained unchanged. What changed a lot was the level of complexity, in particular in what self-description (e.g., XML Schema) is concerned. It should be noted that schema languages do not describe data structures, but rather text documents (data serialized as text, or text patterns). The goal of interoperability is to meaningfully convey data, information and knowledge, which means that the serialization should be handled transparently and limited to ordered data structures, such as lists, and not a central part of the description language. XML is verbose and complex, has limited support for binary formats, is inefficient in computer terms due to parsing and exhibits symmetric interoperability, based on both sender and receiver using the same schema, which constitutes a relevant coupling problem.

JSON (JavaScript Object Notation) appeared as a simpler alternative to XML and, in spite of a lower expressive power, its success is a testimony to the relevance given by the market to simplicity in detriment of complex capabilities. Nevertheless, there is now a proposal for a JSON Schema (Galiegue & Zyp, 2013), which seems to be following the philosophy of XML Schema, but at a lower level of expressive power and complexity.

HTTP is an application level protocol, synchronous and committed to the client-server paradigm. In particular, it does not support full duplex, long running sessions required by general services such as those found at the enterprise level. This has spurred workaround technologies such as AJAX (Asynchronous JavaScript And XML) (Holdener, 2008) and Comet (Crane & McCarthy, 2008). Web Sockets, now part of the HTML5 world (Lubbers, Albers & Salim, 2010), removed this restriction, added binary support and increased performance.

Web Services were the first distributed interoperability solution for services, based on the data interoperability provided by XML to add support for behavioral interfaces. Operations are described just by their signature (name, parameters and result) in the data-oriented syntax of XML, yielding WSDL (Web Services Description Language) documents with a cumbersome syntax. The actual behavior of a Web Service must be done by a separate mechanism, either a general programming language or an orchestration language such as BPEL (Business Process Execution Language) (Juric & Pant, 2008). Web Services are intended only as a wrapping mechanism for services, with emphasis on distributed interoperability, and do not support the notion of structured resources.

SOAP (originally Simple Object Access Protocol, but not an acronym since version 1.2) is the protocol used by Web Services and constitutes another source of complexity and performance overheads, with specific solutions for non-functional data (such as security) and routing. Designed to overcome some of the limitations of HTTP for generic service interoperability, achieves generality at the expense of simplicity and performance.

Heralded as a universal service interoperability solution, Web Services became more a legacy integration and business-level application interoperability mechanism than a true and native service oriented solution. Their universality comes at the price of complexity, with schemas and all the associated standards. Tools automate and simplify a lot, but they just hide the complexity and do not eliminate it.

This has spurred a movement towards simpler, more manageable systems, in the form of a resource oriented architectural style, REST (Fielding, 2000), promoting what is known as RESTful applications (Laitkorpi, Selonen and Systa, 2009; Li and Chou, 2010), usually coupled with the simpler data format JSON.

Whereas SOA emphasizes behavior and rich interfaces, the guiding aspects of REST are state, structure and uniform interfaces. All resources implement the same service, with the same set of operations, although with different semantics. These typically exhibit CRUD style (Create, Read, Update and Delete) and are mapped onto HTTP verbs (GET, PUT, POST and DELETE). Functionality that in SOA would be modeled as an operation is modeled in REST as a resource. The simplicity of REST comes at the price of having to model applications at a lower level than SOA, with a higher semantic gap between the problem and solution spaces. Rich services cannot be modeled as directly in REST as they can be in SOA.

All these technologies have been conceived for the Web, in which interacting applications have to endure reasonably long interaction times, or at least substantially higher than within modules of the same application. In addition, application granularity cannot be too small and the number of interacting applications cannot be very high, to keep overheads comparatively manageable.

The Web was not conceived for the era of Big Data (Zikopoulos, 2012) and of the Internet of Things (Gubbi, Buyya, Marusic & Palaniswami, 2013). The latter is an attempt to extend the Internet protocols to smaller systems, essentially with REST (to keep things simple), but even so having to adapt the protocol to reduce system requirements and protocol overheads. The CoAP (Constrained Application Protocol) (Castellani et al., 2011) is an example, including a subset of the features of HTTP, but adding asynchronous messages, binary headers and UDP (User Datagram Protocol) binding. Since small systems (sensors and actuators, mainly) involve other types of

Table 3. Main limitations of relevant interoperability technologies

Technology	Main Limitations
XML	Text-based, verbose, complex, poor support for binary, data description only (no behavior), syntax-level only (higher levels require other languages), high coupling (interoperability achieved by schema sharing)
JSON	Simpler but less powerful than XML and the same limitations. Coupling is also high since data types have to be agreed prior to data interaction
HTTP	Optimized for Web browsing (scalable retrieval of hypermedia information), but not for generic and distributed service-based interactions. Inefficient and specific text-based control information format. Synchronous, committed to the client-server paradigm, lack of support for the push model (server-initiated interactions) and for binary data
SOAP	Complex, significant performance overheads, XML-based (thus inheriting XML's problems), too high-level, with specific solutions for non-functional data and routing
Web Services (SOA)	Complex (based on WSDL, SOAP and XML), many standards to cover distributed interaction aspects, high coupling (interoperability achieved by sharing the WSDL document), lack of support for structure (flat service space)
REST	Forces a CRUD approach to model real-world entities, causing a significant semantic gap in generic service modeling. Coupling is disguised under the structured data and the fixed syntactic interface. Structure of data returned by the server may vary freely, but the client needs to have prior knowledge of the data schemas and of the expected behavior of the server

networks, not necessarily IP-based, heterogeneity is another source of inadequacy from web-based solutions, which in practice assume a homogenous, IP-based network.

Table 3 summarizes the main limitations of existing technologies that are particularly relevant for interoperability.

AN ALTERNATIVE INTEROPERABILITY SOLUTION

Although the world can live with all these limitations, removing or reducing them to improve interoperability constitutes a very interesting goal. This chapter contends that this entails:

- A new model to describe interacting applications, with support for both rich services and structured resources, instead of forcing one (SOA) or the other (REST);
- A new description language, capable of describing both data structures and behavior, including self-description without separate schema documents or markup syntax, much like a traditional programming language;

- A new interaction protocol, which separates the various levels of interoperability, according to the systematization shown in Table 2, instead of mixing them up. For example, HTTP ties the message level protocol with the service interface.

The following sections detail these issues.

A Resource-Based Model

As argued above, the interaction of modules belonging to different applications cannot simply use names, because the contexts are different and only by out-of-band agreements (such as sharing a common ontology) will a given name have the same meaning in interacting applications.

XML-based systems, for example, solve this problem by sharing the same schema. However, this is a strong coupling constraint and contemplates data only. Behavior (operations) need to be simulated by data declarations, as in WSDL documents describing Web Services.

The goal of this chapter is to conceive a more dynamic and general model of applications and their interactions, which supports interoperability without requiring to share the specification of the application interface (schema). The strategy relies on structural type matching, rather than nominal type matching. This approach entails:

- A small set of primitive types, shared by all applications (universal upper ontology);
- Common structuring mechanisms, to build complex types from primitive ones;
- A mechanism for structurally comparing types from interacting applications.

Applications are structured and, in the model described below, their modules are designated resources. Since applications are distributed by definition, sending each other messages through an interconnecting channel is the only form of interaction. To make intra-application interactions as similar as possible to inter-application interactions,

all resources interact by messages, even if they belong to the same application. Resources are the foundation artifacts of the model of applications and their interactions that is depicted in Figure 5.

This model can be briefly described in the following way:

- A *resource* is an entity of any nature (material, virtual, conceptual, noun, action, and so on) that embodies a meaningful, complete and discrete concept, making sense by itself while being distinguishable from, and able to interact with, other entities;
- Resources that interact do so by sending each other messages. A message is itself a resource that migrates (through some channel, usually a network, using some protocol) from the context of the resource that sends it to the context of the resource that receives it;

Figure 5. A structural model of resources and of their interactions

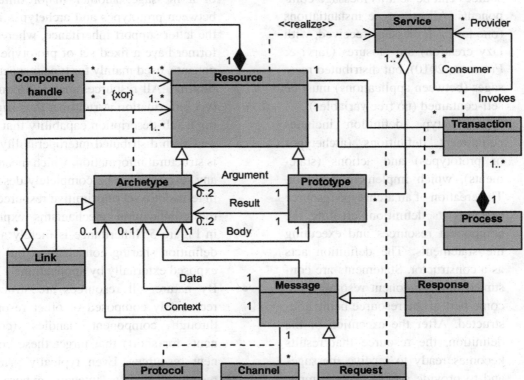

- There are two kinds of resource definitions: *prototypes* and *archetypes*:
  ○ A prototype resource models the concept of an operation (similar to a method in an object), by including the definition of a body and optionally an argument and a result, all archetypes. When the prototype resource receives a message (which must match its argument), the archetypes are used to create the corresponding resources, which together implement an execution context of that prototype resource. The behavior of a prototype stems from executing its body's definition, during its creation. The advantage of using full-fledged resources instead of methods or functions is uniformity of treatment (everything is a resource) and support for high-order programming. Prototype resources can be sent as message components. All prototype instantiations (one for each message received, with lazy creation) are closures (Järvi & Freeman, 2010), but distributed messages (between applications) must be self-contained (no free variables);
  ○ An archetype definition includes component definitions (archetypes or prototypes) and actions (statements), which implement behavior. The creation of an archetype resource executes its definition, creating the component resources and executing the statements. The definition acts as a constructor. Statements are consumed but component resources become part of the resource being constructed. After the execution of the definition, the resource that results becomes ready to receive messages and to provide access to its components. If a message is sent to it, its reaction is to scan its prototypes and to forward the message to the one with an argument that structurally matches the message. If not found, it can delegate the message to another resource or send back an exception response. Archetype-based resources can be dynamically created by reproducing any existing resource (cloning it or creating one anew by executing its definition again);

- Messages have two component resources, both optional: functional data and non-functional context. Arguments and results from prototype instantiations, received and sent as messages, have the same capability, which means that contextual information can be passed on to (or received from) prototypes. This provides support for context-aware programming;

- Besides the basic reaction to the reception of a message, another major difference between prototypes and archetypes is that the latter support inheritance, whereas the former have a fixed set of prototype components, used mainly for type inspection at runtime. All resources maintain complete type information at runtime, thus supporting a self-description capability that is essential in distributed interoperability. This is structural information, which means that any resource can be completely described in terms of a set of primitive resources and the composition mechanisms expressed in Figure 5. Inheritance is merely a local definition sharing convenience, but is not exposed externally by applications;

- By nature, all resources are structured, recursively composed of other resources, through component handles (components for short) that target these component resources. Even typically primitive resources, such as integers, expose a set of prototype components that implement their operations. Since prototypes are resources, they can also expose their components. At some point this must stop, with black box resources that do not expose any components. For this purpose, component handles in Figure 5 can restrict access to the targeted resources, namely with read, change, send and detail access. A resource can thus be prevented from being cloned or changed, receiving a message or having a component accessed. Prototypes from primitive resources must be labeled with *send* access only;

- In addition, a component can specify if the targeted resource is public or private (accessible only from the interior of the resource), and how it can be changed in assignment statements:
  ○ **Atomically:** As an indivisible whole, completely replaced by another resource);
  ○ **Structurally:** Changing only the components of that resource that are matched by corresponding components in the new resource. Structural assignment is important in distributed systems to increase interoperability and to reduce application coupling;
- Within a given application, a component can target a resource with a simple pointer. However, resources must also be able to refer to remote resources (in other applications), in which case the component targets a local link resource, which contains a URI or some other type of remote reference (depends on the channel and protocol used). This model is not limited to the Web. Sending a message to a link has an automatic forwarding effect to the targeted remote resource;
- A link can target more than one resource, constituting a list of remote references. Depending on how it is used, this can express a multicast (sending a message to

all targeted resources) or consumer-side redundancy (if a resource targeted by the link is unavailable, the support system can automatically try to resend the message to the next in the list);
- Component can be named or unnamed. Named components are similar to XML tags, JSON attribute strings, or Description Logic role names (Baader et al., 2010). Component names need not be unique. A component name defines a relation between the resource that holds it and one or more component resources, corresponding to a list of handles to the targeted resources under that name. Unnamed components are similar, considering that the name of these relations is empty;
- In addition to names, the relation between two resources expressed by a component can also be described by an archetype resource, instead of being limited to just the semantics implicit to a name. For example, suppose that a resource A is related to another B by a relation named *managerof*, expressing that A is the manager of B, or performs the role of manager with respect to B. In that case, the features that characterize a manager can be expressed explicitly by a specific resource, instead of a simple name. A component is either a simply named relation or has an associated resource that describes that relation;
- A *service* is a set of logically related reactions of a resource to the messages it can receive and react to (depends on its prototypes). A service can be seen as pure behavior, albeit the implementation of concrete reactions may depend on state, which needs a resource as an implementation platform, or have side effects, changing that state;
- Stating that a resource A sends a message to a resource B is in fact a simplified way of stating that an instantiation of a prototype

in a service implemented by resource *A* invokes a prototype in a service implemented by resource *B*. This constitutes a *service transaction* between these two resources, in which the resources *A* and *B* perform the roles of service consumer and service provider, respectively. A service transaction can entail other service transactions, as part of the chain reaction to the message on part of the service provider. A service is defined in terms of reactions to messages (external view) and not in terms of state transitions or activity flows (internal view);

- A *process* is a graph of all service transactions that can occur, starting with a service transaction initiated at some resource *A* and ending with a final service transaction, which neither reacts back nor initiates new service transactions. The process corresponds to a use case of resource *A* and usually involves other resources as service transactions flow.

This model, depicted by Figure 5, has been conceived to cover the main levels of interoperability described in Table 2 and to contribute to solving the limitations of existing technologies, summarized in Table 3.

Interoperability today is based on data description languages such as XML and JSON, which cover just the syntactic category of Table 2. Semantics has been an afterthought, with languages such as RDF (Resource Description Framework) and OWL (Web Ontology Language) (Grau et al., 2008). Pragmatics (behavior) has been dealt with generic programming languages or, under the process paradigm, with BPEL (Juric & Pant, 2008). Services have been modeled essentially with WSDL documents, which are no more than an interface specification simulated on top of a data description language (XML). The REST architectural style uses a fixed syntax-level service specification and restricts variability to resources and their structure. In essence, no solution today covers Table 2 adequately.

The rationale underlying the model of Figure 5 has been to endow it with the necessary artifacts to cover all levels, with the exception of the symbiotic and environmental categories. The former is still very high-level, largely a matter for documentation. The latter entails a still young domain, with many vendor-specific features and in which the foundation artifacts have yet to be determined.

Resources in Figure 5 model real-world entities, with their interfaces modeled as services. Dynamically, services interact by messages, requests and responses, over some channel with some protocol. These constitute transactions that build up processes. Structured resources refer to others by links. Component handles are roles, in the sense of Description Logic (Baader et al., 2010), and allow semantics to be incorporated in the model from scratch. Operations (prototypes) are modeled as resources, in the same manner as entities typically modeled by a class (archetypes). This makes the model simpler, more canonic, and allows a finer grain of application modeling.

A Distributed Service Interoperability Language

The usefulness of the model described in the previous section needs to be assessed by implementing it, which could be done in several ways, such as:

- Extending WSDL files with another section (e.g., Structure), in which component resources and links could be exposed, thereby introducing structure into Web Services;
- Allowing REST resources to have their own service description document, thereby allowing the coexistence of the uniform and non-uniform interface approaches in REST;
- Using a general-purpose language to program a library of classes to implement the UML (Unified Modeling Language) classes in Figure 5.

However, this would inevitably lead to syntactic and semantic adaptations and compromises, to bridge the gap between the model of Figure 5 and that of the chosen language and/or platform. The basic goal is simplicity for the application architects and programmers, which means that a language conceived from scratch to implement this model, providing native support for its characteristics, will be the best match.

This section presents just a very simple example of this language, SIL (Service Interoperability Language), to give an idea of its look and feel regarding the description of resources and of their services (Delgado, 2013). The example chosen is a car rental system, with just two resources, one performing the role of provider (server, in classical terms) and the other the role of consumer (client), both involved in a car rental transaction. Box 1 depicts the provider and Box 2 the consumer. Resources are distributed (each is an application with a single module).

Box 1 describes a resource, myCarRental, the online reservation system of a car rental enterprise. A resource in SIL has the look and feel of a JSON data structure (components with brackets, {...}), but component names are not strings and there are prototype resources (operations, with statements).

The first declarations (date, carClass, carInfo and car) are archetype definitions, not actual resources, and their purpose is to avoid repeating the definitions whenever a resource with these structures need to be created. Each time they are used, a resource with that structure is created. The keyword union means that carClass can have one of the string values indicated.

The first real resource component, fleet, is a list of resources describing the various cars that compose the fleet. These are described by the car definition and have three archetype (data) components and three prototype (operations) resources. The component fleet is accessible from outside myCarRental, by using the resource path myCarRental.fleet.

Operations are first-class resources (prototypes), recognized by the keyword operation and the optional argument and return declaration between curved parentheses before the body, specified between brackets. Operations can be accessed by a resource path and be sent messages (with

Box 1. Provider (server) side of the car rental system

```
myCarRental: {
  date: definition {day: [1..31]; month: [1..12]};
  carClass: definition union {"economy"; "compact"; "standard"; minivan"};
  carInfo: definition {class: carClass; rate: float; linkCar: link to car};
  car: definition {
    class: carClass;
    occupied: list of date; // days already reserved
    rate: float; // daily rate
    getInfo: operation (-> carInfo) { reply {class; rate; self}; };
    reserve: operation (day: date ->) { occupied.add <- day };
    cancel: operation (day: date ->) { occupied.remove <- day };
  };
  fleet: list of car; // exposed resource structure
  getFleet: (class: carclass = any -> info: list of carInfo) {
    for (i: [0..fleet.size-1]) {
      if (fleet[i].class ==> class) // if the car's class complies
        info.add <- (fleet[i]<-); // invoke the nameless operation in "car"
    reply info;
  };
  getFleetSize: (-> int) { reply fleet.size; };
  };
```

the operator "<-"), just like any other resource. Adding a new car to the fleet can be done by using the expression myCarRental.fleet.add <- ..., sending the description of the new car as message argument. This is also illustrated in Box 2, with access from the consumer side.

When a resource receives a message, it searches among its operations for one with an argument with which the message complies (and with a result that complies with the result expected), forwarding the message to that operation. If the receiving resource is an operation, it reacts by executing its body (creates the resource that the body defines), assuming that compliance has been verified, otherwise an exception occurs. Operations can only have one input argument and one result value, but these can be arbitrarily structured. In the operation's declaration heading, they are separated by "->". Any of them may be non-existent.

Each car offers the functionality of providing information on it, by sending it a message without an argument, as illustrated in operation getFleet in myCarRental, or by specifying operation getInfo explicitly. This information includes the car's class and rate, as well as a link that can later be used to execute operations (creating prototype instantiations) on the car description in the fleet. This corresponds to the hypermedia style advocated by REST. The keyword self indicates a reference to the resource that contains the operation in which it appears.

The operation getFleet returns a list with information on each car (class, rate and a link to each car descriptor in the fleet), allowing the client to navigate through this list and use the link of the chosen car to make the reservation. This is illustrated by Box 2, in which the first car with daily rate below 40 is reserved.

Note the heading of getFleet in Box 1, which declares an input argument (class) that is optional and has value any by default, specified by the operator "=". This means that this argument gets the value passed, is specified, or any, if omitted.

Then, the compliance check operator ("==>") indicates whether each car's class complies with the class required. If omitted, and since all resources comply with any, by definition, the entire fleet is returned.

Box 2 illustrates the use of the myCarRental reservation system, from the consumer side. It includes the SPID (SIL Public Interface Descriptor), designated mcrSPID, which performs the same role as WSDL files (to provide a description of the interface). SPIDs are generated automatically from the program, by eliminating private parts such as the body of operations. The availability of a service description is in line with the SOA style, since the consumer can obtain this description from some resource/service registry. This is also equivalent to declaring a media type in REST, which must be previously agreed upon by both client and server.

A link to the server application (mcr) is used, which must be obtained by the client somehow (specified in the program or found in a registry). In SIL, a link is not necessarily a URI. It is a resource with a structure previously agreed between the interacting applications or compatible by compliance and confirmation. An URI is just one of the possibilities.

Box 2 also illustrates how car descriptors can be added, reflecting the growth of the fleet, and how to retrieve a list of information structure on each car, as described above, both for the entire fleet and just for some of car classes. The operation invoked is the same and all is based on compliance. Finally, a small loop runs through the list and makes a reservation for May 30, for the first car with a daily rate under 40.

Naturally, these are very simple examples and many things are not tested, such as whether the car is free on that day. In a more complete and robust program, these tests would have to be performed.

SIL is a compiled language. The text source is compiled into binary form, which is used for message transmission and program execution, with an interpreter. Connection to other languages (Java,

Box 2. Consumer (client) side of the car rental system

```
mcrSPID: definition {
  date: definition {day: [1..31]; month: [1..12]};
  carClass: definition union {"economy"; "compact"; "standard"; "minivan"};
  carInfo: definition {class: carClass; rate: float; linkCar: link to car};
  car: definition {
    class: carClass;
    occupied: list of date; // days already reserved
    rate: float; // daily rate
    getInfo: operation (-> carInfo);
    reserve: operation (date ->);
    cancel: operation function (date ->);
  };
  fleet: list of car; // exposed resource structure
  getFleet: operation (carclass:=any -> list of carInfo);
  getFleetSize: operation (-> int);
};
mcr: link to mcrSPID; // initialized with a link to myCarRental
mcr.fleet.add <- {class: "economy"; rate: 30}; // add cars
mcr.fleet.add <- {class: "standard"; rate: 50};
numberOfCars: mcr.getFleetSize <-; // invokes operation getFleetSize
carFleet: mcr <-;  // invokes operation getFleet and returns
                   // the entire fleet (class in getFleet
                   // is "any" by default)
minivanCars: mcr <- "minivan"; // returns only the fleet of minivans
smallCars: mcr <- union {"economy"; "compact"}; // returns only the fleet of
                   // economy and compact cars
for (j: [0.. smallCars.size-1]) {
  c: smallCars [j]; // car information. Brings a link to the resource
  if (c.rate < 40){
    c.linkCar <- {30; 5}; // Use the link to reserve the car for May 30
    break;
  };
};
```

C#, Python, and so on), is done in a similar way to XML. There must be a mapping between primitive resource types in SIL and each programming language, an adapting layer, and a dynamic class load mechanism to support changes to resources.

The existence of the myCarRental's SPID in Box 2 is not essential. At the consumer, mcr could have been declared as any, which switches off compiler verifications and defers compliance checks entirely to runtime, which is done structurally and without previous knowledge of the resource types. This is much slower than SPID-based compile-time verifications but, after the first time of each compliance check, the corresponding resource structural mapping can be cached and reused in subsequent messages.

Other features of SIL, not illustrated here for simplicity, include:

- **Delegation:** An operation can execute some statements and then delegate the rest of the execution of the request to another resource, by forwarding either the received message or another one. The delegate will respond directly to the first sender, the one that originated the request;

- **Asynchronous Communication:** Messages can be sent asynchronously, in which a case a *future* (Schippers, 2009) will be immediately returned and execution proceeds concurrently, at the sender and receiver resources. The future will be automatically replaced by the response value, when it arrives at the sender. If in the meantime the sender tries to read the future, it will get suspended until the future is replaced and then automatically resumed.

The receiver can send a promise when it receives the request, which acts as pre-response to confirm that the request has been received and accepted. The promise replaces the future, but it will also suspend the sender if it tries to read its value. The receiver can perform a non-blocking test of whether a given resource component (the equivalent of a variable) contains a future, a promise or a normal value;

- **Context-Awareness:** Messages can be sent in two parts, data and context. The latter is typically used to pass non-functional information. Both parts are normal resources and obey the same compliance and conformance rules as other resources. This applies to both request and response messages, which means that SIL supports forward and backward context passing. The latter is useful both in normal responses and exceptions;

- **Reliability:** The links in Box 1 and 2 can target multiple resources. If for some reason the protocol fails to communicate with the first resource in the link, it will try automatically the following one. An exception is generated if all alternatives fail. There is opportunity for recovery, at the level of the exception handler (covering a set of statements) or at the application level.

A Simple Message-Level Protocol

Unlike HTTP, which goes down from the transport level up to the service level, with verbs such as GET or PUT, the SIL protocol deals only with messages, addressed to resources. Its goal is to support message-level interaction. What to do with the message is the receiver's responsibility. Unlike SOAP, which defines headers for additional information such as security, the SIL protocol delegates to higher interoperability levels the responsibility to add extra information. This is done by wrapping simple messages within other messages, with the

extra information, in what constitutes an open extension to the basic protocol. Both interacting applications need to support the protocol extension mechanism, which may be standardized or be specific to a pair of applications. The basic protocol remains simple.

The SIL protocol requires only an underlying addressable message-level transport protocol, which does not have to be reliable. Message level reliability, if not provided by the transport protocol, can be implemented at the resource or application level. This is intended as a means to support heterogeneity, namely in non-TCP/IP protocols, such as those used in sensor networks (Potdar, Sharif & Chang, 2009), or even in the Internet of Things, at the UDP level, with protocols such as CoAP (Castellani et al., 2011). In the opposite direction, security can be provided by the underlying protocol itself, if it is complex enough to support secure transport.

Table 4 illustrates some of the message types in this protocol, which implements basic transactions in an universal way. Any resource can be both sender and receiver of messages.

There is no notion of session. Messages are independent of each other, with coherence maintained by higher interoperability levels, namely the Pragmatic and Symbiotic categories in Table 2. However, the underlying transport protocol can open a channel, such as a socket in the Web Socket protocol (Lubbers, Albers & Salim, 2010), and maintain it open for some predefined time (TTL, Time To Live) or until some consecutive inactivity period occurs. These timings can be defined by any of interacting applications (each can close the channel). If subsequently a message needs to be sent between the interacting applications, the channel is open again, automatically. Timings can be adaptive, depending on message traffic.

The correlation between request and response messages is made by a token value generated at the sender's server (by a pseudo-random number generator) for each message sent. It is meaningful

Table 4. Examples of message types

Message Category/Type	Description
Request	**Initial Request in Each Transaction**
React	React to message, no answer expected
React & respond	React to message and answer/notify
Asynchronous react & respond	Asynchronous data message. Return future immediately
Amendment	**Further Information on an Already Sent Request**
Cancel	Cancel the execution of the request
Response	**Response to the Request**
Answer	Data returned as a response
Resource fault	Data returned as the result of an exception
Protocol fault	Error data resulting from protocol or partner failure
Notification	**Information of Completion Status**
Promise	Confirm reception of asynchronous request and intention to honor it. Return promise to replace future
Denial	Confirm rejection of request
Done	Request completed but has no value to reply
Cancelled	Confirm cancellation of request

in the context of that server only. The receiver of the request must copy this token to the response and forward it in delegation messages, so that the delegate can also include it in the response. The implementation of futures also uses this mechanism.

Implementation

Regarding the status of implementation of SIL, there is a prototype (completely written in Java) with basic functionality, encompassing:

- A compiler based on ANTLR (ANother Tool for Language Recognition) (Parr, 2007), to check the syntax and semantics of resource descriptions and to generate a binary representation;

- An interpreter and a runtime support system (including a service directory), to manage resources and to implement the service behavior;
- Web Sockets (Lubbers, Albers & Salim, 2010) as the underlying transport protocol, with automatic session management;
- A Jetty-based server to support resource links and message based communication.

These constitute the fundamental components of a SIL server, the unit of distributed operation and management. A network of SIL applications must be deployed using SIL servers, just like web applications usually interact by resorting to web servers.

Although SIL is compiled, the code generated is interpreted, much in the line of a Java virtual machine. The instructions generated are binary and are designated *silcodes*. The format of a compiled resource is exactly the same for sending it in a message and for storing it in a persistent medium. A silcode is a sequence of bytes with predefined format, in which the first byte determines the meaning of the bytes that follow, using a modified version of the TLV (Tag, Length, and Value) scheme used by ASN.1 (Dubuisson, 2000).

SIL uses the byte stream as the lowest common denominator for resource serialization and the unit of processing and migration (including communication). This is even more universal than text, with all its variability of formats. The compiler maintains the synchronization between the source (textual) description and silcodes.

There is also a need to retain a degree of compatibility with existing technologies, namely those based on XML, JSON and HTTP. A stream is merely a sequence of bytes, with no format or *endianness* (byte order) defined. The *theme* of a stream is the set of format and organization rules that define the contents of the stream and allow a software processor to interpret its meaning and do something useful with it. A theme may be iden-

Table 5. Comparison of the sizes (in bytes) of several resource representations, from source to binary only

Names	XML	JSON	Silcodes with Source	Silcodes with Ontology	Silcodes without Metadata
Long	2595	1631	1432	953	382
Short	1972	1193	1014	621	382

tified by a specific sequence of bytes (probably using UTF-8 encoding, such as "SIL" or "<?xml") or may require some deeper content inspection.

When a message is received by the SIL server, it checks with each of the defined handlers (for SIL, XML, and so on) whether it recognizes its theme. The first to achieve it gets the message for further processing. In this way, if a message is XML or if it has some other non-SIL format, the platform is still able to process it, as long as a corresponding handler (an XML parser, for example) is available.

The platform is also able to deal with both HTTP and Web Sockets, so that a given URI can be used for both current market technologies and SIL. Although this is far from backwards compatibility, it is nonetheless a step towards an always desirable evolutionary migration path. Delgado (2013) provides additional details on the language and its implementation.

The current implementation of the silcodes interpreter, in pure Java, is optimized for flexibility rather than performance and is roughly 50-100 times slower than a JVM (Java Virtual Machine). Much of that time is spent just on virtual method dispatch, the mechanism used to execute the various silcodes. A C/C++ based interpreter would be faster but less portable and harder to develop and to maintain. Given the need for flexibility and control of implementation, we chose not to use the JVM as a compilation target.

The silcodes format to represent serialized resources supports three levels of metadata (self-description) information, in addition to the data itself: source code, ontology (names and relationships), and no metadata. The latter is used when a previous data type checking was cached by the message receiver and a token returned to the sender, to be used in subsequent messages. The protocol returns an error if metadata is absent and there is no valid token in the message. The sender should then repeat the message, this time with metadata. The ontology-level metadata is the usual case without cache optimization. The source code can be included, if desired, to provide user-level readability.

Table 5 gives an idea of the size of resource representations in various situations. The example refers to a data-only resource, so that XML and JSON can be used for comparison. The two lines refer to the same resource, but with longer and shorter component names, which have an impact on metadata size. That is why the sizes in the last column are the same and the size reduction with less metadata is greater when names are longer. The sizes presented vary with the concrete example, but this gives an idea of the values involved.

An end-to-end application performance comparison with SOA- and REST-based solutions has not been done yet. Trivial examples tend to assess essentially the application servers and network latency, which are not the distinguishing aspects. A meaningful comparison needs to separate concerns, such as protocols, data parsing, platform-agnostic execution (SIL) versus local programming language (e.g., Java), professional versus research implementation, and so on. This will be done in the near future. In the meantime, Sumaray & Makki (2012) have shown that parsing binary data markup (TLV) can be at least an order of magnitude faster than parsing XML text markup.

COMPARISON WITH EXISTING TECHNOLOGIES

Since active interoperability solutions (involving behavior, not just data) are the most relevant for distributed application integration, it is interesting to compare SIL with the two most popular architectural styles in this area, SOA (Erl, 2008) and REST (Webber, Parastatidis & Robinson, 2010). Web Services and REST over HTTP, respectively, are their main market instantiations.

SOA has the goal of a low semantic gap, since it models real-world entities by resources with services that express their capabilities. This is good in modeling terms, but entails a coupling between the provider and the consumer that hampers dynamic changeability and adaptability. If the provider's interface changes, the consumer's needs to change accordingly. There is no apparent structure, since service composition is hidden behind each service's interface.

One of the main goals of REST is to reduce the coupling between consumer and provider, both to increase scalability and adaptability. Real-world entities are modeled in a data-oriented way by resources, all with the same syntactical interface (same set of operations). Semantics are restricted to a set of data types (or schemas), either standardized or previously agreed upon between the interacting entities. The variability of the characteristics of entities is modeled by visible structure (resources composed of other resources) and the semantics of the agreed data types.

Unfortunately, the decoupling claimed by REST is somewhat elusive. Messages cannot be understood simply by exploring their data structure and touching links blindly. Semantics and behavior need to be considered as well, and this is determined by the type of resources used. If, for example, the provider decides to change its data type specifications, the code at the consumer will most likely be unable to cope with that.

What happens, in practice, is that REST over HTTP is simpler to use than Web Services and many applications are simple enough to adopt a data-oriented interface, REST style. This means that, although REST represents a modeling shift from real-world entities (lowering the modeling level and increasing the semantic gap), it is still simpler to use than a full-blown SOA environment. The exceptions are applications sufficiently complex to make the semantic gap visible and relevant enough. This is why REST is preferable in simpler applications and SOA constitutes a better match for complex, enterprise-level applications.

Nevertheless, REST is right about one thing: in a distributed context, interoperability has to be based on structural composition of previously known resource types and not by sharing specific service interfaces. Forcing these to have one single set of operations, however, does not increase adaptability in the general sense; it only leads applications to adopt a data-oriented style (CRUD), which is not adequate for all classes of applications.

This is why SIL supports both application-specific service interfaces and resource structure. On the one hand, services have a user-defined interface that can be published, discovered, and used. On the other hand, services are implemented by resources, which have structure (composed of other resources). Operations are first class resources and messages are themselves resources, able to include references to other resources. As a result, applications can be designed in either SOA or REST styles or, most likely, as a combination of the two, according to the needs of the application. SIL's underlying architectural style is designated *Structural Services*, to reflect both slants.

The SIL approach does not really entail new concepts, but rather a new way to combine those that already exist in SOA and REST. These styles have been compared (Adamczyk, Smith, Johnson & Hafiz, 2011; Castillo et al., 2013) and attempts to combine both styles in one application have been described (Muracevic & Kurtagic, 2009; Li

& Svard, 2010). However, the theme is usually brought up as a decision on which style is the most adequate (Pautasso, Zimmermann & Leymann, 2008) or as a transformation of one style to the other (Peng, Ma & Lee, 2009; Erl, Balasubramanians, Pautasso & Carlyle, 2011; Upadhyaya, Zou, Xiao, Ng & Lau, 2011). SIL aims to solve this problem by providing an architectural style and an integration technology that readily support both SOA and REST styles.

Another fundamental difference is that SIL provides a complete solution, by allowing not only data but also behavior and service interfaces to be specified. The current solutions to implement behavior include external programming languages (e.g., a Web Service or a REST resource implemented in Java) and BPEL (Juric & Pant, 2008), an XML-based language. Services are described separately (e.g., in a WSDL file). Several languages and specifications are needed to implement the full solution. Just like XML, SIL is able to interface other languages, with either static stubs or reflection. However, the programmer has now the possibility of implementing behavior in SIL, at a platform-agnostic level and under the service paradigm.

The coupling inherent to data description languages such as XML and JSON is seldom emphasized. XML supports arbitrary data types, but only as long as their schema are shared by both interacting parties. The same happens with WSDL documents. A client will only be able to access the Web Service for which it has been designed. JSON usually resorts to a simpler method: the data types need to be previously agreed upon by the interacting parties or be standardized. In both the XML and JSON cases, coupling resulting from this data type sharing prevents a client from using another server, or a server from using a client not designed for it.

SIL follows another approach, in which types are checked structurally and dynamically for compliance and conformance. As long as the required components are present, interaction is possible by mapping the components of one interacting party to the matching components of the other. This is a slow operation, but this mapping can be cached and reused in future interactions, which is particularly effective in repetitive interactions that invoke a given operation.

Compliance and conformance extend to the ontology level, usually based in Description Logic (Baader et al., 2010). OWL (Grau et al., 2008) is the most common language, but constitutes an add-on to interoperability solutions. Based on XML, OWL has to specify individuals, concepts, roles and axioms in a cumbersome syntax, not designed for this purpose. As illustrated by Figure 5, SIL has been conceived to specify individual resources (named components), concepts (archetype definitions), roles (relations established between resources and their components) and axioms and rules, introduced as statements. Unlike OWL, the knowledge base can be structured. Each resource, with its internal structure of definitions, constitutes an ontology, with all public definitions accessible by paths (using dot notation). Like OWL, in accordance with Description Logic, SIL uses the open world assumption, in which a concept is not necessarily described completely by a type but rather is consistent (compatible) with that type. This allows having more features than those described by that type. That is the underlying philosophy of compliance and conformance, which are also the foundation for ontology mapping, a concept fundamental for interoperability. Instead of qualifying names of components with namespaces, as XML does, SIL qualifies names by using full-fledged ontologies (which can be imported by each resource).

As a distributed programming language, SIL cannot exist without a communication protocol, which has been briefly described in Table 4. This is a minimalist specification, encompassing only what is needed for generic message-based interaction. All other higher-level features, such as security, routing, or other application-specific transformation, need to be built on top of the basic protocol, by encapsulating messages in more complex ones, with additional information. Essentially, it just adds a message processing layer to an underlying transport-level protocol, which depends on the network used but must support binary messages and asynchronous, full duplex interaction.

In contrast, HTTP is an application-level protocol, synchronous and committed to the client-server paradigm, which does not support full duplex, long running sessions required by general service interoperability. Workaround technologies such as AJAX (Holdener, 2008) and Comet (Crane & McCarthy, 2008) now have an alternative approach, Web Sockets (Lubbers, Albers & Salim, 2010). Unsurprisingly, HTTP also mixes several levels of Table 2, given that it was conceived for a specific problem and not as a general-purpose interoperability solution. SOAP is more general than HTTP but is more complex and also includes several higher-level features, namely non-functional information and routing. The SIL protocol decouples all these features and deals with them above the transport and message levels, either by endowing messages with contextual information, either by forwarding them to other services. This allows the message protocol to remain simple and independent from the underlying transport protocol and from higher-level features, which should be based on the normal message mechanisms and not be included in the message protocol itself.

SIL can also be used to implement distributed interoperability platforms, namely involving clouds. The typical solution for cloud portability and cloud API interoperability is to use shared specifications, but this usually leads to vendor lock-in. OVF (DTMF, 2012) is a standard that allows applications to be packaged and deployed to virtualized systems. It uses a compressed archive file that includes the binary images to be deployed and a manifest file with a description of the contents of the archive. It is a file-based solution, which needs specific treatment. Since SIL supports binary data, images can be included directly in a single SIL program, which can also include install scripts that can detect the target platform and select the binary image automatically. Data and scripts can be protected by security mechanisms, at the message and authentication levels. In addition, compliance and conformance can be applied to check whether a given SIL program (containing an application to deploy) is compliant with a given cloud's server or if that server is conformant to what the application requires, without additional specific mechanisms. Regarding cloud API portability, the support of SIL to both rich-interface services and rich-structure resources enables resource-by-resource cloud management, including only the features actually required by each resource. The trick is to add management operations to each resource. This does not affect in any way the type of that resource, since these extra operations are qualified by a management ontology and SIL uses the open world assumption (based on structural compliance and conformance).

Table 6 summarizes the main characteristics of integration solutions based on SOA, REST and SIL.

FUTURE RESEARCH DIRECTIONS

The work that this chapter described follows an approach that entails defining a new language, with the basic goal of minimizing the constraints and limitations of current interoperability solutions. This goal is pursued with a single language, adequate to most of the levels of the interoperability stack (Table 2), instead of a plethora of languages and specifications.

A new language means opportunity for innovation but also risk and much work, since there is a complete world to discover without experience and tools on which development can be based. Therefore, the goal of SIL is not to replace the existing technologies, but rather

Table 6. Comparison between SIL and integration solutions based on SOA and REST

Characteristic	SOA (Web Services)	RESTful Applications	SIL (Structural Services)
Basic tenet	Behavior	Hypermedia (structure + links)	Tunable between pure behavior and pure hypermedia
Distinguishing features	Resource-specific interface; Operations are entry points to a service; Design-time service declaration	Uniform interface; Operations are resources; Clients react to structure received (do not invoke resource interfaces)	Variable resource interface; Resources are structured; Operations are resources; Links are resources; Resource types need not be known at design time
Best applicability	Large-grained resources (application integration)	Small-grained resources (CRUD-oriented APIs)	Wide range (small to large, behavior to structured-oriented)
Structure exposed	Behavior	State and behavior	State and behavior
Interoperability based on	Schema sharing	Predefined media types	Structural compatibility (compliance and conformance)
Coupling	Significant	Significant	Minimum
Self-description	Repository (e.g., WSDL document)	Content type declaration in resource representations	Included in each resource, message or application resource
Design time support	High	Low	High
Complexity	High	Low	Low
Main advantages	Low semantic gap (resources model closely real-world entities)	Structured resources, with links to other resources (hypermedia)	Low semantic gap + structured resources with links + structural compatibility
Main fallacy	Resource structure is unimportant	Hypermedia increases decoupling	None identified
Main limitation	No polymorphism (coupling higher than needed)	Fixed interface (semantic gap higher than needed)	None identified

to constitute a means to research a new path to the old problem of interoperability, without the constraint of compatibility with existing specifications.

The work on this approach is in its infancy and much remains to be done before it can be realistically tested and its capabilities demonstrated. Future research will include the following activities and approaches:

- Carrying out a comparative study, with qualitative and quantitative assessment, between SIL, its platform and the Structural Services architectural style, on one side, and all the current technologies, specifications, models and architectural styles for the interoperability of web applications, on the other;

- Compliance and conformance are basic concepts in interoperability and can be applied to all domains and levels of abstraction and complexity. Although work exists on its formal treatment in specific areas, such as choreographies (Adriansyah, van Dongen & van der Aalst, 2010), an encompassing and systematic study needs to be conducted regarding what is the formal meaning of compliance and conformance in each of the levels of Table 2;

- Cloud interoperability (Loutas, Kamateri, Bosi & Tarabanis, 2011) is a huge problem with ever-increasingly importance. Cloud providers favor standardization but not homogeneity, since they need differentiation as a marketing argument. A study needs to be carried out on the suitability of compliance and conformance as a partial interoperability solution in cloud computing, including the possibility of defining APIs at the resource level, as discussed above;

- Extending SIL with constructs to support the definition of choreographies (Bravetti & Zavattaro, 2007) and to be able to search for compatible services. The basic idea is to specify the definition of a choreography with interactions that require service roles and form an automaton, which choreography participants must comply with and conform to, at the choreography level in Table 2. Compatibility (compliance and conformance) must hold at all interoperability levels;

- The current compliance and conformance algorithms are implemented just at design time, by the compiler. These algorithms also need to be implemented at the binary level, so that messages can be checked upon arrival, with cache-based mechanisms to optimize message exchange and dynamic resource type checking. The effectiveness of these mechanisms needs to be assessed;

- Completing the implementation, since some aspects have been designed but are not implemented yet, such as structural ontology mapping;

- An assessment of application scenarios. One idea concerns bringing together a SIL server and a conventional browser, working in tight cooperation, which is designated a *browserver* (Delgado, 2012). This has been conceived to replace the browser as a Web access device (at the user's laptop, tablet, or smart phone) with the goal of turning the user into a first class Web citizen. This aims at improving the interactivity experience and allowing to automatically offer services (including private information for customization, context awareness, ambient intelligence, authentication, gathering statistics and information on usage patterns,

direct browserver to browserver interaction, and so on). Distributed applications will no longer be an exclusive of computer-to-computer interaction. WebRTC (Johnston, Yoakum & Singh, 2013; Becke, M. et al., 2013) is an effort to add real-time voice and video communication capabilities to browsers, enabling browser-to-browser communication. However, this is limited in scope, based on current technologies and their constraints, and does not entail generic service or resource models;

- In spite of all its diversity, the Web is a rather homogenous network (all web devices use HTTP as the underlying protocol and text-based data description languages), with a very reliable backbone. This is not particularly suitable for newer networks and environments, such as the Internet of Things (Luigi, Iera & Morabito, 2010) and mesh network applications (Benyamina, Hafid & Gendreau, 2012). Dynamic and adaptive protocols, using messages with binary formats, constitute a better match. The interoperability problem in heterogeneous environments acquires completely new proportions and innovative solutions need to be envisaged.

CONCLUSION

This chapter has discussed the interoperability problem, in particular in distributed and heterogeneous environments. The conclusions drawn from the arguments and ideas presented can be briefly described along the following lines:

1. Current technologies for distributed interoperability are essentially supported, in one way or another, on textual data description languages (XML and JSON) and on a stateless and connectionless protocol (HTTP). Their roots lie in the original problem of

human-level interaction (browsing) and no longer constitute a good match to the current range of global interoperability problems, now dominated by computers and involving binary data and real-time communications, in heterogeneous environments and networks;

2. XML and JSON are too low level, forcing all kinds of specifications, such as WDSL, SOAP, BPEL and semantic descriptions, to adopt verbose and inefficient mappings to their syntax. HTTP is too high level, with many application-level decisions taken in the context for which it was designed, but not adequate to current contexts. The protocol should be layered and readily support binary data, generic message-level processing and asynchronous, full-duplex communication;

3. Currently, there seem to be too many specifications and languages to cover the various levels of interoperability in Table 2. This is a consequence of using description languages defined before tackling some of these more seriously, such as semantics, but also of using a passive artifact (the document) as a foundation for the Web, instead of an active one (service implemented by a resource). A paradigm shift, in this respect, may make all the difference;

4. Coupling between distributed applications is higher than needed. Typically, either schemas are fully shared between interacting applications, the approach followed by Web Services, or schemas are limited to predefined types (standardized or previously agreed upon), the approach taken by RESTful applications;

5. There is a dichotomy between rich service interfaces (offered by Web services) and structured resources (offered by RESTful applications). There is no support for structured resources with rich service interfaces, to better tune the applications to the nature and requirements of the real-world problem to solve;

6. The typical evolution of technologies is to start simple and well matched to the problem they intend to solve, but then grow more powerful, more complex and not always better matched to the problem. This is what happened with the XML and Web Services world. The growing popularity of JSON and RESTful applications and APIs clearly shows that people prefer to lose expressive power to keep things simple enough and manageable. This also means that established technologies, with good support from commercially available tools, can be displaced by alternative solutions if these are simpler, effective and provide a good match to the problem to solve.

The advices that this chapter provides to these challenges can be summarized as follows:

1. Use text for human-level descriptions, but add a compiler to convert it to binary format. To people what is human-level, to computers what is binary. Change from the client-server model to peer-level interactions, with reversible roles and a full-duplex protocol that supports structured binary data;

2. Describe interacting applications by active resources, offering services, with a description language that natively supports them, in a more familiar programming kind of syntax. Use a protocol that clearly separates the various levels at which interaction needs to occur, using Table 2 as a guideline;

3. Include (in the description language) support for the various levels of interoperability, including structure, messaging, semantics, services, actions and multiple transaction interaction (choreographies). This way, one language will be enough to cater for most of the interoperability issues and aspects;

4. Use structural compatibility (compliance and conformance), coupled with ontology support, as the foundation artifact to ensure

interoperability. This will provide just enough coupling to solve the problem while increasing the consumer and provider base available to interact with a given application. Compliance and conformance are universal concepts, involved in all interactions at all levels;

5. Provide support for both rich service interfaces and structured resources. This needs to be a central feature of the description language. The best of SOA and REST will be possible in the same application;

6. Structure the description language and protocol according to a framework such as the one provided by Table 2, with vertical extensions (in complexity level) done by moving up one level in the interoperability ladder (typically, by wrapping or composing artifacts in the level below) instead of mixing several custom solutions. This will maximize the extensibility of specifications without compromising simplicity or suitability to a wide range of problems to solve.

REFERENCES

Adamczyk, P., Smith, P., Johnson, R., & Hafiz, M. (2011). REST and web services: In theory and in practice. In E. Wilde & C. Pautasso (Eds.), *REST: From research to practice* (pp. 35–57). New York, NY: Springer. doi:10.1007/978-1-4419-8303-9_2

Adriansyah, A., van Dongen, B., & van der Aalst, W. (2010). Towards robust conformance checking. In M. Muehlen & J. Su (Eds.), *Business process management workshops* (pp. 122–133). Berlin, Germany: Springer.

Aggarwal, C., & Han, J. (2013). A survey of RFID data processing. In C. Aggarwal (Ed.), *Managing and mining sensor data* (pp. 349–382). New York, NY: Springer US. doi:10.1007/978-1-4614-6309-2_11

Armbrust, M., Stoica, I., Zaharia, M., Fox, A., Griffith, R., Joseph, A. D., & Rabkin, A. et al. (2010). A view of cloud computing. *Communications of the ACM, 53*(4), 50–58. doi:10.1145/1721654.1721672

Athanasopoulos, G., Tsalgatidou, A., & Pantazoglou, M. (2006). Interoperability among heterogeneous services. In *Proceedings of International Conference on Services Computing* (pp. 174-181). Piscataway, NJ: IEEE Society Press.

Baader, F et al. (Eds.). (2010). *The description logic handbook: theory, implementation, and applications* (2nd ed.). Cambridge, UK: Cambridge university press.

Becke, M., Rathgeb, E. P., Werner, S., Rungeler, I., Tuxen, M., & Stewart, R. (2013). Data channel considerations for RTCWeb. *IEEE Communications Magazine, 51*(4), 34–41. doi:10.1109/MCOM.2013.6495758

Benyamina, D., Hafid, A., & Gendreau, M. (2012). Wireless mesh networks design – A survey. *IEEE Communications Surveys and Tutorials, 14*(2), 299–310. doi:10.1109/SURV.2011.042711.00007

Berners-Lee, T. (1999). *Weaving the web: The original design and ultimate destiny of the world wide web by its inventor.* New York, NY: HarperCollins Publishers.

Berre, A. (2007). The ATHENA interoperability framework. In R. Gonçalves, J. Müller, K. Mertins, & M. Zelm (Eds.), *Enterprise interoperability II* (pp. 569–580). London, UK: Springer. doi:10.1007/978-1-84628-858-6_62

Binz, T., Breiter, G., Leyman, F., & Spatzier, T. (2012). Portable cloud services using Tosca. *IEEE Internet Computing, 16*(3), 80–85. doi:10.1109/MIC.2012.43

Bist, M., Wariya, M., & Agarwal, A. (2013). Comparing delta, open stack and Xen cloud platforms: A survey on open source IaaS. In KalraB. GargD.PrasadR.KumarS. (Eds.) *3rd International Advance Computing Conference* (pp. 96-100). Ghaziabad, India: IEEE Computer Society Press. doi:10.1109/IAdCC.2013.6514201

Bravetti, M., & Zavattaro, G. (2007). Towards a unifying theory for choreography conformance and contract compliance. In LumpeM.VanderperrenW. (Eds.) *6th International Symposium on Software Composition* (pp. 34-50). Berlin, Germany: Springer. doi:10.1007/978-3-540-77351-1_4

Castellani, A. (2011). Web Services for the Internet of Things through CoAP and EXI. In *Proceedings of International Conference on Communications Workshops* (pp. 1-6). Kyoto, Japan: IEEE Computer Society Press.

Castillo, P. (2013). Using SOAP and REST web services as communication protocol for distributed evolutionary computation. *International Journal of Computers & Technology*, *10*(6), 1659–1677.

Chen, D. (2006). Enterprise interoperability framework. In MissikoffM.De NicolaA.D'AntonioF. (Eds.) *Open interop workshop on enterprise modelling and ontologies for interoperability*. Berlin, Germany: Springer-Verlag.

Crane, D., & McCarthy, P. (2008). *Comet and reverse Ajax: The next-generation Ajax 2.0.* Berkeley, CA: Apress.

Delgado, J. (2012). The user as a service. In D. Vidyarthi (Ed.), *Technologies and protocols for the future of internet design: Reinventing the web* (pp. 37–59). Hershey, PA: IGI Global. doi:10.4018/978-1-4666-0203-8.ch003

Delgado, J. (2013). Service interoperability in the internet of things. In N. Bessis (Eds.), *Internet of things and inter-cooperative computational technologies for collective intelligence* (pp. 51–87). Berlin, Germany: Springer. doi:10.1007/978-3-642-34952-2_3

Demchenko, Y., Makkes, M., Strijkers, R., & de Laat, C. (2012). Intercloud architecture for interoperability and integration. In *Proceedings of 4th International Conference on Cloud Computing Technology and Science* (pp. 666-674). Taipe, Taiwan: IEEE Computer Society Press. doi:10.1109/CloudCom.2012.6427607

DTMF. (2012). *Open virtualization format specification*. Document Number: DSP0243, version 2.0.0. Portland, OR: Distributed Management Task Force, Inc. Retrieved May 30, 2014 from http://www.dmtf.org/sites/default/files/standards/documents/DSP0243_2.0.0.pdf

DTMF. (2013). *Cloud infrastructure management interface (CIMI) model and REST interface over HTTP specification*. Document Number: DSP0263, version 1.1.0. Portland, OR: Distributed Management Task Force, Inc. Retrieved May 30, 2014 from http://www.dmtf.org/sites/default/files/standards/documents/DSP0263_1.1.0.pdf

Dubuisson, O. (2000). *ASN.1 communication between heterogeneous systems*. San Diego, CA: Academic Press.

Edmonds, A., Metsch, T., & Papaspyrou, A. (2011). Open cloud computing interface in data management-related setups. In S. Fiore & G. Aloisio (Eds.), *Grid and cloud database management* (pp. 23–48). Berlin, Germany: Springer. doi:10.1007/978-3-642-20045-8_2

EIF. (2010). *European interoperability framework (EIF) for European public services, annex 2 to the communication from the commission to the European Parliament, the council, the European economic and social committee and the committee of regions towards interoperability for European public services.* Retrieved May 30, 2014 from http://ec.europa.eu/isa/documents/isa_annex_ii_eif_en.pdf

El Raheb, K. (2011). Paving the way for interoperability in digital libraries: The DL.org project. In A. Katsirikou & C. Skiadas (Eds.), *New trends in qualitive and quantitative methods in libraries* (pp. 345–352). Singapore: World Scientific Publishing Company.

Erl, T. (2008). *SOA: Principles of service design.* Upper Saddle River, NJ: Prentice Hall PTR.

Erl, T., Balasubramanians, R., Pautasso, C., & Carlyle, B. (2011). *Soa with rest: Principles, patterns & constraints for building enterprise solutions with REST.* Upper Saddle River, NJ: Prentice Hall PTR.

Euzenat, J., & Shvaiko, P. (2007). *Ontology matching.* Berlin, Germany: Springer.

Fernando, N., Loke, S., & Rahayu, W. (2013). Mobile cloud computing: A survey. *Future Generation Computer Systems, 29*(1), 84–106. doi:10.1016/j.future.2012.05.023

Fielding, R. (2000). *Architectural styles and the design of network-based software architectures.* (Doctoral dissertation). University of California, Irvine, CA.

Galiegue, F., & Zyp, K. (Eds.). (2013). *JSON schema: Core definitions and terminology.* Internet Engineering Task Force. Retrieved May 30, 2014 from https://tools.ietf.org/html/draft-zyp-json-schema-04

Gottschalk, P., & Solli-Sæther, H. (2008). Stages of e-government interoperability. *Electronic Government: International Journal (Toronto, Ont.), 5*(3), 310–320.

Grau, B., Horrocks, I., Motik, B., Parsia, B., Patel-Schneider, P., & Sattler, U. (2008). OWL 2: The next step for OWL. *Web Semantics: Science, Services, and Agents on the World Wide Web, 6*(4), 309–322. doi:10.1016/j.websem.2008.05.001

Gubbi, J., Buyya, R., Marusic, S., & Palaniswami, M. (2013). Internet of things (IoT): A vision, architectural elements, and future directions. *Future Generation Computer Systems, 29*(7), 1645–1660. doi:10.1016/j.future.2013.01.010

Hartenstein, H., & Laberteaux, K. (Eds.). (2010). *VANET: Vehicular applications and inter-networking technologies.* Chichester, UK: Wiley. doi:10.1002/9780470740637

Holdener, A. III. (2008). *Ajax: The definitive guide.* Sebastopol, CA: O'Reilly Media, Inc.

Hughes, D., Coulson, G., & Walkerdine, J. (2010). A survey of peer-to-peer architectures for service oriented computing. In Handbook of research on P2P and grid systems for service-oriented computing: Models, methodologies and applications (pp. 1-19). Hershey, PA: IGI Global. doi:10.4018/978-1-61520-686-5.ch001

ISO/IEC. (2012). *Information technology -- Cloud data management interface (CDMI): ISO/IEC standard 17826:2012.* Geneva, Switzerland: International Organization for Standardization.

Iyengar, S., & Brooks, R. (Eds.). (2012). *Distributed sensor networks: Sensor networking and applications.* Boca Raton, FL: CRC Press. doi:10.1201/b12988

Jackson, K. (2012). *OpenStack cloud computing cookbook.* Birmingham, UK: Packt Publishing Ltd.

Jardim-Goncalves, R., Agostinho, C., & Steiger-Garcao, A. (2012). A reference model for sustainable interoperability in networked enterprises: Towards the foundation of EI science base. *International Journal of Computer Integrated Manufacturing, 25*(10), 855–873. doi:10.1080/0951192X.2011.653831

Jardim-Goncalves, R., Grilo, A., Agostinho, C., Lampathaki, F., & Charalabidis, Y. (2013). Systematisation of interoperability body of knowledge: The foundation for enterprise interoperability as a science. *Enterprise Information Systems, 7*(1), 7–32. doi:10.1080/17517575.2012.684401

Järvi, J., & Freeman, J. (2010). C++ lambda expressions and closures. *Science of Computer Programming, 75*(9), 762–772. doi:10.1016/j.scico.2009.04.003

Jeong, B., Lee, D., Cho, H., & Lee, J. (2008). A novel method for measuring semantic similarity for XML schema matching. *Expert Systems with Applications, 34*(3), 1651–1658. doi:10.1016/j.eswa.2007.01.025

Johnston, A., Yoakum, J., & Singh, K. (2013). Taking on WebRTC in an enterprise. *Communications Magazine, IEEE, 51*(4), 48–54. doi:10.1109/MCOM.2013.6495760

Juric, M., & Pant, K. (2008). *Business process driven SOA using BPMN and BPEL: From business process modeling to orchestration and service oriented architecture.* Birmingham, UK: Packt Publishing.

Keyes, J. (2013). *Bring your own devices (BYOD) survival guide.* Boca Raton, FL: CRC Press. doi:10.1201/b14050

Khadka, R. (2011). Model-driven development of service compositions for enterprise interoperability. In Enterprise interoperability (pp. 177-190). Berlin, Germany: Springer-Verlag. doi:10.1007/978-3-642-19680-5_15

Kim, D., & Shen, W. (2007). An approach to evaluating structural pattern conformance of UML models. In *Proceedings of ACM Symposium on Applied Computing* (pp. 1404-1408). New York, NY: ACM Press. doi:10.1145/1244002.1244305

Kokash, N., & Arbab, F. (2009). Formal behavioral modeling and compliance analysis for service-oriented systems. In F. Boer, M. Bonsangue, & E. Madelaine (Eds.), *Formal methods for components and objects* (pp. 21–41). Berlin, Germany: Springer-Verlag. doi:10.1007/978-3-642-04167-9_2

Laitkorpi, M., Selonen, P., & Systa, T. (2009). Towards a model-driven process for designing ReSTful web services. In *Proceedings of International Conference on Web Services* (pp. 173-180). Los Angeles, CA: IEEE Computer Society Press. doi:10.1109/ICWS.2009.63

Lewis, G. (2012). *The role of standards in cloud-computing interoperability.* Software Engineering Institute. Retrieved May 30, 2014 from http://repository.cmu.edu/sei/682

Li, L., & Chou, W. (2010). Design patterns for RESTful communication. In *Proceedings of International Conference on Web Services* (pp. 512-519). Piscataway, NJ: IEEE Computer Society Press.

Li, W., & Svard, P. (2010). REST-based SOA application in the cloud: A text correction service case study. In *Proceedings of 6th World Congress on Services* (pp. 84-90). Piscataway, NJ: IEEE Society Press. doi:10.1109/SERVICES.2010.86

Loutas, N., Kamateri, E., Bosi, F., & Tarabanis, K. (2011). Cloud computing interoperability: the state of play. In *Proceedings of International Conference on Cloud Computing Technology and Science* (pp. 752-757). Piscataway, NJ: IEEE Computer Society Press. doi:10.1109/CloudCom.2011.116

Loutas, N., Peristeras, V., & Tarabanis, K. (2011). Towards a reference service model for the web of services. *Data & Knowledge Engineering, 70*(9), 753–774. doi:10.1016/j.datak.2011.05.001

Lubbers, P., Albers, B., & Salim, F. (2010). *Pro HTML5 programming: Powerful APIs for richer internet application development.* New York, NY: Apress. doi:10.1007/978-1-4302-2791-5

Luigi, A., Iera, A., & Morabito, G. (2010). The internet of things: A survey. *Computer Networks, 54*(15), 2787–2805. doi:10.1016/j.comnet.2010.05.010

Mell, P., & Grance, T. (2011). *The NIST definition of cloud computing.* National Institute of Standards and Technology. Retrieved May 30, 2014 from http://csrc.nist.gov/publications/nistpubs/800-145/SP800-145.pdf

Muracevic, D., & Kurtagic, H. (2009). Geospatial SOA using RESTful web services. In *Proceedings of 31st International Conference on Information Technology Interfaces* (pp. 199-204). Piscataway, NJ: IEEE Society Press.

Mykkänen, J., & Tuomainen, M. (2008). An evaluation and selection framework for interoperability standards. *Information and Software Technology, 50*(3), 176–197. doi:10.1016/j.infsof.2006.12.001

Nurmi, D. (2009). The eucalyptus open-source cloud-computing system. In *Proceedings of 9th IEEE/ACM International Symposium on Cluster Computing and the Grid* (pp. 124-131). Shanghai, China: IEEE Computer Society Press.

Palm, J., Anderson, K., & Lieberherr, K. (2003). *Investigating the relationship between violations of the law of demeter and software maintainability.* Paper presented at the Workshop on Software-Engineering Properties of Languages for Aspect Technologies. Retrieved May 30, 2014 from http://www.daimi.au.dk/~eernst/splat03/papers/Jeffrey_Palm.pdf

Parr, T. (2007). *The definitive ANTLR reference.* Raleigh, NC: The Pragmatic Bookshelf.

Pautasso, C., Zimmermann, O., & Leymann, F. (2008). Restful web services vs. "big" web services: Making the right architectural decision. In *Proceedings of International Conference on World Wide Web* (pp. 805-814). ACM Press.

Peng, Y., Ma, S., & Lee, J. (2009). REST2SOAP: A framework to integrate SOAP services and RESTful services. In *Proceedings of International Conference on Service-Oriented Computing and Applications* (pp. 1-4). Piscataway, NJ: IEEE Computer Society Press. doi:10.1109/SOCA.2009.5410458

Potdar, V., Sharif, A., & Chang, E. (2009). Wireless sensor networks: A survey. In *Proceedings of International Conference on Advanced Information Networking and Applications Workshops* (pp. 636-641). Bradford, UK: IEEE Computer Society Press. doi:10.1109/WAINA.2009.192

Rimal, B., Choi, E., & Lumb, I. (2009). A taxonomy and survey of cloud computing systems. In *Proceedings of Fifth International Joint Conference on INC, IMS and IDC* (pp. 44-51). Seoul, Korea: IEEE Computer Society Press. doi:10.1109/NCM.2009.218

Sabharwal, N., & Shankar, R. (2013). *Apache cloudstack cloud computing.* Birmingham, UK: Packt Publishing Ltd.

Schippers, H. (2009). Towards an actor-based concurrent machine model. In *Proceedings of 4th Workshop on the Implementation, Compilation, Optimization of Object-Oriented Languages and Programming Systems* (pp. 4-9). New York, NY: ACM Press.

Seinstra, F. (2011). Jungle computing: Distributed supercomputing beyond clusters, grids, and clouds. In M. Cafaro & G. Aloisio (Eds.), *Grids, clouds and virtualization* (pp. 167–197). London, UK: Springer.

Sumaray, A., & Makki, S. (2012). A comparison of data serialization formats for optimal efficiency on a mobile platform. In *Proceedings of 6th International Conference on Ubiquitous Information Management and Communication* (article no. 48). New York, NY: ACM Press. doi:10.1145/2184751.2184810

Tolk, A. (2006). What comes after the semantic web - PADS implications for the dynamic web. In *Proceedings of 20th Workshop on Principles of Advanced and Distributed Simulation* (pp. 55-62). Beach Road, Singapore: IEEE Computer Society Press. doi:10.1109/PADS.2006.39

Toshniwal, R., & Agrawal, D. (2004). Tracing the roots of markup languages. *Communications of the ACM*, *47*(5), 95–98. doi:10.1145/986213.986218

Upadhyaya, B., Zou, Y., Xiao, H., Ng, J., & Lau, A. (2011). Migration of SOAP-based services to RESTful services. In *Proceedings of 13th IEEE International Symposium on Web Systems Evolution* (pp. 105-114). Piscataway, NJ: IEEE Society Press. doi:10.1109/WSE.2011.6081828

Villegas, D. (2010). The role of grid computing technologies in cloud computing. In B. Furht & A. Escalante (Eds.), *Handbook of cloud computing* (pp. 183–218). New York, NY: Springer US. doi:10.1007/978-1-4419-6524-0_8

Wang, W., Tolk, A., & Wang, W. (2009). The levels of conceptual interoperability model: Applying systems engineering principles to M&S. In *Proceedings of Spring Simulation Multiconference* (article no.: 168). San Diego, CA: Society for Computer Simulation International.

Webber, J., Parastatidis, S., & Robinson, I. (2010). *REST in practice: Hypermedia and systems architecture*. Sebastopol, CA: O'Reilly Media, Inc. doi:10.1007/978-3-642-15114-9_3

Weber-Jahnke, J., Peyton, L., & Topaloglou, T. (2012). eHealth system interoperability. *Information Systems Frontiers*, *14*(1), 1–3. doi:10.1007/s10796-011-9319-8

Wyatt, E., Griendling, K., & Mavris, D. (2012). Addressing interoperability in military systems-of-systems architectures. In *Proceedings of International Systems Conference* (pp. 1-8). Piscataway, NJ: IEEE Computer Society Press.

Zhang, Q., Cheng, L., & Boutaba, R. (2010). Cloud computing: State-of-the-art and research challenges. *Journal of Internet Services and Applications*, *1*(1), 7–18. doi:10.1007/s13174-010-0007-6

Zikopoulos, P. (2012). *Understanding big data*. New York, NY: McGraw-Hill.

ADDITIONAL READING

Amundsen, M. (2012, April). From APIs to affordances: a new paradigm for web services. In *Proceedings of the Third International Workshop on RESTful Design* (pp. 53-60). ACM Press. doi:10.1145/2307819.2307832

Bravetti, M., & Zavattaro, G. (2009). A theory of contracts for strong service compliance. *Journal of Mathematical Structures in Computer Science*, *19*(3), 601–638. doi:10.1017/S0960129509007658

Chandler, D. (2007). *Semiotics: the basics*. New York, NY: Routledge.

Diaz, G., & Rodriguez, I. (2009). Automatically deriving choreography-conforming systems of services. In *IEEE International Conference on Services Computing* (pp. 9-16). Piscataway, NJ: IEEE Society Press.

Dillon, T., Wu, C., & Chang, E. (2007). Reference architectural styles for service-oriented computing. In LiK. (Eds.) *IFIP International Conference on Network and parallel computing* (pp. 543–555). Berlin, Germany: Springer-Verlag. doi:10.1007/978-3-540-74784-0_57

Ehrig, M. (2007). Ontology alignment: bridging the semantic gap (Vol. 4). New York, NY: Springer Science+Business Media, LLC.

Erl, T. (2005). *Service-oriented architecture: concepts, technology and design*. Upper Saddle River, NJ: Pearson Education.

Fielding, R. (2008). REST APIs must be hypertext-driven. *Roy Fielding's blog: Untangled*. Retrieved May 30, 2014 from http://roy.gbiv.com/untangled/2008/rest-apis-must-be-hypertext-driven

Fielding, R., & Taylor, R. (2002). Principled Design of the Modern Web Architecture. *ACM Transactions on Internet Technology*, 2(2), 115–150. doi:10.1145/514183.514185

Gray, N. (2004). Comparison of Web Services, Java-RMI, and CORBA service implementations. In SchneiderJ.HanJ. (Eds.) *The Fifth Australasian Workshop on Software and System Architectures* (pp. 52-63). Melbourne, Australia: Swinburne University of Technology.

Graydon, P., Habli, I., Hawkins, R., Kelly, T., & Knight, J. (2012). Arguing Conformance. *IEEE Software*, 29(3), 50–57. doi:10.1109/MS.2012.26

Greefhorst, D., & Proper, E. (2011). *Architecture principles: the cornerstones of enterprise architecture*. Berlin, Germany: Springer-Verlag. doi:10.1007/978-3-642-20279-7

Haslhofer, B., & Klas, W. (2010). A survey of techniques for achieving metadata interoperability. *ACM Computing Surveys*, 42(2), 7:1-37.

Henkel, M., Zdravkovic, J., & Johannesson, P. (2004). Service-based Processes– Design for Business and Technology. In *International Conference on Service Oriented Computing* (pp. 21-29). New York, NY: ACM Press.

ISO/IEC/IEEE. (2010). *Systems and software engineering – Vocabulary. International Standard ISO/IEC/IEEE 24765:2010(E)* (1st ed., p. 186). Geneva, Switzerland: International Organization for Standardization.

Jardim-Goncalves, R., Grilo, A., Agostinho, C., Lampathaki, F., & Charalabidis, Y. (2013). Systematisation of Interoperability Body of Knowledge: The foundation for Enterprise Interoperability as a science. *Enterprise Information Systems*, 7(1), 7–32. doi:10.1080/17517575.2012.684401

Jardim-Goncalves, R., Popplewell, K., & Grilo, A. (2012). Sustainable interoperability: The future of Internet based industrial enterprises. *Computers in Industry*, 63(8), 731–738. doi:10.1016/j.compind.2012.08.016

Läufer, K., Baumgartner, G., & Russo, V. (2000). Safe Structural Conformance for Java. [Oxford, UK: Oxford University Press.]. *The Computer Journal*, 43(6), 469–481. doi:10.1093/comjnl/43.6.469

Loreto, S., & Romano, S. (2012). Real-time communications in the web: Issues, achievements, and ongoing standardization efforts. *IEEE Internet Computing*, 16(5), 68–73. doi:10.1109/MIC.2012.115

Mooij, A., & Voorhoeve, M. (2013). Specification and Generation of Adapters for System Integration. In van de Laar, P., Tretmans, J. & Borth, M. (Eds.) Situation Awareness with Systems of Systems (pp. 173-187). New York, NY: Springer. doi:10.1007/978-1-4614-6230-9_11

Ostadzadeh, S., & Fereidoon, S. (2011). An Architectural Framework for the Improvement of the Ultra-Large-Scale Systems Interoperability. In *International Conference on Software Engineering Research and Practice*. Las Vegas, NV.

Pautasso, C. (2009). RESTful Web service composition with BPEL for REST. *Data & Knowledge Engineering*, 68(9), 851–866. doi:10.1016/j.datak.2009.02.016

Popplewell, K. (2011). Towards the definition of a science base for enterprise interoperability: A European perspective. *Journal of Systemics, Cybernetics, and Informatics*, 9(5), 6–11.

Severance, C. (2012). Discovering JavaScript Object Notation. *IEEE Computer, 45*(4), 6–8. doi:10.1109/MC.2012.132

Shadbolt, N., Hall, W., & Berners-Lee, T. (2006). The semantic web revisited. *IEEE Intelligent Systems, 21*(3), 96–101. doi:10.1109/MIS.2006.62

Sheth, A., Gomadam, K., & Lathem, J. (2007). SA-REST: Semantically interoperable and easier-to-use services and mashups. *IEEE Internet Computing, 11*(6), 91–94. doi:10.1109/MIC.2007.133

Uram, M., & Stephenson, B. (2005). Services are the Language and Building Blocks of an Agile Enterprise. In N. Pal & D. Pantaleo (Eds.), *The Agile Enterprise* (pp. 49–86). New York, NY: Springer. doi:10.1007/0-387-25078-6_4

KEY TERMS AND DEFINITIONS

Architectural Style: A set of constraints on the concepts of an architecture and on their relationships.

Compliance: Asymmetric property between a consumer C and a provider P (C is compliant with P) that indicates that C satisfies all the requirements of P in terms of accepting requests.

Conformance: Asymmetric property between a provider P and a consumer C (P conforms to C) that indicates that P fulfills all the expectations of C in terms of the effects caused by its requests.

Consumer: A role performed by a resource A in an interaction with another B, which involves making a request to B and typically waiting for a response.

Distributed Interoperability: Interoperability between systems that have independent lifecycles. This means that they can evolve (to a new version) without having to change, to suspend or to stop the behavior or interface of the other. Distribution does not necessarily imply geographical dispersion.

Interoperability: Asymmetric property between a consumer C and a provider P (C is compatible with P) that holds if C is compliant with P and P is conformant to C.

Provider: A role performed by a resource B in an interaction with another A, which involves waiting for a request from A, honoring it and typically sending a response to A.

Resource: An entity of any nature (material, virtual, conceptual, noun, action, and so on) that embodies a meaningful, complete and discrete concept, makes sense by itself and can be distinguished from, although able to interact with, other entities.

Service: The set of operations supported by a resource and that together define its behavior (the set of reactions to messages that the resource exhibits).

Transaction: Primitive pattern (predefined sequence) of messages exchanged between two interacting systems, one in the role of consumer, which initiates the pattern by a request, and the other in the role of provider, which honors that request and typically provides a response.

Section 2
Resource Management

Chapter 2
Network–Aware Virtual Machine Placement and Migration in Cloud Data Centers

Md Hasanul Ferdaus
Monash University, Australia

Rodrigo N. Calheiros
The University of Melbourne, Australia

Manzur Murshed
Federation University, Australia

Rajkumar Buyya
The University of Melbourne, Australia

ABSTRACT

With the pragmatic realization of computing as a utility, Cloud Computing has recently emerged as a highly successful alternative IT paradigm. Cloud providers are deploying large-scale data centers across the globe to meet the Cloud customers' compute, storage, and network resource demands. Efficiency and scalability of these data centers, as well as the performance of the hosted applications' highly depend on the allocations of the data center resources. Very recently, network-aware Virtual Machine (VM) placement and migration is developing as a very promising technique for the optimization of compute-network resource utilization, energy consumption, and network traffic minimization. This chapter presents the relevant background information and a detailed taxonomy that characterizes and classifies the various components of VM placement and migration techniques, as well as an elaborate survey and comparative analysis of the state of the art techniques. Besides highlighting the various aspects and insights of the network-aware VM placement and migration strategies and algorithms proposed by the research community, the survey further identifies the benefits and limitations of the existing techniques and discusses on the future research directions.

INTRODUCTION

Cloud Computing is a recently emerged computing paradigm that promises virtually unlimited compute, communication, and storage resources where customers are provisioned these resources according to their demands following a pay-per-use business model. In order to meet the increasing consumer demands, Cloud providers are deploying large-scale data centers across the world, consisting of hundreds of thousands of servers. Cloud applications deployed in these data centers such as

DOI: 10.4018/978-1-4666-8213-9.ch002

Copyright © 2015, IGI Global. Copying or distributing in print or electronic forms without written permission of IGI Global is prohibited.

web applications, parallel processing applications, and scientific workflows are primarily composite applications comprised of multiple compute (e.g., Virtual Machines or VMs) and storage components (e.g., storage blocks) that exhibit strong communication correlations among them. Traditional research works on network communication and bandwidth optimization mainly focused on rich connectivity at the edges of the network and dynamic routing protocols to balance the traffic load. With the increasing trend towards more communication intensive applications in the Cloud data centers, the inter-VM network bandwidth consumption is growing rapidly. This situation is aggravated by the sharp rise in the size of the data that are handled, processed, and transferred by the Cloud applications. Furthermore, the overall application performance highly depends on the underlying network resources and services. As a consequence, the network conditions have direct impact on the Service Level Agreements (SLAs) and revenues earned by the Cloud providers.

Recent advancement in virtualization technologies emerges as a very promising tool to address the above mentioned issues and challenges. Normally, VM management decisions are made by using various capacity planning tools such as VMware Capacity Planner ("VMware Capacity Planner", 2014) and their objectives are set to consolidate VMs for higher utilization of compute resources (e.g., CPU and memory) and minimization of power consumption, while ignoring the network resource consumption and possible prospects of optimization. As a result, this often leads to situations where VM pairs with high mutual traffic loads are placed on physical servers with large network cost between them. Such VM placement decisions not only put stress on the network links, but also have adverse effects on the application performance. Several recent measurement studies in operational data centers reveal the fact that there exists low correlation between the average pairwise traffic rates between the VMs and the end-to-end network costs of the hosting servers

(Meng, Pappas, & Zhang, 2010). Also because of the heterogeneity of the deployed workloads, traffic distribution of individual VMs exhibit highly uneven patterns. Moreover, there exists stable per-VM traffic at large timescale: VM pairs with relatively heavier traffic tend to exhibit the higher rates whereas VMs pairs with relatively low traffic tend to exhibit the lower rates. Such observational insights of the traffic conditions in data centers have opened up new research challenges and potentials. One such emerging research area is the network-aware VM placement and migration that covers various online and offline VM placement decisions, scheduling, and migration mechanisms with diverse objectives such as network traffic reduction, bandwidth optimization, data center energy consumption minimization, network-aware VM consolidation, and traffic-aware load balancing.

Optimization of VM placement and migration decisions has been proven to be practical and effective in the arena of physical server resource utilization and energy consumption reduction, and a plethora of research contributions have already been made addressing such problems. Until recently, a handful of research attempts are made to address the VM placement and migration problem focusing on inter-server network distance, run-time inter-VM traffic characteristics, server load and resource constraints, compute and network resource demands of VMs, data storage locations, and so on. These works not only differ in the addressed system assumptions and modeling techniques, but also vary considerably in the proposed solution approaches and the conducted performance evaluation techniques and environments. As a consequence, there is a rapidly growing need for elaborate taxonomy, survey, and comparative analysis of the existing works in this emerging research area. In order to analyze and assess these works in a uniform fashion, this chapter presents an overview of the aspects of Cloud data center management as background information, followed by various state-of-the-art data center network architectures, inter-VM traffic patterns observed in production data centers followed by an elaborate taxonomy and survey of notable research contributions.

The rest of this chapter is organized as follows: Section 2 presents the necessary background information relevant to network-aware VM placement and migration in Cloud data centers; Section 3 presents a detailed taxonomy and survey of the VM placement and migration strategies and techniques with elaborate description on the significant aspects considered during the course of the classification; a comprehensive comparative analysis highlighting the significant features, benefits, and limitations of the techniques has been put forward in Section 4; Section 5 focuses on the future research outlooks; and finally, Section 6 summarizes the chapter.

BACKGROUND

Cloud Infrastructure Management Systems

While the number and scale of Cloud Computing services and systems are continuing to grow rapidly, significant amount of research is being conducted both in academia and industry to determine the directions to the goal of making the future Cloud Computing platforms and services successful. Since most of the major Cloud Computing offerings and platforms are proprietary or depend on software that is not accessible or amenable to experimentation or instrumentation, researchers interested in pursuing Cloud Computing infrastructure questions as well as future Cloud service providers have very few tools to work with (Nurmi et al., 2009). Moreover, data security and privacy issues have created concerns for enterprises and individuals to adopt public Cloud services (Armbrust et al., 2010). As a result, several attempts and ventures of building open-source Cloud management systems came

out of both academia and industry collaborations including Eucalyptus (Nurmi et al., 2009), OpenStack, OpenNebula (Sotomayor, Montero, Llorente, & Foster, 2009), and Nimbus ("Nimbus is cloud computing for science", 2014). These Cloud solutions provide various aspects of Cloud infrastructure management such as:

1. Management services for VM life cycle, compute resources, networking, and scalability.
2. Distributed and consistent data storage with built-in redundancy, failsafe mechanisms, and scalability.
3. Discovery, registration, and delivery services for virtual disk images with sup-port of different image formats (VDI, VHD, qcow2, VMDK).
4. User authentication and authorization services for all components of Cloud management.
5. Web and console-based user interface for managing instances, images, crypto-graphic keys, volume attachment/detachment to instances, and similar functions.

Figure 1 shows the four essential layers of Cloud Computing environment from the architectural perspective. Each layer is built on top of the lower layers and provides unique services to the upper layers.

1. **Hardware Layer:** This layer is composed of the physical resources of typical data centers, such as physical servers, storage devices, load balancers, routers, switches, communication links, power systems, and cooling systems. This layer is essentially the driving element of Cloud services and as a consequence, operation and management of the physical layer incurs continuous costs for the Cloud providers. Example includes the numerous data centers of Cloud providers such as Amazon, Rackspace, Google, Microsoft, Linode, and GoGrid that spread all over the globe.

Figure 1. The Cloud Computing architecture

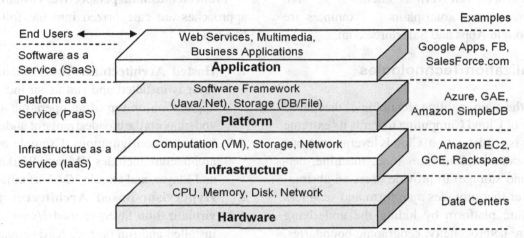

2. **Infrastructure Layer:** This layer (also known as Virtualization Layer) creates a pool of on-demand computing and storage resources by partitioning the physical resources utilizing virtualization technologies such as Xen (Barham et al., 2003) and VMware. Efficient allocation and utilization of the virtual resources in accordance with the computing demands of Cloud users are important to minimize the SLA violations and maximize revenues.

3. **Platform Layer:** Built on top of the infrastructure layer, this layer consists of customized operating systems and application frameworks that help automate of application development, deployment, and management. In this way, this layer strives to minimize the burden of deploying applications directly on the VM containers.

4. **Application Layer:** This layer consists of the actual Cloud applications which are different from traditional applications and can leverage the on-demand automatic-scaling feature of Cloud Computing to achieve better performance, higher availability and reliability, as well as operating cost minimization.

In alignment with the architectural layers of Cloud infrastructure resources and services, the following three services models evolved and used extensively by the Cloud community:

- **Infrastructure as a Service (IaaS):** Cloud provides provision computing resources (e.g., processing, network, storage) to Cloud customers in the form of VMs, storage resource in the form of blocks, file systems, databases, etc., as well as communication resources in the form bandwidth. IaaS provides further provide management consoles or dashboards, APIs (Application Programming Interfaces), advanced security features for manual and autonomic control and management of the virtual resources. Typical examples are Amazon EC2, Google Compute Engine, and Rackspace Cloud Servers.

- **Platform as a Service (PaaS):** PaaS providers offer a development platform (programming environment, tools, etc.) that allows Cloud consumers to develop Cloud services and applications, as well as a deployment platform that hosts those services and applications, thus supports full software lifecycle management. Examples include Google App Engine and Windows Azure platform.

- **Software as a Service (SaaS):** Cloud consumers release their applications on a hosting environment fully managed and controlled by SaaS Cloud providers and the applications can be accessed through

Internet from various clients (e.g., web browser and smartphones). Examples are Google Apps and Salesforce.com.

Virtualization Technologies

One of the main enabling technologies that paved the way of Cloud Computing towards its extreme success is virtualization. Clouds leverage various virtualization technologies (e.g., machine, network, and storage) to provide users an abstraction layer that provides a uniform and seamless computing platform by hiding the underlying hardware heterogeneity, geographic boundaries, and internal management complexities (Zhang, Cheng, & Boutaba, 2010). It is a promising technique by which resources of physical servers can be abstracted and shared through partial or full machine simulation by time-sharing and hardware and software partitioning into multiple execution environments each of which runs as complete and isolated system. It allows dynamic sharing and reconfiguration of physical resources in Cloud Computing infrastructure that makes it possible to run multiple applications in separate VMs having different performance metrics. It is virtualization that makes it possible for the Cloud providers to improve utilization of physical servers through VM multiplexing (Meng, Isci, Kephart, Zhang, Bouillet, & Pendarakis, 2010) and multi-tenancy (i.e. simultaneous sharing of physical resources of the same server by multiple Cloud customers). It also enables on-demand resource pooling through which computing resources like CPU and memory, and storage resources are provisioned to customers only when needed (Kusic, Kephart, Hanson, Kandasamy, & Jiang, 2009). This feature helps avoid static resource allocation based on peak resource demand characteristics. In short, virtualization enables higher resource utilization, dynamic resource sharing, and better energy management, as well as improves scalability, availability, and reliability of Cloud resources and services (Buyya, Broberg, & Goscinski, 2010).

From architectural perspective, virtualization approaches are categorized into the following two types:

1. **Hosted Architecture:** The virtualization layer is installed and run as an individual application on top of an operating system and supports the broadest range of underlying hardware configurations. Example of such architecture includes VMware Workstation and Player, and Oracle VM VirtualBox.
2. **Hypervisor-Based Architecture:** The virtualization layer, termed *Hypervisor* is installed and run on bare hardware and retains full control of the underlying physical system. It is a piece of software that hosts and manages the VMs on its *Virtual Machine Monitor* (VMM) components (Figure 2). The VMM implements the VM hardware abstraction, and partitions and shares the CPU, memory, and I/O devices to successfully virtualize the underlying physical system. In this process, the Hypervisor multiplexes the hardware resources among the various running VMs in time and space sharing manner, the way traditional operating system multiplexes hardware resources among the various processes (Smith & Nair, 2005). VMware ESXi and Xen Server (Barham et al., 2003) are examples of this kind of virtualization. Since Hypervisors have direct access to the underlying hardware resources rather than executing instructions via operating systems as it is the case with hosted virtualization, a hypervisor is much more efficient than a hosted virtualization system and provides greater performance, scalability, and robustness.

Among the different processor architectures, the Intel x86 architecture has been established as the most successfully, widely adopted, and highly inspiring. In this architecture, different privilege level instructions are executed and controlled

Figure 2. Hypervisor-based virtualization architecture

Application	Application	Application	
Operating System	Operating System	Operating System	
VM (Virtual CPU, RAM, NIC, Disk)	VM (Virtual CPU, RAM, NIC, Disk)	VM (Virtual CPU, RAM, NIC, Disk)	
VMM	VMM	VMM	Enhanced Features
Basic Functionality (e.g., scheduling, memory management)			

Hypervisor

through the four privilege rings: Ring 0, 1, 2, and 3, with 0 being the most privileged (Figure 3) in order to manage access to the hardware resources. Regular operating systems targeted to run over bare-metal x86 machines assume full control of the hardware resources and thus are placed in Ring 0 so that they can have direct access to the underlying hardware, while typical user level applications run at ring 0.

Virtualization of the x86 processor required placing the virtualization layer between the operating system and the hardware so that VMs can be created and managed that would share the same physical resources. This means the virtualization layer needs to be placed in Ring 0; however unmodified operating systems assumes to be run in the same Ring. Moreover, there are some sensitive instructions that have different semantics when

Figure 3. The x86 processor privilege rings without virtualization

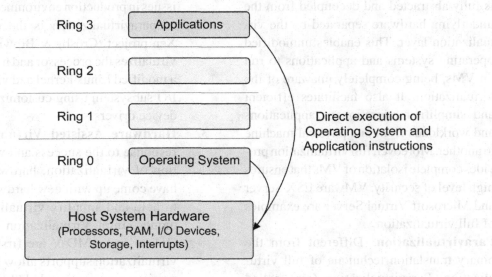

47

they are not executed in Ring 0 and thus cannot be effectively virtualized. As a consequence, the industry and research community have come up with the following three types of alternative virtualization techniques:

1. **Full Virtualization:** This type of virtualization technique provides full abstraction of the underlying hardware and facilitates the creation of complete VMs in which guest operating systems can execute. Full virtualization is achieved through a combination of binary translation and direct execution techniques that allow the VMM to run in Ring 0. The binary translation technique translates the OS kernel level code with alternative series of instructions in order to substitute the non-virtualizable instructions so that it has the intended effect on the virtual hardware (Figure 4(a)). As for the user level codes, they are executed directly on the processor to achieve high performance. In this way, the VMM provides the VM with all the services of the physical machine like virtual processor, memory, I/O devices, BIOS, etc. This approach have the advantage of providing total virtualization of the physical machine as the guest operating system is fully abstracted and decoupled from the underlying hardware separated by the virtualization layer. This enables unmodified operating systems and applications to run on VMs, being completely unaware of the virtualization. It also facilitates efficient and simplified migration of applications and workloads from one physical machine to another. Moreover, full virtualization provides complete isolation of VMs that ensures high level of security. VMware ESX Server and Microsoft Virtual Server are examples of full virtualization.

2. **Paravirtualization:** Different from the binary translation technique of full virtualization, Paravirtualization (also called OS Assisted Virtualization) works through the modification of the OS kernel code by replacement of the non-virtualizable instructions with hypercalls that communicate directly with the hypervisor virtualization layer (Figure 4(b)). The hypervisor further provides hypercall interfaces for special kernel operations such as interrupt handling, memory management, timer management, etc. Thus, in paravirtualization each VM is presented with an abstraction of the hardware that is similar but not identical to the underlying physical machine. Since paravirtualization requires modification of guest OSs, they are not fully un-aware of the presence of the virtualization layer. The primary advantage of paravirtualization technique is lower virtualization overhead over full virtualization where binary translations affect instruction executing performance. However, this performance advantage is dependent on the types of workload running on the VMs. Paravirtualization suffers from poor compatibility and portability issues since every guest OS running on it top of paravirtualized machines needs to be modified accordingly. For the same reason, it causes significant maintenance and support issues in production environments. Example of paravirtualization is the open source Xen project (Crosby & Brown, 2006) that virtualizes the processor and memory using a modified Linux kernel and virtualizes the I/O subsystem using customized guest OS device drivers.

3. **Hardware Assisted Virtualization:** In response to the success and wide adaptation of virtualization, hardware vendors have come up with new hardware features to help and simplify virtualization techniques. Intel Virtualization Technology (VT-x) and AMD-V are first generation virtualization supports allow the VMM to run in a new root mode below Ring 0 by

Figure 4. Alternative virtualization techniques: (a) full virtualization through binary translation, (b) paravirtualization, and (c) hardware assisted virtualization

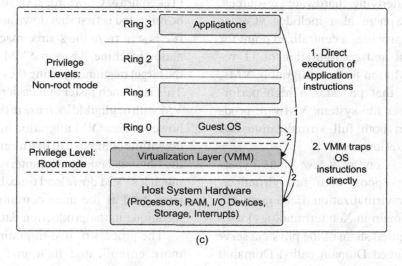

the introduction of a new CPU execution mode. With this new hardware assisted feature, privileged and critical system calls are automatically trapped by the hypervisor and the guest OS state is saved in Virtual Machine Control Structures (VT-x) or Virtual Machine Control Blocks (AMD-V), removing the need for either binary translation (full virtualization) or paravirtualization (Figure 4 (c)). The hardware assisted virtualization has the benefit that unmodified guest OSs can run directly and access to virtualized re-sources without any need for modification or emulation. With the help of the new privilege level and new instructions, the VMM can run at Ring -1 (between Ring 0 and hardware layer) allowing guest OS to run at Ring 0. This reduces the VMM's burden of translating every privileged instruction, and thus helps achieve better performance compared to full virtualization. The hardware assisted virtualization requires explicit virtualization support from the physical host processor, which is available only to modern processors.

Among the various virtualization systems, VMware, Xen (Barham et al., 2003), and KVM (Kernel-based Virtual Machine) (Kivity, Kamay, Laor, Lublin, & Liguori, 2007) have proved to be the most successful by combing features that make them uniquely well suited for many important applications:

- VMware Inc. is the first company to offer commercial virtualization technology. It offers VMware vSphere (formerly VMware Infrastructure 4) for computer hardware virtualization that includes VMware ESX and ESXi hypervisors that virtualize the underlying hardware resources. VMware vSphere also includes vCenter Server that provides a centralized point for management and configuration of IT resources, VMotion for live migrating VMs, and VMFS that provides a high performance cluster file system. VMware products support both full virtualization and paravirtualization.
- Xen Server is one of a few Linux hypervisors that support both full virtualization and paravirtualization. Each guest OS (termed Domain in Xen terminology) uses a pre-configured share of the physical server. A privileged Domain called Domain0 is a bare-bone OS that actually controls physical hardware and is responsible for the creation, management, migration, and termination other VMs.
- KVM also provides full virtualization with the help of hardware virtualization support. It is a modification to the Linux kernel that actually makes Linux into a hypervisor on inserting a KVM kernel module. One of the most interesting KVM features is that each guest OS running on it is actually executed in user space of the host system. This approach makes each guest OS look like a normal process to the underlying host kernel.

Virtual Machine Migration Techniques

One of the most prominent features of the virtualization system is the *VM Live Migration* (Clark et al., 2005) which allows for the transfer of a running VM from one physical machine to another, with little downtime of the services hosted by the VM. It transfers the current working state and memory of a VM across the network while it is still running. Live migration has the advantage of transferring a VM across machines without disconnecting the clients from the services. Another approach for VM migration is the *Cold* or *Static VM Migration* (Takemura & Crawford, 2009) in which the VM to be migrated is first shut down and a configuration file is sent from the source machine to the destination machine. The same VM can be started on the target machine by using the configuration file. This is a much faster and easier way to migrate a VM with negligible increase in the network traffic; however static VM migration incurs much higher downtime compared to live migration. Because of the obvious benefit of uninterrupted service and much less VM download time, live migration has been used as the most common VM migration technique in the production data centers.

The process of live-migrating a VM is much more complicated than just transferring the memory pages of the VM from the source machine to the destination machine. Since a running VM can execute write instructions to memory pages in the source machine during the memory copying process, the new dirty pages must also be copied to the destination. Thus, in order to ensure a consistent state of the migrating VM, copying process for all the dirty pages must be carried out until the migration process is completed. Furthermore, each active VM has its own share and access to the physical resources such as storage, network, and I/O devices. As a result, the VM live migration process needs to ensure that the corresponding physical resources in the destination machine must be attached to the migrated VM.

Transferring VM memory from one machine to another can be carried out in many different ways. However, live migration techniques utilize one or more of the following memory copying phases (Clark et al., 2005):

- **Push Phase:** The source host VMM pushes (i.e. copies) certain memory pages across the network to the destination host while the VM is running. Consistency of VM's execution state is ensured by resending any modified (i.e. dirty) pages during this process.
- **Stop-and-Copy Phase:** The source host VMM stops the running VM on certain stop condition, copies all the memory pages to the destination host, and a new VM is started.
- **Pull Phase:** The new VM runs in the destination host and, if a page is accessed that has not yet been copied, a page fault occurs and this page is copied across the network from the source host.

Performance of any VM live migration technique depends on the balance of the following two temporal parameters:

1. **Total Migration Time:** The duration between the time when the migration is initiated and when the original VM may be discarded after the new VM is started in the destination host. In short, the total time required to move the VM between the physical hosts.
2. **VM Downtime:** The portion of the total migration time when the VM is not running in any of the hosts. During this time, the hosted service would be unavailable and the clients will experience service interruption.

Incorporating the above three phases of memory copying, several VM live migration techniques are presented by the research communities with tradeoffs between the total migration time and VM downtime:

- **Pure Stop-and-Copy:** The VM is shut down at the source host, all the memory pages are copied to the destination host, and a new VM is started. This technique is simple and, the total migration time is relatively small compared to other techniques and directly proportional to the size of the active memory of the migrating VM. However, the VM can experience high VM downtime, subject to the memory size, and as a result, this approach can be impractical for live services (Sapuntzakis, Chandra, Pfaff, Chow, Lam, & Rosenblum, 2002).
- **Pure Demand-Migration:** The VM at the source host is shut down and essential kernel data structures (CPU state, registers, etc.) are transferred to the destination host using a short stop-and-copy phase. The VM is then started in the destination host. The remaining pages are transferred across the network when they are first referenced by the VM at the destination. This approach has the advantage of much shorter VM downtime; however the total migration time is generally much longer since the memory pages are transferred on-demand upon page fault. Furthermore, post-migration VM performance is likely to be hampered substantially due to large number of page faults and page transfers across the network (Zayas, 1987).
- **Post-Copy Migration:** Similar to the pure demand-migration approach, the VM is suspended at the source host, a minimal VM kernel data structure (e.g., CPU execution state, registers values, and non-pageable memory) is transferred to the destination host, and the VM is booted up. Unlike of pure demand-migration, the source VMM actively sends the remaining memory pages to the destination host, an activity termed *pre-paging*. When the running VM at the destination attempts to access a page that is not copied yet, a page

fault occurs (known as *network faults*) and the faulted page is transferred from the source host to the destination host over the communication network. As in the case of pure demand-migration, post-copy migration suffers from VM performance degradation due to on-demand page transfer upon page fault. However, pre-paging technique can help reduce the performance degradation by adapting the page transmission order dynamically in response to the network faults by pushing the pages near the last page fault (Hines, Deshpande, & Gopalan, 2009).

- **Pre-Copy Migration:** Unlike the above approaches, the VM continues running in the source host while the VMM iteratively transfers memory pages to the destination host. Only after a substantial amount of memory pages are copied, or a predefined number of iterations are completed, or any other terminating condition is met, the VM is stopped at the source, the remaining pages are transferred to the destination, and the VM is restarted. Pre-copy migration has the obvious benefit of short stop-and-copy phase since most of the memory page would be copied to the destination by this time. So, the VM downtime is comparatively much shorter than other live migration techniques, making this approach suitable for live services. Furthermore, pre-copy migration offers higher reliability since it retains an up-to-date state of the VM in the source machine during the migration process, an added advantage absent in other migration approaches. However, pre-copy migration can suffers from longer total migration time since the same memory pages can be transmitted multiple time in several rounds depending on page dirty rate. For the same reason, it can generate much higher network traffic compared to other techniques (Clark et al., 2005).

Almost all the modern virtualization environments offers VM live migration feature, including Xen Server, VMware ESX Server (through VMotion (Nelson, Lim, & Hutchins, 2005)), KVM, Microsoft Hyper-V, Oracle VM VirtualBox, and OpenVZ. A high level flow chart of the logical steps followed during the pre-copy migration technique implemented in Xen Server is depicted in Figure 5 (Clark et al., 2005). Focusing primarily on high reliability against system failure, the Xen pre-copy migration takes a transactional approach between the source and target hosts:

Stage 0 (Pre-Migration): Source host A has an active VM to be migrated. The target host B can be pre-selected in advance in order to speed up future migrations through guaranteed resources required for the migration process.

Stage 1 (Reservation): The request to migrate the VM from source host A to target host B is issued. Host B confirms that it has the required resources and reserves a VM container of that size. If host B fails to secure enough resources, the migration request is discarded and the VM runs on host A without any changes.

Stage 2 (Iterative Pre-Copy): In the first iteration, all the memory pages are transmitted (i.e. copied) from host A to host B. In the remaining iterations, only the pages that have been modified during the previous iteration are transmitted.

Stage 3 (Stop-and-Copy): The VM is shut down in host A and all the network traffic is redirected to host B. Then, the critical kernel data structures (e.g., CPU states and registers) and the remaining dirty pages are transmitted. At the end of this stage, the two copies of the VM at both host A and B are consistent; however, the copy at A is still considered primary and is resumed in the incident of failure.

Figure 5. Stages of the pre-copy VM live migration technique
(Clark et al., 2005).

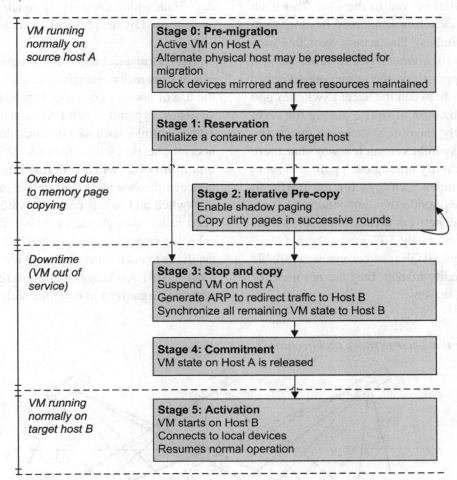

Stage 4 (Commitment): Host B notifies host A that it has a consistent VM image. Upon receipt, host A sends the acknowledgment message indicating the commitment of the total migration transaction. After this point, the original VM at host A can be abandoned and host B is considered as the primary host of the VM.

Stage 5 (Activation): Host B activates the migrated VM. The post-migration code runs in order to reattach the device drivers at host B and advertise the moved IP addresses.

Data Center Network Architectures

Modern data centers are built primarily according to the generic multi-tier architecture ("Cisco Data Center Infrastructure 2.5 Design Guide", 2014). The most common network topologies follow the three-tier architecture (Figure 6), where each tier has specific responsibility and goal in the design and traffic handling. In the bottom tier, known as the *Access Tier* every physical server is connected to one or two (in case of redundancy to increase reliability) access switches, in the *Aggregation Tier*, each access switch is connected to one or two aggregation switches, and in the *Core Tier* each aggregation switch is connected to more than one core switches. The access switches provide the servers connectivity to other servers and to the upper tiers, the aggregate switches interconnects between the access switches and enables localization of traffic among the servers, and finally, the core switches connects the aggregation switches in such a way that there exists connectivity among each pair of servers and also includes gateways for the traffic to communicate outside the data center.

In three-tier network architectures, the access tier links are normally 1 Gigabit Ethernet (GE) links. Although 10 GE transceivers are available in the commodity market, they are not used for the following reasons:

1. Very high price, and
2. Bandwidth capacity is much more than needed by the physical servers.

Servers in data centers are normally grouped in ranks and rack connectivity is achieved through the use of not-so-expensive Top-of-Rack (ToR) switches. Typically, such ToR switches have two 10 GE uplinks with 48 GE links that interconnects the servers within the rack. *Oversubscription Ratio* of a switch is defined the difference between the downlink and uplink capacities of the switch and in this case it is 48:20 or 2.4: 1. As a result, though each access link has 1 GE capacity, under full load, only 416 Mb/s will be available to each server (Kliazovich, Bouvry, & Khan, 2013). At the aggregation and core tier, the racks are organized in *modules* with a couple of

Figure 6. The three-tier network architecture

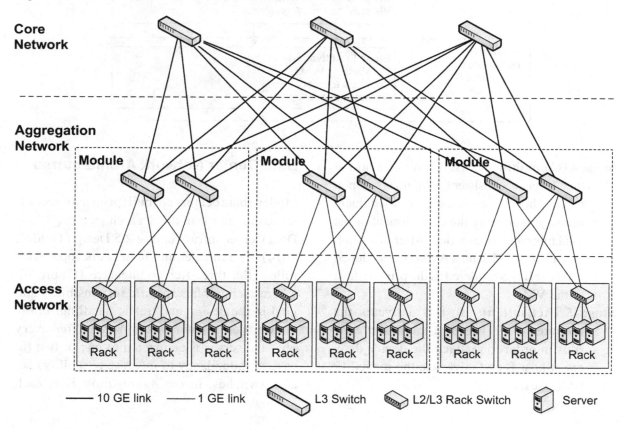

aggregation switches and oversubscription ratio for these switches is around 1.5:1. Therefore, the available bandwidth for each server is reduced to 277 Mb/s.

Though such network architectures have multi-rooted forest topology at the physical level, because of the extensive use of *Virtual LANs* (VLANs) and *Spanning Tree* algorithm the network packets are forwarded according to the logical layer-2 topology. Such layer-2 logical topology always takes the form of a tree, normally rooted at one of the core switches.

Scalability issue of three-tier architecture is normally addressed through scaling up each individual switches by increasing their fan-outs, not by the scaling out of the network topology. For example, according to the Cisco Data Center Infrastructure 2.5 Design Guide, the core tier can have a maximum of 8 switches. Because of such scalability issues regarding topology scaling, high oversubscription ratio, as well as requirement for flat address space, several recent research endeavors produced complex network architectures for the large scale modern data centers and among these, the following are considered as the standard-de-facto solutions:

1. **Fat-Tree:** This is a three-tier architecture based on bipartite graphs (Al-Fares et al., 2008) and basic building block of this topology is called pods which are collections of access and aggregation switches connected in a complete bipartite graph. Every pod is connected to all the core switches; however links that connect pods to core switches are uniformly distributed between the aggregation switches contained within the pods. Such connection pattern results in a new bipartite graph between aggregation and core switches. In this topology, all the switches need to have same number of ports. The primary advantage of fat-tree topology is that $N^2/4$ paths are available to route the traffic between any two servers.

2. **VL2:** Somewhat similar to fat-tree, VL2 (Greenberg et al., 2009) is also a three-tier topology having a complete bipartite graph between core and aggregation switches, rather than between access and aggregation switches. Moreover, access switch traffic is forwarded through the aggregation and core switches using valiant load balancing techniques that forwards the traffic first to a randomly selected core switch and then back to the actual destination switch. The advantage of such routing is that when traffic is unpredictable, the best way to balance load across all the available network links is to forward the packets to a randomly selected core switch as an intermediate destination.

3. **PortLand:** This is also a three-tier architecture that shares the same bipartite graph feature with VL2, however at different levels (Mysore et al., 2009). It makes use of fat-tree topologies (Leiserson, 1985) and uses the concept of pods. Such pods are collections of access and aggregations switches that form complete bipartite graphs. Furthermore, each pod is connected to all the core switches, by uniformly distributing the up-links between the aggregation switches of the pod. As a result, another level of bipartite graph is formed between the pods and the core switches. Portland requires that the number of ports of all the switches is same. The number of ports per switch is the only parameter that determines the total number of pods in the topology, and consequently the total number of switches and hosts machines.

4. **BCube:** It is a multi-level network architecture for the data center defined in a recursive fashion (Guo et al., 2009). Host machines are considered as part of the network architecture and they forward packets on behalf of other host machines. It is based on the generalized hypercube architecture (Bhuyan & Agrawal, 1984) with the main difference that the neighboring hosts instead of forming a full

mesh network with each other, they connect through switches. In a BCube topology, the total number of connected hosts machines and the total number of required switches is a function of the total number of ports of each switch.

Cloud Applications and Data Center Traffic Patterns

With the increasing popularity of Cloud hosting platforms (e.g., Amazon AWS and Microsoft Azure) due to the benefits of pay-as-you-go business model, high availability and reliability, as well as extensive computing and storage services, Cloud platforms are enjoying deployment of a wide variety of composite applications, including scientific applications, social networks, video streaming, medical services, search engines and web browsing, various content delivery applications, and so on (Chen et al., 2011; Huang, Yang, Zhang, & Wu, 2012; Vaquero, Rodero-Merino, Caceres, & Lindner, 2008). Such composite applications are generally composed of multiple compute VMs backed by huge amount of data. As more and more communication-intensive applications are being deployed in data centers, the amount of inter-VM traffic is increasing with rapid pace. Based on the dynamics on computational and communicational requirements, the commonly deployed Cloud application workloads are categories into the following three groups (Kliazovich et al., 2013):

1. **Data-Intensive Workloads:** Such workloads require less computational resources, but cause heavy data transfers. For example, video file sharing where each user request generates a new video streaming process. For such applications, it is the interconnection network that can be a bottleneck rather than the computing power. In order to maintain the application performance and respect the SLAs, a continuous feedback mechanism

need to be present between the network devices (e.g. switches) and the centralized workload scheduler or placement manager. Based on feedbacks, the scheduler will decide the placement of the workloads with consideration of the run-time network status and congestion levels of communication links. In this way, placement of workloads over congested network links can be avoided even though corresponding servers have enough computing capacity to accommodate the workloads. As a result, data center traffic demands can be distributed over the network in a balanced way and minimize network latency and average task completion time.

2. **Computationally Intensive Workloads:** CIWs represent the High Performance Computing (HPC) applications that are used to solve advanced and computationally expensive problems. These applications require very high amount of computing capacity, but causes little data transfer over the communication network. Such applications can be grouped together and placed in a minimum number of computing servers through VM consolidation mechanisms in order to save energy. Because of low data traffic among the VMs, there is very less probability of network congestion and most of network switches can be turned into lower power states (e.g., in sleep mode) and thus help reducing energy consumption in the data center.

3. **Balanced Workloads:** Applications that require both computing power and data transfer among the computing nodes (i.e. VMs) as represented by BWs. For example, Geographic Information Systems (GISs) need to transfer large volume of graphical data as well as huge computing resources to process these data. With this type of workloads, the average compute server load is proportional to the amount of data volume transferred over the communication

networks. VM placement and scheduling policies for such application need to account for both current state of compute servers' load and traffic loads on the network switches and links.

Since Cloud data centers host heterogeneous services and application, communication patterns exhibit wide spectrum of variations, ranging from one-to-one and all-to-all traffic matrixes. Based on trace analysis of network usage from production data centers, the following trends of network traffic are found to be pre-dominant (Ersoz, Yousif, & Das, 2007; Kandula, Sengupta, Greenberg, Patel, & Chaiken, 2009; Meng et al., 2010):

1. **Highly Non-Uniform Distribution of Traffic Volume Among VMs:** VMs running on servers exhibit uneven traffic volume among themselves across different VMs. The trace analysis reports show that 80% of the VMs have relatively low traffic rate (800Kbyte/min) over a period of two-weeks, 4% of the VMs have a rate ten times higher. This concludes that the inter-VM traffic rate varies significantly and it is quite hard for the data center administration to estimate the amount of inter-VM traffic accurately and consistently.
2. **Stable Inter-VM Traffic Volume:** For a long duration, the average inter-VM traffic rate is found to be relatively stable in spite of the highly skewed traffic rate among VMs. The work of Meng et al. (2010) shows that for the majority of the VMs, the standard deviation of their traffic rates is less than the double of the mean of the traffic rates. This consistent traffic volume among VMs implies that the run-time communication patterns among the VMs can be estimated and known a priory from the users deploying the VMs in the Clouds.

3. **Weak Correlation between Traffic Rate and Network Latency:** It is further reported from the measurement-based study that there is no any dependency or relationship between inter-VM traffic volume and the network distance between the servers hosting the VMs. That means VM pairs with high traffic rate do not necessarily correspond to low latency and vice versa.

TAXONOMY AND SURVEY OF THE NETWORK-AWARE VM PLACEMENT AND MIGRATION TECHNIQUES

With the various intricacies of virtualization technologies, enormous scale of modern data centers, and wide spectrum of hosted applications and services, different VM placement strategies and algorithms are proposed with various assumptions and objectives. Figure 7 presents a full taxonomy of the various aspects of network-aware VM placements and migrations. A brief description of the identified aspects of the research works used in the course of taxonomy is given below:

1. **System Assumption:** Physical servers and network resources in data centers or IT infrastructures are primarily modeled as homogeneous, and often times as heterogeneous as well. Homogeneous cluster of servers normally represent servers with same capacity for certain fixed types of resources (e.g., CPU, memory, and storage), whereas heterogeneous cluster of servers can either mean servers having different capacities of resources or different types of resources (e.g., virtualized servers powered by Xen or VMware hypervisor, and servers with Graphics Processing Units or GPUs). In practice, commercial data centers evolve over time and thus different parts of the data center can have devices with different capabilities and properties. It is quite common

Figure 7. Taxonomy of network-aware VM placement and migration

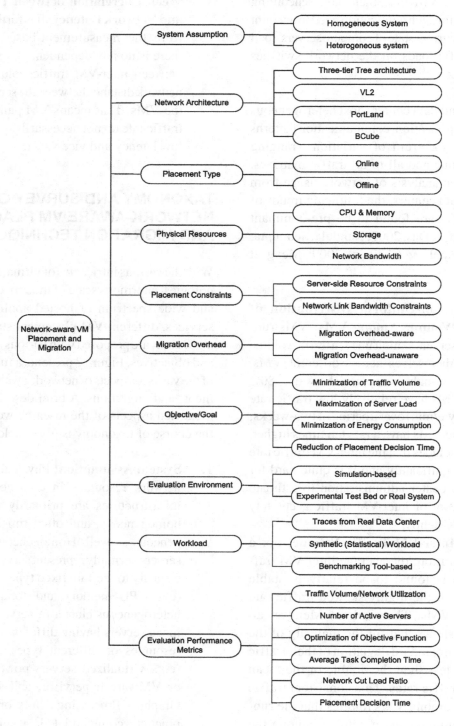

that a recent server installed in a data center would have much higher computing power compared to the old ones; similarly a network switch can be more recent than others and thus can have lower network latency and higher I/O throughput capacity. Moreover, recently there is growing trends towards deploying multi-purpose hardware devices that increase the degree of heterogeneity in data centers. Example of such devices can be some storage devices, such as IBM DS8000 series that have built-in compute capability (POWER5 logical portioning LPAR) that can host applications (Adra et al., 2004; Korupolu, Singh, & Bamba, 2009) and network switches, such as Cisco MDS 9000 switches ("Cisco MDS 9000 SANTap", 2014) that have additional x86 processors capable of executing applications. Efficiency and effectiveness of VM placement and migration strategies are highly dependent on the assumed system assumptions and properties. VM placement techniques that consider the heterogeneity of the devices in data centers can efficiently utilize various capabilities of the divergent resources and optimize the placements, and thus can reduce the traffic burden and energy consumption.

2. **Network Architecture/Topology:** With the variety of proposed data center network architectures and intricacies of traffic patterns, different VM placement approaches are proved to be efficient for different types of network topologies and inter-VM traffic patterns. Such effectiveness is sometimes subject to the specific analytic or modeling technique used in the proposed placement and migration schemes. Since different network topologies are designed independently focusing on different objectives (e.g., VL2 is good for effective load balancing while BCube has higher degree of connectivity and network distances among hosts), different VM placement techniques see different levels performance gains for existing network topologies. For example, the TVMPP (Traffic-aware VM Placement Problem) optimization technique (Meng et al., 2010) gains better performance for multi-layer architecture such as BCube, compared to VL2.

3. **Placement Types:** VM placement problems can be broadly categorized into two groups: online VM placement and offline VM placement. Online VM placement, including VM migrations indicate VM placement and migration actions during the run-time of the data centers where different production applications and services are active and customers are continuously requesting services (Shrivastava, Zerfos, Lee, Jamjoom, Liu, & Banerjee, 2011; Song, Huang, Zhou, & You, 2012; Takouna, Rojas-Cessa, Sachs, & Meinel, 2013; Zhang, Qian, Huang, Li, & Lu, 2012). On the other hand, offline VM placements normally indicate initial VM placements that will be actively running in subsequent phases of the system administration (Biran et al., 2012; Georgiou, Tsakalozos, & Delis, 2013; Korupolu et al., 2009; Piao & Yan, 2010; Zhang, Qian, Huang, Li, & Lu, 2012). One very important difference between online and offline VM placements is the fact that online VM placements require potential VM live migrations and large amount of extra network traffic due performing the VM migrations and can have detrimental effects on the hosted applications performance SLAs subject to the VM downtime and types of hosted services.

4. **Modeling Technique:** Effectiveness and applicability of different VM placement and migration schemes are highly contingent on the applied analytic and modeling approaches. Since different models have specific system assumptions and objectives, VM placement problems are presented using various optimizations modeling techniques, such as Quadratic Assignment Problem (QAP) (Meng et al., 2010), Convex Optimization

Problem (Huang, Gao, Song, Yang, & Zhang, 2013), Knapsack Problem (Korupolu et al., 2009), Integer Quadratic Programming (Biran et al., 2012), and so on.

5. **Physical Resources:** Generally, optimization across different ranges of resources (i.e. CPU, memory, network I/O, storage, etc.) is harder than single resource optimization. Often various mean estimators (such as L1 norm, vector algebra, etc.) are used to compute equivalent scalar estimation while trying to optimize across multiple types of server resources. Inter-VM communication requirement is often modeled as Virtual Links (VL) that is characterized by the bandwidth demand. VM cluster forming an application environment with mutual traffic demand is represented as graph with VMs denoting vertices and VLs denoting edges of the graph.

6. **VM Placement Constraints:** Individual VM placement feasibility or practicality involves a server resource capacity constraint which means that the remaining resource (e.g., CPU cycles, memory, and storage) capacities of the hosting servers need to be enough in order to accommodate the VM. Similarly, while placing two VMs with mutual communication requirement, the bandwidth demand of the VL connecting the two VMs need to match with the remaining bandwidth capacities of the corresponding physical network links connecting the two hosting servers.

7. **Migration Overhead-Awareness:** During VM live migration process, additional network traffic is generated during the whole migration period since hypervisor need to transfer in-memory states of the running VM to the target machine. Furthermore, VM migration causes unavailability of hosted applications due to the VM downtime factor. As a consequence VM living migration is identified as an expensive data center operation that should not be triggered very often

(Mann, Gupta, Dutta, Vishnoi, Bhattacharya, Poddar, & Iyer, 2012). Therefore, efficiency of a VM migration policy also dependents on the number of required VM migration commands issued. While network-aware VM migration strategies opt for optimizing overall network usage and reduce the inter-VM communication delays through migrating communicating VMs into nearly hosts, most of the strategies do not consider the associated VM migration overheads and resulting application performance degradation.

8. **Goal/Objective:** Network-aware VM placement and migration policies primarily target on minimizing overall network traffic overhead within the data center. The obvious way to achieve such goal is to place VMs with large amount of traffic communication in neighboring servers with minimum network delays and enough available bandwidth, most preferably in the same server where the VMs can communicate through memory rather than network links. With this goal in mind, VM placement and migration problem is generally modeled as mathematical optimization framework with minimization objective function. Such objective function can be a measure of total amount of network traffic transferred with the data center, or network utilization of the switches at the different tiers of the network architecture. Since VM placement and migration decision needs to be taken during run-time, reduction of the placement decision time (i.e. problem solving time or algorithm execution time) is also considered as an objective.

9. **Algorithm/Solution Approach:** Given the above mentioned placement constraints, VM placement problem is in fact an NP-complete problem since it requires combinatorial optimization to achieve the goals. As a consequence, most of the research works attempt to solve the problem through heuristic methods so that the algorithms terminate in a reasonable amount

of time. Such heuristics are not guaranteed to produce optimal placement decision; however from time constraints perspective exhaustive search methods that guarantee the generation of optimal solutions are not practical, especially considering the scale of modern data centers. Several metaheuristic-based approaches such as Ant Colony Optimization (ACO), Genetic Algorithms (GA), and Simulated Annealing (SA) have been proven to be effective in the area of VM consolidation. Nevertheless, adaptation and utilization of these problem solving techniques are still open to explore to address the network-aware VM placement and migration problem.

10. **Evaluation/Experimental Platform:** Most of the proposed works presentation evaluation based on simulation based experimentation. This, however, makes sense given the complexity and scale of modern data centers and the hosted applications. Several works have attempted to validate their proposed placement policies through testbed-based experiments and have reported various run-time dynamics across different performance metrics, that is otherwise would be impossible to report though simulation-based evaluations. However, such evaluations are performed on small scale testbeds with 10 to 20 physical machines (or PMs) and thus do not necessarily forecast the potential behavior and performance for large scale data centers.

11. **Competitor Approaches:** Comparison of the performance results among the various competitor placement approaches highly depends on the goals of the competitor approaches. Since network-aware VM placement is a relatively new area of research, proposed approaches are often compared to other placement approaches that are agnostic to network traffic and network topologies and have different goals set in the underlying algorithms (e.g., power consumption minimization or SLA violation reduction).

12. **Workload/VM Cluster:** Because of the lack of enough VM workload data sets from large scale Cloud data centers or other production data centers due to their proprietary nature, statistical distribution-based VM load (compute resource and network bandwidth demands) generation is the most common approach adopted in the simulation-based evaluations. Among others, normal, uniform, and exponential distributions are usually used most. Such synthetic workload data characterize randomness based on particular trend (e.g., through setting mean and variance in case of normal distribution). Subject to accessibility, workload traces from real data centers of often used to feed data to the simulation based evaluation to imply the effectiveness of the proposed approaches in real workload data. Furthermore, testbed-based evaluations often use various benchmarking tools to generate and feed runtime workload data to the algorithms under evaluation.

13. **Evaluation Performance Metrics:** Depending of the goals of the VM placement solutions, various performance metrics are reported in proposed research works. Most common performance metric used is the overall network traffic in the data center. Placement schemes that have multiple objectives, often try to balance between network performance gain and energy consumption reduction, and report evaluations based on both traffic volume reduction and number of active servers. From energy savings point of view, minimization of the number of active servers in data center through VM consolidation is always an attractive choice.

Figure 8 provides a categorization of the various published research works based on the addressed and analyzed subareas of the VM placement problem and the ultimate objectives of the VM placement and migration strategies.

Figure 8. Categorization of network-aware VM placement and migration approaches

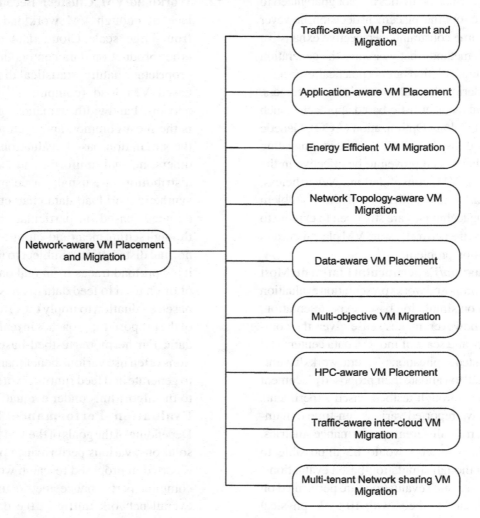

The next four subsections are dedicated to thorough review, analysis, and remarks on the recent prominent research works.

Traffic-Aware VM Placement and Migration Techniques

Network Topology-Aware VM Cluster Placement in IaaS Clouds

Georgiou et al. (2013) have investigated the benefits of user-provided hints regarding inter-VM communication patterns and bandwidth demands during the actual VM placement decisions phase. The authors have proposed two offline VM-cluster placement algorithms with the objective to minimize the network utilization at physical layer, provided that the physical server resource capacity constraints are met. VM deployment request is modeled as Virtual Infrastructure (VI) with specification of the number and resource configuration (CPU core, memory, and storage demands) of VMs, bandwidth demands of inter-VM communication within the VI, modeled as Virtual Links (VLs), as well as possible anti-colocation constraint for pairs of VMs. The underlying physical infrastructure is modeled as a homogeneous cluster of servers organized according to the PortLand (Mysore et al., 2009) network architecture. The authors have argued that conventional tree-like network topologies often suffer from over-subscription and network resource contention primarily at the core top-levels, leading to bottlenecks and delays in services, PortLand network architecture can play a significant role in effective management of computational resources and network bandwidth in Cloud data centers.

The authors have also presented a framework comprising of two layers: physical infrastructure consisting of homogeneous servers organized as PortLand network topology and a middleware on top of the infrastructure. The middleware layer is composed of the following two main components: Planner and Deployer. As input, the Planner gets VM deployment request as VI specification (in XML format), and possible suggestions regarding desired features in VI from user as well as the current resource state information of the infrastructure layer, executes the VM placement algorithms to determine the VM-to-PM and VL-to-physical link mappings, and finally passes over the placement decision to the Deployer. The Deployer can be a third-party provided component that takes care of the VMs deployment on the physical layer components.

With the goal of minimizing network utilization of the physical layer during the VI deployment decision, the authors have proposed two algorithms based on greedy approach. The first algorithm, Virtual Infrastructure Opportunistic fit (VIO) tries to place the communicating VMs near to each other in the physical network. Starting with a sorted list of VLs (in decreasing order of their bandwidth demands) connecting the VMs, the VIO picks up the front VL from the list and attempts to place the VMs connected by the VL in the nearest possible physical nodes (preferably in the same node when anti-colocation is not set), provided that physical node resource capacity constraints, network link bandwidth capacity constraints, as well as user provided constraints are met. In case VIO reaches a dead-end state where

the VL at hand cannot be placed on any physical link, VIO employs a backtracking process where VLs and corresponding VMs are reverted back to unassigned state. Such VL placement inability can occur due to three reasons:

1. No physical node with enough resource is found to host a VM of the VL,
2. No physical path with enough bandwidth is found to be allocated for the VL, and
3. Anti-colocation constraint is violated.

Backtracking process involves de-allocation of both server resource and network bandwidth of physical links. In order to limit the number of reverts for a VL and terminate the algorithm with a reasonable amount of time, a revert counter is set for each VL. When the maximum amount of reverts has been reached for a VL, the VI placement request is rejected and the VIO terminates gracefully. The second algorithm, Vicinity-BasEd Search (VIBES) based on the PortLand network architecture characteristics, tries to detect an appropriate PortLand neighborhood to accommodate all the VMs and VLs of the requested VI, and afterward applies VIO within this neighborhood. In order to identify fitting neighborhood, VIBES exploits PortLand's architectural feature of pods (cluster of physical nodes under the same edge-level switch). The authors also presented formula for ranking all neighborhoods based on the available resources in the servers and bandwidth of the physical links within each neighborhood. VIBES starts with the pod with the most available resources and invokes VIO. Upon rejection from VIO, VIBES expands the neighborhood further by progressively merging the next most available pod to the set of already selected pods. The search for a large enough neighborhood proceeds until a neighborhood with enough available resources is found or the search window is growing beyond a customizable maximize size in which case the VI placement request is rejected.

Performance evaluation of VIO and VIBES is conducted through simulation of physical infrastructures and compared against network-agnostic First Fit Decreasing (FFD) algorithm. Online VI deployment and removal is simulated using three different data flow topologies: Pipeline, Data Aggregation, and Epigenomics (Bharathi et al., 2008). The simulation results show that the proposed algorithms outperforms FFD with respect to network usage: VIO trims down the network traffic routed through the top-layer core switches in the PortLand architecture by up to 75% and incorporation of VIBES attains a further 20% improvement. The authors have also suggested future research directions such as optimization of the power usage of network switches through exploitation of reduced network utilization, testing VIO and VIBES for other network topologies such as BCube (Guo et al., 2009) and VL2 (Greenberg et al., 2009).

Stable Network-Aware VM Placement for Cloud Systems

With focus on communication pattern and dynamic traffic variations of modern Cloud applications, as well as non-trivial data center network topologies, Biran et al. (2012) have addressed the problem of VM placement with the objective to minimize the maximum ratio of bandwidth demand and capacity across all network cuts and thus maximize unused capacity of network links to accommodate sudden traffic bursts. The authors have identified several important observations regarding network traffic and architectures:

1. Due to several factors such as time-of-day effects and periodic service load spikes, run-time traffic patterns undergo high degree of variations,
2. Modern data centers are architected following non-trivial topologies (e.g., Fat-tree (Al-Fares, Loukissas, & Vahdat, 2008) and VL2 (Greenberg et al., 2009)) and employ various adaptations of dynamic multi-path routing protocols.

Considering the above mentioned points, the authors presented two VM placement algorithms that strive to satisfy the forecasted communication requirements as well as be resistant to dynamic traffic variations.

The authors have introduced the Min Cut Ratio-aware VM Placement (MCRVMP) problem and formally formulated using the Integer Quadratic Programming model considering both the server side resource capacity constraints and network resource constraints evolving from complex network topologies and dynamic routing schemas. Since the MCRVMP problem definition works only for tree topology, the authors have also proposed graph transformation techniques so that MCRVMP can be applied to other complex network topologies, for example VL2 and Fat-tree. Considering the fact the MCRVMP is a NP-hard problem, the authors have proposed two separate heuristic algorithms for solving the placement problem and compared these against optimal and random placements.

Both the proposed VM placement heuristic algorithms utilize the concept of Connected Components (CCs) of the running VMs in the data center. Such a CC is formed by the VMs that exchange data only between themselves or with the external gateway (e.g., VMs comprising a multi-tier application) and thus clustering VMs in this way helps minimize the complexity of the problem. First algorithm, termed 2-Phase Connected Component-based Recursive Split (2PCCRS) is a recursive, integer programming technique-based algorithm that utilizes the tree network topology to define and solve small problem instances on one-level trees. By adopting a two-phase approach, 2PCCRS places the CCs in the network and then expands them to place the actual VMs on the servers. Thus, 2PCCRS reduces the larger MCRVMP problem into smaller sub-problems and solves them using mixed integer programming solver in both the phases. Second algorithm, called Greedy Heuristic (GH) entirely avoids using mathematical programming and greedy places each VM individually. Similar to 2PCCRS, GH works in two phases. In the first phase, GH sorts all the traffic demands in decreasing values and sorts all CCs in decreasing order based on the accumulated traffic demands among the VMs within a CC. In the second phase, GH iteratively processes the ordered traffic demands by placing each VM on the physical server that results in minimum value of the maximum cut load values.

The efficiency of the proposed algorithms is evaluated in two phases. In the first phase, 2PC-CRS and GH algorithms were compared to random and optimal placement approaches with focus on placement quality in terms of worst and average cut load ratio and solution computation time. As reported by the authors, for small problem instances both 2PCCRS and GH reach worst case and average cut load ratio very close to optimal algorithm with nearly zero solving time; whereas for larger problem sizes, 2PCCRS significantly outperforms GH, while requiring much higher solving time due its use of mathematical programming techniques. In the second phase, the authors have validated the resilience of MCRVMP-based placements under time-varying traffic demands with NS2-based simulations focusing on the percentage of dropped packets and average packet delivery delay. Simulation results show that with no dropped packets, both 2PCCRS and GH can absorb traffic demands up to three times the nominal values. Furthermore, placements produced by the 2PCCRS algorithm have average packet delivery delays lower than GH-based ones due to the less loaded network cuts.

The authors have also remarked that the proposed MCRVMP problem formulation is not meant for online VM placement where new VM requests are served for data center having already placed VMs. In addition, the authors have ignored the potential VM migration costs entirely.

As per future works, the authors have indicated potential extension of MCRVMP by incorporating traffic demand correlation among VMs to further cut down the amount of dropped packets and by preventing MCRCMP to produce solutions with very high local compute-resource overhead due to inter-memory communications.

Scalability Improvement of Data Center Networks with Traffic-Aware VM Placement

Meng et al. (2010) have addressed the scalability problem of modern data center networks and proposed solution approaches through optimization of VM placement on physical servers. Different from existing solutions that suggest changing of network architecture and routing protocols, the authors have argued that scalability of network infrastructures can be improved by reducing the network distance of communicating VMs. In order to observe the dominant trend of data center traffic-patterns, the authors have claimed to have conducted a measurement study in operational data centers resulting with the following insights:

1. There exists low correlation between average pairwise traffic rate and the end-to-end communication cost,
2. Highly uneven traffic distribution for individual VMs, and
3. VM pairs with relatively heavier traffic rate tend to constantly exhibit the higher rate and VM pairs with low traffic rate tend to exhibit the low rate.

The authors have formally defined the Traffic-aware VM Placement Problem (TVMPP) as a combinatorial optimization problem belonging to the family of Quadratic Assignment Problems (Loiola, de Abreu, Boaventura-Netto, Hahn, & Querido, 2007) and proved its computational complexity to be NP-hard. TVMPP takes the traffic matrix among VMs and communication cost matrix among physical servers as input, and its optimal solution would produce VM-to-PM mappings that would result in minimum aggregate traffic rates at each network switch. The cost between any two communicating VMs is defined as the number of switches or hops on the routing path of the VM pair. The authors have also introduced a concept of slot to refer to one CPU/memory allocation on physical server where multiple such slots can reside on the same server and each slot can be allocated to any VM.

Since TVMPP is NP-hard and existing exact solutions cannot scale to the size of current data centers, the authors have proposed two-tier approximate algorithm Cluster-and-Cut based on two design principles:

1. Finding solution of TVMPP is equivalent to finding VM-to-PM mappings such that VM pairs with high mutual traffic are placed on PM pairs with low-cost physical links and
2. Application of the divide-and-conquer strategy.

The Cluster-and-Cut heuristic is composed of two major components: SlotClustering and VMMinKcut. SlotClustering partitions a total of n slots in the data center into k clusters using the cost between slots as the partition criterion. This component produces a set of slot-clusters sorted in decreasing order of their total outgoing and incoming cost. The VMMinKcut partitions a total of n VMs into k VM-clusters such that VM pairs with high mutual traffic rate are placed within the same VM-cluster and inter-cluster traffic is minimized. This component uses the minimum k-cut graph algorithm (Saran & Vazirani, 1995) partition method and produces k clusters with the same set of size as the previous k slot-clusters. Afterwards, Cluster-and-Cut maps each VM-cluster to a slot-cluster and for each VM-cluster and slot-cluster pair, it maps VMs to slots by solving the much smaller sized TVMPP problem. Furthermore, the authors have shown that the computational complexity of SlotClustering and VMMinKcut are $O(nk)$ and $O(n^4)$, respectively, with total complexity of $O(n^4)$.

The performances evaluation of Cluster-and-Cut heuristic is performed through trace-driven simulation using hybrid traffic model on inter-VM traffic rates (aggregated incoming and outgoing) collected from production data centers. The results show that Cluster-and-Cut produces solution with objective function value 10% lower than its competitors across different network topologies and the solution computation time is halved.

However, the proposed approach considers some assumptions that cannot be hold in the context of real data centers. TVMPP does not incorporate the link capacity constraints that can lead to VM placement decisions with congested links into the data center (Biran et al., 2012). Furthermore, Cluster-and-Cut algorithm places only one VM per server that can result in high amount of resource wastage. Additionally, it is assumed that static layer 2 and 3 routing protocols are deployed in the data center. Finally, VM migration overhead incurred due to the offline VM shuffling is not considered.

Through discussion the authors have indicated the potential benefit of combining the goals of both network resource optimization and server resource optimization (such as power consumption or CPU utilization) during the VM placement decision phase. They also emphasized that reduction of total energy consumption in a data center requires combined optimization of the above mentioned resources. The authors have also mentioned potential of performance improvement by employing dynamic routing and VM migration, rather than using simple static routing.

Network-Aware Energy-Efficient VM Placement and Migration Approaches

Multi-Objective Virtual Machine Migration in Virtualized Data Center Environments

Huang et al. (2013) have addressed the problem of overloaded VM migration in data centers having inter-VM communication dependencies. Indicating the fact that most of the existing works on VM migrations focus primarily on the server-side resource constraints with the goal of consolidating VMs on minimum number of servers and thus improving overall resource utilization and reducing energy-consumption, the authors have argued that VMs of modern applications have mutual communication dependencies and traffic patterns. As a result, online VM migration strategies need to be multi-objective focusing both on maximizing resource utilization and minimizing data center traffic overhead.

Following a similar approach as in (Huang et al., 2012), the authors have presented three stages of the joint optimization framework:

1. Based on the dominant resource share and max-min fairness model, the first optimization framework tries to maximize the total utilities of the physical servers; in order words tries to minimize the number of used servers and thus reduce power consumption,
2. Considering the complete application context with inter-VM traffic dependencies, the second optimization framework strives to minimize the total communication costs among VM after necessary VM migrations, and
3. Based on the above two frameworks, the third optimization framework combines the above goals subject to the constraints that the allocated resources from each server is not exceeded its capacity and the aggregated communication weight of a server is lower or equal to its bandwidth capacity.

The authors have further proposed a two-stage greedy heuristic algorithm to solve the defined optimization problem: Base Algorithm and Extension Algorithm. The Base Algorithm takes as input the set of VMs, set of servers, and the dominant resource share of user servers, and the set of overloaded VMs. Then, it sorts the overloaded VMs in decreasing order of their dominant resource share before migration. After incorporation of application dependencies (i.e. inter-VM communication dependencies), the Extension Algorithm selects candidate destination

server for migration to the server with the minimum dominant resource share and application-dependent inter-VM traffic. The VM migration effect is computed as the impact based on both distance effect and inter-VM traffic pattern-based network cost after migration. For each overloaded VM, the total communication weight is computed as the sum of all related inter-VM communication weights and the overloaded VM is migrated to the server with minimum migration impact.

The authors have shown simulation-based evaluation of the proposed multi-objective VM placement approach with comparison to AppAware (Shrivastava et al., 2011) application-aware VM migration policy. The following four different network topologies are used as data center network architecture: Tree, Fat-Tree (Al-Fares et al., 2008), VL2 (Greenberg et al., 2009), and BCube (Guo et al., 2009). Data center server capacity, VM resource demand, and inter-VM traffic volume is generated synthetically based on normal distribution with varying mean. The results show that the achieved mean reduction in traffic of the proposed algorithm is higher for BCube compared to Tree topology. Compared to AppAware, the proposed algorithm can achieve larger reduction in data center network traffic volume, by generating migrations that decreased traffic volume transported by the network up to 82.6% (for small number of VMs). As per average impact of migration, it decreases with the increase of server resource capacity. It is attributed that since the multiplier factor in the migration impact formulation includes dominant resource share of the migrating VM and it is decreased after migration. However, with the increase of VM resource demands, the average impact of migration is increased. This is attributed for the fact that the demand of VMs has a direct impact on the inter-dependencies among the VMs of multi-tier applications. Finally, with the increase of inter-VM communication weights, the average impact of migration increases since communication weights influence the cross-traffic burden between network switches.

Communication Traffic Minimization with Power-Aware VM Placement in Data Centers

Zhang et al. (2012) have addressed the problem of static greedy allocations of resources to VMs, regardless of the footprints of resource usage of both VMs and PMs. The authors have suggested that VMs with high communication traffic can be consolidated into minimum number of servers so as to reduce the external traffic of the host since co-located VMs can communicate using memory copy. With goal of minimizing communication traffic within a data center, the authors have defined dynamic VM placement as an optimization problem. The solution of the problem would be a mapping between VMs and servers, and such a problem is presented to be reduced from a minimum k-cut problem (Xu & Wunsch, 2005) that is already proved to be NP-hard. Since an idle server uses more than two-third of the total power when the machine is fully utilized (Kusic et al., 2009), the authors set power-consumption minimization as a second objective of their proposed VM placement scheme.

The authors have provided formal presentation of the optimization problem using mathematical framework that is set to minimize the total communication traffic in the data center, provided that various server-side resource constraints should be satisfied. Such problem can be solved by partitioning the VMs into clusters in such a way that VMs with heavy communication can be placed in the same server. As a solution, the author proposed the use of K-means clustering algorithm (Xu & Wunsch, 2005) that would generate VM-to-server placement mappings. Utilizing the K-means clustering approach, the authors proposed a greedy heuristic named K-means Clustering for VM consolidation that starts by considering each server as a cluster. Such cluster definition has got some benefits:

1. The number K and the initial clusters can be fixed to minimize the negative impact from randomization,
2. There is an upper-bound for each cluster that corresponds to the capacity constraints of each server, and
3. Fixed clusters can reduce the number of migrations.

In each iteration of the K-means Clustering for the VM Consolidation algorithm, the distance between a selected VM and a server is determined. Using this, the VM is placed in the server with minimum distance. This step is repeated until every VM has a fixed placement on its destination server. The authors have further reported that the greedy algorithm has a polynomial complexity of $O(tmn)$, where t is the number of iterations, n is the number of VMs, and m is the number of servers in the data centers. The authors have further presented algorithms for computing the distance between a VM and a cluster, and for online scenarios where greedy heuristic handles new VM requests.

Performance evaluation based on simulation and synthetic data center load characteristics is reported with superior performance gain by the proposed algorithm compared to its three competitors:

1. Random placement,
2. Simple greedy approach (puts the VM on the server which communicates most with current VM), and
3. First Fit (FF) heuristic.

Both the random placement and FF heuristics are unaware of inter-VM communication. The results show that the proposed greedy algorithm achieved better performance for both performance metrics:

1. Total communication traffic in data center, and
2. Number of used server (in other words, measure of power cost) after consolidation.

For the online VM deployment scenario, the clustering algorithm is compared against greedy algorithm and it is reported that the greedy algorithm can perform very close to the clustering method where the number of migrations is significantly larger than the greedy method and the greedy method can deploy new VM requests rapidly without affecting other nodes.

As for future work directions, the authors expressed plan to introduce the SLA to approach a better solution where the data center can provide better performance for the applications because of less communication traffic. This metric would be included in the cost model. Furthermore, the migration cost would be taken as a metric of the proposed distance model.

Energy-Aware Virtual Machine Placement in Data Centers

Huang et al. (2012) have presented a joint physical server and network device energy consumption problem for modern data centers hosting communication-intensive applications. The authors have staged several data center facts in order to signify the importance of multi-objective VM placement:

1. Increasing deployment of wide spectrum of composite applications consisting of multiple VMs with large amount of inter-VM data transfers,
2. Continuous growth in the size of data centers,
3. Existing VM placement strategies lack multiple optimizations, and
4. Rise of electricity cost.

In response to the above issues, the authors have investigated the balance between server energy consumption and energy consumption of data center transmission and switching network.

The multi-objective VM placement problem is modeled as an optimization problem in three stages. Considering server resource capacities (CPU, memory, and storage) and VM resource demands, the first optimization framework is targeted on VM placement decisions that would maximize server resource utilizations and eventually reduce energy consumption (by turning idle servers to lower power state, e.g., standby) following proportional fairness and without considering inter-VM communication pattern. The second optimization framework considers inter-VM data traffic patterns and server-side bandwidth capacity constraints, and is modeled as a Convex Programming Problem that tries to minimize the total aggregated communication costs among VMs. Finally, the energy-aware joint VM placement problem is modeled using fuzzy-logic system with trade-off between the first two objectives that can be in conflict when combined together. The authors have further proposed a prototype implementation approach for the joint VM placement following a two-level control architecture with local controllers installed in every VM and a global controller at the data center level responsible to determining VM placement and resource allocations.

As solution approach, the authors have put forward two algorithmic steps: VMGrouping and SlotGrouping. VMGrouping finds VM-to-server mappings such that VM pairs with high traffic communication are mapped to server pairs with low cost physical link. Such VM-to-server mappings are modeled as Balanced Minimum K-cut Problem (Saran & Vazirani, 1995) and a k-cut with minimum weight is identified so that the VMs can be partitioned into k disjoint subsets of different sizes. Afterwards, SlotGrouping maps each VM group to appropriate servers in closest neighborhood respecting the server side resource constraints.

The authors have validated the proposed multi-objective VM placement approach using simulation-based evaluation under varying traffic demands, and load characteristics of VMs and physical servers using normal distribution under different means as well as for different network architectures (e.g., Tree (Al-Fares et al., 2008),

VL2 (Greenberg et al., 2009), Fat-tree (Guo et al., 2008), and BCube (Guo et al., 2009)). Focusing on the formulated objective function value and total data center traffic volume as performance metrics, the proposed joint VM placement policy is compared against random placement and First Fit Decreasing (FFD) heuristic-based placement policies. The results show that the joint VM placement achieves higher objective values and much reduced traffic flow (up to 50% to 81%) compared to other approaches, resulting in lower communication cost and resource wastage. In order to assess performance from energy-consumption reduction point of view, the proposed placement approach is compared against Grouping Genetic Algorithm (GGA) (Agrawal, Bose, & Sundarrajan, 2009), FFD, two-stage heuristic algorithm (Gupta, Bose, Sundarrajan, Chebiyam, & Chakrabarti, 2008), random placement, and optimal placement considering the number of used PMs as performance metric. It is reported that the proposed energy-aware joint placement method achieves better performance over random placement, GGA, and the two stage heuristic algorithm, and inferior performance over FFD and optimal placement. Such performance pattern is rationalized by the trade-offs between multiple objectives (i.e. minimizing both resource wastage and traffic volume simultaneously) that the joint VM placement policy strives to achieve.

In this research work, the authors have brought about a very timely issue of balancing both energy- and network-awareness while VM placement decisions are made. Most of the existing works focus on either one of the objectives, not both at the same time. However, this work has not considered the impact of the necessary VM live migrations and reconfigurations on both the network links and hosted applications performance, which can have substantially detrimental effects on both applications SLAs and network performance given that the new VM placement decision requires large number of VM migrations.

Network- and Data-Aware VM Placement and Migration Mechanisms

Coupled Placement in Modern Data Centers

Korupolu et al. (2009) have addressed the problem of placing both computation and data components of applications among the physical compute and storage nodes of modern virtualized data centers. The authors have presented several aspects that introduce heterogeneity in modern data centers and thus make the optimization problem of compute-data pairwise placement non-trivial:

1. Enterprise data centers evolve over time and different parts of the data center can have performance variations (e.g., one network switch can be more recent than others and have lower latency and greater I/O throughput),
2. Wide spread use of multi-purpose hardwire devices (e.g., storage devices with built-in compute resources), and
3. Large variance of the I/O rates between compute and data components of modern applications.

Taking into considering the above factors, the Coupled Placement Problem (CPP) is formally defined as an optimization problem with the goal of minimizing the total cost over all applications, provided that compute server and storage node capacity constraints are satisfied. The cost function can be any user defined function and the idea behind it is that it captures the network cost that is incurred due placing the application computation component (e.g., VM) in a certain compute node and the data component (e.g., data block or file system) in a certain storage node. One obvious cost function can be the I/O rate between compute and data components of application multiplied by the corresponding network distance between the compute and storage nodes.

After proving the CPP as a NP-hard problem, the authors proposed three different heuristic algorithms to solve it:

1. Individual Greedy Placement (INDV-GR), following greedy approach, tries to place the application data storages sorted by their I/O rate per unit of data storage where storage nodes are ordered by the minimum distances to any connected compute node. Thus, INDV-GR algorithm places highest throughput applications on storage nodes having the closest compute nodes.
2. Another greedy algorithm, Pairwise Greedy Placement (PAIR-GR) considers the compute-storage node affinities and tries to place both compute and data components of each application simultaneously by assigning applications sorted by their I/O rate normalized by their CPU and data storage requirements on storage-compute node pairs sorted by the network distance between the node pairs.
3. Finally, in order to avoid early sub-optimal placement decisions resulting due to the greedy nature of the first two algorithms, the authors proposed Coupled Placement Algorithm (CPA) where CPP is shown to have properties very similar to the Knapsack Problem (Pisinger, 1997) and the Stable-Marriage Problem (McVitie & Wilson, 1971). Solving both the Knapsack and the Stable-Marriage Problem, the CPA algorithm iteratively refines placement decisions to solve the CPP problem in three phases:
   a. CPA-Stg phase where data storage placement decision is made,
   b. CPA-Compute phase where computation component placement decision is taken provided the current storage placements, and
   c. CPA-Swap phase that looks for pairs of applications for which swapping their storage-compute node pairs improves the cost function and performs the swap.

The performance of INDV-GR, PAIR-GR, and CPA is compared against the optimal solutions through simulation-based experimentations. The authors have used CPLEX ILP solver for small problem instances and MINOS solver based on LP-relaxation for larger problems. Cost function values and placement computation times are considered as performance metrics and the experiments are carried out across four different dimensions:

1. Problem size/complexity through variations in simulated data center size,
2. Tightness of fit through variations of mean application compute and data demands,
3. Variance of application compute and data demands, and
4. Physical network link distance factor.

Through elaborate analysis of results and discussion, the proposed CPA algorithm is demonstrated to be scalable both in optimization quality and placement computation time, as well as robust with varying workload characteristics. On average, CPA is shown to produce placements within 4% of the optimal lower bounds obtained by LP formulations.

However, the optimization framework takes some simplistic view of the application models and resource capacity constraints. Firstly, the CPP has considered each application as having one compute and one data storage components whereas modern applications usually have composite view with multiple compute components with communications among themselves as well as communication with multiple data storage components. Secondly, on the part of compute resource demand, only CPU is considered whereas memory and other OS-dependent features make the problem multi-dimensional (Ferdaus, Murshed, Calheiros, & Buyya, 2014). Thirdly, no assumption is made regarding the overhead or cost of reconfiguration due to the new placement decision, in which VM migrations and data movement would be dominating factors. Finally, no network link bandwidth capacity constraint is no taken into account during the CPP formulation.

Nonetheless, the authors have pointed out couple of future research outlooks: inclusion of multi-dimensional resource capacity constraints and other cost models focusing on different data center objectives like and energy utilization.

Network and Data Location-Aware VM Placement and Migration Approach in Cloud Computing

Piao et al. (2010) have addressed the problem of achieving and maintaining expected performance level of data-intensive Cloud applications that need frequent data transmission from storage blocks. The studied scenario is focused on modern Cloud data centers comprising of both compute Clouds (e.g., Amazon EC2) and storage Clouds (e.g., Amazon S3) where hosted applications access the associated data across the Internet or Intranet over communication links that can either be physical or logical. Moreover, the authors have suggested that under current VM allocation policy, the data can be stored arbitrarily and distributed across single storage Cloud or even over several storage Clouds. Furthermore, the brokers allocate the applications without consideration of the data access time. As a consequence, such placement decisions can lead to data access over unnecessary distance.

In order to overcome the above mentioned problem, the authors have proposed two algorithms based on exhaustive search: VM placement approach and VM migration approach. For both the solutions, the per application data is modeled as a set of data blocks distributed across different physical storage nodes with varying distances (either logical or physical) from physical compute nodes. Network speed between physical compute node and storage node is modeled using *Speed(s, Δt)* function that depends on the size of the data *s* and packet transfer time slot *Δt*. Finally, for each physical compute node, the corresponding data

access time is formulated as the sum of product of each data block size and the inverse of the corresponding network speed value. The VM placement algorithm handles each new application deployment request and performs an exhaustive search over all the feasible compute nodes to find the one with minimum data access time for the corresponding data blocks for the submitted VM, subject to the compute node resource capacity constraints are satisfied. The VM migration algorithm is triggered when the application execution time exceeds the SLA specified threshold. In such a situation, a similar exhaustive search over all the feasible compute nodes is performed to find the one with minimum data access time for the corresponding data blocks for the migrating VM, subject to the compute node resource capacity constraints as satisfied.

The efficacy of the proposed algorithms is validated through simulation based on the CloudSim (Buyya, Ranjan, & Calheiros, 2009) simulation toolkit. The evaluation is focused on the average task completion time and the proposed algorithms are compared against the default VM placement policy implemented in CloudSim 2.0, namely VMAllocationPolicySimple that allocates the VM on the least utilized host following a load-balancing approach. The simulation is setup with small scale data centers comprising of 3 VMs, 3 data blocks, 2 storage nodes, and 3 compute nodes with fixed resource capacities. It is shown that the proposed approaches needed shorter average task completion time, which is emphasized as due to the optimized location of hosted VMs. In order to trigger the proposed VM migration algorithm, the network status matrix is changed and as a consequence some of the VMs are migrated to hosts that resulted in lower average task completion time.

Besides considering very simplistic view of federated Cloud data centers, the proposed VM placement and migration algorithms take an exhaustive search approach that may not scale for very large data centers. Moreover, the experimental evaluation is performed in a tiny scale and compared with a VM placement that is fully network-agnostic. Furthermore, VM migration or reconfiguration overhead is not considered in the problem formulation or solution schemes.

As for future work directions, the authors suggested inclusion of negotiation between service provider and user in terms of data access time to guarantee SLA enforcement. In order to avoid some users' tasks always occupying a faster network link, priority-based scheduling policy is recommended through extension of the payment mechanisms.

Application-Aware VM Placement and Migration Strategies

Communication-Aware Scheduling for Parallel Applications in Virtualized Data Centers

Takouna et al. (2013) have introduced the problem of scheduling VMs that are part of HPC applications and communicate through shared memory bus (when placed in the same server) and shared networks (when placed in different servers). The authors have identified some limitations of existing VM placement and migration approaches with regards to the HPC and parallel applications:

1. VM placement approaches that optimize server-side resources (e.g., CPU and memory) are unaware of the inter-VM communication patterns, and as a result are less efficient from network utilization and ultimately from application performance point of view, and
2. Recent network-aware VM placement approaches focus on optimal initial VM placement and overlook the real-time communication patterns and traffic demands, and thus are not reactive to changes.

In order to address the above shortcomings, the authors have proposed communication-aware and energy-efficient VM scheduling technique focusing on parallel applications that use different programming models for inter-VM communication (e.g. OpenMP and Message Passing Interface (MPI)). The proposed technique determines the run-time inter-VM bandwidth requirements and communication patterns and upon detection of inefficient placement, reschedules the VM placement through VM live migrations.

In order to handle potential VM migration requests, the authors have presented a brief overview of the system framework consisting of VMs with peer-VM information (i.e. VMs that have mutual communication) and a central Migration Manager (MM). HPC jobs are executed in individual VMs and each VM have a list of its peer-VMs at run-time. It is the responsibility of the MM to determine the communication pattern of the whole parallel application. It is further assumed that each physical server have enough free resources (10% to 20% of CPU) to handle potential VM migration. The authors have further proposed an iterative greedy algorithm, namely Peer VMs Aggregation (PVA) that would be run by the MM upon getting migration requests from VMs. The ultimate goal of the PVA algorithm is to aggregate the communicating VMs with mutual traffic into the same server so that they can communicate through the shared memory bus, so as to reduce the inter-VM traffic flow in the network. This would both localize the traffic (and thus reduce network utilization) and minimize the communication delays among VMs with mutual communication dependencies (and thus improving application performance). The PVA algorithm is composed of the following four parts:

1. **Sort:** The MM ranks the VMs that are requesting migration in a decreasing order based on the number of input/output traffic flows while ignoring the requests of VMs assigned on the same server),
2. **Select:** MM selects the highest ranked VM to be migrated to the destination server where its peer VMs are assigned,

3. **Check:** MM examines the feasibility of VM migrations to the destination servers in terms of server resource (CPU, memory, and network I/O) capacity constraints, and

4. **Migrate:** If MM finds the server suitable for the migrating VM, it directly migrates the selected VM to that server; otherwise the MM tries to migrate a VM from the destination server to free enough resources for the selected VM to be placed in the same server of its peer VMs (in that case the selected VM should also be suitable to be migrated). However, if the destination server does not host any VM, the MM can assign the selected VM on a server that shares the same edge switch with the server of its peer VMs.

The PVA approach is reported to minimize the total data center traffic significantly by reducing the network utilization traffic by 25%. The authors have claimed to have implemented the network topology and memory subsystem on the popular CloudSim simulation toolkit (Calheiros, Ranjan, Beloglazov, De Rose, & Buyya, 2011) and used the NAS Parallel Benchmarks (NPB) as HPC application which is divided into two groups: kernel benchmarks and pseudo-applications (Takouna, Dawoud, & Meinel, 2012). While compared to CPU utilization-based random placement algorithm, PVA is reported to have aggregated all the VMs belonging to an application into the same server and thus produced perfect VM placement after determining the traffic pattern of the communicating VMs. Moreover, the proposed approach have been shown to have outperformed the CPU-based placement in terms of reducing network link utilization through transferring inter-VM communication from shared network to shared memory by aggregating communicating VMs. In addition, the application performance degradation is computed and compared against the ideal execution time of the individual jobs and it is reported that 18% of the VMs suffer performance degradation while using PVA, whereas 20% performance degradation is experienced in the case of CPU-based placements.

Though PVA approach mentions where to migrate a VM, it does not make it clear when a VM requests for migration. Moreover, the associated VM migration overhead is not taken into account. Furthermore, it would not be always the case that all the VMs consisting of a parallel/HPC application can be aggregated into a single server. Finally, the evaluation lacks the reporting of the energy-efficiency aspect of the proposed approach.

The authors have presented a few future research work directions: 1) performance evaluation using different number of VMs for each application and 2) comparison with communication- and topology-aware VM placement approaches.

Application-Aware VM Placement in Data Centers

Song et al. (2012) have presented an application-aware VM placement problem focusing on energy-efficiency and scalability of modern data centers. The authors have pointed out several factors of modern data center management:

1. Increasing use of large-scale data processing services deployed in data centers,

2. Due to the rise of inter-VM bandwidth demands of modern applications, several recent network architecture scalability research works have been conducted with the goal of minimizing data center network costs by increasing the degree of network connectivity and adopting dynamic routing schemes,

3. Focusing on energy- and power-consumption minimization, several other recent works proposed mechanisms to improve server resource utilization and turning inactive servers to lower power states to save energy, and

4. Existing VM placement tools (e.g., VMware Capacity Planner ("VMware Capacity Planner", 2014) and Novell PlateSpin

Recon ("Novell PlateSpin Recon", 2014)) are unaware of inter-VM traffic patterns, and thus can lead to placement decisions where heavily communicating VMs can be placed in physical servers with long distance network communication.

Similar to the work by Huang et al. (2012), Song et al. (2012) have expounded a VM placement problem based on proportional fairness and convex optimization to address the combined problem of reducing energy-consumption and data center traffic volume in order to improve scalability. During the problem formulation, both server-side resource capacity constraints and application-level inter-VM traffic demands are considered. However, given the problem definition, no algorithm or placement mechanism is presented in the work in order to solve the problem. Furthermore, simulation-based evaluation is presented and it is claimed that the combined VM placement algorithm outperforms random and FFD-based VM placement algorithms.

Application-Aware VM Migration in Data Centers

Shrivastava et al. (2011) have addressed the load balancing problem in virtualized data centers trough migration of overloaded VMs to underloaded physical servers such that the migration would be network-aware. The authors have argued that when VMs (part of multi-tier applications) are migrated to remove hot spots in data centers can introduce additional network overhead due to the inherent coupling between VMs based on communication, especially when moved to servers that are distant in terms of network distance. With the goal of finding destination servers for overloaded VMs that would result in minimum network traffic after the migration, the authors have formulated the VM migration as an optimization problem and proposed a network topology-aware greedy heuristic.

The proposed optimization problem is called application-aware since the complete application context running on top of the overloaded VM is considered during the migration decision. A view of the interconnections of the VMs comprising a multi-tier application is modeled as a dependency graph consisting of VMs as vertices and inter-VM communications as edges of the graph. The authors have also modeled the network cost function as a product of traffic demand of edge and network distance of the corresponding host servers, where such network distance can be defined as latency, delay, or number of hops between any two servers. Furthermore, server-side resource capacity constraint is also included in the problem formulation.

Since such optimization problem is NP-complete, the authors have proposed a greedy approximate solution named AppAware that attempts to reduce the cost during each migration decision step while considering both application-level inter-VM dependencies and underlying network topology. AppAware has the following four stages:

1. **Base Algorithm:** for each overloaded VM in the system, the total communication weight is computed and based on this the overloaded VMs are sorted in decreasing order, and then for each feasible destination server, the migration impact factor is computed. The impact factor gives a measure of the migration overhead based on the defined cost function due to the potential migration. Finally, the base algorithm selects the destination host for which the migration impact factor is the minimum, provided that the destination host has enough resources to accommodate the migrating VM.

2. **Incorporation of Application Dependency:** this part of AppAware computes the total cost to migrate a VM to a destination server as the sum of its individual cost corresponding to each of its peer VM that the migrating VM has communication.

3. **Topology Information and Server Load:** this part of AppAware considers network topology and neighboring server load while making migration decisions since a physical server that is close (in terms of topological distance) to other lightly loaded servers would be of higher preference as destination for a VM due to its potential for being capable of accommodating it dependent VMs to nearly servers.

4. **Iterative Refinements:** AppAware is further improved by incorporating two extensions to minimize the data center traffic. The first extension computes multiple values of the migration impact over multiple iterations of the AppAware base algorithm and the second extension further refines upon the previous extension by considering expected migration impact of future mappings of other VMs for a given candidate destination server at each iteration.

Based on numerical simulations, the authors have reported performance evaluation of AppAware by comparing with the optimal solution and Sandpiper black-box and grey-box migration scheme (Wood, Shenoy, Venkataramani, & Yousif, 2007). Run-time server-side remaining resource capacity (CPU, memory, and storage) and VM resource demands are generated using normal distribution, whereas inter-VM communication dependencies are generated using normal, exponential, and uniform distributions with varying mean and variance. Since the formulated migration problem is NP-hard, the performance of AppAware and Sandpiper are compared with optimal migration decisions only for small scale data centers (with 10 servers) and AppAware is reported to have produced solutions that are very close to the optimal solutions. For large data centers (with 100 servers), AppAware is compared against Sandpiper and it is reported that AppAware outperformed Sandpiper consistently by producing migration decisions that decreased

traffic volume transported by the network by up to 81%. Moreover, in order to assess the suitability of AppAware against various network topologies, AppAware is compared to optimal placement decisions for Tree and VL2 network topologies. It is reported that AppAware performs close to optimal placement for Tree topology, whereas the gap is increased for VL2.

AppAware considered server-side resource capacity constraints during VM migration, but it does not consider the physical link bandwidth capacity constraints. As a consequence, subsequent VM migrations can cause network links of low distance to get congested.

COMPARATIVE ANALYSIS OF THE VM PLACEMENT AND MIGRATION TECHNIQUES

Besides resource capacity constraints on the physical computer servers, scalability and performance of data centers also depends on the efficient network resource allocations. With the growing complexity of the hosted applications and rapid rise in the volume of data associated to the application tasks, network traffic rates among the VMs running inside the data centers are increasing sharply. Such inter-VM data traffic exhibits non-uniform patterns and can change dynamically. As a result, this can cause bottlenecks and congestions in the underlying communication infrastructure. Network-aware VM placement and migration decisions have been considered as an effective tool to address this problem by assigning VMs to PMs with consideration of different data center characteristics and features, as well as traffic demands and patterns among the VMs.

The existing VM placement and migration techniques proposed by both academia and industry consider various system assumptions, problem modeling techniques and the features of the data centers and applications, as well as different solution and evaluation approaches. As

Table 1. Comparative analysis of the traffic-aware VM placement and migration techniques

Project	Network Topology-Aware VM Cluster Placement in IaaS Clouds
Salient Features	• VMs deployment as composite virtual infrastructure. • Physical server resource capacity constraints. • User provided prospective traffic patterns and bandwidth requirements among VMs in the form of XML configuration. • Possible anti-colocation condition among VMs. • Physical infrastructure interconnection following PortLand network topology. • Two-layered framework: physical infrastructure and middleware.
Advantages	• Suggested VIBES algorithm incrementally searches for a neighborhood by utilizing PortLand's topological features with sufficient physical resources and VIO places the virtual infrastructure within the neighborhood. This approach has the advantage that all the VMs of the whole virtual infrastructure are placed in near proximity within the network topology. • Use of greedy heuristics ensures fast placement decisions. • Placements of VMs with higher inter-VM traffic demands in topologically near physical servers suggests lower network utilization and possible accommodation of higher number of VMs.
Drawbacks	• VM Placement decisions focusing on network utilization may result in significant compute resource wastage and less energy efficient. • Expected inter-VM traffic demands may not always be readily available to Cloud users and dynamic traffic patterns can different from the initial estimation. • In a dynamic data center, VMs are deployed and terminated at runtime and the initial traffic-aware VM placement decisions may not remain network efficient as time passes. Such approaches can be complemented through the use of dynamic (periodic or event triggered) VM migration and reconfiguration decisions.
Project	Stable Network-Aware VM Placement for Cloud Systems

Salient Features	• Graph transformation techniques to convert complex network topologies (e.g., Fat-tree and VL2) to plain tree topology.
	• Minimization of the ratio between the inter-VM bandwidth requirements and physical link bandwidth capacities.
	• Integer Quadratic Programming model-based Min Cut Ratio-aware VM Placement (MCRVMP) problem definition with server and network resource capacities constraints.
	• Grouping of communicating VMs in data center as connected components and dynamic relocation of the connected components in order to minimize network overhead on physical network infrastructure.
	• Two VM placement heuristic algorithms:
	    o Integer Programming-based recursive algorithm, and
	    o Iteration-based greedy placement algorithm.

Advantages	• Grouping of communicating VMs into smaller-sized connected components ensure faster VM placement decision. • Though the proposed VM placement algorithms works on tree topology, by the use of topology conversion techniques the algorithms can be applied for much complex network architectures. • As reported by the experimental evaluation using NS2 network simulator, the proposed VM placement techniques experience zero dropped packets and can absorb time-varying traffic demands up to three times the nominal values.
Drawbacks	• Cost or overhead of necessary VM migrations are not considered in the problem formulation and solution techniques. • The quality of the VM placement solutions were compared to random and optimal solutions only for small problems and not evaluated against other placement techniques for larger data centers.

continued on following page

a consequence, comparative analysis in a uniform fashion of such techniques becomes quite tricky. Moreover, VM placement and migration is a broad area of research with various optimization and objectives. Some of the techniques strive for single-objective optimization, while others try to incorporate multiple objectives while making VM placement and relocation decisions. Taking into account the various aspects and features considered and proposed in the network-aware VM placement and migration strategies, detailed comparative analyses are presented in Tables 1, 2, 3, and 4 grouped by the subdomains they are categorized in.

Table 1. Continued

Project	Scalability Improvement of Data Center Networks with Traffic-Aware VM Placement
Salient Features	• Three observed dominant trends of data center traffic patterns: 　o Low correlation between mean traffic rates of VM pairs and the corresponding end-to-end physical communication distance/cost. 　o Highly non-uniform traffic distribution for individual VMs. 　o Traffic rates between VM pairs tend to remain relatively constant. • Definition of the traffic-aware VM placement problem as a NP-hard combinatorial optimization problem belonging to the family of the Quadratic Assignment Problems. • The goal of the defined problem is minimization of aggregate traffic rates at each network switch. • The cost of placing any two VMs with traffic flows is defined as the number of hops or switches on the routing path of the VM pairs. • A concept of slot is incorporated to represent one CPU/memory allocation on physical server. Multiple such slots can reside on the same server and each slot can be allocated to any VM.
Advantages	• Adaptation of divide-and-conquer strategy to group all the slots based on the cost among the slots. This approach helps reduce the problem space into smaller sub-problems. • The proposed Cluster-and-Cut algorithm finds VM-to-PM assignment decisions to place VM pairs with high mutual traffic on PM pairs with low cost communication links. • Trace-driven simulation using global and partitioned traffic model, as well as hybrid traffic model combining real traces from production data centers with classical Gravity model.
Drawbacks	• The formulated Traffic-aware VM Placement Problem does not consider the physical link capacity constraints. • It is assumed that static layer 2 and 3 routing protocols are deployed in the data center. • VM migration overhead incurred due to the offline VM shuffling is not considered. • The proposed Cluster-and-Cut algorithm places only one VM per server that can result in high amount of resource wastage.

Finally, Table 5 illustrates the most significant aspects of the reviewed research projects that are highly relevant to network-aware VM placement and migration techniques.

FUTURE RESEARCH DIRECTIONS

VM consolidation and resource reallocation through VM migrations with focus on both energy-awareness and network overhead is yet another area of research that requires much attention. VM placement decisions focusing primarily on server resource utilization and energy consumption reduction can produce data center configurations that are not traffic-aware or network optimized, and thus can lead to higher SLA violations. As a consequence, VM placement strategies utilizing both VM resource requirements information and inter-VM traffic load can come up with placement decisions that are more realistic and efficient.

Cloud environments allow their consumers to deploy any kind of applications in an on-demand fashion, ranging from compute intensive applications such as HPC and scientific applications, to network and disk I/O intensive applications like video streaming and file sharing applications. Co-locating similar kinds of applications in the same physical server can lead to resource contentions for some types of resources while leaving other types under-utilized. Moreover, such resource contention will have adverse effects on application performance, thus leading to SLA violations and profit minimization. Therefore, it is important to understand the behavior and resource usage patterns of the hosted applications in order to efficiently place VMs and allocate resources to the applications. Utilization of historical workload data and application of appropriate load prediction mechanisms need to be integrated with VM consolidation techniques to minimize resource contentions among applications and increase resource utilization and energy efficiency of data centers.

Table 2. Comparative analysis of the network-aware energy-efficient VM placement and migration techniques

Project	**Multi-Objective Virtual Machine Migration in Virtualized Data Center Environments**

Salient Features	• Definition of VM migration problem as multi-objective optimization with the goal of maximization of resource utilization and minimization of network traffic.
	 • Three levels of joint optimization framework:
	    o **Server Consolidation:** Minimization of the number of active physical servers and reduce energy consumption.
	    o Minimization of the total communication cost after necessary VM migrations.
	    o Combined goal of minimizing energy consumption and total communication costs.
	 • Two-staged greedy heuristic solution to compute overloaded VM migration decisions:
	    o Application of dominant resource share of servers.
	    o Selection of destination server for migration with minimum dominant resource share and communication traffic among VMs.

Advantages	• VM migration decisions consider minimum migration impact of overloaded VMs. • Combined optimization of energy consumption and network traffic.
Drawbacks	• Exhaustive search-based solution generation.
Project	**Communication Traffic Minimization with Power-Aware VM Placement in Data Centers**

Salient Features	• VMs located in same server would communicate using memory copy rather than network links, thus reduce total network traffic.
	 • Definition of dynamic VM placement problem as a reduced minimum k-cut problem (NP-hard).
	 • Two-fold objectives of minimizing total network traffic and energy consumption through VM consolidation.
	 • Server side resource capacity constraints as VM placement constraints.
	 • Solution approach utilizes K-means clustering algorithm with following distinguishing features:
	    o Minimization of the negative impact of placement randomization
	    o Reduction of the number of migration
	 • Method for computing the communication distance between a VM and a cluster.

Advantages	• Suggested solutions address both online dynamic VM migration and offline deployment of new VM requests. • Evaluation using workload traces from production data centers. • Multiple goals of reducing power consumption and network traffic.
Drawbacks	• Most of the compared VM placement approaches are network-agnostic.
Project	**Energy-Aware Virtual Machine Placement in Data Centers**

Salient Features	• Balanced optimization between server power consumption and network-infrastructure power consumption.
	 • Definition of three-phased optimization framework:
	    o Maximization of server resource utilization and reduction of power consumption.
	    o Minimization of total aggregated communication costs.
	    o Fuzzy-logic system-based energy-aware joint VM placement with trade-off between the above two optimizations.
	 • Clustering of VMs and PMs based on the amount of communication traffic and network distances.
	 • Broad range of experimental evaluation comparing with multiple existing VM placement approaches using different network topologies.

Advantages	• Multiple objectives focusing on optimizations of resource utilization, data center power consumption, and network resource utilization. • Partitioning of VMs into disjoint sets helps reduce the problem space and find solutions in reduced time.

Drawbacks	• Impacts of necessary VM migrations and reconfigurations are not considered in the modeled problem and proposed solution approaches:
	    o Increased traffic due to required VM migrations could impose overhead in network communication.
	    o VM migrations can have detrimental effects on hosted applications SLA due to VM download time.

Table 3. Comparative analysis of the network- and data-aware VM placement and migration techniques

Project	Coupled Placement in Modern Data Centers
Salient Features	• Network-focused joint (pair-wise) compute and data component placement. • Heterogeneous data center comprised of storage and network devices with built-in compute facilities and diversified performance footprints. • User defined network cost function. • Joint compute and data component placement problem modeled as Knapsack Problem and Stable-Marriage Problem. • Proposed Couple Placement Algorithm based on iterative refinement using pair-wise swap of application compute and storage components.
Advantages	• Incorporation of data components associated with application compute components and the corresponding traffic rates in application placement. • Incorporation of physical storage nodes and the corresponding network distances to the compute servers in cost definition. • Featured advanced properties and features of modern data center devices.
Drawbacks	• Compared to modern Cloud applications (composite and multi-tiered), the proposed Couple Placement Problem (CPP) assumes simplistic view of the application having only one compute and one data component. • CPP considers the server side resource capacity constraint as single dimensional (only CPU-based), whereas this is in fact a multi-dimensional problem (Ferdaus et al., 2014). • Network link bandwidth capacity is not considered. • VM and data components reconfiguration and relocation overhead is not considered in the problem formulation.
Project	**Network- and Data Location-Aware VM Placement and Migration Approach in Cloud Computing**
Salient Features	• Cloud applications with associated data components spread across one or more storage Clouds. • Single VM placement (initial) and overloaded VM migration decisions. • Initial fixed location of data components. • Modeled network link speed depends on both the size of the data transmitted and the packet transfer time. • Allocations of application compute components (i.e. VMs) with consideration of the associated data access time.
Advantages	• Consideration of data location during VM placement and migration decisions.
Drawbacks	• Over simplified view of federated Cloud data centers. • Exhaustive search-based solution approaches that can be highly costly as data center size increases. • VM migration and reconfiguration overheads are not considered. • Over simplified and small scale evaluation of the proposed VM placement and migration algorithms comparing with network-agnostic VM placement algorithm of CloudSim simulation toolkit.

Centralized VM consolidation and placement mechanisms can suffer from the problems of scalability and single-point-of-failure, especially for Cloud data centers. One possible solution approach would be replication of VM consolidation managers; however such decentralized approach is non-trivial since VMs in the date centers are created and terminated dynamically through on-demand requests of Cloud consumers, and as a consequence consolidation managers need to have updated information about the data center. As initial solution, servers can be clustered and assigned to the respective consolidation managers and appropriate communication and synchronization among the managers need to be ensured to avoid possible race conditions.

VM migration and reconfiguration overhead can have adverse effect on the scalability and bandwidth utilization of data centers, as well as application performance. As a consequence, VM placement and scheduling techniques that are

Table 4. Comparative analysis of the application-aware VM placement and migration techniques

Project	Communication-Aware Scheduling for Parallel Applications in Virtualized Data Centers
Salient Features	• Network-aware VM placement with focused on Parallel and HPC applications. • Dynamic VM reconfiguration through VM migrations based on communication patterns with peer-VMs of HPC applications. • Proposed approach iteratively refines the VMs placement through VM migrations with the goal of accumulating VMs (with traffic dependencies) of the same HPC application in the same server. • VM migration follows a ranking system based on the total number of input/output traffic flows.
Advantages	• Reactive VM scheduling approach to dynamic (run-time) changes of the inter-VM communication patterns. • Multiple objectives to optimization communication overhead and delay, as well as energy consumption.
Drawbacks	• It is unclear when a VM triggers it migration request. • Associated VM migration overhead is not considered in the problem statement. • Depending on the size of the HPC applications and the resource capacities of the physical servers, it is not guaranteed that all the VMs of a HPC application can be placed in a single server. • The reported experimental evaluation does not show improvement in terms of energy consumption.
Project	**Application-Aware VM Placement in Data Centers**
Salient Features	• Combined optimization of data center power consumption and network traffic volume. • Proposed modeling considers server-side resource capacity constraints and application-level communication dependencies among the VMs.
Advantages	• Multiple optimizations of both network traffic and power consumption.
Drawbacks	• Presented work lacks sufficient information regarding VM placement algorithm or scheduling. • Simulation-based evaluation considers network-agnostic competitors.
Project	**Application-Aware VM Migration in Data Centers**
Salient Features	• Load balancing through network-aware migration of overloaded VMs. • VM migration decisions considers complete application context in terms of peer VMs with communication dependencies. • Network cost is modeled as a product of traffic demands and network distance. • Server side resource capacity constraints are considered during VM migration decisions.
Advantages	• Network topology-aware VM migration decisions. • Iterative improvement is suggested to minimize data center traffic volume.
Drawbacks	• Physical link capacity constraints are not considered while mapping overloaded VMs to underloaded physical servers.

unaware of VM migration and reconfiguration overhead can effectively congest the network and cause SLA violations unbeknown. Incorporation of the estimated migration overhead with the placement strategies and optimization of VM placement and migration through balancing the utilization of network resources, migration overhead, and energy consumption are yet to explore areas of data center virtual resource management. With various trade-offs and balancing tools, data center administrators can have the freedom of tuning the performance indicators for their data centers.

CONCLUSION

Cloud Computing is quite a new computing paradigm and from the very beginning it has been growing rapidly in terms of scale, reliability, and availability. Because of its flexible pay-as-you-go business model, virtually infinite pool of on-demand resources, guaranteed QoS, and almost perfect reliability, consumer base of Cloud Computing is increasing day-by-day. As a result, Cloud providers are deploying large data centers across the globe. Such data centers extensively use virtualization technologies in order to utilize the

Table 5. Aspects of the notable research works on network-aware VM placement and migration

Research Project	System Assumption	Net. Arch/Topology	Placement Type	Modeling/Analysis Technique	Physical Resources	VM Placement Constraints	Objective/Goal	Solution Approach/Algorithm	Evaluation/Experimental Platform	Competitor Approaches	Workload/VM-Cluster in Experiments/Evaluation	Evaluation Performance Metrics
Multi-objective Virtual Machine Migration in Virtualized Data Center Environments (Huang et al., 2013)	Homogeneous data center	Tree, VL2, Fat-tree, BCube	Online	Max-min fairness and convex optimization framework	CPU, memory, and storage	Server resource capacity and inter-VM bandwidth requirement	Maximize utilization of physical servers and minimize data center network traffic	Two-staged greedy heuristic (exhaustive search based)	Simulation based on synthetic data center and load characteristics	AppAware: Application-aware VM Migration (Shrivastava et al., 2011)	Normal distribution-based load characteristics for VMs and servers, and inter-VM traffic demands	Reduction in network traffic and average impact of migration
Communication Traffic Minimization with Power-aware VM Placement in Data Centers (Zhang et al., 2012)	Homogeneous data center	N/A	Online and Offline	Mathematical optimization (minimization)	CPU, memory, network, and I/O	Server resource capacity	Minimization of communication traffic and power cost	Greedy heuristic	Simulation based on synthetic data center and load characteristics	Random placement, simple greedy, and First Fit (FF)	Workload traces from production data center	Total communication traffic and number of active servers
Energy-aware Virtual Machine Placement in Data Centers (Huang et al, 2012)	Homogeneous data center	Tree, VL2, Fat-tree, BCube	Online	Mathematical Optimization Framework [Proportional Fairness and (Convex Optimization)]	CPU, memory, and storage	Server resource capacity and inter-VM bandwidth requirement	Reduction of data Transmission and minimization of energy consumption of server and network device	Greedy approach	Simulation based on synthetic data center and load characteristics	Random placement, First Fit Decreasing (FFD), Grouping Genetic Algorithm (GGA), two stage heuristic algorithm, optimal placement	Normal distribution-based load characteristics for VMs and servers, and inter-VM traffic demands	Objective function value, reduction rate of traffic volume, and number of used servers
Network-aware VM Placement and Migration Approach in Cloud Computing (Piao & Yan, 2010)	IaaS Compute and Storage Data Center	Federated and Distributed Cloud Data Centers	Offline and Online		CPU and Memory	Server resource capacity constraints	Minimization of data transfer time consumption	Exhaustive search	Fixed simulation scenario implemented in CloudSim (Buyya, Ranjan, & Calheiros, 2009)	Default VM placement policy of CloudSim	Small-scale fixed valued workload data	Average task completion time
Coupled Placement in Modern Data Centers (Korupolu et al., 2009)	Heterogeneous data center	SAN Data Center using Core-Edge design pattern	Offline	Knapsack Problem and Stable Marriage Problem	CPU and Storage	Server node CPU and storage node capacity	Minimization of total network cost across all application communication links	Individual and pairwise Greedy heuristic, and iterative refinement-based heuristic	Heterogeneous SAN data center and synthetic workload-based simulation	LP-based optimal placement	Normal distribution-based compute and storage resource demands and network I/O rates	Defined network cost function value and placement computation time
Network Topology-aware VM Cluster Placement in IaaS Clouds (Georgiou et al., 2013)	IaaS Cloud Data Center, Homogeneous	PortLand	Offline	Graph search	CPU, Memory, and Storage	VM Anti-colocation, server resource capacity constraints	Minimization of network utilization, Low decision time overhead regardless of infrastructure size	Greedy Approach, Recursive, Backtracking	Simulation (JgraphT lib)	First Fit Decreasing (FFD)	Workflow structures (Pipeline, Data Aggregation, and Epigenomics)	Network utilization,

continued on following page

Table 5. Continued

Research Project	System Assumption	Net. Arch/Topology	Placement Type	Modeling/Analysis Technique	Physical Resources	VM Placement Constraints	Objective/Goal	Solution Approach/Algorithm	Evaluation/Experimental Platform	Competitor Approaches	Workload/VM-Cluster in Experiments/Evaluation	Evaluation Performance Metrics
Improving the Scalability of Data Center Networks with Traffic-aware VM Placement (Meng et al., 2010)	N/A	Tree, VL2, Fat-tree, BCube	Both Offline and Online	NP-hard Combinatorial Optimization Problem, instance of Quadratic Assignment Problem (QAP)	CPU and Memory	Maximum placement of one VM per PM	Improvement of scalability by minimizing the aggregated traffic rates at each network switch	Greedy approximate heuristic employing divide-and-conquer strategy and minimum k-cut graph algorithm	Trace-driven simulation using global and partitioned traffic model, as well as hybrid traffic model combining real traces with classical Gravity model	Local Optimal Pairwise Interchange (LOPI) (Armour & Buffa, 1963) and Simulated Annealing (Burkard & Rendl, 1984)	Inter-VM traffic rates (aggregated incoming and outgoing) collected from production data centers.	Worst case and average network cut load ratio (utilization), placement solving time, % of dropped packets, and avg. packet delivery delay
Stable Network-aware VM Placement for Cloud Systems (Biran et al., 2012)	Homogeneous Data Center	Tree, Fat-tree, VL2	Offline	NP-hard Integer Quadratic Programming	CPU and Memory	Server resource capacity constraints, physical link bandwidth capacity constraints	Minimization of the maximum ratio of the demand and capacity across all network cuts	Integer Programming Techniques employing divide-and-concur strategy and Greedy heuristics	Simulation-based using IBM ILOG CPLEX mixed integer mathematical solver.	Random and optimal placement	Gaussian distribution based inter-VM and VM-gateway traffic demands. Equal server resource capacity and VM resource demand.	Uniformity of VM placement on servers, average utilization of network links, and application performance degradation
Communication-Aware and Energy-Efficient Scheduling for Parallel Applications in Virtualized Data Centers (Takouna et al., 2013)	Homogeneous data center	Tree topology based on core-aggregation-edge model	Online	Simple peer-based inter-VM communication pattern	CPU, memory, and network I/O	Server resource capacity and inter-VM bandwidth requirement	Minimization of energy consumption by servers and network components, as well as average network utilization	Iterative greedy that ranks VMs based on the number of in/out traffic flow	Simulation-based (network and memory subsystem implemented on CloudSim (Calheiros et al., 2011))	Simple CPU utilization-based random VM placement	NPB parallel application benchmark used as HPC application	
Application-aware VM Placement in Data Centers (Song et al., 2012)	Homogeneous Data Center	Tree, VL2, Fat-tree, BCube	Online	Proportional Fairness and Convex Optimization	CPU, memory, and storage	Inter-VM bandwidth requirement and server resource capacity	Reduction of data transmission and energy consumption	N/A	Simulation based on synthetic data center and load characteristics	Random placement and First Fit Decreasing (FFD)	Normal distribution-based load characteristics for VMs and servers, and inter-VM traffic demands	Objective function value and reduction rate of traffic volume
Application-aware VM Migration in Data Centers (Shrivastava et al., 2011)	Homogeneous data center	Tree and VL2	Online	Mathematical optimization, multiple knapsack problem	CPU, memory, and storage	Server resource capacity	Minimization of network overhead due to VM migration	Greedy heuristic (exhaustive)	Simulation based on synthetic data center and load characteristics	Optimal placement (CPLEX solver) and Sandpiper VM migration scheme (Wood et al., 2007)	Normal distribution-based server resource and VM demands and, Normal, exponential, and uniform distribution-based inter-VM traffic demands	Objective function value and reduction in data center traffic

underlying effectively and with much higher reliability. With increasing deployment of data- and communication-intensive composite applications in the virtualized data centers, traffic volume transferred through the network devices and links are also increasing rapidly. Performance of these applications is highly dependent on the communication latencies and thus can have tremendous effects on the agreed SLA guarantees. Since SLA violations result in direct revenue reduction for the Cloud data center providers, efficient utilization of the network resources is highly important. Intelligent VM placement and migration is one of the key tools to maximize utilization of data center network resources. When coupled with effective prediction mechanism of inter-VM communication pattern, VM placement strategies can be utilized to localize bulk of the intra-data center traffic. This localization would further help in reducing packet switching and forwarding load in the higher level switches, which will be helpful in reducing energy consumption of the data center network devices.

This chapter has presented the motivation and background knowledge related to the network-aware VM placement and migration in data centers. Afterwards, a detailed taxonomy and characterization on the existing techniques and strategies have been expounded followed by an elaborate survey on the most notable recent research works. A comprehensive comparative analysis highlighting the significant features, benefits, and limitations of the techniques has been put forward, followed by a discussion on the future research outlooks.

REFERENCES

Adra, B., Blank, A., Gieparda, M., Haust, J., Stadler, O., & Szerdi, D. (2004). Advanced power virtualization on ibm eserver p5 servers: Introduction and basic configuration. IBM Corp.

Agrawal, S., Bose, S. K., & Sundarrajan, S. (2009). Grouping genetic algorithm for solving the server consolidation problem with conflicts. In *Proceedings of the First ACM/SIGEVO Summit on Genetic and Evolutionary Computation*. ACM. doi:10.1145/1543834.1543836

Al-Fares, M., Loukissas, A., & Vahdat, A. (2008). A scalable, commodity data center network architecture. *Computer Communication Review*, *38*(4), 63–74. doi:10.1145/1402946.1402967

Armbrust, M., Fox, A., Griffith, R., Joseph, A. D., Katz, R., & Konwinski, A. (2010). A view of cloud computing. *Communications of the ACM*, *53*(4), 50–58. doi:10.1145/1721654.1721672

Armour, G. C., & Buffa, E. S. (1963). A heuristic algorithm and simulation approach to relative location of facilities. *Management Science*, *9*(2), 294–309. doi:10.1287/mnsc.9.2.294

Barham, P., Dragovic, B., Fraser, K., Hand, S., Harris, T., Ho, A., & Warfield, A. et al. (2003). Xen and the art of virtualization. *Operating Systems Review*, *37*(5), 164–177. doi:10.1145/1165389.945462

Bharathi, S., Chervenak, A., Deelman, E., Mehta, G., Su, M.-H., & Vahi, K. (2008). Characterization of scientific workflows. In *Proceedings of Third Workshop on Workflows in Support of Large-Scale Science*. Academic Press.

Bhuyan, L. N., & Agrawal, D. P. (1984). Generalized hypercube and hyperbus structures for a computer network. *IEEE Transactions on Computers*, *100*(4), 323–333.

Biran, O., Corradi, A., Fanelli, M., Foschini, L., Nus, A., Raz, D., & Silvera, E. (2012). A stable network-aware VM placement for cloud systems. In *Proceedings of the 2012 12th IEEE/ACM International Symposium on Cluster, Cloud and Grid Computing* (CCGRID 2012) (pp 498-506). IEEE. doi:10.1109/CCGrid.2012.119

Burkard, R. E., & Rendl, F. (1984). A thermodynamically motivated simulation procedure for combinatorial optimization problems. *European Journal of Operational Research, 17*(2), 169–174. doi:10.1016/0377-2217(84)90231-5

Buyya, R., Broberg, J., & Goscinski, A. M. (2010). *Cloud computing: Principles and paradigms* (Vol. 87). John Wiley & Sons.

Buyya, R., Ranjan, R., & Calheiros, R. N. (2009). Modeling and simulation of scalable cloud computing environments and the CloudSim toolkit: Challenges and opportunities. In *Proceedings of High Performance Computing & Simulation.* Academic Press.

Calheiros, R. N., Ranjan, R., Beloglazov, A., De Rose, C. A., & Buyya, R. (2011). CloudSim: A toolkit for modeling and simulation of cloud computing environments and evaluation of resource provisioning algorithms. *Software, Practice & Experience, 41*(1), 23–50. doi:10.1002/spe.995

Chen, M., Zhang, H., Su, Y.-Y., Wang, X., Jiang, G., & Yoshihira, K. (2011). Effective vm sizing in virtualized data centers. In *Proceedings of Integrated Network Management* (pp. 594-601). Academic Press. doi:10.1109/INM.2011.5990564

Cisco, M. D. S. 9000 SANTap. (2014). Retrieved from http://www.cisco.com/c/en/us/products/collateral/storage-networking/mds-9000-santap/data_sheet_c78-568960.html

Cisco Data Center Infrastructure 2.5 Design Guide. (2014). Retrieved from http://www.cisco.com/c/en/us/td/docs/solutions/Enterprise/Data_Center/DC_Infra2_5/DCI_SRND_2_5a_book/DCInfra_1a.html

Clark, C., Fraser, K., Hand, S., Hansen, J. G., Jul, E., Limpach, C., . . . Warfield, A. (2005). Live migration of virtual machines. In *Proceedings of the 2nd Conference on Symposium on Networked Systems Design & Implementation* (vol. 2, pp. 273-286). Academic Press.

Crosby, S., & Brown, D. (2006). The virtualization reality. *Queue, 4*(10), 34–41. doi:10.1145/1189276.1189289

Ersoz, D., Yousif, M. S., & Das, C. R. (2007). Characterizing network traffic in a cluster-based, multi-tier data center. In *Proceedings of Distributed Computing Systems* (pp. 59-59). Academic Press. doi:10.1109/ICDCS.2007.90

Ferdaus, M. H., Murshed, M., Calheiros, R. N., & Buyya, R. (2014). Virtual machine consolidation in cloud data centers using ACO metaheuristic. In Proceedings of Euro-Par 2014 Parallel Processing (pp. 306-317). Springer. doi:10.1007/978-3-319-09873-9_26

Georgiou, S., Tsakalozos, K., & Delis, A. (2013). Exploiting network-topology awareness for VM placement in IaaS clouds. In *Proceedings of Cloud and Green Computing* (CGC) (pp. 151-158). Academic Press. doi:10.1109/CGC.2013.30

Greenberg, A., Hamilton, J. R., Jain, N., Kandula, S., Kim, C., Lahiri, P., & Sengupta, S. et al. (2009). VL2: A scalable and flexible data center network. *Computer Communication Review, 39*(4), 51–62. doi:10.1145/1594977.1592576

Guo, C., Lu, G., Li, D., Wu, H., Zhang, X., Shi, Y., & Lu, S. et al. (2009). BCube: A high performance, server-centric network architecture for modular data centers. *Computer Communication Review, 39*(4), 63–74. doi:10.1145/1594977.1592577

Guo, C., Wu, H., Tan, K., Shi, L., Zhang, Y., & Lu, S. (2008). Dcell: A scalable and fault-tolerant network structure for data centers. *Computer Communication Review*, *38*(4), 75–86. doi:10.1145/1402946.1402968

Gupta, R., Bose, S. K., Sundarrajan, S., Chebiyam, M., & Chakrabarti, A. (2008). A two stage heuristic algorithm for solving the server consolidation problem with item-item and bin-item incompatibility constraints. In *Proceedings of Services Computing* (Vol. 2, pp. 39-46). IEEE. doi:10.1109/SCC.2008.39

Hines, M. R., Deshpande, U., & Gopalan, K. (2009). Post-copy live migration of virtual machines. *Operating Systems Review*, *43*(3), 14–26. doi:10.1145/1618525.1618528

Huang, D., Gao, Y., Song, F., Yang, D., & Zhang, H. (2013). Multi-objective virtual machine migration in virtualized data center environments. In *Proceedings of Communications* (ICC) (pp. 3699-3704). IEEE. doi:10.1109/ICC.2013.6655129

Huang, D., Yang, D., Zhang, H., & Wu, L. (2012). Energy-aware virtual machine placement in data centers. In *Proceedings of Global Communications Conference* (GLOBECOM). IEEE.

Kandula, S., Sengupta, S., Greenberg, A., Patel, P., & Chaiken, R. (2009). The nature of data center traffic: Measurements & analysis. In *Proceedings of the 9th ACM SIGCOMM Conference on Internet Measurement* (pp. 202-208). ACM. doi:10.1145/1644893.1644918

Kivity, A., Kamay, Y., Laor, D., Lublin, U., & Liguori, A. (2007). KVM: The Linux virtual machine monitor. In *Proceedings of the Linux Symposium* (*Vol. 1,* pp. 225-230). Academic Press.

Kliazovich, D., Bouvry, P., & Khan, S. U. (2013). DENS: Data center energy-efficient network-aware scheduling. *Cluster Computing*, *16*(1), 65–75. doi:10.1007/s10586-011-0177-4

Korupolu, M., Singh, A., & Bamba, B. (2009). Coupled placement in modern data centers. In *Proceedings of Parallel & Distributed Processing* (pp. 1-12). IEEE. doi:10.1109/IPDPS.2009.5161067

Kusic, D., Kephart, J. O., Hanson, J. E., Kandasamy, N., & Jiang, G. (2009). Power and performance management of virtualized computing environments via lookahead control. *Cluster Computing*, *12*(1), 1–15. doi:10.1007/s10586-008-0070-y

Leiserson, C. E. (1985). Fat-trees: Universal networks for hardware-efficient supercomputing. *IEEE Transactions on Computers*, *100*(10), 892–901.

Lo, J. (2005). *VMware and CPU virtualization technology*. World Wide Web Electronic Publication.

Loiola, E. M., de Abreu, N. M. M., Boaventura-Netto, P. O., Hahn, P., & Querido, T. (2007). A survey for the quadratic assignment problem. *European Journal of Operational Research*, *176*(2), 657–690. doi:10.1016/j.ejor.2005.09.032

Mann, V., Gupta, A., Dutta, P., Vishnoi, A., Bhattacharya, P., Poddar, R., & Iyer, A. (2012). Remedy: Network-aware steady state VM management for data centers. In Proceedings of Networking 2012 (pp. 190-204). Springer.

McVitie, D. G., & Wilson, L. B. (1971). The stable marriage problem. *Communications of the ACM*, *14*(7), 486–490. doi:10.1145/362619.362631

Meng, X., Isci, C., Kephart, J., Zhang, L., Bouillet, E., & Pendarakis, D. (2010). Efficient resource provisioning in compute clouds via VM multiplexing. In *Proceedings of the 7th International Conference on Autonomic Computing* (pp. 11-20). Academic Press. doi:10.1145/1809049.1809052

Meng, X., Pappas, V., & Zhang, L. (2010). Improving the scalability of data center networks with traffic-aware virtual machine placement. In Proceedings of INFOCOM (pp. 1-9). IEEE. doi:10.1109/INFCOM.2010.5461930

Mysore, R. N., Pamboris, A., Farrington, N., Huang, N., Miri, P., Radhakrishnan, S., & Vahdat, A. et al. (2009). Portland: A scalable fault-tolerant layer 2 data center network fabric. *Computer Communication Review*, *39*(4), 39–50. doi:10.1145/1594977.1592575

Nelson, M., Lim, B.-H., Hutchins, G., & Associates. (2005). Fast transparent migration for virtual machines. In *Proceedings of USENIX Annual Technical Conference, General Track* (pp. 391-394). Academic Press.

Nimbus is Cloud Computing for Science. (2014). Retrieved from http://www.nimbusproject.org/

Novell PlateSpin Recon. (2014). Retrieved from https://www.netiq.com/products/recon/

Nurmi, D., Wolski, R., Grzegorczyk, C., Obertelli, G., Soman, S., Youseff, L., & Zagorodnov, D. (2009). The eucalyptus open-source cloud-computing system. In *Proceedings of Cluster Computing and the Grid* (pp. 124-131). IEEE. doi:10.1109/CCGRID.2009.93

Piao, J. T., & Yan, J. (2010). A network-aware virtual machine placement and migration approach in cloud computing. In *Proceedings of Grid and Cooperative Computing* (GCC) (pp. 87-92). Academic Press. doi:10.1109/GCC.2010.29

Pisinger, D. (1997). A minimal algorithm for the 0-1 knapsack problem. *Operations Research*, *45*(5), 758–767. doi:10.1287/opre.45.5.758

Sapuntzakis, C. P., Chandra, R., Pfaff, B., Chow, J., Lam, M. S., & Rosenblum, M. (2002). Optimizing the migration of virtual computers. *ACM SIGOPS Operating Systems Review, 36*(SI), 377-390.

Saran, H., & Vazirani, V. V. (1995). Finding k cuts within twice the optimal. *SIAM Journal on Computing*, *24*(1), 101–108. doi:10.1137/S0097539792251730

Shrivastava, V., Zerfos, P., Lee, K.-W., Jamjoom, H., Liu, Y.-H., & Banerjee, S. (2011). Application-aware virtual machine migration in data centers. In Proceedings of INFOCOM, 2011 (pp. 66–70). IEEE. doi:10.1109/INFCOM.2011.5935247

Smith, J., & Nair, R. (2005). *Virtual machines: Versatile platforms for systems and processes*. Elsevier.

Song, F., Huang, D., Zhou, H., & You, I. (2012). Application-aware virtual machine placement in data centers. In *Proceedings of Innovative Mobile and Internet Services in Ubiquitous Computing* (IMIS) (pp. 191-196). Academic Press. doi:10.1109/IMIS.2012.119

Sotomayor, B., Montero, R. S., Llorente, I. M., & Foster, I. (2009). Virtual infrastructure management in private and hybrid clouds. *IEEE Internet Computing*, *13*(5), 14–22. doi:10.1109/MIC.2009.119

Takemura, C. & Crawford, L. S. (2009). *The book of Xen: A practical guide for the system administrator*. No Starch Press.

Takouna, I., Dawoud, W., & Meinel, C. (2012). Analysis and simulation of HPC applications in virtualized data centers. In *Proceedings of Green Computing and Communications* (GreenCom) (pp. 498-507). IEEE. doi:10.1109/GreenCom.2012.80

Takouna, I., Rojas-Cessa, R., Sachs, K., & Meinel, C. (2013). Communication-aware and energy-efficient scheduling for parallel applications in virtualized data centers. In *Proceedings of Utility and Cloud Computing* (UCC) (pp. 251-255). IEEE. doi:10.1109/UCC.2013.50

Vaquero, L., Rodero-Merino, L., Caceres, J., & Lindner, M. (2008). A break in the clouds: Towards a cloud definition. *Computer Communication Review*, *39*(1), 50–55. doi:10.1145/1496091.1496100

VMware Capacity Planner. (2014). Retrieved from http://www.vmware.com/products/capacity-planner

Wood, T., Shenoy, P. J., Venkataramani, A., & Yousif, M. S. (2007). *Black-box and gray-box strategies for virtual machine migration.* NSDI.

Xu, R., & Wunsch, D. (2005). Survey of clustering algorithms. *IEEE Transactions on Neural Networks*, *16*(3), 645–678.

Zayas, E. (1987). Attacking the process migration bottleneck. *Operating Systems Review*, *21*(5), 13–24. doi:10.1145/37499.37503

Zhang, B., Qian, Z., Huang, W., Li, X., & Lu, S. (2012). Minimizing communication traffic in data centers with power-aware VM placement. In *Proceedings of Innovative Mobile and Internet Services in Ubiquitous Computing* (IMIS) (pp. 280-285). Academic Press. doi:10.1109/IMIS.2012.71

Zhang, Q., Cheng, L., & Boutaba, R. (2010). Cloud computing: State-of-the-art and research challenges. *Journal of Internet Services and Applications, 1*(1), 7-18.

ADDITIONAL READING

Al-Fares, M., Radhakrishnan, S., Raghavan, B., Huang, N., & Vahdat, A. (2010). Hedera: Dynamic Flow Scheduling for Data Center Networks. In NSDI (Vol. 10, pp. 19-19).

Ballani, H., Jang, K., Karagiannis, T., Kim, C., Gunawardena, D., & O'Shea, G. (2013). Chatty Tenants and the Cloud Network Sharing Problem. In NSDI (pp. 171-184).

Bansal, N., Lee, K. W., Nagarajan, V., & Zafer, M. (2011). Minimum congestion mapping in a cloud. In *Proceedings of the 30th annual ACM SIGACT-SIGOPS symposium on Principles of distributed computing* (pp. 267-276). ACM. doi:10.1145/1993806.1993854

Benson, T., Akella, A., Shaikh, A., & Sahu, S. (2011). CloudNaaS: a cloud networking platform for enterprise applications. In *Proceedings of the 2nd ACM Symposium on Cloud Computing* (p. 8). ACM. doi:10.1145/2038916.2038924

Bose, S. K., & Sundarrajan, S. (2009). Optimizing migration of virtual machines across datacenters. In Parallel Processing Workshops, 2009. ICPPW'09. International Conference on (pp. 306-313). IEEE. doi:10.1109/ICPPW.2009.39

Calcavecchia, N. M., Biran, O., Hadad, E., & Moatti, Y. (2012). VM placement strategies for cloud scenarios. In Cloud Computing (CLOUD), 2012 IEEE 5th International Conference on (pp. 852-859). IEEE. doi:10.1109/CLOUD.2012.113

Chaisiri, S., Lee, B. S., & Niyato, D. (2009). Optimal virtual machine placement across multiple cloud providers. In Services Computing Conference, 2009. APSCC 2009. IEEE Asia-Pacific (pp. 103-110). IEEE. doi:10.1109/APSCC.2009.5394134

Cruz, J., & Park, K. (2001). Towards communication-sensitive load balancing. In Distributed Computing Systems, 2001. 21st International Conference on. (pp. 731-734). IEEE. doi:10.1109/ICDSC.2001.919011

Fan, P., Chen, Z., Wang, J., Zheng, Z., & Lyu, M. R. (2012). Topology-aware deployment of scientific applications in cloud computing. In Cloud Computing (CLOUD), 2012 IEEE 5th International Conference on (pp. 319-326). IEEE. doi:10.1109/CLOUD.2012.70

Ferreto, T. C., Netto, M. A., Calheiros, R. N., & De Rose, C. A. (2011). Server consolidation with migration control for virtualized data centers. *Future Generation Computer Systems*, *27*(8), 1027–1034. doi:10.1016/j.future.2011.04.016

Gupta, A., Kalé, L. V., Milojicic, D., Faraboschi, P., & Balle, S. M. (2013). HPC-Aware VM Placement in Infrastructure Clouds. In Cloud Engineering (IC2E), 2013 IEEE International Conference on (pp. 11-20). IEEE.

Gupta, A., Milojicic, D., & Kalé, L. V. (2012). Optimizing VM Placement for HPC in the Cloud. In *Proceedings of the 2012 workshop on Cloud services, federation, and the 8th open cirrus summit* (pp. 1-6). ACM. doi:10.1145/2378975.2378977

Hyser, C., Mckee, B., Gardner, R., & Watson, B. J. (2007). Autonomic virtual machine placement in the data center. Hewlett Packard Laboratories, Tech. Rep. HPL-2007-189, 2007-189.

Jung, G., Hiltunen, M. A., Joshi, K. R., Schlichting, R. D., & Pu, C. (2010). Mistral: Dynamically managing power, performance, and adaptation cost in cloud infrastructures. In Distributed Computing Systems (ICDCS), 2010 IEEE 30th International Conference on (pp. 62-73). IEEE.

Kozuch, M. A., Ryan, M. P., Gass, R., Schlosser, S. W., O'Hallaron, D., Cipar, J., & Ganger, G. R. (2009). Tashi: location-aware cluster management. In *Proceedings of the 1st workshop on Automated control for datacenters and clouds* (pp. 43-48). ACM. doi:10.1145/1555271.1555282

Machida, F., Kim, D. S., Park, J. S., & Trivedi, K. S. (2008). Toward optimal virtual machine placement and rejuvenation scheduling in a virtualized data center. In Software Reliability Engineering Workshops, 2008. ISSRE Wksp 2008. IEEE International Conference on (pp. 1-3). IEEE. doi:10.1109/ISSREW.2008.5355515

Mann, V., Gupta, A., Dutta, P., Vishnoi, A., Bhattacharya, P., Poddar, R., & Iyer, A. (2012). Remedy: Network-aware steady state VM management for data centers. In NETWORKING 2012 (pp. 190-204). Springer Berlin Heidelberg.

Mann, V., Kumar, A., Dutta, P., & Kalyanaraman, S. (2011). VMFlow: leveraging VM mobility to reduce network power costs in data centers. In *NETWORKING 2011* (pp. 198–211). Springer Berlin Heidelberg. doi:10.1007/978-3-642-20757-0_16

Mogul, J. C., & Popa, L. (2012). What we talk about when we talk about cloud network performance. *Computer Communication Review*, *42*(5), 44–48. doi:10.1145/2378956.2378964

Nakada, H., Hirofuchi, T., Ogawa, H., & Itoh, S. (2009). Toward virtual machine packing optimization based on genetic algorithm. In Distributed Computing, Artificial Intelligence, Bioinformatics, Soft Computing, and Ambient Assisted Living (pp. 651-654). Springer Berlin Heidelberg. doi:10.1007/978-3-642-02481-8_96

Rodrigues, H., Santos, J. R., Turner, Y., Soares, P., & Guedes, D. (2011). Gatekeeper: Supporting Bandwidth Guarantees for Multi-tenant Datacenter Networks. In WIOV.

Shieh, A., Kandula, S., Greenberg, A. G., Kim, C., & Saha, B. (2011). Sharing the Data Center Network. In NSDI.

Sonnek, J., Greensky, J., Reutiman, R., & Chandra, A. (2010). Starling: Minimizing communication overhead in virtualized computing platforms using decentralized affinity-aware migration. In Parallel Processing (ICPP), 2010 39th International Conference on (pp. 228-237). IEEE.

Stage, A., & Setzer, T. (2009). Network-aware migration control and scheduling of differentiated virtual machine workloads. In *Proceedings of the 2009 ICSE Workshop on Software Engineering Challenges of Cloud Computing* (pp. 9-14). IEEE Computer Society. doi:10.1109/CLOUD.2009.5071527

Tsakalozos, K., Roussopoulos, M., & Delis, A. (2011). VM placement in non-homogeneous IaaS-Clouds. In *Service-Oriented Computing* (pp. 172–187). Springer Berlin Heidelberg. doi:10.1007/978-3-642-25535-9_12

Wang, S. H., Huang, P. P. W., Wen, C. H. P., & Wang, L. C. (2014). EQVMP: Energy-efficient and QoS-aware virtual machine placement for software defined datacenter networks. In Information Networking (ICOIN), 2014 International Conference on (pp. 220-225). IEEE.

Xu, J., & Fortes, J. (2011). A multi-objective approach to virtual machine management in datacenters. In *Proceedings of the 8th ACM international conference on Autonomic computing* (pp. 225-234). ACM. doi:10.1145/1998582.1998636

Zhang, Y., Su, A. J., & Jiang, G. (2011). Understanding data center network architectures in virtualized environments: A view from multi-tier applications. *Computer Networks*, 55(9), 2196–2208. doi:10.1016/j.comnet.2011.03.001

KEY TERMS AND DEFINITIONS

Cloud Computing: A computing paradigm that enables on-demand, ubiquitous, convenient network access to a shared pool of configurable and highly reliable computing resources (such as servers, storage, networks, platforms, applications, and services) that can be readily provisioned and released with minimal management effort or service provider interaction.

Data Center: An infrastructure or facility (either physical or virtual) that accommodates servers, storage devices, networking systems, power and cooling systems, and other associated IT resources that facilitates the storing, processing, and serving of large amounts of mission-critical data to the users.

Network Topology: Physical or logical arrangement of various computing and communication elements (nodes such as servers, storage devices, network switches/routers, and network links). It defines how the nodes are interconnected with each other (physical topology); alternately, it defines how data is transmitted among the nodes (logical topology).

Virtual Machine: A software computer (emulation of physical machine) that is comprised of a set of specification and configuration files backed by the physical resources of a host machine and runs an operating system and applications. A Virtual Machine has virtual devices with similar functionality as the underlying physical devices having additional advantages in relation to manageability, security, and portability.

Virtualization: The creation, management, and termination of virtual version of a resource or device (such as computer hardware, storage device, operating system, or computer network) where the framework partitions the resource into one or more virtual execution environments.

VM Live Migration: The process of moving a running VM from one host machine to another with little downtime of the services hosted by the VM. It enables server maintenance, upgrade, and resource optimization without subjecting the service users to downtime.

VM Placement: The selection process that identifies of the most suitable physical machine during the VM deployment in a data center. During placement, hosts are ranked based on their resource conditions and the VM's resource requirements and additional deployment conditions. VM placement decisions also consider the placement objectives such as maximization of physical compute-network resource utilization, energy efficiency, and load balancing.

Chapter 3
Cloudlet-Based Cyber-Foraging in Resource-Limited Environments

Grace A. Lewis
Carnegie Mellon Software Engineering Institute, USA

Soumya Simanta
Carnegie Mellon Software Engineering Institute, USA

Sebastián Echeverría
Carnegie Mellon Software Engineering Institute, USA

James Root
Carnegie Mellon Software Engineering Institute, USA

Ben Bradshaw
Carnegie Mellon Software Engineering Institute, USA

ABSTRACT

First responders and others operating in crisis environments increasingly make use of handheld devices to help with tasks such as face recognition, language translation, decision making, and mission planning. These resource-limited environments are characterized by dynamic context, limited computing resources, high levels of stress, and intermittent network connectivity. Cyber-foraging is the leverage of external resource-rich surrogates to augment the capabilities of resource-limited devices. In cloudlet-based cyber-foraging, resource-intensive computation is offloaded to cloudlets: discoverable, generic servers located in single-hop proximity of mobile devices. This chapter presents several mechanisms for cloudlet-based cyber-foraging that consider a tradeoff space beyond energy, performance, and fidelity of results. It demonstrates that cyber-foraging in resource-limited environments can greatly benefit from moving cloud computing concepts and technologies closer to the edge so that surrogates, even if disconnected from the enterprise, can provide offload capabilities that enhance the computing power of mobile devices.

DOI: 10.4018/978-1-4666-8213-9.ch003

Copyright © 2015, IGI Global. Copying or distributing in print or electronic forms without written permission of IGI Global is prohibited.

1. INTRODUCTION

Mobile applications are increasingly used by first responders and others operating in crisis and hostile environments in support of their missions. These environments are not only at the edge of the network infrastructure, but are also resource limited due to dynamic context, limited computing resources, intermittent network connectivity, and high levels of stress. Applications that are useful to field personnel include speech and image recognition, natural language processing, and situational awareness. These are all computation-intensive tasks that take a heavy toll on the device's battery power and computing resources.

Cyber-foraging is the leverage of external resource-rich surrogates to augment the capabilities of resource-limited mobile devices (Satyanarayanan, Bahl, Caceres, & Davies, 2009). Most existing cyber-foraging solutions rely on conventional Internet for connectivity to the cloud or strategies that tightly couple mobile clients with servers at deployment time. These solutions are not appropriate for resource-limited environments because of their dependence on multi-hop networks to the cloud and static deployment. Cloudlet-based cyber-foraging relies on discoverable, generic, stateless servers located in single-hop proximity of mobile devices. These characteristics make cloudlets a good match for the characteristics of resource-limited environments. However, most cyber-foraging solutions identified in the literature do not address the challenges of "being at the edge."

The goal of this chapter is to propose cloudlet-based cyber-foraging as a solution for supporting mobile systems in resource-limited environments. Section 2 presents a summary of related work in cyber-foraging. Section 3 describes cloudlet-based cyber-foraging. Section 4 describes cloudlet discovery. Section 5 presents five mechanisms for cloudlet provisioning. Section 6 describes the generic process for mobile application execution. Section 7 presents experimental data that shows the pros and cons of each cloudlet provisioning mechanism. Section 8 presents future research directions. Finally, Section 9 concludes the chapter.

2. RELATED WORK

Multiple cyber-foraging systems have been developed that differ in terms of the strategy that they use to leverage remote resources — where to offload, when to offload, and what to offload.

Where to offload varies between remote clouds (Kosta, Aucinas, Hui, Mortier, & Zhang, 2012), local servers located in proximity of mobile devices (often called surrogates; Satyanarayanan et al., 2009), or local servers that are connected to remote clouds for provisioning (Xiao, Simoens, Pillai, Ha, & Satyanarayanan, 2013) or as intermediaries to the cloud (Rahimi, Venkatasubramanian, Mehrotra, & Vasilakos, 2012).

When to offload varies between a runtime decision or an "always offload" strategy. To support runtime offload decisions, one strategy is to manually or automatically partition code into portions that either run on the mobile device or on a remote machine. At runtime an optimization engine — typically targeted at optimizing energy efficiency, performance, or network usage — decides whether the code should execute locally or be offloaded to a remote machine. An example of such a cyber-foraging system is MAUI (Cuervo et al., 2010). CloneCloud (Chun, Ihm, Maniatis, Naik, & Patti, 2011) follows the same code partitioning principle but automatically partitions code at the process level without the need for manual code annotation. Other cyber-foraging solutions assume that the computation-intensive code exists in a remote machine and the cyber-foraging task therefore becomes one of service discovery and composition. ThinAV (Jarabek, Barrera, & Aycock, 2012) is an example of this "always offload" strategy.

Figure 1. Three-tier cloudlet architecture

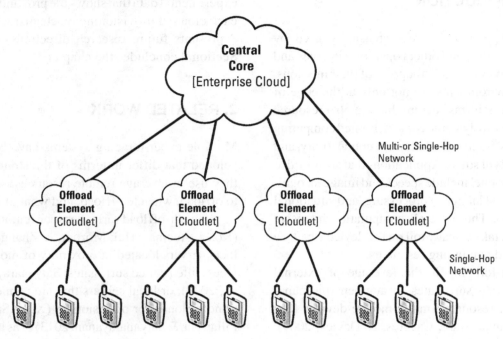

What to offload involves the most variation, ranging from processes (Chun et al., 2011), to methods (Cuervo et al., 2010), to modules (Iyer & Roopa, 2012), to services (Jarabek, Barrera, & Aycock, 2012), to full applications (Satyanarayanan et al., 2009), with other options in between.

Despite all the work in cyber-foraging, results of a systematic literature review show that (1) there is emphasis on the algorithms to support computation offload and state synchronization with minimal focus on software architecture and quality attributes beyond energy efficiency and performance, and (2) there is minimal guidance on how to support system-level quality attributes such as survivability, resilience, trust and ease of deployment, which are critical in resource-limited environments.

3. CLOUDLET-BASED CYBER-FORAGING

Cloudlets are discoverable, generic, stateless servers, located in single-hop proximity of mobile devices, that can operate in disconnected mode

and are virtual-machine (VM) based to promote flexibility, mobility, scalability, and elasticity (Satyanarayanan et al., 2009). A high-level, three-tier architecture that includes cloudlets was first proposed by Ha and colleagues (Ha, Lewis, Simanta, & Satyanarayanan, 2011) and is shown in Figure 1. This architecture includes cloudlets as part of an intermediate layer between the central core (i.e., public or private enterprise cloud or data center) and the mobile devices. The cloudlets are dispersed and located close to the mobile devices they serve. This architecture decreases latency by using a single-hop network and potentially lowers battery consumption by using WiFi or short-range radio instead of broadband wireless, which typically consumes more energy (Balasubramanian, Balasubramanian, & Venkataramani, 2009; Lehr & McKnight, 2002). A key attribute of this architecture is that cloudlets are stateless. A mobile device does not need to communicate with the core during an offload operation; it only needs to communicate with its physically closest cloudlet. Communication between the cloudlet and the central core is only needed during setup and provisioning. Once a cloudlet is provisioned, its connection to the core can be disrupted without affecting offload service to mobile devices. Adding a new cloudlet or replacing an existing one involves little setup or configuration effort.

In the proposed implementation of cloudlets, applications are statically partitioned into a very thin Client that runs on the mobile device and a

computation-intensive Server that runs inside a Service VM. For example, for a speech recognition application the Client would simply capture voice using the microphone on the mobile device, save it to an audio file, send the file as input to the Service VM, receive the results, and display these results to the user. The Service VM contains all the complex speech recognition algorithms as

Figure 2. Reference architecture for cloudlet-based cyber-foraging

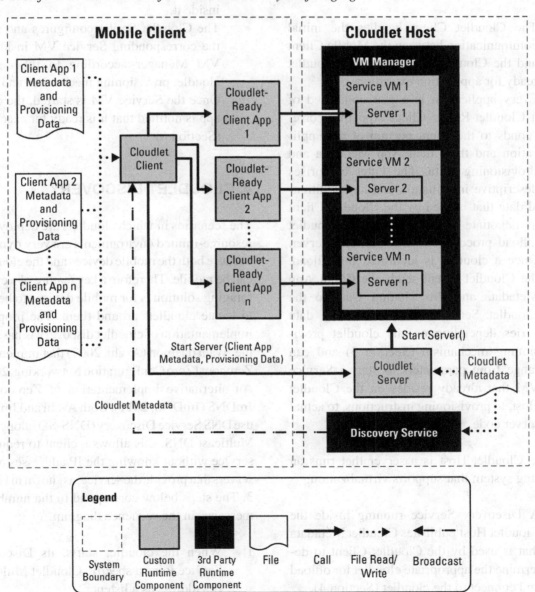

well as the training data. It would take an audio file as input and produce a text string as output that corresponds to the audio.

A reference architecture for cyber-foraging is presented in Figure 2. The main elements of the architecture are the Mobile Client and the Cloudlet Host. Instantiations of this reference architecture will be presented in Section 5.

The Mobile Client is a smartphone that runs the Cloudlet Client and any Cloudlet-Ready Apps installed by the user.

- The Cloudlet Client handles the initial communication between the Mobile Client and the Cloudlet Host to get the cloudlet ready for application execution.
- Every application is a pair composed of a Cloudlet-Ready Client App that corresponds to the client portion of the application and the Client App Metadata and Provisioning Data. The latter comprises descriptive information and any additional data that is used by the Cloudlet Client to negotiate and carry out the cloudlet offload process with the Cloudlet Server. Once a cloudlet is identified for offload, the Cloudlet Client sends the Client App Metadata and Provisioning Data to the Cloudlet Server. The provisioning data varies depending on the cloudlet provisioning mechanism (Section 5) and can range from parameters to start a Service VM that already resides on the Cloudlet Host, to provisioning instructions, to actual server code.

The Cloudlet Host is a server that runs an operating system that supports virtualization.

- A Discovery Service running inside the Cloudlet Host publishes Cloudlet Metadata that is used by the Cloudlet Client to determine the appropriate cloudlet for offload and connect to the cloudlet (Section 4).

- Cloudlet Metadata can range from a simple IP address and port to connect to the Cloudlet Server to more complex data structures describing cloudlet capabilities such as current load, available memory, and connectivity to the cloud.
- The VM Manager is any virtual machine management software such as KVM, Virtual Box or VMWare.
- A Service VM is a guest VM with the Server portion of the application running inside it.
- The Cloudlet Server configures and starts the corresponding Service VM inside the VM Manager according to the defined cloudlet provisioning mechanism and data. Once the Service VM is started, the client app is notified that it is ready for execution (Section 6).

4. CLOUDLET DISCOVERY

The scenarios in which cloudlets are deployed in resource-limited environments are very dynamic because both the mobile devices and the cloudlets can be mobile. Therefore a key feature of a cyber-foraging solution is for mobile devices to be able to locate cloudlets around them. The proposed implementation of cloudlet discovery is based on the Avahi daemon (Avahi, 2007) that implements Zeroconf (Zero Configuration Networking, 2014). An alternative implementation of Zeroconf is JmDNS (JmDNS, 2011). Both Avahi and JmDNS use DNS Service Discovery (DNS-SD) along with Multicast DNS; this allows a client to request a service without knowing the IP addresses of the servers that provide the service, as shown in Figure 3. The steps below correspond to the numbered messages in the sequence diagram.

1. When the cloudlet starts, its Discovery Service joins a specific Cloudlet Multicast IP Address as a listener.

Figure 3. Cloudlet discovery

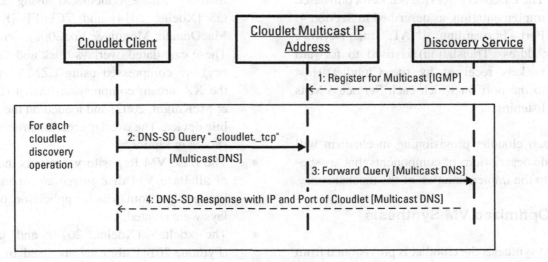

2. When the Cloudlet Client wants to discover cloudlets, it sends a DNS-SD Query for cloudlet services (defined as a "_cloudlet._tcp" service) through Multicast DNS to the Cloudlet Multicast IP Address.
3. The query reaches the Discovery Service of any cloudlets in the network through Multicast DNS.
4. The Discovery Service replies with a DNS-SD Response indicating the IP address and port of the cloudlet.

After the Cloudlet Client receives the response (IP address and port) from one or more cloudlets, it selects an appropriate cloudlet and starts the Cloudlet Provisioning process explained in Section 5.

5. CLOUDLET PROVISIONING

In addition to cloudlet discovery, a key aspect of cloudlet-based cyber-foraging is cloudlet provisioning—configuring and deploying the Service VM that contains the server code (i.e., server portion of the application) on the cloudlet so that it is ready to use by the client running on the mobile device.

The cloudlet provisioning mechanisms that will be described in the next subsections share a set of common components described as follows.

- The Mobile Client is an Android-based smartphone
- The Cloudlet Client and Cloudlet-Ready Apps are implemented as Android apps (Java)
- The VM Manager is QEMU-KVM. KVM (KVM, 2014) arbitrates access to the CPU and memory and QEMU (QEMU, 2014b) creates and manages VMs using the KVM kernel module.
- The API used to interact with QEMU is libvirt (Libvirt, 2014a).
- The qemu-img tool is a QEMU disk image utility (Bellard, 2013).
- Each Service VM is a guest VM in QEMU-KVM that runs the Application Server that corresponds to the server portion of the Cloudlet-Ready App.
- The Cloudlet Server is implemented as an HTTP Server using CherryPy (CherryPy, 2014) for most mechanisms, except for Application Virtualization, which uses Jetty (Eclipse, 2014).

- The Discovery Service is a Zeroconf-based implementation, as described in Section 4.
- Port Forwarding (NAT; for Network Address Translation) is used to forward packets received by the Cloudlet Host to the port on which each Service VM is listening.

Each cloudlet provisioning mechanism will include descriptions of components that are specific to the implementation of the mechanism.

5.1 Optimized VM Synthesis

In VM synthesis the cloudlet is provisioned from the mobile device at runtime. The original implementation of VM synthesis is fully described by Simanta (Simanta, Ha, Lewis, Morris, & Satyanarayanan, 2013).

In the Optimized VM Synthesis implementation the goal is to reduce application-ready time – time between the cloudlet provisioning request and the notification that the server is ready for execution. The high-level architecture for cloudlet provisioning using Optimized VM Synthesis is shown in Figure 4. Details specific to this provisioning mechanism are below:

- An Application Overlay that corresponds to the server portion of a client-server application is created once offline by starting a VM instance from a Base VM disk image file (that uses QEMU copy on write 2 [qcow2]; McLoughlin, 2008) as the VM disk image file format) and a base memory image, installing the server on the base VM image, and suspending the VM. When a VM is suspended, two files are created as part of the application overlay: one that corresponds to the disk image differences between the suspended VM and the base VM (the qcow2 file) and another that corresponds to the binary difference between the suspended memory image and the base memory image (calculated using xdelta3 [Xdelta, 2014] and VCDIFF [Korn, MacDonald, Mogul, & Vo, 2002] format). These calculated overlays (disk and memory) are compressed using LZMA2 with the XZ stream compression format (Lehr & McKnight, 2002) and loaded on the mobile device. The overlay creation process is shown in Figure 5.
- The Base VM Repository contains the set of all Base VM disk image and memory image files from which application overlays were created.
- The xdelta3 (Xdelta, 2014) and lzma (Python, 2014) libraries are used by the Cloudlet Server at runtime to decompress and apply the received application overlay to its corresponding Base VM (details in Figure 6).

The details of the offload process are shown in Figure 6. For simplification, error conditions are not included. The steps below correspond to the numbered messages in the sequence diagram.

1-3: The Cloudlet Client checks whether the cloudlet has the Base VM from which the overlay was created.

4-5: If it does, then the compressed application overlay disk image is sent in chunks to the Cloudlet Server.

6-9: Each chunk is placed in a queue, decompressed, and appended to a qcow2 file. This optimization, called pipelining, enables overlay decompression to be done incrementally as opposed to having to wait until the complete overlay is received.

10-15: The compressed application overlay memory image is also sent in chunks to the Cloudlet Server. Each chunk is placed in a queue, decompressed, and appended to a VCDIFF file.

16-17: Client App Metadata that is used to set up the Service VM is sent to the Cloudlet Server.

Figure 4. High-level architecture for VM synthesis

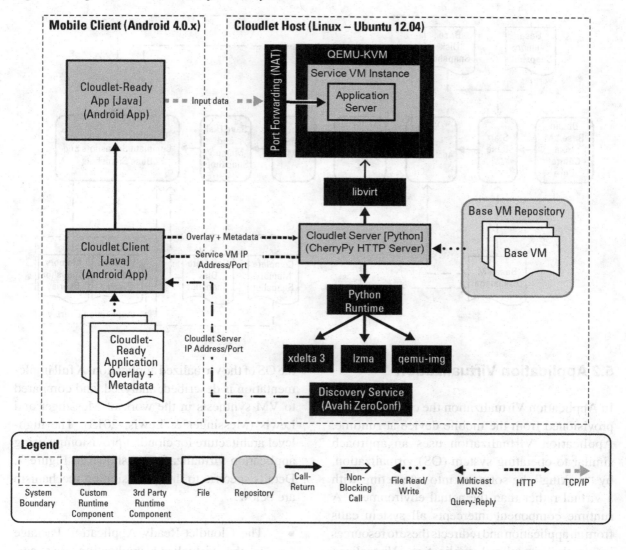

18-20: In the Synthesize Disk step, because of the optimization to use qcow2 as the VM file image format, the disk overlay that is received already corresponds to the changes with respect to the Base VM, which means that there is no need for extra processing after decompression, other than pointing the disk overlay to the Base VM.

21-22: In the Synthesize Memory step, the received memory overlay is applied to the base memory overlay in order to create the complete memory image (the opposite of what was done in the memory overlay creation process).

23: The Cloudlet Client indicates that it is ready to start the new Service VM.

24: The Cloudlet Server sets up port forwarding between a free port on the Cloudlet Host and the port indicated in the Client App Metadata on the new Service VM.

25-26: The Service VM is started.

27: The IP address and port to connect to the Service VM are sent back to the Cloudlet Client.

Figure 5. Application overlay creation process for VM synthesis

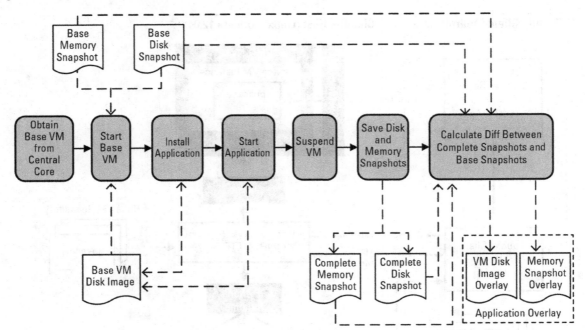

5.2 Application Virtualization

In Application Virtualization the cloudlet is also provisioned from the mobile device at runtime. Application Virtualization uses an approach similar to operating system (OS) virtualization, by "tricking" the software into interacting with a virtual rather than the actual environment. A runtime component intercepts all system calls from an application and redirects these to resources inside the virtualized application. Virtualized applications are created in advance for server portions of applications using tools that package the application with all its dependencies. CDE (short for Code, Data and Environment) was used as the application virtualizer for Linux (Guo & Engler, 2011) and Cameyo was used for Windows (Cameyo, 2013). CDE virtualizes applications by monitoring their execution and Cameyo by monitoring their installation process. Both tools produce virtualized applications that are loaded on the mobile device and at runtime are sent to the cloudlet to be deployed in a VM that matches

the OS of the virtualized application. A full implementation is described, analyzed, and compared to VM synthesis in the work of Messinger and Lewis (Messinger & Lewis, 2013). The high-level architecture for cloudlet provisioning using application virtualization is shown in Figure 7. Details specific to this provisioning mechanism are below:

- The Cloudlet-Ready Application Package is the virtualized application that corresponds to the server portion of the Cloudlet-Ready App and is created using the process just described.
- The Guest VM Repository contains VM disk image files for each operating system supported by the cloudlet.

The details of the offload process are shown in Figure 8. For simplification, error conditions are not included. The steps below correspond to the numbered messages in the sequence diagram.

Figure 6. Sequence diagram for the VM synthesis process

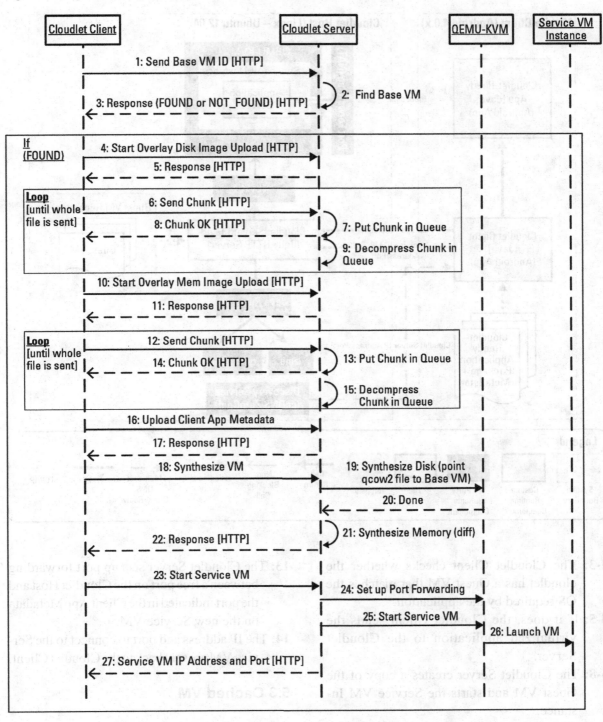

Figure 7. High-level architecture for application virtualization

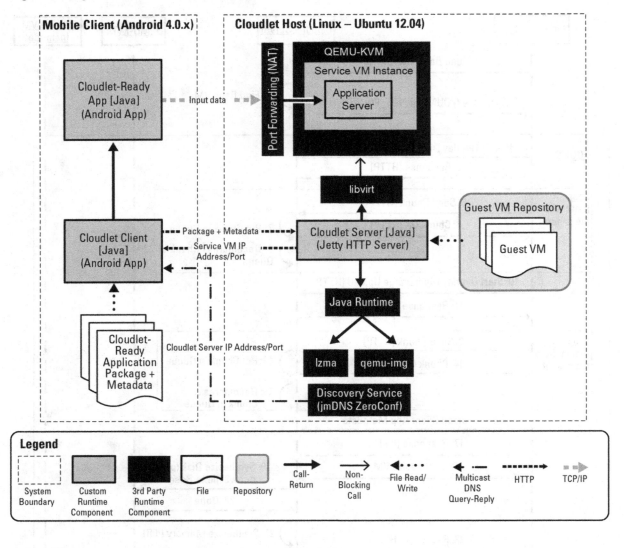

1-3: The Cloudlet Client checks whether the cloudlet has a Guest VM that matches the OS required by the application.

4-5: If it does, the Cloudlet Client sends the virtualized application to the Cloudlet Server.

6-8: The Cloudlet Server creates a copy of the Guest VM and starts the Service VM Instance.

9-10: The application is deployed in the Service VM Instance.

11-12: The application is started.

13: The Cloudlet Server sets up port forwarding between a free port on the Cloudlet Host and the port indicated in the Client App Metadata on the new Service VM.

14: The IP address and port to connect to the Service VM are sent back to the Cloudlet Client.

5.3 Cached VM

In Cached VM the cloudlet is pre-provisioned with Service VMs that correspond to capabilities that match the client apps on the mobile

Figure 8. Sequence diagram for the application virtualization process

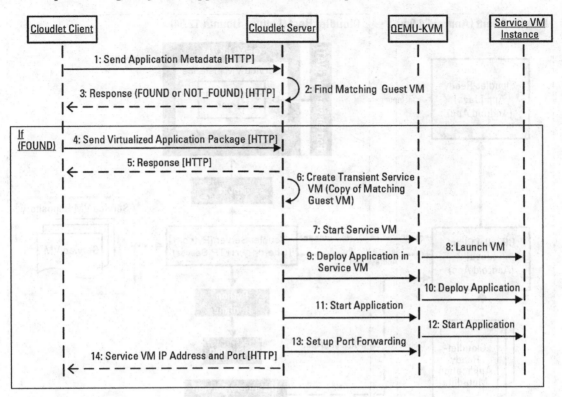

device. The high-level architecture for cloudlet provisioning using Cached VM is shown in Figure 9. Details specific to this provisioning mechanism are:

- Each Service VM has a unique service identifier and is stored in the Service VM Repository as a set of files:
  - **Service VM Metadata File (.jsons-vm):** JSON[1] file with the following fields:
    - **serviceId:** Unique identifier for the service provided by the VM
    - **servicePort:** Port on which the server inside the VM will be listening for connections
  - **Disk Image File (.qcow2):** qcow2 file that contain the VM disk image and contains the server portion of the application.

  - **VM State Image File (.lqs):** VM state image in the format that libvirt.save() generates when saving a memory image. This format is called Libvirt Qemu Saved (lqs), and includes both the description of the VM that was suspended, as well as the memory state of the VM that includes the running server (Libvirt, 2014b).
- The Service VM Repository is set up as a set of folders, each of which uses the following naming convention:
  - <serviceId>
    - <serviceId>.jsonsvm
    - <serviceId>.qcow2
    - <serviceId>.qcow2.lqs

Similar to what is done in the application overlay process shown in Figure 5, a Service VM is created by installing the application server inside

Figure 9. High-level architecture for cached VM

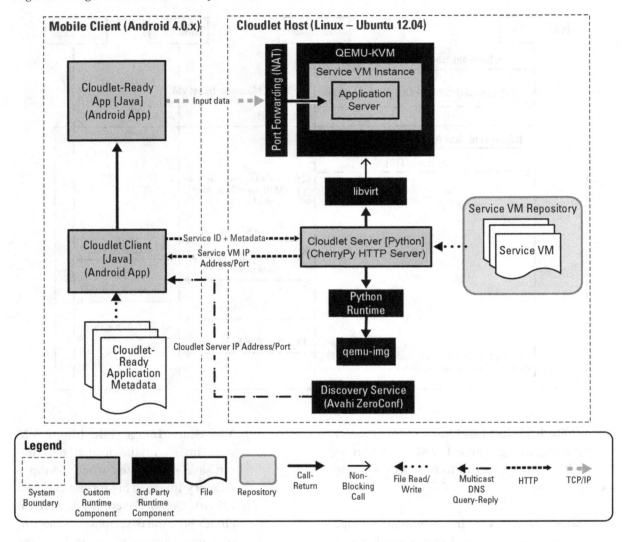

a VM and then suspending it. The JSON file is created automatically by the script that we use to create the Service VM and is stored in the same directory as the disk and memory image files. These three files are used to launch a Service VM so that it starts from the point at which it was suspended, therefore reducing application-ready time.

The details of the offload process are shown in Figure 10. For simplification, error conditions are not included. The steps below correspond to the numbered messages in the sequence diagram.

1-3: The Cloudlet Client checks whether the cloudlet has a Service VM with a given Service ID.

4: If it does, the Cloudlet Server creates a copy of the Service VM.

5: The Cloudlet Server sets up port forwarding between a free port on the Cloudlet Host and the port indicated in the Service VM metadata.

6-7: The Service VM is started.

8: The IP address and port to connect to the Service VM are sent back to the Cloudlet Client.

Figure 10. Sequence diagram for the cached VM process

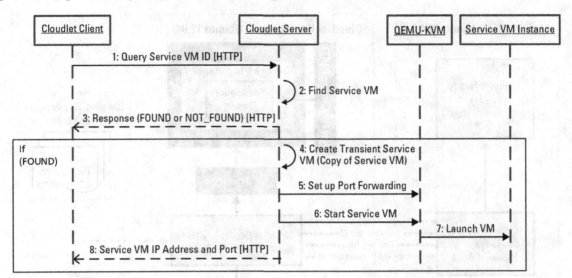

5.4 Cloudlet Push

In Cloudlet Push, the cloudlet is not only pre-provisioned with Service VMs, but also mobile client apps that can use the Service VMs. The high-level architecture for cloudlet provisioning using Cloudlet Push is shown in Figure 11. Details specific to this provisioning mechanism are below:

- Each Cloudlet-Ready App has a unique identifier and additional metadata that is stored in the Cloudlet-Ready App Repository. The Cloudlet Server uses this information to build a Cloudlet-Ready App List that is sent to the Cloudlet Client upon request, similar to accessing an app store. It is important to note that the only element that is needed on the Mobile Client is the Cloudlet Client.
- The Cloudlet-Ready App and its Cloudlet-Ready Application Metadata are obtained from the cloudlet at runtime and saved on the Mobile Client.

Once the app is installed, the process is the same as Cached VM (see Section 5.3). Details of the process are shown in Figure 12. For simplification, error conditions are not included. The steps below correspond to the numbered messages in the sequence diagram.

1-2: The Cloudlet Client obtains a list of available applications on the cloudlet.

3-4: The user selects an application and the Cloudlet Client requests the selected application for the mobile device's operating system.

5-7: If there is a matching client app, the Cloudlet Client receives the APK[2] file for the app, installs it on the mobile device, and saves its Metadata.

8: The Cloudlet Client requests to start a Service VM that corresponds to the installed app.

9: The Cloudlet Server locates and creates a copy of the Service VM.

10: The Cloudlet Server sets up port forwarding between a free port on the Cloudlet Host and the port indicated in the Service VM metadata.

11-12: The Service VM is started.

13: The IP address and port to connect to the Service VM are sent back to the Cloudlet Client.

Figure 11. High-level architecture for cloudlet push

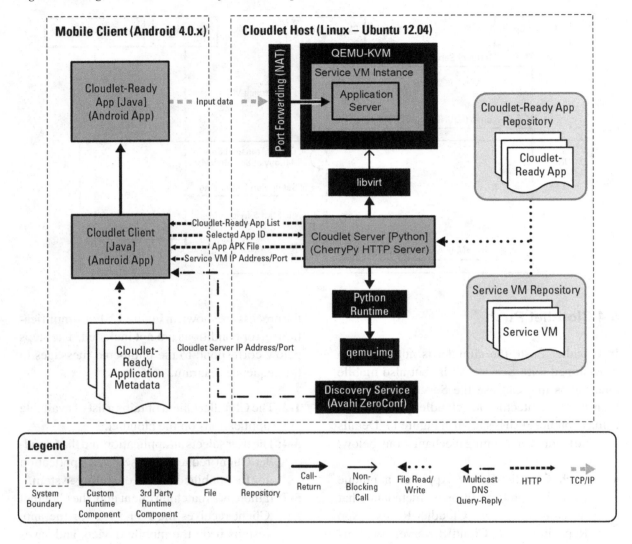

5.5 On-Demand VM Provisioning

In On-Demand VM Provisioning a commercial cloud provisioning tool is used to assemble a Service VM. In this case the cloudlet has access to all the elements to put together a Service VM based on a provisioning script. The experimental prototype uses Puppet (Puppet Labs, 2014b) and the provisioning script is a manifest that is written in Puppet's declarative language. The high-level architecture for cloudlet provisioning using On-

Demand VM Provisioning is shown in Figure 13. Below the figure are details specific to this provisioning mechanism:

A Baseline VM is a suspended VM that is used as a template for the construction of Service VMs. It is important to note that unlike Base VMs in VM Synthesis (see Section 5.1), Baseline VMs can be modified, updated, and maintained continuously without affecting the provisioning process. Each Baseline VM is stored in the Baseline VM Repository as a set of files:

Figure 12. Sequence diagram for the cloudlet push process

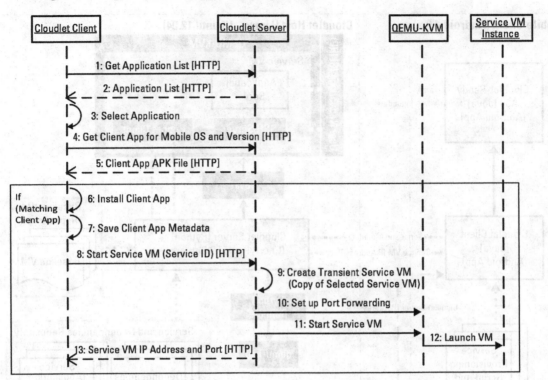

- Disk Image file (.qcow2): qcow2 file that corresponds to the VM disk image of the Baseline VM. It should contain a basic OS installation plus any components and libraries commonly used by Service VMs. In the experimental prototype that uses Puppet, the following components must be part of the Baseline VM:
  - SSH Server for the Cloudlet Server to send files and commands. In this provisioning mechanism *QEMU-KVM* is set up with User Networking (QEMU, 2014a) so that the Cloudlet Server can send SSH commands to the Service VM.
  - Puppet Client for the execution of Puppet manifests inside the VM.
  - Link to the Cloudlet Server so that the Service VM can download pack-

ages and dependencies that are stored locally on the Cloudlet (via HTTP with the Cloudlet Server acting as an HTTP file server).

- VM State Image file (.lqs): VM state image in the format that libvirt.save() generates when saving a memory image
- Baseline VM Metadata file (.jsonbmd): JSON file with the following fields that describes the basic features of the Baseline VM
  - **osFamily (string):** Basic OS family (e.g., "Linux", "Windows")
  - **os (string):** Name of the OS or distribution (e.g., "Windows 7", "Ubuntu")
  - **osVersion (string):** OS version (e.g., "SP1", "8.1", "12.10")
  - **osISA:** Instruction set (e.g., "x86-32" or "x86-64")

Figure 13. High-level architecture for on-demand provisioning

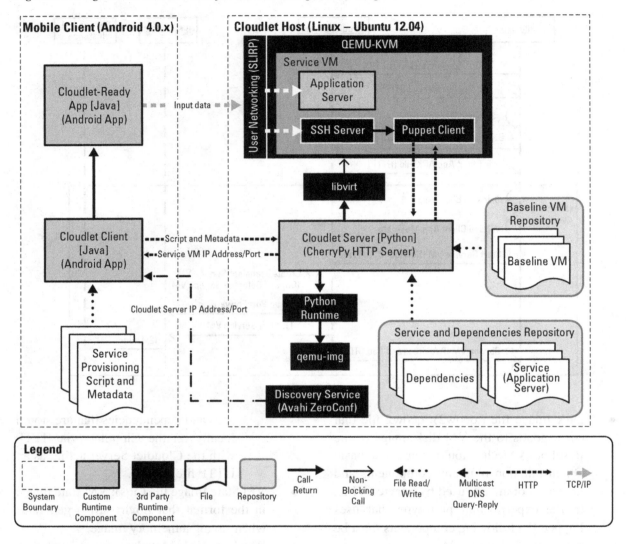

The Baseline VM Repository is set up as a set of folders, each of which uses the following naming convention:

- <baseline-vm-id>
  ○ <baseline-vm-id>.jsonbmd
  ○ <baseline-vm-id>.qcow2
  ○ <baseline-vm-id>.qcow2.lqs

Each Cloudlet-Ready App has a corresponding Service Provisioning Script and Metadata that are used to set up the corresponding Service VM on the cloudlet.

- **Baseline VM Metadata File (.jsonbmd):** JSON file that describes the basic features of the Baseline VM that is needed to create the Service VM. The format is the same as the Baseline VM Metadata file described above and is used during the provisioning process to find matching Baseline VMs.
- **Service VM Metadata File (.jsonsvm):** JSON file with the same structure defined in Section 5.3 to describe a Service VM
- **Puppet Manifest:** Script with instructions on what must be provisioned inside the Service VM, such as the application server

to install, dependencies, and libraries. The script follows the standard for Puppet manifests (Puppet Labs, 2014a).

The Services and Dependencies Repository contains two sets of files. Although in the experimental prototype these files are retrieved from the Cloudlet Host using HTTP download, they could also be obtained from an external URL if there were connectivity.

- **Services:** Files that compose the actual service to be provided by the Service VM (implemented in the Application Server).
- **Dependencies:** Files that compose any dependencies/libraries that could be used by Services. In the experimental prototype it is implemented for Ubuntu as an APT-GET repository and for Windows as MSI packages.

The details of the process are shown in Figure 14. For simplification, error conditions are not included. The steps below correspond to the numbered messages in the sequence diagram.

1-3: The Cloudlet Client checks whether the cloudlet has a Baseline VM that matches the given metadata.

4: If it does, the Cloudlet Client sends the provisioning script to the Cloudlet Server.

5-6: The Cloudlet Server creates a copy of the Baseline VM and starts it as the Service VM.

7-8: The Cloudlet Server transfers the Provisioning Script (Puppet manifest) to the running Service VM Instance and notifies it to start its execution.

9: The Service VM Instance instructs Puppet to execute the Provisioning Script.

10-11: Puppet obtains the files for the Service and Dependencies from the Cloudlet Host via the Cloudlet Server.

12-15: Puppet installs the Service and its Dependencies, starts the Service, and notifies the Cloudlet Server that the installation is complete.

16: The Cloudlet Server sets up port forwarding between a free port on the Cloudlet Host and the port indicated in the Service VM metadata.

17: The IP address and port to connect to the Service VM are sent back to the Cloudlet Client.

6. MOBILE APP EXECUTION

After the cloudlet has been provisioned and it has a running Service VM, the Cloudlet-Ready App has to be started from the Cloudlet Client so that it can start using the service. The details for mobile app execution are shown in Figure 15. For simplification, error conditions are not included. The steps below correspond to the numbered messages in the sequence diagram.

0: The Cloudlet-Ready App, once at compile time, indicates in its manifest that it will be listening to a particular type of intent.

1: The Cloudlet Client receives the Service VM IP Address and Port after executing any of the cloudlet provisioning mechanisms to indicate that the server is ready for execution.

2-3: The Cloudlet Client obtains the app id from the Client App Metadata and builds an intent of the type indicated in Step 0 that includes the Service VM IP Address and Port.

4: Android will forward that Intent to the appropriate Cloudlet-Ready App.

5-6: The Cloudlet-Ready App opens a socket on the Cloudlet Host with the Service VM IP Address and Port and forwards the request to the appropriate Service VM that it has mapped through port forwarding.

7-11: The Cloudlet Ready-App sends a request to the Application Server and receives a response. This request-response interaction continues until the Cloudlet-Ready App is closed.

Figure 14. Sequence diagram for the on-demand provisioning process

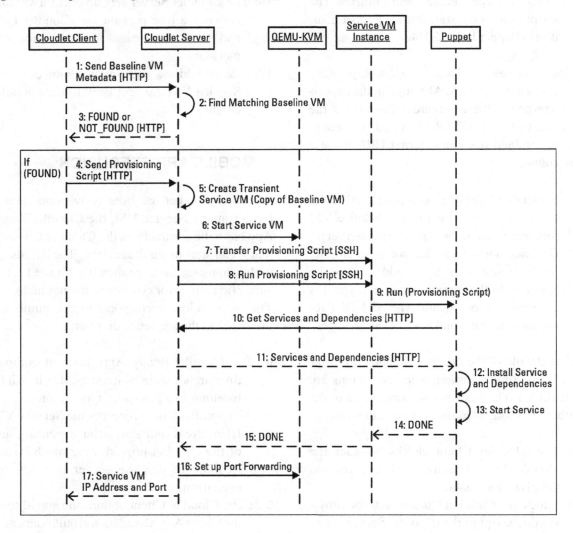

The interaction depicted in Figure 15 is simple request-response. Even though other types of interaction could be supported by cloudlets, this is the most energy-efficient type of interaction because it limits communication between the mobile device and the cloudlet. In general, offloading is beneficial when large amounts of computation are needed with relatively small amounts of communication (Kumar & Lu, 2010). Also, even though not shown in Figure 15, an optional step after the Cloudlet-Ready App is closed is to stop the Service VM on the cloudlet to promote elasticity. This would release resources on the cloudlet that could be used by other mobile devices.

7. QUANTITATIVE AND QUALITATIVE COMPARISON OF CLOUDLET PROVISIONING MECHANISMS

To perform a quantitative and qualitative comparison of the five different cloudlet provisioning mechanisms, we conducted a set of experiments using three computation-intensive applications: face recognition (FACE), speech recognition (SPEECH), and object recognition (OBJECT). We used a Galaxy Nexus with Android 4.3 as a mobile device and a Core i7-3960x based server with 32 GB of RAM running Ubuntu 12.04 as

Figure 15. Sequence diagram for cloudlet-ready mobile app execution

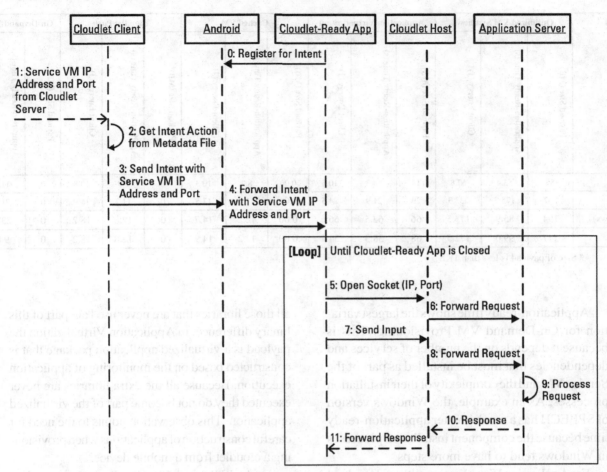

the cloudlet. We created a self-contained wireless network (using Wi-Fi 802.11n at 2.4 GHz, 65 Mbps) to be able to isolate network traffic effects. Energy was measured using a Power Monitor from Monsoon Solutions (Monsoon Solutions, 2014).

The results of the experiments are shown in Table 1. The first column under each mechanism is the size of the payload in MB that is sent from the mobile device to the cloudlet for provisioning. The second column is application-ready time, measured as the time in seconds from the start of the provisioning process until the cloudlet responds that it is ready. The third column is the energy consumed on the mobile device during application-ready time.

Table 1 shows that the largest amount of energy is consumed by VM Synthesis and On-Demand VM Provisioning. In VM Synthesis this consumption is due to the large payload size that also leads to high application-ready times because of communication time. Our experiments confirm that payload size is directly proportional to energy consumption, as has been stated by many others. In On-Demand VM Provisioning, although the payload is very small, the high energy consumption is due to the longer application-ready time. Unfortunately, the external power monitor used in the experiments measures total energy consumption and does not distinguish between energy consumed during communication and during idle time.

Table 1. Experiment data for cloudlet provisioning mechanisms

Applications	Optimized VM Synthesis			Application Virtualization			Cached VM			Cloudlet Push			On-Demand VM Provisioning		
	Payload Size (MB)	Application-Ready Time (s)	Client Energy (J)	Payload Size (MB)	Application-Ready Time (s)	Client Energy (J)	Payload Size (MB)	Application-Ready Time (s)	(Client Energy (J)	Payload Size (MB)*	Application-Ready Time (s)	Client Energy (J)	Payload Size (MB)*	Application-Ready Time (s)	Client Energy (J)
FACE (Windows)	55	53.4	57.8	14	14.3	10.5	0.00	8.2	10.3	0	7.9	13.8	0	112.7	129.1
OBJECT (Linux)	332	175.7	333.3	29	21.9	24.5	0.00	11.6	13.5	0	11.7	16.9	0	211.0	244.0
SPEECH (Windows)	194	85.9	175.5	66	62.5	66.6	0.00	12.2	14.7	0	12.8	18.2	0	237.6	269.2
SPEECH (Linux)	147	99.0	172.5	68	38.3	54.2	0.00	12.2	14.9	0	12.8	18.2	0	94.1	109.3

* Size of payload is less than 1KB.

Application-ready time shows the largest variation for On-Demand VM Provisioning. This is because it depends on the number of services and dependencies that must be installed as part of the Service VM and the complexity of their installation processes. As an example, the Windows version of SPEECH has a much greater application-ready time because the component installation processes in Windows tend to have more steps.

For Application Virtualization, although payload size is between 8% and 46% of the payload for VM Synthesis, it is still quite large for transmission in resource-limited environments. In addition, the size of the payload is highly variable because it depends on the OS and the number of external dependencies of the application that is being virtualized. An interesting observation is the difference in the payload size between Application Virtualization and Optimized VM Synthesis for OBJECT: OBJECT has the largest payload size for Optimized VM Synthesis but one of the smallest for Application Virtualization. The reason for this difference is that the OBJECT application, as it was written, contains many libraries that are never used. Because the payload in Optimized VM Synthesis is the binary difference between a Base VM and that VM with the installed application,

all those libraries that are never used are part of this binary difference. In Application Virtualization the payload is a virtualized application package that is constructed based on the monitoring of application execution. Because all the extra libraries are never executed they do not become part of the virtualized application. This observation points to the need for careful construction of applications when provisioning a cloudlet from a mobile device.

Cached VM and Cloudlet Push consume less energy because payload size is smaller, which in turn leads to shorter and more consistent application-ready times across applications. In Cached VM the payload size is very small (Service ID) and application-ready time is the time that it takes to start the corresponding Service VM. In Cloudlet Push the payload is small (client app from cloudlet to mobile device) and the application-ready time is the time that it takes to install the app on the mobile device and then start the corresponding Service VM.

Simply based on this quantitative data, one would assume the Cached VM and Cloudlet Push are the better option. However, it is important to look at qualitative data as well. Table 2 shows a qualitative comparison of the cloudlet provisioning mechanisms.

Table 2. Qualitative comparison of cloudlet provisioning mechanisms

	Optimized VM Synthesis	Application Virtualization	Cached VM	Cloudlet Push	On-Demand VM Provisioning
Cloudlet Content[c]	Exact base VM	VM compatible with server code	Service (VM) repository	Repository of paired VMs (server code) and client apps	• VM provisioning software • Server code components
Mobile Device Content	• Application overlay • Client app and metadata	• Virtualized server code • Client app and metadata	Client app and metadata	None	• VM provisioning script • Client app and metadata
Payload	Application overlay	Virtualized server code	Service ID	Client app and metadata	VM provisioning Script
Advantages	Cloudlet can run any server code that can be installed on a Base VM.	Portability across OS distribution boundaries	Supports server code updates as long as service interface remains the same	Supports most client mobile devices with distribution at runtime	Service VM with server code can be assembled at runtime.
Constraints	Requires exact base VM, which limits distributions and patches	All server code dependencies have to be captured at packaging time.	Cloudlet is provisioned with service VMs required by client apps (or has access to them).	Cloudlet has a client app version that matches mobile client OS version.	Cloudlet has all required server code components (or access to them).

[c] In addition to Cloudlet Server and Metadata.

For Optimized VM Synthesis the advantage is that the cloudlet can run any server code that can be installed in a VM. In addition, because the cloudlet is provisioned from the mobile device, the cloudlet does not have to be pre-provisioned with any server code. However, as noted earlier, the large payload size is a disadvantage for resource-limited environments. In addition, because the VM synthesis process requires the exact base VM from which the overlay was created, any changes to the base VM, due to, for example, security patches, would require changes to every application overlay that was created with that base VM.

For Application Virtualization the advantage is also that the cloudlet can be provisioned from the mobile device, with an advantage over VM synthesis with respect to payload size. In addition, the dependency is on the operating system running inside the VM, which enables portability across OS distribution boundaries. As long as the cloudlet has a VM with an OS that is compatible

with the server code, it is possible to offload the application. However, all server code dependencies have to be captured at packaging time, which is a challenge for any application virtualization tool (Messinger & Lewis, 2013).

For Cached VM, in addition to the small payload size, the advantage is that it supports server code updates as long as service interface remains the same. However, the assumption is that the cloudlet is provisioned with Service VMs required by client apps or has access to them, either at deployment time or at runtime (i.e., through an enterprise-level Service VM repository).

For Cloudlet Push, in addition to the small payload size, the advantage is that it supports most client mobile devices with distribution at runtime. However, similar to Cached VM, the assumption is that the cloudlet is provisioned with Service VMs as well as Client Apps. In addition, the cloudlet would need to have a client app version that matches the mobile client OS version.

Finally, for On-Demand VM Provisioning, in addition to small payload size, the advantage is that the Service VM can be assembled at runtime, which provides the greatest flexibility. However, as noted earlier, in addition to longer application-ready time the constraint is that the cloudlet has all required service and dependency components, or access to the components from enterprise repositories or code distribution sites.

8. FUTURE RESEARCH DIRECTIONS

The results of the experiments show that the combination of Cached VM with Cloudlet Push as the cloudlet provisioning mechanism is the best fit for resource-limited environments because it enables lower energy consumption on the mobile device, places less requirements on mobile devices, and simplifies provisioning in the environments experienced by first responders and others operating in crisis situations. An additional advantage of combining both mechanisms is that if the mobile device already has the client app it can simply invoke the matching Service VM; if not, it can obtain the client app from the cloudlet, similar to accessing an app store, and then invoke the matching Service VM. The tradeoff is that it relies on cloudlets that are pre-provisioned with server capabilities that might be needed for a particular mission, or that the cloudlet is connected to the enterprise, even if just at deployment time, to obtain the capabilities. We argue that this requirement is not unreasonable in these environments and that it makes cloudlet deployment in the field easier and faster while leveraging the state of art and best practices from the cloud computing industry. A pre-provisioned-VM-based solution also promotes resilience and survivability by supporting rapid live VM migration in case of cloudlet mobility, discovery of more powerful or less-loaded cloudlets, or unavailability due to disconnection or disruption. It supports scalability and elasticity by starting and stopping VMs as needed based on the number of active users (which is typically bounded in these environments because group size is known). In addition, the request-response nature of many of the operations needed in the field also lends itself to an asynchronous form of interaction in which the cloudlet can continue processing and send results back to a mobile device (directly or by re-routing) as network conditions change.

In addition, the results of a systematic literature review show that in current research in cyber-foraging, there is very little understanding of system qualities beyond energy, performance, network usage, and fidelity of results. Many of the cyber-foraging systems, especially those that perform runtime partitioning and offloading decisions, have very complex algorithms for guaranteeing fidelity of results and for optimizing energy consumption, network bandwidth usage, and performance. Disconnected operations and fault tolerance are supported by some systems in which the local computation is a fallback mechanism should the remote computation fail. However, there is very little consideration of other system qualities that are relevant to cyber-foraging systems, such as ease of distribution and installation, resiliency, and security. Related to this point, the systems in the studies tend to focus on enabling cyber-foraging between one mobile device and one offload target, but there is very little discussion of system-level attributes that must be considered when moving from experimental prototypes to operational systems. For example,

- How does the system perform when multiple devices are trying to offload to the same target?
- If there are multiple offload targets available, how does the mobile device select the target that best fits its requirements?
- What happens if the mobile device loses connectivity to the offload target?
- What are the mechanisms for ensuring currency and compatibility of mobile-device-side and server-side components if these may not have the same distribution mechanisms?

The current and future focus of the research presented in this chapter is on these system-level quality attributes that will enable more widespread adoption of cyber-foraging as a standard feature to support computation-intensive applications.

- **Standard Packaging of Service VMs:** Service VMs can be easily installed from the cloudlet manager (web-based interface to the Cloudlet Server and Service VM repository), an enterprise Service VM repository, a thumb drive, or the mobile device connected via USB to the cloudlet to enable deployability and ease of distribution.

- **Optimal Cloudlet Selection:** The cloudlet discovery protocol has been extended to use metadata from the client app, Service VM, and the cloudlet so that, in the case where there is more than one cloudlet in range, the mobile device can automatically select the cloudlet that maximizes a pluggable utility function. This function can be based on cloudlet load, signal strength, or any other parameter. Optimal cloudlet selection further optimizes resources and increases survivability of the system because the cloudlet that is selected is the one that more quickly and reliably performs the task at hand before the mobile device moves out of range.

- **Manual and Automated Cloudlet Handoff:** The goal is to implement VM migration capabilities that enable manual and automated handoff of data and computation between cloudlets that are within range of each other. Manual handoff would enable scenarios in which a user is migrating capabilities from a fixed cloudlet to a mobile cloudlet to support field operations, as well as reintegration back to the fixed cloudlet. Automated migration would enable load balancing, similar to that done in cloud data centers for resource optimization.

- **Data Synchronization between Cloudlets and the Enterprise:** Although cloudlets can operate fully-disconnected from the enterprise if they are pre-provisioned at deployment time, there are situations when cloudlet capabilities (Service VMs) need access to a master data source located in the enterprise. Support for integration with distributed, networked file systems such as Coda (Coda File System, 2014) enables disconnected operations with opportunistic synchronization when connectivity becomes available.

9. CONCLUSION

Forward-deployed, discoverable, virtual-machine-based cloudlets can be hosted on vehicles or other platforms to provide infrastructure to offload computation, provide forward data-staging for a mission, perform data filtering to remove unnecessary data from streams intended for mobile users, and serve as collection points for data heading for enterprise repositories. The forward-deployed, single-hop proximity to mobile devices promotes energy efficiency as well as lower latency (faster response times). If cloudlets are pre-provisioned, there are many applications that can function disconnected from the enterprise or can synchronize with the enterprise if and when there is connectivity. The fact that cloudlets are discoverable enables mobile devices to locate mission-specific capabilities as personnel and cloudlets move and missions change. Finally, virtual machine technology not only simplifies the distribution and rapid deployment of capabilities, but also enables the leverage of any legacy application that can be packaged inside a VM.

Going forward, cyber-foraging has applicability beyond resource-limited mobile environments. As sales of mobile devices grow and smartphones and tablets become, for many, the preferred way of interacting with the Internet, social media, and the enterprise, organizations are striving to push content and functionality out to mobile users. However, mobile devices still do not have the computing power and battery life that will allow them to perform effectively. Cyber-foraging is likely going to become the mechanism to support the mobile applications of the present and the future. These large-scale deployments will require the consideration of system-level qualities like the ones presented in this chapter.

REFERENCES

Avahi. (2007). *Avahi daemon* [Computer software]. Retrieved from http://avahi.org

Balasubramanian, N., Balasubramanian, A., & Venkataramani, A. (2009). Energy consumption in mobile phones: A measurement study and implications for network applications. In *Proceedings of IMC '09: The 9th ACM SIGCOMM Internet Measurement Conference* (pp. 280–293). New York, NY: ACM. doi:10.1145/1644893.1644927

Bellard, F. (2013). *qemu-img(1): Linux man page*. Retrieved from http://linux.die.net/man/1/qemu-img

Cameyo [Computer software]. (2013). Retrieved from http://www.cameyo.com/

CherryPy: A Minimalist Python Web Framework [Computer software]. (2014). Retrieved from http://www.cherrypy.org/

Chun, B. G., Ihm, S., Maniatis, P., Naik, M., & Patti, A. (2011). CloneCloud: Elastic execution between mobile device and cloud. In *Proceedings of the Sixth Conference on Computer Systems* (pp. 301–314). New York, NY: ACM. doi:10.1145/1966445.1966473

Coda File System. (2014). *What is CODA?* Retrieved from http://www.coda.cs.cmu.edu

Cuervo, E., Balasubramanian, A., Cho, D. K., Wolman, A., Saroiu, S., Chandra, R., & Bahl, P. (2010). MAUI: Making smartphones last longer with code offload. In *Proceedings of the 8th International Conference on Mobile Systems, Applications, and Services* (pp. 49–62). New York, NY: ACM. doi:10.1145/1814433.1814441

Eclipse. (2014). *Jetty: Servlet engine and http server* [Computer software]. Retrieved from http://www.eclipse.org/jetty/

Guo, P. J., & Engler, D. (2011). CDE: Using system call interposition to automatically create portable software packages. In *Proceedings of the 2011 Annual Technical Conference on USENIX* (p. 21). Berkeley, CA: USENIX Association.

Ha, K., Lewis, G., Simanta, S., & Satyanarayanan, M. (2011). *Code offload in hostile environments (CMU-CS-11-146)*. Pittsburgh, PA: Carnegie Mellon University.

Iyer, A. N., & Roopa, T. (2012). Extending Android application programming framework for seamless cloud integration. In *Proceedings of 2012 IEEE First International Conference on Mobile Services* (pp. 96–104). Washington, DC: IEEE Computer Society Press. doi:10.1109/MobServ.2012.22

Jarabek, C., Barrera, D., & Aycock, J. (2012). ThinAV: Truly lightweight mobile cloud-based anti-malware. In *Proceedings of the 28th Annual Computer Security Applications Conference* (pp. 209–218). New York, NY: ACM.

JmDNS [Computer software]. (2011). Retrieved from http://jmdns.sourceforge.net/

Korn, D., MacDonald, J., Mogul, J., & Vo, K. (2002). *RFC 3284: The VCDIFF generic differencing and compression data format* [Computer software]. Retrieved from http://tools.ietf.org/html/rfc3284

Kosta, S., Aucinas, A., Hui, P., Mortier, R., & Zhang, X. (2012). ThinkAir: Dynamic resource allocation and parallel execution in the cloud for mobile code offloading. In *Proceedings IEEE INFOCOM* (pp. 945–953). Washington, DC: IEEE Computer Society Press.

Kumar, K., & Lu, Y. H. (2010). Cloud computing for mobile users: Can offloading computation save energy? *Computer*, *43*(4), 51–56. doi:10.1109/MC.2010.98

KVM. (2014). *Kernel based virtual machine* [Computer software]. Retrieved from http://www.linux-kvm.org/

Lehr, W., & McKnight, L. (2002). Wireless internet access: 3G vs. WiFi? Cambridge, MA: Center for eBusiness @ MIT.

Libvirt. (2014a). *Libvirt: The virtualization API* [Computer software]. Retrieved from http://libvirt.org/

Libvirt. (2014b). *Snapshot XML format* [Computer software]. Retrieved from http://libvirt.org/formatsnapshot.html

McLoughlin, M. (2008). *The QCOW2 image format* [Computer software]. Retrieved from https://people.gnome.org/~markmc/qcow-image-format.html

Mell, P., & Grance, T. (2011). *The NIST definition of cloud computing (Special Publication 800-145)*. Gaithersburg, MD: National Institute of Standards and Technology.

Messinger, D., & Lewis, G. (2013). *Application virtualization as a strategy for cyber foraging in resource-constrained environments (CMU/SEI-2013-TN-007)*. Pittsburgh, PA: Software Engineering Institute, Carnegie Mellon University.

Monsoon Solutions, Inc. (2014). *Power monitor* [Apparatus]. Retrieved from http://www.msoon.com/LabEquipment/PowerMonitor/

Puppet Labs. (2014a). *Learning puppet—Manifests*. Retrieved from http://docs.puppetlabs.com/learning/manifests.html

Puppet Labs. (2014b). *Puppet enterprise* [Computer software]. Retrieved from http://puppetlabs.com/puppet/puppet-enterprise

Python. (2014). *LZMA – Compression using the LZMA algorithm*. Retrieved from https://docs.python.org/dev/library/lzma.html

QEMU. (2014a). *Documentation/networking*. Retrieved from http://wiki.qemu.org/Documentation/Networking

QEMU: *Open Source Processor Emulator* [Computer software]. (2014b). Retrieved from http://wiki.qemu.org

Rahimi, M. R., Venkatasubramanian, N., Mehrotra, S., & Vasilakos, A. V. (2012). MAPCloud: Mobile applications on an elastic and scalable 2-tier cloud architecture. In *Proceedings of the 2012 IEEE/ACM Fifth International Conference on Utility and Cloud Computing* (pp. 83–90). Washington, DC: IEEE Computer Society Press. doi:10.1109/UCC.2012.25

Satyanarayanan, M., Bahl, P., Caceres, R., & Davies, N. (2009). The case for VM-based cloudlets in mobile computing. *IEEE Pervasive Computing*, *8*(4), 14–23. doi:10.1109/MPRV.2009.82

Simanta, S., Ha, K., Lewis, G., Morris, E., & Satyanarayanan, M. (2013). A reference architecture for mobile code offload in hostile environments. In *Proceedings of the 5th International Conference on Mobile Computing, Applications, and Services* (pp. 274–293). Berlin, Germany: Springer. doi:10.1007/978-3-642-36632-1_16

Xdelta [Computer software]. (2014). Retrieved from http://xdelta.org

Xiao, Y., Simoens, P., Pillai, P., Ha, K., & Satyanarayanan, M. (2013). Lowering the barriers to large-scale mobile crowdsensing. In *Proceedings of the 14th Workshop on Mobile Computing Systems and Applications* (p. 9). New York, NY: ACM. doi:10.1145/2444776.2444789

Zeroconf: Zero Configuration Networking [Computer software]. (2014). Retrieved from http://www.zeroconf.org/

ADDITIONAL READING

Abolfazli, S., Sanaei, Z., Ahmed, E., Gani, A., & Buyya, R. (2014). Cloud-based augmentation for mobile devices: Motivation, taxonomies, and open challenges. *IEEE Communications Surveys and Tutorials*, *16*(1), 337–368. doi:10.1109/SURV.2013.070813.00285

Angin, P., & Bhargava, B. (2013). An agent-based optimization framework for mobile-cloud computing. *Journal of Wireless Mobile Networks, Ubiquitous Computing, and Dependable Applications*, *4*(2), 1–17.

Armstrong, T., Trescases, O., Amza, C., & de Lara, E. (2006). Efficient and transparent dynamic content updates for mobile clients. In *Proceedings of the 4th International Conference on Mobile Systems, Applications, and Services* (pp. 56–68). New York, NY: ACM. doi:10.1145/1134680.1134687

Bahrami, A., Wang, C., Yuan, J., & Hunt, A. (2006). The workflow based architecture for mobile information access in occasionally connected computing. In *IEEE International Conference on Services Computing*, 2006 (pp. 406–413). Washington, DC: IEEE Computer Society Press. doi:10.1109/SCC.2006.105

Balan, R. K., Gergle, D., Satyanarayanan, M., & Herbsleb, J. (2007). Simplifying cyber foraging for mobile devices. In *Proceedings of the 5th International Conference on Mobile Systems, Applications and Services, MobiSys '07* (pp. 272–285). New York, NY: ACM. doi:10.1145/1247660.1247692

Chen, G., Kang, B.-T., Kandemir, M., Vijaykrishnan, N., Irwin, M. J., & Chandramouli, R. (2004). Studying energy trade offs in offloading computation/compilation in Java-enabled mobile devices. *IEEE Transactions on Parallel and Distributed Systems*, *15*(9), 795–809. doi:10.1109/TPDS.2004.47

Chu, H.-, Song, H., Wong, C., Kurakake, S., & Katagiri, M. (2004). Roam, a seamless application framework. *Journal of Systems and Software*, *69*(3), 209–226. doi:10.1016/S0164-1212(03)00052-9

Dinh, H. T., Lee, C., Niyato, D., & Wang, P. (2011). A survey of mobile cloud computing: Architecture, applications, and approaches. *Wireless Communications and Mobile Computing*, *13*(18), 1587–1611. doi:10.1002/wcm.1203

Fernando, N., Loke, S. W., & Rahayu, W. (2013). Mobile cloud computing: A survey. *Future Generation Computer Systems*, *29*(1), 84–106. doi:10.1016/j.future.2012.05.023

Fjellheim, T., Milliner, S., & Dumas, M. (2005). Middleware support for mobile applications. *International Journal of Pervasive Computing and Communications*, *1*(2), 75–88. doi:10.1108/17427370580000114

Flinn, J. (2012). Cyber foraging: Bridging mobile and cloud computing. In M. Satyanarayanan (Ed.), *Synthesis Lectures on Mobile and Pervasive Computing* [Series]. San Rafael, CA: Morgan & Claypool Publishers. doi:10.2200/S00447ED-1V01Y201209MPC010

Flinn, J., Park, S., & Satyanarayanan, M. (2002). Balancing performance, energy, and quality in pervasive computing. In *Proceedings of the 22nd International Conference on Distributed Computing Systems* (pp. 217–226). Washington, DC: IEEE Computer Society Press. doi:10.1109/ICDCS.2002.1022259

Flinn, J., Sinnamohideen, S., Tolia, N., & Satyanarayanan, M. (2003). Data staging on untrusted surrogates. In *Proceedings of FAST'03: The 2nd USENIX Conference on File and Storage Technologies* (pp. 15–28). Berkeley, CA: USENIX Association.

Giurgiu, I., Riva, O., Juric, D., Krivulev, I., & Alonso, G. (2009). Calling the cloud: Enabling mobile phones as interfaces to cloud applications. In *Proceedings of the ACM/IFIP/USENIX 10th International Conference on Middleware* (pp. 83–102). Berlin, Germany: Springer. doi:10.1007/978-3-642-10445-9_5

Ha, K., Pillai, P., Lewis, G., Simanta, S., Clinch, S., Davies, N., & Satyanarayanan, M. (2013). The impact of mobile multimedia applications on data center consolidation. In *Proceedings of IC2E 2013: The 2013 IEEE International Conference on Cloud Engineering* (pp. 166–176). Washington, DC: IEEE Computer Society Press.

Kemp, R., Palmer, N., Kielmann, T., & Bal, H. (2012). *Cuckoo: A computation offloading framework for smartphones. Mobile Computing, Applications, and Services* (pp. 59–79). New York, NY: Springer.

Kovachev, D., & Klamma, R. (2012). Framework for computation offloading in mobile cloud computing. *International Journal of Interactive Multimedia and Artificial Intelligence, 1*(7), 6–15. doi:10.9781/ijimai.2012.171

Kumar, K., Liu, J., Lu, Y.-H., & Bhargava, B. (2013). A survey of computation offloading for mobile systems. *Mobile Networks and Applications, 18*(1), 129–140. doi:10.1007/s11036-012-0368-0

Kundu, S., Mukherjee, J., Majumdar, A. K., Majumdar, B., & Sekhar Ray, S. (2007). Algorithms and heuristics for efficient medical information display in PDA. *Computers in Biology and Medicine, 37*(9), 1272–1282. doi:10.1016/j.compbiomed.2006.11.015 PMID:17222816

Kwon, Y.-W., & Tilevich, E. (2013). Reducing the energy consumption of mobile applications behind the scenes. In *Proceedings of the 29th IEEE International Conference on Software Maintenance* (pp. 170–179). Washington, DC: IEEE Computer Society Press. doi:10.1109/ICSM.2013.28

Lee, B.-D. (2012). A framework for seamless execution of mobile applications in the cloud. In Z. Qian, L. Cao, W. Su, T. Wang, & H. Yang (Eds.), Lecture Notes in Electrical Engineering: Vol. 126. Recent Advances in Computer Science and Information Engineering (pp. 145–153). New York, NY: Springer. doi:10.1007/978-3-642-25766-7_20

Matthews, J., Chang, M., Feng, Z., Srinivas, R., & Gerla, M. (2011). Powersense: Power aware dengue diagnosis on mobile phones. In *Proceedings of the First ACM Workshop on Mobile Systems, Applications, and Services for Healthcare* (p. 6). New York, NY: ACM. doi:10.1145/2064942.2064951

O'Sullivan, M. J., & Grigoras, D. (2013). The cloud personal assistant for providing services to mobile clients. In *SOSE 2013: The IEEE 7th International Symposium on Service Oriented System Engineering* (pp. 478–485). Washington, DC: IEEE Computer Society Press.

Ok, M., Seo, J.-W., & Park, M.-s. (2007). A distributed resource furnishing to offload resource-constrained devices in cyber foraging toward pervasive computing. In T. Enokido, L. Barolli, & M. Takizawa (Eds.), Lecture Notes in Computer Science: Vol. 4658. *Network-Based Information Systems* (pp. 416–425). New York, NY: Springer. doi:10.1007/978-3-540-74573-0_43

Park, S., Choi, Y., Chen, Q., & Yeom, H. (2012). SOME: Selective offloading for a mobile computing environment. In *2012 IEEE International Conference on Cluster Computing* (pp. 588–591). Washington, DC: IEEE Computer Society Press. doi:10.1109/CLUSTER.2012.49

Phokas, T., Efstathiades, H., Pallis, G., & Dikaiakos, M. (2013). Feel the world: A mobile framework for participatory sensing. In *Proceedings of the 10th International Mobile Web Information Systems Conference* (pp. 143–156). Berlin, Germany: Springer. doi:10.1007/978-3-642-40276-0_12

Ra, M.-R., Sheth, A., Mummert, L., Pillai, P., Wetherall, D., & Govindan, R. (2011). Odessa: Enabling interactive perception applications on mobile devices. In *Proceedings of MobiSys '11: The 9th International Conference on Mobile Systems, Applications, and Services* (pp. 43–56). New York, NY: ACM.

Satyanarayanan, M., Lewis, G., Morris, E., Simanta, S., Boleng, J., & Ha, K. (2013). The role of cloudlets in hostile environments. *IEEE Pervasive Computing / IEEE Computer Society [and] IEEE Communications Society*, *12*(4), 40–49. doi:10.1109/MPRV.2013.77

Silva, J. N., Veiga, L., & Ferreira, P. (2008). SPADE: Scheduler for parallel and distributed execution from mobile devices. In *Proceedings of the 6th International Workshop on Middleware for Pervasive and Ad-Hoc Computing* (pp. 25–30). New York, NY: ACM. doi:10.1145/1462789.1462794

Su, Y.-Y., & Flinn, J. (2005). Slingshot: Deploying stateful services in wireless hotspots. In *Proceedings of MobiSys '05: The 3rd International Conference on Mobile Systems, Applications, and Services* (pp. 79–92). New York, NY: ACM. doi:10.1145/1067170.1067180

Yang, K., Ou, S., & Chen, H.-H. (2008). On effective offloading services for resource-constrained mobile devices running heavier mobile internet applications. *IEEE Communications Magazine*, *46*(1), 56–63. doi:10.1109/MCOM.2008.4427231

Yang, L., Cao, J., Yuan, Y., Li, T., Han, A., & Chan, A. (2013). A framework for partitioning and execution of data stream applications in mobile cloud computing. *Performance Evaluation Review*, *40*(4), 23–32. doi:10.1145/2479942.2479946

Yu, P., Ma, X., Cao, J., & Lu, J. (2013). Application mobility in pervasive computing: A survey. *Pervasive and Mobile Computing*, *9*(1), 2–17. doi:10.1016/j.pmcj.2012.07.009

Zhang, X., Jeon, W., Gibbs, S., & Kunjithapatham, A. (2012). Elastic HTML5: Workload offloading using cloud-based web workers and storages for mobile devices. In *Proceedings of the 4th International Conference on Mobile Computing, Applications, and Services* (pp. 373–381). New York, NY: Springer. doi:10.1007/978-3-642-29336-8_26

Zhang, X., Kunjithapatham, A., Jeong, S., & Gibbs, S. (2011). Towards an elastic application model for augmenting the computing capabilities of mobile devices with cloud computing. *Mobile Networks and Applications*, *16*(3), 270–284. doi:10.1007/s11036-011-0305-7

Zhang, Y., Guan, X.-t., Huang, T., & Cheng, X. (2009). A heterogeneous auto-offloading framework based on web browser for resource-constrained devices. In *ICIW'09: The Fourth International Conference on Internet and Web Applications and Services* (pp. 193–199). Washington, DC: IEEE Computer Society Press. doi:10.1109/ICIW.2009.35

Zhang, Y., Huang, G., Zhang, W., Liu, X., & Mei, H. (2012). Towards module-based automatic partitioning of java applications. *Frontiers of Computer Science*, 6, 725–740.

KEY TERMS AND DEFINITIONS

Cloud Computing: Based on the definition from the National Institute of Standards and Technology (NIST) that has become the de facto definition (Mell & Grance, 2011), cloud computing is a model for enabling on-demand access to a shared pool of configurable computing resources, such as servers, storage, and applications, that can be rapidly provisioned and released with minimal management effort or service provider interaction.

Cloudlet: Cloudlets are discoverable servers located in single-hop proximity of mobile devices on which those mobile devices can offload expensive computation or stage data. The single-hop proximity enables lower battery consumption on the mobile device and faster response times. Another simple way to define a cloudlet is as a "data center in a box" or very small private cloud.

Computation Offload: Offload of expensive computation in order to extend battery life and increase computational capability.

Cyber-Foraging: Cyber-foraging is the leverage of external resource-rich surrogates to augment the capabilities of resource-limited mobile devices. Examples of cyber-foraging are computation offload and data staging.

Data Staging: Data staging is the use of intermediate storage and processing resources to temporarily stage data in transit to and from mobile devices and data centers. Examples of data staging are pre-fetching, in-bound pre-processing and out-bound pre-processing.

Mobile Cloud Computing: Mobile cloud computing is a model for mobile devices to leverage mobile networks and cloud computing resources to enable execution of rich mobile application with improved user experience. Examples of mobile cloud computing include (1) extending access to cloud services to mobile devices, (2) enabling mobile devices to work collaboratively as cloud resource providers, and (3) cyber-foraging.

Reference Architecture: A reference architecture is a software architecture that generalizes and abstracts common connectors, components, and configurations that promote certain system qualities and functions, from which concrete systems can be instantiated.

ENDNOTES

[1] JSON stands for JavaScript Object Notation and is a widely used lightweight data-interchange format.
[2] APK stands for Android Application Package and is the file format used to distribute and install applications on the Android operating system.

Chapter 4
Energy–Saving QoS Resource Management of Virtualized Networked Data Centers for Big Data Stream Computing

Nicola Cordeschi
"Sapienza" University of Rome, Italy

Danilo Amendola
"Sapienza" University of Rome, Italy

Mohammad Shojafar
"Sapienza" University of Rome, Italy

Enzo Baccarelli
"Sapienza" University of Rome, Italy

ABSTRACT

In this chapter, the authors develop the scheduler which optimizes the energy-vs.-performance trade-off in Software-as-a-Service (SaaS) Virtualized Networked Data Centers (VNetDCs) that support real-time Big Data Stream Computing (BDSC) services. The objective is to minimize the communication-plus-computing energy which is wasted by processing streams of Big Data under hard real-time constrains on the per-job computing-plus-communication delays. In order to deal with the inherently nonconvex nature of the resulting resource management optimization problem, the authors develop a solving approach that leads to the lossless decomposition of the afforded problem into the cascade of two simpler sub-problems. The resulting optimal scheduler is amenable of scalable and distributed adaptive implementation. The performance of a Xen-based prototype of the scheduler is tested under several Big Data workload traces and compared with the corresponding ones of some state-of-the-art static and sequential schedulers.

INTRODUCTION

Energy-saving computing through Virtualized Networked Data Centers (VNetDCs) is an emerging paradigm that aims at performing the adaptive energy management of virtualized Software-as-a-Service (SaaS) computing platforms. The goal is to provide QoS Internet services to large populations of clients, while minimizing the overall computing-plus-networking energy consumption (Cugola & Margara, 2012; Baliga, Ayre, Hinton, & Tucker, 2011; Mishra, Jain, & Durresi, 2012). As recently pointed out in (Mishra et al. 2012; Azodomolky, Wieder, & Yahyapour, 2013; Wang

DOI: 10.4018/978-1-4666-8213-9.ch004

Copyright © 2015, IGI Global. Copying or distributing in print or electronic forms without written permission of IGI Global is prohibited.

et al. 2014), the energy cost of communication gear for current data centers may represent a large fraction of the overall system cost and it is induced primarily by switches, LAN infrastructures, routers and load balancers.

However, actual virtualized data centers subsume the (usual) Map/Reduce-like batch processing paradigm and they are not designed for supporting networking-computing intensive real-time services, such as, for example, emerging Big Data Stream Computing (BDSC) services (Cugola et al. 2012). In fact, BDSC services retain the following (somewhat novel and unique) characteristics (Cugola et al. 2012; Scheneider, Hirzel, & Gedik, 2013; Qian, He, Su, Wu, Zhu, & Zhang, 2013; Kumbhare, 2014):

1. The incoming data (i.e., the offered workload) arrive continuously at volumes that far exceed the storage capabilities of individual computing machines. Furthermore, all data must be timely proceed but, typically, a few of data require to be stored. This means that the (usual) storing-then-computing batch paradigm is no longer feasible;
2. Since BDSC services acquire data from massive collections of distributed clients in a stream form, the size of each job is typically unpredictable and also its statistics may be quickly time-varying; and,
3. The offered workload is a real-time data stream, which needs real-time computing with latencies firmly limited up to a few of seconds (Qian et al. 2013; Kumbhare, 2014). Imposing hard limits on the overall per-job delay requires, in turn, that the overall VNetDC is capable to quickly adapt its resource allocation to the current (a priori unpredictable) size of the incoming big data.

In order to attain energy saving in such kind harsh computing scenario, the joint balanced provisioning and adaptive scaling of the networking-plus-computing resources is demanded. This is the focus of this work, whose main contributions may be so summarized. First, the contrasting objectives of low consumptions of both networking and computing energies in delay and bandwidth-constrained VNetDCs are cast in the form of a suitable constrained optimization problem, namely, the Computing and Communication Optimization Problem (CCOP). Second, due to the nonlinear behavior of the rate-vs.-power-vs.-delay relationship, the CCOP is not a convex optimization problem and neither guaranteed-convergence adaptive algorithms nor closed-form formulas are, to date, available for its solution. Hence, in order to solve the CCOP in exact and closed-form, we prove that it admits a loss-free (e.g., optimality preserving) decomposition into two simpler loosely coupled sub-problems, namely, the CoMmunication Optimization Problem (CMOP) and the ComPuting Optimization Problem (CPOP). Third, we develop a fully adaptive version of the proposed resource scheduler that is capable to quickly adapt to the a priori unknown time-variations of the workload offered by the supported Big Data Stream application and converges to the optimal resource allocation without the need to be restarted.

RELATED WORK

Updated surveys of the current technologies and open communication challenges about energy-efficient data centers have been recently presented in (Mishra et al. 2012; Balter, 2013). Specifically, power management schemes that exploit Dynamic Voltage and Frequency Scaling (DVFS) techniques for performing resource provisioning are the focus of (Chen & Kuo, 2005; Kim, Buyya, & Kim, 2007; Li, 2008). Although these contributions consider hard deadline constraints, they do not consider, indeed, the performance penalty and the energy-vs.-delay tradeoff stemming from the finite capacity of the utilized network infrastructures and do not deal with the issues arising from perfect/imperfect Virtual Machines (VMs) isolation in VNetDCs.

Energy-saving dynamic provisioning of the computing resources in virtualized green data centers is the topic of (Liu, Zhao, Liu, & He, 2009; Mathew, Sitaraman, & Rowstrom, 2012; Padala, You, Shin, Zhu, Uysal, Wang, Singhal, & Merchant, 2009; Kusic & Kandasamy, 2009; Govindan, Choi, Urgaonkar, Sasubramanian, & Baldini, 2009; Zhou, Liu, Jin, Li, Li, & Jiang, 2013; Lin, Wierman, Andrew, & Thereska, 2011; Laszewski, Wang, Young, & He, 2009). Specifically, (Padala et al. 2009) formulates the optimization problem as a feedback control problem that must converge to an a priori known target performance level. While this approach is suitable for tracking problems, it cannot be employed for energy-minimization problems, where the target values are a priori unknown. Roughly speaking, the common approach pursued by (Mathew et al. 2012; Kusic et al. 2009; Govindan et al. 2009) and (Lin et al. 2011) is to formulate the afforded minimum-cost problems as sequential optimization problems and, then, solve them by using limited look-ahead control. Hence, the effectiveness of this approach relies on the ability to accurately predict the future workload and degrades when the workload exhibits almost unpredictable time fluctuations. In order to avoid the prediction of future workload, (Zhou et al. 2013) resorts to a Lyapunov-based techniques, that dynamically optimizes the provisioning of the computing resources by exploiting the available queue information. Although the pursued approach is of interest, it relies on an inherent delay-vs.-utility tradeoff that does not allow us to account for hard deadline constraints.

A suitable exploitation of some peculiar features of the network topology of current NetDCs is at the basis of the capacity planning approach recently proposed in (Wang et al. 2014). For this purpose, a novel traffic engineering-based approach is developed, which aims at reducing the number of active switches, while simultaneously balancing the resulting communication flows. Although the attained reduction of the energy consumed by the networking infrastructures is,

indeed, noticeable, the capacity planning approach in (Wang et al. 2014) does not consider, by design, the corresponding energy consumed by the computing servers and, which is the most, it subsumes delay-tolerant application scenarios.

The joint analysis of the computing-plus-communication energy consumption in virtualized NetDCs which perform static resource allocation is, indeed, the focus of (Baliga et al. 2011; Tamm, Hersmeyer, & Rush, 2010), where delay-tolerant Internet-based applications are considered. Interestingly, the main lesson stemming from these contributions is that the energy consumption due to data communication may represent a large part of the overall energy demand, especially when the utilized network is bandwidth-limited. Overall, these works numerically analyze and test the energy performance of some state-of-the-art static schedulers, but do not attempt to optimize it through the dynamic joint scaling of the available communication-plus-computing resources. Providing computing support to the emerging BDSC services is the target of some quite recent virtualized management frameworks such as, S4 (Neumeyer, Robbins, & Kesari, 2010), D-Streams (Zaharia, Das, Li, Shenker, & Stoica, 2012) and Storm (Loesing, Hentschel, & Kraska, 2012). While these management systems are specifically designed for the distributed runtime support of large scale BDSC applications, they do not still provide automation and dynamic adaptation to the time-fluctuations of Big Data streams. Dynamic adaptation of the available resources to the time-varying rates of the Big Data streams is, indeed, provided by the (more recent) Time Stream (Qian et al. 2013) and PLAStiCC (Kumbhare, 2014) management frameworks. However, these frameworks manage only the computing resources and do not consider the simultaneous management of the networking resources.

The rest of this chapter is organized as follows. After modeling in Section 2 the considered virtualized NetDC platform, in Section 3 we formally state the afforded CCOP and, then, we solve it and provide the analytical conditions for its feasibility. In Section 4, we present the main structural properties of the resulting optimal scheduler and analytically characterize the (possible) occurrence of hibernation phenomena of the instantiated VMs. Furthermore, we also develop an adaptive implementation of the optimal scheduler and prove its convergence to the optimum. In Section 5, we test the sensitivity of the average performance of the proposed scheduler on the Peak-to-Mean Ratio (PMR) and time-correlation of the (randomly time-variant) offered Big Data workload and, then, we compare the obtained performance against the corresponding ones of some state-of-the-art static and sequential schedulers. After addressing some possible future developments and hints for incoming research in Section 6, the conclusive Section 7 recaps the main results.

About the adopted notation, $[x]_a^b$ indicates $\min\{\max\{x; a\}; b\}$, $[x]_+$ indicates $\max\{x; 0\}$, $\triangleq$ means equality by definition, while $1_{[A]}$ is the (binary-valued) indicator function of the A event (that is, $1_{[A]}$ is unit when the A event happens, while it vanishes when the A event does not occur).

THE CONSIDERED VNetDC PLATFORM

A networked virtualized platform for real-time parallel computing is composed by multiple clustered virtualized processing units interconnected by a single-hop virtual network and managed by a central controller (see, for example, Figure 1 of (Azodomolky et al. 2013)). Each processing unit executes the currently assigned task by self-managing own local virtualized storage/computing resources. When a request for a new job is submitted to the VNetDC, the central resource controller dynamically performs both admission control and allocation of the available virtual resources (Almeida, Almeida, Ardagna,

Cunha, & Francalanci, 2010). Hence, according to the emerging communication-computing system architectures for the support of real-time BDSC services (see, for example, Figs. 1 of (Azodomolky et al. 2013) and (Ge, Feng, Feng, & Cameron, 2007)), a VNetDC is composed by multiple reconfigurable VMs, that operate at the Middleware layer of the underlying protocol stack and are interconnected by a throughput-limited switched Virtual Local Area Network (VLAN). The topology of the VLAN is of star-type, and, in order to guarantee inter-VM communication, the Virtual Switch of Figure 1 acts as a gather/scatter central node. The operations of both VMs and VLAN are jointly managed by a Virtual Machine Manager (VMM), which performs task scheduling by dynamically allocating the available virtual computing-plus-communication resources to the VMs and Virtual Links (VLs) of Figure 1. A new job is initiated by the arrival of a data of size L_{tot} *(bit)*. Due to the (an aforementioned) hard real-time nature of the supported BDSC services, full processing of each input job must be completed within *assigned* and *deterministic* processing time which spans T_t seconds.

Hence, in our framework, a real-time job is characterized by:

1. The size L_{tot} of the data segment to be processed;
2. The maximum tolerated processing delay T_t; and,
3. The job granularity, that is, the (integer-valued) maximum number $M_T \geq 1$ of independent parallel tasks embedded into the submitted job.

Let $M_V \geq 1$ be the maximum number of VMs which are available at the Middleware layer of Figure 1. In principle, each VM may be modeled as a virtual server that is capable to process f_c bits per second (Portnoy, 2012). Depending on the size L *(bit)* of the task to be currently processed by the

Figure 1. A typical VNetDC architecture for the support of real-time BDSC services

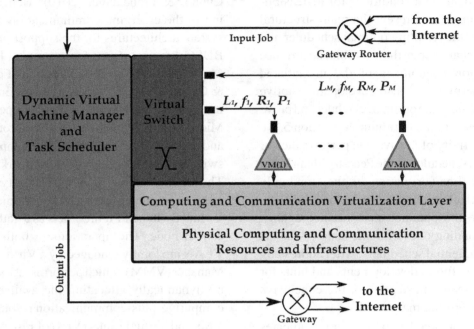

VM, the corresponding processing rate f_c may be adaptively scaled at runtime, and it may assume values over the interval $\left[0, f_c^{\max}\right]$, where $f_c^{\max}$ *(bit/s)* is the per-VM maximum allowed processing rate[1]. Furthermore, due to the real-time nature of the considered application scenario, the time allowed the VM to fully process each submitted task is fixed in advance at $\Delta(s)$, regardless from the actual size L of the task currently assigned to the VM. In addition to the currently assigned task (of size L), the VM may also process a background workload of size $L_b(bit)$, that accounts for the programs of the guest Operating System (Portnoy, 2012).

Hence, by definition, the utilization factor η of the VM equates (Portnoy, 2012):

$$\eta \triangleq \frac{f_c}{f_c^{\max}} \in \left[0, 1\right].$$

Then, as in (Kim et al. 2009; Almeida et al. 2010; Koller, Verma, & Neogi, 2010), let $E_c = E_c(f_c)$ *(Joule)* be the overall energy consumed by the VM

to process a single task of duration Δ at the processing rate f_c, and let $E_c^{\max} = E_c\left(f_c^{\max}\right)$ *(Joule)* be the corresponding maximum energy when the VM operates at the maximum processing rate $f_c^{\max}$. Hence, by definition, the (dimensionless) ratio is the so-called Normalized Energy Consumption of the considered VM (Warneke & Kao, 2011). From an analytical point of view, $\Phi(\eta) : [0,1] \rightarrow [0,1]$ is a function of the actual value η of the utilization factor of the VM. Its analytical behavior depends on the specific features of the resource provisioning policy actually implemented by the VMM of Figure 1 (Kim, Beloglazov, & Buyya, 2009; Zhu, Melhem, & Childers, 2003).

$$\Phi(\eta) \triangleq \frac{E_c\left(f_c\right)}{E_c^{\max}} = \Phi\left(\frac{f_c}{f_c^{\max}}\right). \qquad (1)$$

Specifically, the following three main conclusions are widely agreed by several recent studies (Kansal, Zhao, Liu, Kothari, & Bhattacharya, 2010; Ge et al. 2007; Cordeschi, Shojafar, & Baccarelli, 2013; Stoess, Lang, & Bellosa, 2007), (Laszewski et al. 2009). First, under the assumption of isolation of the VMs, the energy consumed by the physical servers is the summation of the energies wasted by the hosted VMs. Second, in practice, the per-VM normalized energy consumption $\Phi(\eta)$ follows the c-powered behavior:

$$\Phi(\eta) = (1 - b)\eta^c + b, \quad 0 \leq \eta \leq 1, \qquad (2)$$

In (2), the exponent parameter $c \geq 1$ is application-depending and it is empirically evaluated at runtime (e.g., $c=1$ in (Kansal et al. 2010) and $c=2$ in (Lin et al. 2011)), while $b \in [0,1)$ is the fraction of the per-VM maximum energy consumption E_c^{max} which is wasted by the VM in the idle state, that is, $E_c^{idle} = \dfrac{b}{E_c^{max}}$.

Third, from an application point of view, the aforementioned per-VM energy parameters E_c^{max}, E_c^{idle} and c may be estimated at runtime. In particular, the *Joulemeter* system described in section 5 of (Kansal et al. 2010) is a practical tool that estimates at runtime the per-VM energy parameters by performing suitable measurements atop the VMM of Figure 1. Finally, before proceeding, we anticipate that the validity of the analytical developments of Sections 3 and 4 is not limited up to the energy model in (2) and it extends, indeed, to the more general case in which $\Phi(\eta)$ is an increasing and convex function of η.

In Figure 1, the Virtual LAN (VLAN) is atop the Virtualization Layer. Black boxes indicate Virtual Network Interface Cards (VNICs) ending point-to-point TCP-based connections. Physical Ethernet adapters connect the VLAN to the underlying physical network (Azodomolky et al. 2013). The reported architecture is instantiated at the Middleware layer.

Big Data Streaming Workload and Power-Limited Virtualized Communication Infrastructures

Let $M = min \{M_V, M_T\}$ be the degree of concurrency of the submitted job, let L_{tot} be the overall size of the job currently submitted to the VNetDC, and let $L_i \geq 0, i = 1, ..., M$, be the size of the task that the Scheduler of Figure 1 assigns to the i-th VM, e.g., *VM(i)*. Hence, the following constraint: $\sum_{i=1}^{M} L_i = L_{tot}$ guarantees that the overall job L_{tot} is partitioned into (at the most) M parallel tasks. In order to hold at the minimum the transmission delays from (to) the Scheduler to (from) the connected VMs of Figure 1, as in (Baliga et al. 2011), (Azodomolky et al. 2013), we assume that *VM(i)* communicates to the Scheduler through a dedicated (i.e., contention-free) reliable virtual link, that operates at the transmission rate of R_i *(bit/s)*, $i=1,..., M$ and it is equipped with suitable Virtual Network Interface Cards (VNICs) (see Figure 1). The one-way transmission-plus-switching operation over the i-th virtual link drains a (variable) power of P_i^{net} *(Watt)*, where P_i^{net} is the summation: $P_i^{net} \triangleq P_T^{net}(i) + P_R^{net}(i)$ of the power $P_i^{net}(i)$ consumed by the transmit VNIC and Switch and the corresponding power P_i^{net} wasted by the receive VNIC (see Figure 1).

About the actual value of P_i^{net}, we noted that, in order to limit the implementation cost, current data centers utilize off-the-shelf rackmount physical servers which are interconnected by commodity Fast/Giga Ethernet switches. Furthermore, they implement legacy TCP suites (mainly, the TCPNewReno one) for attaining end-to-end (typically, multi-hop) reliable communication (Mishra et al. 2012). At this regard, we note that the data center-oriented versions of the legacy TCPNewReno suite proposed in (Vasudevan, Phanishayee, & Shah, 2009; Alizadeh, Greenberg,

Maltz, & Padhye, 2010; Das & Sivalingam, 2013) allow the managed end-to-end transport connections to operate in the Congestion Avoidance state during 99.9% of the working time, while assuring the same end-to-end reliable throughput of legacy TCPNewReno protocol. This means, in turn, that the average throughput R_i *(bit/s)* of the i-th virtual link of Figure 1 (i.e., the i-th end-to-end transport connection) equates (Kurose & Ross, 2013, section 3.7; (Jin, Guo, Matta, & Bestavros, 2003)

$$R_i = \sqrt{\frac{3}{2v}} \frac{MSS}{RTT_i \sqrt{\overline{P_i}^{Loss}}}, \quad i = 1, ..., M, \quad (3)$$

As it is well-known, *MSS (bit)* in (3) is the maximum segment size, $v \in \{1, 2\}$ is the number of per-ACK acknowledged segments, $\overline{RTT_i}$ is the average round-trip-time of the i-th end-to-end connection (e.g., $\overline{RTT_i}$ less than *1 (ms)* in typical data centers (Vasudevan et al. 2009)), and $\overline{P_i}^{Loss}$ is the average segment loss probability experienced by the i-th connection section 3.7 in (Kurose et al. 2013). At this regard, several studies point out that $\overline{P_i}^{Loss}$ scales down for increasing $\overline{P_i}^{net}$ as in (Liu, Zhou, &Giannakis, 2004); Cordeschi et al 2012a; Baccarelli, Cordeschi, & Patriarca, 2012b; Baccarelli & Biagi, 2003; Baccarelli, Biagi, Pelizzoni, &Cordeschi, 2007)

$$\overline{P_i}^{Loss} = \left(g_i P_i^{net}\right)^{-d}, \quad i = 1, ..., M, \quad (4)$$

where $g_i \left(W^{-1}\right)$ is the coding gain-to-receive noise power ratio of the i-th end-to-end connection, while the positive exponent d measures the diversity gain provided by the frequency-time interleavers implemented at the Physical layer. Explicit closed-form expressions for g_i and d are reported, for example, in (Liu et al. 2004; Cordeschi, Pa-

triarca, & Baccarelli, 2012a) and (Baccarelli et al. 2012b) for various operating settings. Hence, after introducing (4) into (3), we obtain

$$P_i^{net} = \Omega_i (\overline{RTT_i R_i})^{\alpha}, \quad i = 1, ..., M, \quad (5)$$

with

$$\alpha \triangleq \left(\frac{2}{d}\right) \geq 1,$$

and

$$\Omega_i \equiv \frac{1}{g_i} \left(\frac{1}{MSS} \sqrt{\frac{2v}{3}}\right)^{\alpha}, \quad i = 1, ..., M.$$

Hence, since the corresponding one-way transmission delay equates: $D(i) = \left(\frac{L_i}{R_i}\right)$, the corresponding one-way communication energy $E^{net}(i)$ needed for supporting the i-th virtual link of Figure 1 is: $E^{net}(i) = P_i^{net} \left(\frac{L_i}{R_i}\right)$.

Before proceeding, we point out that the α-powered (convex) formula in (5) featuring the power-vs.-throughput relationship of the i-th virtual link of Figure 1 holds regardless from the actual (possibly, multi-hop) topology of the adopted physical network (e.g., Fat-tree, BCube, DCell (Wang et al. 2014)). Formally speaking, the validity of (5) relies on the (minimal) assumption that TCP-based transport connections working in the Congestion Avoidance state are used for implementing the virtual links of Figure 1.

Reconfiguration Cost in VNetDCs

Under the per-job delay constraints imposed by Big Data stream services (Zhou et al. 2013), the VMM of Figure 1 must carry out two main operations at runtime, namely, Virtual Machine management and load balancing. Specifically, goal of the Virtual Machine management is to adaptively control the Virtualization Layer of Figure 1. In particular, the set of the (aforementioned) VM's attributes:

$$\left\{ \Delta, f_c^{max}(i), \Phi_i(\eta_i), E_c^{max}(i), L_b(i), i = 1, ..., M \right\}, \tag{6}$$

are dictated by the Virtualization Layer and, then, they are passed to the VMM of Figure 1. It is in charge of the VMM to implement a suitable frequency-scaling policy, in order to allow the VMs to scale up/down in real-time their processing rates f_c's at the minimum cost (Warneke et al. 2011).

At this regard, we note that switching from the processing frequency f_1 to the processing frequency f_2 entails an energy cost of $\varepsilon(f_1; f_2)$ *(Joule)* (Laszewski et al. 2009; Kim et al. 2007). Although the actual behavior of the function $\varepsilon(f_1; f_2)$ may depend on the adopted VMM and the underlying DVFS technique and physical CPUs (Portnoy, 2012), any practical $\varepsilon(f_1; f_2)$ function typically retains the following general properties (Laszewski et al. 2009; Kim et al. 2007): *i)* it depends on the absolute frequency gap $|f_1-f_2|$; *ii)* it vanishes at $f_1=f_2$ and is not decreasing in $|f_1-f_2|$; and, *iii)* it is jointly convex in $|f_1-f_2|$. A quite common practical model which retains the aforementioned formal properties is the following one:

$$\varepsilon(f_1; f_2) = k_e(f_1 - f_2)^2 \quad (Joule) \tag{7}$$

where k_e *(Joule/(Hz)²)* dictates the resulting per-VM reconfiguration cost measured at the Middleware layer (see Figure 1). For sake of concreteness, in the analytical developments of the following section 3, we directly subsume the quadratic model in (6). The generalization to the case of $\varepsilon(.;.)$ functions that meet the aforementioned (more general) analytical properties is, indeed, direct.

On the Virtual-to-Physical QoS Resource Mapping in VNetDCs

Due to the hard delay-sensitive feature of Big Data stream services, the Virtualization Layer of Figure 1 must guarantee that the demands for the computing f_i and communication R_i resources done by the VLAN are mapped onto adequate (i.e., large enough) computing (e.g., CPU cycles) and communication (e.g., link bandwidths) physical supplies.

In our setting, efficient QoS mapping of the virtual demands f_i for the computing resources may be actually implemented by equipping the Virtualization Layer of Figure 1 with a per-VM queue system that implements the (recently proposed) *mClock* scheduling discipline section 3 in (Gulati, Merchant, & Varman, 2010). Interestingly enough, Table 1 of (Gulati et al. 2010) points out that the *mClock* scheduler works on a per-VM basis and provides:

1. Resource isolation;
2. Proportionally fair resource allocation; and,
3. Hard (i.e., absolute) resource reservation, by adaptively managing the computing power of the underlying DVSF-enabled physical CPUs (see the Algorithm 1 of (Gulati et al. 2010) for a code of the *mClock* scheduler).

About the TCP-based networking virtualization, several (quite recent) contributions (Ballami, Costa, Karagiannis, & Rowstron, 2011; Greenberg et al. 2011; Guo et al. 2010; Xia, Cui, & Lange, 2012) point out that the most appealing property of emerging data centers for the support of delay-sensitive services is the agility, i.e., the capability to assign arbitrary physical server to any service without experiencing performance degradation. To this end, it is recognized that the virtual network atop the Virtualization Layer should provide a flat networking abstraction (see Figure 1 of (Azodomolky et al. 2013)). The Middleware layer architecture of Figure 1 of the considered

Table 1. Main taxonomy of the paper

Symbol	Meaning/Role
$L_{tot}(bit)$	Job's size
$f_i(bit \, / \, s)$	Computing rate of *VM(i)*
$L_i(bit)$	Task's size of *VM(i)*
$R_i(bit \, / \, s)$	Communication rate of the *i*-th virtual link
$R_t(bit \, / \, s)$	Aggregate communication rate of the VLAN
$\Delta(s)$	Per-job maximum allowed computing time
$T_t(s)$	Per-job maximum allowed computing-plus-communication time
$E_i^{\max}(Joule)$	Per-job maximum energy consumed by *VM(i)*
$f_i^{\max}(bit \, / \, s)$	Maximum computing rate of *VM(i)*
$E_c(i)(Joule)$	Per-job maximum energy consumed by *VM(i)*
$E^{net}(i)(Joule)$	Per-job communication energy consumed by the *i*-th virtual link
$E_{tot}(Joule)$	Per-job total consumed energy

virtualized NetDC is aligned, indeed, with this requirement and, then, it is general enough to allow the implementation of agile data centers.

Specifically, according to (Azodomolky et al. 2013), the VNetDC of Figure 1 may work in tandem with *any* Network Virtualization Layer that is capable to map the rate-demands R_i onto bandwidth-guaranteed end-to-end (possibly, multi-hop) connections over the actually available underlying physical network. Just as examples of practical state-of-the-art Networking Virtualization tools, *Oktopous* (Ballami et al. 2011, Figure 5) provides a contention-free switched LAN abstraction atop tree-shaped physical network topologies, while *VL2* (Greenberg et al. 2011) works atop

physical Clos' networks. Furthermore, *SecondNet*e (Guo et al. 2010, section 3) and *VNET/P* (Xia et al. 2012, section 4.2) provide bandwidth-guaranteed virtualized Ethernet-type contention-free LAN environments atop *any* TCP-based end-to-end connection. For this purpose, *SeconNet* implements Port-Switching based Source Routing (PSSR) (Guo et al. 2010, section 4), while *VNET/P* relies on suitable Layer2 Tunneling Protocols (L2TPs) (Xia et al. 2012, section 4.3).

An updated survey and comparison of emerging contention-free virtual networking technologies is provided by Table 2 of (Azodomolky et al. 2013). Before proceeding, we anticipate that the solving approach developed in section 3.1 still

Table 2. Average energy reductions attained by the proposed and the sequential schedulers one over the static one at k_e=0.005 (Joule/(MHz)²), and $f_i^{max} = 80$ (Mbit/s)

PMR	Proposed Scheduler at Δ = 0.05(s)	SES at Δ = 0.05(s)	Proposed Scheduler at Δ = 0.1(s)	SES at Δ = 0.1(s)
1	0%	0%	0%	0%
1.25	51%	54%	65%	68%
15	45%	48%	62%	65%
1.75	63%	67%	57%	62%
2	57%	62%	50%	56%

holds verbatim when the summation: $\sum_{i=1}^{M} E_i^{net}(i)$ in (7) is replaced by a single energy function $\chi(.)$ which is jointly convex and not decreasing in the variables $\{L_i\}$ (see (15.1)). This generalization could be employed for modeling flow coupling effects that may be (possibly) induced by the *imperfect* isolation provided by the Networking Virtualization Layer (e.g., contentions among competing TCP flows) (Portnoy, 2012).

Remark 1: Discrete DVFS.

Actual VMs are instantiated atop physical CPUs which offer, indeed, only a *finite* set:

$$A \triangleq \left\{ \hat{f}^{(0)}0, \hat{f}^{(1)},..., \hat{f}^{(Q-1)} \triangleq f_c^{max} \right\},$$

of Q discrete computing rates. Hence, in order to deal with both continuous and discrete reconfigurable physical computing infrastructures without} introducing loss of optimality, we borrow the approach formerly developed, for example, in (Neely, Modiano, & Rohs, 2003; Li, 2008). Specifically, after indicating by

$$B \triangleq \left\{ \hat{\eta}^{(0)} \triangleq 0, \hat{\eta}^{(1)},..., \hat{\eta}^{(Q-1)} \triangleq 1 \right\},$$

the discrete values of η which correspond to the frequency set A, we build up a per-VM Virtual Energy Consumption curve $\hat{\Phi}(\eta)$ by resorting to a piecewise linear interpolation of the allowed Q operating points:

$$\left\{ \left(\hat{\eta}^{(j)}, \Phi(\hat{\eta}^{(j)}) \right), j = 0,...,(Q-1) \right\}.$$

Obviously, such virtual curve retains the (aforementioned) formal properties and, then, we may use it as the true energy consumption curve for virtual resource provisioning (Neely et al. 2003). Unfortunately, being the virtual curve of continuous type, it is no longer guaranteed that the resulting optimally scheduled computing rates are still discrete valued. However, as also explicitly noted in (Neely et al. 2003; Li, 2008), any point $\left\{ \left(\hat{\eta}^*, \Phi(\eta^*) \right) \right\}$, with $\hat{\eta}^{(j)} < \eta^* < \hat{\eta}^{(j+1)}$, on the virtual curve may be actually attained by time-averaging over Δ secs (i.e., on a per-job basis) the corresponding surrounding vertex points: $\left\{ \left(\hat{\eta}^{(j)}, \Phi(\hat{\eta}^{(j)}) \right) \right\}$ and $\left\{ \left(\hat{\eta}^{(j+1)}, \Phi(\hat{\eta}^{(j+1)}) \right) \right\}$. Due to the piecewise linear behavior of the virtual curve, as in (Neely et al. 2003; Li, 2008), it is guaranteed that the average energy cost of the discrete DVFS system equates that of the corresponding virtual one over *each* time interval of duration Δ (e.g., on a per-job basis).

OPTIMAL ALLOCATION OF THE VIRTUAL RESOURCES

In this section, we deal with the second functionality of the VMM of Figure 1; namely, the dynamic load balancing and provisioning of the communication-plus-computing resources at the Middleware layer (see Figure 1). Specifically, this functionality aims at properly tuning the task sizes $\{L_i, i = 1,...,M\}$, the communication rates $\{R_i, i = 1,...,M\}$ and the computing rates $\{f_i, i = 1,...,M\}$ of the networked VMs of Figure 1. The goal is to minimize (on a per-slot basis) the overall resulting communication-plus-computing energy:

$$E_{tot} \triangleq \sum_{i=1}^{M} E_c(i) + \sum_{i=1}^{M} E^{net}(i) \quad (Joule) \qquad (8)$$

under the (aforementioned) *hard* constraint T_t on the allowed per-job execution time. This last depends, in turn, on the (one-way) delays *{D(i), i=1,..., M}* introduced by the VLAN and the allowed per-task processing time Δ. Specifically, since the *M* virtual connections of Figure 1 are typically activated by the virtual switch of Figure 1 (e.g., the load dispatcher) in a parallel fashion (Scheneider et al. 2013), the overall two-way communication-plus-computing delay induced by the *i*-th connection of Figure 1 equates: $2D(i) + \Delta$, so that the hard constraint on the overall per-job execution time reads as in:

$$\max_{1 \leq i \leq M}\{2D(i)\} + \Delta \leq T_t \qquad (9)$$

Thus, the overall CCOP assumes the following form:

$$\min_{\{R_i, f_i, L_i\}} \sum_{i=1}^{M} \left\{ \Phi_i\left(\frac{f_i}{f_i^{\max}}\right) E_i^{\max} + k_e(f_i - f_i^0)^2 + 2P_i^{net}(R_i)\left(\frac{L_i}{R_i}\right) \right\} \qquad (10.1)$$

s.t:

$$(L_i + L_b(i)) \leq f_i\Delta, \quad i = 1,...,M, \qquad (10.2)$$

$$\sum_{i=1}^{M} L_i = L_{tot} \qquad (10.3)$$

$$0 \leq f_i \leq f_i^{\max}, \quad i = 1,...,M, \qquad (10.4)$$

$$L_i \geq 0, \quad i = 1,...,M, \qquad (10.5)$$

$$\frac{2L_i}{R_i} + \Delta \leq T_t, \quad i = 1,...,M,, \qquad (10.6)$$

$$\sum_{i=1}^{M} R_i \leq R_t \qquad (10.7)$$

$$R_i \geq 0, \quad i = 1,...,M. \qquad (10.8)$$

About the stated problem, the first two terms in the summation in (10.1) account for the computing-plus-reconfiguration energy $E_c(i)$ consumed by the *VM(i)*, while the third term in (10.1) is the communication energy $E^{net}(i)$ requested by the corresponding point-to-point virtual link for conveying L_i bits at the transmission rate of R_i *(bit/s)*. Furthermore, f_i^0 and f_i in (10.1) represent the current (i.e., already computed and consolidated) computing rate and the target one, respectively. Formally speaking, f_i is the variable to be optimized, while f_i^0 describes the *current* state of the *VM(i)*, and, then, it plays the role of a known constant. Hence, $k_e(f_i - f_i^0)^2$ in (10.1) accounts for the resulting reconfiguration cost. The constraint in (10.2) guarantees that *VM(i)* executes the assigned task within Δ secs, while the (global) constraint in (10.3) assures that the overall job is partitioned into *M* parallel tasks. According to (9), the set of constraints in (10.6) forces the VNetDC of Figure 1 to process the overall job within the assigned hard deadline T_t. Finally, the global constraint in (10.7) limits up to R_t *(bit/s)* the aggregate transmission rate which may be sustained by the underlying VLAN of Figure 1, so that R_t is directly dictated by the actually considered VLAN standard (Azodomolky et al. 2013; Scheneider et al. 2013). Table 1 summarizes the main taxonomy used in this paper.

Remark 2: On the setup cost of turning OFF the idle servers.

Due to the noticeable power drained by idle servers, turning the idle servers OFF is commonly considered an energy-effective policy. However, nothing comes for free, so that, although the above conclusion holds under delay-tolerant application scenarios, it must be carefully re-considered when hard limits on the allowed per-job service time T_t are present (Kim et al. 2009; Almeida et al. 2010; Balter, 2013, Chap. 27; Koller et al. 2010; Gandhi, Balter, & Adam, 2010; Loesing et al. 2012). In fact, the setup time *I* for transitioning a server from the OFF state to the ON one is currently larger than 200 seconds and, during the overall setup time, the server typically wastes power (Balter, 2013, Chap. 27; (Loesing et al. 2012).

Hence, under real-time constrains, there are (at least) two main reasons to refrain to turn the idle servers OFF. First, the analysis recently reported in (Balter, 2013, Chap. 27; Loesing et al. 2012) point out that turning the idle servers OFF *increases*, indeed, the resulting average energy consumptions when the corresponding setup time *I* is larger than $2T_t$, and this conclusion holds also when the

long-run (i.e., not instantaneous) average utilization factor of the servers is low and of the order of about 0.3 (see Table 27.1 of (Balter, 2013)). Second, in order to not induce outage-events, the setup time *I* must be limited up to a (negligible) fraction of the per-job service time T_t (see the hard constraint in (10.6)). Hence, since the tolerated per-job service times of communication-oriented real-time applications are typically limited up to few seconds (see, for example, Tables 1 and 2 of (Zaharia et al. 2012)), the results of the aforementioned performance analysis induce to refrain to turn the idle servers OFF, at least when the setup times *I* is two orders of magnitude larger than the corresponding service times. However, as a counterbalancing aspect, the performance results reported in the (quite recent) contributions (Kim et al. 2009; Almeida et al. 2010, section 3.1; Koller et al. 2010) unveil that, under real-time constraints, there is still large room for attaining energy savings by adaptively setting the set of the utilization factors in (2) of the available VMs, so as to properly track the instantaneous size L_{tot} of the offered workload. This is, indeed, the energy-management approach we pursue in the following sections, where we focus on the (still quasi unexplored) topic of the energy-saving adaptive configuration of the VNetDC of Figure 1.

Remark 3: Generalization of the *CCOP*'s formulation.

Depending on the actually considered VNetDC platform and sustained BDSC services, some generalizations of the reported CCOP's formulation are possible.

First, several reports point out that the energy consumption of other non-IT equipments (e.g., cooling equipments) is roughly proportional to that in (8) through a constant factor PUE, which represents the (measured) ratio of the total energy wasted by the data center to the energy consumed by the corresponding computing-plus-networking equipments (Greenberg, Hamilton, & Maltz, 2009).

Second, the size $\tilde{L}_i^{(0)}(bit)$ of the workload output by *VM(i)* at the end of the computing phase may be different from the corresponding one L_i received in input at the beginning of the computing phase. Hence, after introducing the *i*-th inflating/deflating constant coefficient $\theta_i \triangleq \dfrac{\tilde{L}_i^{(0)}}{L_i} \geq \leq 1$, the basic CCOP's formulation may be generalized by simply replacing the term: *2Li* in (10.1), (10.6) by the following one: $(1+\theta_i)L_i, i=1,...,M$.

Third, the summation in (10.1) of the computing and reconfiguration energies may be replaced by *any* two energy functions: $H(f_1,...,f_M)$ and $V(f_1,...,f_M)$ which are jointly convex in *{f₁, i=1,...,M}*. Just as an application example, as in (Zhou et al. 2013), let us assume that all the VMs are instantiated onto the same physical server and, due to imperfect isolation; they directly compete for acquiring CPU cycles. In this (limit) case, the sum-form in (8) for the computing energy falls short, and the total energy E_{CPU} wasted by the physical host server may be modeled as in (Zhou et al. 2013):

$$E_{CPU} = E_{CPU}^{\max}\left\{(1-b)\left[\sum_{i=1}^{M}\left(\frac{f_i}{f_i^{\max}}\right)\right]^c + b\right\},$$

where $E_{CPU}^{\max}$ is the maximum energy consumed by the physical server, $E_{CPU}^{idle} \triangleq bE_{CPU}^{\max}$ is the corresponding energy consumed by the physical server in the idle state, while the inner summation is the aggregate utilization of the server by all hosted VMs. Since the above expression of E_{CPU} is jointly convex in *{f₁, i=1,...,M}* for $c \geq 1$, the solving approach of the next section 3.1 still applies verbatim.

Solving Approach and Optimal Provisioning of the Virtual Resources

The CCOP in (10) is *not* a convex optimization problem. This due to the fact that, in general, each function: $P_i^{net}(R_i)\left(\dfrac{L_i}{R_i}\right)$ in (10.1) is not jointly convex in L_i, R_i, even in the simplest case when the power function $P_i^{net}(R_i)$ reduces to an assigned constant P_i^{net} that does not depend on R_i. Therefore, neither guaranteed-convergence iterative algorithms nor closed-form expressions are, to date, available to compute the optimal solution $\left\{\hat{L}_i, \hat{R}_i, \hat{f}_i, i=1,...,M\right\}$ of the CCOP.

However, we observe that the computing energy in (10.1) depends on the variables *{f₁}*, while the network energy depends on the variables *{R₁}*. Furthermore, since the variables *{L₁}* are simultaneously present in the sets of constraints in (10.2) and (10.6), they affect both the computing and network energy consumptions. Formally speaking, this implies, that, for any assigned set of values of *{L₁}*, the minimization of the computing and network energies reduces to two uncoupled optimization sub-problems over the variables *{f₁}* and *{R₁}*, respectively. These sub-problems are loosely coupled (in the sense of (Chiang, Low, Calderbank, & Doyle, 2007)), and (10.2), (10.6) are the coupling constraints.

Therefore, in order to compute the optimal solution of the CCOP, in the following, we formally develop a solving approach that is based on the lossless decomposition of the CCOP into the (aforementioned) CMOP and CPOP.

Formally speaking, for any assigned non-negative vector $\vec{L}$ of the task's sizes, the CMOP is a (generally nonconvex) optimization problem in the communication rate variables *{R₁, i=1,... ,M}*, so formulated:

$$\min_{\{R_i\}} \sum_{i=1}^{M} \frac{2P_i^{net}(R_i)}{R_i} L_i \qquad (11.1)$$

s.t:

CCOP's constraints in (10-6)-(10-8) $\qquad (11.2)$

Let $\{R_i^*, (\vec{L}), i = 1,...,M\}$ be the optimal solution of the CMOP in (11), and let

$$S \triangleq \begin{Bmatrix} \vec{L} \in (\Re_0^+)^M : \left(\frac{L_i}{R_i^*(\vec{L})} \right) \leq \frac{(T_i - \Delta)}{2}, i = 1,...,M; \\ \sum_{i=1}^{M} R_i^*(\vec{L}) \leq R_t \end{Bmatrix} \qquad (12)$$

be the region of the nonnegative M-dimensional Euclidean space which is constituted by all $\vec{L}$'s vectors that meet the constraints in (10.6)-(10.8). Thus, after introducing the dummy function:

$$\chi(L_1,...,L_M) \triangleq \sum_{i=1}^{M} \frac{2P_i^{net}(R_i^*)}{R_i^*} L_i,$$

the CPOP is formally stated as in:

$$\min_{\{R_i, f_i, L_i\}} \sum_{i=1}^{M} \left\{ \Phi_i \left(\frac{f_i}{f_i^{max}} \right) E_i^{max} + k_e (f_i - f_i^0)^2 \right\} + \chi(\vec{L}), \qquad (13.1)$$

s.t:

CCOP's constraints in (10-2)-(10-5) and L \in S $\qquad (13.2)$

Let $\{L_i^*, R_i^*, f_i^*, i = 1,...,M\}$ be the (possibly, empty) set of the solutions of the cascade of the CMOP and CPOP. The following Proposition 1 proves that the cascade of these sub-problems is equivalent to the CCOP.

Proposition 1

The CCOP in (10.1)-(10.8) admits the *same* feasibility region and the *same* solution of the cascade of the CMOP and CPOP, that is,

$$\left\{ \hat{L}_i, \hat{R}_i, \hat{f}_i, i = 1,...,M \right\} = \left\{ L_i^*, R_i^*, f_i^*, i = 1,...,M \right\}.$$

Proof

By definition, the region S in (12) fully accounts for the set of the CCOP constraints in (10.6)-(10.8), so that the constraint $\vec{L}$ is equivalent to the set of constraints in (10.6)-(10.8). Since these constraints are also accounted for by the CMOP, this implies that S fully characterizes the coupling induced by the variables $\{L_i, i=1,...,M\}$ between the two sets of constraints in (10.2)-(10.5) and (10.6)-(10.8). Therefore, the claim of Proposition 1 directly arises by noting that, by definition, $\chi(L_1,...,L_M)$ is the result of the constrained optimization of the objective function in (10.1) over the variables $\{R_i, i=1,...,M\}$, and $\chi(L_1,...,L_M)$ is part of the objective function of the resulting CPOP in (13.1).

About the feasibility of the CMOP, the following result holds (see (Cordeschi, Amendola, Shojafar, & Baccarelli, 2014) for the proof).

Proposition 2

Let each function $P_i^{net} \frac{(R_i)}{R_i}$ in (11.1) be continuous and not decreasing for $R_i \geq 0$. Hence, for any assigned vector $\vec{L}$, the following two properties hold:

1.   The CMOP in (11.1) is feasible *if and only if* the vector $\vec{L}$ meets the following condition:

$$\sum_{i=1}^{M} L_i \le \frac{\left(R_t(T_t - \Delta)\right)}{2}. \tag{14}$$

2. The solution of the CMOP is given by the following closed-form expression:

$$R_i^*(\vec{L}) = R_i^*(L_i) = \left(2L_i(T_t - \Delta)\right), i = 1,...,M. \tag{15}$$

Being the condition in (14) necessary and sufficient for the feasibility of the CMOP, it fully characterizes the feasible region S in (12). This last property allows us to recast the CPOP in the following equivalent form:

$$R_i^*(\vec{L}) = R_i^*(L_i) = \left(2L_i(T_t - \Delta)\right), i = 1,...,M. \tag{16.1}$$

s.t.:

CCOP's constraints in (10-2)-(10-5) and (14) (16.2)

where (see (15)):

$$\chi(L_1,...,L_M) = (T_t - \Delta)\sum_{i=1}^{M} P_i^{net}\left(\frac{2L_i}{T_t - \Delta}\right). \tag{17}$$

Since the constraint in (14) involves only the offered workload, it may be managed as a feasibility condition and this observation leads to the following formal feasibility result (proved in the final Appendix A of (Cordeschi et al. 2013)).

Proposition 3

The CCOP in (10) is feasible if and only if the CPOP in (16) is feasible. Furthermore, the following set of *(M+1)* conditions:

$$L_b(i) \le \Delta f_i^{\max}, \quad i = 1,...,M, \tag{18.1}$$

$$L_{tot} \le \min\left\{\sum_{i=1}^{M}\left(f_i^{\max}\Delta - L_b(i)\right); \frac{R_t}{2}(T_t - \Delta)\right\}, \tag{18.2}$$

is necessary and sufficient for the feasibility of the CPOP.

About the solution of the CPOP, after denoting by $\pi_i(.)$ the following dummy function:

$$\pi_i(f_i) \triangleq \left(\frac{E_i^{\max}}{f_i^{\max}}\right)\frac{d\Phi_i}{d\eta}\left(\frac{f_i}{f_i^{\max}}\right) + 2k_e f_i, i = 1,...,M, \tag{19}$$

and by $\pi_i^{-1}(.)$ its inverse, let *TH(i)* be the non-negative threshold so defined:

$$TH(i) \triangleq 2\left(\partial P_i^{net}\frac{(R_i)}{\partial R_i}\right)\Big|_{R_i=0}, i = 1,...,M. \tag{20}$$

Hence, after indicating by $\left(\partial P_i^{net}\frac{(R_i)}{\partial R_i}\right)^{-1}(y)$

the final inverse function of $\partial P_i^{net}\frac{(R_i)}{\partial R_i}$, the following Proposition 4 analytically characterizes the optimal scheduler (see the Appendix A for the proof).

Proposition 4

Let the feasibility conditions in (18) be met. Let the $\chi(.)$ function in (17) be strictly jointly convex and let each function: $P_i^{net}\frac{(R_i)}{R_i}$, $i = 1,...,M$ be continuous and increasing for $R_i \ge 0$. Hence, the global optimal solution of the CPOP is unique, and it is analytically computable as in:

$$f_i^* = \left[\pi_i^{-1}(2k_e f_i^0 + \nu_i^* \Delta)\right]_{f_i^{min}}^{f_i^{max}} \qquad (21.1)$$

$$L_i^* = 1_{[\nu_i^* > 0]}\left((f_i^* \Delta - L_b(i))\right)$$
$$+ 1_{[\nu_i^* = 0]}\left[\frac{(T_t - \Delta)}{2}\left(\frac{\partial P_i^{net}(R_i)}{\partial R_i}\right)^{-1}\left(\frac{\mu^*}{2}\right)\right]_+, \qquad (21.2)$$

where $f_i^{min} \triangleq L_b(i) / \Delta$, and the nonnegative scalar ν_i^* is defined as in

$$\nu_i^* \triangleq \left[\mu^* - \frac{2\partial P_i^{net}}{\partial R_i}\left(R_i = \frac{2L_i^*}{(T_t - \Delta)}\right)\right]_+. \qquad (22)$$

Finally, $\mu^* \in \Re_0^+$ in (21.2) is the unique non-negative root of the following algebraic equation:

$$\sum_{i=1}^{M} L_i^*(\mu) = L_{tot}, \qquad (23)$$

where $L_i^*(.)$ is given by the r.h.s. of (21.2}, with μ^* replaced by the dummy variable μ.

ADAPTIVE IMPLEMENTATION OF THE OPTIMAL SCHEDULER

About the main structural properties and implementation aspects of the optimal scheduler, the following considerations may be of interest.

Hibernation Effects

Formally speaking, the i-th VM is hibernated when $L_i^* = 0$ (i.e., no exogenous workload is assigned to *VM(i)*) and the corresponding processing rate f_i^* is strictly larger than the minimum one: $f_i^{min} \triangleq L_b(i) / \Delta$ requested for processing the background workload $L_b(i)$ (see

(10.2)). In principle, we expect that the hibernation of *VM(i)* may lead to energy savings when k_e, f_i^0 's and the ratios $\{P_i^{net} / R_i\}$'s are large, while the offered workload L_{tot} is small. As proved in the *Appendix B*, this is, indeed, the behavior exhibited by the optimal scheduler, that hibernates *VM(i)* at the processing frequency f_i^* in (21.1) when the following hibernation condition is met:

$$\mu^* \leq TH(i). \qquad (24)$$

Adaptive Implementation of the Optimal Scheduler and Convergence Properties

From an application point of view, remarkable features of the optimal scheduler of Proposition 4 are that:

1. It leads to distributed and parallel computation (with respect to the i-index) of the *3M* variables $\{f_i^*, L_i^*, R_i^* \quad i = 1,...M\}$; and,

2. Its implementation complexity is fully independent from the (possibly, very large) size L_{tot} of the offered workload.

Moreover, in Big Data Streaming environments characterized by (possibly, abrupt and unpredictable) time-fluctuations of the offered workload L_{tot} (see section 5), the per-job evaluation and adaptive tracking of theLagrange multiplier in (23) may be performed by resorting to suitable primal-dual iterates. Specifically, due to the (strict) convexity of the CPOP, Theorem 6.2.6 of (23) guarantees that the Karush-Khun-Tucker (KKT) point of CPOP is unique and coincides with the saddle point of the corresponding Lagrangian function in (A.1) of Appendix B (Bazaraa, Sherali, & Shetty, 2006, pp.272-273). Furthermore, the saddle point is the equilibrium point of the equations' system which is obtained by equating to zero the gradients of the Lagrangian function in (A.1) performed with respect to the primal and dual variables (Bazaraa et al. 2006, Th.6.2.6).

Hence, as in (Srikant, 2004, sections 3.4, 3.8; Zaharia et al. 2012), we apply the primal-dual iterative algorithm for computing the saddle-point of the Lagrangian function in (A.1)[2]. Since the gradient of the Lagrangian function in (A.1) with respect the dual variable μ is:

$$\left(L_{tot} - \sum_{i=1}^{M} L_i \right),$$

and the closed-form KKT relationships in (21.1), (21.2), (22) hold, the primal-dual algorithm reduces to the following quasi-Newton iterates:

$$\mu^{(n)} = \left[\mu^{(n-1)} - \alpha^{(n-1)} \left(\sum_{i=1}^{M} L_i^{(n-1)} - L_{tot} \right) \right]_+$$

(25)

with $\mu^{(0)} \geq 0, L^{(0)} \geq 0$. In (25), $n \geq 1$ is an integer-valued iteration index, $\{\alpha^{(n-1)}\}$ is a (suitable) positive step-size sequence, and the following dummy iterates in the n-index also hold (see (21.1),(21.2) and (22)):

$$\nu_i^{(n)} \equiv \left[\mu^{(n)} - \frac{2\partial P_i^{net}}{\partial R_i} \left(R_i = \frac{2L_i^{(n-1)}}{(T_t - \Delta)} \right) \right]_+ \quad (26.1)$$

$$f_i^{(n)} = \left[\pi_i^{-1}(2k_e f_i^0 + \nu_i^{(n)}\Delta) \right]_{f_i^{min}}^{f_i^{max}} \quad (26.2)$$

$$L_i^{(n)} = 1_{[\nu_i^{(n)}>0]} \left((f_i^{(n)}\Delta - L_b(i)) \right)$$
$$+1_{[\nu_i^{(n)}=0]} \left[\frac{(T_t - \Delta)}{2} \left(\frac{\partial P_i^{net}(R_i)}{\partial R_i} \right)^{-1} \left(\frac{\mu^{(n)}}{2} \right) \right]_+$$

(26.3)

Regarding the asymptotic global convergence to the optimum of the primal-dual iterates in (25), (26), the following formal result holds (see the final Appendix B for the proof).

Proposition 5

Let the feasibility condition in (18) be met and let $\{\alpha^{(n-1)}\}$ in (25) be positive and vanishing for $n \to \infty$, i.e., $\lim_{n\to\infty} \alpha^{(n-1)} = 0^+$. Hence, the primal-dual iterates in (25), (26) converge to the global optimum for $n \to \infty$, regardless of the starting point $\mu^{(0)} \geq 0, L^{(0)} \geq 0$.

Formally speaking, Proposition 5 points out that the adaptive version in (25), (26) of the proposed scheduler attains the global convergence to the solving point in *Proposition 4* of the considered optimization problem. The numerical plots of section 5.2 confirm the actual global convergence of the iterates in (25), (26). In principle, the actual choice of $\{\alpha^{(n-1)}\}$ in (25) also impact on the rate of convergence and the tracking capability of the iterates. At this regard, we note that an effective choice for coping with the unpredictable time-variations of the workload offered by Big Data streaming applications is provided by the gradient-descendant algorithm in (Kushner et al. 1995) for the adaptive updating of the step-size in (25). In our framework, this updating reads as in (Kushner et al. 1995, Equation (2.4)):

$$\alpha^{(n)} = \max\left\{0; \min\left\{\beta; \alpha^{(n-1)} - \gamma V^{(n-1)} \left(\sum_{i=1}^{M} L_i^{(n-1)} - L_{tot} \right)\right\}\right\}$$

(27)

where β and γ are positive constants, while $V^{(n-1)}$ is updated as in (Kushner et al. 1995, Equation (2.5)):

$$V^{(n)} = \left(1 - \alpha^{(n-1)}\right)V^{(n-1)} - \left(\sum_{i=1}^{M} L_i^{(n-1)} - L_{tot} \right),$$

(28)

with $V^{(0)} = 0$.

Figure 3. Time evolution (in the n-index) of $\mu^{(n)}$ in (25) for the application scenario of Section 5.2

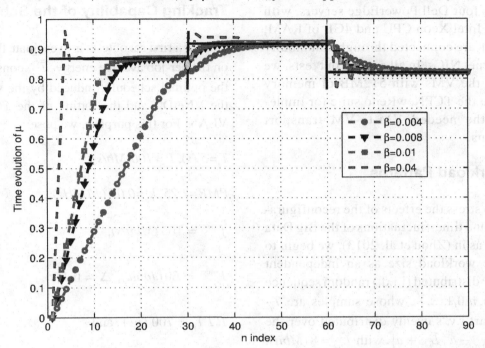

In practice, the iteration index *n must run faster* than the slot-time T_t. Although the actual duration of each *n*-indexed iteration may depend on the considered application, it should be small enough to allow the iterates in (25), (26) to converge to the global optimum within a limited fraction of the slot-time T_t. In fact, at the beginning of each slot, the iterates in (25), (26) are performed by starting from the optimal resource allocation computed at the previous slot. Then, after attaining the convergence, the iterates stop and the corresponding resource reconfiguration takes place. Hence, since a single reconfiguration action is performed during each slot-time T_t, the resulting reconfiguration cost of the adaptive implementation of the scheduler does not depend, indeed, on the convergence times and/or trajectories of the iterates (25), (26) (see Figure 3).

PROTOTYPE AND PERFORMANCE EVALUATION

In order to evaluate the per-job average communication-plus-computing energy $\bar{E}_{tot}^{*}$ consumed by the proposed scheduler, we have implemented a prototype of the adaptive scheduler of section 4.2, with paravirtualized Xen 3.3 as VMM and Linux 2.6.18 as guest OS kernel (see Figure 1). The adaptive scheduler has been implemented at the driver domain (i.e., *Dom0*) of the legacy Xen 3.3. Interestingly enough, out of approximately 1100 lines of SW code needed for implementing the proposed scheduler, 45% is directly reused from existing Xen/Linux code. The reused code includes part of the Linux's TCPReno congestion control suite and Xen's I/O buffer management.

The implemented experimental setup comprises four Dell PowerEdge servers, with 3.06 GHz Intel Xeon CPU and 4GB of RAM. All servers are connected through commodity Fast Ethernet NICs. In all carried out tests, we configure the VMs with 512MB of memory and utilize the TCPNewReno suite for implementing the needed VM-to-VM transport connections.

Test Workload Patterns

In order to stress the effects of the reconfiguration costs and time-fluctuations of the Big Data workload, as in (Zhou et al. 2013), we begin to model the workload size as an independent identically distributed (i.i.d.) random sequence $\{\overline{L}_{tot}(mT_t), m0,1,...,\}$, whose samples are T_t-spaced apart r.v.'s evenly distributed over the interval $[\overline{L}_{tot} - a , \overline{L}_{tot} + a]$, with $\overline{L}_{tot} = 8\,(Mbit)$. By setting the spread parameter a to $0\,(Mbit)$, $2\,(Mbit)$, $4\,(Mbit)$, $6\,(Mbit)$ and $8\,(Mbit)$, we obtain Peak-to-Mean Ratios (PMRs) of 1 (e.g., the offered workload is of constant size), 1.2, 1.5, 1.75 and 2.0, respectively. About the dynamic settings of $\{f_i^0\}$ in (10.1), at the first round of each batch of the carried out tests, all the frequencies f_i^0's are reset. Afterwards, at the m-th round, each f_i^0 is set to the corresponding optimal value f_i^* computed at the previous $(m-1)$-th round.

Since each round spans an overall slot-time T_t, all the reported test results properly *account* for the reconfiguration cost in (7). Furthermore, all the reported test results have been obtained by implementing the adaptive version in (25)-(28) of the optimal scheduler, with the duration of each n-indexed iterate set to $(T_t/30)$ secs. Finally, the performed tests subsume the power-rate function in (5) at $\alpha = 1.2$, together with the computing energy function in (2) with $c=2.0$ and $b=0.5$.

Impact of the VLAN Setup and Tracking Capability of the Scheduler

Goal of a first set of tests is to evaluate the effects on the per-job average energy $\overline{E}_{tot}^*$ consumed by the optimal scheduler induced by the size M of the VNetDC and the setting of the TCP-based VLAN. For this purpose, we pose:

$T_t=5\,(s)$, $R_t=100(Mb/s)$,

$PMR=1.25$, $k_e=0.05\,(J/(MHz)^2$,

$f_i^{\max} = 105\,(Mbit/s)$,

$E_i^{\max} = 60\,(Joule)$, $\Delta = 0.1\,(s)$,

$RTT_i = 700\,(\mu s)$, and

$L_b(i)=0$.

Afterwards, since the quality of the virtual links (e.g., end-to-end TCP connections) of Figure 1 is captured by the corresponding coefficients Ω_i (see (5)), we have evaluated the average consumed energy $\overline{E}_{tot}^*$ under the following settings:

1. $\Omega_i = 0.2$;
2. $\Omega_i = 0.5(W)$;
3. $\Omega_i = [0.5 + 0.25(i-1)](W)$; and,
4. $\Omega_i = [0.5 + 0.5(i-1)](W)$ $i = 1,...M$.

The obtained numerical plots are drawn in Figure 2. As it could be expected, larger Ω_i's penalized the overall energy performance of the emulated VNetDC. Interestingly, since $\overline{E}_{tot}^*$ is, by definition, the minimum energy when up to M VMs may be turned on, at fixed P_i^{net}'s, $\overline{E}_{tot}^*$ decreases for increasing M and, then, it approaches a minimum value, that does not vary when M is further increased (see the flat segments of the two uppermost plots of Figure 2).

Figure 2. Effects of the link quality on $\overline{E}^*_{tot}$ for the application scenario of Section 5.2 at PMR= 1.25

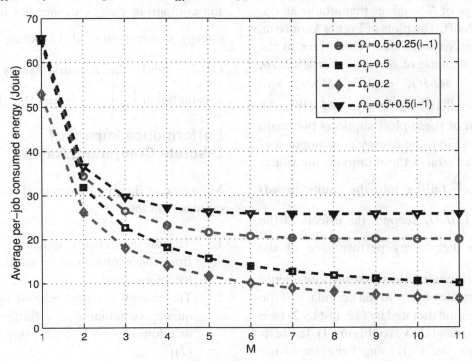

Finally, in order to appreciate the sensitivity to the parameters β, γ of the adaptive version in (27), (28) of the implemented scheduler, Figure 3 reports the measured time-behavior of $\mu^{(n)}$ in (25) when the workload offered by the supported Big Data stream application abruptly passes from L_{tot}=8 (Mbit/s) to L_{tot}=10 (Mbit/s) at n=30 and, then, it falls out to L_{tot}=6 (Mbit/s) at n=60. The application scenario already described at the beginning of this sub-section has been tested at M= 10 and $\Omega_i = 0.5$ (W). The solid piece-wise linear plot of Figure 3 marks the steady-state optimal values of μ. These optimal values have been obtained by directly solving the equation (23) through offline centralized numerical methods. Overall, an examination of the plots of Figure 3 supports two main conclusions. First, the implemented adaptive version of the scheduler quickly reacts to abrupt time-variations of the offered workload, and it is capable to converge to the corresponding steady-state optimum within about

10-15 iterations. Second, virtually indistinguishable trajectories for $\mu^{(n)}$ are obtained for γ ranging over the interval *[0.1, 0.6]*, so that in Figure 3 we report the time-evolutions of $\mu^{(n)}$ at $\beta = 0.004, 0.008, 0.01, 0.04$ and $\gamma = 0.4$.

As already noted in (Kushner et al. 1995), also in our framework, the *sensitivity* of the adaptive version of the optimal scheduler on β, γ is negligible, at least for values of β, γ in (27) ranging over the intervals [10^{-3}, 10^{-1}] and *[0.1, 0.6]*, respectively.

Computing vs. Communication Tradeoff

Intuitively, we expect that small Δ 's values give rise to high per-VM computing frequencies (see (10.2)), while too large Δ 's induce high end-to-end communication rates (see (10.6)). However, we also expect that, due to the adaptive power-rate control provided by the implemented scheduler (see (21.2), (22)), there exists a broad range of Δ's values that attains an optimized tradeoff. The plots of Figure 4 confirm, indeed, these expectations. They refer to the application scenario of section 5.2 at *M=2, 10,* $\overline{L}_{tot} = 4,12$ *(Mbit)*, *a=1,3 (Mbit)* and $\Omega_i = [0.5 + 0.25(i-1)]$ *i=1,..., M (W)*. An examination of these plots supports two main conclusions. First, the energy consumption of the scheduler attains the minimum for values of the ratio $\dfrac{\Delta}{T_t}$ falling into the (quite broad) interval *[0.1, 0.8]*. Second, the effects of the ratio $\dfrac{\Delta}{T_t}$ on the energy performance of the scheduler are negligible when the considered VNetDC operates far from the boundary of the feasibility region dictated by (18.1)-(18.2) (see the two lowermost curves of Figure 4). Interestingly enough, the increasing behavior of the

curves of Figure 4 gives practical evidence that the computing energy dominates the overall energy consumption at vanishing $\dfrac{\Delta}{T_t}$ (see (10.2)), while the network energy becomes substantial at $\left(\dfrac{\Delta}{T_t}\right) \rightarrow 1^-$ (see (10.6)).

Performance Impact of Discrete Computing Rates

Main goal of this set of numerical tests is to acquire insight into:

1. The average energy reduction stemming from the exploitation of multi-frequency techniques; and,

2. The energy penalty induced by the frequency-switching over a finite number Q of allowed per-VM processing rates (see (7)).

Figure 4. Impact on $\overline{E}_{tot}^*$ of the computing vs. communication delay tradeoff

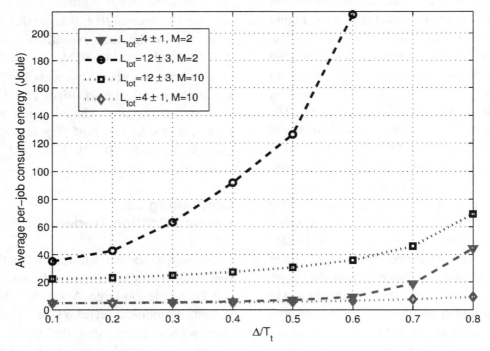

For this purpose, the same operating scenario of the above section 5.2 has been considered at

$$k_e = 5 \times 10^{-4} \; (Joule/(MHz)^2$$

and

$$\Omega_i = \left[0.5 + 0.25(i-1) \right](W) \quad i = 1, ..., M \; .$$

The energy curves obtained at:

1. $Q = +\infty$ (i.e., continuous computing rates);
2. $Q=6$ (i.e., discrete computing rates with six allowed computing frequencies evenly spaced over $\left[0, f_i^{max} \right]$); and,
3. $Q=2$ (i.e., each VM may operate at $f_i=0$ or $f_i = f_i^{max}$), are drawn in Figure 5.

Interestingly, we have ascertained that the not monotonic behavior of the uppermost curve of Figure 5 is the result of two effects that are dominating at $Q=2$. First, at $Q=2$, each active VM is forced to operate at f_i^{max}, so that the increment in the computing energy induced by the activation of an additional VM scales up as E_i^{max}. Second, at $Q=2$, the energy overhead in (8) required for switching from $f_i = 0$ to $f_i = f_i^{max}$ (or vice versa) is maximum.

As a consequence, the plots of Figure 5 support the following three main conclusions. First, at $Q=2$, the activation of only two VMs (if feasible) stems out as the most energy-saving solution. Second, the relative gap in Figure 5 between the uppermost curve (at $M=2$) and the lowermost one (at $M=9$) is very large. Third, the relative gap between the two lowermost curves of Figure 5 is limited up to *15%*.

Figure 5. Effects of continuous/discrete computing rates on the energy performance of the platform of Figure 1; the frequency-switching energy penalty in (7) is explicitly accounted for.

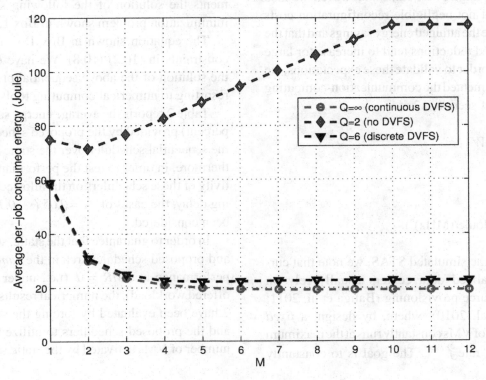

Box 1.

$$\min_{\{R_i(m),f_i(m),L_i(m)\}} \sum_{m=1}^{I} \sum_{i=1}^{M} \left\{ \Phi_i \left(\frac{f_i(m)}{f_i^{\max}} \right) E_i^{\max} + k_e (f_i(m) - f_i(m-1))^2 + 2 P_i^{net}(R_i(m)) \left(\frac{L_i(m)}{R_i(m)} \right) \right\} \quad (29)$$

Performance Comparisons under Synthetic Time-Uncorrelated Workload Traces

Testing the sensitivity of the performance of the implemented scheduler on the PMR of the offered workload is the goal of the tests of this sub-section. Specifically, they aim at unveiling the impact of the PMR of the offered workload on the average energy consumption of the proposed scheduler and comparing it against the corresponding ones of two state-of-the-art schedulers, namely, the STAtic Scheduler (STAS) and the SEquential Scheduler (SES). Intuitively, we expect that the energy savings attained by dynamic schedulers increase when reconfigurable VMs are used, especially at large PMR values. However, we also expect that not negligible reconfiguration costs may reduce the attained energy savings and that the experienced reductions tend to increase for large PMRs. In order to validate these expectations, we have implemented the communication-computing platform of section 5.2 at

$$\Omega_i = 0.9 \big(W \big),$$

and

$$k_e = 0.005 (\text{Joule}/(\text{MHz})^2).$$

About the simulated STAS, we note that current virtualized data centers usually rely on static resource provisioning (Baliga et al. 2011; Tamm et al. 2010), where, by design, a *fixed* number M_s of VMs constantly runs at the maximum processing rate $f^{\max}$. The goal is to constantly provide the exact computing capacity needed for satisfying the peak workload $L_{tot}^{\max} \triangleq \bar{L}_{tot} + a$ *(Mb)*. Although the resulting static scheduler *does not* experience reconfiguration costs, it induces overbooking of the computing resources. Hence, the per-job average communication-plus-computing energy consumption $\bar{E}_{tot}^{(STAS)}$ *(Joule)* of the STAS gives a benchmark for numerically evaluating the energy savings actually attained by dynamic schedulers.

About the simulated SES, it exploits (by design) perfect future workload information over a time-window of size $I \geq 2$ (measured in multiple of the slot period T_t), in order to perform off-line resource provisioning at the minimum reconfiguration cost. Formally speaking, the SES implements the solution of the following sequential minimization problem shown in Box 1.

The equation shown in Box 1` is under the constraints in (10.2)-(10.8). We have evaluated the solution of the above sequential problem by resorting to numerical computing tools.

Table 2 reports the average energy savings (in percent) provided by the proposed scheduler and the sequential scheduler over the static one. Furthermore, in order to test the performance sensitivity of these schedulers on the allowed computing delay, the cases of $\Delta = 0.05$ *(s)*, *0.1 (s)* have been considered.

In order to guarantee that the static, sequential and proposed schedulers retain the *same* energy performance at *PMR = 1* (i.e., under constant offered workload), the numerical results of Table 2 have been evaluated by forcing the sequential and the proposed schedulers to utilize the *same* number of VMs activated by the static scheduler.

Although this operating condition strongly penalizes the resulting performance of the sequential and proposed schedulers, nevertheless, an examination of the numerical results reported in Table 2 leads to four main conclusions.

First, the average energy savings of the proposed scheduler over the static one approaches 65%, even when the VMs are equipped with a limited number $Q=4$ of discrete processing rates and the reconfiguration energy overhead is accounted for. Second, the performance loss suffered by the proposed (adaptive) scheduler with respect to the sequential one tends to increase for growing PMRs, but it remains limited up to 3%-7%. Third, the performance sensitivity of the proposed and sequential schedulers on the allowed computing delay Δ is generally not critical, at least for values of Δ corresponding to the flat segments of the curves of Figure 4. Finally, we have experienced that, when the proposed scheduler is also free to optimize the number of utilized VMs, the resulting average energy saving over the static scheduler approaches 90%-95% (Cordeschi et al. 2014).

Performance Comparisons under Time-Correlated Real-World Workload Traces

These conclusions are confirmed by the numerical results of this subsection, that refer to the *real-world* (e.g., not synthetic) workload trace of Figure 6. This is the same real-world workload trace considered in Figure 14.a of (Urgaonkar, Pacifici, Shenoy, Spreitzer, & Tantawi, 2007). The numerical tests of this subsection refer to the communication-computing infrastructure of Section 5.5 at $k_e=0.5$ *(Joule/ (MHz)^2)* and $\Delta=1.2$ *(s)*. Furthermore, in order to maintain the peak workload still fixed at *16 (Mbit/slot)*, we assume that each arrival of Figure 6 carries out a workload of *0.533(Mbit)*.

Figure 6. Measured workload trace (Urgaonkar et al. 2007, Figure 14 a); the corresponding PMR and covariance coefficient ρ equate 1.526 and 0.966, respectively.

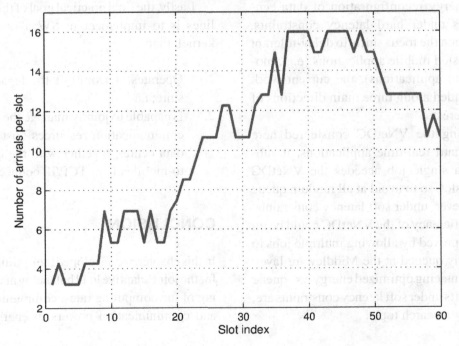

Since the (numerically evaluated) PMR of the workload trace of Figure 6 is limited up to 1.526, and the corresponding time-covariance coefficient ρ is large and approaches 0.966, the workload trace of Figure 6 is smoother (e.g., it exhibits less time-variations) than those previously considered in Section 5.5. Hence, we expect that the corresponding performance gaps of the proposed and sequential schedulers over the static one are somewhat less than those reported in Section 5.5 for the case of time-uncorrelated workload.

However, we have tested that, even under the (strongly) time-correlated workload trace of Figure 6, the average energy reduction of the proposed scheduler over the static one still approach 40%, while the corresponding average energy saving of the sequential scheduler over the proposed one remains limited up to 5.5%-5%.

ONGOING DEVELOPMENTS AND HINTS FOR FUTURE RESEARCH

The focus of this chapter is on the adaptive minimum-energy reconfiguration of data center resources under hard latency constraints. However, when the focus shifts to delay-tolerant Internet-assisted mobile applications (e.g., mobile Big Data applications), the current work may be extended along three main directions of potential interest.

First, being the VNetDC considered here tailored on hard real-time applications, it subsumes that a single job accedes the VNetDC during each slot, so to avoid at all random queue effects. However, under soft latency constraints, the energy efficiency of the VNetDC could be, in principle, improved by allowing multiple jobs to be temporarily queued at the Middleware layer. Hence, guaranteeing optimized energy-vs.-queue delay trade-offs under soft latency constraints are, indeed, a first research topic.

Second, due to the considered hard real-time constrains, in our framework, the size L_{tot} of the incoming job is measured at the beginning of the corresponding slot and, then, it remains constant over the slot duration T_t. As a consequence, the scheduling policy considered here is of clairvoyant-type, and this implies, in turn, that migrations of VMs are not to be considered. However, under soft delay constraints, intra-slot job arrivals may take place. Hence, the optimal resource provisioning policy could be no longer of clairvoyant-type, so that live migrations and VMs replacement could become effective means to further reduce the energy costs. The development of adaptive mechanisms for planning at runtime minimum-energy live migrations of VMs is a second research topic of potential interest.

Third, emerging mobile BDSC applications require that the information processed by data centers is timely delivered to the requiring clients through TCP/IP mobile connections (Cugola et al. 2012). In this application scenario, the energy-efficient adaptive management of the delay-vs.-throughput trade-off of TCP/IP mobile connections becomes an additional topic for further research.

Lastly, the final practical goal of these research lines is to implement in SW a revised VMM kernel, that:

1. Operates at Dom0 of the legacy Xen 3.3 suite; and,
2. Is capable to jointly manage the computing/communication resources hosted onto the data center, together with the data center-to-mobile client TCP/IP connections.

CONCLUSION

In this chapter, we developed the optimal scheduler for the joint adaptive load balancing and provisioning of the computing rates, communication rates and communication powers in energy-efficient virtualized NetDCs which support real-time Big Data streaming services. Although the resulting optimization problem is inherently nonconvex, we unveil and exploit its loosely coupled structure for attaining the analytical characterization of the optimal solution. The carried out performance comparisons and sensitivity tests highlight that the average energy savings provided by our implemented scheduler over the state-of-the-art static one may be larger than 60%, even when the PMR of the offered workload is limited up to 2 and the number Q of different processing rates equipping each VM is limited up to 4-5. Interestingly, the corresponding average energy loss of our scheduler with respect to the corresponding sequential one is limited up to 4%-6%, especially when the offered workload exhibits not negligible time-correlation.

REFERENCES

Alizadeh, M., Greenberg, A., Maltz, D. A., & Padhye, J. (2010). Data center TCP (DCTCP). In *Proceedings of ACM SIGCOMM*. ACM.

Almeida, J., Almeida, V., Ardagna, D., Cunha, I., Francalanci, C., & Trubian, M. (2010). Joint admission control and resource allocation in virtualized servers. *Journal of Parallel and Distributed Computing*, 70(4), 344–362. doi:10.1016/j.jpdc.2009.08.009

Azodomolky, S., Wieder, P., & Yahyapour, R. (2013). Cloud computing networking: Challanges and Opportunities for Innovations. *IEEE Comm. Magazine*, 54-62.

Baccarelli, E., & Biagi, M. (2003). Optimized power allocation and signal shaping for interference-limited multi-antenna 'ad hoc' networks. *Personal Wireless Communications*, 138-152.

Baccarelli, E., Biagi, M., Pelizzoni, C., & Cordeschi, N. (2007). Optimized power allocation for multiantenna systems impaired by multiple access interference and imperfect channel estimation. *IEEE Transactions on Vehicular Technology*, 56(5), 3089–3105. doi:10.1109/TVT.2007.900514

Baccarelli, E., Cordeschi, N., & Patriarca, T. (2012). QoS stochastic traffic engineering for the wireless support of real-time streaming applications. *Computer Networks*, 56(1), 287–302. doi:10.1016/j.comnet.2011.09.010

Baliga, J., Ayre, R. W. A., Hinton, K., & Tucker, R. S. (2011). Green Cloud Computing: Balancing Energy in Processing, Storage and Transport. *Proceedings of the IEEE*, 99(1), 149–167. doi:10.1109/JPROC.2010.2060451

Ballami, H., Costa, P., Karagiannis, T., & Rowstron, A. (2011). Towards predicable datacenter networks. In *Proceedings of SIGCOMM '11*. ACM.

Balter, M. H. (2013). *Performance modeling and design of computer systems*. Cambridge Press.

Bazaraa, M. S., Sherali, H. D., & Shetty, C. M. (2006). *Nonlinear programming* (3rd ed.). Wiley. doi:10.1002/0471787779

Chen, J. J., & Kuo, T. W. (2005). Multiprocessor energy-efficient Scheduling for real-time tasks with different power characteristics. *ICCP*, 05, 13–20.

Chiang, M., Low, S. H., Calderbank, A. R., & Doyle, J. C. (2007). Layering as optimization decomposition: A mathematical theory of network architectures. *Proceedings of the IEEE*, 95(1), 255–312. doi:10.1109/JPROC.2006.887322

Cordeschi, N., Amendola, D., Shojafar, M., & Baccarelli, E. (2014). Performance evaluation of primary-secondary reliable resource-management in vehicular networks. In *Proceedings of IEEE PIMRC 2014*. Washington, DC: IEEE.

Cordeschi, N., Patriarca, T., & Baccarelli, E. (2012). Stochastic traffic engineering for real-time applications over wireless networks. *Journal of Network and Computer Applications, 35*(2), 681–694. doi:10.1016/j.jnca.2011.11.001

Cordeschi, N., Shojafar, M., & Baccarelli, E. (2013). Energy-saving self-configuring networked data centers. *Computer Networks, 57*(17), 3479–3491. doi:10.1016/j.comnet.2013.08.002

Cugola, G., & Margara, A. (2012). Processing flows of information: From data stream to complex event processing. *ACM Computing Surveys, 44*(3), 1–62. doi:10.1145/2187671.2187677

Das, T., & Sivalingam, K. M. (2013). TCP improvements for data center networks. *Communication Systems and Networks (COMSNETS)*, 1-10.

Gandhi, A., Balter, M. H., & Adam, I. (2010). Server farms with setup costs. *Performance Evaluation, 11*(67), 1123–1138. doi:10.1016/j.peva.2010.07.004

Ge, R., Feng, X., Feng, W., & Cameron, K. W. (2007). CPU miser: A performance-directed, run-time system for power-aware clusters. In Proceedings of IEEE ICPP07. IEEE.

Govindan, S., Choi, J., Urgaonkar, B., Sasubramanian, A., & Baldini, A., (2009). Statistical profiling-based techniques for effective power provisioning in data centers. In *Proc of EuroSys*. Academic Press.

Greenberg, A., Hamilton, J., Maltz, D. A., & Patel, P. (2009). The cost of a cloud: Research problems in data center networks. *ACM SIGCOMM, 39*(1), 68–73. doi:10.1145/1496091.1496103

Greenberg, A., Hamilton, J. R., Jain, N., Kandula, S., Kim, C., Lahiri, P., & Sengupta, S. et al. (2011). VL2: A scalable and flexible data center Network. *Communications of the ACM, 54*(3), 95–104. doi:10.1145/1897852.1897877

Gulati, A., Merchant, A., & Varman, P.J. (2010). mClock: Handling throughput variability for hypervisor IO scheduling. In *Proceedings of OSDI'10*. Academic Press.

Guo, C. (2010). SecondNet: A data center network virtualization architecture with bandwidth guarantees. In Proceedings of ACM CoNEXT. ACM; doi:10.1145/1921168.1921188

Jin, S., Guo, L., Matta, I., & Bestavros, A. (2003). A spectrum of TCP-friendly window-based congestion control algorithms. *IEEE/ACM Transactions on Networking, 11*(3), 341–355. doi:10.1109/TNET.2003.813046

Kansal, A., Zhao, F., Liu, J., Kothari, N., & Bhattacharya, A. (2010). Virtual machine power metering and provisioning. *SoCC, 10*, 39–50.

Kim, K. H., Beloglazov, A., & Buyya, R. (2009). Power-aware provisioning of cloud resources for real-time services. In *Proc. of ACM MGC'09*. ACM.

Kim, K. H., Buyya, R., & Kim, J. (2007). Power aware scheduling of bag-of-tasks applications with deadline constraints on DVS-enabled clusters. In *Proceedings of IEEE International Symposium of CCGRID* (pp. 541-548). IEEE. doi:10.1109/CCGRID.2007.85

Koller, R., Verma, A., & Neogi, A. (2010). WattApp: An application aware power meter for shared data centers. In Proceedings of ICAC'10. IEEE; doi:10.1145/1809049.1809055

Kumbhare, A. (2014). *PLAstiCC: Predictive look-ahead scheduling for continuous data flaws on clouds*. IEEE.

Kurose, J. F., & Ross, K. W. (2013). *Computer networking - A top-down approach featuring the internet* (6th ed.). Addison Wesley.

Kushner, H. J., & Yang, J. (1995). Analysis of adaptive step-size SA algorithms for parameter tracking. *IEEE Transactions on Automatic Control, 40*(8), 1403–1410. doi:10.1109/9.402231

Kusic, D., & Kandasamy, N. (2009). Power and performance management of virtualized computing environments via look-ahead control. In *Proc. of ICAC*. Academic Press.

Laszewski, G., Wang, L., Young, A. J., & He, X. (2009). Power-aware scheduling of virtual machines in DVFS-enabled clusters. In *Proceeding of CLUSTER'09*. IEEE. doi:10.1109/CLUS-TR.2009.5289182

Li, K. (2008). Performance analysis of power-aware task scheduling algorithms on multiprocessor computers with dynamic voltage and speed. *IEEE Tr. On Par. Distr. Systems, 19*(11), 1484–1497. doi:10.1109/TPDS.2008.122

Lin, M., Wierman, A., Andrew, L., & Thereska, E. (2011). Dynamic right-sizing for power-proportional data centers. In *Proceedings of INFOCOM*. IEEE.

Liu, J., Zhao, F., Liu, X., & He, W. (2009). Challenges towards elastic power management in internet data centers. In *Proc. on IEEE Conf. Distr. Comput. Syst. Workshops*. Los Alamitos, CA: IEEE. doi:10.1109/ICDCSW.2009.44

Liu, Q., Zhou, S., & Giannakis, G. B. (2004). Cross-layer combining of adaptive modulation and coding with truncated ARQ over wireless links. *IEEE Transactions on Wireless Communications, 3*(5), 1746–1755. doi:10.1109/TWC.2004.833474

Loesing, S., Hentschel, M., Kraska, T., & Kossmann, D. (2012). Storm: An elastic and highly available streaming service in the cloud. *EDBT-ICDT, 12*, 55–60. doi:10.1145/2320765.2320789

Lu, T., Chen, M., & Andrew, L. L. H. (2012). Simple and effective dynamic provisioning for power-proportional data centers. *IEEE Transactions on Parallel and Distributed Systems, 24*(6), 1161–1171. doi:10.1109/TPDS.2012.241

Mathew, V., Sitaraman, R., & Rowstrom, A. (2012). Energy-aware load balancing in content delivery networks. In Proceedings of INFOCOM (pp. 954-962). IEEE.

Mishra, A., Jain, R., & Durresi, A. (2012). Cloud computing: Networking and communication challenges. *IEEE Comm. Magazine*, 24-25.

Neely, M.J., Modiano, E., & Rohs, C.E. (2003). Power allocation and routing in multi beam satellites with time-varying channels. *IEEE/ACM Tr. on Networking, 19*(1), 138-152.

Neumeyer, L., Robbins, B., & Kesari, A. (2010). S4: Distributed stream computing platform. In *Proceedings of Intl. Workshop on Knowledge Discovery Using Cloud and Distributed Computing Platforms*. IEEE.

Padala, P., You, K.Y., Shin, K.G., Zhu, X., Uysal, M., Wang, Z., … Merchant, M. (2009). Automatic control of multiple virtualized resources. In *Proc. of EuroSys*. Academic Press.

Portnoy, M. (2012). *Virtualization essentials*. Wiley.

Qian, Z., He, Y., Su, C., Wu, Z., Zhu, H., Zhang, T. (2013). TimeStream: Reliable stream computation in the cloud. In *Proceedings of EuroSys* (pp. 1-14). Academic Press.

Scheneider, S., Hirzel, M., & Gedik, B. (2013). Tutorial: Stream processing optimizations. In *Proceedings of ACM DEBS* (pp. 249-258). ACM.

Srikant, R. (2004). *The mathematics of internet congestion control*. Birkhauser. doi:10.1007/978-0-8176-8216-3

Stoess, J., Lang, C., & Bellosa, F. (2007). Energy management for hypervisor-based virtual machines. *USENIX Annual Technical*, 1-14.

Tamm, O., Hersmeyer, C., & Rush, A. M. (2010). Eco-sustainable system and network architectures for future transport networks. *Bell Labs.Techn. J.*, *14*(4), 311–327. doi:10.1002/bltj.20418

Urgaonkar, B., Pacifici, G., Shenoy, P., Spreitzer, M., & Tantawi, A. (2007). Analytic modeling of multitier Internet applications. *ACM Tr. on the Web*, *1*(1).

Vasudevan, V., Phanishayee, A., & Shah, H. (2009). Safe and effective fine-grained TCP stream retransmissions for datacenter communication. In Proceedings of ACM SIGCOMM (pp. 303-314). ACM.

Wang, L., Zhang, F., Aroca, J.A., Vasilakos, A.V., Zheng, K., Hou, C., …, Liu, Z. (2014). Green DCN: A general framework for achieving energy efficiency in data denter networks. *IEEE JSAC, 32*(1).

Warneke, D., & Kao, O. (2011). Exploiting dynamic resource allocation for efficient parallel data processing in the cloud. *IEEE Tr. on Paral. and Distr. Systems*, *22*(6), 985–997.

Xia, L., Cui, Z., & Lange, J. (2012). *VNET/P: Bridging the cloud and high performance computing through fast overaly networking*. IEEE. doi:10.1145/2287076.2287116

Zaharia, M., Das, T., Li, H., Shenker, S., & Stoica, I. (2012). *Discretized streams: an efficient and fault-tolerant model for stream processing on large clusters*. Hotcloud.

Zhou, Z., Liu, F., Jin, H., Li, B., & Jiang, H. (2013). On arbitrating the power-performance tradeoff in SaaS clouds. In *Proceedings of INFOCOM* (pp. 872–880). IEEE.

Zhu, D., Melhem, R., & Childers, B. R. (2003). Scheduling with dynamic voltage/rate adjustment using slack reclamation in multiprocessor real-time systems. *IEEE Transactions on Parallel and Distributed Systems*, *14*(7), 686–700. doi:10.1109/TPDS.2003.1214320

KEY TERMS AND DEFINITIONS

Cloud Brokers: They accept risk associated with reserving dynamically priced resources in return for charging higher but stable prices.

Data Center: A data center is a facility used to house computer systems and associated components, such as telecommunications and storage systems.

Dynamic Voltage and Frequency Scaling (DVFS): DVFS is applied in most of the modern computing units, such as cluster computing and supercomputing, to reduce power consumption and achieve high reliability and availability.

Load Balancing: Algorithms seek to distribute workloads across a number of servers in such a manner that the average time taken to complete execution of those workloads is minimized.

Network Virtualization: Network virtualization is categorized as either external virtualization, combining many networks or parts of networks into a virtual unit, or internal virtualization, providing network-like functionality to software containers on a single network server.

Reconfiguration Cost: Reconfiguration cost measured at the Middleware layer of VNetDc and refer to the cost of changing the frequency of each VM while it loaded for new workload compare to its frequency for the previous workload.

Stream Computing: A high-performance computer system that analyzes multiple data streams from many sources live. The word stream in stream computing is used to mean pulling in streams of data; processing the data and streaming it back out as a single flow.

Virtual Machine Manager (VMM): Virtual Machine Manager allows users to create, edit, start and stop VMs, view and control of each VM's console and see performance and utilization statistics for each VM.

ENDNOTES

[1] Since L_{tot} is expressed in *(bit)*, we express f_c^{max} *(bit/s)*. However, all the presented developments and formal properties still hold verbatim when L_{tot} is measured in *Jobs* and, then, f_c is measured in *(Jobs/cycle)*. Depending on the considered application scenario, a Job may be a bit, frame, datagram, segment, or an overall file.

[2] Formally speaking, the primal-dual algorithm is an iterative procedure for solving convex optimization problems, which applies quasi-Newton methods for updating the primal-dual variables simultaneously and moving towards the saddle-point [23, pp.407-408]

[3] Proposition 4 proves that, for any assigned $\mu^{(n)}$, the relationship in (26.3) gives the corresponding optimal $L_i^{(n)}, i = 1, ..., M$. This implies, in turn, that $U^{(n-1)}(.)$ in (B.1) vanishes if and *only* if the global optimum is attained, that is, at $L_i^{(n-1)} = L_i^*$, for any $i = 1, ..., M$.

[4] About this point, the formal assumption of section 2 guarantees that: 1. $\pi^{-1}(.)$ in (26.2) is continuous and strictly increasing in $v_i^{(n)}$ over the feasible set $\left[f_i^{min}, f_i^{max} \right]$; 2. $\left(\partial P_i^{net} \dfrac{\left(R_i \right)}{\partial R_i} \right)^{-1} (.)$ in (26.3) is continuous and strictly increasing in $\Delta(s)$; and, 3. $v_i^{(n)}$ in (26.1) is continuous for $\mu^{(n)} \geq 0$ and strictly increasing in η for $\dfrac{f_c}{f_c^{max}} \in [0,1]$. Hence, the condition: $E_c = E_c(f_c)$ guarantees that: Δ, for any $i = 1, ..., M$.

APPENDIX A: DERIVATIONS OF EQUATIONS (21.1)-(23)

Being the constraint in (10.7) already accounted for by the feasibility condition in (18.2), without loss of optimality, we may directly focus on the resolution of optimization problem in (16) under the constraints in (10.2)-(10.5). Since this problem is strictly convex and all its constraints are linear, the Slater's qualification conditions hold (Bazaraa et al. 2006, Chap.5, 23), so that the KKT conditions (Bazaraa et al. 2006, Chap.5) are both necessary and sufficient for analytically characterizing the corresponding unique optimal global solution. Before applying these conditions, we observe that each power-rate function in (17) is increasing for $L_i \geq 0$, so that, without loss of optimality, we may replace the equality constraint in (10.3) by the following equivalent one: $\sum_{i=1}^{M} L_i \geq L_{tot}$. In doing so, the Lagrangian function of the afforded problem reads as in

$$
\ell(\{L_i, f_i, \nu_i, \mu\})
= Z(\{L_i, f_i\}) \sum_{i=1}^{M} \nu_i \left(L_i - f_i \Delta + L_b(i) \right) + \mu \left(L_t - \sum_{i=1}^{M} L_i \right),
\tag{A.1}
$$

where $Z(L_i, f_i)$ indicates the objective function in (16.1), ν_i's and μ are nonnegative Lagrange multipliers and the box constraints in (10.4), (10.5) are managed as implicit ones. The partial derivatives of $\ell(.;.)$ with respect to f_i, L_i are given by

$$
\frac{\partial \ell(.)}{\partial f_i} = \frac{E_i^{\max}}{f_i^{\max}} \frac{\partial \Phi_i \left(\frac{f_i}{f_i^{\max}} \right)}{\partial \eta_i} + 2k_e(f_i - f_i^0) - \nu_i \Delta,
\tag{A.2}
$$

$$
\frac{\partial \ell(.)}{\partial L_i} = 2 \frac{\partial P_i^{net}}{\partial R_i} \left(\frac{2L_i}{T_t - \Delta} \right) + \nu_i - \mu, i = 1, ..., M,
\tag{A.3}
$$

while the complementary conditions (Bazaraa et al. 2006, Chap.4) associated to the constraints present in (A.1) read as in

$$
\nu_i \left(L_i - f_i \Delta + L_b(i) \right) = 0, i = 1, ..., M; \mu \left(L_t - \sum_{i=1}^{M} L_i \right) = 0.
\tag{A.4}
$$

Hence, by equating (A.2) to zero, we directly arrive at (21.1), that also account for the box constraint: $f_i^{\min} \leq f_i \leq f_i^{\max}$ through the corresponding projector operator. Moreover, a direct exploitation of the last complementary condition in (A.4) allows us to compute the optimal μ^* by solving the algebraic equation in (23). In order to obtain the analytical expressions for L_i^* and ν_i^*, we proceed to consider the two cases of $\nu_i^* > 0$ and $\nu_i^* = 0$. Specifically, when ν_i^* is positive, the i-th constraint in (10.2) is bound (see (A.4)), so that we have:

$$L_i^* = f_i^* \Delta - L_b(i), at\ \nu_i > 0\ .$$

(A.5)

Hence, after equating (A.3) to zero, we obtain the following expression for the corresponding optimal ν_i^*:

$$\nu_i^* = \mu^* - 2\left[\frac{\partial P_i^{net}}{\partial R_i}\left(\frac{2L_i^*}{T_t - \Delta}\right)\right], at\ \nu_i^* > 0,$$

(A.6)

Since L_i^* must fall into the closed interval $[0, \Delta f_i^* - L_b(i)]$ for feasible CPOPs (see (10.2), (10.5)), at $\nu_i^* = 0$, we must have: $L_i^* = 0$ or $0 < L_i^* < \Delta f_i^* - L_b(i)$. Specifically, we observe that, by definition, vanishing L_i^* is optimal when $\left[\frac{\partial \ell}{\partial L_i}\right]_{L_i=0} \geq 0$. Therefore, by imposing that the derivative in (A.3) is non-negative at $L_i^* = \nu_i^* = 0$, we obtain the following condition for the resulting optimal μ_i^*:

$$\mu_i^* \leq 2\left[\partial P_i^{net}\frac{(R_i)}{\partial R_i}\right]_{R_i=0}$$

$$\equiv TH(i), at\ \nu_i^* = L_i^* = 0, \quad i = 1, ..., M,$$

(A.7)

Passing to consider the case of $\nu_i^* = 0$ and $L_i^* \in]0, \Delta f_i^* - L_b(i)[$, we observe that the corresponding KKT condition is unique; it is necessary and sufficient for the optimality and requires that (A.3) vanishes (Bazaraa et al. 2006, Chap.4). Hence, the application of this condition leads to the following expression for the optimal L_i^* (see (A.3)):

$$L_i^* = \frac{(T_t - \Delta)}{2}\left[\frac{\partial P_i^{net}}{\partial R_i}\right]^{-1}(\mu^* / 2), at\ \nu_i^*$$

$$= 0\ and\ 0 < L_i^* < (\Delta f_i^* - L_b(i))$$

(A.8)

Equation (A.8) vanishes at $\mu^* \leq TH(i)$ (see (A.7)), and this proves that the function: $L_i^*(\mu^*)$ vanishes and is continuous at $\mu^* \leq TH(i)$. Therefore, since (A.7) already assures that vanishing L_i^* is optimal at $\nu_i^* = 0$ and $\mu^* \leq TH(i)$, we conclude that the expression in (A.8) for the optimal L_i^* must hold when $\nu_i^* = 0$ and $\mu^* \leq TH(i)$. This structural property of the optimal scheduler allows us to merge (A.7), (A.8) into the following equivalent expression:

$$L_i^* = \frac{(T_i - \Delta)}{2}\left[\left[\frac{\partial P_i^{net}}{\partial R_i}\right]^{-1}(\mu^*/2)\right]_+ \quad for \ v_i^* = 0,$$

(A.9)

so that Equation (21.2) directly arises from (A.5), (A.9). Finally, after observing that v_i^* cannot be negative by definition, from (A.6) we obtain (22), where the projector operator accounts for the non-negative value of v_i^*. This completes the proof of Proposition 4.

APPENDIX B: PROOF OF PROPOSITION 5

The reported proof exploits arguments based on the Lyapunov Theory which are similar, indeed, to those already used, for example, in sections 3.4, 8.2 in (Srikant, 2004). Specifically, after noting that the feasibility and strict convexity of the CPOP in (16) guarantees the existence and uniqueness of the equilibrium point of the iterates in (25) and (26), we note that Proposition 4 assures that, for any assigned $\mu^{(n)}$ and $\{L_i^{(n-1)}\}$, Equations (26.1)-(26.3) give the corresponding (unique) optimal values of the primal and dual variables $\{f_i^{(n)}, v_i^{(n)}, L_i^{(n)}\}$. Hence, it suffices to prove the global asymptotic convergence of the iteration in (25).

To this end, after posing

$$U^{(n-1)}\left(\{L_i^{(n-1)}\}\right) \equiv U^{(n-1)} \triangleq \left[\sum_{i=1}^{M} L_i^{(n-1)} - L_{tot}\right]^2$$

(B.1)

we observe that $U^{(n-1)} > 0$ for $\{L_i^{(n-1)}\} \neq \{L_i^*\}$ and $U^{(n-1)} = 0$ at the optimum, i.e., for $\{L_i^{(n-1)}\} = \{L_i^*\}$ [3]. Hence, since $U^{(n-1)}(.)$ in (B.1) is also radially unbounded (that is, $U^{(n-1)}(.) \to \infty$ as $\left\|\sum_{i=1}^{M} L_i^{(n-1)} - L_{tot}\right\| \to \infty$), we conclude that (B.1) is an admissible Lyapunov's function for the iterate in (25). Hence, after posing

$$U^{(n)}\left(\{L_i^{(n)}\}\right) = U^{(n)} \triangleq \left[\sum_{i=1}^{M} L_i^{(n)} - L_{tot}\right]^2,$$

according to the Lyapunov's Theorem (Srikant, 2004, section 3.10), we must prove that the following (sufficient) condition for the asymptotic global stability of (25) is met:

$$U^{(n)} < U^{(n-1)}, for \ n \to \infty.$$

(B.2)

To this end, after assuming $U^{(n-1)} > 0$, let us consider, at first, the case of

$$\left(\sum_{i=1}^{M} L_i^{(n-1)} - L_{tot} \right) > 0 . \tag{B.3}$$

Hence, since $\alpha^{(n-1)}$ is positive, we have (see (25)): $\mu^{(n)} < \mu^{(n-1)}$, that, in turn, leads to (see (26.3)): $L_i^{(n)} < L_i^{(n-1)}$, for any $i=1,...,M$[4]. Therefore, in order to prove (B.2), it suffices to prove that the following inequality holds for large n:

$$\left(\sum_{i=1}^{M} L_i^{(n)} - L_{tot} \right) \geq 0 . \tag{B.4}$$

To this end, we observe that:

1. $\{\alpha(n-1)\}$ in (25) vanishes (by assumption) for $n \rightarrow \infty$; and,
2. $L_i^{(n)}$ is limited up to $\Delta f_i^{\max}$, for any $i=1,..., M$ (see the constraints in (10.2), (10.4)).

As a consequence, the difference: $(\mu^{(n)} - \mu^{(n-1)})$ may be done vanishing (i.e., as small as desired) as $n \rightarrow \infty$. Hence, after noting that the functions in (25), (26) are continuous by assumption (see the footnote 4), a direct application of the Sign Permanence Theorem guarantees that (B.4) holds when the difference in (B.3) is positive.

By duality, it is direct to prove that (B.2) is also met when the difference in (B.3) is negative. This completes the proof of Proposition 5. From an application point of view, we have numerically ascertained that, in our setting, the step-size sequence in (27) leads to the global convergence in the steady-state and allows fast tracking in the transient-state.

Section 3
Control and Monitoring

Chapter 5
Application-Level Monitoring and SLA Violation Detection for Multi-Tenant Cloud Services

Vincent C. Emeakaroha
University College Cork, Ireland

Ivona Brandic
Vienna University of Technology, Austria

Marco A. S. Netto
IBM Research, Brazil

César A. F. De Rose
PUCRS, Brazil

ABSTRACT

Keeping the quality of service defined by Service Level Agreements (SLAs) is a key factor to facilitate business operations of Cloud providers. SLA enforcement relies on resource and application monitoring— a topic that has been investigated by various Cloud-related projects. Application-level monitoring still represents an open research issue, especially for billing and accounting purposes. Such a monitoring is becoming fundamental, as Cloud services are multi-tenant, thus having users sharing the same resources. This chapter describes key challenges on application provisioning and SLA enforcement in Clouds, introduces a Cloud Application and SLA monitoring architecture, and proposes two methods for determining the frequency that applications needs to be monitored. The authors evaluate their architecture on a real Cloud testbed using applications that exhibit heterogeneous behaviors. The achieved results show that the architecture is low intrusive, able to monitor resources and applications, detect SLA violations, and automatically suggest effective measurement intervals for various workloads.

INTRODUCTION

Cloud computing facilitates on-demand and scalable resource provisioning as services in a pay-as-you-go manner (Buyya, Yeo, Venugopal, Broberg, & Brandic, 2009) thereby making resources available at all times from every location. Like in other business engagements, resource and ser-

vice provisioning in Clouds are based on Service Level Agreements (SLAs), which are contracts signed between providers and their customers detailing the terms of the provisioning including non-functional requirements, such as Quality of Service (QoS) and penalties in case of violations (Comuzzi, Kotsokalis, Spanoudkis, & Yahyapour, 2009; Buyya et al., 2009).

DOI: 10.4018/978-1-4666-8213-9.ch005

Copyright © 2015, IGI Global. Copying or distributing in print or electronic forms without written permission of IGI Global is prohibited.

To establish Cloud computing as a reliable state of the art form of on-demand computing, Cloud vendors have to offer scalability, reliable resources, competitive prices, and minimize interactions with the customers in case of failures or environmental changes. However, ensuring SLAs for different Cloud actors at different layers (i.e., resource, platform, and application) is a challenging task, especially for the application layer. Monitoring at this layer is necessary as several applications may share the same VMs (e.g., to reduce energy consumption and cost) or one application may run on multiple Virtual Machines (VMs) (e.g., large scale distributed or parallel applications).

Although a large body of work considers the development of reliable Cloud management infrastructure (Koller & Schubert, 2007; Frutos & Kotsiopoulos, 2009; Boniface, Phillips, Sanchez-Macian, & Surridge, 2007), there is still a lack of efficient application monitoring infrastructures capable of monitoring and detecting SLA violations of different customer applications that share the same Cloud resources—mostly virtual machines. Since monitoring might be intrusive and drive down the overall performance of the system, determination of the optimal monitoring intervals is another important issue. The application level monitoring is particularly relevant when considering provisioning of multi-tenant Cloud resources and services.

This chapter describes the current challenges on application monitoring in Clouds, introduces the design and implementation details of a Cloud Application and SLA monitoring architecture, and proposes two methods for determining the frequency that applications need to be monitored. Furthermore, it analyzes the cost of missing SLA violation detections from the customer perspective as initially proposed in our previous work (Emeakaroha, Ferreto, Netto, Brandic, & Rose, 2012). The core component of the architecture is the application-level monitor, which is capable of monitoring application metrics at runtime to determine their resource consumption behaviors and performance. The main contributions of this chapter are:

1. Identification and discussion of challenges facing application provisioning and SLA enforcement especially in multi-tenant Cloud services,
2. Design choices and implementation details of the proposed architecture,
3. Empirical evaluation of two methods for optimal monitoring interval determination: one based on a utility model that considers provider's profit and SLA objectives and another based on the balance of provider's penalty costs for violating SLAs and customer's business impact for missing SLA violation detections; and
4. Evaluation of the impact of multi-tenancy on both the architecture monitoring intrusiveness and provider's net utility.

The rest of the chapter is organized as follows: Section 2 presents views on application provisioning and SLA enforcement in Clouds. It also discusses the current challenges and research efforts. In Section 3, we describe the proposed architecture and give details of its design and implementation. Section 4 presents evaluations of the architecture functions using three ray-tracing applications representing customers' services with different SLAs. We also present intrusion analysis using different monitoring frequencies. Section 5 presents further evaluations to determine the effective measurement interval to detect SLA violations in order to increase provider's profit, and also to make a comparison between the provider's and customer's costs. Finally, in Section 6, we present the conclusions.

BACKGROUND

Cloud computing facilitates efficient service provisioning mechanisms at different layers. The three well-known delivery models for service provisioning in Clouds are Infrastructure-as-a-service (IaaS), Platform-as-a-Service (PaaS), and Software-as-a-Service (SaaS) as shown in Figure 1.

Figure 1. Cloud delivery models

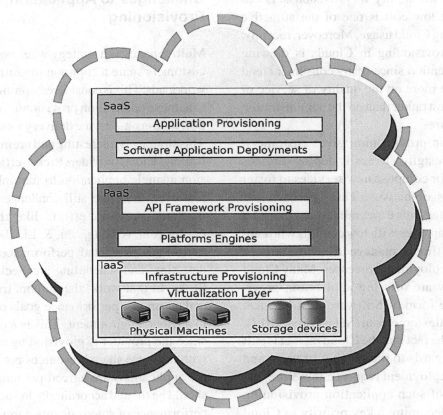

The models provide different granularities for provisioning services in Clouds. There exist some other delivery models in Cloud but they are specialized forms of these basic ones. For a quick overview, we describe these models as follows:

- The IaaS delivery model provides the consumer full access to use fundamental computing resources such as CPU, storage, memory, network devices. The consumer has the ability to control the operating system, hardware, networking infrastructure, and the deployed applications. In the industry, this is the type of service Amazon is providing to its customers.
- In PaaS model, a hosting environment, consisting of software APIs and frameworks, is made available to the consumers for host-

ing their applications. They are granted the capability of controlling the applications in the host environment. However, the consumer has a limited control of the operating system, hardware, and network devices of the hosting environment. An example is the Google AppEngine service platform.
- In the SaaS delivery model, a consumer uses only a Cloud application as a service but does not control the operating system, hardware, and network devices of the environment provisioning the application. This removes the issues associated with infrastructure maintenances and platform configurations from the consumers. This is one of the core strength of this model and it is gradually attracting users. Our research work in this chapter is focused on this model.

Generally, the ability to provision services on-demand at low cost is one of the attractive features driving Cloud usage. Moreover, recently, application provisioning in Clouds is drawing increasing attention since many consumers tend to concentrate more on the quality of service of their application rather than on the administration of infrastructures.

Application provisioning gives customers/enterprises the agility to easily deploy services on the Cloud or compose new services to foster their business objectives. This approach has proven advantageous especially to startups and small size companies with low capitals who cannot afford the time to manage infrastructures or application deployment processes. Many Cloud vendors today are offering application provisioning in the form of Software-as-a-Service, for example salesforce.com (SalesForce, 2014). Considering the fact that the Cloud market is still growing as regards to the number of users and application deployment requests, therefore, the management of such application provisioning scenarios is becoming a key priority to Cloud providers.

Service Level Agreement (SLA) establishment and enforcement are core issues in the management of Cloud application provisioning since it requires distinct per customer supervision of the agreed SLAs. The means and strategies to address these issues at this layer differs from resource provisioning at the infrastructural layer, where there are currently offers of stringent SLAs by Cloud providers such as Amazon. Most of the existing commercial Cloud providers offering application provisioning services do not offer stringent SLA enforcement. Even some do not offer SLAs at all. This is a serious problem hindering the adoption progress and the establishment of Cloud technology. As a result, there is a need for further research in this area. The next section further highlights the challenges of application monitoring.

Challenges to Application Provisioning

Multi-tenancy is a strategy where several clients/customers share a common platform to run their workloads. This is considered a promising strategy to achieve application provisioning in the form of Software-as-a-Service delivery model in Clouds. This strategy is interesting and promising because it allows Cloud providers to cost-efficiently provision a single application to multiple customers. However, there are still challenges in realizing it. Some previous efforts like the one from Cheng et al. (Cheng, Shi, & Li, 2009) discuss a multi-tenant oriented performance monitoring, detecting, and scheduling architecture based on SLAs. In that work, the authors tried to isolate and ensure the performance goals of each tenant in a Cloud environment. This is a complex task, since the provider is provisioning all the tenants with the same shared resources but the SLAs for the applications are agreed per tenant basis and should be treated accordingly. In such a setup, the performance of some customer applications may be affected by greedy resource consumption by others as they all share the same Cloud hardware. Cheng et al. (Cheng et al., 2009) proposed a solution to this issue by presenting a customized dynamic SLA management infrastructure able to monitor, discover abnormalities, and schedule resources to ensure tenants' SLA objectives. But the approach is not generic and cannot easily be ported into a new Cloud environment.

The above-described work depicts the serious issues facing application provisioning in Clouds. This is worsen especially by the propositions of proprietary solutions by Cloud providers, which do not allow interoperability among different Cloud platforms. Lack of interoperability causes vendor lock-in and do not encourage competitive market that helps to drive down the provisioning cost. Openness and standardized interfaces are required in solving this problem. However, most of the existing commercial Cloud vendors are reluctant in adopting standardized Cloud interfaces or platform-neutral data formats due to the associated cost or fear of loosing competitiveness against their competitors. We foresee the pressure from customers/application developers on the vendors to turn this trend in the future.

Another problem facing application provisioning is the performance of the application being provisioned. Factors, such as resource allocation, hardware/software failure, and different performance of identical virtual machines results in performance loss in Clouds. This problem has been known to Bonvin et al. (Bonvin, Papaioannou, & Aberer, 2011), who presents an autonomic SLA-driven provisioning for Cloud applications. Their work focused on cost-effective resource allocation to adaptively satisfy SLAs for performance and availability of shared resources in application provisioning. In an effort to realize this objective, a prototype was developed for placing and migrating applications according to their requirements as well as allocating resources to maintain the agreed SLA objectives. The aspect of scalability is missing in this work, which is relevant as Cloud resources keep increasing in size and geographical locations.

Scalable means of guaranteeing performance and enforcing agreed SLAs are essential for the success of Clouds at a whole not only regarding application provisioning. These factors play major roles in supporting the provisioning of mission critical applications in Clouds. SLA enforcement plays an important role in different management areas in Clouds such as runtime configuration management. In the next section, we discuss the current research efforts in this area.

Current Research Efforts

Cloud application provisioning is fast growing and attracting many customers in the commercial and business sectors. The vendors of these services are mostly public Cloud providers using proprietary tools to manage their services. This poses problems for enterprises and academic institutions in terms of monitoring and managing hybrid application deployments using their private and these public Cloud platforms.

In this section, we discuss the basic concepts of monitoring and then analyze the pervious research efforts on monitoring in Grids, Clouds and other related technologies. Furthermore, we analyze the previous efforts in developing SLA management strategies, which should guide service provisioning.

Monitoring Concept

The concept of monitoring to support management strategies is not new and dates back to previous technologies such as Clusters and Grids. Monitoring can be defined as the art of actively or passively supervising a device/software artifacts or service in order to make an informed decision (Fatema, Emeakaroha, Healy, Morrison, & Lynn, 2014). Figure 2 presents a basic general monitoring architecture.

As shown in Figure 2, monitoring mechanisms employ mostly agents for probing or supervising the monitored object. The monitored objects vary and in most cases, the monitoring could be configured based on the technology involved and the deployment environment. There is usually a back-end database for storing or persisting the monitored data for historical purposes. These data could be visualized as graphs for easy human consumption. Monitoring can be specialized for different technologies based on their requirements. In the next sections, we analyze the existing monitoring approaches.

Grid Monitoring Approaches

In this section, we present some previous research efforts on Grid monitoring.

Grid computing is considered as a predecessor technology to Cloud computing. Thus, the consideration of Grid monitoring concepts is relevant

Figure 2. Basic monitoring architecture

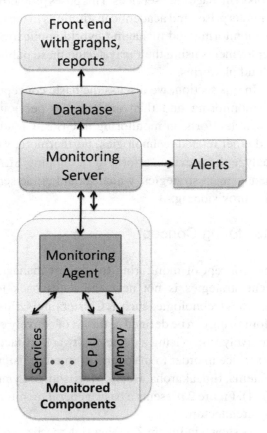

for this work since most of the Cloud monitoring tools is based on their mechanisms. The discussed literatures in this section are focused on Grid application monitoring.

Balis et al. (Balis, Bubak, Funika, Szepieniec, & Wismller, 2002) present an infrastructure for Grid application monitoring called OCM-G. The infrastructure is meant to facilitate the investigation and manipulation of parallel distributed applications executing on Grids. Its objective is to support the building of management tools for parallel applications in Grids. It uses run-time instrumentations to supervise and gather status information during application execution. The OCM-G is designed to be an on-the-fly tool, which delivers the monitored information to its consumers without storing it anywhere for later use or post-processing. As an autonomous monitoring

infrastructure, the OCM-G provides abstraction and increases modularity. In designing the architecture of this monitoring infrastructure, the authors first considered the requirements imposed on monitoring system in Grids such as reliability, scalability and efficiency. The OCM-G consists of three core components:

1. Service Manager (SM),
2. Local Monitor (LM), and
3. Application Monitor (AM).

The SM receives monitoring request from external tool and provide responses. It interacts directly with the LMs. The LMs reside on each node of the target system. It accepts requests from the service manager, executes them and passes back responses. The application monitor is embedded in each process of the monitored application. It executes performance request directly in the application context and passes data to the higher layers. This approach considers mainly Grid specific applications.

Another work from Balis et al. discuss the monitoring of Grid applications with Grid-Enabled On-line Monitoring Interface Specification (OMIS) monitor, which provides a standardized interface for accessing services. In OMIS, the target system is viewed as a set of objects hierarchically organized. The defined objects are node, processes, threads, messages, and message queues. They are identified by token symbols. The monitoring system exposes services through which its functionalities can be accessed. These services are grouped into three categories: information services to obtain information about objects; manipulation services to manipulate objects and event services to detect events and arrange actions to be executed on their occurrences. The OMIS interface facilitated the monitoring system to fit well into the Grid environment and support monitoring of interactive applications. The monitoring goal in this work is focused toward application development and the authors did not consider detecting application SLA violations, which enables the management of deployed applications.

In further Grid monitoring efforts, Balaton et al. (Balaton, Kacsuk, & Podhorszki, 2001) propose application monitoring in Grid with GRM and PROVE, which were originally developed as part of the P-GRADE graphical program development environment running on Clusters. In their work, they showed how they transformed GRM and PROVE into a standalone Grid monitoring tool. GRM is a semi-online monitor that gather information about applications executing in a distributed heterogeneous system and deliver them to the PROVE graphical visualization tool. The gathered information can either be event traced data or statistics of an application behavior. The monitoring in GRM is event-driven utilizing software tracing as measurement method that is achieved with direct source code instrumentation. The monitor is aimed to be portable among different UNIX operating systems by using only standardized UNIX programming solutions in the implementations. GRM is a distributed monitor consisting of three main components:

1. A client library to instrument request in the application execution;
2. A local monitor that handles trace events from processes on the same host and
3. A main monitor, which co-ordinates the local monitors and collects event traces from them on user request. PROVE can periodically request event traces from the main monitor for visualization. This approach, however, does not consider SLA enforcement and finding of effective measurement intervals to dynamically monitor the diverse application types being deployed as tenants.

A broader Grid monitoring solution is presented by Balaton et al. (Balaton & Gombs, 2003). In that work, they discuss resource and job monitoring in the Grid. The approach is based on the Grid Monitoring Architecture (GMA) proposed by the Global Grid Forum (GGF). The inputs of the monitoring system consist of measurement data generated by sensors. The sensors implement the measurement of a single or many measurable quantities that are represented in the monitoring system as metrics. A measurement corresponding to a metric is known as metric value, which contains a timestamp and the measured data. This monitoring system includes actuators that are analogue to sensors but instead of taking measurements of metrics; they implement controls, which can be used to interact with the monitored entity or the external environment. The use of metrics and controls makes the monitoring system very general and flexible. However, their motivations toward application monitoring are to understand its internal operations and detect failure situations. They do not consider the effects of monitoring intervals.

Cloud Monitoring Approaches

Moving forward from Grid monitoring mechanisms, this section presents some existing monitoring efforts in Clouds. We consider both the infrastructure level and software/application level monitoring approaches.

Towards Cloud management, Clayman et al. (2010) present Lattice framework for Cloud service monitoring in the RESERVOIR EU project. It is a tool capable of monitoring physical resources, virtual machines and customized applications embedded with probes. Compared to our approach in this chapter, the Lattice framework is not generic because its application monitoring capabilities are restricted to applications preconfigured with probes. This makes it proprietary and constraints its wider usage by application developers to monitor the execution of their applications in Clouds. In another effort, Ferrer et al. (Ferrer, 2011) present the fundamentals for a toolkit for service platform architecture management that enable flexible and dynamic provisioning of Cloud services within the

OPTIMIS EU project. The focus of the toolkit is aimed at optimizing the whole service lifecycle management including service construction, deployment, and operation. It does neither detail the application monitoring strategy nor consider the determination of effective measurement intervals to detect SLA violations. For monitoring at the Cloud infrastructure layer, Emeakaroha et al. (Emeakaroha, Calheiros, Netto, Brandic, & De Rose, 2010) propose DeSVi, an architecture for monitoring and detecting SLA violation of services deployed at the Cloud infrastructure layers. It consists of many components including a host monitor, a run-time monitor and a machine configurator. The DeSVi monitor targets monitoring virtual machines and physical host in a Cloud environment. Its architecture, however, does not consider the monitoring and detection of SLA violations at the Cloud application layers.

At the Cloud application layer, Rak et al. (Rak, Venticinque, M andhr, Echevarria, & Esnal, 2011) propose Cloud application monitoring using the mOSAIC approach. The mOSAIC project aims to offer a set of APIs to enable developers build up Cloud applications in a very flexible and portable manner. It provides a provisioning system, which enables developers to decouple Cloud applications from Cloud providers by providing abstractions that offer uniform access independent of the provider and the technologies it supports. In mOSAIC, the monitoring framework is a set of tools whose goal is to generate warning when the target application and its associated resources are not in the desired state. The approach is focused towards gathering information that can be used to perform manual or automatic load-balancing, increase/decrease the number of virtual machines or calculate the total cost of application execution. It does not consider the determination of effective monitoring intervals and moreover, it monitors only applications developed using the mOSAIC API.

The issue of generic solutions has been described as a top priority in the Cloud application levels. This is mostly attributed to the diverse nature of applications and lack of sufficient knowledge about their characteristics. Application profiling and proper documentation of their characteristics are required to address this issue. Furthermore, Shao et al. (Shao & Wang, 2011) present a performance guarantee for Cloud applications based on monitoring. The authors extract performance model from runtime monitored data using data mining techniques, which is then used to adjust the provisioning strategy to achieve a certain performance goals. The focus of this work was on the performance model. Thus, they do not consider finding effective measurement intervals.

SLA Management Approaches

This section describes the previous efforts on SLA management strategies. SLA provides a contract that aims to enforce the agreed quality of service between a consumer and a provider. There are different aspects of SLA managements including negotiation, establishment, enforcement and cancelation. This area is basically technology agnostic. This means that it is not only applicable in Clouds but also in Grids and other technologies as well. Monitoring mechanisms are important components of SLA management since they provide the insight for supervising QoS status during service deployments.

In this area, Boniface et al. (Boniface et al., 2007) discuss dynamic service provisioning using GRIA SLAs. They describe service provisioning based on SLAs to avoid violations. In their approach, they try to model services and allocate resources in a manner to avoid violating the agreed SLAs. This mechanism lacks the ability to supervise multiple applications executing on a single host, as it is the case with multi-tenancy deployments. Another effort by Koller et al. (Koller & Schubert, 2007) discuss autonomous QoS management using a proxy-like approach. Its implementation is based on WS-Agreement with which SLAs can be exploited to define certain QoS parameters that a service has to maintain during its interaction with specific customers. This approach however, is limited to Web services and could not be applied to other applications types. For SLA management in Grids, Frutos et al. (Frutos & Kotsiopoulos, 2009) present the main approach of the EU project BREIN (Brein, 2009) to develop a framework that extends the characteristics of computational Grids by driving their usage inside new target areas in the business domain for advanced SLA management. BREIN applies SLA management to Grids, whereas we target SLA management in Clouds.

Further research efforts are presented by Dobson et al. (Dobson & Sanchez-Macian, 2006). In their approach, they described a unified QoS ontology applicable to QoS-based Web services selection, QoS monitoring, and QoS adaptation. The main goal of the approach is to identify the strength and weakness of the existing ontologies. Comuzzi et al. (Comuzzi et al., 2009) in another effort define the process for SLA establishment adopted within the EU project SLA@SOI framework. The authors propose an architecture for monitoring SLAs considering two requirements introduced by SLA establishment: the availability of historical data for evaluating SLA offers and the assessment of the capability to monitor the terms in an SLA offer. But, they do not consider application monitoring to guarantee the agreed SLA parameter objectives. In a previous effort, Emeakaroha et al. (Emeakaroha, Ferreto, et al., 2012) introduced a Cloud Application SLA Violation Detection (CASViD) architecture for monitoring at the application layers and detecting SLA violations. In that work, they addressed application monitoring and the impact of SLA violation detection from only a provider perspective. The broad challenges facing application provisioning and the effects of missing SLA violations from the customer perspective were not analyzed. This chapter presents an extension of that work to address many open issues.

The analysis of these previous research efforts has shown that the issues of interoperability, scalability and generic solution to application monitoring in Clouds are still challenging. Therefore, further research efforts are required to address them. In the next section, we discuss our proposed framework, which is an example solution geared towards addressing these challenges.

ADDRESSING APPLICATION MONITORING CHALLENGES

This section describes our proposed architecture framework designed to demonstrate a means of addressing the identified application monitoring challenges. The architecture is capable of handling the whole service provisioning lifecycle in a Cloud environment, which includes resource allocation to services, service scheduling, application monitoring, and SLA violation detection.

Figure 3 presents the architecture and its internal operating mechanisms. Customers place their service requests through a defined interface (Service Interface) to the front-end node (step 1), which acts as the management node in the Cloud environment. The VM Configurator sets up the Cloud environment by deploying preconfigured VM images (step 2) on physical machines and making them accessible for service provisioning. The request is received by the Service Interface and delivered to the SLA Management Framework for validation (step 3), which is done to ensure that the request comes from the right customer. In the next step, the service request is passed to the Application Deployer (step 4), which allocates resources for the service execution and deploys it in the Cloud environment (step 5). After deploying the service applications, the Monitor Framework monitors them and sends the monitored information to the SLA Management Framework (step 6) for processing and detection of SLA violations.

Figure 3. System architecture

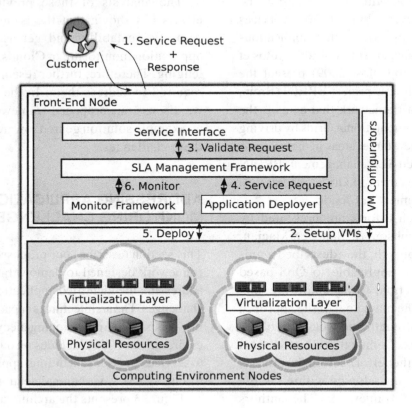

The proposed architecture is generic enough to support a wide range of applications, varying from traditional web services to parameter sweep and bag-of-task applications. The SLA management framework can handle the provisioning of all application types based on the pre-negotiated SLAs. Description of the negotiation process and components is out of scope of this chapter and is discussed by Brandic et al. (Brandic, 2009). The architecture components are discussed in the next sections.

SERVICE INTERFACE

The service interface is the first instance in our architecture. It is responsible for managing the acceptance of customer application provisioning requests, forwarding them for further processing, and handling notifications of success/failures

to the customers. The functions of the service interface resemble those of a service container in coordinating service provisioning (Chappell, 2004). However, it has detailed knowledge of the system and the agreed service level objectives for customer applications.

This component is made up internally of two parts: a service checker and a service forwarder. The service checker does the first-level validation by checking the format of the request and whether SLAs have been properly established for this particular request. It does that by querying the SLA database using the customer credentials and the particular application ID. In case of failure at this checking, the service request is rejected outright and a notification with the details of the failure is sent to the customer. Otherwise (i.e., in case of success) the service forwarder initiates communication with the SLA management framework and forwards the service request accordingly.

The service interface is implemented in Java language and uses the Java Management eXtensions (JMX) (JMX, 2014) to realize the input, output, and notification functions. The usage of JMX in the implementation makes it generic and easy to interact with popular application servers such J2EE for receiving and forwarding application requests.

VM CONFIGURATOR AND APPLICATION DEPLOYER

The VM Configurator and Application Deployer are components for allocating resources and deploying applications in our Cloud testbed. They are included in the architecture to show our complete solution. The Application Deployer is responsible for managing the execution of user applications, similar to brokers in the Grid literature (Elmroth & Tordsson, 2004; Abramson, Buyya, & Giddy, 2002; Krauter, Buyya, & Maheswaran, 2002; Netto & Buyya, 2009), focusing on parameter sweeping executions (Casanova, Obertelli, Berman, & Wolski, 2000). It simplifies the processes of transferring application input data to each VM, starting the execution, and collecting the results from the

VMs to the front-end node. A scheduler located in the Application Deployer performs the mapping of application tasks to VMs dynamically—each slave process consumes tasks whenever the VM is idle. The execution of the applications and the monitoring process can be done automatically by the Cloud provider, or can be incorporated into a Cloud Service that can be instantiated by the users.

Figure 4 illustrates the main modules of the Application Deployer. The task generator receives as input the service request and a generated machine file containing the list of VMs (step 1). The scheduler uses this machine file and a list of all tasks (step 2) in order to map tasks to VMs (step 3). The mapping is performed dynamically since each VM hosts a slave process, which consumes tasks whenever the VM is idle. A list of tasks for each VM is transferred from the task manager to the VMs (step 4). The task manager is also responsible for triggering the executions on VMs (step 5) and collecting the results at the end of tasks execution.

The application deployer is written in Python. It receives a machine file (in plain ASCII format) as one of its input. The file contains the list of hostnames or IPs of the VMs allocated for the execution of the user applications. It supports multiple

Figure 4. Application deployer

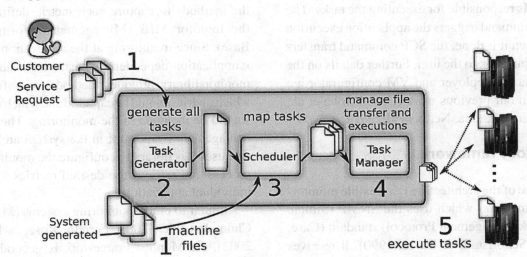

Figure 5. Monitor framework overview

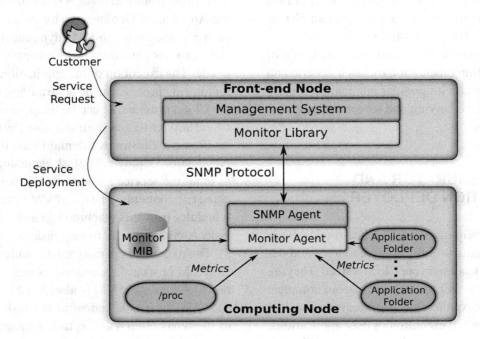

users sharing the same VMs. For instance, if a set of users requires little CPU capacity and privacy is not an issue, there is no reason why each one of these users should have exclusive VM access.

The application deployer defines a script to split the work to be done into a list of tasks that are mapped to the VMs. Once the mapping of tasks to VM is complete, it uses the Linux SCP command to transfer the application related files to the VMs responsible for executing the tasks. The SSH command triggers the application execution and when it is done, the SCP command transfers the output back to the user. Further details on the Application Deployer and VM configurator are found in our previous work (Emeakaroha et al., 2010; Emeakaroha, Netto, et al., 2012).

Monitor Framework

The core of the architecture is a flexible monitoring framework, which uses the SNMP (Simple Network Management Protocol) standard (Case, Fedor, Schoffstall, & Davin, 1990). It receives instructions to monitor applications from the SLA management framework and delivers the monitored information. It is based on the traditional manager/agent model used in network management. Figure 5 presents the monitor architecture. The manager, located in the front-end node, polls periodically each agent in the cluster to get the monitored information. The monitor is composed of a library and an agent. The agent implements the methods to capture each metric defined in the monitor MIB (Management Information Base). Since monitoring at the application layer is application-dependent, at the manager side, the monitor library provides methods to configure, which metrics should be captured and which nodes should be included in the monitoring. The SLA management framework in the system architecture uses this library to configure the monitoring process and retrieve the desired metrics for the individual applications.

Similar to other monitoring systems (Massie, Chun, & Culler, 2004; Ferreto, Rose, & Rose, 2002), the Monitor Framework is general purpose and supports the acquisition of common application metrics as a new added feature to the monitoring of system metrics such as CPU and memory utilization.

The monitor library is implemented in Java and uses the SNMP4J library, which provides access to all functionalities of the SNMP protocol for Java applications. The communication is performed using asynchronous requests to enhance the scalability. Each request to an agent creates a listener process, which is automatically called when the message arrives.

The monitor agent is implemented in Python and receives the SNMP request through the net-snmp daemon6 that is installed on each node. The net-snmp daemon forwards all requests for metrics defined in the monitor MIB to the monitor agent. The monitor agent periodically processes the requests, which are instructions to probe the application metrics and returns the obtained results to be packaged in an SNMP message and sent back to the manager by the net-snmp daemon.

System metrics are obtained through the standard /proc directory which enables the gathering of kernel information regarding the underlying system including current configuration and performance metrics.

We capture the application metrics by probing the processes, which execute the applications and by analyzing their generated log files.

We use SNMP in the Monitor Framework to realize a generic solution deployable in various platforms and operating systems. SNMP is well established, and even many hardware devices today are being managed based on SNMP protocol.

SLA Management Framework

The service provisioning management and detection of application SLA objective violations are performed by the SLA Management Framework component. This component is central and interacts with the Service Interface, Application Deployer, and Monitor Framework as shown in Figure 3. This component receives the monitored information from the monitor agents embedded in the computing nodes where the applications are executing in order to manage the SLA violations. It is designed to access the SLA database containing the originally agreed SLAs between the customer and the provider. From this database, it retrieves the SLA objectives, which are used together with the predefined thresholds to calculate future SLA violation threat or detect real violation situation.

To detect SLA violations, predefined threat thresholds, which are more restrictive than the violation thresholds are used. A violation threshold is a value indicating the least acceptable performance level for an application. For example, Response time $\leq$ 2ms. In this case, 2ms is the violation threshold and the threat threshold could be about 1.5ms, which allows the system to have 0.5ms of reaction time. In this work, the violation thresholds are derived from the SLA documents and the Cloud provider defines the threat thresholds manually by applying his experiences with the various workloads running in his environment.

When the threat threshold values are exceeded, they indicate an imminent occurrence of SLA violations. With this information the system can react quickly to avert the violation threat and save the Cloud provider from costly SLA violation penalties. In case the violation threat cannot be averted and the real violation threshold is exceeded, the system logs the necessary information for calculating the appropriate SLA violation penalties.

The whole of this component is implemented in Java language. To realize the SLA violation detection, the framework interacts with the monitor component through a defined interface implemented with Java Messaging Service (JMS) (JMS, 2014). Through this service, it receives a data structure holding the metric-value pairs monitored by the monitor agents. The JMS is used together with Apache ActiveMQ (ActiveMQ, 2014) to realize a scalable communication mechanism for the framework.

Table 1. Cloud environment composed of 36 virtual machines

Machine Type = Physical Machine				
OS	CPU	Cores	Memory	Storage
OVM Server	AMD Opteron 2GHz	2	8GB	250GB
Machine Type = Virtual Machine				
OS	CPU	Cores	Memory	Storage
Linux/Ubuntu	AMD Opteron 2GHz	1	2GB	50GB

In passing the messages between the components, they go through ESPER engine (ESPER, 2014), which filters out identical monitored values so that only changed values between measurements are delivered for the evaluations against the predefined thresholds. The filtering reduces the number of messages to be processed in order to increase the scalability of the framework. We use MySQL DB to store the processed messages. In this respect, we use HIBERNATE to map our Java classes into DB tables for easy storing and retrieving of information.

This framework is designed to be highly scalable. The JMS and ActiveMQ are used because they are platform independent and due to the scalability of the underlying ActiveMQ queues. Furthermore, the application of ESPER to filter out identical monitored information reduces drastically the number of messages to be processed. Especially in situations where the agents are monitoring in short intervals. In the next section, we present some evaluations of the proposed system architecture.

EVALUATION OF ARCHITECTURE FUNCIONALITIES

The primary goal of this evaluation is to provide a proof of concept considering the proposed architecture functionalities. We evaluate two aspects:

1. The ability of the architecture to monitor applications at runtime to detect SLA violations and
2. The capability of automatically determining the effective measurement interval for efficient monitoring.

The evaluation is carried out using real world application provisioning scenarios executed on a real Cloud testbed. The monitoring intrusion results of the Monitor Framework are also shown here. In Section 5, we discuss the finding of effective measurement interval and the provisioning costs for both Cloud providers and customers. The monitoring in our evaluation is done from the provider's perspective.

Testbed

The basic hardware and virtual machine components of our experimental Cloud testbed are shown in Table 1. We use Xen 3.4.0 virtualization technology on top of Oracle Virtual Machine (OVM). This testbed is located at the High Performance Computing Lab at Catholic University of Rio Grande do Sul, Brazil.

We have in total nine physical machines and, based on the resource capacities presented in Table 1, we host 4 VMs on each physical machine. The hypervisor uses over-provisioning strategy in allocating the virtual CPU cores to maximize the utilization of the physical CPU cores. The VM

Figure 6. Experimental testbed

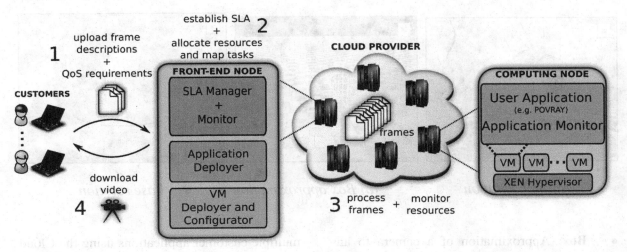

configurator deploys the VMs onto the physical hosts, thus creating a virtualized Cloud environment with up to 36 nodes capable of provisioning resources to applications.

Figure 6 depicts the experimental testbed. It shows the processes of provisioning a user application. The front-end node serves as the control entity. Application are uploaded through the front-end node and executed on the computing nodes. After the execution, the output is transferred back to the front-end node.

We deploy the components in two hierarchy levels:

1. In front-end node, and
2. In computing nodes.

This separation makes the system scalable because we run the management processes on the front-end nodes and the actual application provisioning on the computing nodes. The front-end and computing nodes are virtual machines and the computing nodes are the ones to be monitored. The monitor agents, running on the computing nodes, monitor the application metrics at execution, and send back the monitored information to a front-end node. The monitor agents are light

weighted and consume little computing capacity. With this setup, one can easily manage many computing nodes.

Workload

Our experimental workload comprises applications based on the Persistence of Vision Raytracer (POV-Ray) (Glassner et al., 1989), which is a ray tracing program available for several computing platforms. For the experiments, we designed three workload applications that can be executed sequentially or simultaneously on our Cloud testbed environment. With the three workloads, we cover different application behaviours thereby realizing heterogeneous load in the experiments. The workloads are based on three POV-Ray applications with different characteristics of time for rendering frames, as shown in Figure 7 and their behaviour illustrated in Figure 8. Each workload contains approximately 2000 tasks. Each task has an execution time that varies from 10 to 40 seconds.

- **Fish:** Rotation of a fish on water as shown in Figure 7a. Time for rendering frames is variable.

Figure 7. POV-Ray application animation images

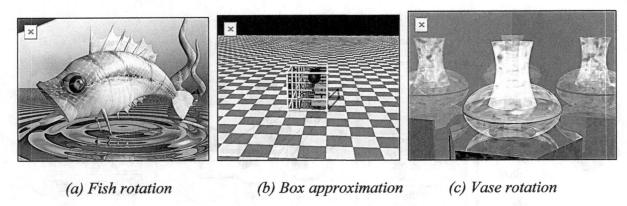

(a) Fish rotation *(b) Box approximation* *(c) Vase rotation*

- **Box:** Approximation of a camera to an open box with objects inside as shown in Figure 7b. Time for rendering frames increases during execution.
- **Vase:** Rotation of a vase with mirrors around as shown in Figure 7c. Time for processing different frames is constant.

Our architecture handles simultaneous customer provisioning. Therefore, the experiments contain three scenarios, where each scenario has a given number of customers. These scenarios represent real world provisioning situations where a provider is simultaneously provisioning one or

multiple customer applications using the Cloud infrastructure. Furthermore, it shows the ability of the architecture to independently monitor the application performance of each customer.

Each customer has a distinct SLA document for his/her workload application. The SLAs must be guaranteed for each application to avoid costly penalties. Table 2 presents the SLA objectives for the applications. These SLA objectives are defined based on historical data and experiences with these specific application types. The response time is expressed in seconds and the throughput in frames per second (f/s). Here, response time means the time between the submission time for

Table 2. SLA objective thresholds specification

Scenario 1			
SLA Parameter	**Customer 1**		
Response Time	265s		
Throughput	2.75 f/s		
Scenario 2			
SLA Parameter	**Customer 1**	**Customer 2**	
Response Time	430s	540s	
Throughput	3.99 f/s	1.35 f/s	
Scenario 3			
SLA Parameter	**Customer 1**	**Customer 2**	**Customer 3**
Response Time	795s	430s	1030s
Throughput	0.965 f/s	2.31 f/s	0.709 f/s

executing an application and its completion. The customer application stack to be provisioned on the Cloud environment is made up of

1. The SLA document specifying the quality of service for the application, and
2. The application files to be executed.

Monitored SLA Violation Detection Results

Five measurement intervals were defined and used to monitor the application workloads in this experiment. Table 3 shows the achieved results of the three scenarios for each measurement interval. The applications run for about 12 minutes in scenario 1, 22 minutes in scenario 2, and 30 minutes in scenario 3. The different execution length of the scenarios is necessary to investigate the application behaviors in each case.

Table 3 shows the number of SLA violations detected with each measurement interval for the two SLA parameters: Response Time and Throughput. These numbers at first sight seem logically obvious because the faster the measurements, the higher the number of detected violations. However, the main objective of presenting these results is to determine how profitable the measurement with each of these intervals would be for the provider. This is investigated with the analysis in Section 4.4. These two SLA

parameters are monitored in this evaluation because they define the desirable quality of service for the user applications. In case of different application types, the parameters to be monitored might differ.

In Table 3 the 5-second measurement interval is a reference interval currently used by the provider to monitor application executions. To explain the results for example in scenario 1, the customer application provisioning length was 12 minutes. With 10 seconds interval, we made 72 measurements within this provisioning period. From these measurements, 51 response time SLA violations and 16 throughput SLA violations were detected. The number of detected SLA violations decreases as the measurement interval increases. This is due to the missed SLA violation detection in between the measurement interval. This illustrates the risk involved with larger measurement intervals. We analyze these results in Section 5.2 to show the effective measurement interval.

Analysis of Monitoring Intrusion

One of the issues that are typically evaluated in a monitoring system is its intrusion, i.e., what is the overhead incurred in the system when the monitoring is used. The intrusion of a monitoring system is usually related to the sampling or measurement frequency used. Higher frequencies result in a higher intrusion.

Figure 8. Behaviour of execution time for each POV-Ray application

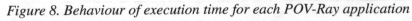

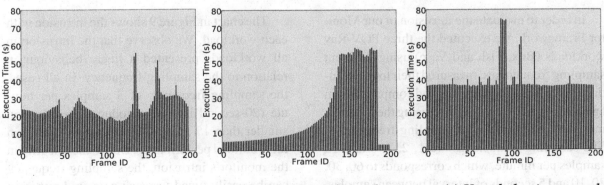

(a) Fish behaviour graph　　　*(b) Box behaviour graph*　　　*(c) Vase behaviour graph*

Table 3. Number of detected SLA violations

Scenario 1						
	Intervals	5s	10s	20s	30s	60s
	Nr. of Measurements	144	72	36	24	12
	Customer 1	**Nr. of Violations**				
SLA Parameters	Response Time	5s	10s	20s	30s	60s
	Throughput	54	16	4	3	1
Scenario 2						
	Intervals	5s	10s	20s	30s	60s
	Nr. of Measurements	264	132	66	44	22
	Customer 1	**Nr. of Violations**				
SLA Parameters	Response Time	5s	10s	20s	30s	60s
	Throughput	128	54	27	16	4
	Customer 2	**Nr. of Violations**				
SLA Parameters	Response Time	5s	10s	20s	30s	60s
	Throughput	90	49	14	8	2
Scenario 3						
	Intervals	5s	10s	20s	30s	60s
	Nr. of Measurements	360	180	90	60	30
	Customer 1	**Nr. of Violations**				
SLA Parameters	Response Time	5s	10s	20s	30s	60s
	Throughput	141	73	14	7	2
	Customer 2	**Nr. of Violations**				
SLA Parameters	Response Time	5s	10s	20s	30s	60s
	Throughput	137	92	42	26	12
	Customer 3	**Nr. of Violations**				
SLA Parameters	Response Time	5s	10s	20s	30s	60s
	Throughput	190	87	77	14	6

In order to evaluate the intrusion of our Monitor Framework, we executed the three POV-Ray workloads (Box, Fish and Vase) using different sampling frequencies, measured their total execution time without monitoring, and compared them against the total execution time using the monitoring system and the same sampling frequencies. The sampling frequencies are 1, 2, 3, 6 and 12 samples per minute, which corresponds to 60, 30, 20, 10 and 5 seconds of interval between samples.

The chart in Figure 9 shows the intrusion with each workload. We observe that the intrusion in all workloads presented a linear behaviour in relation to the sampling frequency. In all cases, the sampling frequency of 3 samples per minute (20-second interval) produced an intrusion smaller than 1%, resulting in a small impact in the workload performance. Due to the linearity in the monitor's intrusion, the sampling frequency can be easily tuned to reach a desired intrusion

Figure 9. Monitor framework's intrusion with different sampling frequencies

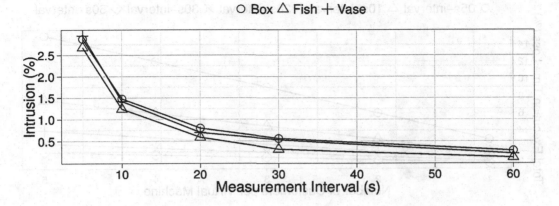

boundary. Naturally, if multiple customers share the same virtual machine, the overhead increases accordingly. For instance, Figure 10 shows that if five customers require a service to be hosted on the same virtual machine using a very short monitoring measurement interval (5-second interval), the total execution time loss becomes quite significant. Therefore, the monitoring strategy used by the provider needs to also takes this factor into account.

EVALUATIONS: VARIABLE MONITORING FREQUENCY BASED ON UTILITY MODEL

In this section, we propose a utility function to manually determine the best monitoring frequency that results in maximal provider's profit. In a further step, we present and discuss an algorithm to automatically address this issue thereby increasing the efficiency of our application monitoring architecture. We also evaluate the impact on the customer side, and analyze the drawbacks based on the ratio between the cost incurred on the provider and customer sides.

Utility Function Definition

The effective measurement interval is an economic factor. The goals of the provider are i) to achieve the maximal profit; and ii) to maintain the agreed SLA objectives for the applications while efficiently utilizing resources. The trade-off between these two factors determines the effective measurement interval. To derive such an interval, we define a utility function (U) for the provider, which is based on experiences gained from existing utility functions discussed by Lee et al. (K. Lee, Paton, Sakellariou, & Alvaro, 2009). The utility function considers on the one hand the provider profit and on the other hand the cost associated with the effort of detecting SLA violations and the penalty cost of the violations. Equation 1 presents the utility function.

$$U = \sum_{\beta \in \{customer\}} P_c(\beta) * P_t(\beta) - (\mu * M_c + \sum_{\psi \in \{RT, TP\}} \alpha(\psi) * V_p)$$

(1)

where P_c is the service provisioning cost, P_t is the duration of provisioning in minutes, μ is the number of measurements, M_c is the measurement

Figure 10. Intrusion overhead for multiple customers

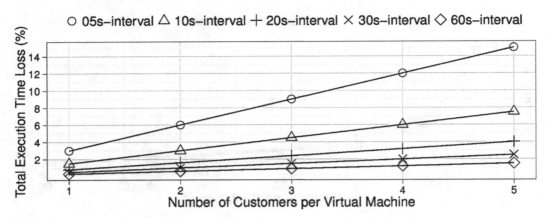

cost, α (ψ) is the number of detected SLA violations of the SLA objectives, RT is response time, TP is throughput, and V_p is the SLA violation penalty. Pc * Pt is equal to the provider profit. Defining the service provisioning cost is subject to negotiations between the customer and the service provider. In our experiments, we defined service provisioning costs based on experiences from existing approaches (Yeo & Buyya, 2007; C. B. Lee & Snavely, 2006). This utility function is not a configuration for the experimentations rather it is used to analyze the achieved results. The measurement cost is derived based on the intrusiveness/overhead effects of the monitoring framework on the system as described in Section 4.4. The values of the parameters are different for each customer/application type as described in the next section.

Analysis of Monitored Results using the Utility Function

In this section, we first manually analyze the achieved results to determine the effective measurement interval using the utility function defined in Section 5.1. Then, we demonstrate the method to automatically determine this interval using Figure 12 in Section 5.3. The experimental scenarios are analyzed separately.

The first scenario (as described in Table 2) deals with provisioning and monitoring of one customer application. In this case the customer pays a provisioning cost of $0.6 per minute (i.e., the service price) and the provisioning time length is 12 minutes. The SLA penalty cost is $0.04 and the measurement cost for the system is $0.02. Note that the cost values are experimental values. The idea is derived from existing approaches presented in literature (Yeo & Buyya, 2007; C. B. Lee & Snavely, 2006).

Figure 11 (a) presents the analyzed results of scenario 1. The 5-second interval is the reference measurement interval to capture all SLA violations for the applications in each case.

The analyzed results show the net utility (in dollar) of the provider with each measurement interval. The net utility translates into the profit of the provider in provisioning the customer application. The 10-second measurement interval has the highest net utility and is considered the effective one. The later intervals miss several SLA violations and thereby incur high penalty cost.

In Scenario 2, the provider provisions and monitors two customer applications using their specified SLA objectives as shown in Table 2. The first customer pays a provisioning cost of $0.5 per minute while the second customer pays $0.4 per minute. SLA penalty cost of $0.045 was

Figure 11. Analyzed results from monitoring over three scenarios

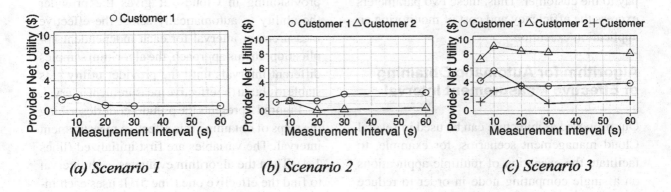

(a) Scenario 1   (b) Scenario 2   (c) Scenario 3

agreed for customer 1 and $0.038 for customer 2. The measurement cost is the same for both applications and is specified to be $0.037. Applying these values in the utility function of Equation 1 we achieve the results presented in Figure 11(b).

As depicted in Figure 11(b), for customer 1, the 60-second measurement interval has the highest net utility and in our opinion the effective measurement interval for the provider to adequately monitor the application of this customer. The other intervals provide lesser utility for the provider. For customer 2, the 10-second measurements interval proves to be the effective one with the highest net utility. In this case it can be seen that the reference measurement interval provides a negative utility meaning that the provider loses revenues

in his current situation. Therefore, finding another measurement interval is essential for the business continuity of the provider.

Scenario 3 consists of the provisioning and monitoring of three different customer applications based on their respective SLA objectives. Customer 1 pays a provisioning cost of $0.5 per minute and customer 2 pays $0.6 per minute while customer 3 pays $0.4 per minute. The agreed SLA penalty for customer 1 is $0.035, for customer 2 is $0.038, and for customer 3 is $0.025. The customer applications execute simultaneously on the testbed, thus there is only one measurement cost of $0.03. Figure 11(c) presents the analyzed results of this scenario. For customer 1 and 2, the 10-second measurement interval provides the highest net utility and therefore is the effective interval for the provider to cost-efficiently monitor the application of these customers at runtime. In the case of customer 3, the 20-second interval provides the highest net utility and is considered the effective measurement interval for the customer applications.

Generally, the effective measurement interval determined by the total net utility is a trade-off between the monitoring cost and the number of detected SLA violation at runtime (see Equation 1). The monitoring cost represents the efforts and overheads in monitoring the applications while the number of detected SLA violations determines

Figure 12. Pseudo-code for obtaining the effective measurement intervals

```
1  intervalList ← set list of possible intervals;
2  effectiveInterval ← intervalList[0];
3  maxTime ← MAXTIME;
4  netUtility ← 0;
5  for ∀interval ∈ intervalList do
6      tmpNetUtility ← monitorApp(maxTime);
7      if tmpNetUtility > netUtility then
8          netUtility ← tmpNetUtility;
9          effectiveInterval ← interval;
10  return effectiveInterval;
```

the amount of penalty cost the provider has to pay to the customer. Thus, these two parameters express the efficiency and cost of monitoring an application execution.

Algorithm for Automatic Obtaining of Effective Measurement Interval

Our proposed architecture can be used in several Cloud management scenarios, for example, to facilitate the execution of multiple applications on a single computing node in order to reduce cost and save energy in a Cloud environment. It can also assist management systems to migrate applications between computing nodes in order to shutdown some nodes to save energy. The applications could belong to different customers and provisioned based on their agreed SLA terms. The architecture measures the resource consumption and performance of each application to detect SLA violations. In order to achieve this, there is a need for finding an interval for effective measurements.

The effective measurement interval depends on the application and its input, and such interval has to be determined automatically. Therefore, to improve our manual approach discussed in the previous section, we present in this section an algorithm to automatically determine the effective measurement interval. This algorithm increases

the efficiency of managing multiple application provisioning in Clouds. It gives the provider the ability to automatically select the effective measurement interval for each independent application. In this approach, the algorithm samples different intervals until the provider utility gets stable to obtain the effective measurement interval.

Figure 12 presents the pseudo-code describing the steps of obtaining this effective measurement interval. The variables are first initialized (lines 1-4). Then the algorithm evaluates each interval to find the effective one (line 5). It uses each interval to monitor the application for a maximum specified time (line 6) after which it checks if the net utility gained with the current interval is higher than the highest net utility so far (line 7). If yes, this net utility gain becomes the highest net utility (line 8) and this interval is set to be the current effective interval (line 9). If no, the previous highest net utility is retained. The algorithm goes back to step 5 and checks the other interval using the same procedure. At the end, the interval with the highest net utility is returned as the effective measurement interval (line 10).

Based on our experiments, the proposed architecture proved to be efficient in monitoring and detecting application SLA violation situations. To demonstrate our automatic method of finding the effective measurement interval, we present in

Figure 13. Behaviour of provider net utility for the 10-sec measurement interval

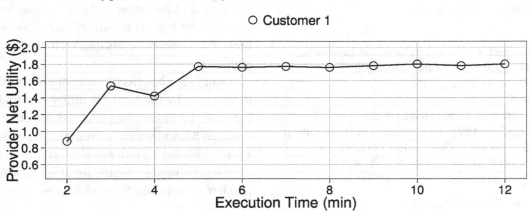

Figure 14. Pseudo-code for obtaining the effective measurement intervals considering provider and customer costs

```
 1  intervalList ← set list of possible intervals;
 2  effectiveInterval ← intervalList[0];
 3  maxTime ← MAXTIME;
 4  penaltyPerViolation ← setupPenaltyCost();
 5  costPerMissedDetection ← setupBusinessImpactCost();
 6  numViolations ← monitorApp(maxTime);
 7  for ∀interval ∈ intervalList do
 8      missedDetections, violations ← monitorApp(maxTime);
 9      providerCost ← violations * penaltyPerViolation;
10      customerCost ← missedDetections * costPerMissedDetection;
11      if customerCost > providerCost then
12          return effectiveInterval ← interval;
13  return effectiveInterval;
```

Figure 13 the behavior of the provider net utility for the 10-second measurement interval over the execution of the entire application of scenario 1. From the figure, it can be observed that after 5 minutes, the metric gets steady. As the net utility reaches this stability, it is possible to have a good prediction on this metric for this interval. Therefore, by doing so for other intervals, it is possible to automatically find the one that provides best cost-benefit value for measuring and detecting SLAs. The basic idea is that the provider would specify a range of possible intervals and the monitoring architect would detect the suitable measurement interval via figure 12.

Provider vs. Customer Costs

Until now, we have analyzed the impact of the measurement intervals considering the provider's side. As we can observe from the results presented so far, the shorter the measurement interval the higher the number of SLA violations and the amount of penalties to be paid by provider. This happens because the high rate of monitoring degrades the provider overall system performance that invariably affects the application performance. This behaviour motivates providers to use longer

measurement intervals. However, by doing so, the customer tends to have more violations that are not detected, thus impacting on his/her business. Figure 14 summarizes the pseudo-code for determining the measurement interval considering provider and customer costs.

Based on this figure, we analyze the measurement intervals considering the penalty costs for the provider to violate an SLA and the impact (cost) of missing an SLA violation detection for the customer. We analyzed three scenarios where:

1. The costs are the same for both provider and customer;
2. The cost for the customer is three times higher than the cost for the provider; and
3. The cost for the provider is three times higher than the cost for the customer.

The results of these scenarios are presented in Figures 15 (a), (b), and (c) respectively, and they are based on the number of violations for one customer.

We can observe that for all scenarios there is a point where the lines for both provider and customer costs cross. Such point represents the balance where the measurement interval brings

Figure 15. Provider's cost of violating SLAs and customer's cost of missing SLA violation detection

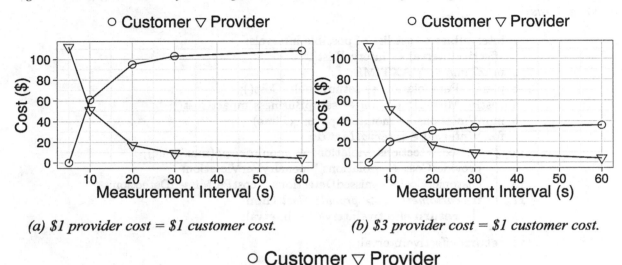

(a) $1 provider cost = $1 customer cost.

(b) $3 provider cost = $1 customer cost.

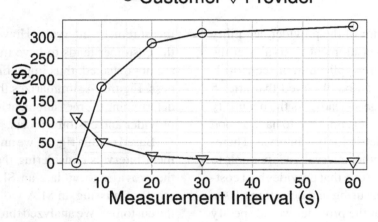

(c) $1 provider cost = $3 customer cost.

benefits for both provider and customer. The higher the cost for the customer in relation to the provider the shorter needs to be the measurement interval (Figure 15(b)). This happens because any violation detection miss has a great impact on the customer business. On the other hand, the lower the cost for the customer in relation to the provider the longer needs to be the measurement interval (Figure 15(c)), which improves his overall system performance. In this scenario, the provider pays a high price when monitoring at high rate.

FUTURE RESEARCH DIRECTIONS

Cloud service provisioning especially at the application levels is bound to increase in the coming years. Based on the insight drawn from our work presented in this chapter and from the current industrial trends, we envisage numerous future research efforts in the area of Cloud application provisioning and SLA management.

This is partly supported by the growing numbers of different application types in health science, medicine, ICT and other disciplines.

Cloud technology provides cheap, flexible and on-demand resources that are capable for deploying and executing these applications. In the light of this, many startup companies are relying on Cloud resources to setup and run their businesses. Such customers do not have enough capital to buy and maintain their own infrastructures. This is one of the key factors driving the interest in Cloud service provisioning and the need for future researches in this area.

Given the fact that the business relationship between a Cloud provider and a customer is being guided by an established service level agreement document. The negotiations, establishment, enforcement of agreed terms and the management of this document are other areas that are going to experience lots of research efforts in the near future. The research objectives will include: the automation of SLA negotiation processes, definition of new metrics for evaluating the quality of service for the new emerging applications, interoperable means of managing Cloud provider offers and their associated SLAs, automating SLA penalty calculations and compensation procedures, etc.

Currently, there are many Cloud vendors like IBM, Amazon, Microsoft and Google that are provisioning services using their proprietary platforms. However, this causes vendor-lockin and less flexibility for the customers. As the numbers of customers are increasing, we foresee for the future considerable research and industrial efforts in developing interoperable deployments and platform-independent APIs for accessing services.

With the increase in smart devices, electronic transactions and social platforms like Facebook, Twitter, etc, enormous amount of data are being generated, which requires appropriate analytic tools and applications to process. Cloud services provide adequate resources for such applications. Thus, in the future, more of such applications will be moving to the Cloud and there will be need for further monitoring techniques to supervise their executions.

CONCLUSION

This chapter presented the current challenges on application monitoring in Clouds. It introduced Cloud Application and SLA monitoring architecture, and proposed two methods for determining the frequency that applications need to be monitored. The two methods for determining the application measurement intervals consider provider's profit, SLA objectives, and the balance of provider's penalty costs for violating SLAs and customer's business impact for missing SLA violation detections. Furthermore, we analyzed the cost of missing SLA violation detection from the customer perspective. We evaluated our architecture on a real Cloud testbed using three types of image rendering application workloads with heterogeneous behaviors necessary to investigate different application provisioning scenarios and to determine the effective measurement intervals to monitor the provisioning processes. From our experiments, the proposed architecture proved to be efficient in monitoring and detecting application SLA violations.

Based on our defined contributions, we draw the following lessons:

- One of the most serious issues facing application monitoring is the lack of generic solutions that are portable to different platforms and application types. Most of the existing approaches are application and platform dependent, which severely restricts usability;
- An efficient design and implementation of application monitoring and SLA enforcement could be realized by appropriate utilization of already existing tools and technology with some extensions;
- Regarding the methods to determine the monitoring intervals, a key lesson is that it is relevant to consider the costs from the perspective of both the provider and customers. This is because of the tradeoff between monitoring overhead and penalty for missing SLAs;

- The implementation of an efficient monitoring tool for multi-tenant Cloud services requires special attention on its intrusiveness. This is because of the performance effects of monitoring multiple tenants considering the heterogeneous monitoring frequencies that generate different levels of intrusiveness.

The investigations presented in this chapter on application monitoring strategies and SLA violation detection are important for Cloud providers considering the provisioning of multi-tenant services. The marketing of such services have become more pervasive due to the increased number of companies moving their workloads to the Cloud to exploit the advantages of cheap modern servers with high numbers of computing cores.

ACKNOWLEDGMENT

This work is supported by the Vienna Science and Technology Fund (WWTF) under the grant agreement ICT08-018 Foundations of Self-governing ICT Infrastructures (FoSII) and by the Irish Centre for Cloud Computing and Commerce (IC4), an Irish National Technology Centre funded by Enterprise Ireland and the Irish Industrial Development Authority. The experiments were performed in the High Performance Computing Lab at Catholic University of Rio Grande do Sul (LAD-PUCRS) Brazil.

REFERENCES

Abramson, D., Buyya, R., & Giddy, J. (2002). A computational economy for grid computing and its implementation in the Nimrod-G resource broker. *Future Generation Computer Systems*, *18*(8), 1061–1074. doi:10.1016/S0167-739X(02)00085-7

Active, M. Q. (2014). *Messaging and integration pattern provider*. Retrieved from http://activemq.apache.org/

Balaton, Z., & Gombs, G. (2003). Resource and job monitoring in the grid. In *Proceedings of Europar'03* (Vol. 2790, pp. 404–411). Springer Berlin Heidelberg. doi:10.1007/978-3-540-45209-6_59

Balaton, Z., Kacsuk, P., & Podhorszki, N. (2001). Application monitoring in the grid with GRM and prove. In *Proc. of ICCS* (*Vol. 2073*, pp. 253-262). Springer Berlin Heidelberg. doi:10.1007/3-540-45545-0_34

Balis, B., Bubak, M., Funika, W., Szepieniec, T., & Wismller, R. (2002). An infrastructure for grid application monitoring. In Recent advances in parallel virtual machine and message passing interface (pp. 41 - 49). Academic Press.

Balis, B., Bubak, M., Funika, W., Szepieniec, T., Wismller, R., & Radecki, M. (2004). Monitoring grid applications with grid-enabled omis monitor. In *Grid computing* (Vol. 2970, pp. 230–239). Springer Berlin Heidelberg. doi:10.1007/978-3-540-24689-3_29

Boniface, M., Phillips, S. C., Sanchez-Macian, A., & Surridge, M. (2007). Dynamic service provisioning using GRIA SLAs. In Proc. of icsoc'07. Academic Press.

Bonvin, N., Papaioannou, T. G., & Aberer, K. (2011). Autonomic SLA-driven provisioning for cloud applications. In *Proceedings of the 2011 11th IEEE/ACM International Symposium on Cluster, Cloud and Grid Computing* (pp. 434–443). IEEE.

Brandic, I. (2009). Towards self-manageable cloud services. In *Proceedings of the 33rd Annual IEEE International Computer Software and Applications Conference* (compsac'09). IEEE. doi:10.1109/COMPSAC.2009.126

Brein. (2009). *Business objective driven reliable and intelligent grids for real business*. Retrieved from http://www.eu-brein.com/

Buyya, R., Yeo, C. S., Venugopal, S., Broberg, J., & Brandic, I. (2009). Cloud computing and emerging IT platforms: Vision, hype, and reality for delivering computing as the 5th utility. *Future Generation Computer Systems*, 25(6), 599–616. doi:10.1016/j.future.2008.12.001

Casanova, H., Obertelli, G., Berman, F., & Wolski, R. (2000). The AppLeS parameter sweep template: User-level middleware for the Grid. In Proc. of the Supercomputing (SC'00). Academic Press.

Case, J. D., Fedor, M., Schoffstall, M. L., & Davin, J. (1990). *Simple network management protocol (SNMP)*. RFC Editor.

Chappell, D. A. (2004). *Enterprise service bus*. O'Reilly Media.

Cheng, X., Shi, Y., & Li, Q. (2009, December). A multi-tenant oriented performance monitoring, detecting and scheduling architecture based on SLA. In *Proceedings of 2009 Joint Conferences on Pervasive Computing (JCPC)* (pp. 599 - 604). Academic Press.

Clayman, S., Galis, A., Chapman, C. L. R M., Vaquero, L. M., Nagin, K., et al. (2010, April). Monitoring future internet service clouds. In Towards the future internet - A European research perspective book (pp. 115 - 126). Academic Press.

Comuzzi, M., Kotsokalis, C., Spanoudkis, G., & Yahyapour, R. (2009). Establishing and monitoring SLAs in complex service based systems. In *Proceedings of the 7th International Conference on Web Services* (icws'09). Academic Press. doi:10.1109/ICWS.2009.47

Dobson, G., & Sanchez-Macian, A. (2006). Towards unified QoS/SLA ontologies. In Proc. of SCW'06. Academic Press.

Elmroth, E., & Tordsson, J. (2004). A grid resource broker supporting advance reservations and benchmark-based resource selection. In *Proc. of the Workshop on State-of-the-Art in Scientific Computing (para'04)*. Academic Press. doi:10.1007/11558958_128

Emeakaroha, V. C., Calheiros, R. N., Netto, M. A. S., Brandic, I., & De Rose, C. A. F. (2010). DeSVi: An architecture for detecting SLA violations in cloud computing infrastructures. In *Proc. of the 2nd International ICST Conference on Cloud Computing* (cloudcomp'10). Academic Press.

Emeakaroha, V. C., Ferreto, T. C., Netto, M. A. S., Brandic, I., & Rose, C. A. D. (2012). CASViD: Application level monitoring for SLA violation detection in clouds. In *Proc. of the 36th Annual IEEE Computer and Application International Conference* (compsac12) (p. 499 - 508). Academic Press.

Emeakaroha, V. C., Netto, M. A. S., Calheiros, R. N., Brandic, I., Buyya, R., & De Rose, C. A. F. (2012). Towards autonomic detection of SLA violations in cloud infrastructures. *Future Generation Computer Systems*, 28(7), 1017–1029. doi:10.1016/j.future.2011.08.018

ESPER. (2014). Event stream processing. http: / / esper .codehaus .org/

Fatema, K., Emeakaroha, V. C., Healy, P. D., Morrison, J. P., & Lynn, T. (2014). A survey of cloud monitoring tools: Taxonomy, capabilities and objectives. *Journal of Parallel and Distributed Computing*, 74(10), 2918–2933. doi:10.1016/j.jpdc.2014.06.007

Ferrer, A. J. (2011). Optimis: a holistic approach to cloud service provisioning. http: / / www. optimis -project. eu/.

Ferreto, T. C., Rose, C. A. F. D., & Rose, L. D. (2002). Rvision: An open and high configurable tool for cluster monitoring. In CCgrid'02.

Frutos, H. M., & Kotsiopoulos, I. (2009). BREIN: Business objective driven reliable and intelligent grids for real business. *International Journal of Interoperability in Business Information Systems*, *3*(1), 39–42.

Glassner, A. S. (1989). *An introduction to ray tracing*. Academic Press London.

JMS. (2014). *Java messaging service*. Retrieved from http://java.sun.com/products/jms/

JMX. (2014). *Java management extenstions*. Retrieved from http://www.oracle.com/technetwork/java/javase/tech/javamanagement-140525.html

Koller, B., & Schubert, L. (2007). Towards autonomous SLA management using a proxy-like approach. *Multiagent Grid Systems*, *3*(3), 313–325.

Krauter, K., Buyya, R., & Maheswaran, M. (2002). A taxonomy and survey of grid resource management systems for distributed computing. *Software, Practice & Experience*, *32*(2), 135–164. doi:10.1002/spe.432

Lee, C. B., & Snavely, A. (2006). On the user-scheduler dialogue: Studies of user-provided runtime estimates and utility functions. *International Journal of High Performance Computing Applications*, *20*(4), 495–506. doi:10.1177/1094342006068414

Lee, K., Paton, N. W., Sakellariou, R., & Alvaro, A. A. F. (2009). Utility driven adaptive workflow execution. In *Proc. of the 9th International Symposium on Cluster Computing and the Grid* (CCgrid'09). Academic Press.

Massie, M. L., Chun, B. N., & Culler, D. E. (2004). The Ganglia distributed monitoring system: Design, implementation and experience. *Parallel Computing*, *30*(7), 817–840. doi:10.1016/j.parco.2004.04.001

Netto, M. A. S., & Buyya, R. (2009). Offer-based scheduling of deadline-constrained bag-of-tasks applications for utility computing systems. In *Proc. of the 18th International Heterogeneity in Computing Workshop (hcw'09), in Conj. with the 23rd IEEE International Parallel and Distributed Processing Symposium (IPDPS'09)*. IEEE. doi:10.1109/IPDPS.2009.5160910

Rak, M., Venticinque, S., Mandhr, T. A., Echevarria, G., & Esnal, G. (2011). Cloud application monitoring: The mosaic approach. In *Proceedings of Cloud Computing Technology and Science* (cloudcom) (pp. 758 - 763). IEEE.

SalesForce. (2014). *Service cloud*. Retrieved from http://www.salesforce.com/

Shao, J., & Wang, Q. (2011, July). A performance guarantee approach for cloud applications based on monitoring. In Proceedings of Computer Software and Applications Conference Workshops (compsacw) (pp. 25 - 30). IEEE. doi:10.1109/COMPSACW.2011.15

Yeo, C. S., & Buyya, R. (2007). Pricing for utility-driven resource management and allocation in clusters. *International Journal of High Performance Computing Applications*, *21*(4), 405–418. doi:10.1177/1094342007083776

ADDITIONAL READING

Andreozzi, S., De Bortoli, N., Fantinel, S., Ghiselli, A., Rubini, G. L., Tortone, G., & Vistoli, M. C. (2005). GridICE: A monitoring service for grid systems. *Future Generation Computer Systems*, *21*(4), 559–571. doi:10.1016/j.future.2004.10.005

Buyya, R., Garg, S. K., & Calheiros, R. N. (2011). Sla-oriented resource pro- visioning for cloud computing: Challenges, architecture, and solutions. In Cloud and service computing (CSC), 2011 international conference on (pp. 1–10).

Cheng, X., Shi, Y., & Li, Q. (2009, December). A multi-tenant oriented performance monitoring, detecting and scheduling architecture based on sla. In 2009 joint conferences on pervasive computing (jcpc) (p. 599 - 604).

Comuzzi, M., Kotsokalis, C., Spanoudakis, G., & Yahyapour, R. (2009). Establishing and monitoring SLAs in complex service based systems. In Web services, 2009. ICWS 2009. IEEE international conference on (pp. 783–790). doi:10.1109/ICWS.2009.47

De Chaves, S., Uriarte, R., & Westphall, C. (2011). Toward an architecture for monitoring private clouds. *Communications Magazine, IEEE, 49*(12), 130–137. doi:10.1109/MCOM.2011.6094017

Foster, I., Zhao, Y., Raicu, I., & Lu, S. (2008). Cloud computing and grid computing 360-degree compared. In Grid computing environments workshop, 2008. GCE'08 (pp. 1–10).

Gogouvitis, S. V., Alexandrou, V., Mavrogeorgi, N., Koutsoutos, S., Kyriazis, D., & Varvarigou, T. (2012). A monitoring mechanism for storage clouds. In Cloud and green computing (CGC), 2012 second international conference on (pp. 153–159). doi:10.1109/CGC.2012.26

Haiteng, Z., Zhiqing, S., Hong, Z., & Jie, Z. (2012). Establishing service level agreement requirement based on monitoring. In Cloud and green computing (CGC), 2012 second international conference on (p. 472-476). doi:10.1109/CGC.2012.75

Imamagic, E., & Dobrenic, D. (2007). Grid infrastructure monitoring system based on nagios. In *Proceedings of the 2007 workshop on grid monitoring* (pp. 23–28). New York, NY, USA: ACM. doi:10.1145/1272680.1272685

Iori, E., Simitsis, A., Palpanas, T., Wilkinson, K., & Harizopoulos, S. (2012). Cloudalloc: a monitoring and reservation system for compute clusters. In *Proceedings of the 2012 ACM sigmod international conference on management of data* (pp. 721–724). New York, NY, USA: ACM. doi:10.1145/2213836.2213942

Jones, W. M., Daly, J. T., & DeBardeleben, N. (2012). Application monitoring and checkpointing in HPC: looking towards exascale systems. In *Proceedings of the 50th annual southeast regional conference* (pp. 262–267). doi:10.1145/2184512.2184574

Krizanic, J., Grguric, A., Mosmondor, M., & Lazarevski, P. (2010). Load testing and performance monitoring tools in use with ajax based web applications. In Mipro, 2010 proceedings of the 33rd international convention (pp. 428– 434).

Kutare, M., Eisenhauer, G., Wang, C., Schwan, K., Talwar, V., & Wolf, M. (2010). Monalytics: online monitoring and analytics for managing large scale data centers. In *Proceedings of the 7th international conference on autonomic computing* (pp. 141–150). New York, NY, USA: ACM. doi:10.1145/1809049.1809073

Liu, F., Tong, J., Mao, J., Bohn, R., Messina, J., & Badger, L. et al.. (2011). Nist cloud computing reference architecture. *NIST Special Publication, 500*, 292.

Milojičíc, D., Llorente, I., & Montero, R. (2011). Opennebula: A cloud management tool. Internet Computing, IEEE, 15(2), 11–14.

Rellermeyer, J. S., Alonso, G., & Roscoe, T. (2007). Building, deploying, and monitoring distributed applications with eclipse and R-OSGI. In Proceedings of the 2007 oopsla workshop on eclipse technology exchange (pp. 50–54). Available from http://doi.acm.org/10.1145/1328279.1328290

Somasundaram, T., & Govindarajan, K. (2011, dec.). Cloud monitoring and discovery service (CMDS) for IaaS resources. In Advanced computing (ICOAC), 2011 third international conference on (p. 340-345).

Tovarnak, D., & Pitner, T. (2012). Towards multi-tenant and interoperable monitoring of virtual machines in cloud. In Symbolic and numeric algorithms for scientific computing (synasc), 2012 14th international symposium on (p. 436-442). doi:10.1109/SYNASC.2012.55

Tsai, C., Ruan, Y., Sahu, S., Shaikh, A., & Shin, K. (2007). Virtualization- based techniques for enabling multi-tenant management tools. *Managing Virtualization of Networks and Services*, 171–182.

Zanikolas, S., & Sakellariou, R. (2005). A taxonomy of grid monitoring systems. *Future Generation Computer Systems*, *21*(1), 163–188. doi:10.1016/j.future.2004.07.002

Zhou, W., Chen, C., & Li, S. (2011). Monitoring system for the campus card based on cacti and nagios. *Shiyan Jishu yu Guanli*, 28(4), 246–249.

KEY TERMS AND DEFINITIONS

Measurement Interval: The rate at which the performance of a system or service is being supervised.

Monitoring Intrusion: The amount of performance degradation caused by the monitoring activities on a system.

Monitoring: Gathering of data, such as CPU, memory, and network usage.

Multi-Tenancy: Multiple users/clients sharing the same resources.

Quality of Service: Establishes the measure of performance in a system to promote user satisfaction.

Service Level Agreement (SLA): Contract between service provider and users.

SLA Violation: Contract is broken for not meeting a specified criterion in the SLA.

Utility Function: The measure of profit in relation to operation conditions by a service provider.

Chapter 6
Self–Management of Operational Issues for Grid Computing:
The Case of the Virtual Imaging Platform

Rafael Ferreira da Silva
University of Southern California, USA

Tristan Glatard
University of Lyon, France & McGill University, Canada

Frédéric Desprez
University of Lyon, France

ABSTRACT

Science gateways, such as the Virtual Imaging Platform (VIP), enable transparent access to distributed computing and storage resources for scientific computations. However, their large scale and the number of middleware systems involved in these gateways lead to many errors and faults. This chapter addresses the autonomic management of workflow executions on science gateways in an online and non-clairvoyant environment, where the platform workload, task costs, and resource characteristics are unknown and not stationary. The chapter describes a general self-management process based on the MAPE-K loop (Monitoring, Analysis, Planning, Execution, and Knowledge) to cope with operational incidents of workflow executions. Then, this process is applied to handle late task executions, task granularities, and unfairness among workflow executions. Experimental results show how the approach achieves a fair quality of service by using control loops that constantly perform online monitoring, analysis, and execution of a set of curative actions.

DOI: 10.4018/978-1-4666-8213-9.ch006

Copyright © 2015, IGI Global. Copying or distributing in print or electronic forms without written permission of IGI Global is prohibited.

INTRODUCTION

Distributed computing infrastructures such as campus clusters, Grids, and now Clouds have become daily instruments of scientific research. As collections of independent computers linked by a network presented to the users as a single coherent system (e.g. Open Science Grid, XSEDE, EGI, and Amazon EC2), they enable easy collaboration among researchers, enhanced reliability and availability, and high-performance computing (Romanus et al., 2012). Increasingly, these systems are becoming more complex, heterogeneous, and prone to failures that can affect the productivity of their users.

In the meantime, science gateways, such as the Virtual Imaging Platform (VIP) (Ferreira da Silva et al., 2011; Glatard et al., 2013), are emerging as user-level platforms to facilitate the access to distributed computing and storage resources for scientific computations. Their high-level interface allows scientists to transparently run their analyses on large sets of computing resources. However, their large scale and the number of middleware systems involved in these gateways lead to many errors and faults. Applications running on these infrastructures are also growing in complexity and volume. Moreover, many scientists now formulate their computational problems as scientific workflows (Taylor, 2007). Workflows allow researchers to easily express multi-step computational tasks, for example: retrieve data from an instrument or a database, reformat the data, and run an analysis. Scientists expect such gateways to deliver high quality of service (QoS), where the workload and resources are efficiently and automatically handled, and the system is fault-tolerant. In order to provide fair QoS, scientific workflow executions are often backed by substantial human intervention that requires constantly monitoring of the running experiments and infrastructure to prevent or handle faults and ensure successful application completion.

Automating fault prevention, detection, and handling is challenging in such platforms. Science gateways have no *a-priori* model of the execution time of their applications because

1. Task costs depend on input data with no explicit model, and
2. Characteristics of the available resources depend on background load (Ferreira da Silva, Juve, et al., 2013).

Modeling application execution time in these conditions requires cumbersome experiments, which cannot be conducted for every new application in the platform. As a consequence, such platforms operate in non-clairvoyant conditions, where little is known about executions before they actually happen. Such platforms also run in online conditions, i.e. users may launch or cancel applications at any time and resources may leave at any time too.

In this chapter, we propose a general self-management process for autonomous detection and handling of operational incidents in scientific workflow executions on grids (Ferreira da Silva, Glatard, & Desprez, 2012, 2013b). Our process is described as a MAPE-K loop (Kephart & Chess, 2003), which consists of monitoring (M), analysis (A), planning (P), execution (E), and knowledge (K). Self-management techniques, generally implemented as MAPE-K loops, provide an interesting framework to cope with online non-clairvoyant problems. They address non-clairvoyance by using a-priori knowledge about the platform (e.g. extracted from traces), detailed monitoring, and analysis of its current behavior. They can also cope with online problems by periodical monitoring updates. Our ultimate goal is to reach a general model of such a scientific gateway that could autonomously detect and handle operational incidents, and control the behavior of non-clairvoyant, online platforms to limit human intervention required for their operation. Performance optimization is a target but the main point is to ensure that correctly-defined executions are completed, that performance is acceptable, and that misbehaving runs (e.g. failures coming from user errors or unrecoverable infrastructure downtimes) are quickly detected and handled before they consume too many resources.

BACKGROUND

In this section, we introduce definitions necessary to understand the rest of this chapter, and present the relevant work regarding strategies to address the operational incidents proposed in this chapter: task replication, task grouping, and fairness among workflow executions.

Scientific Gateways

Some Software-as-a-Service platforms, commonly called scientific gateways, integrate application software with access to computing and storage resources via web portals or desktop applications, where users can process their own data with predefined applications. Science-gateways are used in different scientific domains such as multi-disciplinary, climate, and medical imaging.

Scientific Workflows

Scientific workflows allow users to easily express multi-step computational tasks, for example retrieve data from an instrument or a database, reformat the data, and run an analysis. A scientific workflow describes the dependencies between the tasks. In most cases the workflow is described as a directed acyclic graph (DAG), where the nodes are tasks (or group of tasks) and the edges denote the task (or group of tasks) dependencies. Sometimes control structures (e.g. loops, ifs) are also used within workflows. Scientific workflows are described as high-level abstraction languages that conceal the complexity of execution infrastructures to the user. Workflow language

formalism is a formalism expressing the causal/temporal dependencies among a number of tasks to execute. Workflow interpretation and execution are handled by a workflow engine that manages the execution of the application on the distributed computing infrastructure. In addition, scientific workflows facilitate application management by assembling dependencies on deployment, and by enabling automatic interface generation in a scientific gateway.

Grid Computing

Computational grids emerged in the middle of the past decade as a paradigm for high-throughput computing for scientific research and engineering, through the federation of heterogeneous resources distributed geographically in different administrative domains (Foster, 2001). Resource sharing is governed by virtual organizations (VO), which are a set of individuals or institutions defined around a set of resource-sharing rules and conditions. Grid computing infrastructures are federations of cooperating resource infrastructure providers, working together to provide computing and storage services for research communities. These infrastructures can be characterized into research and production infrastructures. Research infrastructures are designed to support computer-science experiments related to parallel, large-scale or distributed computing, and networking. Production infrastructures, on the other hand, are designed to support large scientific experiments. They can be classified into HPC (High-Performance Computing) and HTC (High throughput computing). HPC systems focuses on tightly coupled parallel tasks, while HTC focuses on the efficient execution of a large number of loosely coupled tasks. The grid middleware enables users to submit tasks to store data and execute computation on grid infrastructures. Task scheduling, resources management, data storage, replication, and transfers are handled by the middleware. It also enables security functions, such as authentication and authorization.

Task Replication

Task replication, a.k.a. redundant requests, is commonly used to address non-clairvoyant problems (Cirne, Brasileiro, Paranhos, Góes, & Voorsluys, 2007), but it should be used sparingly, to avoid overloading the middleware and degrading fairness among users (Casanova, Desprez, & Suter, 2010). For instance, (Litke, Skoutas, Tserpes, & Varvarigou, 2007) propose a task replication strategy to handle failures in mobile grid environments. Their approach is based on the Weibull distribution to estimate the number of replicas to guarantee a specific fault-tolerance level. In (Ramakrishnan et al., 2009), task replication is enforced as a fault-tolerant mechanism to increase the probability to complete a task successfully. Recently, (Ben-Yehuda, Schuster, Sharov, Silberstein, & Iosup, 2012) proposed a framework for dynamic selection of Pareto-efficient scheduling strategy, where tasks are replicated only in the tail phase when task completion rate is low. All the proposed approaches make strong assumptions on task and resource characteristics, such as the expected duration and resource performance. An important aspect to be evaluated when replicating task is the resource waste, a.k.a. the cost of task replication. (Cirne et al., 2007) evaluate the waste of resources by measuring the percentage of wasted cycles among all the cycles required to execute the application.

Task Grouping

The low performance of fine-grained tasks is a common problem in widely distributed platforms where the scheduling overhead and queuing times are high, such as grid and cloud systems. Several works have addressed the control of task granularity of bag of tasks. For instance, (Muthuvelu et al., 2005) proposed an algorithm to group bag of tasks based on their granularity size--defined as the processing time of the task on the resource. Resources are ordered by their decreasing values of capacity (in MIPS) and tasks are grouped up to the resource capacity. This process continues until all tasks are grouped and assigned to resources. Then, (Ng Wai Keat, 2006) and (Ang, Ng, Ling, Por, & Liew, 2009) extended the previous work by introducing bandwidth in the scheduling framework to enhance the performance of task scheduling. Resources are sorted in decreasing order of bandwidth, then assigned to grouped tasks downward ordered by processing requirement length. Later, (Muthuvelu, Chai, & Eswaran, 2008) extended (Muthuvelu et al., 2005) to determine task granularity based on QoS requirements, task file size, estimated task CPU time, and resource constraints. Meanwhile, (Liu & Liao, 2009) proposed an adaptive fine-grained job scheduling algorithm (AFJS) to group lightweight tasks according to processing capacity (in MIPS) and bandwidth (in Mb/s) of the current available resources. To accommodate with resource dynamicity, the grouping algorithm integrates monitoring information about the current availability and capability of resources. (Zomaya & Chan, 2004) studied limitations and ideal control parameters of task clustering by using genetic algorithms. Their algorithm performs task selection based on the earliest task start time and task communication costs; it converges to an optimal solution of the number of clusters and tasks per cluster. Although the reviewed works significantly reduce communication and processing time, neither of them is non-clairvoyant and online at the same time. Recently, (Muthuvelu, Chai, Chikkannan, & Buyya, 2010) proposed an online scheduling algorithm to determine the task granularity of compute-intensive bag-of-tasks applications. The granularity optimization is based on task processing requirements, resource-network utilization constraint, and users QoS requirements (user's budget and application deadline). Submitted tasks are categorized according to their file sizes, estimated CPU times, and estimated output file sizes, and arranged in a tree structure. The scheduler selects a few tasks from these categories to perform resource benchmarking. In a collaborative work (Chen, Ferreira da Silva, Deelman, & Sakellariou, 2013), we presented three balancing methods to address the load balancing problem when clustering scientific workflow tasks. We defined three imbalance metrics to quantitative measure workflow characteristics based on task runtime variation (HRV), task impact factor (HIFV), and task distance variance (HDV). Although these are online approaches, the solutions are still clairvoyant.

Fairness

Fairness among scientific workflow executions has been addressed in several studies considering the scheduling of multiple scientific workflows. For instance, (Henan Zhao & Sakellariou, 2006) address fairness based on the slowdown of DAGs; they consider a clairvoyant problem where the execution time and the amount of data transfers are known. Similarly, (N'Takpe & Suter, 2009) propose a mapping procedure to increase fairness among parallel tasks on multi-cluster platforms; they address an offline and clairvoyant problem where tasks are scheduled according to the critical path length, maximal exploitable task parallelism, or amount of work to execute. (Casanova et al., 2010) evaluate several scheduling online algorithms of multiple parallel task graphs (PTGs) on a single, homogeneous cluster. Fairness is measured through the maximum stretch (a.k.a. slowdown) defined by the ratio between the PTG execution time on a dedicated cluster, and the PTG execution time in the presence of competition with other PTGs. (C.-C. Hsu, Huang, & Wang, 2011) and (Sommerfeld & Richter, 2011) propose an online HEFT-based algorithm to schedule multiple workflows; they address a clairvoyant problem where tasks are ranked based on the length of their critical path, and tasks are mapped to the resources with the earliest finish time. (Hirales-Carbajal et al., 2012) schedule multiple parallel workflows on a Grid in a non-clairvoyant but

offline context, assuming dedicated resources. Their multi-stage scheduling strategies consist of task labeling and adaptive allocation, local queue prioritization and site scheduling algorithm. Fairness among workflow tasks is achieved by task labeling based on task run time estimation. Recently, (Arabnejad & Barbosa, 2012) proposed an algorithm addressing an online but clairvoyant problem where tasks are assigned to resources based on their rank values; task rank is determined from the smallest remaining time among all remaining tasks of the workflow, and from the percentage of remaining tasks. Finally, in their evaluation of non-preemptive task scheduling, (Sabin, Kochhar, & Sadayappan, 2004) assess fairness by assigning a fair start time to each task, defined by the start time of the task on a complete simulation of all tasks whose queue time is lower than that one. If a task has started its execution after its fair start time, it is considered unfairly treated. Results are trace-based simulations over a period of one month, but the study is performed in a clairvoyant context. (Skowron & Rzadca, 2013) proposed an online and non-clairvoyant algorithm to schedule sequential jobs on distributed systems. They consider a non-clairvoyant model where job's processing time is unknown until the job completes. However, they assume that resources are homogeneous (what is not the case on Grid computing). In contrast, our method considers resource performance, the execution of concurrent activities, and task dependency in scientific workflow executions.

THE VIRTUAL IMAGING PLATFORM

The Virtual Imaging Platform (VIP) (Ferreira da Silva et al., 2011; Glatard et al., 2013) is an openly-accessible platform for scientific workflow executions on a production grid. Figure 1 show the overall VIP architecture for workflow execution. It is composed of

Figure 1. VIP architecture for workflow execution

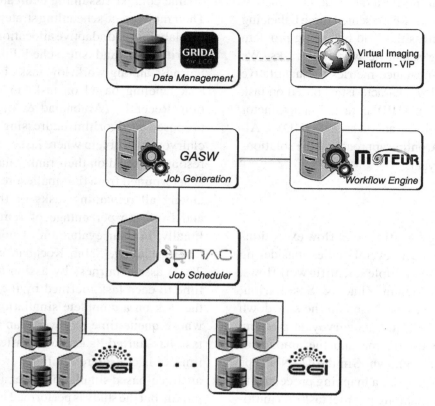

1. A web portal which interfaces users to applications described as workflows,
2. A data management tool to handle transfer operations between users machines and the Grid storage,
3. A workflow engine to process user inputs and spawn computational tasks,
4. A workload management system for resource provisioning and task scheduling, and
5. An execution infrastructure.

In VIP, users authenticate to a web portal with login and password, and they are then mapped to X.509 robot credentials. From the portal, users transfer data and launch applications workflows to be executed on the Grid. Workflows are compositions of activities defined independently from the processed data and that only consist of a program description and requirements. At runtime, activi-

ties receive data and spawn invocations from their input parameter sets. Invocations are independent from each other (bag of tasks) and executed on the computing resource as single-core tasks, which can be resubmitted in case of failures. VIP applications are executed on the biomed virtual organization (VO) of the European Grid Infrastructure (EGI). EGI is a federation of over 350 resources centers (sites) across more than 50 countries, which has access to more than 320,000 logical CPUs and 152 PB of disk space. The biomed VO has access to some 90 computing sites of 22 countries, offering 190 batch queues and approximately 4 PB of disk space.

For a user, a typical application execution consists of the following steps:

1. Select an application,
2. Upload input data,

3. Launch a workflow, and

4. Download results.

hese steps are shown in steps 1, 2 and 11 from Figure 2. For the platform, it consists of performing a workflow execution. A workflow description and a set of input parameters is received and processed by the workflow engine, which produces invocations. In VIP, workflows are interpreted and executed using the MOTEUR workflow engine (Glatard, Montagnat, Lingrand, & Pennec, 2008), which provides an asynchronous grid-aware enactor. From invocations the workflow engine generates Grid tasks, and submits to the DIRAC (Tsaregorodtsev et al., 2010) workload management system, which implements a late binding between tasks and resources. DIRAC deploys pilot jobs on computing resources; pilot jobs run special

agents that fetch user tasks from the task queue, set up their environment and steer their execution; task execution consists of downloading input data, executing the application, and uploading results. Figure 2 summarizes this process.

SELF-MANAGEMENT OF WORKFLOW EXECUTIONS ON GRIDS

The resource heterogeneity of production Grids, such as EGI, raises workflow execution issues, for instance, input and output data transfers may fail because of network glitches or limited site inter-communication; application executions may fail because of corrupted executable files, missing dependencies, or incompatibility; ap-

Figure 2. Workflow execution flow in VIP

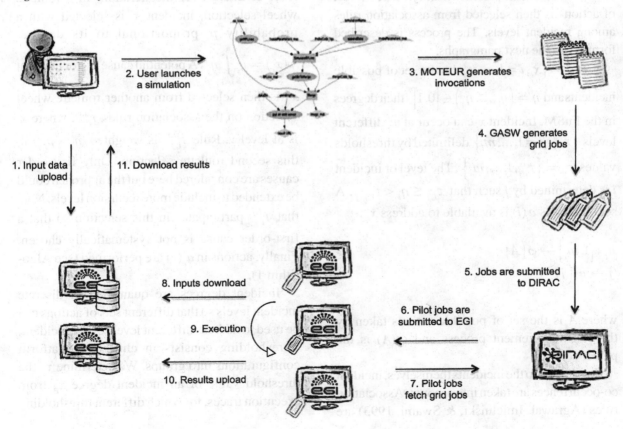

plication executions may slowdown because of resources with poorer performance. Furthermore, the high communication overhead and queuing time intrinsic to such infrastructures may delay the workflow execution.

In this section, we propose a general self-management process (Ferreira da Silva et al., 2012; Ferreira da Silva, Glatard, et al., 2013b) to autonomously handle operational incidents on workflow executions. Instances involved in a workflow execution are modeled as Fuzzy Finite State Machines (FuSM) (Malik, Mordeson, & Sen, 1994) where state degrees of membership are determined by an external process. Degrees of membership are computed from metrics assuming that incidents have outlier performance, e.g. a site or a particular invocation behaves differently than the others. These metrics make little assumptions on the application or resource characteristics. Based on incident degrees, the process identifies incident levels using thresholds determined from the platform history. A specific set of actions is then selected from association rules among incident levels. The process is described formally in the next paragraphs.

Let $I = \{x_i, i = 1, ..., n\}$ be the set of possible incidents and $\eta = (\eta_1, ..., \eta_\eta) \in [0,1]^n$ their degrees in the FuSM. Incident x_i can occur at m_i different levels $\{x_{i,j}, j = 1, ..., m_i\}$ delimited by thresholds values $\tau_j = \{\tau_{i,j}, 1, ..., m_i\}$. The level of incident i is determined by j such that $\tau_{i,j} \leq \eta_i < \tau_{i,j+1}$. A set of actions $a_i(j)$ is available to address $x_{i,j}$:

$$a_i : [1, m_i] \rightarrow \wp(A)$$
$$j \rightarrow a_i(j) \tag{1}$$

where A is the set of possible actions taken by the self-management process and $\wp(A)$ is the power set of A.

In addition to the incidents themselves, incident co-occurrences are taken into account. Association rules (Agrawal, Imieliński, & Swami, 1993) are used to identify relations between levels of different incidents. Association rules to $x_{i,j}$ are defined as $R_{i,j} = \{r_{i,j}^{u,v} = (x_{u,v}, x_{i,j}, p_{i,j}^{u,v})\}$. Rule $r_{i,j}^{u,v}$ means that when $x_{u,v}$ happens then $x_{i,j}$ also happens with confidence $\rho_{i,j}^{u,v} \in [0,1]$. The confidence of a rule is an estimate of probability $P(x_{i,j} \mid x_{u,v})$. For the sake of completeness, $r_{i,j}^{i,j} \in R_{i,j}$ and $\rho_{i,j}^{i,j} = 1$. We also define $R = U_{i \in [1,n], j \in [1,m]} R_{i,j}$. The inference made by an association rule does not necessarily imply causality. Instead, it quantifies co-occurrence between the rule's terms (Tan, 2006).

Algorithm 1 presents the algorithm used at each iteration of the self-management process. Incident degrees are determined based on metrics and incident levels j are obtained from historical data. A roulette wheel selection (De Jong, 1975) based on η is performed to select $x_{i,j}$ the incident level of interest for the iteration. In a roulette wheel selection, incident x_i is selected with a probability p_i proportional to its degree:

$$p(x_i) = \eta_i \int_{j=1}^{n} \eta_j.$$ A potential cause $x_{u,v}$ for incident $x_{i,j}$ is then selected from another roulette wheel selection on the association rules $r_{i,j}^{u,v}$, where x_u is at level v. Rule $r_{i,j}^{u,v}$ is weighted $\eta_u \times \rho_{i,j}^{u,v}$ in this second roulette selection. Only first-order causes are considered here but the approach could be extended to include more recursion levels. Note that $r_{i,j}^{i,j}$ participates in this selection so that a first-order cause is not systematically chosen. Finally, actions in $a_u(v)$ are performed (see Algorithm 1).

Incident degrees are quantified in discrete incident levels so that different sets of actions can be used to address different levels of the incident. Thresholding consists in clustering platform configurations into groups. We determine τ_i, the threshold value of an incident degree x_i, from execution traces, for which different thresholding

Algorithm 1. One iteration of the self-managing process

```
1. Input: History of η
2. Output: Set of actions a
3. Wait for event or timeout
4. Determine incident degrees η ∈ [0,1]based on metrics
5. Determine incident levels j such that τ_{i,j} ≤ η_i < τ_{i,j+1}
6. Select incident x_i by roulette wheel selection based on η
7. Select rule r_{i,j}^{u,v} = (x_{u,v}, x_{i,j}, ρ_{i,j}^{u,v}) ∈ R_{i,j} by roulette wheel selection based on
   η_u × ρ_{i,j}^{u,v}, where x_u is at level v.
8. a=a_u(v)
9. Perform actions in a.
```

approached can be used. For instance, we could consider that x% of the platform configurations are inappropriate while the rest are acceptable. The choice of x, however, would be arbitrary. Instead, we inspect the modes of the distribution of η_i to determine a threshold. Thresholds τ_i are determined from visual mode clustering. The number m_i of incident levels associated to incident i is set as the number of modes in the observed distribution of η_i. Incidents levels and thresholds are determined offline; thus they do not create any overhead on the workflow execution. The process is parameterized on real application traces acquired in production on the European Grid Infrastructure (EGI) (Ferreira da Silva & Glatard, 2013).

In the rest of this chapter, we show the instantiation of our self-management process to address two workflow activity-level incidents: the long tail effect issue, and the task granularity problem; and an incident at platform level: unfairness among workflow executions.

HANDLING BLOCKED ACTIVITIES

The long-tail effect is a common frustration for users who have to wait to retrieve the last pieces of their computation. This issue happens due to execution on slow machines, poor network con-

nection, or communication issues, and leads to substantial speed-up reductions. In this section, we propose an algorithm to handle the long-tail effect and to control task replication (Ferreira da Silva et al., 2012; Ferreira da Silva, Glatard, et al., 2013b). Our method identifies blocked activities as the ones whose tasks are performing worse than the median of already completed tasks. Tasks are assumed of identical costs. This assumption considers that the variation of task durations of correct executions due to resource heterogeneity is negligible compared to the variation when an incident happens. Algorithm 2 describes our activity blocked control process.

Incident Degree and Levels

Activity Blocked Degree η_b

We define the incident degree η_b of an activity from the maximum of the performance coefficients p_i of its n tasks, which relate the task phase durations (setup, inputs download, application execution, and outputs upload) to their medians:

$$\eta_b = 2 \cdot \max \left\{ p_i = p(t_i, \tilde{t}) = \frac{t_i}{\tilde{t} + t_i}, i \in [1,n] \right\} - 1$$

(2)

Algorithm 2. Main loop for activity blocked control

```
1.Input: m workflow executions
2.While there is an active workflow do
3.Wait for timeout or task status change in any workflow
4.Determine blocked degree η_b
5.     If η_b > τ_b then
6.          Replicate late tasks
7.     End if
8.End while.
```

where

$$t_i = t_{i\_setup} + t_{i\_input} + t_{i\_exec} + t_{i\_output}$$

is the estimated duration of task i and

$$\tilde{t}_i = \tilde{t}_{i\_setup} + \tilde{t}_{i\_input} + \tilde{t}_{i\_exec} + \tilde{t}_{i\_output}$$

is the sum of the median durations of tasks 1 to n. Note that

$$\max\left\{ p_i, i \in [1,n] \right\} \in [0.5,1]$$

so that $\eta_b \in [0,1]$. Moreover, $\lim_{t_i \to +\infty} p_i = 1$ and $\max\left\{ p_i, i \in [1,n] \right\} = 0.5$ when all the tasks behave like the median. When less than 2 tasks are completed, medians remain undefined and the control process is inactive.

The estimated duration t_i of a task is computed phase by phase, as follows:

1. For completed task phases, the actual consumed resource time is used;
2. For ongoing task phases, the maximum value between the current consumed resource time and the median consumed time is taken; and
3. For unstarted task phases, the time slot is filled by the median value.

Figure 3 illustrates the task estimation process where the actual durations are used for the two first completed phases (42s for setup and 300s for inputs download), the application execution phase uses the maximum value between the current value of 20s and the median value of 400s, and the last phase (outputs upload) is filled by the median value of 5s, as it is not started yet. Table 1 shows a summary of the symbols used in this section.

Threshold Value τ_b

The threshold value for η_b separates configurations where the activity has acceptable performance ($\eta_b \le \tau_b$) from configurations where the

Figure 3. Task estimation based on median values

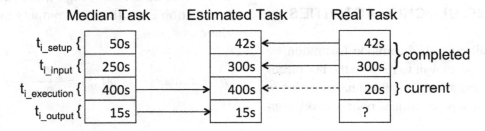

Table 1. Explanation of the symbols used in this section

Parameter	Description
η_b	Activity blocked incident degree.
p	Performance coefficient of a task.
$t, \tilde{t}$	Estimated duration of a task and sum of the median estimated durations of tasks.
τ_b	Threshold value for η_b.
R	Set of replicas.
w	Waste coefficient.

activity is blocked ($\eta_b > \tau_b$). We determine τ_b from observed distributions of η_b. The blocked degree η_b was computed after each event found in the platform historical data (Ferreira da Silva & Glatard, 2013), and as shown in Figure 4. Since the modes are not clearly separable visually, we used K-Means to determine the threshold value $\tau_b = 0.35$. We assume that values in the lowest mode correspond to acceptable performance, and values in the highest mode correspond to low performance. Thus, for $\eta_b > 0.35$ task replication will be triggered.

Algorithm 3. Replication process for one task

```
1. Input: Set of replicas R of a task i
2. Rep = true
3. For r ∈ R do
4.     For j ∈ R, j ≠ r do
5.         If p(t_r, t_j) > τ_b and j is a step further than r then
6.             Abort r
7.         End if
8.     End for
9.     If (r is started and p(t_r, t_j) ≤ τ_b) or r is queued then
10.        Rep = false
11.    End if
12. End for
13. If rep == true then
14.     Replicate r
15. End if.
```

Task Replication

Blocked activities are addressed by task replication. To limit resource waste, the replication process for a particular task is controlled by two mechanisms. First, a task is not replicated if a replica is already queued. Second, if replica j has better performance than replica r (i.e. $p(t_r, t_j) > \tau_b$, see Equation 2) and replica j is in a more advanced phase than replica r, then replica r is aborted. Algorithm 3 presents the algorithm of the replication process. It is applied to all tasks with $p_i > \tau_b$, as defined on Equation 2.

EXPERIMENTS AND RESULTS

The experiment presented hereafter evaluate the ability of the activity blocked control process to improve workflow makespan without wasting resources in case of tasks are late.

Experiment Conditions

The self-management control process was implemented as a plug-in of the MOTEUR workflow engine, receiving notifications about

Figure 4. Histogram of activity-blocked degree sampled in bins of 0.05

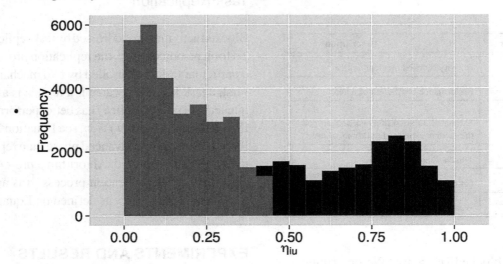

task status changes and task phase durations. Task replication is performed by resubmitting running tasks to DIRAC. To avoid concurrency issues in the writing of output files, a simple mechanism based on file renaming is implemented. To limit infrastructure overload, running tasks are replicated up to 5 times. MOTEUR is configured to resubmit failed tasks up to 5 times in all runs.

This experiment uses a correct execution where the application is supposed to run properly and produce the expected results. Five repetitions are performed for each workflow activity. Two workflow activities are considered for the experiment: FIELD-II/pasa and Mean-Shift/hs3. FIELD is a program to simulate ultrasound transducer fields and ultrasound imaging using linear acoustics. Mean-Shift is an image processing technique used to implement filtering, cluster-

ing, and segmentation in a d-dimensional space. Table 2 summarizes their main characteristics. A workflow execution using our method (Self-Management) is compared to a control execution (No-Management). Executions are launched on the biomed VO of the EGI, in production conditions. Self-Management and No-Management are both launched simultaneously to ensure similar grid conditions. The DIRAC scheduler is configured to equally distribute resources among executions.

Task replication may waste resources, i.e., resources are consumed by a set of tasks that compute the same operations. Here, resource waste is measured by the amount of resource time consumed by Self-Management executions related to the amount of resource time consumed by control executions. We use the waste coefficient (w), defined as follows:

Table 2. Workflow activity characteristics

Workflow Activity	#Tasks	CPU Time	Input	Output
FIELD-II (data-intensive)	122	Few seconds to 15 minutes	~208 MB	~40 KB
Mean-Shift (CPU-intensive)	250	Few minutes to 1 hour	~182 MB	~1KB

$$w = \frac{\sum_{i=1}^{n} h_i + \sum_{j=1}^{m} rj}{\sum_{i=1}^{n} c_i} - 1 \qquad (3)$$

where h_i and c_i are the resource time consumed (CPU time + data transfers time) by n completed tasks for Self-Management and No-Management executions respectively, and r_i is the resource time consumed by m unused replicas. Note that task replication usually leads to $h_i \leq c_i$. If $w > 0$, Self-Management wastes resources compared to the control execution. Otherwise, Self-Management consumes fewer resources than No-Management, which can happen when faster resources are selected.

Results and Discussion

Figures 5 and 6 and Tables 3 and 4 show the makespan and waste coefficient values of FIELD-II/pasa (left) and Mean-Shift/hs3 (right) for the 5 repetitions, respectively. The makespan was considerably reduced in all repetitions of both activities. Speed-up values yielded by Self-Management ranged from 1.7 to 4.5 for FIELD-II/pasa and from 1.5 to 3.2 for Mean-Shift/hs3. The Self-Management process also reduces resource consumption up to 35% when compared to the control execution. This happens because replication increases the probability to select a faster resource. The total number of replicated tasks

Figure 5. Execution makespan values for FIELD-II/pasa

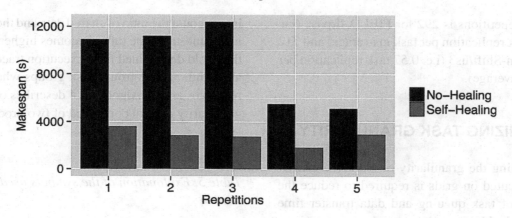

Figure 6. Execution makespan values for mean-shift/hs3

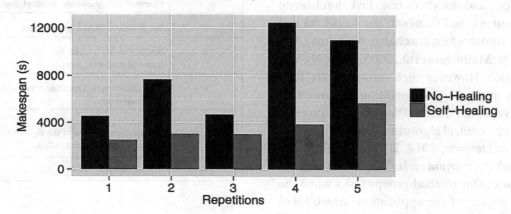

Table 3. Waste coefficient values (w) for FIELD-II/pasa

Repetition	h	r	c	w
1	41,338s	23,823s	71,853s	-0.09
2	37,190s	28,251s	66,435s	-0.01
3	40,209s	25,068s	68,792s	-0.05
4	39,009s	32,973s	78,723s	-0.08
5	38,847s	37,393s	78,988s	-0.03

Table 4. Waste coefficient values (w) for mean-shift/hs3

Repetition	h	r	c	w
1	97,875s	17,709s	116,853s	-0.01
2	85,100s	19,086s	161,801s	-0.35
3	98,736s	25,162s	125,615s	-0.01
4	107,071s	62,746s	204,456s	-0.17
5	126,344s	2,195s	131,446s	-0.02

for all repetitions is 292 for FIELD-II/pasa (i.e. 0.48 task replication per task in average) and 712 for Mean-Shift/hs3 (i.e. 0.57 task replication per task in average).

OPTIMIZING TASK GRANULARITY

Controlling the granularity of workflow activities executed on grids is required to reduce the impact of task queuing and data transfer time overheads. Most existing granularity control approaches assume extensive knowledge about the applications and resources (e.g. task duration on each resource), and that both the workload and available resources do not change over time (Ang et al., 2009; Muthuvelu et al., 2005, 2010; Ng Wai Keat, 2006). However such estimates are hard to obtain in production conditions (Ferreira da Silva, Juve, et al., 2013). Therefore, we propose a granularity control algorithm (Ferreira da Silva, Glatard, & Desprez, 2014, 2013a) for platforms where such clairvoyant and offline conditions are not realistic. Our method groups tasks when the fineness degree of the application, which takes

into account the ratio of shared data and the queuing/round-trip time ratio, becomes higher than a threshold determined from execution traces. The algorithm also ungroups task groups when new resources arrive. Algorithm 4 describes our task granularity control composed of two processes:

Table 5. Explanation of the symbols used in this section

Parameter	Description
η_f, η_c	Fineness and coarseness incident degrees.
T	Set of tasks within a grouped task.
d	Ratio between transfer time of input shared data and execution time.
r	Ratio between task queuing times and task turnaround time.
$\tilde{t}_{shared}$	Median transfer time of the input data shared among all tasks of an activity.
τ_f, τ_c	Threshold values for η_f and η_c.

Algorithm 4. Main loop for granularity control

```
1. Input: m waiting tasks
2. Create n 1-task groups T_i
3. While there is an active task group do
4.     Wait for timeout or task status change
5.     Determine fineness degree η_f
6.     If η_f > τ_f then
7.         Group task groups using Algorithm 5
8.     End if
9.     Determine coarseness degree η_c
10.     If η_c > τ_c then
11.         Ungroup coarsest task groups
12.     End if
13. End while.
```

1. Fineness control groups too fine task groups for which the fineness degree η_f is greater than threshold τ_f, and
2. Coarseness control ungroups too coarse task groups for which the coarseness degree η_c is greater than threshold τ_c. Table 5 shows a summary of the symbols used in this section.

INCIDENT DEGREE AND LEVELS

Fineness Control

Fineness Degree η_f

Let *n* be the number of waiting tasks in a workflow activity, and *m* the number of task groups. Tasks of an activity are assumed independent, but with similar costs (bag of tasks). Initially, 1 group is created for each task ($n = m$). T_i is the set of tasks in group *i*, and n_i is the number of tasks in T_i. Groups are a partition of the set of waiting tasks: $T_i \cap_{i \neq j} T_j = \varnothing$ and $\sum_{i=1}^{m} n_i = n$. The activity fineness degree η_f is the maximum of all group fineness degrees f_i:

$$n_f = \max_{i \in [1,m]} (f_i) \qquad (4)$$

All η_f are in [0,1], and high fineness degrees indicate fine granularities. We use a *max* operator in this equation to ensure that *any* task group with a too fine granularity will be detected. The fineness degree f_i of group *i* is defined as:

$$f_i = d_i \cdot r_i \qquad (5)$$

where d_i is the ratio between the transfer time of the input data shared among all tasks in the activity, and the total execution time of the group:

$$d_i = \frac{\tilde{t}_{\_shared}}{\tilde{t}_{\_shared} + n_i(\tilde{t} - \tilde{t}_{\_shared})} \qquad (6)$$

where $\tilde{t}_{\_shared}$ is the median transfer time of the input data shared among all tasks in the activity, and $\tilde{t}$ is the sum of its median task phase durations corresponding to application setup, input data transfer, application execution and output data transfer: $\tilde{t} = \tilde{t}_{\_setup} + \tilde{t}_{\_input} + \tilde{t}_{\_exec} + \tilde{t}_{\_output}$. Median values $\tilde{t}_{\_shared}$ and $\tilde{t}$ are computed from values measured on completed tasks. When less than 2 tasks are completed, medians remain undefined and the control process is inactive. This online estimation makes our process non-clairvoyant with respect to the task duration, which is progressively estimated as the workflow activity runs. Yet, it assumes that all tasks in an activity have similar costs.

In Equation 5, r_i is the ratio between the maximum of the task queuing times q_i in the group, and the total round-trip time (queuing + execution) of the group:

$$r_i = \frac{\max_{j \in [1,n_i]} q_j}{\max_{j \in [1,n_i]} q_j + \tilde{t}_{\_shared} + n_i(\tilde{t} - \tilde{t}_{\_shared})} \quad (7)$$

Group queuing time is the max of all task queuing times in the group; group execution time is the time to transfer shared input data and the time to execute all task phases in the group except for the transfers of shared input data. Note that d_i, r_i, and therefore f_i and η_f are in [0,1]. η_f tends to 0 when there is little shared input data among the activity tasks or when the task queuing times are low compared to the execution times; in both cases, grouping tasks is indeed useless. Conversely, η_f tends to 1 when the transfer time of shared input data becomes high, and the queuing time is high compared to the execution time; grouping is needed in this case.

Threshold Value τ_f

The threshold value for η_f separates configurations where the activity's fineness is acceptable ($\eta_f \leq \tau_f$) from configurations where the activity is too fine ($\eta_f > \tau_f$). We determine τ_f from execution traces (Ferreira da Silva & Glatard, 2013), inspecting the distribution modes of η_f. Values of η_f in the highest mode of the distribution, i.e. which are clearly separated from the others, will be considered too fine. Figure 7 shows the histogram of these values. The histogram appears bimodal, which indicates that η_f separates platform configurations in two distinct groups. We assume that these groups correspond to acceptable fineness (lowest mode) and too fine granularity (highest mode), and thus we choose $\tau_f = 0.55$. For $\eta_f \geq 0.55$, task grouping will therefore be triggered.

Task Grouping

We assume that running tasks cannot be preempted, i.e. only waiting tasks can be grouped. Algorithm 5 describes our task grouping algorithm. Groups where $f_i > \tau_f$ are grouped pairwise until $\eta_f \leq \tau_f$ or until the amount of waiting groups Q is smaller or equal to the amount of running groups R. Although η_f ignores scattering (Equation 4 uses a *max* operator), the algorithm considers

Figure 7. Histogram of fineness incident degree sampled in bins of 0.05

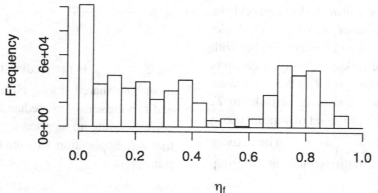

Algorithm 5. Task grouping

```
1. Input: f₁ to fₘ          // group fineness degrees, sorted in decreasing order
2. Input: Q, R        // number of queued and running task groups
3. For i = 1 to m - 1 do
4.      j = i + 1
5.      While fᵢ > τf and Q > R and j ≤ m do
6.          If fᵢ > τf then
7.              Group all tasks of Tⱼ into Tᵢ
8.              Recalculate fᵢ using Equation 5
9.              Q = Q - 1
10.         End if
11.         j = j + 1
12.     End while
13.     i = j
14. End for
15. Delete all empty task groups.
```

it by grouping tasks in all groups where $f_i > \tau_f$. Ordering groups by decreasing f_i values tends to equally distribute tasks among groups. The grouping process stops when $Q \leq R$ to avoid parallelism loss. This condition also avoids conflicts with the ungrouping process described in the next sub-section.

Coarseness Control

Condition $Q > R$ used in Algorithm 5 ensures that all resources will be exploited if the number of available resources is stationary (i.e., constant). In case the number of available resources decreases, the fineness control process may further reduce the number of groups. However, if the number of available resources increases, task groups may need to be ungrouped to maximize resource exploitation. This ungrouping is implemented by our coarseness control process. The process monitors the value of η_c defined as:

$$n_c = \frac{R}{Q + R} \tag{8}$$

The threshold value τ_c is set to 0.5 so that $\eta_c > \tau_c \Leftrightarrow Q < R$.

When an activity is considered too coarse, its groups are ordered by increasing values of η_f and the first groups (i.e. the coarsest ones) are split until $\eta_c < \tau_c$. Note that ungrouping increases the number of queued tasks, therefore tends to reduce η_c.

Experiments and Results

The experiments presented hereafter evaluate, in a production environment, the fineness control process under stationary load, and the interest of controlling coarseness under non-stationary load.

Experiment Conditions

The granularity control process was implemented as a plugin of the MOTEUR workflow manager, receiving notifications about task status changes and task phase durations. The plugin then uses this data to group and ungroup tasks according to Algorithm 4, where the timeout value is set to 2 minutes. To ensure resource limitation without overloading the production system with test tasks,

Table 6. Workflow activity characteristics

Workflow Activity	#Tasks	CPU Time	Input	Output	$\dfrac{\tilde{t}_{\_shared}}{\tilde{t}}$
SimuBloch (data-intensive)	25	Few seconds	~15 MB	< 5 MB	~0.9
FIELD-II (data-intensive)	122	Few seconds to 15 minutes	~208 MB	~40 KB	[0.4,0.6]
Mean-Shift (CPU-intensive)	250	Few minutes to 1 hour	~182 MB	~1KB	[0.5,0.8]

experiment executions are limited to 3 sites of different countries. As no online task modification is possible in the DIRAC workload management system, we implemented task grouping by canceling queued tasks and submitting grouped tasks as a new task.

Three workflow activities (summarized in Table 6), implementing different types of medical image simulation, are used in the experiments: SimuBloch, FIELD-II, and PET-Sorteo/emission. SimuBloch is a simulator made for fast simulation of MRIs based on Bloch equation. Two sets of experiments are conducted under different load patterns. The first experiment evaluates the fineness control process only under stationary load. It consists of separated executions of SimuBloch, FIELD-II, and PET-Sorteo/emission. A workflow activity using our task grouping mechanism (Fineness) is compared to a control activity (No-Granularity). Resource contention on the 3 execution sites is maintained high and constant so that no ungrouping is required. The second experiment evaluates the interest of using the ungrouping control process under non-stationary load. It uses activity FIELD-II. An execution using both fineness and coarseness control (Fineness-Coarseness) is compared to an execution without coarseness control (Fineness) and to a control execution (No-Granularity). Executions are started under resource contention, but the contention is progressively reduced during the experiment. This is done by submitting a heavy workflow before the experiment starts, and canceling it when half of the control tasks are completed.

Results and Discussion

Figure 8 shows the makespan of SimuBloch, FIELD-II, and PET-Sorteo/emission executions. Fineness yields a significant makespan reduction for all repetitions. Table 5 shows the makespan (*M*) values and the final number of task groups. The task grouping mechanism is not able to group all SimuBloch tasks in a single group because 2 tasks must be completed for the process to have enough information about the application (i.e. $\tilde{t}_{\_shared}$ and $\tilde{t}$ can be computed). This is a constraint of our non-clairvoyant conditions, where task durations cannot be determined in advance. FIELD-II tasks are initially not grouped, but as the queuing time becomes important, tasks are considered too fine, thus they are grouped. PET-Sorteo/emission is an intermediary case where only a few tasks are grouped. Results show that the task grouping mechanism speeds up Simu-Bloch and FIELD-II executions up to a factor of 2.6, and PET-Sorteo/emission executions up to a factor of 2.5.

Figure 9 shows the evolution of task groups for FIELD-II executions under non-stationary load (resources arrive during the experiment). Makespan values are reported in Table 8. In the first three repetitions, resources emerge progressively during workflow executions. Fineness and Fineness-Coarseness speed up executions up to a factor of 1.5 and 2.1. Since Fineness does not benefit from newly arrived resources, it has a lower speed up compared to No-Granularity

Figure 8. Makespan for fineness and no-granularity executions under stationary load

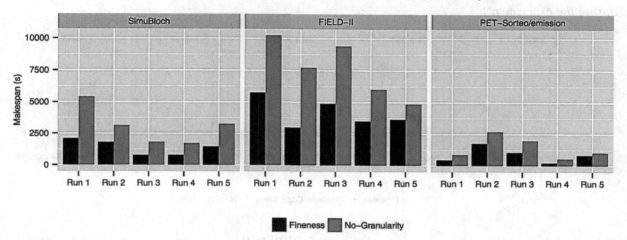

due to parallelism loss. In the two last repetitions (where resources appear suddenly), the ungrouping process in Fineness-Coarseness has similar performance than No-Granularity since the execution maximizes the parallelism, while Fineness is penalized by its lack of adaptation: a slowdown of 20% is observed compared to No-Granularity.

Our task granularity control process works best under high resource contention, when the amount of available resources is stable or de-

creases over time. Coarseness control can cope with soft increases in the number of available resources, but fast variations remain difficult to handle. In the worst-case scenario, tasks are first grouped due to resource limitation, and resources suddenly appear once all task groups are already running. In this case the ungrouping algorithm has no group to handle, and granularity control penalizes the execution. Task pre-emption should be added to the method to address this scenario.

Table 7. Makespan (M) and number of task groups for SimuBloch, FIELD-II, and PET-Sorteo/emission executions for the 5 repetitions

		SimuBloch		FIELD-II		PET-Sorteo	
		M (s)	Groups	M (s)	Groups	M (s)	Groups
1	No-Granularity	5421	25	10230	122	873	80
	Fineness	2118	3	5749	80	451	57
2	No-Granularity	3138	25	7734	122	2695	80
	Fineness	1803	3	2982	75	1766	40
3	No-Granularity	1831	25	9407	122	1983	80
	Fineness	780	4	4894	73	1047	53
4	No-Granularity	1737	25	6026	122	552	80
	Fineness	797	6	3507	61	218	64
5	No-Granularity	3257	25	4865	122	1033	80
	Fineness	1468	4	3641	91	831	71

Figure 9. Evolution of task groups for FIELD-II executions under non-stationary load (resources arrive during the experiment)

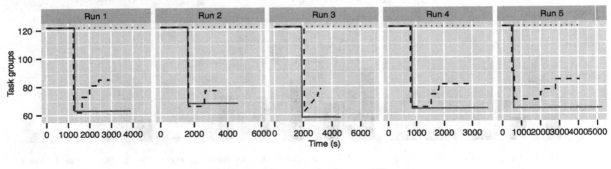

Table 8. Makespan (M) and average queuing time (ē) for FIELD-II workflow execution for the 5 repetitions

Workflow Activity	Run 1		Run 2		Run 3		Run 4		Run 5	
	M (s)	$\bar{e}$ (s)	M (s)	$\bar{e}$ (s)	M (s)	$\bar{e}$ (s)	M (s)	$\bar{e}$ (s)	M (s)	$\bar{e}$ (s)
No-Granularity	4617	2011	5934	2765	6940	3855	3199	1863	4147	2295
Fineness	3892	2036	4607	2090	4602	2631	3567	1928	5247	2326
Fineness-Coarseness	2927	1708	3335	1829	3247	2091	2952	1586	4073	2197

CONTROLLING FAIRNESS AMONG WORKFLOW EXECUTIONS

Fairly allocating distributed computing resources among workflow executions is critical to multi-user platforms such as VIP. However, this problem remains mostly studied in clairvoyant and offline conditions, where task durations on resources are known, or the workload and available resources do not vary along time. We consider a non-clairvoyant, online fairness problem where the platform workload, task costs and resource characteristics are unknown and not stationary. We propose a fairness control loop which assigns task priorities based on the fraction of pending work in the workflows (Ferreira da Silva et al., 2014; Ferreira da Silva, Glatard, & Desprez, 2013c). Workflow characteristics and performance on the target resources are estimated progressively, as information becomes available during the execution. Workflows consist of linked

activities spawning tasks for which the executable and input data are known, but the computational cost and produced data volume are not. Algorithm 6 summarizes our fairness control process. Fairness is controlled by allocating resources to workflows according to their fraction of pending work. It is done by re-prioritizing tasks in workflows where the unfairness degree η_u is greater than a threshold τ_u. Table 9 shows a summary of the symbols used in this section.

Incident Degree and Levels

Unfairness Degree η_u

Let m be the number of workflows with an active activity; a workflow activity is active if it has at least one waiting (queued) or running task. The unfairness degree η_u is the maximum difference between the fractions of pending work:

$$\eta_u = W_{\max} - W_{\min} \qquad (9)$$

with

$$W_{\min} = \min\left\{W_i, i \in [1,m]\right\}$$

and

$$W_{\max} = \max\left\{W_i, i \in [1,m]\right\}.$$

All W_i are in [0,1]. For $\eta_u = 0$, we consider that resources are fairly distributed among all workflows; otherwise, some workflows consume more resources than they should. The fraction of pending work W_i of a workflow $i \in [1,m]$ is defined from the fraction of pending work $w_{i,j}$ of its n_i active activities:

$$W_i = \max_{j \in [1,n_i]}(w_{i,j}) \qquad (10)$$

All $w_{i,j}$ are between 0 and 1. A high $w_{i,j}$ value indicates that the activity has a lot of pending work compared to the others. We define $w_{i,j}$ as:

$$w_{i,j} = \frac{Q_{i,j}}{Q_{i,j} + R_{i,j}P_{i,j}} \cdot T_{i,j} \qquad (11)$$

Table 9. Explanation of the symbols used in this section

Parameter	Description
η_u	Unfairness incident degree.
W, w	Fraction of pending work.
Q, R	Number of queued and running tasks.
P	Performance of the activity.
T	Relative observed duration.
$\tilde{t}$	Sum of the median task execution times.
τ_u	Threshold value for η_u.
Δ	Number of waiting tasks of an activity.
μ	Area under the curve η_u during the execution.

where $Q_{i,j}$ is the number of waiting tasks in the activity, $R_{i,j}$ is the number of running tasks in the activity, $P_{i,j}$ is the performance of the activity, and $T_{i,j}$ is its relative observed duration. $T_{i,j}$ is defined as the ratio between the median duration $t_{i,j}$ of the completed tasks in activity j and the maximum median task duration among all active activities of all running workflows:

$$T_{i,j} = \frac{\tilde{t}_{i,j}}{\max\limits_{v \in [1,m], w \in [1,n_i^*]}\left(\tilde{t}_{u,w}\right)} \qquad (12)$$

Algorithm 6. Main loop for fairness control

```
1. Input: m workflow executions
2. While there is an active workflow do
3.     Wait for timeout or task status change in any workflow
4.     Determine unfairness degree η_u
5.     If η_u > τ_u then
6.         Re-prioritize tasks using Algorithm 7
7.     End if
8. End while.
```

Tasks of an activity all consist of the following successive phases: setup, inputs download, application execution, and outputs upload; $\tilde{t}_{i,j}$ is computed as

$$\tilde{t}_{i,j} = \tilde{t}_{i,j}^{setup} + \tilde{t}_{i,j}^{input} + \tilde{t}_{i,j}^{exec} + \tilde{t}_{i,j}^{output}.$$

Medians are progressively estimated as tasks complete. At the beginning of the execution, $T_{i,j}$ is initialized to 1 and all medians are undefined; when two tasks of activity j complete, $\tilde{t}_{i,j}$ is updated and $T_{i,j}$ is computed with Equation 12. In this equation, the *max* operator is computed only on $n_i^* \leq n_i$ activities with at least 2 completed tasks, i.e. for which $\tilde{t}_{i,j}$ can be determined. We are aware that using the median may be inaccurate. However, without a model of the applications' execution time, we have to rely on observed task durations. Using the whole time distribution (or at least its few first moments) may be more accurate but it would make the method more complex.

In Equation 11, the performance $P_{i,j}$ of an activity varies between 0 and 1. A low $P_{i,j}$ indicates that resources allocated to the activity have bad performance for the activity; in this case, the contribution of running tasks is reduced and $w_{i,j}$ increases. Conversely, a high $P_{i,j}$ increases the contribution of running tasks, therefore decreases $w_{i,j}$. For an activity j with k_j active tasks, we define $P_{i,j}$ as:

$$P_{i,j} = 2 \cdot \left(1 - \max_{u \in [1,k_j]} \left\{ \frac{t_u}{\tilde{t}_{i,j} + t_u} \right\} \right) \quad (13)$$

where $t_u = t_u^{setup} + t_u^{input} + t_u^{exec} + t_u^{output}$ is the sum of the estimated durations of task u's phases. Estimated task phase durations are computed as the max between the current elapsed time in the task phase (0 if the task phase has not started) and the median duration of the task phase. $P_{i,j}$ is ini-

tialized to 1, and updated using Equation 13 only when at least 2 tasks of activity j are completed. Note that computing $P_{i,j}$ is equivalent to computing the complement of the activity blocked degree $1 - \eta_b$ for activity j of workflow i.

If all tasks perform as the median, i.e. $t_u = \tilde{t}_{i,j}$, then

$$\max_{u \in [1,k_j]} \left\{ \frac{t_u}{\left(\tilde{t}_{i,j} + t_u \right)} \right\} = 0.5$$

and $P_{i,j} = 1$. Conversely, if a task in the activity is much longer than the median, i.e. $t_u \gg \tilde{t}_{i,j}$, then

$$\max_{u \in [1,k_j]} \left\{ \frac{t_u}{\left(\tilde{t}_{i,j} + t_u \right)} \right\} \approx 1$$

and $P_{i,j} \approx 0$. This definition of $P_{i,j}$, considers that bad performance results in a few tasks blocking the activity. Indeed, we assume that the scheduler does not deliberately favor any activity and that performance discrepancies are manifested by a few *unlucky* tasks slowed down by bad resources. Performance, in this case, has a relative definition: depending on the activity profile, it can correspond to CPU, RAM, network bandwidth, latency, or a combination of those. We admit that this definition of $P_{i,j}$ is a bit rough. However, under our non-clairvoyance assumption, estimating resource performance for the activity more accurately is hardly possible because

1. We have no model of the application, therefore task durations cannot be predicted from CPU, RAM or network characteristics, and

2. Network characteristics and even available RAM are shared among concurrent tasks running on the infrastructure, which makes them hardly measurable.

Algorithm 7. Task re-prioritization

```
1. Input: W₁ to Wₘ          // fractions of pending works
2. maxPriority = max task priority in all workflows
3. For i = 1 to m do
4.     If Wᵢ − W_min > τᵤ then
5.         For j = 1 to aᵢ do
6.             // aᵢ is the number of active activities in workflow i
7.             If wᵢ,ⱼ − W_min > τᵤ then
8.                 Compute Δᵢ,ⱼ from Equation 15
9.                 For p = 1 to Δᵢ,ⱼ do
10.                    If ∃waiting task q in activity j with priority ≤
maxPriority then
11.                        q.priority = maxPriority + 1
12.                    End if
13.                End for
14.            End if
15.        End for
16.    End if
17. End for.
```

Thresholding Unfairness τᵤ

Task prioritization is triggered when the unfairness degree is considered critical, i.e $\eta_u > \tau_u$. Inspecting the modes of the distribution of η_u we determine that values of η_u in the highest mode of the distribution, i.e. which are clearly separated from the others, will be considered unfair. Figure 10 shows the histogram of these values, where only $\eta_u \neq 0$ values are represented. This histogram is clearly bi-modal, which is a good property since it reduces the influence of τ_u. From this histogram, we choose $\tau_u = 0.2$. For $\eta_u > 0.2$, task prioritization is triggered.

Figure 10. Histogram of the unfairness degree η_u sampled in bins of 0.05

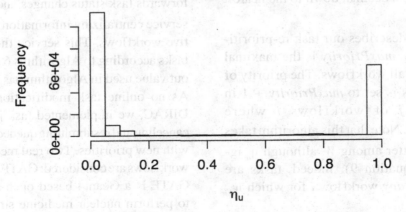

Table 10. Workflow characteristics

Workflow Activity	#Tasks	CPU Time	Input	Output
GATE (CPU-intensive)	100	Few minutes to 1 hour	~115 MB	~40 MB
SimuBloch (data-intensive)	25	Few seconds	~15 MB	< 5 MB

Task Prioritization

Task priority is an integer initialized to 1. The action taken to cope with unfairness is to increase the priority of $\Delta_{i,j}$ waiting tasks for all activities j of workflow i where $w_{i,j} - W_{\min} > \tau_u$. Running tasks cannot be pre-empted. $\Delta_{i,j}$ is determined so that $\tilde{w}_{i,j} = W_{\min} + \tau_u$, where $\tilde{w}_{i,j}$ is the estimated value of $w_{i,j}$ after $\Delta_{i,j}$ tasks are prioritized. We approximate $\tilde{w}_{i,j}$ as:

$$\tilde{w}_{i,j} = \frac{Q_{i,j} - \Delta_{i,j}}{Q_{i,j} + R_{i,j} P_{i,j}} \cdot \hat{T}_{i,j} \qquad (14)$$

which assumes that $\Delta_{i,j}$ tasks will move from status queued to running, and that the performance of new resources will be maximal. It gives:

$$\Delta_{i,j} = Q_{i,j} - \left\lfloor \frac{(\tau_u + W_{\min})(Q_{i,j} + R_{i,j} P_{i,j})}{\hat{T}_{i,j}} \right\rfloor \qquad (15)$$

where $\lfloor \ \rfloor$ rounds a decimal down to the nearest integer value.

Algorithm 7 describes our task re-prioritization algorithm. *maxPriority* is the maximal priority value in all workflows. The priority of $\Delta_{i,j}$ waiting tasks is set to *maxPriority* + 1 in all activities j of workflows i where $w_{i,j} - W_{\min} > \tau_u$. Note that this algorithm takes into account scatter among W_i although η_u ignores it (see Equation 9). Indeed, tasks are re-prioritized in *any* workflow i for which $w_{i,j} - W_{\min} > \tau_u$.

The method also accommodates online conditions. If a new workflow i is submitted, then $R_{i,j} = 0$ for all its activities and $\hat{T}_{i,j}$ is initialized to 1. This leads to $W_{\max} = W_i = 1$, which increases η_u. If η_u goes beyond τ_u, then $\Delta_{i,j}$ tasks of activity j of workflow i have their priorities increased to restore fairness. Similarly, if new resources arrive, then $R_{i,j}$ increase and η_u is updated accordingly.

Experiments and Results

The experiments presented hereafter evaluate our method on a set of identical workflows, where the variability of the measured makespan can be used as a fairness metric. In addition, we add a very short workflow to this set of identical workflow, which was one of the configurations motivating this study.

Experiment Conditions

Fairness control was implemented as a MOTEUR plug-in receiving notifications about task and workflow status changes. Each workflow plug-in forwards task status changes and $\tilde{t}_{i,j}$ values to a service centralizing information about all the active workflows. This service then re-prioritizes tasks according to Algorithms 6 and 7. The time-out value used in Algorithm 6 is set to 3 minutes. As no online task modification is possible in DIRAC, we implemented task prioritization by canceling and resubmitting queued tasks to DIRAC with new priorities. Two real medical simulation workflows are considered: GATE and SimuBloch. GATE is a Geant4-based open-source software to perform nuclear medicine simulations, especially for TEP and SPECT imaging, as well for radiation therapy. Table 10 summarizes their main characteristics.

Three different fairness metrics are used in the experiments. First, the standard deviation of the makespan, written σ_m, is a straightforward metric that can be used when identical workflows are executed. Second, we define the unfairness μ_u as the area under the curve η_u (see Equation 9) during the execution:

$$\mu = \sum_{i=2}^{M} \eta_u(t_i) \cdot (t_i - t_{i-1}) \tag{16}$$

where M is the number of time samples until the makespan. This metric measures if the fairness process can indeed minimize its own criterion η_u. In addition, the slowdown s of a completed workflow execution is measured as:

$$s = \frac{M_{multi}}{M_{own}} \tag{17}$$

where M_{multi} is the makespan observed on the shared platform, and M_{own} is the estimated makespan if it was executed alone on the platform. In our conditions, M_{own} is estimated as:

$$M_{own} = \max_{p \in \Omega} \sum_{u \in p} t_u \tag{18}$$

where Ω is the set of task paths in the workflow, and t_u is the measured duration of task u. This assumes that concurrent executions only impact task waiting time. For instance, network congestion or changes in performance distribution resulting from concurrent executions are ignored. We use σ_s, the standard deviation of the slowdown to quantify unfairness. The standard deviation of the makespan (σ_m) is also used.

Results and Discussion

Figure 11 shows the makespan for the set of identical workflows. The unfairness degree η_u is shown in Figure 12, while the makespan standard deviation σ_m, slowdown standard deviation σ_s and unfairness μ_u for the 4 repetitions using the set of identical workflows is shown in Table 11. The difference among makespans and unfairness degree values are significantly reduced in all repetitions of Fairness. Both Fairness and No-Fairness behave similarly until η_u reaches the threshold value $\tau_u = 0.2$. Unfairness is then detected and the mechanism triggers task prioritization. Paradoxically, the first effect of task prioritization is a slight increase of η_u. Indeed, $P_{i,j}$ and $\hat{T}_{i,j}$, that are initialized to 1, start changing earlier in Fairness than in No-Fairness due to the availability of task duration values to compute $\tilde{t}_{i,j}$. Note that η_u reaches similar maximal values in both cases, but reaches them

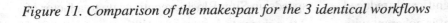

Figure 11. Comparison of the makespan for the 3 identical workflows

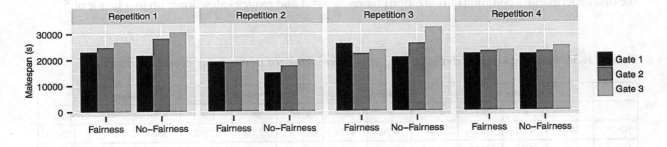

Figure 12. Unfairness degree η_u for the set of identical workflows

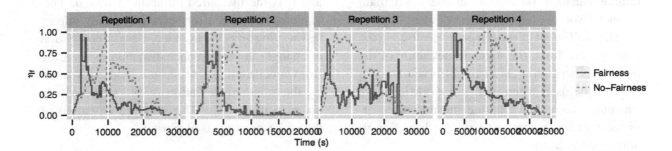

Figure 13. Comparison of the makespan for 3 identical workflows and a very short workflow

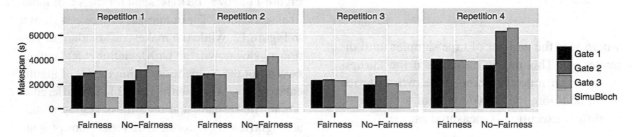

faster in Fairness. The fairness mechanism then manages to decrease η_u back under 0.2 much faster than it happens in No-Fairness when tasks progressively complete. Quantitatively, the fairness mechanism reduces σ_m up to a factor of 15, σ_s up to a factor of 7, and μ_u by about 2.

Figure 13 shows the makespan for the case where a very short workflow is introduced. Unfairness degree η_u is shown in Figure 14. Table 12 shows unfairness μ_u and slowdown standard deviation σ_s. In all cases, the makespan of the very short SimuBloch executions is significantly reduced for Fairness. The evolution of η_u is coherent with the first experiment: a common initialization phase

followed by an anticipated growth and decrease for Fairness. Fairness reduces σ_s up to a factor of 5.9 and unfairness up to a factor of 1.9. Table 13 shows the execution makespan (m), average wait time ($\overline{w}$) and slowdown (s) values for the SimuBloch execution launched after the 3 GATE. As it is a non-clairvoyant scenario where no information about task execution time and future task submission is known, the fairness mechanism is not able to give higher priorities to SimuBloch tasks in advance. Despite that, the fairness mechanism speeds up SimuBloch executions up to a factor of 2.9, reduces task average wait time up to factor of 4.4 and reduces slowdown up to a factor of 5.9.

Table 11. Makespan standard deviation σ_m, slowdown standard deviation σ_s and unfairness μ_u

	Repetition 1			Repetition 2			Repetition 3			Repetition 4		
	$\sigma_m(s)$	σ_s	$\mu(s)$	$\sigma_m(s)$	σ_s	$\mu(s)$	$\sigma_m(s)$	σ_s	$\mu(s)$	$\sigma_m(s)$	σ_s	$\mu(s)$
NF	4666	1.03	8758	2541	0.50	4154	5791	2.10	13392	1567	0.87	12283
F	1884	0.40	5292	167	0.84	2367	2007	0.84	7243	706	0.24	6070

Figure 14. Unfairness degree η_u for a set of identical workflows and a very short workflow

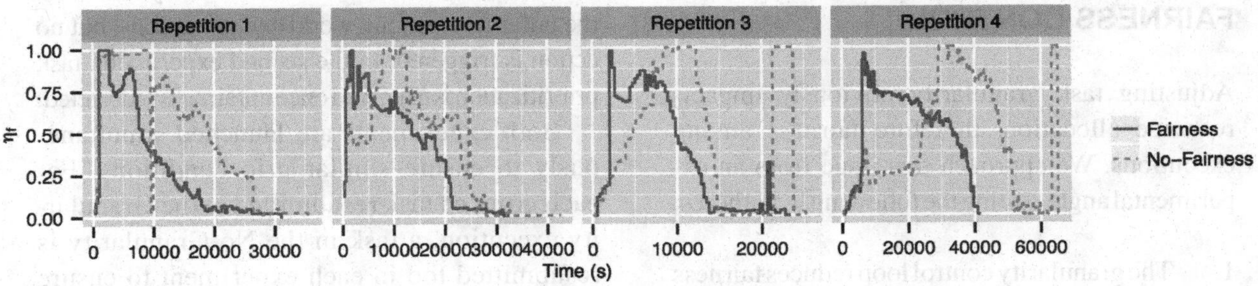

In all experiments, fairness optimization takes time to begin because the method needs to acquire information about the applications, which are totally unknown when a workflow is launched. We could think of reducing the time of this information-collecting phase, e.g. by designing initialization strategies maximizing information discovery, but it could not be totally removed. Currently, the method works best for applications with a lot of short tasks because the first few tasks can be used for initialization, and optimization can be exploited for the remaining tasks. The worst-case scenario is a configuration where the number of available resources stays constant and equal to the number of tasks in the first submitted workflow: in this case, no action could be taken until the first workflow completes, and the method would not do better than first-come-first-served. Pre-emption of running tasks should be considered to address that.

Table 12. Slowdown standard deviation σ_s and unfairness μ_u

	Repetition 1		Repetition 2		Repetition 3		Repetition 4	
	σ_s	$\mu(s)$	σ_s	$\mu(s)$	σ_s	$\mu(s)$	σ_s	$\mu(s)$
NF	94.88	7269	100.05	16048	87.93	11331	213.60	28190
F	15.95	9085	42.94	12543	57.62	7721	76.69	21355

Table 13. SimuBloch's makespan, average wait time and slowdown

Run	Type	m (Secs)	$\bar{w}$ (Secs)	s
1	No-Fairness	27854	18983	196.15
	Fairness	9531	4313	38.43
2	No-Fairness	27784	19105	210.48
	Fairness	13761	10538	94.25
3	No-Fairness	14432	13579	182.48
	Fairness	9902	8145	122.25
4	No-Fairness	51664	47591	445.38
	Fairness	38630	27795	165.79

INTERACTIONS BETWEEN TASK GRANULARITY AND FAIRNESS CONTROL

Adjusting task granularity obviously impacts resource allocation, therefore fairness among executions. We approach this issue from an experimental angle, testing the following hypotheses:

1. The granularity control loop reduces fairness among executions; and
2. The fairness control loop avoids this reduction (Ferreira da Silva et al., 2014).

Two experiments are conducted. The first experiment tests whether the task granularity control process penalizes fairness among workflow executions; and the second tests whether the fairness control process mitigates the unfairness created by the granularity control process. For each experiment, a workflow set where one workflow uses the granularity control process (Granularity, G) is compared to a control workflow set (No-Granularity, NG). A workflow set consists of three SimuBloch workflows submitted sequentially. In the Granularity set, the first workflow has the granularity control process

enabled, and the others do not. The first experiment has a fairness service, which only measures the unfairness among workflow executions, but no action is triggered. In the second experiment, task prioritization is triggered once unfairness is detected.

Both experiments are launched simultaneously to ensure similar grid conditions. For each grouped task resubmitted in the Granularity execution, a task in the No-Granularity is resubmitted too in each experiment to ensure equal race conditions for resource allocation. Similarly, for each task prioritized in the first experiment, a task in the second is also prioritized to ensure equal race conditions. Again, experiment results are not influenced by the submission process overhead since both Granularity and No-Granularity of both experiments experience the same overhead. Therefore, performance results obtained in both experiments can be compared to each other.

Results and Discussion

Figure 15 shows the comparison of the slowdown for the first experiment. Unfairness degree η_u is shown in Figure 16. Table 14 shows the

Figure 15. Granularity without fairness: comparison of the slowdowns

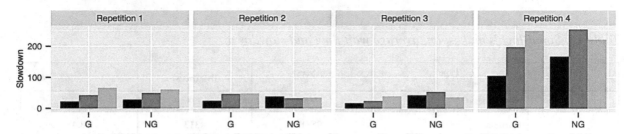

Table 14. Granularity without fairness: unfairness and standard deviation of the makespan and slowdown

	Repetition 1			Repetition 2			Repetition 3			Repetition 4		
	$\sigma_m(s)$	σ_s	$\mu(s)$	$\sigma_m(s)$	σ_s	$\mu(s)$	$\sigma_m(s)$	σ_s	$\mu(s)$	$\sigma_m(s)$	σ_s	$\mu(s)$
NF	2446	16.55	823	15	3.24	503	1273	8.91	998	1364	38.70	1040
F	2962	21.94	1638	1015	13.15	527	2566	11.01	1212	2017	73.90	1250

Figure 16. Granularity without fairness: unfairness degree η_u

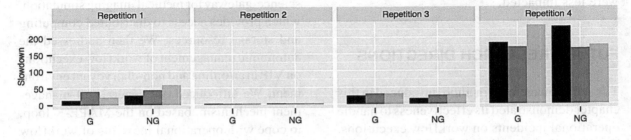

Figure 17. Granularity with fairness: comparison of the slowdowns

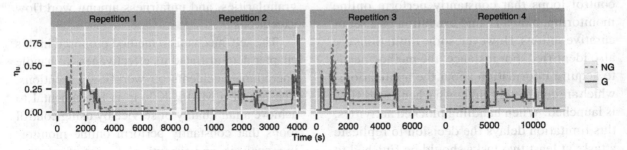

Figure 18. Granularity with fairness: unfairness degree η_u

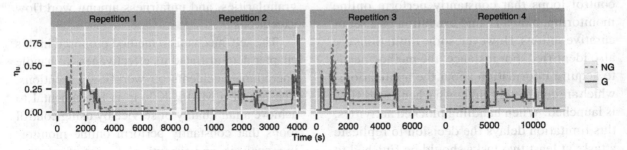

makespan standard deviation σ_m, slowdown standard deviation σ_s, and unfairness μ_u. Both Granularity and No-Granularity executions behave similarly until η_f reaches the threshold value $\tau_f = 0.55$. Tasks are considered too fine and the mechanism triggers task grouping. In all cases, the slowdown of the workflow executed with granularity (the first one on the Granularity set) is the lowest, i.e. its execution benefits of the grouping mechanism by saving waiting times and data transfers of shared input data. In the workflow set where the granularity control process is enabled, the unfairness value is up to a factor of 2 higher when compared to the workflow set where the granularity is disabled (No-Granularity).

Figure 17 shows the comparison of slowdown for the second experiment. Unfairness degree η_u is shown in Figure 18. Table 15 shows makespan standard deviation σ_m, slowdown standard deviation σ_s, and unfairness μ_u. Both Granularity and No-Granularity executions have similar unfairness values. The same behavior is observed in σ_m and σ_s for repetitions 1, 3, and

Table 15. Granularity with fairness: unfairness and standard deviation of the makespan and slowdown

	Repetition 1			Repetition 2			Repetition 3			Repetition 4		
	$\sigma_m(s)$	σ_s	$\mu(s)$	$\sigma_m(s)$	σ_s	$\mu(s)$	$\sigma_m(s)$	σ_s	$\mu(s)$	$\sigma_m(s)$	σ_s	$\mu(s)$
NF	2548	15.41	445	78	0.11	501	2768	6.11	718	1044	35.37	826
F	2384	13.47	335	456	0.23	455	1674	3.11	712	1028	34.53	754

4. This is not the case of repetition 2, in which resources suddenly appeared while tasks were being grouped. This resulted in parallelism loss for some workflow executions while the others were less impacted.

FUTURE RESEARCH DIRECTIONS

The self-management method introduced in this chapter demonstrated its effectiveness to handle operational incidents on workflow executions. The use of a MAPE-K loop is fundamental to achieve a fair quality of service by using control loops that constantly perform online monitoring, analysis, and execution of a set of curative actions. However, some limitations are also identified. For instance, the method needs to acquire information about the applications, which are completely unknown when a workflow is launched. When handling blocked activities, this limitation delays the decision to replicate a task; at least two tasks should be finished to estimate the median durations of each phase. The same delay is observed when handling the granularity of tasks, where tasks are grouped once an estimation of the duration is available. For the fairness process, the relative observed duration parameter also depends on task duration estimations, thus the metric does not consider this parameter while the estimations are not available. One approach to circumvent this issue could be to initialize such estimations according to observed distributions of these values, adjusting the estimations along the workflow execution.

CONCLUSION

In this chapter, we introduced the Virtual Imaging Platform (VIP), an openly accessible online science-gateway for medical imaging simulation, which provides access to distributed computing and storage resources. We then addressed the autonomic management of workflow executions on VIP in an online and non-clairvoyant environment. We introduced our general self-management mechanism, based on the MAPE-K loop, to cope with operational incidents of workflow executions. Then, we showed the application of our method to handle late task executions, task granularities, and unfairness among workflow executions.

The self-mechanism method proposed in this chapter demonstrated its effectiveness to handle operational incidents on workflow executions. The use of a MAPE-K loop is fundamental to achieve a fair quality of service by using control loops that constantly perform online monitoring, analysis, and execution of a set of curative actions. Although we showed the application of the self-management method in a medical imaging science-gateway using a grid infrastructure, the method is general enough to be used by other platforms and infrastructures.

REFERENCES

Agrawal, R., Imieliński, T., & Swami, A. (1993). Mining association rules between sets of items in large databases. *SIGMOD Record, 22*(2), 207–216. doi:10.1145/170036.170072

Ang, T. F., Ng, W. K., Ling, T. C., Por, L. Y., & Liew, C. S. (2009). A bandwidth-aware job grouping-based scheduling on grid environment. *Information Technology Journal, 8*(3), 372–377. doi:10.3923/itj.2009.372.377

Arabnejad, H., & Barbosa, J. (2012). *Fairness resource sharing for dynamic workflow scheduling on heterogeneous systems*. IEEE. doi:10.1109/ISPA.2012.94

Ben-Yehuda, O. A., Schuster, A., Sharov, A., Silberstein, M., & Iosup, A. (2012). *ExPERT: Pareto-efficient task replication on grids and a cloud*. IEEE. doi:10.1109/IPDPS.2012.25

Casanova, H., Desprez, F., & Suter, F. (2010). On cluster resource allocation for multiple parallel task graphs. *Journal of Parallel and Distributed Computing, 70*(12), 1193–1203. doi:10.1016/j.jpdc.2010.08.017

Chen, W., Ferreira da Silva, R., Deelman, E., & Sakellariou, R. (2013). *Balanced task clustering in scientific workflows*. IEEE. doi:10.1109/eScience.2013.40

Cirne, W., Brasileiro, F., Paranhos, D., Góes, L. F. W., & Voorsluys, W. (2007). On the efficacy, efficiency and emergent behavior of task replication in large distributed systems. *Parallel Computing, 33*(3), 213–234. doi:10.1016/j.parco.2007.01.002

De Jong, K. A. (1975). *An analysis of the behavior of a class of genetic adaptive systems*. University of Michigan.

Ferreira da Silva, R., Camarasu-Pop, S., Grenier, B., Hamar, V., Manset, D., Montagnat, J., ... Glatard, T. (2011). Multi-infrastructure workflow execution for medical simulation in the virtual imaging platform. In Proceedings of 2011 Health-Grid Conference. Academic Press.

Ferreira da Silva, R., & Glatard, T. (2013). A science-gateway workload archive to study pilot jobs, user activity, bag of tasks, task sub-steps, and workflow executions. In I. Caragiannis, M. Alexander, R. M. Badia, M. Cannataro, A. Costan, M. Danelutto, ... J. Weidendorfer (Eds.), *Euro-Par 2012: Parallel Processing Workshops* (pp. 79–88). Springer Berlin Heidelberg. Retrieved from http://link.springer.com/chapter/10.1007/978-3-642-36949-0_10

Ferreira da Silva, R., Glatard, T., & Desprez, F. (2012). *Self-healing of operational workflow incidents on distributed computing infrastructures*. IEEE. doi:10.1109/CCGrid.2012.24

Ferreira da Silva, R., Glatard, T., & Desprez, F. (2013a). On-line, non-clairvoyant optimization of workflow activity granularity on grids. In F. Wolf, B. Mohr, & D. Mey (Eds.), *Euro-Par 2013 Parallel Processing* (pp. 255–266). Springer Berlin Heidelberg. doi:10.1007/978-3-642-40047-6_28

Ferreira da Silva, R., Glatard, T., & Desprez, F. (2013b). Self-healing of workflow activity incidents on distributed computing infrastructures. *Future Generation Computer Systems, 29*(8), 2284–2294. doi:10.1016/j.future.2013.06.012

Ferreira da Silva, R., Glatard, T., & Desprez, F. (2013c). Workflow fairness control on online and non-clairvoyant distributed computing platforms. In F. Wolf, B. Mohr, & D. an Mey (Eds.), *Euro-Par 2013 Parallel Processing* (pp. 102–113). Springer Berlin Heidelberg. doi:10.1007/978-3-642-40047-6_13

Ferreira da Silva, R., Glatard, T., & Desprez, F. (2014). Controlling fairness and task granularity in distributed, online, non-clairvoyant workflow executions: Controlling fairness and task granularity in workflows. *Concurrency and Computation: Practice and Experience*. doi:10.1002/cpe.3303

Ferreira da Silva, R., Juve, G., Deelman, E., Glatard, T., Desprez, F., Thain, D., ... Livny, M. (2013). *Toward fine-grained online task characteristics estimation in scientific workflows*. ACM Press. doi:10.1145/2534248.2534254

Foster, I. (2001). The anatomy of the grid: Enabling scalable virtual organizations. *International Journal of High Performance Computing Applications*, *15*(3), 200–222. doi:10.1177/109434200101500302

Glatard, T., Lartizien, C., Gibaud, B., Ferreira da Silva, R., Forestier, G., Cervenansky, F., & Friboulet, D. et al. (2013). A virtual imaging platform for multi-modality medical image simulation. *IEEE Transactions on Medical Imaging*, *32*(1), 110–118. doi:10.1109/TMI.2012.2220154 PMID:23014715

Glatard, T., Montagnat, J., Lingrand, D., & Pennec, X. (2008). Flexible and efficient workflow deployment of data-intensive applications on grids with MOTEUR. *International Journal of High Performance Computing Applications*, *22*(3), 347–360. doi:10.1177/1094342008096067

Hirales-Carbajal, A., Tchernykh, A., Yahyapour, R., González-García, J. L., Röblitz, T., & Ramírez-Alcaraz, J. M. (2012). Multiple workflow scheduling strategies with user run time estimates on a grid. *Journal of Grid Computing*, *10*(2), 325–346. doi:10.1007/s10723-012-9215-6

Hsu, C.-C., Huang, K.-C., & Wang, F.-J. (2011). Online scheduling of workflow applications in grid environments. *Future Generation Computer Systems*, *27*(6), 860–870. doi:10.1016/j.future.2010.10.015

Kephart, J. O., & Chess, D. M. (2003). The vision of autonomic computing. *Computer*, *36*(1), 41–50. doi:10.1109/MC.2003.1160055

Litke, A., Skoutas, D., Tserpes, K., & Varvarigou, T. (2007). Efficient task replication and management for adaptive fault tolerance in mobile grid environments. *Future Generation Computer Systems*, *23*(2), 163–178. doi:10.1016/j.future.2006.04.014

Liu, Q., & Liao, Y. (2009). *Grouping-based fine-grained job scheduling in grid computing*. IEEE; doi:10.1109/ETCS.2009.132

Malik, D. S., Mordeson, J. N., & Sen, M. K. (1994). On subsystems of a fuzzy finite state machine. *Fuzzy Sets and Systems*, *68*(1), 83–92. doi:10.1016/0165-0114(94)90274-7

Muthuvelu, N., Chai, I., Chikkannan, E., & Buyya, R. (2010). On-line task granularity adaptation for dynamic grid applications. In C.-H. Hsu, L. T. Yang, J. H. Park, & S.-S. Yeo (Eds.), Algorithms and architectures for parallel processing (Vol. 6081, pp. 266–277). Berlin: Springer Berlin Heidelberg. Retrieved from http://www.springerlink.com/index/10.1007/978-3-642-13119-6_24

Muthuvelu, N., Chai, I., & Eswaran, C. (2008). *An adaptive and parameterized job grouping algorithm for scheduling grid jobs*. IEEE. doi:10.1109/ICACT.2008.4493929

Muthuvelu, N., Liu, J., Soe, N. L., Venugopal, S., Sulistio, A., & Buyya, R. (2005). A dynamic job grouping-based scheduling for deploying applications with fine-grained tasks on global grids. In Proceedings of the 2005 Australasian Workshop on Grid Computing and e-Research (Vol. 44, pp. 41–48). Darlinghurst, Australia: Australian Computer Society, Inc. Retrieved from http://dl.acm.org/citation.cfm?id=1082290.1082297

N'Takpe, T., & Suter, F. (2009). *Concurrent scheduling of parallel task graphs on multi-clusters using constrained resource allocations*. IEEE. doi:10.1109/IPDPS.2009.5161161

Ng Wai Keat, T. A. (2006). Scheduling framework for bandwidth-aware job grouping-based scheduling in grid computing. *Malaysian Journal of Computer Science, 19*.

Open Science Grid. (2014). Retrieved from http://www.opensciencegrid.org

Ramakrishnan, L., Huang, T. M., Thyagaraja, K., Zagorodnov, D., Koelbel, C., Kee, Y.-S., … Mandal, A. (2009). *VGrADS: Enabling e-science workflows on grids and clouds with fault tolerance*. ACM Press. doi:10.1145/1654059.1654107

Romanus, M., Mantha, P. K., McKenzie, M., Bishop, T. C., Gallichio, E., & Merzky, A., … Jha, S. (2012). The anatomy of successful ECSS projects: Lessons of supporting high-throughput high-performance ensembles on XSEDE. In *Proceedings of the 1st Conference of the Extreme Science and Engineering Discovery Environment: Bridging from the eXtreme to the Campus and Beyond* (pp. 46:1–46:9). New York, NY: ACM. doi:10.1145/2335755.2335843

Sabin, G., Kochhar, G., & Sadayappan, P. (2004). *Job fairness in non-preemptive job scheduling*. IEEE. doi:10.1109/ICPP.2004.1327920

Skowron, P., & Rzadca, K. (2013). *Non-monetary fair scheduling: A cooperative game theory approach*. ACM Press. doi:10.1145/2486159.2486169

Sommerfeld, D., & Richter, H. (2011). *Efficient grid workflow scheduling using a two-tier approach*. Paper presented at the HealthGrid 2011.

Tan, P.-N. (2006). *Introduction to data mining* (1st ed.). Boston: Pearson Addison Wesley.

Taylor, I. J. (2007). Workflows for e-science scientific workflows for grids. London: Springer. Retrieved from http://public.eblib.com/EBLPublic/PublicView.do?ptiID=337445

Tsaregorodtsev, A., Brook, N., Ramo, A. C., Charpentier, P., Closier, J., Cowan, G., & Zhelezov, A. et al. (2010). DIRAC3 – The new generation of the LHCb grid software. *Journal of Physics: Conference Series, 219*(6), 062029. doi:10.1088/1742-6596/219/6/062029

XSEDE. (2014). Retrieved from http://www.xsede.org

Zhao, H., & Sakellariou, R. (2006). *Scheduling multiple DAGs onto heterogeneous systems*. IEEE. doi:10.1109/IPDPS.2006.1639387

Zomaya, A. Y., & Chan, G. (2004). *Efficient clustering for parallel tasks execution in distributed systems*. IEEE. doi:10.1109/IPDPS.2004.1303164

ADDITIONAL READING

Callaghan, S., Deelman, E., Gunter, D., Juve, G., Maechling, P., Brooks, C., & Jordan, T. et al. (2010). Scaling up workflow-based applications. *Journal of Computer and System Sciences, 76*(6), 428–446. doi:10.1016/j.jcss.2009.11.005

Callaghan, S., Maechling, P., Small, P., Milner, K., Juve, G., Jordan, T. H., & Brooks, C. et al. (2011). Metrics for heterogeneous scientific workflows: A case study of an earthquake science application. *International Journal of High Performance Computing Applications*, 1094342011414743.

Camarasu-Pop, S., Glatard, T., Da Silva, R. F., Gueth, P., Sarrut, D., & Benoit-Cattin, H. (2013). Monte Carlo simulation on heterogeneous distributed systems: A computing framework with parallel merging and checkpointing strategies. *Future Generation Computer Systems, 29*(3), 728–738. doi:10.1016/j.future.2012.09.003

Camarasu-Pop, S., Glatard, T., Mościcki, J. T., Benoit-Cattin, H., & Sarrut, D. (2010). Dynamic partitioning of GATE Monte-Carlo simulations on EGEE. *Journal of Grid Computing*, 8(2), 241–259. doi:10.1007/s10723-010-9153-0

Chen, W., & Deelman, E. (2011). Workflow overhead analysis and optimizations. In *Proceedings of the 6th workshop on Workflows in support of large-scale science* (pp. 11-20). ACM. doi:10.1145/2110497.2110500

Deelman, E., Gannon, D., Shields, M., & Taylor, I. (2009). Workflows and e-Science: An overview of workflow system features and capabilities. *Future Generation Computer Systems*, 25(5), 528–540. doi:10.1016/j.future.2008.06.012

Deelman, E., Juve, G., Malawski, M., & Nabrzyski, J. (2013). Hosted science: Managing computational workflows in the cloud. *Parallel Processing Letters*, 23(02), 1340004. doi:10.1142/S0129626413400045

Ferreira da Silva, R., Chen, W., Juve, G., Vahi, K., & Deelman, E. (2014) Community Resources for Enabling Research in Distributed Scientific Workflows. 10th IEEE International Conference on e-Science.

Gil, Y., González-Calero, P. A., & Deelman, E. (2007). On the black art of designing computational workflows. In *Proceedings of the 2nd workshop on Workflows in support of large-scale science* (pp. 53-62). ACM. doi:10.1145/1273360.1273370

Glatard, T., Rousseau, M. E., Camarasu-Pop, S., Rioux, P., Sherif, T., Beck, N., ... & Evans, A. C. (2014) Interoperability between the CBRAIN and VIP web platforms for neuroimage analysis.

Hoffa, C., Mehta, G., Freeman, T., Deelman, E., Keahey, K., Berriman, B., & Good, J. (2008). On the use of cloud computing for scientific workflows. In eScience, 2008. eScience'08. IEEE Fourth International Conference on (pp. 640-645). IEEE. doi:10.1109/eScience.2008.167

Juve, G., Chervenak, A., Deelman, E., Bharathi, S., Mehta, G., & Vahi, K. (2013). Characterizing and profiling scientific workflows. *Future Generation Computer Systems*, 29(3), 682–692. doi:10.1016/j.future.2012.08.015

Kandaswamy, G., Mandal, A., & Reed, D. A. (2008). Fault tolerance and recovery of scientific workflows on computational grids. In Cluster Computing and the Grid, 2008. CCGRID'08. 8th IEEE International Symposium on (pp. 777-782). IEEE.

Kumar, V. S., Sadayappan, P., Mehta, G., Vahi, K., Deelman, E., Ratnakar, V., & Saltz, J. et al. (2009). An integrated framework for performance-based optimization of scientific workflows. In *Proceedings of the 18th ACM international symposium on High performance distributed computing* (pp. 177-186). ACM. doi:10.1145/1551609.1551638

Malawski, M., Juve, G., Deelman, E., & Nabrzyski, J. (2012). Cost-and deadline-constrained provisioning for scientific workflow ensembles in iaas clouds. In *Proceedings of the International Conference on High Performance Computing, Networking, Storage and Analysis* (p. 22). IEEE Computer Society Press. doi:10.1109/SC.2012.38

Montagnat, J., Isnard, B., Glatard, T., Maheshwari, K., & Fornarino, M. B. (2009). A data-driven workflow language for grids based on array programming principles. In *Proceedings of the 4th Workshop on Workflows in Support of Large-Scale Science* (p. 7). ACM. doi:10.1145/1645164.1645171

Olabarriaga, S. D., Jaghoori, M. M., Korkhov, V., van Schaik, B., & van Kampen, A. (2013, November). Understanding workflows for distributed computing: nitty-gritty details. In *Proceedings of the 8th Workshop on Workflows in Support of Large-Scale Science* (pp. 68-76). ACM. doi:10.1145/2534248.2534255

Plankensteiner, K., Prodan, R., & Fahringer, T. (2009). A new fault tolerance heuristic for scientific workflows in highly distributed environments based on resubmission impact. In e-Science, 2009. e-Science'09. Fifth IEEE International Conference on (pp. 313-320). IEEE. doi:10.1109/e-Science.2009.51

Russell, N., van der Aalst, W., & ter Hofstede, A. (2006, January). Workflow exception patterns. In *Advanced Information Systems Engineering* (pp. 288–302). Springer Berlin Heidelberg. doi:10.1007/11767138_20

Samak, T., Gunter, D., Goode, M., Deelman, E., Mehta, G., Silva, F., & Vahi, K. (2011). Failure prediction and localization in large scientific workflows. In *Proceedings of the 6th workshop on Workflows in support of large-scale science* (pp. 107-116). ACM. doi:10.1145/2110497.2110510

Shahand, S., Benabdelkader, A., Jaghoori, M. M., Mourabit, M. A., Huguet, J., Caan, M. W., & Olabarriaga, S. D. et al. (2014). A data-centric neuroscience gateway: Design, implementation, and experiences. *Concurrency and Computation*.

Singh, G., Vahi, K., Ramakrishnan, A., Mehta, G., Deelman, E., Zhao, H., & Katz, D. S. et al. (2007). Optimizing workflow data footprint. *Science Progress*, 15(4), 249–268.

Vöckler, J. S., Juve, G., Deelman, E., Rynge, M., & Berriman, B. (2011). Experiences using cloud computing for a scientific workflow application. In *Proceedings of the 2nd international workshop on Scientific cloud computing* (pp. 15-24). ACM. doi:10.1145/1996109.1996114

Wieczorek, M., Hoheisel, A., & Prodan, R. (2008). Taxonomies of the multi-criteria grid workflow scheduling problem. In Grid Middleware and Services (pp. 237-264). Springer US. doi:10.1007/978-0-387-78446-5_16

Zhang, Y., Mandal, A., Koelbel, C., & Cooper, K. (2009). Combined fault tolerance and scheduling techniques for workflow applications on computational grids. In Cluster Computing and the Grid, 2009. CCGRID'09. 9th IEEE/ACM International Symposium on (pp. 244-251). IEEE. doi:10.1109/CCGRID.2009.59

KEY TERMS AND DEFINITIONS

Grid Computing: Federation of heterogeneous resources distributed geographically in different administrative domains to provide computing and storage services for research communities.

Scientific Gateway: Integrates application software with access to computing and storage resources via web portals or desktop applications.

Scientific Workflow: Allows users to easily express multi-step computational tasks, for example retrieve data from an instrument or a database, reformat the data, and run an analysis.

Task Grouping: Groups fine-grained tasks into coarse-grained tasks to reduce the scheduling and queuing time overheads inherent to distributed computing platforms.

Task Replication: Common technique to increase the probability of successfully complete task executions in distributed computing platforms.

Task Resubmission: Most common technique to address failures on task executions in distributed computing platforms.

Unfairness Among Workflow Executions: Computing resources are not fairly (i.e. proportionally) allocated to workflow applications. It occurs when the demand is higher than the offer, that is, when some workflows are slowed down by concurrent executions.

Chapter 7
On Controlling Elasticity of Cloud Applications in CELAR

Georgiana Copil
Vienna University of Technology, Austria

Daniel Moldovan
Vienna University of Technology, Austria

Hung Duc Le
Vienna University of Technology, Austria

Hong-Linh Truong
Vienna University of Technology, Austria

Schahram Dustdar
Vienna University of Technology, Austria

Chrystalla Sofokleous
University of Cyprus, Cyprus

Nicholas Loulloudes
University of Cyprus, Cyprus

Demetris Trihinas
University of Cyprus, Cyprus

George Pallis
University of Cyprus, Cyprus

Marios D. Dikaiakos
University of Cyprus, Cyprus

Ioannis Giannakopoulos
National University of Athens, Greece

Nikolaos Papailiou
National University of Athens, Greece

Ioannis Konstantinou
National University of Athens, Greece

Craig Sheridan
FLEXIANT, UK

Christos K. K. Loverdos
Greek Research and Technology Network, Greece

Evangelos Floros
Greek Research and Technology Network, Greece

DOI: 10.4018/978-1-4666-8213-9.ch007

Copyright © 2015, IGI Global. Copying or distributing in print or electronic forms without written permission of IGI Global is prohibited.

ABSTRACT

Today's complex cloud applications are composed of multiple components executed in multi-cloud environments. For such applications, the possibility to manage and control their cost, quality, and resource elasticity is of paramount importance. However, given that the cost of different services offered by cloud providers can vary a lot with their quality/performance, elasticity controllers must consider not only complex, multi-dimensional preferences and provisioning capabilities from stakeholders but also various runtime information regarding cloud applications and their execution environments. In this chapter, the authors present the elasticity control approach of the EU CELAR Project, which deals with multi-dimensional elasticity requirements and ensures multi-level elasticity control for fulfilling user requirements. They show the elasticity control mechanisms of the CELAR project, from application description to multi-level elasticity control. The authors highlight the usefulness of CELAR's mechanisms for users, who can use an intuitive, user-friendly interface to describe and then to follow their application elasticity behavior controlled by CELAR.

1. INTRODUCTION

With the popularity and diversity of cloud-based solutions from cloud providers and application providers/developers, there is a considerable need to customize these solutions and to provide cloud users with fine-grained mechanisms of controlling their cloud applications.

Many existing frameworks allow the specification of various cloud application-related information, like the cloud application complex structure (e.g., Di Nitto et al. (2013)) and functional requirements (e.g., Di Cosmo et al. (2013)) when deploying the cloud application on the cloud. Moreover, many tools are capable of describing and deploying cloud applications (e.g., Binz et al. (2013)) on different cloud infrastructures. The requirements of the cloud application stakeholders differ and depend on a number of variables, e.g., the cost of the cloud application reported to the number of clients, or the various cloud application quality parameters (e.g., a banking cloud application differs greatly in requirements from a scientific cloud application). However, current state-of-the-art on elasticity control techniques require the specification of low-level, detailed information. For instance, Auto Scale applications provided by Amazon, Rackspace, Azure or RightScale enable users to specify, for each Virtual Machine they are using, scaling policies, depending on IaaS-level metrics. Proposed frameworks take into consideration cloud application level metrics, e.g., response time, but do not allow users to specify their requirements, the optimization factor being defined in an ad-hoc manner (e.g., equilibrium between the cost and response time) (e.g., Serrano et al. (2013), Simjanoska et al. (2013)).

The concept of multi-dimensional elasticity, covering resources elasticity, cost elasticity and quality elasticity (see Dustdar et al. (2011)) and the relations among them, shows how complex the elasticity control of cloud applications actually is. Such a concept facilitates custom cloud application elasticity depending on what a cloud application stakeholder (e.g., service provider) actually needs. A visual representation of the elasticity dimensions is shown in Figure 1, each of the main dimensions, cost, resource and quality being further decomposed into storage cost and network cost, CPU and memory, and respectively quality of data and performance. Elasticity is defined as the relationship among these dimensions, in time, which change for fulfilling user's elasticity requirements. Considering that distributed cloud applications have complex structures, each com-

Figure 1. Cloud service elasticity dimensions

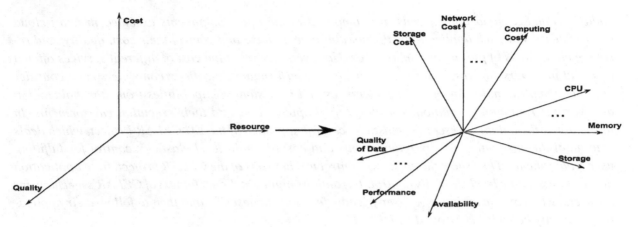

ponent having such complex elasticity behavior in time, we can affirm that elasticity controllers face challenging tasks in managing such applications.

For controlling elasticity of cloud services, several challenges need to be addressed:

1. Enabling the application stakeholders to *specify elasticity requirements*, encapsulating what is a proper application elasticity behavior is, as various users would evaluate subjectively whether their cloud applications are behaving properly (e.g., depending on the business perspective, the allocated cost, or intended QoS for clients).
2. Managing elasticity control at multiple application levels (e.g., components, groups of components or even application level) for fulfilling user's elasticity requirements.
3. Enforcing the elasticity control in a generic manner, on different types of cloud infrastructures, enabling stakeholders to obtain elastic applications on their preferred clouds.

In this chapter, we present elasticity control techniques developed in the EU CELAR Project for addressing above challenges. Our techniques enable cloud application stakeholders to specify the requirements at different levels of granularities, for controlling cloud applications at multiple

levels, applying different types of elasticity control mechanisms suited for data-intensive or compute-intensive parts of the cloud application. CELAR control techniques take real-time decisions for cloud application adaptation to meet user (any application stakeholder, e.g., application developer, or service provider) elasticity requirements, facilitating an automatic adaptation process of the cloud application to "outside" stimuli (e.g., workload, increasing cost, or decreasing quality) without the need of user intervention. Moreover, not only real-time adaptation decisions are enforced but also smart deployment of the cloud application, considering cloud providers applications and estimated cost with respect to quality and performance.

The rest of this chapter is organized as follows: Section 2 presents related work. In Section 3 we present CELAR users and their possible requirements with regard to the elasticity control, in Section 4 we present our elasticity specification language and show how CELAR's user interface component facilitates the description of multi-level elasticity requirements. The next section, Section 5, presents the conceptual architecture of the CELAR elasticity control module, and its techniques. We present experiments in Section 6, a discussion on control frameworks in Section 7 and conclude the chapter in Section 8.

Table 1. Computing resources control mechanisms

Provider	Elasticity Capability	Description
~okeanos	Create New VM	Creates a new Virtual Machine from an existing image
	Start VM	Starts an already created virtual machine, booting the OS
	Shutdown VM	Shuts down the operating system and stops the VM
	Reboot VM	Performs an OS restart
	Destroy VM	Deletes the VM
	Initialize VM Configuration	Number of CPUs, Size of RAM, System disk, OS, Network connectivity (dual IPV4/IPV6),
	Create private virtual L2 network	Creating a subnet (e.g., for constructing arbitrary network topologies)
Flexiant FCO	Create Bento Box	Template entire complex clusters and deploy at the click of a button
	Add/ Remove compute nodes to cluster	Flexiant offers the possibility of grouping compute nodes into clusters which are controlled/monitored as a group
	Initialize Server Configuration	Number of CPUs, Size of RAM, System disk, OS, Network connectivity (dual IPV4/IPV6), user, password, contextualization information
	Create Server	Creates a new server from an existing image
	Start Server	Starts an already creating server, booting the OS
	Duplicate Server	When Server A is duplicated, a new server (Server B) is created, and the initial configuration of Server A is applied to Server B
	Shutdown Server	Shuts down the operating system and stops the Server
	Reboot Server	Performs an OS restart
	Destroy Server	Deletes the Server
	Manage Firewalls	Add/remove/configure firewalls for the server
	Manage Chef Settings for Server	Edit chef account settings
	Create/Manage Virtual Data Center	Virtual Data Center is a logical grouping of servers
Application Specific	Configure software x with configuration y	Configure software which is part of the application or on which the application depends, in order to have different quality/performance/cost parameters for the application.

2. RELATED WORK

In this section, we take a look at current cloud application elasticity status quo regarding cloud application control. We present the elasticity capabilities of cloud providers which are part of the CELAR project, both on data and on computing resources. Next, we focus on computing resource and data resource elasticity control, and compare the state of the art with what we do for controlling elasticity in CELAR. Finally, we take a look at higher, and multiple level application control existent in literature, and compare our approach with them.

2.1 Computing and Data Resources Low-Level Controls

We firstly consider the possibilities of runtime reconfiguration offered by the CELAR cloud providers, Flexiant and ~okeanos. Table 1 presents the fundamental control mechanisms available for computing and network resources, while Table 2 presents data elasticity control mechanisms. Although they have different names for the applications being offered (e.g., VM and Server refer to Virtual Machine), they have similar offerings. For instance, common elasticity control mechanisms are create/start/reboot VM, with minor differences e.g., Flexiant FCO offers Bento Boxes which are complex clusters which can be deployed as a group, while ~okeanos offers the opportunity of constructing arbitrary network topologies. Other big cloud providers (e.g., Google, Azure, or Amazon) typically offer similar capabilities, in the sense of VM and disk level horizontal or vertical scaling, with variations on hot-pluggable capabilities. Although they currently offer low-level capabilities, there is a considerable effort towards offering services between IaaS and PaaS, e.g., Google managed VMs, part of their PaaS services, facilitate automated management similar with the management offered for manually created VMs.

2.2 Computing Resource Elasticity Control

To leverage the low-level elasticity capabilities of cloud infrastructures, several controllers have been developed. Current computing elasticity controllers such as Amazon AutoScaling[i], Paraleap

Table 2. Data elasticity control mechanisms

Provider	Elasticity Capability	Description
~okeanos	Storage Configurations	Local, distributed and centralized, out of which both SAN, NAS
	Volume creation	Create volume with specified size
	Volume deletion	Delete specified volume
	On-the-air attachment of volume	Attach volume to existing computing node (VM), without the need of rebooting the node
	On-the-air de-attachment of volume	De-attach volume from existing computing node (VM) without the need of rebooting the node
	Snapshotting existing volume	Create a snapshot of the specified volume (available copy-on-write of snapshotable volumes)
	Hashing snapshots	Facilitates deduplication, thus reducing the storage cost of each hashed object
	Resizing existing volume	Resize volume to specified size
Flexiant FCO	Storage Configurations	Three types of storage: local, distributed and centralized, out of which both SAN, NAS
	Create disk	Create disk with specified size
	Remove disk	Remove specified disk
	Snapshot disk	Take a snapshot of the disk
	Add the disk to a new or existing deployment instance	Add existing disk to a deployment instance (group of servers)
Data Specific	Clean Data	Remove data which is not valid for improving the data completeness and data access performance
	Move Data	Move data from one disk to another, from one block to another, etc.
	Other Data Specific Control Mechanisms	Reconfigure data in different other ways
Application Specific	Configure software x with configuration y	Configure software which is part of the application or on which the application depends, in order to have different quality/performance/cost parameters for the application.

AzureWatch and RightScale can scale – automatically and seamlessly – large Cloud applications. However, their controlling actions are limited to only scaling horizontally the tiers of an application based on a small number of low-level metrics (e.g., CPU usage and memory usage). For a simple web application, such elasticity controllers are capable of only scaling the application server tier and the distributed database backend by adding/removing virtual instances, when predefined thresholds are violated. Moreover, for large-scale applications, in order to reduce costs and match the current demand, one requires from elasticity controllers to apply various complex adaptation mechanisms, which we refer to as *elasticity control plans*. These mechanisms are required to carefully assess the actual application logic with respect to its internal dependencies and (implicit) requirements towards the cloud provider APIs, including communication, consistency management and scheduling. Overall, managing elasticity of cloud applications by using the most popular mechanisms of computing resources control is not a trivial task. For small-scale application deployments, organizations can (de-) allocate resources manually, but for large-scale distributed applications which require a deployment comprised of multiple virtual instances, which often have complex interdependencies, this task must be done, inevitably, automatically.

To facilitate complex adaptation mechanisms, an elastic compute resource provisioning system must not limit its decisions based on low-level monitoring information. Instead, it is required to assess heterogeneous types of monitoring information of different granularity, from low-level system metrics (e.g., CPU, memory, network utilization) to high-level application specific metrics (e.g., latency, throughput, availability), which are collected across multiple levels (physical, virtualization, application level) in a Cloud environment at different time intervals, as Trihinas et al. (2014) do. To accommodate these limitations, our work

incorporates JCatascopia (presented in detail in Trihinas et al. (2014)), a fully-automated, multi-layer, interoperable cloud monitoring system which provides access to monitoring information through its REST API.

To enforce complex adaptation mechanisms, decisions originating from an elasticity controller must also be aware of what are the offerings and limitations of the underlying IaaS provider. Specifically, the controller must consider:

1. What are the resizing actions permitted per resource, and
2. The quotas for each user/tenant.

Knowing the elasticity capabilities of each IaaS resource is of extreme importance when determining which elasticity mechanism should be enforced. For example, let us consider two IaaS providers (Provider A and Provider B) where only the first provider offers users the capability of vertically scaling virtual instances by allocating more memory, while both offer horizontally scaling capabilities. If we consider a three-tier web application deployed on Provider B, the control mechanism can only scale horizontally the Application Server Tier when memory utilization increases. For Provider A though, the decision-making mechanism can take advantage of Provider A's extra capabilities and decide upon either scaling horizontally the Application Server Tier or, enlarging the allocated memory of existing instances. This approach takes cost into consideration since resizing existing VM(s) may be cheaper than constantly initializing small virtual instances. Additionally, it is important for elasticity controllers to also consider the per tenant quotas such as:

1. The total capacity of resources that a tenant can allocate; and
2. The multiplicity of resources that can be concurrently allocated at any given time.

In continuation of the previous example, if the permitted number of allocated VMs per tenant is low, our application deployed on Provider B will face quota problems when scaling to satisfy very high demands, whereas for Provider A, an intelligent elasticity controller can scale the application both vertically and horizontally to satisfy an even higher demand. To accommodate these limitations, our work constructs an information management tool (described in detail in Trihinas et al. (2013)) which provides access to IaaS specific information.

The inherent dynamicity in the run-time topology of elastic cloud applications raises several issues in run-time control. As elastic applications scale out/in due to elasticity requirements, their underlying virtual infrastructure is subject to run-time changes due to additional/removal of virtual resources (e.g., virtual machines). Thus, cloud application monitoring must avoid associating monitoring information only with virtual resources, as these resources are volatile, and are not present for the whole lifetime of the application. For example, when the application usage is low, one application component could use only one virtual machine, but during peak times would allocate more resources, and deallocate them when load decreases. The other extreme of monitoring just the application level metrics (e.g, response time) is also insufficient, as such high level metrics do not give any indicator on the performance of the underlying virtual infrastructure. Thus, systems for monitoring elastic cloud applications must follow a multi-level monitoring approach. Both virtual infrastructure and application level monitoring data must be collected, and structured according to application's logical structure, as done by Moldovan et al. (2013). Evaluating the cost of an application running in a cloud environment is challenging due to the diversity and heterogeneity of pricing schemes employed by various cloud providers (e.g., Provider A may charge per I/O operation, while Provider B might charge only per storage size). This heterogeneity generates a gap between the monitoring metrics collected by a monitoring system and the metrics targeted by cloud billing schemes. Moreover, evaluating the cost of the application requires information about particular cloud pricing schemes, information that cannot be monitored directly by a cloud monitoring system. To address these issues, our work provides MELA (Moldovan et al. (2013)), which uses monitoring information collected from cloud monitoring tools and the cloud application structure, to provide a cross-layered, multi-level view over the performance and cost of elastic cloud applications.

2.3 Data Resources Elasticity Control

Data-related elasticity controls of cloud application usually entail, at system level, removal/addition of data nodes in clusters of data. Elastically scaling data resources in the cloud requires a data-aware approach in order to obtain the full benefit of extra added resources. The first and most important thing that needs to be addressed during resource adjustment is uneven data distributions: when data nodes join or leave from a data-storage component, they create imbalances in the initial data distribution. Even when resources do not change, unpredictable data access patterns often create unbalanced distributions that degrade performance. In that cases, load balancing approaches that redistribute data between nodes are necessary.

Consistent hashing techniques described by Karger et al. (1997) are a common and effective solution for data control. The majority of modern NoSQL stores (e.g., Lakshman et al. (2010), DeCandia et al. (2007)) make use of such techniques to equally allocate data and incoming requests to the available nodes. Although hashing initially solves the data to machines allocation problem, there are many situations in which this proves suboptimal. Hashing destroys locality and thus, it cannot be employed in situations where semantically close items need to be stored in an order-preserving way. When an order-preserving partitioner is desired, different load balancing schemes need to be devised in order to support range queries. Range queries are present in many popular applications. Therefore, algorithms and systems which handle this case are of great importance. In the literature, there are many load balancing algorithms (e.g., Bharambe et al. (2004), Aspnes et al. (2004), Ganesan et al. (2004), Karger et al (2004), Konstantinou et al. (2011)) which support range queries.

The need to support range queries highlights another problem which belongs to the load balancing family. Although data placement can be balanced, there may be imbalances in the data request load. Ananthanarayanan et al. (2011) show that in a highly skewed data access distribution, where a small portion of popular data may get the majority of the applied load, the system performance may degrade even in over provisioned infrastructures.

DBalancer proposed by Konstantinou et al. (2013) is a generic and automated system, offering load balancing in NoSQL datastores, which we choose to use and extend. DBalancer is a generic distributed module that performs fast and cost-efficient load balancing on top of any distributed NoSQL datastore. The two main features of DBalancer are the datastore and algorithm abstraction. DBalancer is completely independent of the underlying NoSQL datastore.

2.4 Complex Service Elasticity Control

Schatzberg et al. (2012) raise issues that appear in cloud elasticity control and outline that in cloud computing elasticity is an important area of research, which will facilitate the development of applications that would fully benefit from the advantages of cloud computing and from on-demand resources allocation. The different perspectives of cloud applications performance/cost/quality measurement are outlined by Li et al. (2012) who propose a list of categories of metrics which are used for evaluating cloud applications. Their retrieved cloud application evaluation metrics are scattered over three aspects of cloud applications: economics having as subdimensions cost and elasticity evaluation metrics, performance with subdimensions communication, computation, memory, storage evaluation metrics and security evaluation metrics. The abstract metrics are associated to measurable metrics for easier grasp of reality and for being able to actually compute the abstract metrics.

Truong et al. (2010) estimate the cost of application hosting on the cloud considering different sub-costs which may interfere during the lifetime of the application. Villegas et al. [Villegas 2012] propose a framework for conducting empirical research in different IaaS clouds, comparing different allocation and provisioning policies. The authors emphasize the importance of understanding the performance and cost associated with different provisioning or allocation policies, for being able to properly manage their application's workloads.

Gonzalez et al. (2012) propose cloud infrastructure-level virtual machine management for increasing the VM availability. The authors also provide a study on how different properties of the cloud infrastructure affect the VM availability. Chaisiri et al. (2012) focus on the complexity of selecting cloud applications under different provisioning plans, such as reservation and on-demand, defining an optimal cloud resource provisioning algorithm that can provision resources in multiple provisioning stages. Using deterministic equivalent formulation, sample-average approximation, and Benders decomposition, their proposed solution minimizes the total cost of resource provisioning in cloud computing environments.

3. MOTIVATING SCENARIOS

We focus on user scenarios which we encountered in CELAR, namely:

1. The needs of a cancer research application, and
2. The requirements of a gaming application.

For these cases, the applications are designed such that they facilitate as many elasticity capabilities, in order to facilitate better elasticity control.

3.1 Cancer Research Application

The first application, SCAN, shown in Figure 2 and described in detail in Xing et al. (2014), is a cancer research application designed by the Cancer Research UK Manchester Institute, which analyzes large-scale population genome data for helping doctors to determine personalized treatments. The SCAN pipeline consists of four types of data processes:

1. Genome data process;
2. Proteome data process;
3. Cell Image data process;
4. Integrative network analysis.

It employs a set of biological application tools for those various data processes, such as Burrows-Wheeler Aligner (BWA) for gene alignment, Genome Analysis Toolkit (GATK) for e.g., gene variations detection, The Global Proteome Machine for proteomic data analyses, MaxQuant, CellProfiler for cell image analyses, or Cytoscape for data integration.

There are two major challenges regarding cloud-based deployments of such research pipelines. First, different stages of the pipeline may require substantially different levels and types of resources. For example, mapping of deep sequencing data to genome annotation via a relational database such as ENSEMBL relies on the ability to perform frequent joins across multiple tables containing millions of rows, while computation of downstream statistics is often dependent on repeated numerical calculations over permuted data. Second, a specific bio-component within a SCAN stage may have different resource needs due to the size and complexity of the data for different SCAN runs. For example, SCAN mutation detec-

Figure 2. SCAN scientific application

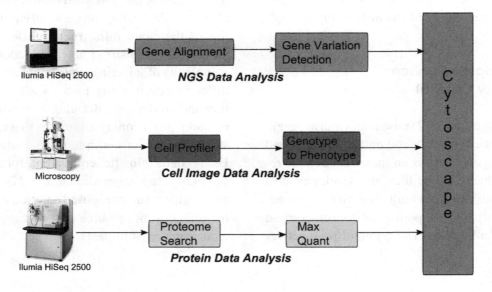

tion process will take different time for various type of genome data, e.g., 4 CPU/hours for Whole Exome Sequencing data (WES) or 10 CPU/hours for Whole Genome Sequencing (WGS) data.

To address the challenges described above, SCAN has been designed as an elasticity-ready bio-computing application so that it can be intelligently orchestrated for adjusting resources to the various situations which can be encountered. For instance, considering the fact that cancer diagnosis and treatment is "time-sensitive", sometimes doctors may need the result of SCAN for a patient in a particular period. Therefore SCAN should be executed according to user specified priories. It is thus important to be able to decide on the adequate amount and type of resources, depending on various metrics, e.g., available money, desired time, or desired accuracy. Moreover, SCAN is comprised of a wide range of bio-applications and may require a large amount of heterogeneous computing resources. The SCAN users may need to query information about execution of bio-applications within different cloud infrastructures in order to assist SCAN users to define, for example, policy of the execution.

Based on the application description above, our control will ensure the following:

1. Deciding the appropriate size of resources,
2. Ensuring predefined levels of service quality,
3. Ensuring that the SCAN pipeline runs within desired costs, and
4. Deciding the concurrency level and appropriate time periods of different stages.

Moreover, since SCAN is comprised of pipes (i.e., components grouped together), the control needs to facilitate the fulfillment of multi-level requirements (e.g., a specific pipe needs to finish executing, with certain quality, before another pipe), and controlling high level metrics (e.g., overall application cost, quality indicators over specific pipes).

The SCAN application needs to benefit from the on-demand storage capabilities offered by the IaaS providers (~okeanos[vii] or Flexiant[vi]), as well as application-specific control mechanisms, this way offering personalized treatments within time and cost constraints. SCAN performance and cost can be customized according to real-time elasticity metrics, thus resulting in a personalized control of the application. For understanding the relation between requirements regarding SCAN execution, and the performance/cost obtained, CELAR's user interface component can be used to browse historical execution data. Moreover, cost and functionalities offered by different IaaS providers can be compared and elasticity control actions taken during the execution of the SCAN pipeline can be analyzed.

3.2 Gaming Application

Playgen's Data Play is a gaming application, shown in Figure 3 and described in detail in Cox et al. (2014). The DataPlay application is designed with elasticity in mind. The main elasticity capabilities designed and embedded in DataPlay are horizontal and vertical scaling of game components, such as the Game Server, the Data Processing component, and the Data Access layer. For enforcing such capabilities, implemented elasticity actions target both the virtual infrastructure (e.g., adding/removing virtual machines), and the application level (e.g., reconfiguring load balancers or data storage).

Starting from industry known guidelines, Data Play requirements are response time<1.5 seconds, I/O Performance >= 100 MBps, and cost as small as possible. CELAR will analyze the behavior of all Data Play components' instances, and, leveraging on the embedded elasticity capabilities of the Data Play, take appropriate actions to ensure the performance and reduce cost of running the Data Play in cloud. Starting from the game requirements, our controller will extract system-level require-

Figure 3. DataPlay application

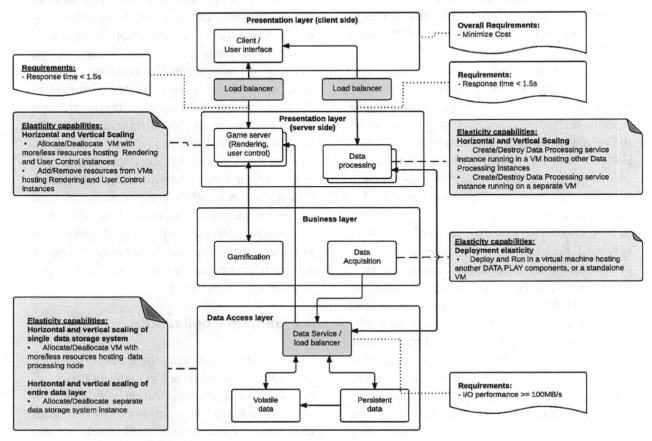

ments (e.g., CPU usage, memory usage, disk I/O performance) and application level requirements for the individual game components. Having a complete view over system and application level requirements, CELAR will monitor and enforce the supplied requirements using the game's elasticity capabilities. DataPlay is centered on users exploring data (Volatile and Persistent data), thus introducing data-related elasticity concerns. Persistent data is static, or changed with a very low frequency (a couple times a year), but it is frequently accessed, highlighting the need for data consistency. Volatile data is created for each DataPlay user, and, for performance, holds temporary data .If a client is manipulating a dataset, then the application

treats that as a different table for speed reasons, but if the client's session expires then that table is destroyed. Therefore, for this application we have a continuous increase/decrease in data depending on the client number, on the size of the datasets they are interested in and on the time they use that data for.

Large volumes of data can also come in at any time, for instance from tweets and RSS feed updates. However, the volatile data is copied for individual users depending on their interest and gameplay. For this kind of data usage, data freshness is an important factor, as one needs to have as fresh as possible trending-related data, especially if the data s/he uses has been cached for performance reasons.

4. ELASTICITY REQUIREMENTS SPECIFICATION

4.1 SYBL Overview

For describing what types of elasticity controls could be required, considering the complexity of CELAR user's elasticity requirements, we examine various types of elasticity requirements from different stakeholders, at different granularities, presented in detail in Copil et al. (2013a). Elasticity requirements are abstract or high level demands formulated by application stakeholders (e.g., application provider, application developer) which affect the application pathway in the elasticity space presented in detail in Moldovan et al. (2013). Although current state of the art (e.g., Amazon AutoScale) facilitates description of low-level, infrastructure-related requirements, the application stakeholder should to be able to specify requirements concerning more abstract metrics (e.g., the cost per application user that the stakeholder needs to pay per hour).

SYBL is a language for elasticity requirements specification, having three types of constructs at its core, enabling the specification of elasticity requirements:

1. **Monitoring:** Enables the designation of different metrics or formulas of metrics which should be monitored;
2. **Constraint:** Specifies the desired state of the application; while
3. **Strategy:** Specifies the desired behavior of the application or of different application parts.

More information regarding the SYBL language is available in Copil et al. (2013a). SYBL allows the specification of elasticity requirements at three levels: application unit level for component related elasticity requirements, service topology elasticity requirements related to groups of components and application level for application related elasticity requirements. At service unit level, the SYBL user (e.g., service provider, or service developer) can specify requirements for the component which is of interest (e.g., for a business unit we can have STRATEGY CASE NumberOfClients<100 AND small(ResponseTime): minimize (cost)). For service topology level, SYBL user can specify higher level goals which target higher level metrics (e.g., CONSTRAINT DataAccessSkewness < 90%), while at cloud service level s/he can specify complex requirements for the entire cloud service, targeting the overall behavior of the cloud service (e.g., STRATEGY maximize (cost/clientNb))

The SYBL language is not tied to any specific implementation language (e.g., SYBL elasticity requirements can be seen as Java annotations, C# annotations, or Python decorators). Moreover, the SYBL elasticity requirements can be injected into any cloud application description language (e.g., TOSCA standard proposed by OASIS (2013)) or can be specified separately through XML description. The current language interpretation mechanism is implemented in Java, and supports TOSCA-injected, XML-based, or Java annotation-based elasticity requirements specification.

Figure 4 shows an excerpt from a TOSCA policy based specification, describing the constraint that the cost for the PilotCloudService should be below 100$. The SYBL elasticity requirements can be easily integrated within TOSCA policies, and interpreted by the CELAR Decision Module. When discovering that this requirement is violate, the Decision Module will evaluate a series of possible actions to be enforced for ensuring that the user's requirements are fulfilled, as we show in Section 5.

We therefore facilitate the user to specify SYBL elasticity requirements with the help of CELAR user interface, as part of the process of cloud application description, as presented below.

Figure 4. SYBL elasticity requirement in TOSCA

```
<tosca:ServiceTemplate name="PilotCloudService">
    <tosca:Policy name="Co1" policyType="SYBLConstraint">
        Co1:CONSTRAINT Cost &lt 100\$
    </tosca:Policy>
    -
</tosca:ServiceTemplate>
```

4.2 SYBL Elasticity Requirements Specification with c-Eclipse

To simplify the task of the developer, we integrate elasticity requirement specification into c-Eclipse, which facilitates the user to describe his/her application, requirements for it and monitor application evolution at runtime (c-Eclipse is described in detail in Sofokleous et al. (2014)). C-Eclipse enables the specification of SYBL elasticity requirements and their injection into TOSCA XML application descriptions. The TOSCA language does not directly specify how to define elasticity requirements for Cloud applications. The way c-Eclipse achieves elasticity specification in TOSCA is by making use of TOSCA's Policy element. TOSCA defines "Policies" as the means by which we can express non-functional behavior or quality-of-services for an application (see OASIS TOSCA Specification (2013)). Thus, we make use of the two types of elasticity requirements defined in the SYBL XML schema (Constraint and Strategy), and inject them into TOSCA as Policy elements of the corresponding types.

Figure 5 presents the Properties View of c-Eclipse, specifically the Elasticity Tab, through which users can define the elasticity requirements of their application in an intuitive, user-friendly manner. Users can use simple low level metrics offered by the platform, such as CPU Usage, to complex user-defined metrics (e.g., cost/client/h), and specify the desired requirements for these metrics. They can also define more complex metrics by combining simple metrics with mathematical operators to design new metrics. Both types of metrics can be used to formulate the Constraints

and Strategies for an application, using the SYBL language defined in Copil et al. (2013). In this case, the user chooses to specify a strategy which should be applied when a condition holds, i.e., when cost is sufficiently small, 1$, the strategy of minimizing throughput should be applied. This takes into account that the throughput cannot be minimized indefinitely, and that the stakeholders have a strict upper bound for the cost per hour which shouldn't be exceeded.

The user-specified elasticity requirements are automatically translated into XML SYBL requirements which in turn are injected into the XML TOSCA description of the application. The code snippet below reflects the elasticity strategy specified through c-Eclipse, shown in Figure 6. In this strategy, the user wants to maximize throughput for an application component (right side of Figure 5), when the cost is less than 1 $/h (in the center of Figure 5, the "Apply Strategy under Condition" window).

Elasticity requirements can be linked to simple application components, composite components or the entire application, depending on which graphical element from the application description is selected when the user specifies the requirements.

5. MULTI-LEVEL AND MULTI-DIMENSIONAL ELASTICITY CONTROL

In this section we focus on the mechanisms used in CELAR for multi-level control of the cloud application, for fulfilling user's elasticity requirements.

Figure 5. Elasticity requirements specification with c-Eclipse

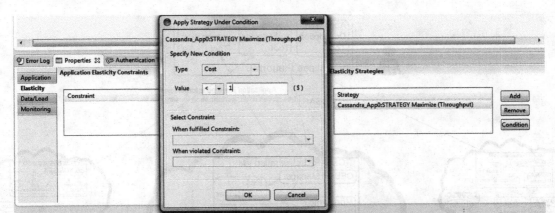

5.1 CELAR Elasticity Control Overview

CELAR proposes application elasticity management, from deployment to runtime control, in an automated fashion. CELAR targets the control of applications deployed in a single cloud. For each cloud where the user has an account and at least one application deployed, consuming cloud provider resources, CELAR deploys an orchestration instance (CELAR Orchestration VM in Figure 7), hosting all CELAR components necessary for deploying, monitoring, analyzing and controlling application's elasticity.

Figure 7 shows a snapshot of a CELAR-based deployment, containing all CELAR components, the application which is being controlled and communication among them, with examples for ~okeanos and Flexiant cloud providers. CELAR user first describes his/her application through c-Eclipse, in the Application Description Tool. This description includes application topology, elasticity requirements at the different levels of the cloud application, and specific artifacts of the application (e.g., web services, or configuration scripts). All information from application description step is described using TOSCA

Figure 6. Elasticity strategy expressed through policy template by c-Eclipse

```
<tosca:PolicyTemplate type="pol:ElasticityStrategy" id="Throughput_Strategy">
    <tosca:Properties>
            <sybl:StrategyProperties>
                    <Condition>
                            <BinaryRestrictionsConjunction Type="LessThan">
                                    <LeftHandSide>
                                            <Metric>cost</Metric>
                                    </LeftHandSide>
                                    <RightHandSide>
                                            <Number Metric="$/h" >1</Number>
                                    </RightHandSide>
                            </BinaryRestrictionsConjunction>
                    </Condition>
                    <ToEnforce ActionName="Maximize" Parameter="Throughput"/>
            </sybl:StrategyProperties>
    </tosca:Properties>
</tosca:PolicyTemplate>
```

Figure 7. Communication among CELAR components

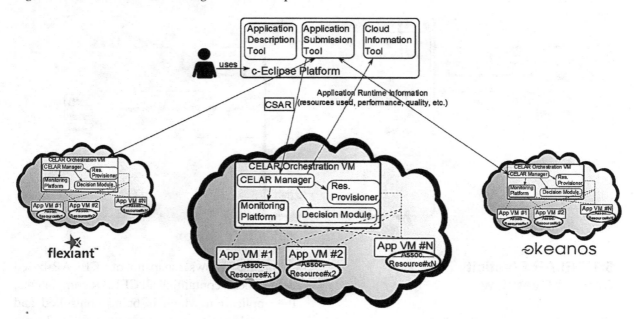

standard defined by OASIS Technical Committee (2013), the description together with the artifacts being packed into a Cloud Application Archive (CSAR) and using the c-Eclipse Application Submission Tool, the cloud provider is selected, the authentication information set and the cloud application deployment call is sent to the CELAR Manager from the CELAR Orchestration VM on the selected cloud. For the same user, we can have a single orchestration instance per cloud provider, which controls and monitors all the user's applications. The CELAR Manager has the mission of coordinating the communication among CELAR modules:

1. It receives the cloud application archive from c-Eclipse, forwards it to decision module in case the user needs suggestions regarding application configurations, and then sends it to Resource Provisioner for allocating the necessary resources,

2. Whenever the Decision Module, which controls the cloud application, decides that control processes need to be enforced for fulfilling user-specified requirements, the CELAR Manager coordinates the enforcement of the generated action plan with the Resource Provisioner.

Figure 8. Elasticity control process – from description to control

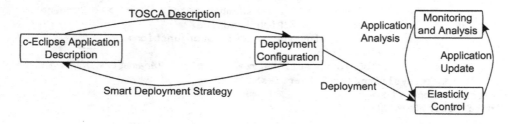

The process of controlling the cloud application is depicted in Figure 8, from c-Eclipse application description, to deployment configuration and elasticity control. Whenever the CELAR user would like a more complex application configuration describing the resources used or with the software artifacts to be deployed, it can ask, through c-Eclipse, for a smart deployment strategy, containing complete information for deployment (e.g., resource configuration, or missing artifacts). After the deployment, the application is monitored and analyzed continuously, and elasticity control is enforced for fulfilling elasticity requirements.

For analyzing and controlling the cloud service, we model various application-related information into a dependency graph, based on the model published in Copil et al. (2013b), depicted in Figure 9. At runtime, the information is represented as a dependency graph, with each concept instance (e.g., Composite Component) from the model being a node, while the relationships (e.g., hasElasticityCapabilities in Figure 9) are edges connecting them.

Figure 9. Cloud application model
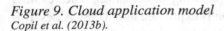
Copil et al. (2013b).

The structural information captures components (e.g., NoSQL database node, or a tool in the SCAN pipeline) and groups of semantically connected components into composite components (e.g., business layer, or a SCAN stage). To each of these, during runtime, are associated resources like processes, virtual machines (equivalent to servers on Flexiant cloud), virtual clusters (equivalent to virtual data centers in Flexiant).

5.2 Cloud Application Deployment Configuration

For configuring cloud application deployment, we have developed a service, SALSA (Le et al. (2014)), generating smart deployment configurations, by analyzing application structure and elasticity requirements. This service takes a high level application description, application profiling information, and available cloud description information and generates a deployment configuration.

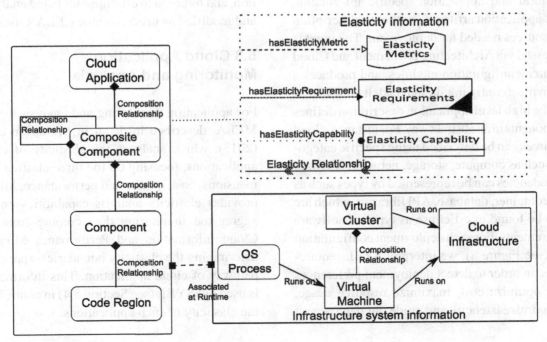

Figure 10. Flow of deployment configuration

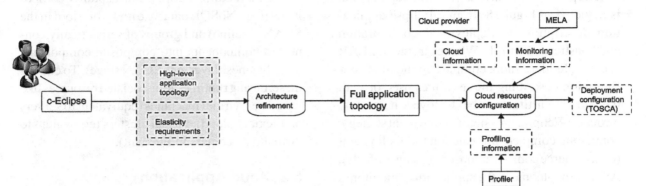

Figure 10 depicts the simple flow of generating a deployment plan from the high level application description. When deciding whether or not they want to use smart deployment, the CELAR users consider how complex the application is, and how familiar they are with the application. The trigger for a smart deployment and necessary information is sent by c-Eclipse when a new application deployment or a re-deployment of running components is needed.

The input for SALSA Service is a TOSCA description from c-Eclipse which consists of a high level application description, containing only structural and application-specific information (e.g., application artifacts), without a description of resources needed for deployment. The input is processed via Architecture refinement and Cloud resource configuration modules, and produces a deployment configuration and sends it to c-Eclipse.

The high level application description defines components in an abstract way. For instance, cloud resources can be described using specific categories such as compute, storage, network; software dependencies can be represented by types such as web container, database, API libraries, which are all to be found in c-Eclipse as types of software requirements. For each deployment configuration step (see Figure 8), we interpret SYBL requirements, in order to detect deployment preferences (e.g., optimize cost, maximize resource usage, or maximize latency), and guide our deployment

configuration with identified preferences. The architecture refinement step in Figure 10 aims to enrich the application topology with artifacts/software using CELAR repository of existing artifacts (e.g., Tomcat web server). The output of this step is a full application topology with all the needed artifacts. Moreover, in the cloud resource configuration step of Figure 10, we associate the required resources to each components/artifacts previously selected, using cloud provider and application profiling information. The resulted configuration is expressed as a TOSCA description, and returned to c-Eclipse for being analyzed and modified as needed by the CELAR user.

5.3 Cloud Application Monitoring and Analysis

For application monitoring and analysis we use MELA, described in detail in Moldovan et al. (2013), which analyzes the elasticity of cloud applications, focusing on the three elasticity dimensions: cost, quality and performance. MELA provides elasticity analysis capabilities on the aggregated monitoring data coming from the Cloud Information and Performance Monitor, determining the elasticity boundaries, space and pathway of cloud application. This information is used by rSYBL (see Section 5.4) in controlling the elasticity of such applications.

Figure 11. Flow of elasticity control

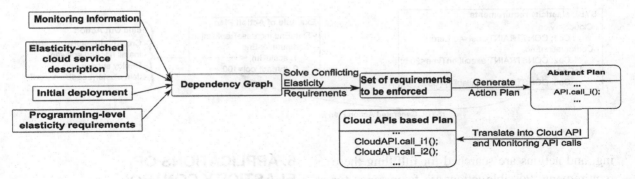

For analyzing and controlling the cloud application, elasticity space boundaries are determined for all application components, composite components, and whole application, and are equal to the maximum and minimum encountered metric values when the elasticity requirements were respected. Thus, starting from supplied user requirements, MELA determines and continuously updates requirements for the rest of the application components, requirements then enforced by rSYBL, as described in Section 5.4.

For elasticity control of cloud applications we also use the elasticity pathway function, which gives an indicator on the historical behavior of the cloud application and correlations between the application's metrics. The elasticity pathway information provides a base for refining user-defined requirements, and validating the Decision Module's control strategy. In the current prototype of the MELA we adapt as elasticity pathway function an unsupervised behavior learning technique using self-organizing maps (SOMs) proposed by Dean et al. (2012). We classify monitoring snapshots by encountering rate in DOMINANT, NON-DOMINANT, and RARE. Such a pathway is important for understanding if the regular behavior of the application fulfills user-defined elasticity requirements.

5.4 Cloud Application Elasticity Control

Considering the model of the application described through the runtime dependency graph presented in the previous subsection, we use rSYBL elasticity control, described in detail in Copil et al. (2013b), to enable multiple levels elasticity control of the described application, based on the flow shown in Figure 11. The flow presented in Figure 11 is executed continually, and is based on the monitoring information, application description, initial deployment and different types of elasticity requirements (left hand side of Figure 11). The elasticity requirements are evaluated and conflicts which may appear among them are resolved. The dependency graph, populated with this information, is continually analyzed, to evaluate whether there are ways of improving requirements fulfillment. Based on this analysis, we use a map coverage approach described in detail in Copil et al. (2013b) for generating an action plan which is composed of abstract actions, which are mapped into infrastructure or application level actions and then enforced with the help of used cloud infrastructure APIs.

Let us consider a simple example shown in Figure 12 of controlling the entire application, e.g., by the system designer. The described elasticity requirements, Co1, Co2, and Co3 are not conflict-

Figure 12. Action plan example

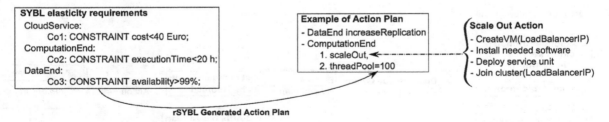

ing, and actions are searched for fulfilling these requirements. Possible actions are, for instance, for the case the running time is higher than 10 hours and the cost is still in acceptable limits, to scale-out for the computation composite component, increasing the processing speed. An example of an action plan, shown in Figure 12 could be:

$$ActionPlan1 = [\,[\,increaseReplication\,],[\,scaleOut,\\ setThreadPool = 100\,]\,].$$

This action plan would address performance issues for the second elasticity requirement Co2, and availability issues for the third elasticity requirement Co3. Each of the generated abstract actions are mapped into complex API calls. For instance, increaseReplication action would consist of calls for adding and configuring a new database node and configuring the cluster for higher replication, while the scaleOut action would be the addition of a new virtual machine, deployment of the ComputationEnd component on the new machine, and necessary calls for the new instance of the component to join the computation topology cluster.

6. APPLICATIONS OF ELASTICITY CONTROL

The two applications described in Section 3 are currently being developed. Therefore we choose to showcase CELAR control approach on a Machine-to-Machine (M2M) DaaS Service. The M2M DaaS Service is quite complex, containing two composite components, one application server-based and one which is a NoSQL. This is similar to the gaming application presented in Section 3.2, which also has requirements regarding application-level metrics like response time and latency. Moreover, the M2M DaaS composite components are similar to pipes in SCAN application presented in Section 3.1, in which the SCAN developer wants to introduce requirements at pipe-level as well as at component level, thus having multi-level elasticity control for the SCAN application.

Considering a CELAR user that wants to deploy this M2M DaaS in the cloud and expects an elastic application behavior, the CELAR user needs to describe two types of information: structural information regarding application artifacts, and

Figure 13. Application used for evaluation

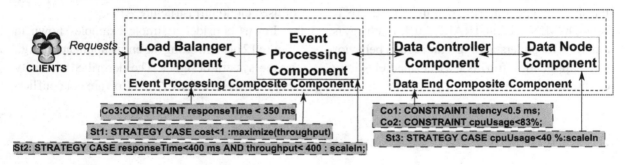

elasticity requirements at the different application level. The M2M DaaS, shown in Figure 13, is comprised of two composite components, an Event Processing Composite Component and a Data End Composite Component. Each composite component consists of two components, one with a processing goal, and the other acting as the composite component balancer/controller. To stress this application we generate random sensor event information which is processed by the Event Processing Composite Component, and stored/retrieved from the Data End Composite Component.

Moreover, the CELAR user is interested in specifying a number of elasticity requirements, both at component, composite component, and at whole application level. The requirement specified at whole application level (St1) specifies as a strategy to increase as much as possible the throughput, but under specific cost condition. In the upper part of Figure 13 shows the various elasticity requirements which we associate to the different levels of M2M application. For having the application elasticity controlled by CELAR, the M2M application as well as these elasticity requirements need to be described with c-Eclipse, as we describe in Section 6.1. After describing the application and pressing the deploy button, the application is controlled following the approach presented in Section 5, control results being presented in Section 6.2.

6.1 Application Description with c-Eclipse

The c-Eclipse framework provides an intuitive, user-friendly interface through which users can describe their applications for deployment over cloud platforms. The c-Eclipse user interface is depicted in Figure 14. At the left-hand side, the CELAR user can see the CELAR Project View where all the files related to an application description are organized in a hierarchy. The Palette, shown at the right-hand side, includes most of the elements

required for creating application descriptions, categorized under different Palette sections. By simply dragging and dropping pictorial elements from the Palette onto the center Canvas, users can create a graphical representation of an application. Additional information can be provided for each element via the Properties View (see in Figure 14). Application descriptions are translated on the fly into XML, according to the open TOSCA specification for cloud applications.

The first step in describing an application is to define the application's structure/topology, following the abstract application composition-based model described in Section 5.2.1. To do so, the user must use components and composite components from the Palette's Components section and then create the relationships between these components by using relationships from the Palette's Connections section. Once the application structure is defined, the user can define the application's properties such as the VM images (shown in the Palettes Images section) and other executables to be installed on the defined application components (Palette's Deployment Scripts section). Moreover, s/he can describe the important monitoring metrics at each application level (Palette's Monitoring Probes section), together with the elasticity actions to be applied when scaling the application's deployment (Palette's Elasticity Actions section), and the time when these actions should be applied. Specifically:

- At Component Level, the user can define the following:
  - **VM Image:** That will be used by the underlying platform when materializing instances of the component (green color box).
  - **Key Pairs:** Generated by the user that will be used by the underlying platform when deploying the component. Thus, a user can make use of the key pair later to access the deployed component (yellow color box).

Figure 14. Application used for evaluation described in c-Eclipse

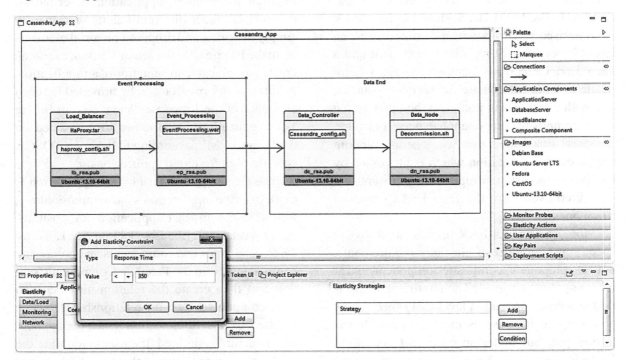

- ◦ **User Applications:** Such as .jar and .war files, that will be used by the underlying platform when materializing instances of the component (orange color box).
- At Application, Component and Composite Component Level, the user can define the following:
  - ◦ **Deployment Scripts:** That will be executed by the underlying platform when initializing instances of the component (pink color box).
  - ◦ **Monitoring Probes:** That will be used by the Monitoring System to capture and return the corresponding metrics to the user. Furthermore, the metrics referred by the probes can be used in the specification of elasticity policies.
  - ◦ **Elasticity Actions:** That can be applied to the components. Elasticity actions can also be used in the specification of elasticity policies.

Figure 14 shows the c-Eclipse application description, following the structure depicted in Figure 13. For achieving this c-Eclipse application description, the user will first drag a composite component from the Palette's Components section onto the Canvas to create the Event Processing component. Then, he will drag two simple components and drop them inside the composite component one for the Load Balancer component and one for the Event Processing component. In a similar way the user can create the Data End composite component with the two simple components inside it for the Data Controller and the Data Node.

Apart from the structure of the application, the user can specify other application properties, such as its elasticity policies. For example, by using the Properties View of c-Eclipse (bottom of Figure 14) the user can define the constraint of keeping the Response Time for the Event Processing Composite Component below 350 ms.

Figure 15. Example of visual cloud application elasticity control enforcement

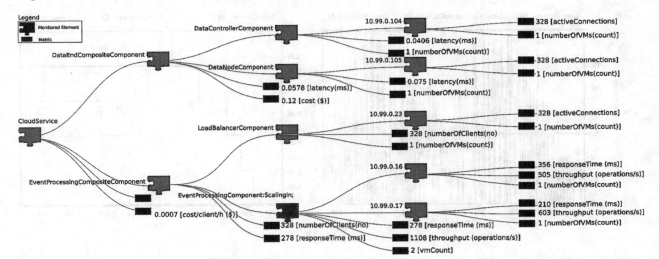

6.2 Controlling the Application with CELAR Decision Module

After describing the application as above, with the help of c-Eclipse, the CELAR user chooses the cloud provider to be used, and specifies his/her credentials, and with a simple press of a button, the application, together with all the necessary CELAR tools are deployed in the cloud. After this, the CELAR user can observe the evolution of application metrics, which is being controlled with the approach presented in Section 5.

Figure 15 depicts a view from the MELA user interface, which is integrated into c-Eclipse for CELAR users to be able to follow cloud application behavior during runtime. The CELAR user can observe various metrics, at the different cloud application levels.

By clicking on different components or complex components, the user is lead to a new view, in which s/he can observe various charts showing metrics evolution in time, and statistical data. Due to the scaling actions enforced by the CELAR Decision Module, the response time is able to stay within the required boundaries, as shown in the left side of Figure 14, at a relatively stable value

without increasing more than acceptable for a too high period. The user can observe that due to CELAR control, there is a correlation between the number of VMs and the number of clients, as depicted in Figure 16, thus showing that the Decision Module is able to adapt the application in order to accommodate a varying demand. This is strengthened by the elasticity pathway depicted in Figure 18. From the pathway's "x" axis, the situation encounter rate, i.e., the percentage of time that situation was encountered, one can see that in 90% of the situations, the response time was maintained within acceptable values.

CELAR facilitates the intuitive, user-friendly description of cloud applications to be elastically controlled, together with their elasticity requirements, which can be both expressive for advanced users and simple for inexperienced ones. Using this description, CELAR analyzes and controls the application, managing cloud resources as well as application configurations for fulfilling user's requirements. Moreover, the CELAR user is continually informed on the cloud service behavior, being able to better understand the application and the consequences of different requirement preferences.

Figure 16. Elasticity control shown at event processing composite component

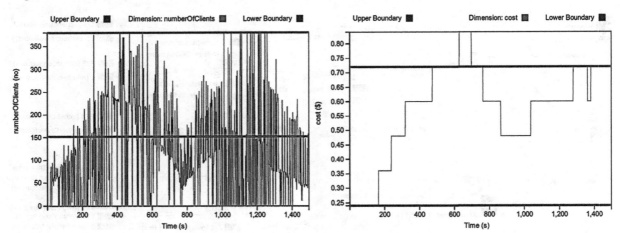

The control provided by CELAR enables applications to fulfill users' requirements, regardless of the highly oscillating load (number of clients metric in Figure 16), as shown in Figure 17 where the response time is kept within user-specified requirements. Moreover, this entire process, which normally would have meant for application stakeholders a lot of manual configurations, is happening automatically and without user intervention, while keeping within user specified requirements, thus avoiding undesirable situations (e.g., very good quality parameters at a much too high cost from application stakeholders perspective).

Figure 17. Response time for event processing composite component

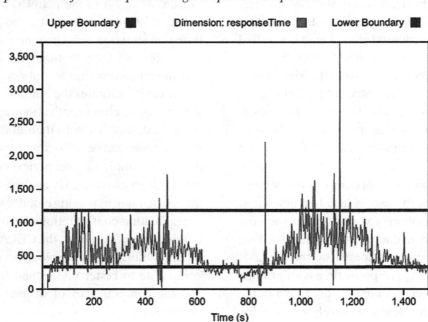

Figure 18. Elasticity pathway for event processing composite component

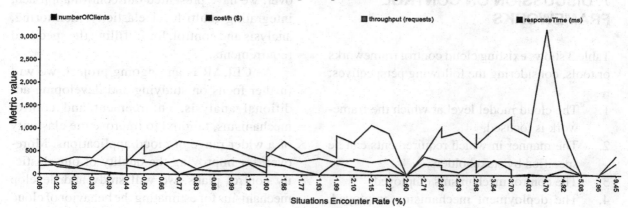

Table 3. Control frameworks for elastic cloud applications

Framework Name/Authors	Addressed Cloud Level	Requirements Specification	Control Mechanisms	Deployment Mechanisms	Application Complexity
CELAR approach	IaaS, PaaS	SYBL language	Elasticity space analysis, map coverage & heuristic based, conflict resolution	c-Eclipse for simple description, discovers missing dependencies, finds best configurations	Multiple hierarchical levels
CloudScale (Shen et al. (2011)) PRESS (Gong et al. (2010))	Hypervisor (Xen)	Low level SLA Los	Online adaptive padding Based on signature/ state driven predictions	No	Single-component application
Kingfisher (Sharma et al. (2011))	Hypervisor (Xen)	No	Integer linear programs	No	Single-component application
Martin et al. (2011)	IaaS	User goals through a goal graph	MAPE-based elasticity management	No	Multi-component application
Buch et al. (2012)	AppScale	Language for configuration and deployment	No	Guided by language	Scientific applications
Malkowski et al. (2011)	IaaS	Low-level SLA	Prediction and SLA driven	No	n-tier application
Naskos et al. (2014)	IaaS	Automatically generated	Markov decision process based	No	NoSQL databases
Almeida et al. (2014)	IaaS	SLA	Uses branch and bound to control services from multiple clouds	No	Multiple components

7. DISCUSSION ON CONTROL FRAMEWORKS

Table 3 shows existing cloud control frameworks or tools, considering the following perspectives:

1. The cloud model level at which the framework is focused,
2. The manner in which requirements can be specified by stakeholders,
3. The control mechanisms employed,
4. The deployment mechanisms employed, and
5. Which is the supported application complexity (e.g., it is assumed that the application consists of a single component, multiple components, or even hierarchical structuring of groups of components).

We can see that, when compared to most frameworks available on the market, CELAR approach encapsulates some powerful features, from elasticity requirements specification language to application components or control/deployment mechanisms used, which could help substantially application stakeholders throughout the application elasticity control lifecycle.

8. CONCLUSION AND FUTURE WORK

In this chapter we presented the CELAR approach to cloud application elasticity control. We have shown that the complexity of cloud application elasticity control is highly dependent on the application complexity, on the underlying infrastructure possibilities, and on the requirements that the cloud application stakeholders have. We have shown how CELAR facilitates the description of cloud applications, and the description of stakeholder requirements with reference to various application parts. More-over, we have presented our control approach, integrating multi-level elasticity monitoring, analysis and control, for fulfilling the specified requirements.

As CELAR is an ongoing project, we will further focus on studying and developing additional analysis, enforcement and control mechanisms, tailored to improve the elasticity of a wider range of cloud applications. Moreover, for improving the quality of our elasticity control plans, we will study and develop mechanisms for estimating the behavior of cloud application and individual components. We plan to provide CELAR both as an integrated platform for designing, deploying, monitoring and controlling elastic cloud services, and as individual components which can be embedded in existing platforms.

ACKNOWLEDGMENT

This work was supported by the European Commission in terms of the CELAR FP7 project (FP7-ICT-2011-8 #317790). We thank Dimitrios Tsoumakos for fruitful discussions.

REFERENCES

Almeida, A., Dantas, F., Cavalcante, E., & Batista, T. (2014). A branch-and-bound algorithm for autonomic adaptation of multi-cloud applications. In *Proceedings of IEEE/ACM International Symposium on Cluster, Cloud and Grid Computing (CCGrid)*. IEEE/ACM. doi:10.1109/CCGrid.2014.25

Ananthanarayanan, G., Agarwal, S., Kandula, S., Greenberg, A., Stoica, I., Harlan, D., & Harris, E. (2011). Scarlett: Coping with skewed content popularity in MapReduce clusters. In *Proceedings of the Sixth Conference on Computer Systems*. ACM. doi:10.1145/1966445.1966472

Aspnes, J., Kirsch, J., & Krishnamurthy, A. (2004). Load balancing and locality in range-queriable data structures. In *Proceedings of the Twenty-Third Annual ACM Symposium on Principles of Distributed Computing*. ACM. doi:10.1145/1011767.1011785

Bharambe, A. R., Agrawal, M., & Seshan, S. (2004). Mercury: Supporting scalable multi-attribute range queries. In *Proceedings of the 2004 Conference on Applications, Technologies, Architectures, and Protocols for Computer Communications*. ACM.

Binz, T., Breitenbücher, U., Haupt, F., Kopp, O., Leymann, F., Nowak, A., & Wagner, S. (2013) OpenTOSCA – A runtime for TOSCA-based cloud services. In *Proceedings of the 11th International Conference*. Academic Press. doi:10.1007/978-3-642-45005-1_62

Bunch, C., Drawert, B., Chohan, N., Krintz, C., Petzold, L., & Shams, K. (2012, March). Language and runtime support for automatic configuration and deployment of scientific computing software over cloud fabrics. *Journal of Grid Computing, 10*(1), 23–46. doi:10.1007/s10723-012-9213-8

Chaisiri, S., Lee, B.-S., & Niyato, D. (2012). Optimization of resource provisioning cost in cloud computing. *IEEE Transactions on Services Computing, 5*(2), 164–177. doi:10.1109/TSC.2011.7

Copil, G., Moldovan, D., Truong, H.-L., & Dustdar, S. (2013a). SYBL: An extensible language for controlling elasticity in cloud applications. In *Proceedings of 13th IEEE/ACM International Symposium on Cluster, Cloud and Grid Computing - CCGRID2013*. IEEE/ACM. doi:10.1109/CCGrid.2013.42

Copil, G., Moldovan, D., Truong, H.-L., & Dustdar, S. (2013b). Multi-level elasticity control of cloud services. In *Proceedings of 11th International Conference on Service Oriented Computing*. Berlin, Germany: Academic Press. doi:10.1007/978-3-642-45005-1_31

Cox, B., Allsopp, J., Moldovan, D., Star, K., Garcia, U., & Le, D. H. (2014). *CELAR deliverable: Cloud policy game design document*. Retrieved from http://www.celarcloud.eu/wp-content/uploads/2014/04/celar_d7.1_finalrelease_1.pdf

DeCandia, G., Hastorun, D., Jampani, M., Kakulapati, G., Lakshman, A., Pilchin, A., & Vogels, W. et al. (2007) Dynamo: Amazon's highly available key-value store. In *Proceedings of Twenty-First ACM SIGOPS Symposium on Operating Systems Principles* (SOSP '07). ACM. doi:10.1145/1294261.1294281

Di Cosmo, R., Mauro, J., Zacchiroli, S., & Zavattaro, G. (2013). Component reconfiguration in the presence of conflict. In *Proceedings of ICALP 2013* (vol. 2, pp. 187 – 198). Springer. doi:10.1007/978-3-642-39212-2_19

Di Nitto, E. (2013). Supporting the development and operation of multi-cloud services: The MODAClouds approach. In *Proceedings of 15th International Symposium on Symbolic and Numeric Algorithms for Scientific Computing (SYNASC)*. Academic Press. doi:10.1109/SYNASC.2013.61

Dustdar, S., Guo Y., Satzger, B., & Truong, H.-L. (2011). Principles of elastic processes. *IEEE Internet Computing, 15*(5), 66-71.

Gambi, A., Moldovan, D., Copil, G., Truong, H.-L., & Dustdar, S. (2013). On estimating actuation delays in elastic computing systems. In *Proceedings of the 8th International Symposium on Software Engineering for Adaptive and Self-Managing Systems* (SEAMS '13). IEEE Press. doi:10.1109/SEAMS.2013.6595490

Gong, Z., Gu, X., & Wilkes, J. (2010, October). Press: Predictive elastic resource scaling for cloud systems. In *Proceedings of Network and Service Management* (CNSM) (pp. 9-16). IEEE.

Gonzalez, A. J., & Helvik, B. E. (2012) System management to comply with SLA availability guarantees in cloud computing. In *Proceedings of 2012 IEEE 4th International Conference on Cloud Computing Technology and Science (CloudCom)* (pp. 325-332). IEEE. http://ieeexplore.ieee.org/stamp/stamp.jsp?tp=&arnumber=6427508&isnumber=6427477

Karger, D., Lehman, E., Leighton, T., Panigrahy, R., Levine, M., & Lewin, D. (1997). Consistent hashing and random trees: Distributed caching protocols for relieving hot spots on the world wide web. In *Proceedings of the Twenty-Ninth Annual ACM Symposium on Theory of Computing* (STOC '97). ACM. doi:10.1145/258533.258660

Karger, D., & Ruhl, M. (2004) Simple efficient load balancing algorithms for peer-to-peer systems. In *Proceedings of the Sixteenth Annual ACM Symposium on Parallelism in Algorithms and Architectures* (pp. 36-43). ACM. doi:10.1145/1007912.1007919

Konstantinou, I., Tsoumakos, D., Mytilinis, I., & Koziris, N. (2011). Fast and cost-effective online load-balancing in distributed range-queriable system. *IEEE Transactions on Parallel and Distributed Systems, 22*(8), 1350–1364. doi:10.1109/TPDS.2010.200

Konstantinou, I., Tsoumakos, D., Mytilinis, I., & Koziris, N. (2013) DBalancer: Distributed load balancing for NoSQL data-stores. In *Proceedings of the 2013 International Conference on Management of Data* (pp. 1037-1040). ACM. doi:10.1145/2463676.2465232

Lakshman, A., & Malik, P. (2010, April). Cassandra: A decentralized structured storage system. *SIGOPS Oper. Syst. Rev., 44*(2), 35–40. doi:10.1145/1773912.1773922

Le, D.-H., Truong, H.-L., Copil, G., Moser, O., Nastic, S., Gambi, A., & Dustdar, S. (2014). SALSA: A dynamic configuration tool for cloud-based applications. In *Proceedings of 6th International Conference on Cloud Computing*. Academic Press.

Li, Z., O'Brien, L., Zhang, H., & Cai, R. (2012). On a catalogue of metrics for evaluating commercial cloud services. In *Proceedings of 2012 ACM/IEEE 13th International Conference on Grid Computing (GRID)* (pp. 164-173). ACM/IEEE. doi:10.1109/Grid.2012.15

Malkowski, S. J., Hedwig, M., Li, J., Pu, C., & Neumann, D. (2011). Automated control for elastic n-tier workloads based on empirical modeling. In *Proceedings of the 8th ACM International Conference on Autonomic Computing (ICAC '11)*. ACM. doi:10.1145/1998582.1998604

Martin, P., Brown, A., Powley, W., & Vazquez-Poletti, J. L. (2011). Autonomic management of elastic services in the cloud. In *Proceedings of 2011 IEEE Symposium on Computers and Communications (ISCC)* (pp. 135-140). IEEE. doi:10.1109/ISCC.2011.5984006

Moldovan, D., Copil, G., Truong, H.-L., & Dustdar, S. (2013). MELA: Monitoring and analyzing elasticity of cloud services. In *Proceedings of 5th International Conference on Cloud Computing*. Academic Press.

Naskos, A., Stachtiari, E., Gounaris, A., Katsaros, P., Tsoumakos, D., Konstantinou, I., & Sioutas, S. (2014). Cloud elasticity using probabilistic model checking. *CoRR abs/1405.4699*

OASIS Topology and Orchestration Specification for Cloud Applications (TOSCA). (2013). Retrieved from http://docs.oasis-open.org/tosca/TOSCA/v1.0/cs01/TOSCA-v1.0-cs01.html

Schatzberg, D., Appavoo, J., Krieger, O., & Van Hensbergen, E. (2012). *Why elasticity matters*. Technical Report BUCS-TR-2012-006. Computer Science Department, Boston University.

Serrano, D., Bouchenak, S., Kouki, Y., Ledoux, T., Lejeune, J., Sopena, J., . . . Sens, P. (2013). Towards QoS-oriented SLA guarantees for online cloud services. In *Proceedings of 13th IEEE/ACM International Symposium on Cluster, Cloud and Grid Computing (CCGrid)*. IEEE/ACM. doi:10.1109/CCGrid.2013.66

Sharma, U., Shenoy, P., Sahu, S., & Shaikh, A. (2011). A cost-aware elasticity provisioning system for the cloud. In *Proceedings of the 2011 31st International Conference on Distributed Computing Systems (ICDCS '11)*. IEEE Computer Society. doi:10.1109/ICDCS.2011.59

Shen, Z., Subbiah, S., Gu, X., & Wilkes, J. (2011). CloudScale: Elastic resource scaling for multi-tenant cloud systems. In *Proceedings of the 2nd ACM Symposium on Cloud Computing (SOCC '11)*. ACM. doi:10.1145/2038916.2038921

Simjanoska, M., Ristov, S., Velkoski, G., & Gusev, M. (2013). Scaling the performance and cost while scaling the load and resources in the cloud. In *Proceedings of 2013 36th International Convention on Information & Communication Technology Electronics & Microelectronics (MIPRO)*. Academic Press.

Sofokleous, C., Loulloudes, N., Trihinas, D., Pallis, G., & Dikaiakos, M. (2014). c-Eclipse: An open-source management framework for cloud applications. In Proceedings of EuroPar 2014. Porto, Portugal: Academic Press.

Trihinas, D., Loulloudes, N., Moldovan, D., Sofokleous, S., Pallis, G., & Dikaiakos, M. D. (2013). *CELAR deliverable: Cloud monitoring tool V1*. Retrieved from http://www.celarcloud.eu/wp-content/uploads/2013/11/Cloud-Monitoring-Tool-V1.pdf

Trihinas, D., Pallis, G., & Dikaiakos, M. D. (2014a). JCatascopia: Monitoring elastically adaptive applications in the cloud. In *Proceedings of 14th IEEE/ACM International Symposium on Cluster, Cloud and Grid Computing*. IEEE/ACM. doi:10.1109/CCGrid.2014.41

Villegas, D., Antoniou, A., Sadjadi, S. M., & Iosup, A. (2012). An analysis of provisioning and allocation policies for infrastructure-as-a-service clouds. In *Proceedings of the 2012 12th IEEE/ACM International Symposium on Cluster, Cloud and Grid Computing (ccgrid 2012) (CCGRID '12)*. IEEE Computer Society. doi:10.1109/CCGrid.2012.46

Xing, W., Tsoumakos, D., Sofokleous, S., Liabotis, I., Floros, V., & Loverdos, C. (2014). *CELAR deliverable: Translational cancer detection pipeline design*. Academic Press.

ADDITIONAL READING

Almeida, A., Dantas, F., Cavalcante, E., & Batista, T. (2014) A Branch-and-Bound Algorithm for Autonomic Adaptation of Multi-cloud Applications, *IEEE/ACM International Symposium on Cluster, Cloud and Grid Computing (CCGrid), 2014 14th*, vol., no., pp.315,323, 26-29 May 2014 doi:10.1109/CCGrid.2014.25

Bersani, M. M., Bianculli, D., Dustdar, S., Gambi, A., Ghezzi, C., & Krstić, S. (2014) Towards the formalization of properties of cloud-based elastic systems. *Proceedings of the 6th International Workshop on Principles of Engineering Service-Oriented and Cloud Systems (PESOS 2014)*. ACM, New York, NY, USA, 38-47. doi:10.1145/2593793.2593798

Binz, T., Breitenbücher, U., Haupt, F., Kopp, O., Leymann, F., Nowak, A., & Wagner, S. (2013) OpenTOSCA – A Runtime for TOSCA-Based Cloud services. In *Proceedings of the 11th International Conference*, ICSOC 2013, Berlin, Germany, December 2-5, 2013, pp 692-695, doi:10.1007/978-3-642-45005-1_62

Copil, G., Moldovan, D., & Truong, H.-L., & Dustdar, S. (2013a) SYBL: an Extensible Language for Controlling Elasticity in Cloud Applications. *13th IEEE/ACM International Symposium on Cluster, Cloud and Grid Computing - CCGRID2013*, Delft, the Netherlands, May 14-16, 2013. doi:10.1109/CCGrid.2013.42

Copil, G., Moldovan, D., Truong, H.-L., & Dustdar, S. (2013b) Multi-level Elasticity Control of Cloud Services, the *11th International Conference on Service Oriented Computing*. Berlin, Germany, on 2-5 December, 2013. doi:978-3-642-45005-1 doi:10.1007/978-3-642-45005-1_31

Copil, G., Trihinas, D., Truong, H.-L., Moldovan, D., Pallis, G., Dustdar, S., & Dikaiakos, M. (2014) ADVISE - a Framework for Evaluating Cloud Service Elasticity Behavior, *12th International Conference on Service Oriented Computing*. Paris, France, 3-6 November, 2014. doi:10.1007/978-3-662-45391-9_19

Dustdar, S. 2014. Principles and methods for elastic computing. *In Proceedings of the 17th international ACM Sigsoft symposium on Component-based software engineering (CBSE '14)*. ACM, New York, NY, USA, 1-2. doi:10.1145/2602458.2611455

Dustdar, S., Guo Y., Satzger, B., & Truong, H.-L. (2011) Principles of Elastic Processes, *Internet Computing, IEEE*, vol.15, no.5, pp.66,71, Sept.-Oct. 2011

Gambi, A., Filieri, A., & Dustdar, S. (2013) Iterative test suites refinement for elastic computing systems. *Proceedings of the 2013 9th Joint Meeting on Foundations of Software Engineering (ESEC/FSE 2013)*. ACM, New York, NY, USA, 635-638. doi:10.1145/2491411.2494579

Guinea, S., Kecskemeti, G., Marconi, A., & Wetzstein, B. (2011) Multi-layered monitoring and adaptation, *Proceedings of the 9th international conference on Service-Oriented Computing, ICSOC'11*, Springer-Verlag, Berlin, Heidelberg, 2011, pp. 359-373. doi:10.1007/978-3-642-25535-9_24

Inzinger, C., Nastic, S., Sehic, S., Vogler, M., Li, F., & Dustdar, S. (2014) Madcat – a methodology for architecture and deployment of cloud application topologies, *8th International Symposium on Service-Oriented System Engineering*, IEEE, 2014.

Konstantinou, I., Tsoumakos, D., Mytilinis, I., & Koziris, N. (2013) DBalancer: distributed load balancing for NoSQL data-stores. In *Proceedings of the 2013 international conference on Management of data* (pp. 1037-1040). ACM. doi:10.1145/2463676.2465232

Kouki, Y., & Ledoux, T. CSLA: a Language for improving Cloud SLA Management, *Proceedings of the International Conference on Cloud Computing and Services Science*, Porto, Portugal, 2012, pp. 586-591.

Kranas, P., Anagnostopoulos, V., Menychtas, A., & Varvarigou, T. (2012) ElaaS: An Innovative Elasticity as a Service Framework for Dynamic Management across the Cloud Stack Layers, *Sixth International Conference on Complex, Intelligent and Software Intensive Systems (CISIS)*, 2012, pp. 1042 -1049. doi:10.1109/CISIS.2012.117

Moldovan, D., Copil, G., Truong, H.-L., & Dustdar, S. (2013) MELA: Monitoring and Analyzing Elasticity of Cloud Services, *5'th International Conference on Cloud Computing*, CloudCom. Bristol, UK, 2-5 December, 2013

Naskos, A., Stachtiari, E., Gounaris, A., Katsaros, P., Tsoumakos, D., Konstantinou, I., Sioutas, S. (2014) Cloud elasticity using probabilistic model checking, *CoRR abs/1405.4699*

OASIS. Topology and Orchestration Specification for Cloud Applications (TOSCA), (2013) http://docs.oasis-open.org/tosca/TOSCA/v1.0/cs01/TOSCA-v1.0-cs01.html

Satzger, B., Hummer, W., Inzinger, C., Leitner, P., & Dustdar, S. (2013). Winds of Change: From Vendor Lock-In to the Meta Cloud. *IEEE Internet Computing, 17*(1), 69–73. doi:10.1109/MIC.2013.19

Serrano, D., Bouchenak, S., Kouki, Y., Ledoux, T., Lejeune, J., Sopena, J., . . . Sens, P. (2013) Towards QoS-Oriented SLA Guarantees for Online Cloud Services, *13th IEEE/ACM International Symposium on Cluster, Cloud and Grid Computing (CCGrid)*, 2013, vol., no., pp.50,57, 13-16 May 2013, doi:10.1109/CCGrid.2013.66

Sharma, U., Shenoy, P., Sahu, S., & Shaikh, A. A Cost-Aware Elasticity Provisioning System for the Cloud, 2011 *31st International Conference on Distributed Computing Systems (ICDCS)*, 2011, pp. 559 - 570. doi:. 59 doi:10.1109/ICDCS.2011

Simjanoska, M., Ristov, S., Velkoski, G., & Gusev, M. (2013) Scaling the performance and cost while scaling the load and resources in the cloud, *2013 36th International Convention on Information & Communication Technology Electronics & Microelectronics (MIPRO)*, vol., no., pp.151,156, 20-24 May 2013

Sofokleous, C., Loulloudes, N., Trihinas, D., Pallis, G., & Dikaiakos, M. (2014) c-Eclipse: An Open-Source Management Framework for Cloud Applications, EuroPar 2014, Porto, Portugal 2014

Tai, S., Leitner, P., & Dustdar, S. Design by Units: Abstractions for Human and Compute Resources for Elastic Systems, *IEEE Internet Computing* 16 (4) (2012) 84-88. doi:http://doi.ieeecomputersociety.org/10.1109/MIC.2012.81

Trihinas, D., Pallis, G., & Dikaiakos, M. D. (2014a) JCatascopia: Monitoring Elastically Adaptive Applications in the Cloud, in *14th IEEE/ACM International Symposium on Cluster, Cloud and Grid Computing*, 2014. doi:10.1109/CCGrid.2014.41

Truong, H.-L., Dustdar, S., Copil, G., Gambi, A., Hummer, W., Le, D.-H., & Moldovan, D. CoMoT – A Platform-as-a-Service for Elasticity in the Cloud *IEEE International Workshop on the Future of PaaS, IEEE International Conference on Cloud Engineering (IC2E 2014)*, Boston, Massachusetts, USA, 10-14 March 2014 doi:10.1109/IC2E.2014.44

Tsoumakos, D., Konstantinou, I., Boumpouka, C., Sioutas, S., & Koziris, N., Automated, Elastic Resource Provisioning for NoSQL Clusters Using TIRAMOLA, (2013) *14th IEEE/ACM International Symposium on Cluster, Cloud and Grid Computing*, pp. 34-41, 2013 13th IEEE/ACM International Symposium on Cluster, Cloud, and Grid Computing, 2013

KEY TERMS AND DEFINITIONS

c-Eclipse: Tool enabling users to describe, deploy and monitor their application. It is published as an Eclipse extension with the name CAMF (Cloud Application Management Framework) – http://eclipse.org/camf. More details are available in Sofokleous et al. (2014).

Elasticity Boundary: The upper and lower bound over a set of metrics, within which the user elasticity requirements are fulfilled.

Elasticity Control: Management of the application using the application capabilities (i.e., available actions) for fulfilling elasticity requirements under varying workload.

Elasticity in Cloud Computing: The property of adapting virtual resources used and application components configurations to varying workloads while fulfilling user requirements.

Elasticity Pathway: Defines a relationship between the metrics captured in the elasticity space, indicating how the elasticity of the service evolved in time.

Elasticity Requirements: User requirements which reference application-specific metrics, driving the application elasticity.

Elasticity Space: The monitored values of all runtime metrics having a user-defined elasticity boundary, and thus believed to offer a good indicator over the elasticity of the service.

MELA: An elasticity monitoring and analysis tool (http://tuwiendsg.github.io/MELA/), offering functionality for logically structuring monitoring information and providing elasticity analytics over historical monitoring data, to be used by elasticity controllers. More details are available in Moldovan et al. (2013).

SYBL: A domain specific language (http://tuwiendsg.github.io/rSYBL) enabling the specification of three types of elasticity requirements: monitoring, constraints and strategies requirements. More details are available in Copil et al. (2013a).

Section 4
Concurrency and Models

Chapter 8
Parallel Programming Models and Systems for High Performance Computing

Manjunath Gorentla Venkata
Oak Ridge National Laboratory, USA

Stephen Poole
Oak Ridge National Laboratory, USA

ABSTRACT

A parallel programming model is an abstraction of a parallel system that allows expression of both algorithms and shared data structures. To accommodate the diversity in parallel system architectures and user requirements, there are a variety of programming models including the models providing a shared memory view or a distributed memory view of the system. The programming models are implemented as libraries, language extensions, or compiler directives. This chapter provides a discussion on programming models and its implementations aimed at application developers, system software researchers, and hardware architects. The first part provides an overview of the programming models. The second part is an in-depth discussion on high-performance networking interface to implement the programming model. The last part of the chapter discusses implementation of a programming model with a case study. Each part of the chapter concludes with a discussion on current research trends and its impact on future architectures.

OVERVIEW OF CURRENT AND EMERGING PROGRAMMING MODELS

Parallel systems, also called supercomputer or clusters, are used for executing a wide range of computationally intensive scientific simulations such as weather forecasting, ocean modeling, combustion simulation, molecular modeling, physical system simulations, and the others. They have evolved from systems built from combining few processors to systems with millions of nodes, each with hundreds of computing cores. The predominant architecture of these systems have either been shared memory (computing nodes with access to the same global memory) or distributed memory (computing nodes with access to the private memory) systems.

DOI: 10.4018/978-1-4666-8213-9.ch008

Copyright © 2015, IGI Global. Copying or distributing in print or electronic forms without written permission of IGI Global is prohibited.

Applications employ parallel computation techniques to exploit the parallelism in the systems and arrive at the solution, quickly. Parallel computation involves dividing the computation into separate computation tasks and mapping each task to an execution context, which is typically managed by an Operating System (OS) process or a thread. A majority of these applications require co-ordination between various computation tasks to arrive at the solution. The coordination involves exchange of data and intermediate results, synchronization between all or some of the processes, spawning of new computation, and restarting some computation.

Achieving parallelism on these systems presents numerous challenges: parallelizing the algorithm to millions of computing cores, controlling the parallel execution contexts, optimizing the computation to reduce communication overhead, handling distributed errors and failures, and optimizing for power usage. These challenges are going to exacerbate as we move towards more extreme-scale systems.

The programming models aim to address these challenges by providing concise, efficient, and scalable abstractions to express the parallel algorithms and shared data structures. They achieve this by making trade-offs and appropriate design choices on: how data is distributed and viewed, execution context is mapped to the physical (system) resources, execution contexts are synchronized, and communication is expressed or controlled. As a consequence of design decisions, there are various programming models, which vary in the abstraction provided to the user, and ideal system architecture required for these abstractions to be highly scalable and high performing. The common variations of these programming models are distributed memory, shared memory, Partitioned Global Address Space (PGAS), and hybrid systems.

Message Passing Model

In the message passing model, computation is organized around execution contexts which co-operate with each other by exchanging explicit messages. The execution contexts are implemented as OS processes or user or kernel threads. In the rest of this chapter, we use execution context and processes interchangeably. A complex problem that requires parallel computation model and supercomputer for arriving at the solution divides the computation into sub-problems. A single or group of processes solves its sub-problem by coordinating with other processes.

Figure 1 shows the programmer view of data and control distribution in the message passing model. The control or execution context has its own data objects encapsulated along with it. The execution context can access other data objects through explicit message exchange. Also, it co-ordinates and exchanges intermediate results with other execution contexts while required through explicit message exchange. The model can be implemented on a single node or on a distributed memory system. The execution context need not necessarily be mapped to a single node. It can be migrated to other nodes, however it must maintain a relation to its data objects.

Figure 1. Programmer's view of the Message Passing Model

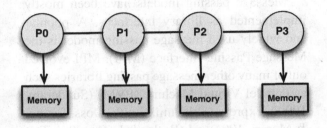

For co-ordination among the execution contexts, the message passing model provides a rich set of synchronization and communication mechanisms. The communication mechanisms can be one-sided, two-sided, or a group. In a two-sided communication, both sender and receiver of data are engaged in the communication. This has an effect of implicit synchronization between the sender and receiver process. In an one-sided communication operation, only sender (initiator) of communication is active, and it does not have the side-effect of synchronization between the sender and receiver. The difference between one-sided or two-sided communication and group communication is that in the later at most two processes are affected. However in group communication more than two processes are involved and affected. Though recent network hardware provides native support for some communication and synchronization operations, these operations are predominantly implemented in software.

The message passing model can be used to implement *Single Program Multiple Data* (SPMD) and Multiple Program Multiple Data (MPMD) parallel models. To implement the SPMD model, the data on which computation is performed is split across the execution contexts and all run the same program. They co-ordinate by using explicit messages and synchronization mechanisms. MPMD, which differs in that each execution context runs different a program, can be implemented similarly.

Message passing models have been mostly implemented as library interfaces. A popular and widely used message passing model is the Message Passing Interface (MPI). MPI evolved out of many other message passing libraries such as Parallel Virutal Machine (PVM) (Sunderam, 1990), Express (Skjellum, Smith, Doss, Leung, & Morari, 1994), p4 (Butler & Lush,1992), TC-GMSG (Harrison, 1993).

Shared-Memory Model

In the *Shared-Memory* (SM) model, multiple execution contexts share a common address space. On modern hardware, the execution context is implemented as a thread, and rarely as a OS process. The execution contexts are co-ordinated by reading and writing the shared variables. This model can be thought of presenting *Single Instruction Multiple Data* (SIMD) mode of parallelism, where sequential control thread is operating on parallel data.

Figure 2 provides a programmer view of control and data distribution in the SM model. All data objects are shared among all control threads presenting share-everything model. Typically, this model is implemented on a shared-memory machine or on a single node. Though there is no restriction for execution contexts to be mapped on to a single node, it is very inefficient for the control threads to be mapped onto different nodes and still manage a single address space. Given that many of the High Performance Computing (HPC) systems are distributed memory systems, this model is inefficient to be implemented on these systems. Another drawback of this model for a Non Uniform Memory Access (NUMA) node is the lack of locality; since all data is shared and global, the process cannot maintain affinity to frequently used data.

Partitioned Global Address Space Model

PGAS presents a programming model, where all execution contexts share a global address space, and have access to private address space. The private address space is managed by a single execution context, while the global address space is managed collectively. The execution contexts can be implemented as an OS process or as a user or kernel thread.

Figure 2. Programmer's view of the Shared-Memory Model

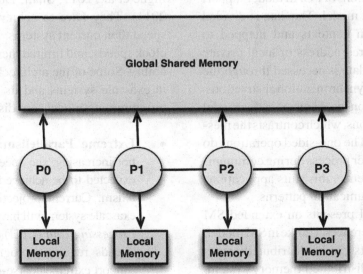

Figure 3 shows the programmer view of data and control distribution in the PGAS programming model. The execution context has its own private address space, which has private control and data objects. It has access to the global address space, which has shared control and data objects. A part of the global address space is co-located with each execution context. As seen in the figure, the

global address space is accessible to all execution contexts. The model can be implemented on a shared memory system or a distributed memory system, and on a single or multiple nodes. The execution context along with its private data and partition of global data can be co-located on a single node, statically mapped to a single node, or migrated during the program execution.

Figure 3. Programmer's view of the Partitioned Global Address Space Model

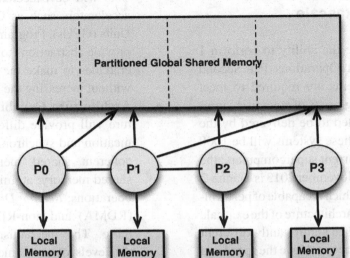

Most implementations of PGAS model support the SPMD execution model. The data is divided among the execution contexts and mapped to either the global shared address or local private address. The global data is accessed through the communication and synchronization abstractions.

The communication mechanisms in this model are one-sided operations, which contrasts the message passing model. The one-sided operations do not involve the receiver process during communication. As a consequence, this suits applications with dynamic communication patterns.

The PGAS model presents an extended SM model with some differences. Unlike in SM model, the execution contexts can be distributed across different nodes in a distributed memory system. It has private address space, which presents a share-everything model.

PGAS programming model is implemented as a language or a library interface. The well known examples of PGAS programming languages are *Unified Parallel C* (UPC) and Co-Array Fortran (CAF) (Coarfa, Dotsenko, Eckhardt, & Mellor-Crummey, 2004), and a popular implementation of PGAS as library interface is *OpenSHMEM* (OpenSHMEM. org, 2011; Chapman et al., 2010) and Global Arrays (Nieplocha, Harrison, & Littlefield, 1994).

Programming Model Challenges for Exascale

Exascale systems have the ability to perform 1 x 10^{18} FLoating-point Operations Per Second (FLOPS). These systems are required to meet the growing computing needs of scientific simulations, and are expected to be delivered by the start of next decade. These systems will be 1000 times faster than the current supercomputers; the fastest computer as of November 2013 is Tianhe-2 (TOP500.org, 2012), which is capable of performing 33.86 FLOPS. The architecture of the exascale systems is expected to be significantly different from current architecture to achieve the speed and operate within the target power budget (Amaras-

inghe et al., 2011; Shalf, Dosanjh, & Morrison, 2011). They have to achieve 1000 times more speed than current systems, with non-increasing clock speeds, and limited increase in power availability. Some of the architecture trends expected in exascale systems and its implications on the programming models are discussed below:

- **Extreme Parallelism:** With clock speed not increasing, the speed of computation is expected to be achieved by increased parallelism. Current projections predict that an exascale system will have millions of *Central Processing Unit* (CPU) cores and billions of threads requiring programming models to support extreme coarse-grained parallelism.
- **Limited Memory:** The amount of memory per computing core is expected to decrease significantly, which in-turns means that the core-level or fine-grained parallelism becomes more dominant and important to be supported by the programming models.
- **Hierarchical Systems:** An application uses registers, caches, on-node memory, flash memory, and disk memory for storing and sharing the data. To achieve the performance and power targets, there will be more memory hierarchies within the CPU. This will be exacerbated with the use of accelerators such as Graphical Processing Units (GPUs). Programming models should provide abstractions to hide the memory hierarchies to make the programming easier without increasing the overhead.
- **Architecture Capabilities:** The architecture will provide different set of communication and synchronization mechanisms: coherent shared memory, non-coherent shared memory; atomic read-modify-write operations; *Remote Direct Memory Access* (RDMA) and non-RDMA channels, and more. The mechanisms differ at different levels of the same system and across systems.

- **Power Consumption:** Current generation of HPC systems consume tens of megawatt of power. Even with technological improvements, the exascale system is expected to consume over hundred megawatt of power. This prohibits many of the current computing centers to operate the HPC system. Hence, there is a need to reduce the power requirements at levels of the stack including hardware and software.

- **Resilience:** The exascale system is expected to have millions of components. These components are expected to have an order of magnitude smaller feature sizes, operate under lower voltages and close to physical thresholds, the component reliability is unlikely to improve, the systems will become more error-prone. To have an effective exascale system, the resiliency must be addressed at every level of the system stack, from circuit design to applications.

- **Heterogeneity:** The exascale system is expected to have diverse computing engines including traditional CPUs and accelerators such as GPUs. This trend will only continue given the FLOPS per watt performance of computing accelerators. The programming model should accommodate this diversity while still maintaining the simplicity of abstractions provided to the users.

PROGRAMMING SYSTEMS AND RECENT RESEARCH TRENDS

The implementation of programming models is referred to as a programming system. The programming systems are implemented as libraries, languages, or compiler directives. Commonly used library based implementations are MPI (The MPI Forum, 1994), a message passing specification which is the defacto standard, and SHMEM

(Chapman et al., 2010). UPC (UPC Consortium, 2005), Fortran (Reid, 2008) and Chapel (Cray Inc, 2013) are language based programming systems, and OpenMP (OpenMP Architecture Review Board, 2013) is a well-known directive-based programming system. In library-based programming system, the abstractions are expressed as library interfaces and thus programmer has explicit control of its usage. However, in language or compiler based programming systems, the abstractions are expressed as variables, types, and language constructs. As a consequence, the expression of abstractions is more implicit. To accommodate the new architectures such as parallel systems with multicore nodes, there is an emergence of hybrid programming systems such as MPI+OpenMP.

This section discusses the broadly used programming systems such as MPI, and *OpenSH-MEM*, and compares their limitations for exascale computing.

Message Passing Interface

MPI is a library interface specification for parallel application communication (The MPI Forum, 1994). It includes function interfaces, macros, and constants. These interfaces are invoked from applications written in languages like C, C++, Fortran, or Java. Though the specification requires support for C and Fortran language bindings, there are C++ and Java language bindings available for MPI specification.

MPI History and MPI Forum

In late eighties and early nineties, many parallel programming models provided abstractions to ease the programming of distributed-memory systems, which were the predominant architecture of supercomputers at that time. They had many similarities and some differences. Intel NX (Pierce, 1988) supported message passing with point-to-point and collective operations.

Zipcode/Express (Skjellum, Smith, Doss, Leung, & Morari, 1994), along with message passing, supported library composition. PVM, which presented a virtual machine abstraction to the programmer, supported fault-aware and fault-tolerant message passing with mechanisms for point-to-point and group communication. IBM-EUI (Bala et al., 1994) supported point-to-point and group communication. Though there were many similarities, the differences in interfaces and semantics required the users to maintain different implementations.

The initial goal of MPI was to consolidate these parallel programming models. The MPI Forum carries out the standardization effort and authoring of the specification; the Forum consists of researchers, hardware vendors, academics, MPI users, and MPI developers. The first MPI specification MPI 1.0 was released in May 1994 (The MPI Forum, 1994), and the latest version, MPI 3.0 (The MPI Forum, 2012), was released in September 2012.

MPI Design

MPI is a widely used programming model by scientific simulations on HPC systems. The popularity of MPI can be attributed to its key design principles such as portability, simplicity, composability, scalability, and completeness. The MPI implementations can compose with other libraries, compilers, and runtimes. The specification aims to provide simple and complete set of interfaces required for parallel programming, and has been largely successful on this. MPI does not restrict implementation to specialized system architectures. It can be implemented for variety of architectures including distributed-memory systems, shared-memory systems, cache-coherent and non-cache-coherent systems, network interface with and without zero-copy support, and on systems with network interfaces with or without RDMA capabilities.

MPI Implements Message Passing Model

In MPI, the execution contexts are MPI processes. The MPI processes can be implemented as an OS process or as a single or group of threads. The MPI processes are identified with a combination of two non-negative integers called *Ranks* and communicator identifier to which the control and data are mapped.

MPI Ranks have local data and control structures and, they co-ordinate with other ranks with explicit messages. It provides interfaces for synchronization, point-to-point, and group communication. MPI provides support for library composition and communication isolation through communicators. These interfaces are explained in detail in Section 2.1.1.

MPI Implementations

MPI is a library interface specification, not an implementation. There are many implementations of the MPI specification. Though the implementations provide the same functionality, they differ in the design, target architecture optimization, and target application domain optimization. The popular open source implementations of MPI are *Open MPI* and *MPICH* (Argonne National Laboratory, 2014). *MVAPICH* (Ohio State University, 2014) is a popular open source implementation of MPI for *InfiniBand* (Hamada & Nakasato, 2005) network interface. Intel, Hewlett-Packard (HP), Silicon Graphics, Inc. (SGI), International Business Machines Corporation (IBM), and Cray all have specialized implementations that are optimized for their systems.

MPI Abstractions and Interfaces

Point-to-Point Communications

Point-to-point communication operations provide interfaces for message passing between two MPI processes in the same communicator. One process is sending the message and other process is receiving the message. An MPI message is identified by (communicator, tag, destination *Rank*). For every message sent (with communicator, tag, Rank) there is a corresponding receive on the receiver process. The communication between the sender and receiver is always ordered and reliable. MPI provides many interfaces for point-to-point communication each varying from other with subtle semantic differences. Some of interfaces are as follows:

- **Standard Send (MPI_SEND):** MPI_SEND will complete when the send buffer can be safely modified. There is no guarantee that the receiver process has received message, but the library ensures that message will be eventually sent and received by the receiver binding to ordering constraints. Figure 4 shows the sender buffer status and completion at the sender process for MPI_SEND. In Figure 4, the transfer of message is shown to start before the completion of send, however, it is also semantically correct if the data is buffered and message transfer starts after the return of MPI_SEND.

- **Synchronous Send (MPI_SSEND):** The send will complete after the receiver receives the send data. Thus, after the synchronous send returns, the send buffer can be modified and the sender can assume that the receiver has received the data. In effect, this operation is a synchronous operation between the sender and receiver process. Figure 5 shows the sender buffer status and completion at the sender and receiver process for a MPI_SSEND.

- **Buffered Send (MPI_BSEND):** The send is returned immediately after buffering the send buffer data. There is no guarantee that the receiver receives the data, but it is safe to modify the send buffer. Figure 6 shows the message exchange between the sender and receiver. The send starts after the completion of MPI_BSEND, sending from the buffered data. The send can start before the completion of MPI_BSEND and this is also semantically correct.

- **Ready Send (MPI_RSEND):** A ready mode send can be started only after the receiver is ready to receive the data. When

Figure 4. The status of sender buffer and the message in an MPI_SEND

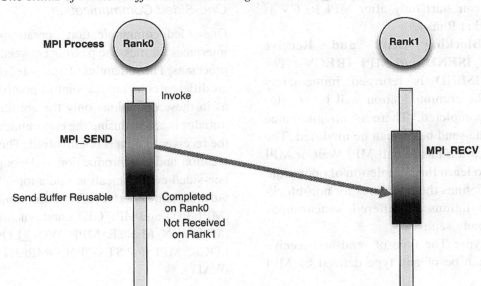

Figure 5. The status of sender buffer and the message in an MPI_SSEND

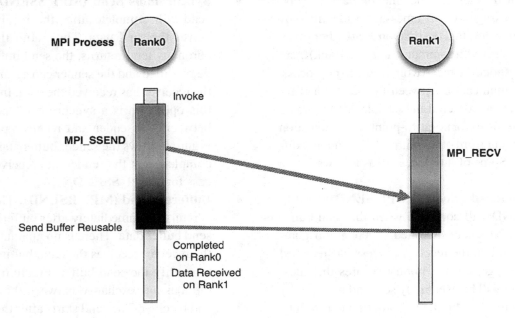

the send completes, the send data buffer can be modified. The completion of send does not necessarily mean that the data is received at the receiver process. Figure 7 shows the message exchange between the sender and receiver for MPI_RSEND. In the figure, you can observe that eventhough the MPI_RSEND is posted; the send can start only after MPI RECV is posted at Rank1.

- **Non-Blocking Send and Receive (MPI_ISEND and MPI_IRECV):** The MPI_ISEND is returned immediately and the communication will be eventually completed. There is no guarantee that the send buffer can be modified. The application has to call MPI Wait or MPI Test to learn the completion of operation. MPI defines the interfaces for non-blocking variations of buffered, synchronous and ready sends.
- **Datatype:** The type of send and receive data can be of any type defined by MPI

Datatype, however they should both match. MPI Datatype includes type for integer, character, float, double, complex, and user-defined types. This provides flexibility to send both contiguous and non-contiguous data, as well as custom data structures of the application.

One-Sided Communication

One-sided communication operations provide interfaces for message passing between two MPI processes. The semantics of one-sided operations are different compared to point-to-point operations as in these operations only the communication initiator is active during the communication, and the receiver of data is not involved. The communication and synchronization is decoupled with one-sided communication operations. MPI provides separate interfaces for both communication (MPI_PUT and MPI_GET), and synchronization (MPI_WIN_FENCE, MPI _WIN _LOCK \UNLOCK, MPI *WIN*START \COMPLETE \POST \WAIT).

Figure 6. The status of sender buffer and the message in an MPI_BSEND

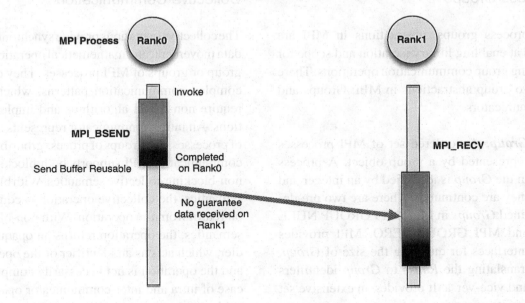

Figure 7. The status of sender buffer and the message in an MPI_RSEND

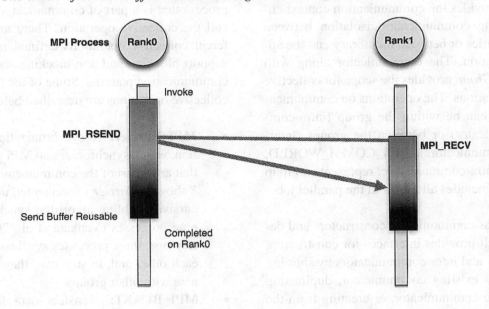

Process Groups

The process groups' abstractions in MPI are aimed at enabling library isolation and scope for defining group communication operations. There are two group abstractions in MPI: Groups and Communicators.

- *Group:* An ordered set of MPI processes represented by a group object. A process in the *Group* is identified by an integer and they are continuous. There are two pre-defined *Groups* in MPI: MPI GROUP NULL and MPI GROUP ZERO. MPI provides interfaces for querying the size of *Group*, translating the *Ranks* to *Group* identifiers and vice-versa. It provides an extensive set of interfaces for creating *Groups* from existing *Groups*.

- **Communicator:** An MPI abstraction that enables dividing the communication space. It provides the communication context enabling communication isolation between libraries or between the library and the application. The communicator along with the *Group* provides the scope for collective operations. The operations on communicators can be within the group (intra-communicator) or between the groups (inter-communicators). MPI_COMM_WORLD, an intra-communicator, represents a group that includes all *Ranks* in the parallel job.

MPI has communicator constructors and destructors. It provides interfaces for constructing both intra- and inter-communicators by splitting an already existing communicator, duplicating an existing communicator, or creating from the *Groups*. It provides interfaces for querying the size of communicator, *Rank* of process, setting or querying the info object. The info objects provides hints and recommendations to the implementations that are applicable only to the *Ranks* in the communicator.

Collective Communication

The collective operations provide synchronization, data movement, and mathematical operations on a group or groups of MPI processes. They capture complex communication patterns, which often require non-trivial algorithms and implementations. An intra-communicator represents a group of processes, and groups of process group by inter-communicator. MPI supports both blocking and non-blocking collective semantics. With blocking semantics, the collective operation is completed on return from the operation. With non-blocking semantics, the operation returns an opaque handler, which acts as an identifier of the operation, and the operation is not necessarily complete. In case of intra and inter-communicator operations or blocking and non-blocking operations, MPI semantics require all processes in the communicator to invoke the collective operation. The collective operation results in an undefined behavior, if any process that is a part of communicator does not call the collective operation. There are 34 different collective operations defined in MPI to support blocking and non-blocking and various communication patterns. Some of the important collective operations are described below:

- **MPI_Barrier:** A synchronization operation, which synchronizes all MPI processes that are a part of the communicator. Figure 8 shows a *Barrier* implemented using a recursive-doubling algorithm synchronizing nine processes (Venkata et al., 2012c). In step one, three processes synchronize with each other and, in step two, they synchronize with other groups.

- **MPI_BCAST:** Transfers data from one process to all other processes. The data can be of any MPI datatype. This is a one-to-all operation. One process acts as a root and other processes acts as non-root with root sending the data and non-root process receiving the data. Figure 9 shows a MPI_

Figure 8. The communication pattern of recursive K'ing Barrier with nine processes

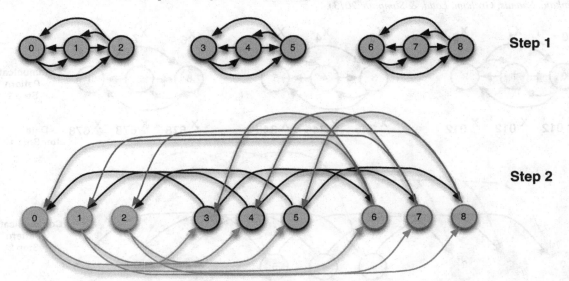

Bcast implemented using a binary tree algorithm. The root process indicated as 0 sends data to 1 and 2, and which in-turn sends data to rest of the processes.

- **MPI_ALLREDUCE:** An all-to-all operation, which combines the data from all processes with an operation, and distributes the results of the operation to all processes. The size and type of data from all the participants is the same, and all participants receive the same results. All processes exchange and reduce data with all processes. Figure 10 shows an example of Allreduce implemented using Recursive K'ing algorithm with nine processes, and with the graph of degree three (k = 3). In the first step, process *X* combines data with process (X + 1 mod 9) and process (X + 2 mod 9). In the second step, it combines data with process (X + 3 mod 9) and process (X + 2 * 3 mod 9).

- **MPI_ALLTOALL:** The process participating in an *All-to-all* collective operation sends and receives data to all other processes participating in the operation. When N processes are participating in an all-to-all operation, the total amount of data sent by each

process is $c\,(N-1)$ data items (a data item is the amount of data sent from one process to another), resulting in a total of $cN(N-1)$ data items exchanged in a single all-to-all operation. Labeling each data item with its originating MPI process, rank i, and destination MPI process, rank j, the MPI definition of all-to-all operation is equivalent to a matrix transpose as shown in Figure 11.

Figure 9. The communication pattern of MPI_ BCAST implemented using a binary tree algorithm

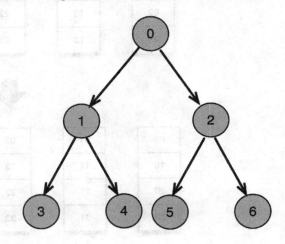

Figure 10. MPI_ALLREDUCE implemented using recursive K'ing algorithm
(Venkata, Shamis, Graham, Ladd, & Sampath, 2013).

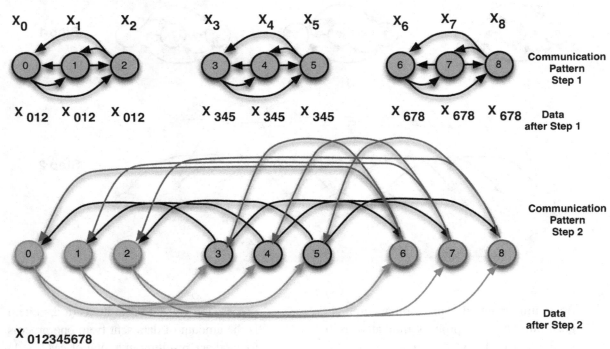

Figure 11. Example showing the data exchange for an MPI_ALLTOALL operation
(Venkata, Graham, Ladd, & Shamis, 2012b).

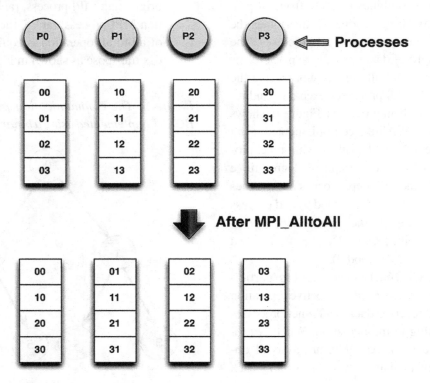

- **MPI_GATHER:** In the MPI_GATHER collective operation, one process acting as root collects data from all other processes in the communicator. Each non-root process in the communicator contributes the same amount and type of data to the result. The size of data at the root process after a *Gather* operation is cN, where c is the size of data, and N is number of processes in the communicator. Figure 12 shows an example of MPI_GATHER for four processes implemented using a simple linear algorithm.

Process Topologies and Neighborhood Collectives

The virtual topology and neighborhood collective abstractions are aimed at providing group communication operations that are mapped well onto the network hardware that the application runs on. The virtual topology interface provides a way to create a mapping between MPI process identifiers (Ranks) and hardware. It is a mechanism, which lets application's communication patterns be specified to the MPI library as hints. The library uses the hints to map processes to processors thereby optimizing for communication patterns. Currently, it supports topologies of type Cartesian and graph supporting both regular and irregular process topologies.

The Neighborhood collective defines group communication operations on the group of processes described by the virtual topology. Like collective operations, all processes call the neighborhood collective operation.

However, unlike the collective operations, the communication is only between the neighbors in the virtual topology. The virtual topology combined with neighborhood collectives is useful for application with sparse communication characteristics. Also, in many HPC systems the nodes are connected to their neighbors. The virtual topology and neighborhood collectives can be efficiently implemented for these systems.

Figure 13 shows an example of MPI_Neighbor_allgather. In this operation, each process sends data to the neighbor process, and receives a distinct element from each neighbor process. The *Process* 4, for example, sends to and receives from *Process* 1, *Process* 3, *Process* 5, and *Process* 7. The *Process* 7, which is on the edge, receives only from *Process* 4, *Process* 6, and *Process* 8.

Process Creation and Management

MPI provides mechanisms to create an initial set of processes, and dynamically add processes to the existing set. The initial set of processes is a part of MPI_COMM_WORLD. The two main

Figure 12. Example showing the data exchange for an MPI_GATHER operation

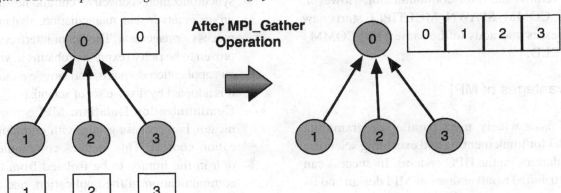

Figure 13. Example showing the data exchange for an MPI_Neighbor_allgather operation

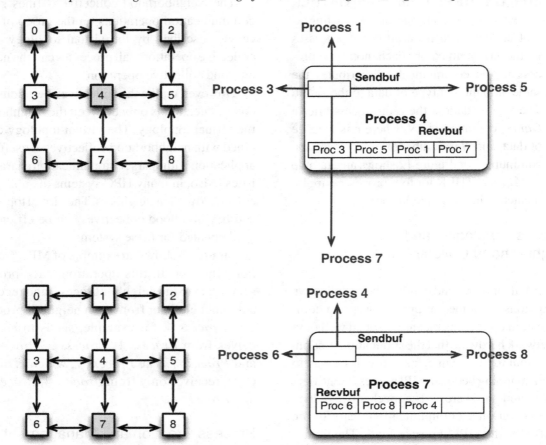

interfaces for starting new processes are MPI_COMM_SPAWN and MPI_COMM_SPAWN_MULTIPLE. MPI_COMM_SPAWN starts new processes, creates new inter-communicator, and returns the inter-communicator. However, MPI_COMM_SPAWN_MULTIPLE starts new processes and adds to the same MPI_COMM_WORLD.

Advantages of MPI

MPI is a widely used parallel programming model for implementing and executing scientific simulations on the HPC systems. Its success can be attributed to advantages of MPI design and its ecosystem which include:

- **Complete and Rich Set of Interfaces:** MPI provides a very rich and complete set of interfaces to express one-sided and two-sided communication, passive and active synchronization, collective communication, group creation and manipulation, dynamic process management. This set of interfaces is proven to be rich to express problems in various application domains, and simple enough it is adopted by diverse set of scientists.

- **Communication Isolation:** MPI communicator is a process group with communication context. This enables communication in the library to be isolated from the communication in the application, and allowing library composition.

- **Distributed Memory Model:** MPI maps well on to a distributed memory systems, a dominant architecture of current supercomputers. The distributed memory systems have many nodes connected through a fast network, and each node is equipped with memory including one or multiple computing engines. The MPI processes can be mapped to the node and use the fast network for message exchange.
- **Performance:** MPI is known to scale and perform well on current supercomputers. The scalability can be attributed to the scalable abstractions and interfaces in the specification, baring few non-scalable interfaces. This followed by high-quality implementations optimized for decades on various architectures have helped achieve scalability.

MPI in Exascale Era

MPI will be one of the dominant programming model in the exascale era (Gropp & Snir, 2013). Researchers have proposed various semantic changes to achieve the scalability and performance required for exascale era, and many of these changes are already incorporated in the recent version of the specification (Hoefler et al., 2006; The MPI Forum, 2012).

- **One-Sided Communication:** MPI should provide interfaces for one-side communication. Historically, MPI is well suited for communications with regular patterns and when two sides are involved in the operation. However, recent trends in applications communication patterns show irregular and require one-sided operations for ease of programming and performance. Though, the recent version of MPI specification has provided the clean one-sided

semantics and functionality, the interfaces are complex and requires deep knowledge to use the interfaces, thus limiting its usability.
- **Heterogeneity Support:** MPI should provide abstractions to handle heterogeneous architecture more seamlessly. Many highly scalable supercomputers have heterogeneous cores on the node, and this trend is becoming more dominant. MPI has been successful in providing the communication abstractions for systems with homogeneous nodes. It has also been successful in composing with other parallel communication libraries such as OpenMP to handle heterogeneity in the nodes. However, for future success, MPI should provide native support for heterogeneous architecture by providing abstractions in the specification.
- **Fault Handling:** MPI should handle hard- and soft-errors. An exascale system with millions of components is expected to have Mean Time Between Interrupts (MTTI) of few hours (Geist, Kale, Kramer, & Snir, 2009; Daly et al., 2012). It is critical for scientific simulations, tools, libraries, and system software ecosystem including MPI implementations to be fault-aware and may be even fault-tolerant. MPI being a critical piece of software should enable its implementations to be fault-aware and fault-tolerant.
- **Active Messages:** It provides a mechanism to trigger callbacks on the receiver process. The message semantics are useful for implementing many higher-level programming models such as task-based programming model and applications in scientific domains such as multi-physics.
- **Communication-Computation Overlap:** MPI should support mechanisms for overlapping communication with computation.

OpenSHMEM

OpenSHMEM Overview

OpenSHMEM is a PGAS library interface specification (OpenSHMEM.org, 2011). It aims to achieve low-latency and high-bandwidth on distributed and shared-memory machines. The specification includes interfaces, constants, environment variables, and macros to implement the PGAS programming model as a library. It also defines bindings in C and Fortran languages enabling the applications to invoke the interfaces.

OpenSHMEM History

OpenSHMEM is an open-source *SHMEM* specification. *SHMEM* is a PGAS programming model specification introduced by Cray Research Inc. for Cray T3D in 1993. Later, SGI acquired Cray's *SHMEM* and integrated it with its Message Passing Toolkit. Currently, SGI owns *SHMEM* and has rights towards *OpenSHMEM* specification. Both Cray and SGI developed implementations for their systems. Cray developed and implemented *SHMEM* for some of its fast and highly scalable systems including Titan (DOE, 2014), Cray T3D, T3E, C90, XMT, and XT. SGI has implemented *SHMEM* for some of its widely used systems such as SGI Origin, Altix 4700, Altix XE, ICE, UV.

A first version of *OpenSHMEM* specification was released in 2011 (OpenSHMEM.org, 2011). It was a effort led by Oak Ridge National Laboratory (ORNL) and University of Houston (UH) along with community input. The second and latest version, *OpenSHMEM* 1.1, will be released in June 2014 (OpenSHMEM.org, 2014). After being dormant for two decades, the open version of *SHMEM* specification is expected to introduce semantics and interfaces to address the programming challenges of extreme-scale systems.

OpenSHMEM Design

OpenSHMEM is a programming model that aims to provide programming abstractions with minimal overhead (performance and scalability), while also providing a very simple view of the parallel machine. The key design principles of *Open-SHMEM* are shared-memory view, simplicity, portability, and one-sided communication. *OpenSHMEM* presents the distributed memory systems as a single node system with the interfaces to access the remote node memory; these interfaces are similar to on-node memory access interfaces simplifying the transition from programming a single node system to multiple node system. Though the SM model is a simpler abstraction than *OpenSHMEM*, it has a scalability and performance drawback that does not constraint the *OpenSHMEM* model. A predominant communication mode of *OpenSHMEM* is one-sided communication. This suits applications with irregular communication patterns, and these semantics are convenient for applications where only one process knows about the data transfer.

OpenSHMEM Implements PGAS Model

OpenSHMEM presents a PGAS view of execution contexts and memory model. The execution context in OpenSHMEM is an OS process identified by non-integer called Processing Element (PE). An *OpenSHMEM* program has private address space and shared address space. A PE allocates and stores its private data and control structures in the private address space. The shared address space in *OpenSHMEM* is presented as symmetric objects, which are accessible by all PEs in an *OpenSHMEM* program. A key characteristic of symmetric object is that a PE can access remote symmetric object through local references. *OpenSHMEM* provides interfaces for communication and synchronization with other PEs. It provides many variants of SHMEM_PUT and SHMEM_GET to access symmetric data objects that are located on remote PEs. It provides synchronization interfaces SHMEM_QUIET and SHMEM_FENCE, which completes and orders the communication, respectively. It provides interfaces for group communication and synchronization. It also provides a rich set of atomic operations interfaces. An important difference between *OpenSHMEM* and MPI is that data transfer functions are one-sided in *OpenSHMEM*. A PE transferring data to a remote PE does not require the participation of the remote PE to complete the operation. The side effect of this is that the communication and computation is decoupled. These semantics are convenient for applications where only one process knows about the data transfer. The *OpenSHMEM* interfaces can be used to implement SPMD style parallel programs. It provides interfaces to start the processes in parallel, and communication and synchronization interfaces to access the data in the remote process address space. In addition, it provides variables, constants, and language bindings in C and Fortran for aiding parallel programming and data sharing.

OpenSHMEM Implementations

OpenSHMEM is a PGAS library interface specification, not an implementation. There are many implementations of *OpenSHMEM*. An open source reference *Open-SHMEM* implementation is provided by ORNL and UH, which is portable across multiple system architectures. Many computer vendors have implemented *Open-SHMEM* that are optimized for their system including SGI, IBM, Mellanox, and HP. Sandia National Laboratory (SNL) has an implementation of *OpenSHMEM* on portal networking abstraction (Sandia National Laboratory, 2014). Argonne National Laboratory (ANL) has an implementation of *OpenSHMEM* on MPI (Hammond, Ghosh, & Chapman, 2014).

OpenSHMEM Abstractions and Interfaces

Symmetric Data Objects

A Symmetric data object is a shared data object in *OpenSHMEM* program that is accessible to all PEs through the *OpenSHMEM* interfaces. The symmetric data objects have a corresponding object with the same name, type, size, and offset (from an arbitrary memory address) on all PEs.

OpenSHMEM provides interfaces for allocating and management of symmetric objects. SHPALLOC, a Fortran interface, allocates symmetric objects from the heap, and a corresponding C interface is SHMALLOC. SHREALLOC, SHMEMALIGN, and SHFREE, extends the symmetric object's memory, allocates byte-aligned memory, and releases the memory, respectively. The symmetric objects can be mapped to a process heap or stack. Fortran arrays allocated with SHPALLOC and data allocated in C and C++ programs by SHMALLOC interfaces are symmetric objects. Global and static C and C++ variables are also symmetric objects. Fortran data objects in common blocks or with the SAVE attribute are symmetric objects.

One-Sided Communication

One-sided communication operations enable manipulating data on target PEs without the involvement of the initiator PE. The operations can only be performed on the symmetric data objects.

- **SHMEM_PUT:** In this operation, the initiator process (active side) writes the local data to the target process' (passive side) memory. The operation is completed only after a synchronization operation such as SHMEM_QUIET, SHMEM_BARRIER or SHMEM_BARRIER_ALL operations. There are two main variants of the *Put* operation. The SHMEM P writes one data item for each invocation, and SHMEM IPUT writes non-contiguous data.

- **SHMEM_GET:** This is an explicit fetch operation, which copies a variable amount of data from a remote PE and stores it locally. The operation is completed upon return. Similar to *Put*, *OpenSHMEM* provides two main variants of *Get* operation. The SHMEM G fetches one data item, and SHMEM IGET fetches variable amount of non-contiguous data.

Collective Communication

Collective operation is a communication or synchronization operation on a group of PEs. The group of PEs called active set is defined by 3-tuple PE Start, logPE Stride, and PE Size. The PE Start is first PE of the Active set. The logPE Stride is distance between PEs in the Active set, and PE Size is equal to number of PEs in the Active set.

All PEs that are a part of collective operation should call the collective operation. A PE that is not a part of Active set but not calling the collective operation results in an undefined behavior. All collective operations are blocking i.e., they are completed on return. *OpenSHMEM* defines six main collective types (and variants) for handling different data types. The six collective operations are as follows:

- **SHMEM_BARRIER_ALL:** This operation synchronizes all PEs in the *Open-SHMEM* job. A variant of SHMEM_BARRIER_ALL is SHMEM_BARRIER. SHMEM_BARRIER takes in Active Set as a parameter, and only synchronizes the PEs in the Active Set.
- **SHMEM_BROADCAST:** It copies a block of data from one PE to one or more remote PEs in the Active Set. The root PE is specified by the input parameter, and it is the source of the data. All other PEs is the destination for the data. C interfaces SHMEM_BROADCAST32 and SHMEM_BROADCAST64 copies 32 and 64 bits of data from the root PE to all other PEs in the Active Set, respectively.

- **SHMEM_FCOLLECT:** This operation combines the data elements from each of PE in the Active Set, and sends the result to all PEs. All PEs contribute the same number of data elements. The number of elements in result is Nc, where N is number of PEs in the Active set and c is number of data elements in input. *OpenSHMEM* provides two interfaces for this operation, one for combining 32 bit data elements and other for combining 64 bit data elements.
- **SHMEM COLLECT:** This operation is similar to SHMEM_FCOLLECT except that each participating PE can contribute varying number of data elements.
- **SHMEM_REDUCTIONS:** This operation combines the data from all processes with a binary operation, and distributes the results of the operation to all processes. All participants in the operation input data that is of same size and type, and receive the same results. The operations supported are logical AND, logical OR, logical XOR, MIN, MAX, SUM, and PRODUCT. These operations are supported on short, integer, long and long long. Besides these datatypes, MIN, MAX, SUM and PRODUCT are supported on float, double, and complex. There is an interface for each of this combination. For example, there is interface for performing logical AND on integer, which is separate from the interface for performing logical AND on short. Overall, there are 44 SHMEM_REDUCTIONS.

Synchronization Mechanisms

- **SHMEM_QUIET:** This operation ensures ordering of *Put* and non-fetch *Atomic Memory Operations* (AMOs) operations from a PE to all PEs. Only after an SHMEM_QUIET operation that a PE can assume previously issued *Put* and AMO operations are completed. Figure 14 shows the completion semantics of SHMEM_PUT in presence of SHMEM_QUIET. The first and second invocation of SHMEM_PUT is completed before the completion of SHMEM_QUIET. Since the third invocation of SHMEM_PUT is after SHMEM_QUIET, its completion is not guaranteed by SHMEM_QUIET.

- **SHMEM_FENCE:** This operation ensures ordering of *Put* and AMOs operations to a specific PE. There is a subtle difference between SHMEM_FENCE and SHMEM_QUIET. The SHMEM_QUIET completes the *Put* and AMOs where as SHMEM_FENCE only orders these operations. If *OpenSHMEM* is implemented on a network interface that orders all its communication and AMO operations, the SHMEM_FENCE can be as simple as a No Operation (NOP).

Atomic Memory Operations

Atomic Memory Operation (AMO) is a one-sided communication (remote memory objects) operation with some guarantees. The guarantees include that accesses to remote memory through the AMO interfaces are exclusive. This guarantee is limited only to AMOs. If an AMO operation is mixed with a non-AMO operation on the same memory location then there are no atomicity guarantees. Similar to one-sided communication operations, AMOs can only be performed on the symmetric memory objects. *OpenSHMEM* defines interfaces for Atomic increment, ADD, SWAP, and conditional SWAP. It also includes interfaces for Fetch-and-ADD. There are two differences between Fetch-and-ADD and ADD interface. 1) Fetch-and-ADD returns the old value on the remote PE, and 2) it does not require SHMEM_QUIET operation for completion. Atomic ADD, SWAP, and conditional SWAP operations are considered complete only after SHMEM_QUIET.

Advantages of *OpenSHMEM*

- **RDMA Supported in Modern Hardware:** A majority of *OpenSHMEM* communication operation is one-sided. The HPC network interfaces natively support RDMA, which translates to native support for one-sided communication operation. Thus, *OpenSHMEM* model can be efficiently implemented on modern HPC hardware.

- **Programmer Productivity:** PGAS model presents the distributed memory systems as a single node with single large memory system. For application scientists, this model presents a lesser complexity to transition from programming a single node system to a parallel node system.

Figure 14. Shows the completion of SHMEM_PUT and SHMEM_GET in presence of SHMEM_QUIET

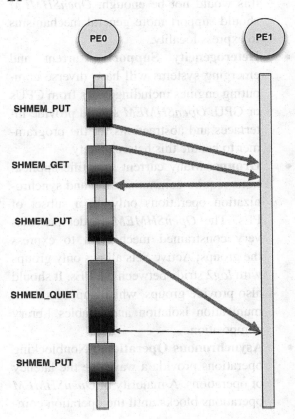

OpenSHMEM in Exascale Era

- **Extreme Parallelism:** The exascale systems are expected to have more than a billion threads. The *OpenSHMEM* model should provide mechanisms for programming such extremely parallel systems. It should support both fine-grained and coarse-grained parallelism.

- **Fault Handling:** The *OpenSHMEM* model does not report any errors for soft-or hard-errors or return any error codes. In exascale era, it would be critical to support various error classes and return error codes. In addition, it would be important to report on failures, function through some of the errors, and recover from some of the errors.

- **Locality:** The *OpenSHMEM* model supports limited hierarchy with local and not-local memory model. However, given the expected complexity of exascale systems this would not be enough. *OpenSHMEM* should support more general mechanisms to express locality.

- **Heterogeneity Support:** Current and emerging systems will have diverse computing engines including cores from CPUs or GPU. *OpenSHMEM* should provide interfaces and abstractions for the programmer to handle this heterogeneity.

- **Groups:** Many current scientific applications require communication and synchronization operations only on a subset of PEs. The *OpenSHMEM* model provides very constrained mechanism to express the groups; Active Sets allows only groups with $log2$ stride between the PEs. It should also provide groups, which supports communication isolation and enables library composition.

- **Asynchronous Operations:** Nonblocking operations provide a way hide the latency of operations. A majority of *OpenSHMEM* operations blocks until the operation completes. A asynchronous and nonblocking operations would enable *OpenSHMEM* programs to hide the latency. *OpenSHMEM* should provide non-blocking one-sided and collective communication operations for performance and handling extreme parallelism.

MODERN HPC NETWORK INTERFACES

HPC network interfaces provide the hardware to implement the communication abstractions of programming models. Often, the programming system provides the functionality that complements the network interface capabilities. Together, they provide the functionality required to implement the programming models. In addition to capabilities provided by non-HPC interfaces such as data transfer and routing, the HPC network interfaces provide capabilities such as OS bypass, offload functionality, optimization for both low-latency and high-bandwidth, flow-control, and optimization for various message sizes. These capabilities are aimed at achieving high performance and scalability required for scientific simulations.

This section discusses capabilities, design issues and trade-offs in Gemini (Alverson, Kaplan, & Roweth, 2010), which is a widely used network in modern supercomputers.

Gemini

Gemini is the network used in newer generation of Cray supercomputers (Alverson, Kaplan, & Roweth, 2010); the fastest and highly scalable non-classified supercomputer in the United States, Titan, uses Gemini for its networking needs (TOP500.org, 2012). In Titan, the Cray nodes are connected in a 3D Torus topology using the Gemini network. Gemini is particularly designed for building such networks, which are known to be highly scalable. The Gemini networks provide low-latency, high-bandwidth, and high throughput transports to efficiently implement the commonly used programming models such as MPI and *OpenSHMEM*.

Hardware Overview

A Gemini ASIC has two NICs and a 48-port router. The processors are connected through Hyper-Transport 3 interface to the NICs, and the NICs are connected the Gemini router via the netlink as in Figure 15. When node issues the commands for transferring the data, the NICs packetizes the data and issues the packets to the network. Gemini's NIC provides two hardware mechanisms for data transfer, Fast Memory Access (FMA) and Byte Transfer Engine (BTE).

Figure 15. Gemini ASIC showing its NIC and router components
(Cray Inc, 2010).

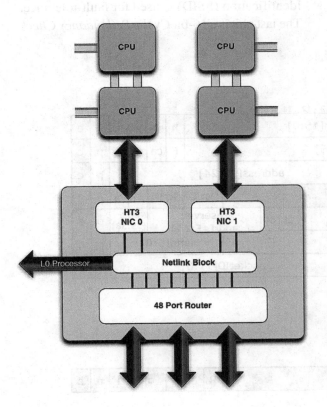

FMA mechanism aims to provide low-latency and high-message rate, while BTE provides high-bandwidth. FMA provides interfaces for *Put*, *Get*, and AMO operations. When the user writes 64 bytes to the put window on NIC, the NIC generates the remote *Put* transaction. When the user writes 8 bytes to the *Get* window, the NIC fetches upto 64 bytes or performs a fetching AMO. Both *Put* and *Get* are one-sided and does not require involvement of the remote node. FMA can generate synchronization events locally, remotely, or globally.

Local synchronization events are generated for completion of *Put*, *Get* or AMO operations. Remote events are generated on remote node (process) on completion of *Put* or AMO completion.

Global synchronization events are generated on the local node indicating the completion on the remote node. For example, when a *Put* transaction is completed on the remote node, the process on the local node receives a synchronization event. BTE provides mechanisms for *Send*, *Put*, and *Get*. Unlike FMA, the data transfer using BTE is asynchronous. The kernel writes the commands to Gemini NIC, and the NIC transfers the data asynchronously. This transfer semantics makes it more suitable for achieving high-bandwidth rather than achieving the low-latency. The *Send* mechanism does not require the receiver buffer address for data transfer. However, it requires the destination node to (process) post a receive buffer. Gemini router is a composition of tiles. A tile consists of one input port, output port, 8*8 switch, and all associated buffers.

Routing a Packet in GEMINI

For the data to be transferred from one node to other, the node issues commands for transferring the data, and writes them across the hypertransport. Then, the NIC packetizes the data and issues the packets to the network. The router tiles routes the packets to the destination NIC.

When a packet arrives at the input link of the tile, it is buffered at the input buffer. Based on the congestion and routing configuration, a column is selected for routing the packet. The packet is driven on the row bus. Then, at a selected column with the aid from the switch, it switches to the column.

At the column, the output port is selected and using the column bus the packet is routed to the output buffer. Gemini routes the packet either using a source routing, adaptive routing, or deterministic hash constructed from source and destination identifiers. The routing used for the data is configurable at the runtime. The diagnostic packets use the source routing, and data packets use either adaptive or deterministic hash. When adaptive routing is used, the routes are decided on per-packet basis, avoiding the congested route, and distributing the load. The deterministic-hash provides lesser flexibility. The details of algorithm are proprietary.

Gemini uses two different mechanisms for flow control. Inside the Gemini ASIC, it uses wormhole flow control to preserve the buffers. However across the network links, it uses the virtual cut-through flow control.

Addressing and Gemini PACKET

Figure 16 shows the Gemini packet with various header and data bits. The Gemini packet for transmission is divided into physical units (phits), which is a 24-bit physical unit. In the diagram, the first phit consists of destination Gemini ASIC identifier of 16-bits. This 16-bit identifier along with two-bit identifier identify the NIC on a node. The three bits h, a, r in the first phit are used for routing. When a bit is set, the packet is routed using adaptive routing, when h is set, the packet is routed using the deterministic-hash, and when r is set, the packet is routed using the source routing. The v bit specifies the virtual channel. Gemini uses one virtual channel for requests and another for responses. The second and third phit mostly used for logical address of the buffer. The Gemini network uses a 3-tuple of PE identifier, a *Memory Descriptor Handle* (MDH), and offset as logical address of buffer on remote user process. The last phit and Synchronization Sequence Identification (SSID) is used for fault-tolerance. The last phit is a 16-bit *Cyclic Redundancy Check*

Figure 16. Details of Gemini packet header (Cray Inc, 2010).

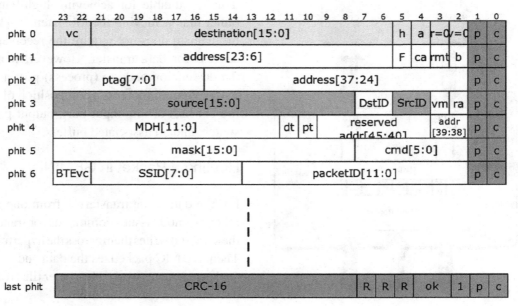

Figure 17. Important components in an MPI implementation for Gemini using the uGNI interface

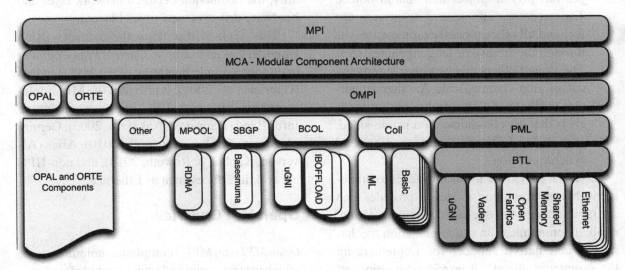

(CRC), which protects up to 64-bytes of data and headers. Gemini considers a set of packets, as a single transaction, and all the packets in a single transaction is identified by the same SSID.

Gemini Network Stack

Gemini provides both user and kernel interfaces for communication. *uGNI* and Distributed Memory Applications (DMAPP) are user-level interfaces, and kGNI is the kernel level interface (Cray Inc, 2011). The user-level processes using *uGNI* or DMAPP does not pass through the kernel for communication. It only requires kernel intervention for initialization. The programming models such as MPI are implemented using *uGNI* and Symmetric Hierarchical Memory (SHMEM) is implemented either using the *uGNI* or DMAPP interface.

- *uGNI*: *uGNI* provides interfaces exposing semantics conducive to message passing programming models (Pritchard, Gorodetsky, & Buntinas, 2011; Venkata, Graham, Hjelm, and Gutierrez, 2012a). In the message passing model, the process in a parallel job communicate via explicit communication. This involves packing the data into message,

transferring via explicit communication interfaces, matching it to the posted receive, and unpacking to the receive buffer. *uGNI* provides interfaces and semantics for implementing the message passing model. To implement this model, *uGNI* provides interfaces for implementing both one-sided and two-sided communication along with per-message completion notification. In addition, it provides FMA interfaces optimized for the small message transfer, and BTE interfaces optimized for the large message transfer. For scalability, it provides connectionless communication and sharing of resources between connections such as shared receive queues. Figure 17 shows different components of MPI implementation over *uGNI*; the components are highlighted. Next section discusses the details of the implementation.

- **DMAPP:** DMAPP (ten Bruggencate & Roweth, 2010) provides interfaces exposing semantics conducive to implementing both library-based one-sided programming models such as SHMEM and language-based one-sided programming models such as UPC and CAF. In the one-sided model, each process that is a part of the job has private object and shared object. The processes can access its private object and all other processes remote objects through the library or language interfaces. The shared object can be either symmetrical or non-symmetrical. Another important attribute of these programming models is that the communication is one-sided, and decoupling of communication and synchronization.

DMAPP provides various interfaces to implement this programming model. It provides rich set of interfaces for one-sided communication, explicit communication synchronization mechanisms, and native support for implementing the symmetric objects. It provides two types of one-sided communication interfaces: explicit one-sided communication and implicit one-sided communication. When an explicit one-sided communication is posted it returns an opaque object called descriptor. The descriptor is used to learn the status of the operation, and for completing the operation. The implicit operation does not return any descriptor. Using an explicit synchronization operation such as SHMEM_WAIT completes the implicit one-sided communication.

PROGRAMMING SYSTEM IMPLEMENTATION: A CASE STUDY WITH *OPEN MPI*

A library-based programming system is typically organized around three layers – protocol, low-level network, and hardware driver. The protocol layer provides the semantics and functionality specific to the programming model. The low-level network layer provides the network functionality abstracting the network interface. This enables the portability of programming system across different network interfaces. The hardware drivers are specific to a particular network interface. In many implementations, though low-level network API and hardware drivers provide different function-

ality, the distinction between network layer and hardware driver is sometimes blurred.

This section discusses these layers using *Open MPI* as an example. *Open MPI* is a popular open source implementation of the MPI standard (Gabriel et al., 2004). It provides the MPI implementation for many HPC interfaces including InfiniBand (Hamada & Nakasato, 2005), Gemini (Alverson, Kaplan, & Roweth, 2010), Aries (Alverson, Kaplan, & Roweth, 2014), and non-HPC network interfaces such as Ethernet.

Open MPI Overview

Open MPI is an MPI-3 complaint implementation, which was designed and implemented after drawing experiences from other MPI implementations such as LAM/MPI (Burns, Daoud, & Vaigl, 1994), LA-MPI (Aulwes et al., 2004), and FT-MPI (Fagg & Dongarra, 2000). Its design goal is to efficiently support various hardware architectures such as supercomputers, clusters of commodity nodes, and grids (nodes on a wide-area network). To efficiently support various architectures, *Open MPI* supports message transfer on various network interfaces which includes Ethernet, Gemini, Aries, and Infiniband; it utilizes available multiple network interfaces to maximize bandwidth availability by network striping and improve fault tolerance by dynamically handling the loss of network devices.

Open MPI uses well-defined component architecture, the Modular Component Architecture (MCA). The component architecture contains three functional areas: MCA, component frameworks, and modules. MCA manages and provides services to the component framework such as passing parameters from a higher layer to components and modules, and configuring, installing and initializing components. Each component framework performs a particular task in *Open MPI*. For example, *Open MPI* includes component frameworks such as a point-to-point transport layer and a point-to-point management layer for managing and implementing point-topoint operations. The component frameworks are also responsible for managing modules.

Modules are self-contained software components that implement communication functionality. Modules, which need to be included, are specified in the *Open MPI* configuration scripts; during *Open MPI* compilation, scripts discover the modules and these modules are compiled with other *Open MPI* code. They can be included in component frameworks either as static libraries or shared libraries; this flexibility provides the ability for including third-party modules that do not provide module source code. The included modules can choose to be enabled at runtime. If enabled, they are initialized and allocated resources.

Point-to-Point Communication in Open MPI

Point-to-point communications are implemented mostly using three component frameworks: Point-to-point Management Layer (PML), Byte Transfer Layer (BTL), and BTL Management Layer (BML). The PML implements all semantics for point-to-point communication including dif-

ferent variations of MPI_SEND and MPI RECV. It implements protocols optimizing for message sizes including eager and rendezvous protocol; eager protocol is an optimized protocol for small message transfer, and rendezvous protocol is an optimized protocol for larger message transfer. The BML is a thin multiplexing layer, which can demultiplex message to multiple BTLs and combine the messages from multiple BTLs. It enables sharing of BTLs by the upper layer. Currently, it has one implementation of BML called R2.

The BTL module exposes a well-defined interface for moving data (in bytes) through the network transport. It provides interfaces to support both two-sided and one-sided communication semantics. A single BTL implementation typically supports one network interface. Though there can be multiple BTL modules of single type of BTL. Currently, there is a BTL implementation for Gemini (*uGNI*) (Gutierrez, Venkata, Hjelm, & Graham, 2012), *InfiniBand* (OpenIB), Ethernet (TCP and usnic), and Shared-memory (SM and Vader) (Gutierrez, Venkata, Hjelm, & Graham, 2012) network interfaces. Decoupling the byte transfer code from the transport protocol code eases the maintenance and portability of code.

Figure 18. Main components of Open MPI to implement MPI

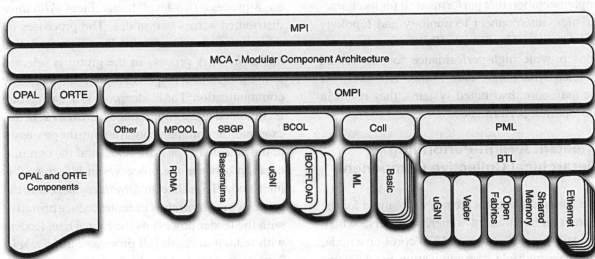

Porting *Open MPI* to the new network interface requires implementing a new BTL. If other programming models such as *OpenSHMEM* is implemented in this infrastructure, only a PML component has to implemented, allowing reuse all of networking code.

COLL: Collective Component Framework

COLL is the main collective component framework of *Open MPI*. There are two main implementations of collective components *Tuned* and Cheetah (Oak Ridge Leadership Computing, 2014). Besides, there is a specialized collective component for Mellanox's *InfiniBand* hardware, and non-blocking implementation of collectives (Hoefler, Lumsdaine, & Rehm, 2007). In this section, we discuss *Tuned, which* is the default collective implementation, and Cheetah, a high-performing collective implementation that supports both blocking and non-blocking collective semantics. *Tuned* is a highly stable collective component in *Open MPI* (Fagg, Pjesivac-grbovic, Bosilca, Dongarra, & Jeannot, 2006). It provides many implementations for each type of collective operation. The main goal of the *Tuned* component was to provide the flexibility to the application (and user) to choose the collective algorithm and implementation that performs well for its characteristics, interconnect technology and topology and data size. The *Tuned* collective implementations provide high-performance for distributed systems with single-core nodes. However, for the multicore distributed systems, they result in sub-optimal performance.

Cheetah: A High-Performing Hierarchical Collective Component

The *Tuned* collectives are not well-suited for the current generation of supercomputers, which typically consist of tens of CPU cores on a node, and have multiple communication mechanisms -multiple cache levels, intra-node communication buses, and network interfaces -with varying performance characteristics. The *Tuned* collectives do not consider these performance variations in communication mechanisms in modern systems, and typically can only use one implementation for any given collective invocation, resulting in sub-optimal performance. Cheetah collectives use the hierarchical design to provide the efficient implementations for the multicore systems (Graham, Ladd, & Venkata, 2010). Cheetah is a framework for building hierarchical collectives in *Open MPI*. It provides support for both blocking and non-blocking MPI collectives.

In Cheetah, the hierarchical collective operations are expressed as a group of independently progressing collective primitives, where each collective primitive is optimized for a specific communication hierarchy. The design of the framework is driven by the goal to provide collective operation implementations tailored to specific communication hardware, while also retaining the re-usability of the collective implementation. In Cheetah, this is achieved by de-coupling the collective operation implementation from the topological organization of the processes.

To understand the hierarchical collective implementations consider an example of hierarchical *Allreduce* operation. Figure 20 shows an 8-process two-level hierarchical *Allreduce* distributed across two nodes. The processes on the same node are grouped into a group called *hierarchy 1*. A process in the group is selected as a leader, and is responsible for inter-hierarchy communication. The leader process of each group is combined into a group called *hierarchy 2*. In this example, the communication among the processes in the *hierarchy 1* is intra-node, and the communication between the processes in *hierarchy 2* is inter-node. To realize an *Allreduce* operation, the processes in *hierarchy 1* execute Reduce primitive with the leader process as the root. Then, leaders with reduction result (all processes in *hierarchy 2*) participate in an *Allreduce* primitive operation,

Figure 19. Cheetah frameworks and components within Open MPI (Venkata, Shamis, Graham, Ladd, & Sampath, 2013).

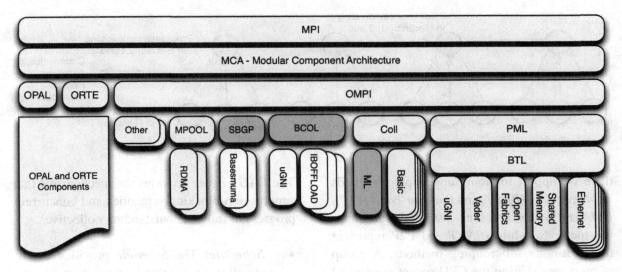

and the result of Allreduce is broadcast to all processes in *hierarchy 1*. Extending this approach to three-level hierarchy is shown in Figure 21. An *n*-level hierarchical *Allreduce* is achieved with *n* − 1 *Reduce* and *Broadcast* primitives, and one *Allreduce* primitive.

Figure 19 shows Cheetah's frameworks and its components to implement the hierarchical collectives. It includes components to create hierarchies (or called as subgroups -SBGP), provide optimized primitives (BCOL), and *Messaging Layer* (ML), which acts as a controller. The ML

provides mapping between primitives and MPI semantics, with the help of enhancements, *DAG Engine* and *Schedule*, it controls and progresses the collectives.

Subgrouping Component (SBGP)

The subgrouping component groups the processes in the job into multiple subgroups based on the communication mechanism shared among them; the hierarchy in Figure 20 is referred as subgroups here, and they are used interchangeably. Currently,

Figure 20. Communication pattern in a two-level Cheetah Allreduce (Venkata, Shamis, Graham, Ladd, & Sampath, 2013).

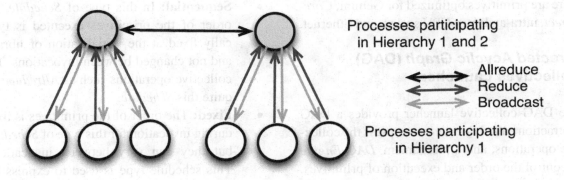

Processes participating in Hierarchy 1 and 2

Allreduce
Reduce
Broadcast

Processes participating in Hierarchy 1

Figure 21. Communication pattern in a three-level Cheetah Allreduce (Venkata, Shamis, Graham, Ladd, & Sampath, 2013).

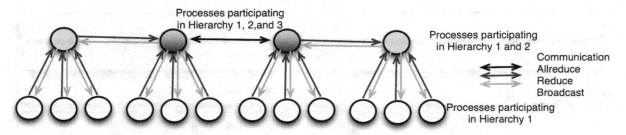

there is support for four subgrouping methods -*UMA*, *Socket*, *IBNET*, and *Point-to-Point* (P2P). *UMA* and *Socket* represents intra-node subgrouping methods, while *IBNET* and P2P represent the inter-node subgrouping methods. A group of processes sharing the CPU socket is grouped into *Socket* subgroup, and processes sharing the CPU node are grouped into *UMA* subgroup. A group of processes connected through Mellanox's *InfiniBand* HCA with *Core-Direct* is grouped into *IBNET* subgroup. The processes connected through none of these communication mechanisms, but other interconnects such as Gemini, SeaStar, Ethernet or any thing else is grouped into a P2P subgroup.

Basic Collective (BCOL) Primitives

The BCOL primitives provide a basic implementation of collective operations, which are not necessarily complaint to the MPI standard. The primitives are optimized implementations for a particular communication mechanism. Currently there are primitives optimized for Gemini, *Core-Direct*, intra-and inter-CPU socket, and Ethernet.

Directed Acyclic Graph (DAG) Collectives Launcher

The DAG collective launcher provides a DAG abstraction called *Schedule* to express the collective operations, and a mechanism, *DAG Engine* to control the order and execution of primitives.

The *DAG Engine* provides the mechanisms that support non-blocking semantics and concurrent progress of multiple outstanding collectives.

- **Schedule:** The *Schedule* provides an abstraction to express combination of collective primitives, and its execution order. For example, the DAG in Figure 22 shows a *Schedule* for *Allreduce* in Figure 22. Each node in the graph represents a collective primitive. The incoming edge describes the list of primitives that have been completed before the collective primitive represented by the node is executed. The outgoing edge imposes a constraint on the target node. In the figure, the *Broadcast* node is required to wait until the *Allreduce* node is completed. Each process in the collective operation has its own *Schedule*. The figure shows the *Schedule* for a leader and non-leader process. Three types of *Schedule*'s can express all collective operations in the MPI standard: Fixed, Sequential, and General.

- **Sequential:** In this type of *Schedule*, the order of the primitives executed is typically fixed at the initialization of library, and not changed between invocations. The collective operations such as *Allreduce* require this *Schedule*.

- **Fixed:** The order of the primitives is fixed during invocation for this type of *Schedule*, but they can vary between invocations. This schedule type is used to express the collective operations that are dependent on the root of the collective operation to determine the order. For example, the *Broadcast* collective operation requires the subgroup containing root to be executed first, and the *Reduce* operation requires the subgroup containing the root to execute last.

- **General:** The order of primitives executed is not fixed in this type of *Schedule*. As a consequence, any primitive that can be progressed is executed. This is used by collective operations such as Barrier, as it does not impose dependencies between the primitives.

- *DAG Engine*: It controls the order and execution of collective primitives expressed by the *Schedule*; it acts as an interpreter of the *Schedule*. *DAG Engine* makes use of two list structures to progress and complete the primitives. When a collective operation is invoked, the *DAG Engine* adds each primitive in the *Schedule* to the progress list, progresses the primitive, and when the primitive is waiting for resources, it removes the collective primitive and adds it to the pending list. A collective primitive could be waiting on network resources, memory resources, or other processes to progress. The *DAG Engine* then progresses the primitive that can be progressed. Thus supporting the non-blocking semantics for the collective operation, and also enabling multiple outstanding primitives.

Other Important Components of *Open MPI*

- **Open Run-time Environment (ORTE):** The ORTE provides the functionality required for bootstrapping *Open MPI* transport components. The bootstrap functionality includes launching of processes on the supercomputer, and provides a basic set of communication interfaces. The communication interfaces are not necessarily designed for performance, but rather for portability and implemented for the commonly available network interfaces.

- **Open Portable Access Layer (OPAL):** The OPAL component framework provides basic network utilities required for implementing the HPC network library. It provides functionality to implement the MCA architecture. In addition, it includes commonly used functionality such as portable implementation of atomic operations, high-resolution timers, processor and memory affinity functionality.

- **HPC Applications and Cloud:** Cloud is an emerging platform for HPC applications (Armbrust et al., 2009). There is growing interest and a large body of research to use Cloud for HPC applications. In this section, we will survey some of the research studies that consider the question "Are Clouds ready for HPC applications"?

Figure 22. Schedule for a two-level Allreduce in Cheetah infrastructure (Venkata, Shamis, Graham, Ladd, & Sampath, 2013).

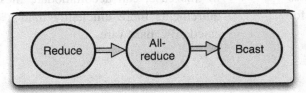

Leader Schedule

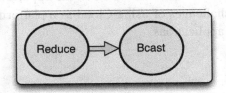

Non-leader Schedule

CLOUDS FOR HPC APPLICATIONS

There are many definitions of Cloud, and there is no community consensus on the definition. For the discussion in this chapter, we will consider the definition of Cloud by National Institute of Standards and Technology (NIST): "Cloud computing is a model for enabling ubiquitous, convenient, on-demand network access to a shared pool of configurable computing resources (e.g., networks, servers, storage, applications, and services) that can be rapidly provisioned and released with minimal management effort or service provider interaction" (Mell & Grance, 2009). Some examples of commercial clouds are Amazon's Elastic Compute Cloud (EC2), Microsoft's Azure, and Google's Cloud Platform. OpenStack (OpenStack, 2014), Eucalyptus (Nurmi et al., 2008), and Nimbus (Nimbus, 2014) are software frameworks that enable Cloud services on HPC systems.

The Clouds are composed of commodity server hardware -commodity processor and network, and have tens of thousands of nodes connected together, typically by a 10-gigabit Ethernet (10GbE). The nodes typically run a commodity operating system, and have multiple Virtual Machines (VMs) running simultaneously. They are connected to the spinning drives for storage. The amount of resources allocated to a user can be varied with very less overhead.

Use of Clouds for HPC applications presents some advantages and some disadvantages. However, it will be shortsighted to dismiss Cloud as a platform for HPC applications. Rather, one should carefully evaluate HPC problems that are suitable for the Cloud. In the rest of the section, we provide a deeper discussion on the opportunities and challenges of using Cloud as a platform for HPC applications.

OPPORTUNITIES

- The operating cost of using Cloud, as infrastructure is considered much lower than the operating cost of HPC centers with low utilization rates. (Fox & Gannon, 2014) estimate that a 3 year Total Cost of Ownership (TCO) for a 512 node HPC cluster is $7 million dollars, and 1024 core Linux instance of Amazon EC2 is about $2.3 million dollars.
- Cloud provides flexible resource provisioning. For applications that have varying resource requirements, the Cloud would be more appropriate than a dedicated HPC cluster as changes in resource requirements can be easily accommodated.
- Clouds can provide a customized environment for applications. The users can customize the OS instances, software stack, and hardware capabilities to suit the needs of the applications. For some applications these customizations might be required for efficiency. For example consider the Genome analysis pipeline, which is a combination of many components (Wang, Lu, Yu, Gibbs, & Yu, 2013). Also, some HPC applications perform simulation and visualize those results using the visualization tools. Both simulation and visualization would require different software stacks and the Cloud infrastructure would provide a better execution environment. The various components of the pipeline can have different OS, system software, and hardware requirements (Brightwell, Oldfield, Maccabe, & Bernholdt, 2013). The Cloud, in this case, can accommodate these requirements more efficiently than a dedicated HPC hardware.

- The Cloud infrastructure is typically enabled to handle hardware and software faults. On failure of the hardware, the Cloud migrates the user workload to a new VM. Scalability of future generation systems are required for satisfying the growing needs of HPC applications. The future generation systems are expected to have more faults (Daly et al., 2012), in this context, the Cloud is an important platform for HPC applications.

- Turnaround time of a job in the Cloud can be an advantage for HPC scientists. The leadership computing systems have very high utilization rate and it could sometimes take days to schedule a job. The Cloud with significant amount of resources, elastic resource provisioning, and resource allocation strategies could be practical for many HPC jobs.

- Performance of embarrassingly parallel applications can be similar to HPC systems. Research shows that for applications such as Genomic studies, the applications performance in Cloud infrastructure is similar to HPC hardware. In general, the researchers observe that scientific applications with low-communication and I/O can use the Cloud without significant performance degradation (Yelick, Coghlan, Draney, & Canon, 2011; Hoffa et al., 2008).

CHALLENGES

- The programming models for HPC-Cloud applications are not well established. Traditional HPC programming models are designed for low latency and high bandwidth networks, and as a result they would perform very poorly (Gupta & Milojicic, 2011; Iosup et al., 2011). The state-of-the-art is rapidly changing in this area with research evaluating the traditional models for Cloud, using MPI for a subset of applications on Cloud, and transforming Cloud applications to use the MPI.

- There are no standard programming model interfaces for HPC applications to use the Cloud infrastructure, resulting in significant porting effort to move from one Cloud infrastructure to the other.

- *MapReduce* (MR) (Dean & Ghemawat, 2008), a parallel programming for the Cloud, is not well suited for HPC applications. Research has shown that MR programming model can be useful for some applications, (Dede, Govindaraju, Gunter, & Ramakrishnan, 2011) classifies the application control flow and argues that for most of HPC applications flows MR would require significant programming effort to convert HPC applications to use the MR model.

- The deployment of a virtual cluster is a time consuming operation because it requires configuring and initializing the VM, virtual network, virtual storage, in addition to application initialization. As a consequence, applications with small runtime would find the overhead negatively impacting the user experience.

- Cloud's system noise and performance interference from other applications can degrade HPC application performance. OS Noise and performance inference from other applications is known to impact the performance of HPC applications (Ferreira, Bridges, Brightwell, & Pedretti, 2010). This will be exacerbated with using the Cloud as computation platform for HPC applications.

- Cloud security could be an issue for some HPC applications. Though security seems like not a concern in general (Yelick, Coghlan, Draney, & Canon, 2011), some applications related to national security, sensitive technology, and privacy would sometimes require a hardware boundary (separation) which Cloud platform lacks.

- Cloud's cost advantage fades away when compared to dedicated HPC centers such as *Oak Ridge Leadership Computing Facility* (OLCF) Argonne Leadership Computing Facility (ALCF) and National Energy Research Scientific Computing Center (NERSC). In these dedicated HPC centers, the systems are highly utilized and they already achieve the advantages of scale and resource consolidation of Clouds (Yelick, Coghlan, Draney, & Canon, 2011).

In conclusion, there are many advantages of using Cloud for some scientific applications such as economy, elastic resource provisioning, customization of environment, and availability. However, for further adoption of scientific applications in Cloud environment there is a need in research and development of programming models, standardizing *Application Programming Interface*s (APIs), research to reduce latency and increase bandwidth of networks, reduce OS noise and performance interference (He, Zhou, Kobler, Duffy, & McGlynn, 2010; Yelick, Coghlan, Draney, & Canon, 2011). This is an evolving area of research; the community should evaluate the answer to the question as technology and economic models of Clouds change.

CONCLUSION

In this chapter, we provide an overview of parallel programming models used for the HPC systems. Particularly, we discuss the message passing model, shared-memory model, and PGAS model with emphasis on the relations among them and also providing some historical significance.

Then, we discuss the implementation of programming models typically called as programming systems, with MPI and OpenSHMEM as examples. For MPI and OpenSHMEM, the chapter provided a discussion on the functionality, interfaces, and semantics of the interfaces.

MPI and OpenSHMEM have been successful in meeting the scalability and performance expectations of the current generation HPC systems and applications. The central challenge for these programming models is to accommodate billion way parallelism, heterogeneity in computing cores, reducing power consumption, abstracting multiple varieties of memory, while still providing an easier user interface for programming the next generation systems. A survey of research shows that there are many advantages of using these programming models. However, these programming models are needed but not sufficient. There are many emerging programming models, however the hybrid programming model is the promising one. It is showing a potential to accommodate the complexity of next generation HPC systems and also does not require complete re-write of legacy applications. The discussion of the programming systems was concluded with a discussion Gemini NIC, Open MPI, and Cheetah; Open MPI is a popular open source implementation of MPI, and Cheetah is collective operation framework.

The chapter concludes with a discussion on the question: Are Clouds ready for HPC applications? A survey of research shows that the some of the HPC applications that have low communication and I/O can take advantage of the Cloud platform. The advantages of Clouds such as low operating cost fades away when compared to dedicated HPC centers, while customizability and flexible resource provisioning remains attractive for adoption of HPC applications.

REFERENCES

Alverson, B., Froese, E., Kaplan, L., & Roweth, D. (2014). *Cray XC series network*. Academic Press.

Alverson, R., Roweth, D., & Kaplan, L. (2010). The gemini system interconnect. In *Proceedings of High Performance Interconnects (HOTI)* (pp. 83–87). IEEE. doi:10.1109/HOTI.2010.23

Amarasinghe, S., Hall, M., Lethin, R., Pingali, K., Quinlan, D., Sarkar, V., & Snir, M. et al. (2011). Exascale programming challenges. In *Proceedings of the Workshop on Exascale Programming Challenges*. U.S Department of Energy, Office of Science, Office of Advanced Scientific Computing Research (ASCR).

Argonne National Laboratory. (2015). *MPICH2: High-performance and widely portable MPI* (version 3.1.4) [Software]. Available from http://www.mcs.anl.gov/research/projects/mpich2/

Armbrust, M., Fox, A., Griffith, R., Joseph, A. D., Katz, R. H., Konwinski, A., Lee, G., Patterson, D. A., Rabkin, A., & Zaharia, M. (2009). *Above the clouds: A Berkeley view of cloud computing*. Technical Report. Academic Press.

Aulwes, R. T., Daniel, D. J., Desai, N. N., Graham, R. L., Risinger, L. D., Taylor, M. A., . . . Sukalski, M. W. (2004). Architecture of LA-MPI, a network-fault-tolerant MPI. In *Proceedings of International Parallel and Distributed Processing Symposium*. Academic Press.

Bala, V., Bruck, J., Bryant, R., Cypher, R., de Jong, P., Elustondo, P., & Snir, M. et al. (1994). The IBM external user interface for scalable parallel systems. *Parallel Computing*, *20*(4), 445–462. doi:10.1016/0167-8191(94)90022-1

Brightwell, R., Oldfield, R., Maccabe, A. B., & Bernholdt, D. E. (2013). Hobbes: Composition and virtualization as the foundations of an extreme-scale OS/R. In *Proceedings of the 3rd International Workshop on Runtime and Operating Systems for Supercomputers*. ACM. doi:10.1145/2491661.2481427

Burns, G., Daoud, R., & Vaigl, J. (1994). *LAM: An open cluster environment for MPI*. University of Toronto.

Butler, R., & Lush, E. (1992). *User's guide to the p4 programming system. Academic Press.*

Chapman, B., Curtis, T., Pophale, S., Poole, S., Kuehn, J., Koelbel, C., & Smith, L. (2010). Introducing OpenSHMEM: SHMEM for the PGAS community. In *Proceedings of the Fourth Conference on Partitioned Global Address Space Programming Model*. New York, NY: Academic Press. doi:10.1145/2020373.2020375

Coarfa, C., Dotsenko, Y., Eckhardt, J., & Mellor-Crummey, J. (2004). Co-array fortran performance and potential: An NPB experimental study. In Languages and Compilers for Parallel Computing (LNCS), (vol. 2958, pp. 177–193). Springer Berlin Heidelberg.

UPC Consortium. (2005). *UPC language specifications, v1.2*. Tech Report LBNL-59208. Lawrence Berkeley National Lab. Available from http://www.gwu.edu/~upc/docs/upc_specs_1.2.pdf

Cray Inc. (2011). *Using the GNI and DMAPP APIs*. Cray Software Document, volume S-2446-4003. Available from http://docs.cray.com/books/S-2446-4003/S-2446-4003.pdf

Cray Inc. (2013). *Chapel language specification version 0.93*. Technical report. Available from http://chapel.cray.com/spec/spec-0.93.pdf

Daly, J., Harrod, B., Hoang, T., Nowell, L., Adolf, B., Shekhar Borkar, S., DeBardeleben, N., ... Woodward, P., (2012). *Inter-agency workshop on HPC resilience at extreme scale*. Technical Report. Available from http://institute.lanl.gov/resilience/docs/Inter-AgencyResilienceReport.pdf

Dean, J., & Ghemawat, S. (2008). MapReduce: Simplified data processing on large clusters. *Communications of the ACM*, *51*(1), 107–113. doi:10.1145/1327452.1327492

Dede, E., Govindaraju, M., Gunter, D., & Ramakrishnan, L. (2011). Riding the elephant: Managing ensembles with Hadoop. In *Proceedings of the 2011 ACM International Workshop on Many Task Computing on Grids and Supercomputers* (pp. 49–58). New York: ACM. doi:10.1145/2132876.2132888

DOE. (2014). *Titan: A Cray XK system at the Oak Ridge National Laboratory*. Retrieved from https://www.olcf.ornl.gov/computing-resources/titan-cray-xk7/

Fagg, G. E., & Dongarra, J. (2000). FT-MPI: Fault tolerant MPI, supporting dynamic applications in a dynamic world. In *Proceedings of the 7th European PVM/MPI Users' Group Meeting on Recent Advances in Parallel Virtual Machine and Message Passing Interface* (pp. 346–353). London, UK: Springer-Verlag. doi:10.1007/3-540-45255-9_47

Fagg, G. E., Pjesivac-grbovic, J., Bosilca, G., Dongarra, J. J., & Jeannot, E. (2006). Flexible collective communication tuning architecture applied to open MPI. In *Proceedings of 2006 Euro PVM/MPI*. Academic Press.

Ferreira, K. B., Bridges, P. G., Brightwell, R., & Pedretti, K. (2010). Impact of system design parameters on application noise sensitivity. In *Proceedings of the 2010 IEEE International Conference on Cluster Computing*. IEEE. doi:10.1109/CLUSTER.2010.41

Fox, G., & Gannon, D. (2014). *Using clouds for technical computing*. Available from http://grids.ucs.indiana.edu/ptliupages/publications/Clouds_Technical_Computing_FoxGannonv2.pdf

Gabriel, E., Fagg, G. E., Bosilca, G., Angskun, T., Dongarra, J. J., Squyres, J. M., Sahay, V. Kambadur, …Woodall, T. S. (2004). Open MPI: Goals, concept, and design of a next generation MPI implementation. In Proceedings, 11th European PVM/MPI Users' Group Meeting. Budapest, Hungary: Academic Press.

Geist, A., Kale, S., Kramer, B., & Snir, M. (2009). Toward exascale resilience. *International Journal of High Performance Computing Applications*, 374–388.

Graham, R. L., Ladd, J. S., & Venkata, M. G. (2010). Hierarchy aware blocking and nonblocking collective communications - The effects of shared memory in the Cray XT environment. In *Proceedings of the 2010 Cray User Group Annual Technical Conference*. Academic Press.

Gropp, W. D., & Snir, M. (2013). *Programming for exascale computers*. Available from http://www.mcs.anl.gov/papers/P4053-0313.pdf

Gupta, A., & Milojicic, D. (2011). Evaluation of HPC applications on cloud. In *Proceedings of the 2011 Sixth Open Cirrus Summit* (pp. 22–26). Washington, DC: IEEE Computer Society. doi:10.1109/OCS.2011.10

Gutierrez, S. K., Venkata, M. G., Hjelm, T. N., & Graham, R. (2012). Performance evaluation of open MPI on Cray XE/XK systems. In *Proceedings of 20th Annual IEEE Symposium on High-Performance Interconnects, HOTI 2012*. Santa Clara, CA: Academic Press. doi:10.1109/HOTI.2012.11

Hamada, T., & Nakasato, N. (2005). InfiniBand trade association, InfiniBand architecture specification. In *Proceedings of International Conference on Field Programmable Logic and Applications* (pp. 366–373). Academic Press. doi:10.1109/FPL.2005.1515749

Hammond, J., Ghosh, S., & Chapman, B. (2014). Implementing OpenSHMEM using MPI-3 one-sided communication. In OpenSHMEM and Related Technologies: Experiences, Implementations, and Tools (LNCS), (vol. 8356, pp. 44–58). Springer International Publishing. doi:10.1007/978-3-319-05215-1_4

Harrison, R. J. (1993). *Tcgmsg send/receive subroutines – Version 4.02 user's manual*. Pacific Northwest Laboratory.

He, Q., Zhou, S., Kobler, B., Duffy, D., & McGlynn, T. (2010). Case study for running HPC applications in public clouds. In *Proceedings of the 19th ACM International Symposium on High Performance Distributed Computing* (pp. 395–401). New York, NY: ACM. doi:10.1145/1851476.1851535

Hoefler, T., Lumsdaine, A., & Rehm, W. (2007). Implementation and performance analysis of non-blocking collective operations for MPI. In *Proceedings of the 2007 International Conference on High Performance Computing, Networking, Storage and Analysis, SC07*. IEEE Computer Society/ACM.

Hoefler, T., Squyres, J., Bosilca, G., Fagg, G., Lumsdaine, A., & Rehm, W. (2006). *Non-blocking collective operations for MPI-2*. Indiana University.

Hoffa, C., Mehta, G., Freeman, T., Deelman, E., Keahey, K., Berriman, B., & Good, J. (2008). On the use of cloud computing for scientific workflows. In *Proceedings of eScience* (pp. 640–645). Academic Press. doi:10.1109/eScience.2008.167

Iosup, A., Ostermann, S., Yigitbasi, N., Prodan, R., Fahringer, T., & Epema, D. (2011). Performance analysis of cloud computing services for many-tasks scientific computing. *IEEE Transactions on Parallel and Distributed Systems, 22*(6), 931–945. doi:10.1109/TPDS.2011.66

Mell, P., & Grance, T. (2011). *The NIST definition of cloud computing (2011, September)*. Available from http://csrc.nist.gov/publications/nistpubs/800-145/SP800-145.pdf

Nieplocha, J., Harrison, R., & Littlefield, R. (1994). Global arrays: A portable shared-memory programming model for distributed memory computers. In Proceedings of Supercomputing (pp. 340–349, 816). Academic Press.

Nimbus. (2014). *Nimbus science cloud* [Software]. Available from http://www.nimbusproject.org/downloads/

Nurmi, D., Wolski, R., Grzegorczyk, C., Obertelli, G., Soman, S., Youseff, L., & Zagorod-nov, D. (2008). The eucalyptus open-source cloud-computing system. In *Proceedings of Cloud Computing and Its Applications*. Academic Press.

Oak Ridge Leadership Computing. (2014). *Cheetah collective library* [Software]. Available from http://www.csm.ornl.gov/cheetah/index.html

Ohio State University. (2014). *MVAPICH: MPI over InfiniBand, 10GigE/iWARP and RoCE*. Retrieved from http://mvapich.cse.ohio-state.edu/download/mvapich2/

OpenMP Architecture Review Board (2013). *OpenMP application program interface specification*. Academic Press.

OpenSHMEM Org. (2011). *OpenSHMEM specification*. Available from http://openshmem.org

OpenSHMEM Org. (2014). *OpenSHMEM specification*. Available from http://openshmem.org

OpenStack. (2014). *OpenStack cloud software* [Software]. Available from https://www.openstack.org/software/

Pierce, P. (1988). The NX/2 operating system. In *Proceedings of the Third Conference on Hypercube Concurrent Computers and Applications* (pp. 384–390). ACM Press.

Pritchard, H., Gorodetsky, I., & Buntinas, D. (2011). A uGNI-based MPICH2 nemesis network module for the cray XE. In *Proceedings of the 18th European MPI Users' Group conference on Recent advances in the message passing interface* (pp. 110–119). Berlin, Germany: Springer-Verlag. doi:10.1007/978-3-642-24449-0_14

Reid, J. (2008). The new features of Fortran 2008. *SIGPLAN Fortran Forum, 27*(2), 8–21.

Sandia National Laboratory. (2014). *Portals-SHMEM* [Software]. Available from https://code.google.com/p/portals-shmem/downloads/list

Shalf, J., Dosanjh, S., & Morrison, J. (2011). Exascale computing technology challenges. In *Proceedings of the 9th International Conference on High Performance Computing for Computational Science*. Springer-Verlag.

Skjellum, A., Smith, S. G., Doss, N. E., Leung, A. P., & Morari, M. (1994). The design and evolution of zipcode. *Parallel Computing, 20*(4), 565–596. doi:10.1016/0167-8191(94)90029-9

Sunderam, V. S. (1990). PVM: A framework for parallel distributed computing. *Concurrency (Chichester, England), 2*(4), 315–339. doi:10.1002/cpe.4330020404

ten Bruggencate, M., & Roweth, D. (2010). DMAPP: An API for one-sided program models on baker systems. In *Proceedings of the 2010 Cray User Group Annual Technical Conference*. Academic Press.

The M. P. I. Forum. (1994). *MPI: A message passing interface*. Technical Report. Available from http://www.mpi-forum.org/docs

The M. P. I. Forum. (2012). *MPI: A message passing interface*. Technical report. Available from http://www.mpi-forum.org/docs/mpi-3.0/mpi30-report.pdf

TOP500.org. (2012). *TOP500 supercomputing sites*. Available from http://www.top500.org/lists/

Venkata, M. G., Graham, R. L., Hjelm, N. T., & Gutierrez, S. K. (2012a). Open MPI for Cray XE/XK systems. In *Proceedings of the 2012 Cray User Group Annual Technical Conference*. Stuttgart, Germany: Academic Press.

Venkata, M. G., Graham, R. L., Ladd, J. S., & Shamis, P. (2012b). Exploring the all-to-all collective optimization space with ConnectX CORE-direct. In *Proceedings of the 41st International Conference on Parallel Processing*. Pittsburgh, PA: Academic Press. doi:10.1109/ICPP.2012.28

Venkata, M. G., Graham, R. L., Ladd, J. S., Shamis, P., Hjelm, N. T., & Gutierrez, S. K. (2012c). Exploiting atomic operations for collective on Cray XE/XK systems. In *EuroMPI 2012: Proceedings of the 19th EuroMPI Conference*. Vienna, Austria: Academic Press.

Venkata, M. G., Shamis, P., Graham, R. L., Ladd, J. S., & Sampath, R. (2013). Optimizing blocking and nonblocking reduction operations for multicore systems: Hierarchical design and implementation. In *Proceedings of IEEE International Conference on Cluster Computing*. Indianapolis, IN: IEEE. doi:10.1109/CLUSTER.2013.6702676

Wang, Y., Lu, J., Yu, J., Gibbs, R. A., & Yu, F. (2013). An integrative variant analysis pipeline for accurate genotype/haplotype inference in population NGS data. *Genome Research, 23*(5), 833–842. doi:10.1101/gr.146084.112 PMID:23296920

Yelick, K., Coghlan, S., Draney, B., & Canon, R. (2011). The Magellan report on cloud computing for science, U.S. Department of Energy. Office of Science, Office of Advanced Scientific Computing Research, Tech. Rep. IEEE.

ADDITIONAL READING

Alverson, R., Roweth, D., & Kaplan, L. (2010). The Gemini System Interconnect. In High Performance Interconnects (HOTI), 2010 IEEE 18th Annual Symposium on, pages 83–87. doi:10.1109/HOTI.2010.23

Brightwell, R., Oldfield, R., Maccabe, A. B., & Bernholdt, D. E. (2013). Hobbes: Composition and virtualization as the foundations of an extreme-scale os/r. In *Proceedings of the 3rd International Workshop on Runtime and Operating Systems for Supercomputers, ROSS '13*, pages 2:1–2:8, New York, NY, USA. ACM. doi:10.1145/2491661.2481427

Dean, J., & Ghemawat, S. (2008). Mapreduce: Simplified data processing on large clusters. *Communications of the ACM*, *51*(1), 107–113. doi:10.1145/1327452.1327492

Dongarra, J., Fox, G., Kennedy, K., Torczon, L., & Gropp, W. (Eds.). (2002). *The Source- book of Parallel Computing. The Morgan Kaufmann Series in Computer Architecture and Design.* Morgan Kaufmann.

Foster, I. (1995). *Designing and Building Parallel Programs: Concepts and Tools for Par- allel Software Engineering.* Boston, MA, USA: Addison-Wesley Longman Publishing Co., Inc.

Fox, G., & Gannon, D. (2014). Using Clouds for Technical Computing. Available from http://grids.ucs.indiana.edu/ptliupages/publications/Clouds_Technical_Computing_FoxGannonv2.pdf

Gabriel, E., Fagg, G. E., Bosilca, G., Angskun, T., Dongarra, J. J., Squyres, J. M., & Sahay, V. Kambadur, …Woodall, T. S. (2004). Open MPI: Goals, Concept, and Design of a Next Generation MPI Implementation. In Proceedings, 11th European PVM/MPI Users' Group Meeting, Budapest, Hungary.

Gavrilovska, A. (2009). *Attaining High Performance Communications: A Vertical Approach* (1st ed.). Chapman & Hall/CRC. doi:10.1201/b10249

Gropp, W., Lusk, E., & Skjellum, A. (1999). Using MPI (2Nd Ed.): Portable Parallel Pro- gramming with the Message-passing Interface. MIT Press, Cambridge, MA, USA.

Nimbus (2014). Nimbus Science Cloud. Available from http://www.nimbusproject.org/

OpenSHMEM Org. (2014). OpenSHMEM specification. Available from http://openshmem.org

OpenStack. (2014). OpenStack Cloud Software. Available from https://www.openstack.org/software/

Pacheco, P. (2011). An Introduction to Parallel Programming. Morgan Kaufmann Publishers Inc., San Francisco, CA, USA, 1st edition. Snir, M., Otto, S., Huss-Lederman, S., Walker, D., and Dongarra, J. (1998). MPI-The Complete Reference, Volume 1: The MPI Core. MIT Press, Cambridge, MA, USA, 2nd.(revised) edition.

Sterling, T., Lusk, E., & Gropp, W. (Eds.). (2003). Beowulf Cluster Computing with Linux. MIT Press, Cambridge, MA, USA, 2 edition. The MPI Forum (Version 3.0., 2012). MPI: A Message Passing Interface. Technical report.

Venkata, M. G., Shamis, P., Graham, R. L., Ladd, J. S., & Sampath, R. (2013). Optimizing Blocking and Nonblocking Reduction Operations for Multicore Systems: Hierarchi- cal Design and Implementation. In *Proceedings of IEEE International Conference on Cluster Computing*, Indianapolis, Indiana, USA. doi:10.1109/CLUSTER.2013.6702676

Yelick, K., Coghlan, S., Draney, B., & Canon, R. (2011). The magellan report on cloud computing for science, u.s. department of energy. In Office of Science, Office of Ad- vanced Scientific Computing Research, Tech. Rep. IEEE.

KEY TERMS AND DEFINITIONS

Collective Operations: Collective operations are a data-exchange operations with complex communication patterns involving more than two process of the parallel job.

HPC: High-performance computing is a practice of achieving higher computing capacity and performance by aggregating many commodity computers (desktops) to solve compute-intensive science, engineering, and business problems.

Message Passing: Message passing is a parallel programming model where computation is organized around execution contexts which co-operate with each other by exchanging explicit messages.

MPI: Message Passing Interface (MPI) is message passing library interface specification.

Open MPI: Open MPI is an open source implementation of MPI specification.

OpenSHMEM: OpenSHMEM is a *PGAS* library interface specification.

Parallel Programming Model: A parallel programming model is an abstraction of a parallel system that allows expression of both algorithms and shared data structures.

PGAS: *Partitioned Global Address Space* (PGAS) presents a programming model, where all execution contexts share a global address space, and have access to private address space.

Section 5
Applications

Chapter 9
Cloud–Based Computing Architectures for Solving Hot Issues in Structural Bioinformatics

Dariusz Mrozek
Silesian University of Technology, Poland

ABSTRACT

Bioinformatics as a scientific domain develops tools that enable understanding the wealth of information hidden in huge volumes of biological data. However, there are several problems in bioinformatics that, although already solved or at least equipped with promising algorithms, still require huge computing power in order to be completed in a reasonable time. Cloud computing responds to these demands. This chapter shows several cloud-based computing architectures for solving hot issues in structural bioinformatics, such as protein structure similarity searching or 3D protein structure prediction. Presented architectures have been implemented in Microsoft Azure public cloud and tested in several projects developed by Cloud4Proteins research group.

INTRODUCTION

Bioinformatics is an interdisciplinary scientific domain, which develops algorithms, methods and software tools for discovering knowledge that is hidden in the wealth of biological data. For example, bioinformatics tools used for comparison of two genes, genomes or proteins help in understanding of evolutionary relationships between two organisms. Such information is not apparent at first glance when looking at raw data and requires appropriate software tools and algorithms in order to become visible. Bioinformatics helps in understanding genetic basis of unique diseases, like Alzheimer's, cancer, diabetes mellitus, providing information on mutations in nucleotide sequences of DNA or RNA strands. Based on the information scientists can distinguish types of particular diseases and medical doctors are able to adjust their therapies to the type of disease. Knowledge of protein structures and other biological molecules is a foundation for the

DOI: 10.4018/978-1-4666-8213-9.ch009

Copyright © 2015, IGI Global. Copying or distributing in print or electronic forms without written permission of IGI Global is prohibited.

creation of new drugs, which translates into better quality of life. Therefore, it is not surprising that bioinformatics has become a part of many areas of biology, medicine and modern pharmacy.

Structural bioinformatics is the branch of bioinformatics, which focuses on the analysis, comparison and modelling of the three-dimensional structures of proteins, DNA and RNA acids, and other molecules and molecular complexes. This sub-discipline of bioinformatics has emerged as a result of rapid increase in the number of three-dimensional macromolecular structures available in databases such as the Protein Data Bank (http://www.pdb.org) (Berman et al., 2000). Structural bioinformatics provides general purpose methods for processing information about biological macromolecules with aim to create new knowledge and a high-resolution understanding of biology. It relies on the belief that having this high-resolution structural information about biological systems will allow scientists to precisely reason about the function of these systems and the effects of modifications or perturbations (Gu & Bourne, 2009). However, performing analyses on such detailed level requires increased computational resources that are sometimes available only in big data centers. Bioinformatics is developing very dynamically in recent years and the development is also supported and accelerated by development of new computing architectures and new computing models. The concept of Cloud computing became one of the elements catalyzing the development of the domain.

Following the definition of NIST, Cloud computing is "a model for enabling convenient, on-demand network access to a shared pool of configurable computing resources (e.g., networks, servers, storage, applications, and services) that can be rapidly provisioned and released with minimal management effort or service provider interaction" (Mell & Grance, 2011). In practice, cloud computing allows to run applications and services on a distributed network using virtualized system and its resources, and at the same time,

allows to abstract away from the implementation details of the system itself. The use of cloud platforms can be particularly beneficial for companies and institutions that need to quickly gain access to a computer system which has a higher than average computing power. In this case, the use of cloud computing services can be more cost effective and faster in implementation than using the owned resources (servers and computing clusters) or buying new ones. For this reason, cloud computing is widely used in business. However, the concept of cloud computing is also becoming increasingly popular in scientific applications for which theoretically infinite resources of the cloud allow to solve the computationally intensive problems. This chapter shows several, tested on Microsoft Azure platform, cloud architecture patterns for solving hot issues in structural bioinformatics, including protein structure similarity searching or 3D protein structure prediction. Presented architectures have been implemented and tested in several projects developed by Cloud4Proteins research group.

BACKGROUND

Today's bioinformatics is struggling with many problems and use a variety of approaches to solve them. This chapter provides broad definitions of the problems, which Cloud4Proteins group tries to solve, and focuses on technologies that are used to achieve the solutions.

Proteins and Computationally-Intensive Problems

From the perspective of biological processes, functioning of living organisms is tightly related to existence and activity of protein molecules. Proteins are important molecules that play a key role in all biochemical reactions in organisms' cells. They are involved in many processes, e.g.: reaction catalysis, energy storage, signal transmission,

Figure 1. Protein sequences: myoglobin (PDB ID: 1MBN) from sperm whale and human hemoglobin (PDB ID: 4HHB, chain A) in the FASTA format

```
>1MBN:A|PDBID|CHAIN|SEQUENCE
VLSEGEWQLVLHVWAKVEADVAGHGQDILIRLFKSHPETLEKFDRFKHLKTEAEMKASEDLKKHGVTVLTALGAILKKKGHHEAEL
KPLAQSHATKHKIPIKYLEFISEAIIHVLHSRHPGDFGADAQGAMNKALELFRKDIAAKYKELGYQG

>4HHB:A|PDBID|CHAIN|SEQUENCE
VLSPADKTNVKAAWGKVGAHAGEYGAEALERMFLSFPTTKTYFPHFDLSHGSAQVKGHGKKVADALTNAVAHVDDMPNALSALSDL
HAHKLRVDPVNFKLLSHCLLVTLAAHLPAEFTPAVHASLDKFLASVSTVLTSKYR
```

maintaining of cell mechanical structure, immune response, stimuli response, cellular respiration, transport of small bio-molecules, regulation of cell growth and division.

Analyzing their general construction proteins are macromolecules with the molecular mass above 10 kDa (1 Da = 1.66×10^{-24}g) built with amino acids (usually more than 100 amino acids). Amino acids are linked in linear chains by peptide bonds. Describing construction of proteins we can use four representation levels: primary structure, secondary structure, tertiary structure and quaternary structure. The last three levels define protein conformation or protein spatial structure. Analyses of protein molecules are usually carried with respect to one of the description levels.

Primary structure is defined by amino acid sequence of a protein linear chain. Examples of sequences of myoglobin and hemoglobin molecules are presented in Figure 1. Each letter in a sequence corresponds to one amino acid in the protein chain. Secondary structure describes spatial arrangement of amino acids located closely in the sequence. This description level distinguishes in the spatial structure some characteristic, regularly folded substructures, like α-helices, β-sheets, loops, turns, and coils (Figure 2b). Tertiary structure (Figure 2a, b, c) refers to spatial relationships and mutual arrangement of amino acids located closely and distantly in the protein sequence. Tertiary structure describes a configuration of the protein structure caused by additional, internal forces, like: hydrogen bonds, disulfide bridges, attractions between positive and negative charges, and hydrophobic and hydrophilic

forces. This description level characterizes the biologically active spatial conformation of a protein. Quaternary structure (Figure 2d) refers to proteins made up of more than one amino acid chain. This level describes the arrangement of subunits and the type of their contact, which can be covalent or not covalent (Lesk, 2010).

Protein molecules are often compared to each other in order to find similarities indicating a common origin or functional similarity. Basic comparison techniques use amino acid sequences for this purpose. However, protein sequences are sometimes insufficient to deliver useful clues. 3D protein structures exhibit higher conservation in the evolution of organisms than sequences, and even if protein sequences diverged significantly, comparison of 3D protein structures and finding structural similarities still allows to draw conclusions on functional similarity of proteins in various, sometimes evolutionary distant organisms. For this reason, 3D protein structure similarity searching is one of the important processes performed in structural bioinformatics, since it allows for protein function identification and reconstruction of phylogeny for weakly related organisms.

3D protein structure similarity searching refers to the process in which a given protein structure is compared to another protein structure or a set of protein structures collected in a database. This is usually done by alignment of protein structures (Figure 3). The aim of the process is to find common fragments of compared protein structures, fragments that match to each other. Matching fragments and protein structure similarities may indicate common ancestry of compared proteins,

Figure 2. Different representations: a) tertiary structure of myoglobin (PDB ID: 1MBN) from sperm whale (Physeter catodon) in atomic display mode; b) tertiary structure of myoglobin (PDB ID: 1MBN) from sperm whale (Physeter catodon) with secondary structures (spiral α helices) visible; c) tertiary structure of the hemoglobin chain A (PDB ID: 4HHB) from Homo sapiens; d) quaternary structure of the whole hemoglobin (PDB ID: 4HHB, all chains) from Homo sapiens

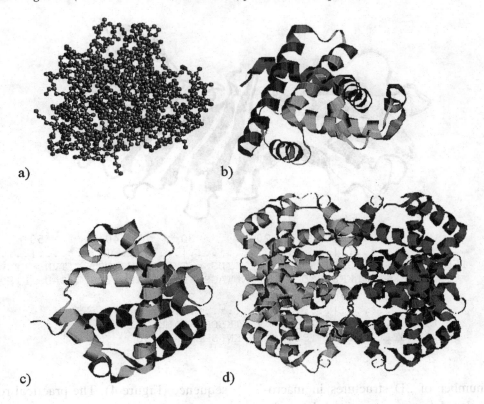

and then organisms, their evolutionary relationships, functional similarities of investigated molecules, existence of common functional regions, and many other things.

Unfortunately, 3D protein structure similarity searching is still very difficult and time-consuming process. The three key factors deciding on this are as follows:

- 3D protein structures are complex. Proteins are built up with hundreds of amino acids, and therefore, thousands of atoms, and sometimes have several chains in their quaternary structures, which make the comparison process difficult.

- Similarity searching, as a process, is computationally intensive; the problem belongs to the NP-hard problems; most of the widely accepted algorithms, like VAST (Gibrat, Madej, & Bryant, 1996), DALI (Holm & Sander, 1993), LOCK2 (Shapiro & Brutlag, 2004), FATCAT (Ye & Godzik, 2003), CE (Shindyalov & Bourne, 1998), FAST (Zhu & Weng, 2005), CASSERT (Mrozek & Małysiak-Mrozek, 2013) have high computational complexity; and the process itself is usually carried out in a pairwise manner comparing a given query structure to successive structures from a collection in pairs, one-by-one.

Figure 3. Protein structure comparison by structure alignment reveals similar fragments of protein structures: a) aligned structures of outer surface proteins OspA mutant (PDB ID: 2I5V, chain O) and OspB (PDB ID: 1RJL, chain C) from Borrelia burgdorferi; b) structural alignment visualized on amino acid sequences showing structurally corresponding residues of both proteins

a)

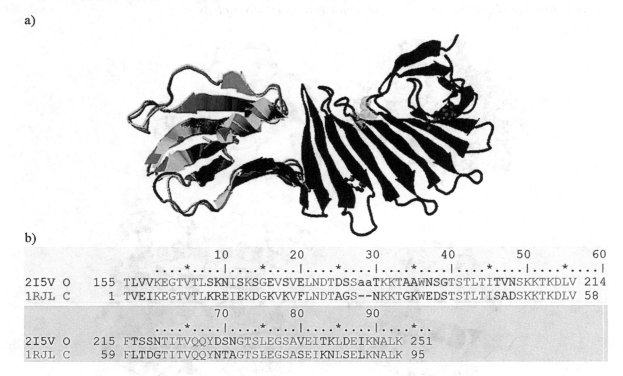

b)

```
                        10        20        30        40        50        60
                ....*....|....*....|....*....|....*....|....*....|....*....|
2I5V O   155    TLVVKEGTVTLSKNISKSGEVSVELNDTDSSaaTKKTAAWNSGTSTLTITVNSKKTKDLV 214
1RJL C     1    TVEIKEGTVTLKREIEKDGKVKVFLNDTAGS--NKKTGKWEDSTSTLTISADSKKTKDLV 58
                        70        80        90
                ....*....|....*....|....*....|....*..
2I5V O   215    FTSSNTITVQQYDSNGTSLEGSAVEITKLDEIKNALK 251
1RJL C    59    FLTDGTITVQQYNTAGTSLEGSASEIKNLSELKNALK 95
```

- The number of 3D structures in macro-molecular data repositories, such as the Protein Data Bank (PDB), grows exponentially; as of Oct 28, 2014 there were 104 537 structures in the PDB.

These factors motivate scientific efforts to build scalable platforms that allow completing the task much faster. Cloud computing provides such a kind of scalable, high-performance computational platform.

Similarly, another computationally-intensive problem related to protein molecules is prediction of their 3D structures. The problem is said to be one of the Holy Grail of science. Protein structure prediction refers to the computational procedure that delivers a three-dimensional structure of a protein based on its amino acid sequence (Figure 4). The practical role of the process becomes very important in the face of dynamically growing number of protein sequences obtained through the translation of DNA sequences coming from large-scale sequencing projects. Experimental methods for determination of protein structures, such as X-ray crystallography or Nuclear Magnetic Resonance (NMR), are lagging behind the number of protein sequences. As a consequence, the number of protein structures in repositories, like the world-wide Protein Data Bank (PDB), is only a small percentage of the number of all known sequences. Therefore, computational procedures that allow for the determination of a protein structure from its amino acid sequence are great alternatives for experimental methods for protein structure determination. There are

Figure 4. Protein structure prediction based on amino acid sequence; amino acid sequence is provided on the input of the modelling software, which returns predicted 3D protein structure.

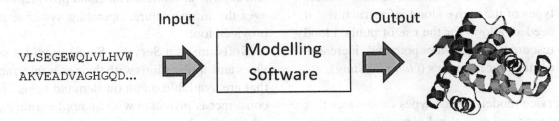

various approaches to the prediction problem and these approaches delivered various methods. These methods generally fall into two groups: physical and comparative. Physical methods rely on physical forces and interactions between atoms in a protein. Most of them try to reproduce the Nature's algorithm and implement it as a computational procedure in order to give proteins their unique 3D native conformations. Physical methods are usually time-consuming, but have strong physical background. Methods that rely on such a physical approach belong to so called *ab initio* protein structure prediction methods. Representatives of the approach include I-TASSER (Wu, Skolnick, & Zhang, 2007), Rosetta@home (Leaver-Fay et al., 2011), Quark (Xu & Zhang, 2012), and WZ (Warecki & Znamirowski, 2004). On the other hand, comparative methods rely on already known structures that are deposited in macromolecular data repositories, such as Protein Data Bank (PDB). They try to predict the structure of the target protein by finding homologues among sequences of proteins of already determined structures and by "dressing" the target sequence in one of the known structures. This group of methods is not so time-consuming as physical methods, but is based on some simplifying assumptions.

This chapter focuses on cloud-based solutions for physical methods, since again, they need an increased computational power in order to complete the task much faster.

CLOUD DEPLOYMENT AND SERVICE MODELS

Developers of applications working in the cloud (not only those developed for bioinformatics) usually adopt one of the deployment models and develop the application to operate in one of the service models. This subchapter explains types of deployment models and service models that can be adopted.

Deployment models decide where the infrastructure of the cloud will be located and managed, and who will use the cloud-based solution. We can distinguish here four widely accepted types (Mell & Grance, 2011):

- **Public Cloud:** The infrastructure of the cloud is available for public use or a large industry group and is owned by an organization selling cloud services.
- **Private Cloud:** The cloud infrastructure is for the exclusive use of a single organization comprising multiple consumers (e.g. the organizational units); it does not matter whether it is a cloud managed by the organization, and it is located in its office; key factors for establishing private clouds seem to be: legal constraints, security, reliability, and lower costs for large organizations and dedicated solutions.
- **Community Cloud:** The cloud infrastructure is made available for the exclusive use of the consumer community from organizations that share common goals or are subjected to common legal restrictions.

- **Hybrid Cloud:** The cloud infrastructure is based on a combination of two or more types of the above cloud infrastructures; if needed, allows for the use of public cloud resources to provide potential increased demand for resources (*cloud bursting*).

Service models define types of services that can be accessed on a cloud computing platform. Among many others, three types of services are universally accepted. They are usually presented in a form of stack as in (Figure 5).

The basis of the stack of services provided in the cloud (Figure 5) is the Infrastructure as a Service (IaaS) layer. IaaS provides basic computing resources in a virtualized form, including: processing power, RAM, storage space and appropriate bandwidth for transferring data over the network, making it possible to deploy and run any application. The IaaS service provider is responsible for the cloud infrastructure and its management.

Platform as a Service (PaaS) allows to create custom applications based on a variety of services delivered by the cloud provider. As an addition to IaaS, PaaS provides operating systems, ap-

plications, development platforms, transactions and control structures. The cloud provider manages the infrastructure, operating systems, and provided tools.

Software as a Service (SaaS) provides services and applications with their user interfaces that are available on an on-demand basis. The consumer is provided with an application running in the cloud infrastructure. The consumer does not take care of the infrastructure, operating systems and other components underlying the application. Its only responsibility is an appropriate interaction with the user interface and entering appropriate data into the application. The user can also change the configuration of the application and customize the user interface, if possible.

Microsoft Azure Public Cloud

Microsoft Azure is Microsoft's cloud platform that delivers services for building scalable web-based applications. Microsoft Azure allows developing, deploying and managing applications and services through a network of data centers located in various countries throughout the world. Microsoft Azure is a public cloud, which means that the infrastructure of the cloud is available for public use and is owned by Microsoft selling cloud services. Microsoft Azure provides computing resources in a virtualized form, including processing power, RAM, storage space and appropriate bandwidth for transferring data over the network, within Infrastructure as a Service (IaaS) service model. Moreover, within Platform as a Service model, Azure also delivers platform and dedicated cloud service programming model for developing applications that should work in the cloud.

Figure 6 shows how a user benefits from the application deployed to the Microsoft Azure cloud. The architecture consists of the following elements:

Figure 5. Cloud services defining types of components that will be delivered to the consumer

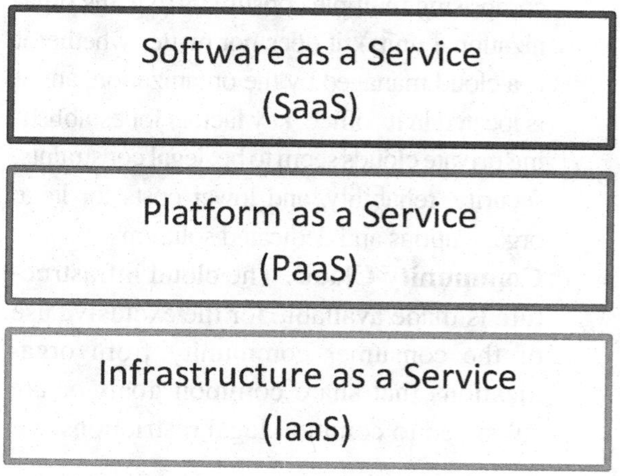

Software as a Service (SaaS)

Platform as a Service (PaaS)

Infrastructure as a Service (IaaS)

Figure 6. Application deployed to Microsoft Azure which serves as a virtualized infrastructure, platform for developers, and gateway for hosting applications

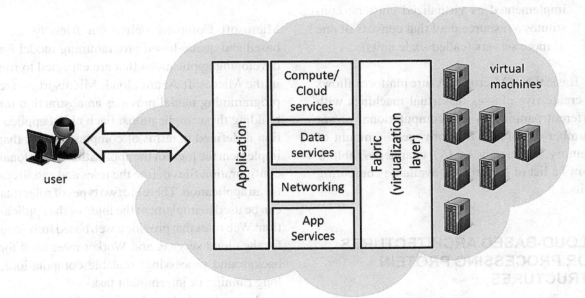

- **Application:** The application that is made available to the community of users in the cloud, usually accessed by its web-based interface, Web service, or mobile interface.
- **Compute/Cloud Services:** Represent applications that are designed to run in the cloud and XML configuration files that define how the cloud service should run. Microsoft Azure programming model provides an abstraction for building cloud applications. Each cloud application is defined in terms of component roles that implement the logic of hosting application. Configuration files define the roles and resources for an application. There are two types of roles that can be used to implement the logic of the application: Web roles that provide a web based front-end for the cloud service, and Worker roles used for background processing, scalable computations, long running or intermittent tasks.

- **Data Services:** For various storage scenarios. These data services enable storing, modifying and reporting on data in Microsoft Azure. The following components of Data Services can be used to store data: BLOBs that allow to store unstructured text or binary data (video, audio and images), Tables that can store large amounts of unstructured non-relational (NoSQL) data, Azure SQL Database for storing large amounts of relational data, HDInsight, which is a distribution of Apache Hadoop, based on the Hortonworks Data Platform.
- **Networking:** Provide general connectivity and routing at the TCP/IP and DNS level.
- **App Services:** Provide multiple services related to security, performance, workflow management, and finally, messaging including Storage Queues and Service Bus providing efficient communication between application tiers running in Microsoft Azure.

- **Fabric:** Entire compute, storage (e.g. hard drives), and network infrastructure, usually implemented as virtualized clusters; constitutes a resource pool that consists of one of more servers (called scale units).

Basic tier of Microsoft Azure platform allows to create five classes of virtual machines with different parameters and computational power (number of cores, CPU/core speed, amount of memory, efficiency of I/O channel). Table 1 shows a list of features for available computing units.

CLOUD-BASED ARCHITECTURES FOR PROCESSING PROTEIN STRUCTURES

Scalable scientific computations require appropriate computing architectures in order to satisfy particular needs or architectures tailored to a specificity of computations. Bioinformatics usually deals with huge amounts of biological data. In order to process and analyze so high volumes of biological data the scientific community creates solutions that are based on parallel computations. And many of the solutions can be implemented as pleasingly parallel ones. This gives an advantage of avoiding costly synchronizations that usually slow down implemented processes. This chapter shows several Microsoft Azure cloud-based architectural solutions for solving some hot issues in bioinformatics.

A Simple Role-Based and Queue-Based Architecture

Microsoft Company delivers a friendly role-based and queue-based programming model for developing applications that are expected to run in the Microsoft Azure cloud. Microsoft Azure programming model provides an abstraction for building these applications. Each cloud application is defined in terms of component roles that implement the logic of the application. Additional configuration files define the roles and resources for an application. There are two types of roles that can be used to implement the logic of the application: Web roles that provide a web based front-end for the cloud service, and Worker roles used for background processing, scalable computations, long running or intermittent tasks.

A simple role-based and queue-based architecture for scientific computations is presented in Figure 7. In this architecture, there are two types of roles: Web role and Worker role, and one queue. Single instance or multiple instances of the Web role consume users' requests and input data and, after finishing computations, provide results. Input data provided by users can be stored in the Storage space available in the cloud, including Storage BLOB, Storage Table, Azure SQL Database, depending on the type of input data. There can be also scenarios, in which input data are already stored in the Storage space of Microsoft Azure cloud and are being used when user performs some operations on them. Such a scenario is typical when the volume of data is huge and is

Table 1. Available sizes of Microsoft Azure virtual machines (VM)

VM/Server Type	Number of Cores	CPU Speed (GHz)	Memory (GB)	Disk Space for Local Storage (GB)
ExtraSmall	shared core	1.0	0.768	19
Small	1	1.6	1.75	224
Medium	2	1.6	3.50	489
Large	4	1.6	7.00	999
ExtraLarge	8	1.6	14.00	2039

Figure 7. Simple role-based and queue-based architecture

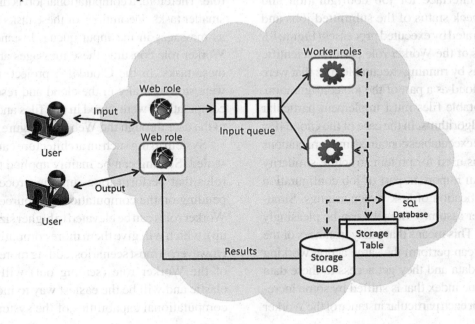

not uploaded every time the user wants to execute the computational procedure. Similarly, results can be stored using one of the Storage technologies depending on the type of output data and the way how users want to see them after processing is finished. For example, some results may have forms of compressed files with some data inside. These files can be stored with the use of BLOBs and can be downloaded by users through available hyperlinks. In other cases, there can be some statistics or measures returned as the output data and they should be presented to the user as tables or grids, where data can be sorted by some selected column. Tables of relational SQL Database or NoSQL Storage Tables are appropriate places, where the data can be stored and retrieved when they are needed.

Roles working in the architecture communicate with each other through Input queue. Queues provide message delivery on First In First Out (FIFO) basis. Messages are typically consumed and processed by instances of the Worker role in the order in which they were added to the queue, and each message is received and processed by only one instance of the Worker role. In such a way, queues allow to achieve temporal decoupling of system components. Web roles and Worker roles do not have to communicate through messages synchronously, because messages are stored durably in the queue. Moreover, Web role does not have to wait for any reply from the Worker roles in order to continue to process users' requests and generate messages.

Such architecture is very simple and common. It can be used while solving many scientific problems. For example, it was implemented in Simulation Runner, the configurable system for scientific computations, provided by Dennis Gannon and Microsoft Research team in the USA. Our group Cloud4Proteins, which develops cloud-based solutions for proteins, had an honor to test the Simulation Runner within the Cloud4Psi (Cloud for Protein Similarity) project.

While performing computations with the Simulation Runner a user has to configure the computational job that will be submitted for execution in the system that implements the architecture presented in Figure 7. The Web role provides the web-based interface for job configuration and allows to check status of the submitted jobs and results generated by executed processes (Figure 8).

Instances of the Worker role perform scientific computations by running executable files that were sent to the cloud as a part of the job configuration. These executable files must implement particular processing algorithms. In the case of the Cloud4Psi project, these executables contained implementations of algorithms used for protein structure similarity searching. An important part of job configuration is also specification of task sweep settings. Simulation Runner assumes that jobs can be pleasingly parallelized. This means that many instances of the Worker role can perform the same action working on different data and they get access to these data based on some index that is shifted by some increment value for each particular instance of the Worker

role. Therefore, a computational job is divided into smaller tasks. Definitions of these tasks are placed as messages in the Input queue. Instances of the Worker role consume these messages and execute these tasks. In the Cloud4Psi project, input data were stored locally in the cloud and results of the computations were stored in text files and provided to the user through the Web role (Figure 9).

System using such an architecture can be easily scaled. Scaling can be mainly applied to Worker roles that perform long-running processes. Depending on the computational resources needed, Worker roles can be elevated to higher sizes (scaled up), which will give them more computing power. However, in most scenarios, adding more instances of the Worker role (scaling out) will be more elastic and will be the easiest way to increase the computational capabilities of the system.

Figure 8. A view of status of the job submitted to the Simulation Runner provided by Web role

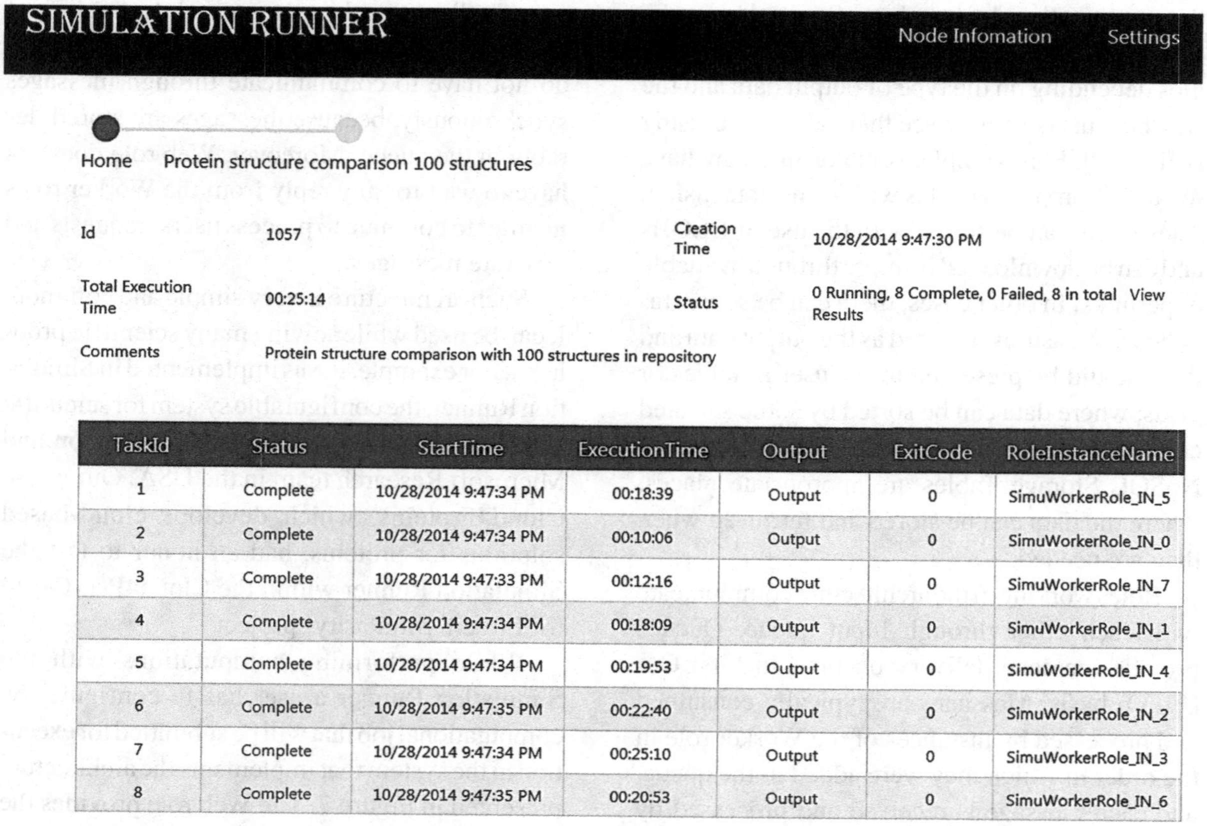

SIMULATION RUNNER

Node Infomation   Settings

Home   Protein structure comparison 100 structures

Id	1057	Creation Time	10/28/2014 9:47:30 PM
Total Execution Time	00:25:14	Status	0 Running, 8 Complete, 0 Failed, 8 in total View Results
Comments	Protein structure comparison with 100 structures in repository		

TaskId	Status	StartTime	ExecutionTime	Output	ExitCode	RoleInstanceName
1	Complete	10/28/2014 9:47:34 PM	00:18:39	Output	0	SimuWorkerRole_IN_5
2	Complete	10/28/2014 9:47:34 PM	00:10:06	Output	0	SimuWorkerRole_IN_0
3	Complete	10/28/2014 9:47:33 PM	00:12:16	Output	0	SimuWorkerRole_IN_7
4	Complete	10/28/2014 9:47:34 PM	00:18:09	Output	0	SimuWorkerRole_IN_1
5	Complete	10/28/2014 9:47:34 PM	00:19:53	Output	0	SimuWorkerRole_IN_4
6	Complete	10/28/2014 9:47:35 PM	00:22:40	Output	0	SimuWorkerRole_IN_2
7	Complete	10/28/2014 9:47:34 PM	00:25:10	Output	0	SimuWorkerRole_IN_3
8	Complete	10/28/2014 9:47:35 PM	00:20:53	Output	0	SimuWorkerRole_IN_6

Figure 9. Partial results of protein structure similarity searching performed on Simulation Runner; structural alignment visible on the level of amino acid sequences of two compared proteins

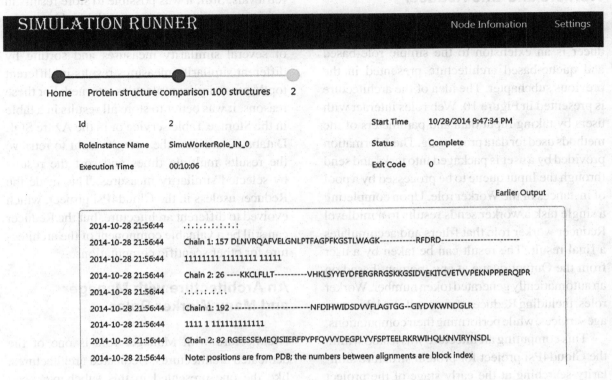

Figure 10. Architecture with many workers and one reducer

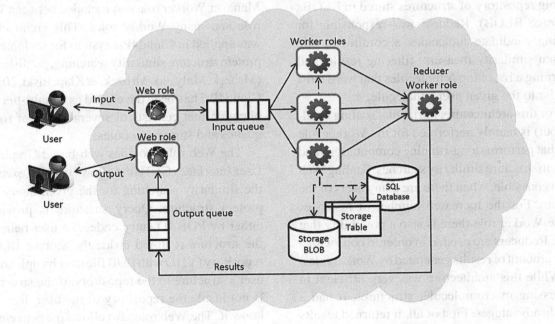

An Architecture with Many Workers and One Reducer

Architecture with many workers and one reducer is an extension to the simple role-based and queue-based architecture presented in the previous subchapter. The idea of the architecture is presented in Figure 10. Web roles interact with users by taking input data and parameters of the methods used for data processing. The information provided by a user is packaged into tasks and send through the Input queue to be processed by a pool of instances of the Worker role. Upon completing a single task a worker sends results to a midlevel Reducer worker role that filters and accumulates a final result. The result can be taken by a user from the Output queue at any moment based on an automatically generated token number. Worker roles, including Reducer, can use all available storage services, while performing their computations.

This computing architecture was tested within the Cloud4Psi project for protein structure similarity searching at the early stage of the project development. Worker roles were responsible for comparing 3D protein structure given by a user (as input data) to all candidate structures from the big repository of structures stored in BLOBs (Storage BLOB). Reducer was responsible for sorting candidate molecules according to one chosen similarity measure, filtering results and returning a list of top N molecules that were most similar to the given user's molecule.

For this architecture, horizontal scaling (scaling out) is mainly performed for the Worker role tier that performs long-running computations and protein structure similarity searches. Scaling Web role is possible, when there are many users of the system. For the increased number of instances of the Worker role there is also a possibility that more Reducers are needed in order to cope with a huge amount of results generated by Worker roles.

While this architecture was very efficient in processing macromolecular structures, it had a few disadvantages. First of all, it returned results directly to the user without storing them for future retrievals. Still, it was possible to store results in one of the storage services available, but results of protein structure similarity searches consist of several similarity measures and sorting by different similarity measures results in different top N, most similar molecules returned. For these reasons, it was better to store all results in a table in the Storage Table service or in the Azure SQL Database, and give the user the right to retrieve the results multiple times and sort the results by selected similarity measures. This made the Reducer useless in the Cloud4Psi project, which evolved to different architecture, but the Reducer can still be a valuable component of the architecture for other scentific computations.

An Architecture with Manager and Many Worker Roles

Architecture with Manager role is one of the dedicated architectures. Dedicated architectures, like the one presented in this subchapter, can be built in special processing circumstances or for solving special scientific problems. In the architecture presented in Figure 11 additional Manager Worker role was included between Web role and many Worker roles. This architecture was applied in Cloud4Psi system for scalable 3D protein structure similarity searching, published in (Mrozek, Małysiak-Mrozek, & Kłapciński, 2014). Cloud4Psi has been developed as a multi-tier application that consists of several types of roles, queues and storage modules:

The Web role provides web-based Graphical User Interface (GUI) that allows users to execute the similarity searching for the given query 3D protein structure. Query structure is provided either by PDB ID entry code, if a user believes the structure is stored inside the Storage BLOB repository (VHD with PDB files), or by uploading user's structure to the repository, if the structure is not inside the repository or the user does not know it. The Web role also allows users to check

Figure 11. Architecture with manager and many worker roles
Reproduced from (Mrozek, 2014).

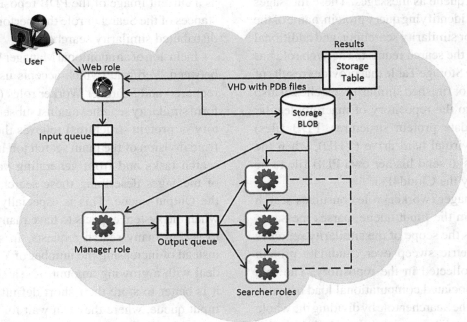

Figure 12. Cloud4Psi web site provided by the Web role

results of their searches. Search requests are placed in the Input queue as messages. These messages contain data identifying query protein, name of the algorithm for similarity searching, and additional metadata of the search request. The Web role has access to the Storage Table that provides results of the ongoing or finished similarity searches. It also has access to the repository of macromolecular data (candidate protein structures, PDB files) located on virtual hard drive (VHD), when the user decides to send his/her own PDB file to be compared by the Cloud4Psi.

The Manager (worker) role consumes search requests from the Input queue, parses messages and arranges the scope of the similarity searches by a parametric sweep over candidate protein structures collected in the repository. The role manages associated computational load between instances of the Searcher role by dividing the whole search process into many tasks. Definitions of these tasks are then placed into the Output queue and asynchronously consumed by Searcher roles.

Many instances of the Searcher role bear the computational load associated with protein comparison. Instances of the Searcher role continuously consume messages from the Output queue. These messages consist of the information on the query protein structure, part of repository that should be processed, the name of the comparison algorithm that should be used, and parameters of the algorithm. After processing a message and comparing query protein structure to a subset of structures defined by the sweep start and width parameters, Searchers enter results to a table in the Storage Table service and listen for new messages.

Table component (from Storage Table service) stores results of similarity searches, a token generated for the user's search request, time stamps of the key moments of the application run and technical parameters used globally by all roles. A page-able BLOB (from Storage BLOBs service) contains the virtual hard drive (VHD). The VHD is mounted by the Web role in the *full* mode, if the user chooses to upload its own protein PDB

file as a query structure, or in the *read-only* mode as a current image of the PDB repository for instances of the Searcher role that perform parallel, distributed similarity searches.

Inclusion of an additional Manager Worker role between Web role (which accepts users' search requests) and Searcher Worker roles (which perform similarity searches against subsets of repository of protein structures) relieves the Web role from division of the main search job into smaller search tasks and from generating vast amount of messages describing these search tasks into the Output queue. This is especially important when the system expects to have many users and to accept many search requests. In such cases, instead of increasing the number of Web roles to deal with a growing amount of search requests, it is better to store their short definitions in the Input queue, where they can wait for being processed by the Manager role. Again, the system benefits from using queues in such a scenario as queues provide load leveling. This enables Web role to send search requests at different rate than Manager role can consume them, since the load of the Cloud4Psi system may vary over time. Assuming that similarity searches performed by each instance of the Searcher role require constant amount of time, it is important just to provision as many compute units as needed to be able to handle average load instead of peak load. This allows to save money with regard to the amount of infrastructure required to service the Cloud4Psi system load. As the number of search requests increases, more instances of the Searcher role can be provisioned to read from the Output queue and handle these requests.

An Architecture with Manager and Many Queues

This architecture is a modification of the architecture presented in previous subchapter with the exception that it contains more queues (Figure 13). The architecture was implemented in the

Figure 13. Architecture with manager role, many instances of worker role, and several queues

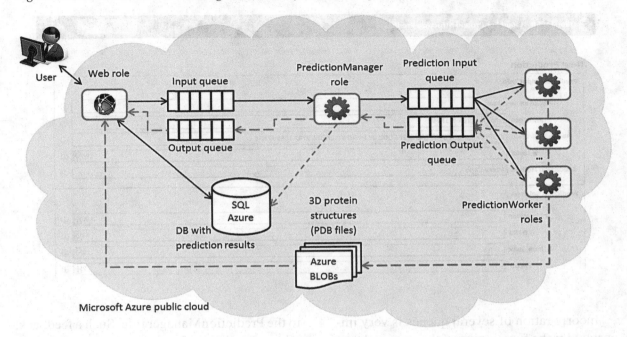

Cloud4PSP (Cloud For Protein Structure Prediction) system, which predicts protein structures by performing thousands independent Monte Carlo simulations. Similarly, to the Cloud4Psi system, the Web role of the Cloud4PSP provides a web site which allows users to interact with the entire system. Through the Web role users input the amino acid sequence of the protein, which structure will be predicted (Figure 14). They also choose the prediction method, specify its parameters, e.g. the number of iterations, and provide a short description of the input molecule.

PredictionManager role distributes the prediction process across many instances of PredictionWorker role. The entire prediction process consists of a vast number of iterations that are performed in parallel by many instances of PredictionWorker role. For testing purposes, the number of iterations can be specified by the user through the Web role. This gives flexibility in choosing the stopping criterion.

Instances of PredictionWorker role execute chosen prediction method, generate successive protein structures, calculate total potential energies for them, store protein structures in PDB files, and then, save these files in Azure BLOBs. Steering instructions that control the entire system and the course of action inside the Cloud4PSP are transferred as messages through the queuing system. There are four queues present in the architecture of the Cloud4PSP: Input queue that collects structure prediction requests (Prediction Job descriptions) generated by users through the Web site, Output queue that collects notifications of prediction completion for particular users (based on generated token number), Prediction Input queue that transfers parameters of the prediction process for a single instance of the PredictionWorker role, among others: amino acid sequence provided by the user, the number of iterations to be performed, parameters of the prediction method, Prediction Output queue that transfers descriptions of results, e.g. PDB file name with protein structure and total energy value for the structure, from each instance of the PredictionWorker role back to the PredictionManager role.

Figure 14. Cloud4PSP main web site provided by the Web role

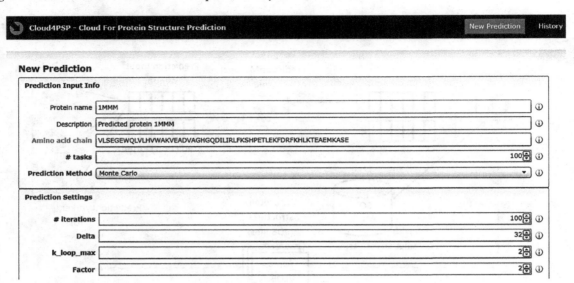

Incorporation of several queues is very important for the functioning of the system. Input queue and Prediction Input queue are needed for buffering prediction requests and steering the prediction process. The prediction process may take several hours and is performed asynchronously. User's requests are being placed in the Input queue with the typical FIFO discipline and they are realized when there are idle instances of the PredictionWorker role that can realize the request. Many users can generate many prediction requests, so there must be a buffering mechanism for these requests. Queues fulfill this task perfectly. One prediction request enqueued in the Input queue causes the creation of many prediction tasks for instances of the PredictionWorker role. The PredictionManager role consumes prediction requests from the Input queue, divides the total number of iterations by the number of PredictionWorker roles available in the system, and generates prediction tasks to the Prediction Input queue. The Prediction Output queue is used by instances of the PredictionWorker role to return description of results to the PredictionManager role. Such a feedback allows PredictionManager role to control if all prediction tasks have been completed. In case of failure in the realization of a prediction task, its completion can be delegated to another PredictionWorker instance. The Output queue allows to notify the Web role that the whole prediction process is already completed.

FUTURE RESEARCH DIRECTIONS

Cloud4Protein group still works on various architectural solutions for processing protein structures. At the moment, the group tests several approaches that use Hadoop cluster and MapReduce computing model for both computational problems, protein structure similarity searching and protein structure prediction. It seems that dynamic scaling provided by Cloud computing is a key concept that will allow to effectively process macromolecular structures and to uncover the knowledge that is hidden in the huge volumes of data.

CONCLUSION

This chapter presented selected computing architectures for processing 3D protein structures, beginning from the simple queue-based and role-based architecture, through the architecture with many workers and one reducer, architecture with one managing role and many workers, and finishing on the architecture with many queues. All of the presented architectures have their own features and provide various capabilities. All of them provide wide scaling capabilities, both vertical and horizontal. Main differences lie in the level of controlling the execution process as a whole.

While the Cloud4Proteins scientific group tested all these architectures within the projects that were realized by the members of the team, these architectures are not narrowed just to processing protein structures. They have general purpose and they can be used in other scientific and also commercial projects. A key feature of the presented architectures is that their components are loosely coupled, which means that roles working in the system do not know anything about the implementation of the other roles. They can even operate at different paces or schedules. Another important feature of presented architectures is statelessness of roles working in the system, which assures fault tolerance. Finally, users' requests are processed asynchronously – they are first send to a queue and processed when the processing tier (worker roles) is ready to do it or has appropriate computing resources. This assures temporal decoupling, load leveling, and load balancing, which are important while using cloud-based applications for performing so long-running scientific computations.

REFERENCES

Berman, H., Westbrook, J., Feng, Z., Gilliland, G., Bhat, T. N., Weissig, H., & Bourne, P. E. et al. (2000). The protein data bank. *Nucleic Acids Research*, 28(1), 235–242. doi:10.1093/nar/28.1.235 PMID:10592235

Gibrat, J., Madej, T., & Bryant, S. (1996). Surprising similarities in structure comparison. *Current Opinion in Structural Biology*, 6(3), 377–385. doi:10.1016/S0959-440X(96)80058-3 PMID:8804824

Gu, J., & Bourne, P. E. (2009). *Structural bioinformatics*. Hoboken, NJ: Wiley-Blackwell.

Holm, L., & Sander, C. (1993). Protein structure comparison by alignment of distance matrices. *Journal of Molecular Biology*, 233(1), 123–138. doi:10.1006/jmbi.1993.1489 PMID:8377180

Leaver-Fay, A., Tyka, M., Lewis, S. M., Lange, O. F., Thompson, J., Jacak, R., & Bradley, P. et al. (2011). ROSETTA3: An object-oriented software suite for the simulation and design of macromolecules. *Methods in Enzymology*, 487, 545–574. doi:10.1016/B978-0-12-381270-4.00019-6 PMID:21187238

Lesk, A. M. (2010). *Introduction to protein science: Architecture, function, and genomics*. Oxford University Press.

Mell, P., & Grance, T. (2011). *The NIST definition of cloud computing*. Special Publication 800-145. Retrieved Oct 20, 2014, from http://csrc.nist.gov/publications/nistpubs/800-145/SP800-145.pdf

Mrozek, D. (2014). *High-performance computational solutions in protein bioinformatics*. Berlin, Germany: Springer. doi:10.1007/978-3-319-06971-5

Mrozek, D., & Małysiak-Mrozek, B. (2013). CASSERT: A two-phase alignment algorithm for matching 3D structures of proteins. In A. Kwiecień, P. Gaj, & P. Stera (Eds.), *Computer Networks: Proceedings of the 20th International Conference (CCIS)* (Vol. 370, pp. 334-343), Berlin, Germany: Springer. doi:10.1007/978-3-642-38865-1_34

Mrozek, D., Małysiak-Mrozek, B., & Kłapciński, A. (2014). Cloud4Psi: Cloud computing for 3D protein structure similarity searching. *Bioinformatics (Oxford, England)*, 30(19), 2822–2825. doi:10.1093/bioinformatics/btu389 PMID:24930141

Shapiro, J., & Brutlag, D. (2004). FoldMiner and LOCK2: Protein structure comparison and motif discovery on the web. *Nucleic Acids Research*, 32(Web Server), 536–541. doi:10.1093/nar/gkh389 PMID:15215444

Shindyalov, I., & Bourne, P. (1998). Protein structure alignment by incremental combinatorial extension (CE) of the optimal path. *Protein Engineering*, 11(9), 739–747. doi:10.1093/protein/11.9.739 PMID:9796821

Warecki, S., & Znamirowski, L. (2004). Random simulation of the nanostructures conformations. In *Computing, Communication and Control Technology, Proceedings of International Conference* (vol. 1, pp. 388-393), Austin, TX: The International Institute of Informatics and Systemics.

Wu, S., Skolnick, J., & Zhang, Y. (2007). Ab initio modeling of small proteins by iterative TASSER simulations. *BMC Biology*, 5(1), 17. doi:10.1186/1741-7007-5-17 PMID:17488521

Xu, D., & Zhang, Y. (2012). Ab initio protein structure assembly using continuous structure fragments and optimized knowledge-based force field. *Proteins*, 80(7), 1715–1735. PMID:22411565

Ye, Y., & Godzik, A. (2003). Flexible structure alignment by chaining aligned fragment pairs allowing twists. *Bioinformatics (Oxford, England)*, 19(2), 246–255. PMID:14534198

Zhu, J., & Weng, Z. (2005). FAST: A novel protein structure alignment algorithm. *Proteins*, 58(3), 618–627. doi:10.1002/prot.20331 PMID:15609341

ADDITIONAL READING

Branden, C., & Tooze, J. (1999). *Introduction to protein structure* (2nd ed.). NY, USA: Garland Science.

Burkowski, F. (2008). *Structural bioinformatics: An algorithmic approach* (1st ed.). London, UK: Chapman and Hall/CRC.

Hazelhurst, S. (2010). PH2: an Hadoop-based framework for mining structural properties from the PDB database. South African Institute of Computer Scientists and Information Technologists, *Proceedings of the 2010 Annual Research Conference* (pp. 104-112). doi:10.1145/1899503.1899515

Hung, C.L., & Hua, G.J. (2013). Cloud computing for protein-ligand binding site comparison. *BioMed Research International, 170356*.

Hung, C.L., & Hua, G.J. (2013). Implementation of a parallel protein structure alignment service on Cloud. *International Journal of Genomics, 439681*, 1–8. PMID:23671842

Kessel, A., & Ben-Tal, N. (2010). *Introduction to proteins: Structure, function, and motion*. London, UK: CRC Press. doi:10.1201/b10456

Krampis, K., Booth, T., Chapman, B., Tiwari, B., Bicak, M., Field, D., & Nelson, K. E. (2012). Cloud BioLinux: Pre-configured and on-demand bioinformatics computing for the genomics community. *BMC Bioinformatics*, *13*(1), 42. doi:10.1186/1471-2105-13-42 PMID:22429538

Małysiak, B., Momot, A., Kozielski, S., & Mrozek, D. (2008). On using energy signatures in protein structure similarity searching. In: L. Rutkowski, et al. (Eds.) Artificial Intelligence and Soft Computing, *Proceedings of 9th International Conference (LNCS)* (vol. 5097, pp. 939-950), Heidelberg, Germany: Springer

Małysiak, B., Momot, A., Mrozek, D., Hera, Ł., Kozielski, S., & Momot, M. (2011). Scalable system for protein structure similarity searching. Computational Collective Intelligence. Technologies and Applications, *Proceedings of 3ʳᵈ International Conference (LNCS)* (vol. 6923, pp. 271-280), Heidelberg, Germany: Springer

Momot, A., Małysiak-Mrozek, B., Kozielski, S., Mrozek, D., Hera, Ł., Górczyńska-Kosiorz, S., & Momot, M. (2010). Improving performance of protein structure similarity searching by distributing computations in hierarchical multi-agent system. Computational Collective Intelligence. Technologies and Applications, *Proceedings of 2ⁿᵈ International Conference (LNCS)* (vol. 6421, pp. 320-329), Heidelberg, Germany: Springer doi:10.1007/978-3-642-16693-8_34

Mrozek, D., Małysiak, B., & Kozielski, S. (2007). An optimal alignment of proteins energy characteristics with crisp and fuzzy similarity awards. Fuzzy Systems (FUZZ-IEEE), *Proceedings of the IEEE International Conference*, (pp. 1508-1513), USA: IEEE doi:10.1109/FUZZY.2007.4295590

Mrozek, D., & Małysiak-Mrozek, B. (2011). An improved method for protein similarity searching by alignment of fuzzy energy signatures. *International Journal of Computational Intelligence Systems*, *4*(1), 75–88. doi:10.2991/ijcis.2011.4.1.7

Sosinsky, B. (2011). *Cloud computing Bible*. Indianapolis, IN, USA: Wiley.

Znamirowski, L. (2004). *Switching. VLSI structures, reprogrammable FPAA structures, nanostructures*. Gliwice, Poland: Studia Informatica.

Zomaya, A. Y. (2006). *Parallel computing for bioinformatics and computational biology: Models, enabling technologies, and case studies*. Hoboken, NJ, USA: Wiley-Interscience.

Zomaya, A. Y., & Talbi, E. G. (2008). *Grid computing for for bioinformatics and computational biology*. Hoboken, NJ: Wiley-Interscience.

Zou, Q., Li, X. B., Jiang, W. R., Lin, Z. Y., Li, G. L., & Chen, K. (2013). Survey of MapReduce frame operation in bioinformatics. *Briefings in Bioinformatics*, *2013*, 1–11. PMID:23396756

KEY TERMS AND DEFINITIONS

3D Protein Structure: An intricate folded, three-dimensional shape that is formed by a protein, important for its function and activity.

Cloud4Proteins: A scientific group that develops cloud-based solutions for processing and analyzing protein structures.

Cloud4Psi: The Cloud for Protein Similarity project that uses cloud resources to find similarities in 3D protein structures. Supported by Microsoft Azure for Research Award.

Protein Data Bank: The most famous data repository for experimentally-determined 3D structures of proteins, nucleic acids, and complex assemblies.

Protein Structure Prediction: Prediction of the three-dimensional structure of a protein from its amino acid sequence.

Proteins: Large biological molecules, built up with amino acids, that play various important functions in cells of living organisms.

Web Role: A virtual machine instance in Microsoft Azure public cloud used for providing a web based front-end for the cloud service.

Worker Role: A virtual machine instance in Microsoft Azure public cloud used for generalized development that performs background processing and scalable computations, accepts and responds to requests, and performs long running or intermittent tasks.

Chapter 10
Cloud–Based Healthcare Systems:
Emerging Technologies and Open Research Issues

Ahmed Shawish
Ain Shams University, Egypt

Maria Salama
British University in Egypt, Egypt

ABSTRACT

Healthcare is one of the most important sectors in all countries and significantly affects the economy. As such, the sector consumes an average of 9.5% of the gross domestic product across the most developed countries; they should invoke smart healthcare systems to efficiently utilize available resources, vastly handle spontaneous emergencies, and professionally manage the population health records. With the rise of the Cloud and Mobile Computing, a vast variety of added values have been introduced to software and IT infrastructure. This chapter provides a comprehensive review on the new Cloud-based and mobile-based applications that have been developed in the healthcare field. Cloud's availability, scalability, and storage capabilities, in addition to the Mobile's portability, wide coverage, and accessibility features, contributed to the fulfillment of healthcare requirements. The chapter shows how Cloud and Mobile opened a new environment for innovative services in the healthcare field and discusses the open research issues.

1. INTRODUCTION

Healthcare provision varies around the world; almost all wealthy nations provide universal healthcare. Health provision is challenging due to the costs required, as well as various social, cultural, political and economic conditions. However, many nations around the world spend considerable resources trying to provide it. Based on the 2012 statistics mentioned in (Organization of economics co-operation and development, 2013), most of the developed countries consumed an average of 9.5%

DOI: 10.4018/978-1-4666-8213-9.ch010

Copyright © 2015, IGI Global. Copying or distributing in print or electronic forms without written permission of IGI Global is prohibited.

of their gross domestic product. For example, The United States (17.6%), Netherlands (12%), France and Germany (11.6%) were the top four spenders in this sector. One of the most critical disease and daily consume a lot of healthcare resources is the diabetes.

Efficient healthcare systems are hence critically important and need to be smartly incorporated. Such systems should fulfill a list of urgent requirements. They should efficiently utilize and allocate the available health resource; i.e., equipments and medications. They also have to be fast enough to effectively cope with spontaneous emergency calls and cases handling. In addition, they should be more flexible to move toward the patients as well as being able to explore critical probes and provide a pro-active model for healthcare crisis management. However, these requirements are not yet totally achieved through the classical healthcare systems that depend on the old technologies.

With the rise of new technologies like Cloud and Mobile Computing, new solutions have been introduced in healthcare field. The smart mobile is emerged as a fast, portable, widely available and efficient connection channel with the patients. Through such channel, data can be vastly acquired from the field with very low expenses. Guiding instructions as well can be also delivered to the patients anywhere and anytime. Developed smart medical mobile applications have hosted and helped patients to fully mange their daily treatment process. The Cloud, on the other hand, has incorporated to accommodate the healthcare system due to its broadly availability, scalability, and storage capability that makes it possible to acquire real updated data and feedbacks from both patients and healthcare managers.

This chapter provides a comprehensive review on the new Cloud-based and Mobile-based applications that have been developed in the healthcare field. Solutions related to Hospital Management System, Emergency Healthcare Systems, Healthcare Records Systems, Social Healthcare Systems,

and Medical Imaging systems are addressed and discussed in details; in terms of their features, functionalities and architecture. As illustrated and discussed along the chapter, these solutions have proven to fulfill the critical healthcare requirements and also Cloud and Mobile have opened a new environment for innovation in the healthcare field. The chapter also covers and discusses the hot research points that need to be addressed in this area.

The rest of this chapter is organized as follows. Section 1, introduces the background on the Cloud-based and mobile-based solutions in the healthcare field. In section 2, cloud-based and mobile-based healthcare systems are presented, and we illustrate their functionalities, features and architectures, along with discussions about their open research points. Finally, the road ahead is discussed in section 3 and the chapter is concluded in section 4.

2. BACKGROUND

This section provides a comprehensive background on the Cloud-based and mobile-based solutions in the healthcare field.

2.1 Cloud Computing and Healthcare

Healthcare and medical services consist of general and emergency medical services. General medical services involve provision of hospital numbers for appointments whereas emergency medical services consist of various pre and in-hospital activities. These activities are performed by various individuals (administrative, hospital staff and paramedical). These individuals differ on grounds of knowledge, experience and status. These activities are interconnected to provide services in case of emergency. Thus, during the process of development of this project, an essential emphasis has to be made over individual and combined processes.

According to the National Institute of Standards and Technology (NIST), Cloud computing is a pay per use model for enabling convenient, on demand network access to a shared pool of configurable computing resources (e.g., networks, servers, storage, applications, and services) that can be rapidly provisioned and released with minimal management effort or service provider interaction (Mell & Grance, 2009).

A cloud provides sharing of data and reducing the amount of local storages required. The advantages of using cloud computing can be mentioned as:

- **Reduced Cost:** Cloud technology is paid incrementally, saving organizations money.
- **Increased Storage:** Organizations can store more data than on private computer systems.
- **Highly Automated:** No need to worry about keeping software up to date.
- **Flexibility:** Cloud computing offers much more flexibility than past computing methods.
- **More Mobility:** Users can access information wherever they are.
- **Allows Shifting Focus:** No need to worry about constant server updates.

Given the characteristics of Cloud Computing and its service models, thus improves the ability of accessing the information by the users being able to rapidly and inexpensively re-provision technological infrastructure resources. Device and location independence enable users to access systems using a web browser regardless of their location or the device they are using. Multi-tenancy enables sharing of resources and costs across a large pool of users thus allowing for centralization of infrastructure in locations with lower costs. Reliability improves through the use of multiple redundant sites, which makes Cloud Computing suitable for business continuity and disaster recovery. Security typically improves due to centralization of data and increased security-focused resources. Sustainability comes about through improved resource utilization, more efficient systems.

2.2 Mobile Cloud Computing and Healthcare

Mobile Cloud Computing is a type of cloud computing in which some of the devices that are used for providing the services, are mobiles. Mobile devices have many constraints imposed upon them because of the desirability of smaller sizes, lower weights, longer battery life and other features. These constraints cause inflexibility in hardware and software development for these devices. Cloud computing can be used to allow the mobile devices to avoid these constraints by making the resource intensive tasks and complex functions to be performed on desktop systems and having the end results sent to the device (Doukas, Pliakas, & Maglogiannis, 2010). This enables the Mobile Cloud Computing to be a very efficient and effective way to develop robust applications in the healthcare sector. The end user will benefit, as they can share resources and applications without high capital expenditure on hardware and software resources. The end users can easily run the applications from the mobile without any costly hardware to run applications as the operations are run within the cloud.

Mobile Cloud Computing (MCC) is gradually becoming a promising technology, which provides a flexible stack of massive computing, storage, and software services in a scalable and virtualized manner at low cost (X. Wang et al., 2013). The integration of WBANs and MCC is expected to facilitate the development of cost-effective, scalable, and data-driven pervasive healthcare systems, which must be able to realize long-term health monitoring and data analysis of patients in different environments (Wan, et al., 2013).

Figure 1. Benefits of emerging cloud computing into healthcare

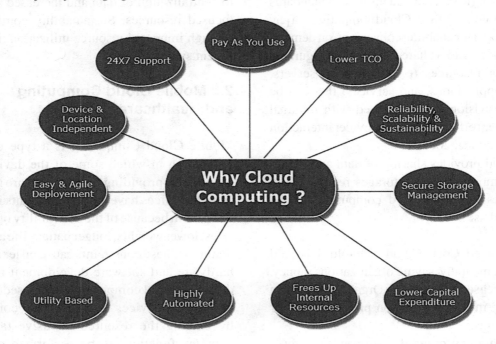

The purpose of applying MCC in medical applications is to minimize the limitations of traditional medical treatment (e.g., small physical storage, security and privacy, and medical errors (Kohn, Corrigan, & Donaldson, 1999), (Kopec, Kabir, Reinharth, & Rothschild, 2003)). Mobile healthcare (m-healthcare) provides mobile users with convenient helps to access resources (e.g., patient health records) easily and quickly. Besides, m-healthcare offers hospitals and healthcare organizations a variety of on-demand services on clouds rather than owning standalone applications on local servers. There are a few schemes of MCC applications in healthcare. For example, five main mobile healthcare applications in the pervasive environment were presented (Varshney, 2007):

- Comprehensive health monitoring services enable patients to be monitored at anytime and anywhere through broadband wireless communications.
- Intelligent emergency management system can manage and coordinate the fleet of emergency vehicles effectively and in time when receiving calls from accidents or incidents.

- Health-aware mobile devices detect pulse-rate, blood pressure, and level of alcohol to alert healthcare emergency system.
- Pervasive access to healthcare information allows patients or healthcare providers to access the current and past medical information.
- Pervasive lifestyle incentive management can be used to pay healthcare expenses and manage other related charges automatically.

3. HEALTHCARE CLOUD-BASED SYSTEMS

In this section, the cloud-based and mobile-based healthcare systems are presented. These solutions are categorized into Hospital Management System, Emergency Healthcare Systems, Healthcare Records Systems, Social Healthcare Systems, and Medical Imaging systems.

Figure 2. Emergence of mobile cloud computing into healthcare

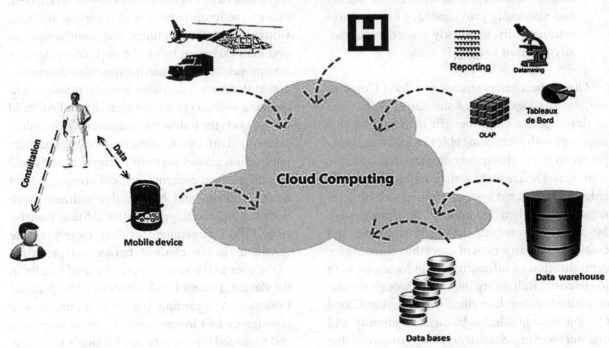

3.1 Hospital Management System

Many studies have demonstrated that there is a very limited access to patient-related information in hospital system which is available, during decision-making and the communication among patient observation team members are usual causes of medical errors in healthcare. Thus, there is a need for the pervasive and ubiquitous access to healthcare data is considered to be most essential for the proper diagnosis and treatment procedure for the patient. Cloud Computing is a model for enabling convenient, on-demand network access to a shared group of configurable computing resources (e.g., networks, servers, storage, applications, and services) that can be rapidly provisioned and released with minimal management effort or service provider interaction. This cloud model promotes availability and is composed of five essential characteristics, three service models, and four deployment models (Vinutha, Raju, & Siddappa, 2012).

The major characteristics of Cloud Computing can be summarized into the following:

1. **On-Demand Self-Service:** A consumer can unilaterally obtain access to computing capabilities, such as server computing time and/or network storage, as needed automatically without requiring human interaction with each service's provider;
2. **Broad Network Access:** Resources are available over the network and accessed through standard mechanisms that promote use by heterogeneous thin or thick client platforms;
3. **Resource Pooling:** The provider's computing resources are pooled to serve multiple consumers using a multi-tenant model, with different physical and virtual resources dynamically assigned and reassigned according to consumer demand. Examples of resources include storage, processing, memory, network bandwidth, and virtual machines;

4. **Rapid Elasticity:** Resources can be rapidly and elastically provisioned, in some cases automatically, to quickly scale out and rapidly released to quickly scale.

Given the characteristics of Cloud Computing and the flexibility of the services that can be developed, a major benefit is the agility that improves with users being able to rapidly and inexpensively re-provision technological infrastructure resources. Device and location independence enable users to access systems using a web browser regardless of their location or the device used. Multi-tenancy enables sharing of resources and costs across a large pool of users thus allowing for centralization of infrastructure in locations with lower costs. Reliability improves through the use of multiple redundant sites, which makes Cloud Computing suitable for business continuity and disaster recovery. Security typically improves due to centralization of data and increased security-focused resources. Sustainability comes about through improved resource utilization, more efficient systems. A number of Cloud Computing platforms are already available for pervasive management of user data, either free; e.g., iCloud, Box, Mozy and DropBox; or commercial; e.g., GoGrid and Amazon AWS. The majority of them however, do not provide to developers, the ability to create their own applications and incorporate Cloud Computing functionality, apart from Amazon AWS (Vinutha, Raju, & Siddappa, 2012).

3.1.1 Electronic Hospital Management System

The prevalent functionality of the application is to provide medical experts and patients with a mobile user interface for managing healthcare information more securely. The latter interprets into storing, querying and retrieving patient health records and patient-related medical data. The data may reside at a distributed Cloud Storage facility, initially uploaded/stored by medical personnel through a Hospital Information System (HIS). In order to be interoperable with a variety of Cloud Computing infrastructures, the communication and data exchange has to be performed through non-proprietary, open and interoperable communication standards. Electronic hospital management utilizing Web Services connectivity and Android OS supports the following functionality: Seamless connection to Cloud Computing storage: The main application allows users to retrieve, modify and upload medical content (medical images, patient health records and biosignals) utilizing Web Services and the Representational State Transfer (REST) API. The content resides remotely into the distributed storage elements but access is presented to the user as the resources are located locally in the device. Patient Health Record Management: Information regarding patient's status, related bio-signals and image content can be displayed and managed through the application's interface. Image viewing support: The Digital Imaging and Communications in Medicine (DICOM) medical image protocol is supported, while the JPEG2000 standard has been implemented to support loss and lossless compression, progressing coding and Region of Interest (ROI) coding. The progressive coding allows the user to decode large image files at different resolution levels optimizing network resources and allowing image acquisition even in cases network availability is limited. The code for performing wavelet decoding on mobile devices in has been modified to support the JPEG2000 standard on the Android platform. Image annotation is also supported, using the multi-touch functions of the Android OS. Proper user authentication and data encryption: User is authenticated at the Cloud Computing Service with SHA1 hashing for message authentication and Secure Sockets Layer (SSL) for encrypted data communication (Vinutha, Raju, & Siddappa, 2012).

Figure 3 illustrates the system architecture for developing and deploying the electronic hospital management system application that utilize Cloud Computing and the VPN connection. The

Figure 3. Electronic hospital management system architecture

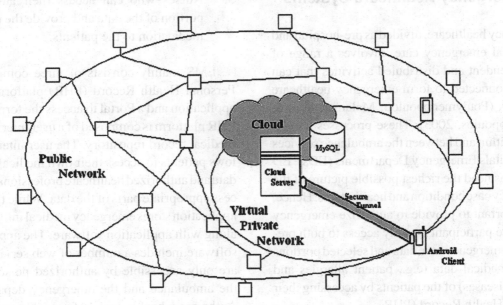

main components of a Cloud Computing Service usually are the platform front-end interface that communicates directly with users and allows the management of the storage content. The interface can be a web client or a standalone application.

The Cloud Storage Facilities manages the physical infrastructure (e.g., storage elements) and is also responsible for performing maintaining operations (e.g., backing up data) The Cloud Platform interface is also connected to the Cloud Service module, which handles and queues user requests. Finally, the Cloud Infrastructure module manages user account, accessibility and billing issues. Electronic hospital management system has been developed based on Google's Android mobile Operating System (OS) (Hung, Shih, Shieh, Lee, & Huang, 2011) using the appropriate Software Development Kit (SDK). Android is a mobile operating system running on the Linux kernel. Several mobile device vendors already support it. The platform is adaptable to larger and traditional smart phone layouts and supports a variety of connectivity technologies (CDMA, EV-DO, UMTS, Bluetooth, and Wi-Fi). It supports a great variety of audio, video

and still image format, making it suitable for displaying medical content. Finally, it supports native multi-touch technology, which allows better manipulation of medical images and generally increases the application's usability. The Cloud Service client running on Android OS consists of several modules. The Patient Health Record application acquires and displays patient records stored into the cloud. Data in Cloud are seamlessly stored and presented to the user as if they reside locally. This means that the Cloud repository is presented as a virtual folder and does not provide the features of a database scheme. In order to provide the user with data querying functionality, medical records and related data are stored into a SQLite file. SQLite is the database platform supported by Android. The file resides into a specific location at the Cloud and is retrieved on the device every time user needs to query data. The query is performed locally and the actual location of the data in the cloud is revealed to the applications. The database file is updated and uploaded into the Cloud every time user modifies data, respectively (Vinutha, Raju, & Siddappa, 2012).

3.2 Emergency Healthcare Systems

Emergency healthcare, divided as pre-hospital and in-hospital emergency care, involves a range of interdependent and distributed activities that can be interconnected to form emergency healthcare processes (Poulymenopoulou, Malamateniou, & Vassilacopoulos, 2003). These processes are executed within and between the ambulance services and hospitals Emergency Departments (EDs). ED physicians need the richest possible picture of the emergency case condition and health status. Hence, it is important to provide to authorize emergency healthcare participants readily access to both pre-hospital emergency case data and selected portions of past medical data (e.g., patient allergies and chronic diseases) of the patients by accessing their Personal Health Record (PHR).

3.2.1 Emergency Medical Systems (EMS) and PHR-Based EMS

Emergency Medical Systems (EMS) are among the most crucial ones as they involve a variety of activities which are performed from the time of a call to an ambulance service till the time of patient's discharge from the emergency department of a hospital and are closely interrelated so that collaboration and coordination becomes a vital issue for patients and for emergency healthcare service performance (Wooten, Klink, Sinek, Bai, & Shar, 2012).

EMS is an emergency medical system that accesses personal health records of patients and helps provide timely care. There are three groups of users in the EMS:

1. Ambulance Paramedics who have access to read and write data regarding paramedic activities performed at an incident site;
2. Emergency department physicians who have access to their respective authorized portions of medical data and can use the data to evaluate medical history, patient allergies and other critical health factors;

3. Nurses who can access their authorized portion of the data and provide the required medication to the patients.

EMS mainly consists of three components, Personal Health Record (PHR) platform, EMS application and a Portal to access the former. The PHR platform is composed of a user interface and medical record repository. The user interface allows patients to access their own medical history data and authorized healthcare professionals to access appropriate parts of the data. While the EMS application stores emergency medical information along with application software. The application software includes a number of web services that are only accessible by authorized personnel in the ambulance and the emergency department. Authorized healthcare professionals can interact with PHR and EMS via mobile phones and personal digital assistants, thus providing timely assistance to patients. This process gets initialized when a telephone operator receives an emergency call and records the patient's demographic and emergency medical information. After that, a physician who requests past medical data of the current patient is given access using a web service invocation. This service takes the doctor's role and the patient's name as input and searches the patient's PHR to retrieve authorized portions of medical data. The case data collected by both the ambulance service personnel and the personnel in the emergency department is captured in two separate XML documents. These XML documents are generated automatically upon ambulance arrival at the emergency department of a hospital and also when the patient is discharged from the emergency department.

EMS uses a private cloud to store data. In particular, PHR data is stored on multiple data centers on the cloud. It helps facilitate a timely access of relevant information by authorized people in case of emergencies (Koufi, Malamateniou, & Vassilacopoulos, 2010). It was developed as a web application using Apache/Tomcat. Its prototype has been implemented on a laboratory cloud computing infrastructure. As of today, usability of the system has not been evaluated (Wooten, Klink, Sinek, Bai, & Shar, 2012).

3.2.2 Cloud-Based Information Support for Emergency Healthcare

Combining cloud computing with Service-Oriented Architectures (SOA) presents a new way for Service-Oriented Integration (SOI) of existing healthcare systems and for developing distributed applications within and between healthcare organizations (Zhou, et al., 2010). Through emergency healthcare process automation, ambulance service and hospital EDs can automate their operations by making information available where and when needed and by providing an infrastructure for the integration of pre-hospital and in-hospital emergency medical care.

At each healthcare organization (e.g. hospitals and ambulance services) there exists an information system. Figure 4 illustrates the information support for emergency healthcare system architecture.

On Amazon EC2 virtual images there exists a SOA platform that consists of a database server, a business process server that hosts the BPEL

processes and an application server that hosts the web services (Poulymenopoulou, Malamateniou, & Vassilacopoulos, 2003). In addition, on Amazon EC2 virtual images a global security server has been installed to enforce the global security policy. Patient data created in the form of XML Clinical Document Architecture (CDA) based documents are stored in and retrieved from the cloud servers with the use of Amazon S3 service and are made available to appropriate authorized recipients through messages sent by the Amazon SQS service.

During pre-hospital emergency healthcare delivery, emergency case data is stored in the ambulance service database servers. Upon ambulance arrival at the ED, a BPEL process is automatically triggered to call web and cloud services that retrieve pre-hospital emergency case data from ambulance service database servers and, optionally, designated portions of medical data from the patient's PHR, transform this data into a CDA document which is stored in the cloud servers and send this document to the ED where it is made readily available to authorized users. In this way, it is assured that timely and accurate patient information is made available at the point of care when needed (e.g. on a tablet pc or mobile phone).

Figure 4. Information support for emergency healthcare system architecture

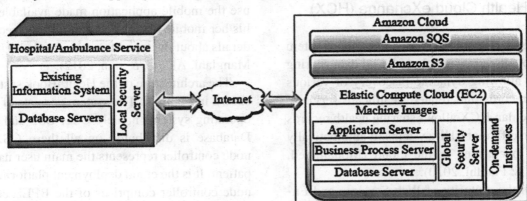

3.2.3 Discussion

Cloud-based services can prove important in emergency care delivery since they can enable easy and immediate access to patient data from anywhere and via almost any device.

3.3 Healthcare Records Systems

Using Cloud Computing, electronic health information is accessed by all the participants of healthcare system such as patients, healthcare providers, healthcare payer using open source cloud which acts as a server that faces several challenges, like data storage and management (e.g., physical storage issues, availability and maintenance), interoperability and availability of heterogeneous resources, security and privacy (e.g., permission control, data anonymity, etc.), unified and ubiquitous access.

On the other hand, mobile applications are used as a client to focus towards achieving two specific goals: the availability of e-health applications and medical information anywhere and anytime and the invisibility of computing. Mobile applications basically support electronic billing and EHR activities of patient and their medical history which can be accessed individually by patient, healthcare provider, healthcare payer by authenticating themselves with the cloud server.

3.3.1 Health Cloud eXchange (HCX)

HCX is a distributed web interactive system that provides a private cloud-based data sharing service allowing dynamic discovery of various health records and related healthcare services. In particular, HCX allows sharing health records between different EHR systems. It automatically adapts to changes in the cloud (Mohammed, Servos, & Fiaidhi, 2010).

With the maturity of Web Services and Enterprise Service Oriented Architectures (SOA), new delivery and Web interaction models are now demonstrating how services can be traded outside traditional ownership and provisioning boundaries. The value of SOA comes from having an architecture that readily accommodates change. The more the business changes, the more SOA pays for itself. However, the initial build-out of SOA, prior to business change or service sharing, is cost-ineffective. By incorporating cloud computing in SOA, the time to value is shortened because you leverage 'other people's work' as well as saving on infrastructure cost by leveraging on demand cloud based infrastructure services. HCX is a distributed web interactive system for sharing health records on the cloud using distributed OSGi services and consumers. This system allows for different health record and related healthcare services to be dynamically discovered and interactively used by client programs running within a federated private cloud (Mohammed, Servos, & Fiaidhi, 2010).

3.3.2 Healthbook

The development of HealthBook provides ease of access to patient's data in case of emergency by any responsible authority. These authorities have access to patient's medical information like previous medical histories, blood group, allergies, uploaded blood and electrocardiogram reports. The patient is initially required to access the web application to register for the service of HealthBook and then use the mobile application made available over his/her mobile device and enter all the required details about the type of service needed (Ujjwal, Manglani, Akarte, & Jain, 2012).

The architecture of the HealthBook system is shown in Figure 5. The system consists of three operating systems namely OS1, OS2 and OS3. Database is distributed on all these OS. The node controller represents the main user namely patient. It is the cloud deployment platform. The node controller comprises of the BPEL engine which has the designed BPEL rules and checks the queries accordingly and processes the output and makes it available over the user's device. The node controller and the database servers are located over the cloud. The user fires a query to the node controller according to the services he/she demands. The node controller which consists of the BPEL engine processes this query using the information stored in the database. The node controller has a complete access to the database servers OS1, OS2 and OS3 (Ujjwal, Manglani, Akarte, & Jain, 2012).

The HealthBook consists of various BPEL-orchestrated services which are usually called by the patient or the ambulance operator or the hospital authority. The entire process begins after a call is made by the patient to the ambulance service. Appropriate web services are used for various services requested. Likewise, if an ambulance operator or hospital doctor requests for previous medical history of the patient then in that case an appropriate web service is invoked. Case history collected by the ambulance service doctor and the hospital doctor form two separate XML documents. These XML documents are automatically generated as the ambulance reaches the hospital and when the patient is discharged, respectively. The applications for HealthBook are licensed for use and these are provided only upon registration to the service. The application

software for PHR and HealthBook component are comprised of various web services which are deployed using BPEL rules. Users can interact with the application either by using desktops or mobile devices.

The HealthBook consists of various BPEL-orchestrated services which are usually called by the patient or the ambulance operator or the hospital authority. The entire process begins after a call is made by the patient to the ambulance service. Appropriate web services are used for various services requested. Likewise, if an ambulance operator or hospital doctor requests for previous medical history of the patient then in that case an appropriate web service is invoked. Case history collected by the ambulance service doctor and the hospital doctor form two separate XML documents. These XML documents are automatically generated as the ambulance reaches the hospital and when the patient is discharged, respectively. The applications for HealthBook are licensed for use and these are provided only upon registration to the service. The application software for PHR and HealthBook component are comprised of various web services which are deployed using BPEL rules. Users can interact with the application either by using desktops or mobile devices (Ujjwal, Manglani, Akarte, & Jain, 2012).

Figure 5. HealthBook architecture

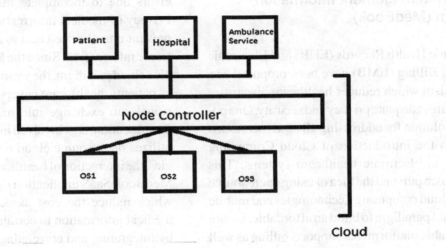

The architecture can be broadly termed consisting of following components:

- **PHR Application:** Responsible for centrally locating the patient information as well as giving the patient privileges to view his/her profile anytime with an access to edit it. Thus, the PHR application consists of a data repository to store the data globally and not locally. The PHR application also consists of a user application which enables user and ambulance or hospital authority to access the patient's information.

- **HealthBook Application:** Stores the hospital and ambulance data which consists of the phone numbers and addresses. This also consists of various BPEL –orchestrated web services. Registered patients only can use these services.

- **Graphical User Interface:** Provides front-end to the services provided by the processes. Users interact with the GUI to access PHR and HealthBook Application. The size of the GUI is flexible so that it can be easily accessed over any device. This property enables the efficient use of GUI in case of emergency when the application has to be accessed through a mobile device.

3.3.3 E-Healthcare Billing and Record Management Information System (MedBook)

Electronic Health Records (EHR) and Electronic Medical Billing (EMB) have been proposed as a mechanism which reduces healthcare disparities and ensures adequate privacy and security. One potential solution for addressing all aforementioned issues is the introduction of Cloud Computing concept in electronic healthcare systems. This mechanism pursued the idea of using open-source public cloud computing Technologies and mobile plus cloud paradigm to build an affordable, secure and scalable platform that supports billing as well as EHR operations. A platform called *MedBook* has been proposed (Vanitha, Narasimha Murthy, & Chaitra, 2013). MedBook is a cloud solution that provides patients, healthcare professionals/providers and healthcare payers a platform for exchange of electronic information about billing activities, benefit inquiries and EHR operations such as insert delete and update record using open source cloud services and Android operating system (OS).

MedBook is Software–as-a-Service (SaaS) platform built on top of open source public cloud technologies and running on the top of an Infrastructure-as-a Service (IaaS) platform. Generally the server applications are implemented as a collection of web services and web applications using MySQL, Tomcat 6or7 server, Apache web server. All the web services run on virtual machines powered by Windows XP or Ubuntu Linux 10.04. These servers are hosted inside an open source cloud which can be Jelastic, Eucalyptus 2.0, Open Stack and so forth. The client applications are mobile apps run from Google's Android Enabled phones. These client applications are built using Java 1.7 or 1.6 and uses REST based API to interact with MedBook SaaS Infrastructure (Vanitha, Narasimha Murthy, & Chaitra, 2013).

MedBook provides a highly reliable and secure electronic billing and record management system. It also helps reduce the occurrences of medical errors due to incomplete medical information. Privacy of medical information is maintained to prevent unauthorized access and misuse of electronic information. Since the MedBook is Mobile plus cloud paradigm, the various participants such as patients, health care payers, healthcare professional can exchange information regardless of time, location, cost involved in it. Since the system utilizes open source cloud computing technologies, the interaction of healthcare participants with MedBook SaaS application can be done globally which reduce the cost associated in accessing medical information to certain limit. In addition, by integrating and correlating the billing system

Figure 6. MedBook system architecture

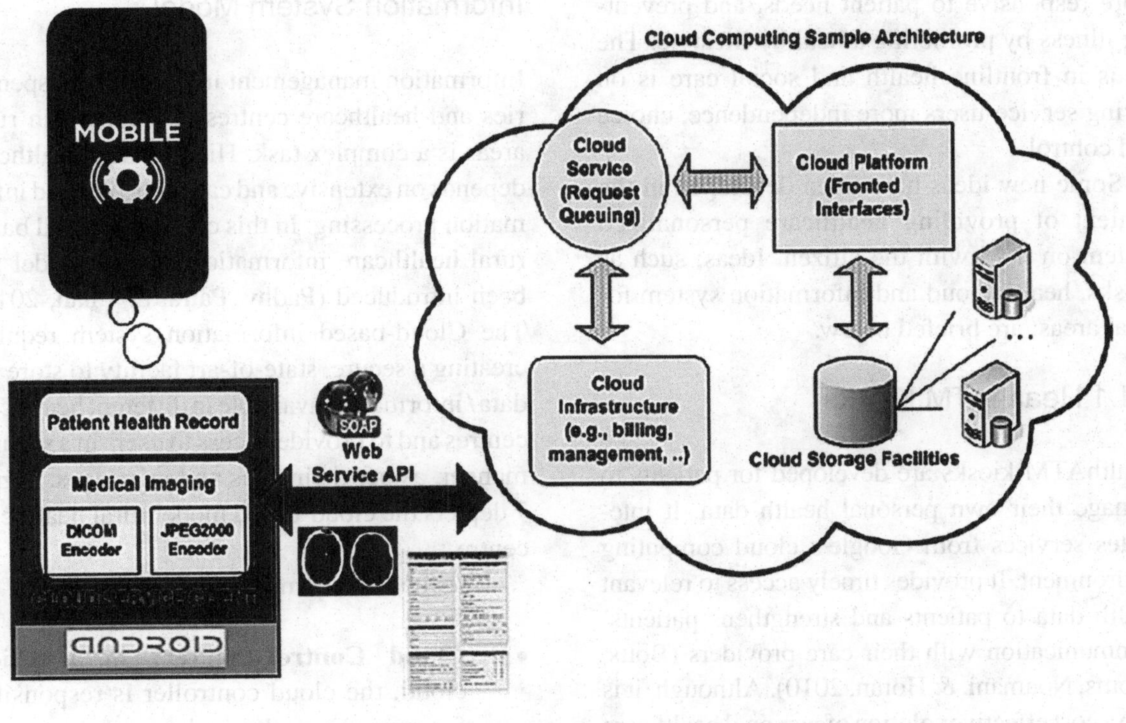

with EHR, it becomes possible to find that a given procedure was actually performed or the medical history of the patient utilized such procedures.

Figure 6 depicts the MedBook system architecture. MedBook SaaS application serves as an integration point between the various participants in the healthcare delivery system. MedBook architecture basically contains two Modules such as Client Module which uses the Mobile apps such as android enabled phones to interact with MedBook application. Server Module which consists of a series of web services and databases residing inside an IaaS cloud that maintains the information about each patient's EHR (Vanitha, Narasimha Murthy, & Chaitra, 2013).

The MedBook Client applications are mobile apps which uses Android enabled phones that connect with the MedBook SaaS infrastructure by means of REST based API. An android enabled phone is an open source and basically supports large number of applications compared to other

Smart phones. Android client application is designed for Patients, Healthcare provider/professional, Healthcare payers to perform billing and EHR activities with MedBook. The MebBook client application is designed for patients, healthcare payers, and healthcare providers/professionals (Vanitha, Narasimha Murthy, & Chaitra, 2013).

MedBook Server Application consists of a series of web services and databases residing inside an IaaS cloud that maintains the information related to each patient's EHR activities. The server module is designed to perform the following activities; service description, submitting Billing Transactions, representing and accessing EHR's (Vanitha, Narasimha Murthy, & Chaitra, 2013).

3.4 Social Healthcare Systems

Health and social care is a vast service sector undergoing rapid change, with new government initiatives giving it a higher profile than ever.

Priorities on the healthcare agenda include being more responsive to patient needs, and preventing illness by promoting a healthy lifestyle. The focus in frontline health and social care is on giving service-users more independence, choice and control.

Some new ideas have been developed in the context of providing healthcare personalized system on hold with the citizen. Ideas; such as kiosks, health cloud and information system for rural areas; are briefed below.

3.4.1 HealthATM Kiosks

HealthATM kiosks are developed for patients to manage their own personal health data. It integrates services from Google's cloud computing environment. It provides timely access to relevant health data to patients and strengthens patients' communication with their care providers (Botts, Thoms, Noamani, & Horan, 2010). Although, it is also a cost effective solution of personal healthcare management; as they makes use of cloud computing architectures, the systems currently cannot be directly handed over to patients; for constant training, outreach, education and collaboration are must.

3.4.2 @HealthCloud

@HealthCloud is a mobile healthcare information management system that is based on cloud computing and Android OS. It enables healthcare data storage, update and retrieval using Amazon Simple Storage Service (S3). It includes a PHR application that acquires and displays patient records stored in the cloud and a medical imaging module to display medical images on the device. It also supports native multi-touch technology which allows better manipulation of medical images and increases the application's usability (Doukas, Pliakas, & Maglogiannis, 2010).

3.4.3 Rural Healthcare Information System Model

Information management in hospitals, dispensaries and healthcare centres particularly in rural areas is a complex task. High quality healthcare depends on extensive and carefully planned information processing. In this context, a cloud based rural healthcare information system model has been introduced (Padhy, Patra, & Chan, 2012). The Cloud-based information system requires creating a secure, state-of-art facility to store the data/information available in different healthcare centres and to provide access to users in a secured manner, as per their roles and privileges. Figure 7 depicts the cloud-based model rural healthcare centre.

The model is composed of:

- **Cloud Control Server:** In a typical cloud, the cloud controller is responsible for managing physical resources, monitoring the physical machines, placing virtual machines, and allocating storage. The controller reacts to new requests or changes in workload by provisioning new virtual machines and allocating physical resources. This server also helps several ways in order to facilitate better control over the network.

- **Authentication Server:** Because in the application and data is hosted outside of the organization in the cloud computing environment, the cloud service provider has to use Authentication and Authorization mechanism. Authentication means that each user has an identity which can be trusted as genuine. This is necessary because some resources may be authorized only to certain users, or certain classes of users.

Figure 7. Architecture of cloud-based model rural healthcare centre

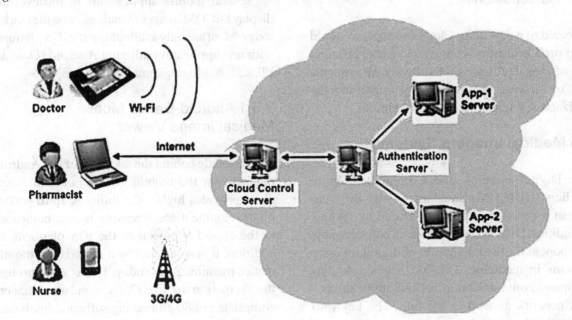

- **Resource Access:** Resource Access means that remote resources can be accessible to Grid users. These resources could mean anything from CPU time to disk storage, to visualization tools and data sets. Everyone should not be able to access all resources.
- **Resource Discovery:** Resource Discovery means that users can access remote resources that they can use.

The connectivity and configuration of the Cloud-based rural healthcare Information system is based on the service provider policy and domain location; i.e. cloud data centre location. Internet is the main communication link between the service provider and the Rural Healthcare centre. Users access cloud computing using networked client devices, such as desktop computers, laptops, tablets and smart phones. Some of these devices - cloud clients - rely on cloud computing for all or a majority of their applications so as to be essentially useless without it. Examples are thin clients and the browser. Many cloud applications do not require specific software on the client and instead use a web browser to interact with the cloud application (Padhy, Patra, & Chan, 2012).

Regarding, the system message flow, a nurse documents a visit of that patient when a patient visits a Rural Healthcare Centre. The Rural Healthcare Centre Information support centre supports an interface that closely used the SOAP protocol for documenting a visit. SOAP is an acronym comprising of the four stages involved; subjective which captures a patient's conditions in her own words, Objective consisting of notes made from measurements, physical examination and tests, Assessment consisting of a summary and differential diagnosis and finally Plan which is the care-provider's recommended course of action that includes prescriptions and referrals. As part of the plan, the care provider also recommends, if she deems necessary, a follow up to be done by the Health Extension Worker. Every visit documented by the nurse goes through an approval by a doctor and, the health care provider can access the history of visits for every patient (Padhy, Patra, & Chan, 2012).

3.4.4 Discussion

Directed to a new area, Cloud Computing would help rural healthcare centres to achieve efficient use of their hardware and software investments and to increase profitability by improving the utilization of resources to the maximum.

3.5 Medical Imaging Systems

The Digital Imaging and Communication in Medicine (DICOM) standard, is the de facto format for medical images produced by various modalities. DICOM has become an indispensable component for the integration of digital imaging systems in medicine. DICOM offers solutions for many communication related applications - in a network as well as off-line. The keyword "DICOM" by itself, however, is no guarantee for a "plug and play" integration of all information systems in a hospital. Such a scenario requires a careful combination of all the partial solutions offered by DICOM.

DICOM image analysis and visualization systems have become important tools that can help to diagnose various pathological disorders affecting human beings. Currently, there are numerous systems that allow medical professionals to access DICOM images located on PACS servers (Pasha, et al., 2012), while some even offer collaborative analysis features for image based discussion with their medical peers via computer networks (Drnasin & Grgic, 2010).

Research and development into advanced medical image analysis and visualization mostly focus on creating algorithms to analyze image features, segment specific soft tissues and ultimately identify lesions. Today, pervasive and cloud computing technology is also receiving widespread acceptance in the healthcare industry (Doukas, Pliakas, & Maglogiannis, 2010) (Vlahu-Gjorgievska & Trajkovik, 2011).

Several mobile applications to retrieve and display DICOM images already exist on the market today. Most are only available on the iOS platform with one application utilizing Android (Doukas, Pliakas, & Maglogiannis, 2010).

3.5.1 Android-Based Mobile Medical Image Viewer

The rationale behind the adoption of the Android platform for the mobile system is because Android provides higher flexibility to third parties on development and licensing issues, compared to the closed approach of the iOS platform. In addition, it is supported by a majority of mobile device manufacturers today. This is seen through the formation of the Open Handset Alliance, comprising of 80 pioneering software, hardware, and telecommunication companies committed to promoting open standards in the mobile technology sector. Thus, the large number and variety of devices running on the Android platform will be advantageous for the mobile solution.

Figure 8 shows the complete architectural design of the mobile system. Overall, it has four major components: the Viewer component, the Preference Store component, the Browse and Import component, and the Collaborative Module (Pasha, et al., 2012). For the database, the SQLite relational embedded database is implemented to store data. In addition, a lightweight collaborative server implementation with infrastructure support for the mobile system collaborative annotation feature is designed.

The Viewer component is basically the main component of the mobile system. It links the other components and manages the data flow between the user and the system. Since the system is designed to run on Android-based devices with touch screens, the viewer component also implements the required touch gestures to control the system. Lastly, it also has three sub-components to provide different functionalities (Pasha, et al., 2012).

Figure 8. Mobile medical image viewer and collaborative annotation system architecture

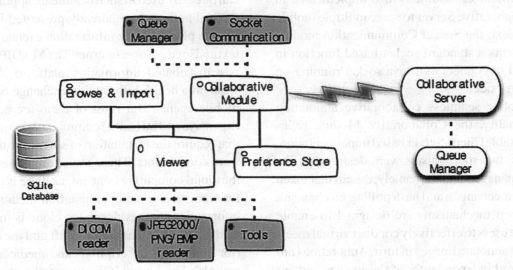

The first sub-component is the DICOM reader, which implements the needed functionality to read DICOM images and the included metadata. The second sub-component is a conventional image reader that focuses on reading compressed lossless JPEG images. And the last sub-component is the tools module providing the needed tools to highlight regions of interest.

The viewer component is linked with the three other components; the Browse and Import component, the Preference store, and the Collaborative Module component. The Browse and Import component is a module designed to scan the mobile device's local directory for DICOM files. It also implements an import function to import local DICOM files and stores its location and metadata into the SQLite database. The Preference store module basically implements the standard system preference settings for storage in mobile devices.

Next, the Collaborative Module component is the core element of the Android-based mobile medical image viewer and collaborative annotation system. It allows multiple experts from different geographical sites, to confer and annotate images in real time without altering the original

data. Medical experts can use this functionality to review the same medical images or radiological reports and conduct discussions in real-time. The Collaborative Module component uses the same drawing tools from the Viewer component's Tools module. The drawings of rectangles, freehand shapes, arrows, or measurement rulers are overlaid upon the images and subsequently displayed on the display screens of all participants in a discussion session.

The Collaborative Module component also provides an alternative way to import medical images from external sources, rather than local DICOM files which can be accessed via the Browse and Import component itself. It downloads medical images from the collaborative server.

Currently this image download feature is designed to only support the collaborative annotation feature, with a single medical image downloadable per instance. There are two sub-components designed to support the collaboration functionality: the Queue Manager and the Socket Communication. The Queue Manager is designed to handle multi-user annotation by queuing up the process of annotations to avoid loss of information due to multiple users annotating at the same time. The

Queue Manager module is also implemented in the Collaborative Server to serve multiple mobile users. Next, the Socket Communication module implements a standard socket based function in Android to connect to a Java socket running on the server side.

To offer seamless collaborative annotation functionality, the Collaborative Module relies upon a stable Client-Server based implementation. For this, two mechanisms were designed in the Queue manager module, namely; the circular token passing mechanism and hash polling mechanism. These two mechanisms are designed to enable multiple users to effectively conduct virtual meetings and annotate images in turn. Annotations are transferred independently of the images and are recombined later to avoid bandwidth issues. To enhance usability and reliability of annotating on relatively small screened mobile devices, an image scaling module was designed for precise annotation. This is to ensure that regardless of the screen size and resolution, annotations drawn will appear in the same precise location and shape for all participants in a session. Via this functionality, users will be able to annotate even a small region of interest within the medical image using only their fingertips. It will also enable the annotation to be shared precisely with other users, regardless of what device they are using.

3.5.2 Medical Image Data Management System

The HMS application is designed to make available the prescriptions and health records, medical image records (like scanned images etc.) of patients, on their Android powered mobile phones. The health records are stored and managed in the cloud OS. The records are transferred from the cloud to the mobile device, where it is displayed. EyeOS is the cloud platform used to build this application. This cloud OS can be easily downloaded for free. Since Android powered mobile devices are available in the market at affordable rates, they can be easily used in such healthcare applications. Several authors have already presented ideas of mobile platforms for information exchange (like text and images) over internet. The MADIP system is a distributed information platform allowing wide-area health information exchange based on mobile agents. But most of them are based on expensive and inflexible communication methods that require the installation of software and hardware components. These issues are solved using the cloud computing concept, as there is no need for extra storage and computation medium. The information that resides in the cloud is managed by the hospital management staff and the doctors (for uploading prescriptions and medical image records). The Android OS supports the connection to the Cloud OS that allows the patient to retrieve, modify, manage and upload medical images and text data using the internet services and REST API concepts like HTTP URLs. The image support is provided by DICOM protocol and the pixel data of images are compressed by the JPEG standard. The progressive coding allows the user to decode large image files at different resolution levels optimizing network resources and allowing image acquisition even in cases network availability is limited. The code for performing wavelet decoding on mobile devices in has been modified to support the JPEG2000 standard on the Android platform. Image annotation is also supported, using the multi-touch functions of the Android OS (Somasundaram, Gitanjali, Govardhani, Priya, & Sivakumar, 2011). The system architecture of the implementation is shown in Figure 9.

The entire process works as follows:

1. The client at the mobile end opens the cloud application as either patient or doctor and is authenticated by the cloud end.
2. The client enters his/her profile details by registering first, and then logging in. The username is the corresponding 'id' and password is the one set by him/her in the cloud server.

Figure 9. Medical image data management system architecture

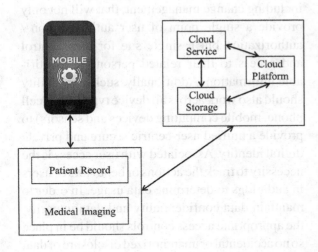

3. Then the Patient id is required to "search" for the records under that id. Then the particulars, diagnosis details and medical images are viewed by selecting the same via the checkbox.

4. When the user requests for an operation in the mobile end, the request is sent via Rest API like HTTP URL to the cloud OS.

5. The cloud OS responds by sending the requested information by searching in the database and sending them back to client.

6. The mobile application checks whether there are any files that were received and are waiting to be downloaded, and will download them and make them viewable to the client.

3.5.3 Discussion

In summary, different cloud-based medical applications and systems are being investigated. As seen above, some systems are designed to maximize the benefits of treatment, while others to assist patients in managing their own care. Yet, the benefits of mobile and cloud computing are not yet interactively used by governments when implementing their e-health solutions.

The healthcare industry is a prominent user of mobile cloud computing. The industry had developed applications which allow patients and doctors access to information anywhere at any time, the ability to monitor patients remotely and enhance emergency response. Due to the sensitive nature of health information, mobile cloud computing for the healthcare industry faces many challenges such as data storage, heterogeneous resources, and last but not least, security (Ahuja & Rolli, 2012).

Nevertheless, mobile cloud computing is being identified as one of the "key factors contributing to better health care for the society." Mobile cloud computing utilized in fields like the healthcare industry offer improved efficiency and improved quality.

4. OPEN RESEARCH ISSUES

The emergence of cloud computing leads to new developments for diverse application domains. This is particularly true for healthcare with its tremendous importance in today's society, thus making it worth to investigate the relevant perspectives and insights. Healthcare, as with any other service operation, has been impacted by the cloud computing phenomenon with the literature reporting both benefits and challenges of cloud computing in the area. However, despite the significant advantages for the utilization of cloud computing as part of Healthcare IT, security and privacy, reliability, integration and data portability are some of the significant challenges and barriers to implementation that are responsible for its slow adoption.

4.1 Privacy and Security

Healthcare data has stringent requirements for security, confidentiality, availability to authorized users, traceability of access, reversibility of data, and long-term preservation. Hence, cloud vendors need to account for all these while conforming to government and industry regulations. Problems in making IT systems interoperable have delayed cloud computing growth in the health care industry.

Data maintained in a cloud may contain personal, private or confidential information; such as healthcare related information that requires the proper safeguards to prevent disclosure, compromise or misuse. Globally, concerns related to data jurisdiction, security, privacy and compliance are impacting adoption by healthcare organizations.

Data leaving a mobile device onto a commercial 3G or 4G network is typically the responsibility of the network operator to ensure that the data is securely transported. All major domestic carriers have developed encryption measures designed to safeguard data flowing through their cellular networks. Without proper data encryption methods in place, sensitive data may be passed through non-secure networks such as the Internet or transmitted through an open Wi-Fi hot spot.

Medical devices also pose potential privacy risks. As medical devices and sensors become more sophisticated, they may allow for not only external monitoring and data gathering for storage in a Big Data cloud but for their control as well. Improper controls or management of these patient medical devices may compromise patient information, or provide a mechanism for inappropriate access to or tampering of the device itself.

Another critical component is the process of correctly identifying and authenticating users along with a comprehensive authorized privilege and role-based access control. Passwords or other safeguards are necessary to confirm the identity of all those seeking to access information. Currently, varying forms of user authentication and authorization are used to provide access to cloud based capabilities with personal access information required for each system or application. This results in a potential plethora of user accounts, account IDs and passwords, which not only makes it challenging for the user but also reduces privacy and security.

Future Identity Management advances should provide for end-to-end full life-cycle capabilities, including change management, that will not only provide a single point of user authentication / authorization but a single site for user control and access to their related personally identifiable information. Additionally, such a capability should also work across all device types (PCs, cell phone, mobile computing devices and sensors) to provide a unified user-centric secure and private digital identity. Associated with user access is the necessity to track the actions or behaviors of users in audit logs to determine data usage. In order to maintain data confidentiality and data integrity, the appropriate access controls should be in place so no accidental or unauthorized disclosure of data takes place or that data does not get unintentionally or maliciously altered.

4.2 Service Reliability

From an operational standpoint, the reality is that all cloud ecosystems and enterprise infrastructures will have disruptions to some degree at some point in time. Mission critical healthcare applications must meet very high performance, availability and reliability standards. The growing reliance on distributed network-based solutions; such as Service-Oriented Architecture (SOA) web services, Cloud-based service providers and Software as a Service (SaaS) solutions, are only increasing the complexities of managing, securing and maintaining these dynamic environments. These types of services may be hosted by multiple heterogeneous, geographically distributed CSPs or in local on-premise data centers. In order to meet overall mission performance goals, the service capabilities may have their workloads shifted across the cloud ecosystem in order to optimize processing and storage resources.

Disaster recovery is a component of service reliability that focuses on processes and technology for resumption of applications, data, hardware, communications (such as networking), and other

IT infrastructure in case of a disaster. The process of devising a disaster recovery plan starts with identifying and prioritizing applications, services and data, and determining for each one the amount of downtime that's acceptable before there is a significant business impact. In general, current cloud Service Level Agreements (SLAs) provide inadequate guarantees in case of a service outage due to a disaster. Most cloud SLAs provide cursory treatment of disaster recovery issues, procedures and processes.

The healthcare industry's dependence on the availability and reliability of information can be a matter of life and death. Performance is another factor that is slowing the pace at which cloud computing is adopted by healthcare organizations. Globally, hospitals, physicians and patients have different types of Internet connections that can impact performance of a healthcare system. For example, many rural healthcare facilities still use modems to connect to the Internet. Uptime and other appropriate service levels should be reviewed and included as part of the service level agreement.

4.3 Integration and Interoperability

A key component to healthcare that transcends the IT domain is the reliable exchange of commonly understood information to facilitate coordinated patient care. Different participants (e.g., surgeons, pediatricians, nurses) in the healthcare ecosystem have different terminologies and requirements. Delivering an end-to-end system that fully integrates all patient information, including emergency and in-patient care, pharmacies, billing, reimbursement and more requires standardization and interoperability. Certain standards are needed to help drive the transfer and storage of data within the cloud through common and unifying components.

Some of the risks associated with migration to the cloud include incompatibilities with the enterprise organization, strategic vision, its business or operational processes, managing a new services-based financial/billing chargeback

model, dealing with the lack of transparency of off-loaded data and applications, or leveraging existing system architecture. A typical cloud computing environment consists of disparate components from multiple participants and legacy on-premise data center applications. Ultimately the legacy system infrastructure, business process improvements, financial management, and operations and maintenance; all need to be an integral part of the cloud strategy.

4.4 Data Portability

Another barrier that impacts some healthcare organizations' willingness to adopt cloud computing is the concern regarding the ability to transition to another cloud vendor or back to the healthcare organization without disrupting operations or introducing conflicting claims to the data. With traditional IT, the healthcare organization has physical control of systems, services and data. The concern is that if a provider were to suspend its services or refuse access to data, a healthcare organization may suddenly be unable to service its patients or customers. Or, if the healthcare organization were given notice that the cloud service would be discontinued, the lack of interoperability across cloud systems could make it very challenging to migrate to a new cloud service provider. This risk highlights the need for provider agreements that address termination rights, rights to access and retrieve data at any time, termination assistance in moving to another provider and cure periods to allow breach of contract to be remedied before the provider terminates or suspends services.

5. CONCLUSION

This chapter provided a comprehensive review on the Cloud-based and Mobile-based applications that have been developed in the healthcare field. The review covered different solutions related to Hospital Management, Emergency Healthcare, Healthcare

Records, Social Healthcare, and Medical Imaging systems, where each solution was addressed and discussed in terms of its features, functionalities and architecture. The chapter discussed how these solutions fulfilled the healthcare requirements and even provide new services. The chapter illustrated how the emergence of both Cloud and Mobile in the healthcare field have reduce the cost overhead, increase the storage capability, keep high level of automation, provide mobility, and eliminate technical administrative burden. The chapter had discussed some open research issues that need to be addressed in this field.

REFERENCES

Ahuja, S., & Rolli, A. (2012, June). Exploring the convergence of mobile computing with cloud computing. *Journal of Network and Communication Technologies*, *1*(1).

Botts, N., Thoms, B., Noamani, A., & Horan, T. (2010). Cloud computing architectures for the underserved: Public health cyberinfrastructures through a network of HealthATMs. In *Proceedings of 43rd Hawaii Int. Conf. on System Sciences (HICSS)* (pp. 1-10). IEEE. doi:10.1109/HICSS.2010.107

Doukas, C., Pliakas, T., & Maglogiannis, I. (2010). Mobile healthcare information management utilizing cloud computing and Android OS. In *Proceedings of 32nd Annual International Conference of the IEEE Engineering in Medicine and Biology Society (EMBC)*. Buenos Aires, Argentina: IEEE.

Drnasin, I., & Grgic, M. (2010). The use of mobile phones in radiology. *ELMAR*, *2010*, 17–21.

Hung, S., Shih, C., Shieh, J., Lee, C., & Huang, Y. (2011). An online migration environment for executing mobile applications on the cloud. In *Proceedings of 2011 5th International Conference on Innovative Mobile and Internet Services in Ubiquitous Computing*. Seoul, Korea: Academic Press.

Kohn, L., Corrigan, J., & Donaldson, S. (1999). *To err is human: Building a safer health system*. Washington, DC: National Academy Press.

Kopec, D., Kabir, M., Reinharth, D., & Rothschild, O. (2003, August). Human errors in medical practice: Systematic classification and reduction with automated information systems. *Journal of Medical Systems*, *27*(4), 297–313. doi:10.1023/A:1023796918654 PMID:12846462

Koufi, V., Malamateniou, F., & Vassilacopoulos, G. (2010). Ubiquitous access to cloud emergency medical services. In *Proceedings of 10th IEEE Int. Conf. on Information Technology and Applications in Biomedicine (ITAB)* (pp. 1-4). Corfu, Greece: IEEE. doi:10.1109/ITAB.2010.5687702

Mell, P., & Grance, T. (2009). *Draft NIST working definition of cloud computing - v15*. National Institutes of Standard and Technology, Information Technology Laboratory.

Mohammed, S., Servos, D., & Fiaidhi, J. (2010). HCX: A distributed OSGi based web interaction system for sharing health records in the cloud. In *Proceedings of IEEE/WIC/ACM Int. Conf. on Web Intelligence and Intelligent Agent Technology (WI-IAT)* (pp. 102-107). Toronto, Canada: IEEE. doi:10.1109/WI-IAT.2010.26

Organization of Economics Co-Operation and Development. (2013). Retrieved from http://www.oecd.org/

Padhy, R., Patra, M., & Chan, S. (2012). Design and implementation of a cloud based rural healthcare information system mode. *UNIASCIT*, *2*(1), 149–157.

Pasha, M., Supramaniam, S., Liang, K., Amran, M., Chandra, B., & Rajeswari, M. (2012, January). An Android-based mobile medical image viewer and collaborative annotation: Development issues and challenges. *International Journal of Digital Content Technology and its Applications*, *6*(1).

Poulymenopoulou, M., Malamateniou, F., & Vassilacopoulos, G. (2003). Emergency healthcare process automation using workflow technology and web services. *Med Inform Internet, 28*(3), 195–207. doi:10.1080/14639230310001617841 PMID:14612307

Somasundaram, M., Gitanjali, S., Govardhani, T., Priya, G., & Sivakumar, R. (2011). Medical image data management system in mobile cloud computing environment. In *Proceedings of International Conference on Signal, Image Processing and Applications (ICSIPA 2011)*. Kuala Lumpur, Malaysia: Academic Press.

Ujjwal, A., Manglani, B., Akarte, D., & Jain, A. (2012, March-April). Healthbook – Ubiquitous solution for heath services. *International Journal of Engineering Research and Applications, 2*(2), 965–967.

Vanitha, T., Narasimha Murthy, M., & Chaitra, B. (2013). E-healthcare billing and record management information system using Android with Cloud. *IOSR Journal of Computer Engineering, 11*(4), 13-19.

Varshney, U. (2007, March). Pervasive healthcare and wireless health monitoring. *Journal on Mobile Networks and Applications, 12*(2-3), 113–127. doi:10.1007/s11036-007-0017-1

Vinutha, S., Raju, C., & Siddappa, M. (2012, July). Development of electronic hospital management system utilizing cloud computing and Android OS using VPN connections. *International Journal of Scientific & Technology Research, 1*(6), 59–61.

Vlahu-Gjorgievska, E., & Trajkovik, V. (2011). Personal healthcare system model using collaborative filtering techniques. *Advances in Information Sciences and Service Sciences, 3*(3), 64–74. doi:10.4156/aiss.vol3.issue3.9

Wan, J., Zou, C., Ullah, S., Lai, C., Zhou, M., & Wang, X. (2013, September-October). Cloud-enabled wireless body area networks for pervasive healthcare. *IEEE Transactions on Network, 27*(5).

Wang, X., et al. (2013, February). AMES-cloud: A framework of adaptive mobile video streaming and efficient social video sharing in the clouds. *IEEE Trans. Multimedia, 10*(1109).

Wooten, R., Klink, R., Sinek, F., Bai, Y., & Shar, M. (2012). Design and implementation of a secure healthcare social cloud system. In *Proceedings of 12th IEEE/ACM Int. Symp. Cluster, Cloud and Grid Computing (CCGRID 2012)* (pp. 805-810). Ottawa, Canada: IEEE/ACM. doi:10.1109/CCGrid.2012.131

Zhou, Y., Liu, X., Xue, L., Liang, X., & Liang, S. (2010). Business process centric platform-as-a-service model and technologies for cloud enabled industry solutions. In *Proceedings of 3rd International Conference on Cloud Computing* (pp. 534-537). Miami, FL: Academic Press. doi:10.1109/CLOUD.2010.52

KEY TERMS AND DEFINITIONS

Cloud Computing: A market-oriented distributed computing paradigm consisting of a collection of inter-connected and virtualized computers that are dynamically provisioned and presented as one or more unified computing resources based on service-level agreements established through negotiation between the service provider and consumers.

Cloud: A large pool of easily usable and accessible virtualized resources (such as hardware, development platforms and/or services). These resources can be dynamically reconfigured to optimum resource utilization. This pool of resources is typically exploited by a pay-per-user model in which guarantees are offered by the Infrastructure Provider by means of customized SLA's.

eHealth: A relatively recent term for healthcare practice supported by electronic processes and communication, dating back to at least 1999. Usage of the term varies: some would argue it is interchangeable with health informatics with a broad definition covering electronic/digital processes in health while others use it in the narrower sense of healthcare practice using the Internet.

Emergency Medical Services: A type of emergency service dedicated to providing out-of-hospital acute medical care, transport to definitive care, and other medical transport to patients with illnesses and injuries which prevent the patient from transporting themselves.

Healthcare System: The organization of people, institutions, and resources to deliver health care services to meet the health needs of target populations.

Hospital Information System: A comprehensive, integrated information system designed to manage all the aspects of a hospital operation, such as medical, administrative, financial, legal and the corresponding service processing.

Hybrid Cloud: A Cloud Computing environment in which an organization provides and manages some resources in-house and has others provided externally.

Infrastructure-as-a-Service (IaaS): A provision model in which an organization outsources the equipment used to support operations, including storage, hardware, servers and networking components, where the service provider owns the equipment and is responsible for housing, running and maintaining it and the client typically pays on a per-use basis.

Medical Imaging: The technique and process used to create images of the human body (or parts and function thereof) for clinical purposes (medical procedures seeking to reveal, diagnose, or examine disease) or medical science (including the study of normal anatomy and physiology).

mHealth: A term used for the practice of medicine and public health, supported by mobile devices. The mHealth field has emerged as a sub-segment of eHealth, the use of information and communication technology (ICT); such as computers, mobile phones, communications satellite, patient monitors; for health services and information. mHealth applications include the use of mobile devices in collecting community and clinical health data, delivery of healthcare information to practitioners, researchers, and patients, real-time monitoring of patient vital signs, and direct provision of care (via mobile telemedicine).

Mobile Cloud Computing (MCC): The state-of-the-art mobile distributed computing paradigm comprises three heterogeneous domains of mobile computing, cloud computing, and wireless networks aiming to enhance computational capabilities of resource-constrained mobile devices towards rich user experience.

Private Cloud: A marketing term for a proprietary computing architecture that provides hosted services to a limited number of people behind a firewall.

Public Cloud: One based on the standard Cloud Computing model, in which a service provider makes resources, such as applications and storage, available to the general public over the Internet. Public Cloud services may be free or offered on a pay-per-usage model.

Software-as-a-Service (SaaS): A software distribution model in which applications are hosted by a vendor or service provider and made available to customers over a network, typically the Internet.

Section 6
Security

Chapter 11
Access Control in Cloud Computing

Qianqian Zhao
Xidian University, China

Yuqing Zhang
Xidian University, China

Maode Ma
Nanyang Technological University, Singapore

Bingsheng He
Nanyang Technological University, Singapore

ABSTRACT

Data sharing as one of the most popular service applications in cloud computing has received wide attention, which makes the consumers achieve the shared contents whenever and wherever possible. However, the new paradigm of data sharing will also introduce some security issues while it provides much convenience. The data confidentiality, the privacy security, the user key accountability, and the efficiency are hindering its rapid expansion. An effective and secure access control mechanism is becoming one way to deal with this dilemma. In this chapter, the authors focus on presenting a detailed review on the existing access control mechanisms. Then, they explore some potential research issues for the further development of more comprehensive and secure access control schemes. Finally, the authors expect that the topic of access control in cloud computing will attract much more attention from academia and industry.

INTRODUCTION

Cloud Computing has emerged as a promising computing paradigm that has drawn extensive attention from both academia and industry recently. By combining a set of existing and new techniques from the research areas including Service-Oriented Architectures (SOA) and virtualization, cloud computing is regarded as a computing paradigm in which resources in the computing infrastructure are provided as a service over the Internet. The

cloud computing provides a platform to cut costs and help the users to focus on their core business instead of being impeded by information technology (IT) obstacles.

Along with this new paradigm, many researchers are engaged in the design of the valuable service applications in cloud computing. Especially, the data storage service based cloud computing has reached an unprecedented development. Cloud storage allows data owners to host the data from their local computing systems to the cloud. First,

DOI: 10.4018/978-1-4666-8213-9.ch011

Copyright © 2015, IGI Global. Copying or distributing in print or electronic forms without written permission of IGI Global is prohibited.

the cloud storage is a model of networked online storage where the data is stored in the virtualized pools of storage which are generally hosted by the third parties such as the storage service providers. Then, the service providers operate some large data centers for the data owners to purchase or lease storage capacity from them in a pay-as-you-go business model. The service providers, in the background, virtualize the resources according to the requirements of the customers and expose them as storage pools, which the customers themselves can use to store files or data objects. Physically, the resource may span across multiple servers. Finally, the cloud storage can provide a comparably low-cost, scalable, location independent platform for managing the users' data, thus more and more data owners start to store their data in the cloud. By hosting their data in the cloud, data owners can avoid the initial investment of expensive infrastructure setup, large equipment, and daily maintenance costs. The data owners only need to pay for the space they actually use described by the cost-per-gigabyte-stored model. Another reason is that data owners can rely on the cloud to provide more reliable services, so that they can access data from anywhere in the world at any time. Individuals or small-sized companies usually do not have the resource to keep their servers as reliable as the cloud does. In a word, the significance of cloud storage is to provide the cloud users with the ample storage resources anywhere anytime at the cost of little investment on their own local servers.

However, this new paradigm of data storage service will introduce some security challenges. It is obvious that the data owners would worry their data be misused or accessed by the unauthorized users in the cloud storage system. Since the cloud storage service separates the roles of the data owners from the data service provider, the data owners cannot interact with the users directly to provide data access services. Therefore, the access control scheme will be an effective way to ensure the data security in the cloud storage. Traditional access control archi-tectures usually assume that the data owners and the servers storing the data are in the same trusted domain, where the servers are fully entrusted as an omniscient reference monitor responsible for defining and enforcing the access control policies. Those existing methods usually delegate the data access control to a trusted server and let it be in charge of defining and enforcing access policies. However, the cloud servers cannot be fully trusted by the data owners because the cloud servers could be allowed to unauthorized users for the data access to make profits. Thus, the traditional server-based data access control mode is no longer suitable for the cloud storage systems. The design of the secure and effective access control mechanisms with the semi-trusted cloud servers will become demanding in the cloud storage systems.

In this book chapter, we mainly investigate the security issues of access control in cloud storage system and introduce some solutions to these security issues in detail. We hope that the topic of access control in cloud computing can attract much more attentions from the academia and industry. We first make a brief description about the definition or the background involved in this topic, which includes the following several aspects, cloud computing, cloud storage, the access control, the security issues and so on. Then, as the main contribution of this chapter, we explore the solutions to these security issues and make a detailed comparison among the existing schemes. In the end, we explore potential future research direction for the design of more secure and effective access control scheme for the cloud storage systems.

BACKGROUND

Cloud Computing

Cloud Computing is the result of evolution and adoption of existing computing technologies and paradigms, which has changed the modern

IT industry. The National Institute of Standards and Technology (NIST) has specified the official definition of cloud computing as follows.

Cloud Computing is a model for enabling ubiquitous, convenient, on-demand network access to a shared pool of configurable computing resources that can be rapidly provisioned and released with minimal management effort or service provider interaction (Mell & Grance, 2011).

The goal of cloud computing is to allow users to take benefit from all of current IT technologies without the need for deep knowledge about or expertise with each one of them. The cloud aims to cut costs, and helps the users focus on their core business instead of being impeded by IT obstacles. As shown in Figure 1, it presents an intuitive understanding on the ways how cloud computing changes the normal rules of daily life.

As we know, the emergence of cloud computing is not accidental, and actually it is gradually evolved from the development of grid computing and parallel computing. However, it has the apparent characteristics different from them. We will analyze specifically the basic characteristic of the cloud computing, which are of great use to develop the service applications based the cloud computing. The cloud computing model holds five essential characteristics, three service models, and four deployment models.

The five essential characteristics are defined as follows.

1. **On-Demand Self-Service:** It indicates that a consumer can be unilaterally provided with computing capabilities, such as server time and network storage, as needed automatically without requiring human interaction with each service provider.
2. **Ubiquitous Network Access:** It indicates that capabilities are available over the network and can be accessed by the standard mechanisms to promote the usage by heterogeneous thin or thick client platforms including mobile phones, tablets, laptops, and workstations.

Figure 1. The architecture of the cloud computing

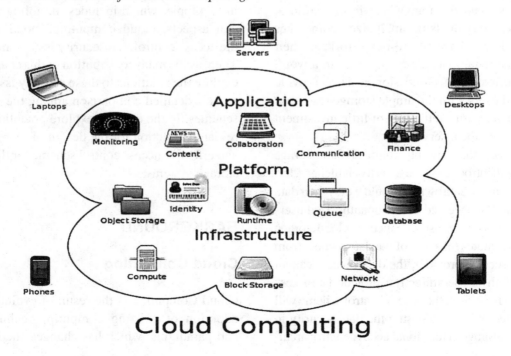

3. **Resource Pooling:** It indicates that the computing resources of the service providers are pooled to serve multiple consumers using a multi-tenant model, with different physical and virtual resources dynamically assigned and reassigned according to consumer demands.

4. **Rapid Elasticity or Expansion:** It implies that the capabilities can be elastically provisioned and released, in some cases, automatically and rapidly to be scaled outward and inward commensurate with demands.

5. **Measured Service:** It means that the cloud systems can automatically control and optimize the usage of the resource by leveraging a metering capability at some level of abstraction appropriate to the type of service. Resource usage can be monitored, controlled, and reported, providing transparency for both the provider and consumer of the utilized service.

At the same time, as shown in the official definition of NIST, the service models of Cloud Computing are defined as follows.

- **Cloud Software as a Service (SaaS):** The capability provided to the consumer is to use the provider's applications running on a cloud infrastructure. The applications are accessible from various client devices through either a thin client interface, such as a web browser (e.g., web-based email), or a program interface. The consumer does not manage or control the underlying cloud infrastructure including network, servers, operating systems, storage, or even individual application capabilities, with the possible exception of limited user-specific application configuration settings.

- **Cloud Platform as a Service (PaaS):** The capability provided to the consumer is to deploy onto the cloud infrastructure consumer -created or acquired applications created using programming languages, libraries, services, and tools supported by the provider. The consumer does not manage or control the underlying cloud infrastructure including network, servers, operating systems, or storage, but has control over the deployed applications and possibly configuration settings for the application-hosting environment.

- **Cloud Infrastructure as a Service (IaaS):** The capability provided to the consumer is to provision processing, storage, networks, and other fundamental computing resources where the consumer is able to deploy and run arbitrary software, which can include operating systems and applications. The consumer does not manage or control the underlying cloud infrastructure but has control over operating systems, storage, and deployed applications; and possibly limited control of select networking components (e.g., host firewalls). Proponents claim SaaS allows a business the potential to reduce IT operational costs by outsourcing hardware and software maintenance and support to the cloud provider. This enables the business to reallocate IT operations costs away from hardware/software spending and personnel expenses, towards meeting other goals. In addition, with applications hosted centrally, updates can be released without the need for users to install new software. One drawback of SaaS is that the users' data are stored on the cloud provider's server. As a result, there could be unauthorized access to the data. For this reason, users are increasingly adopting intelligent third-party key management systems to help secure their data.

Besides the theoretical explanations, we have Figure 2 to provide a more intuitive understanding about the difference and relationship between these three service models.

Figure 2. The architecture of the service model of cloud computing

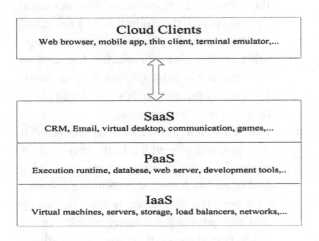

The deployment models, which can be either internally or externally implemented, are summarized in the NIST definition as follows.

- **Private Cloud:** The cloud infrastructure is provisioned for exclusive use by a single organization comprising multiple consumers (e.g., business units). It may be owned, managed, and operated by the organization, a third party, or some combination of them, and it may exist on or off premises.

- **Community Cloud:** The cloud infrastructure is provisioned for exclusive use by a specific community of consumers from organizations that have shared concerns (e.g., mission, security requirements, policy, and compliance considerations). It may be owned, managed, and operated by one or more of the organizations in the community, a third party, or some combination of them, and it may exist on or off premises.

- **Public Cloud:** The cloud infrastructure is provisioned for open use by the general public. It may be owned, managed, and operated by a business, academic, or government organization, or some combination of them. It exists on the premises of the cloud provider.

- **Hybrid Cloud:** The cloud infrastructure is a composition of two or more distinct cloud infrastructures such as private, community, or public, that remain unique entities, but are bound together by standardized or proprietary technology that enables data and application portability (e.g., cloud bursting for load balancing between clouds).

Table 1. The difference of all the cloud models

Model	Advantage	Disadvantage
Private Cloud	The security of this cloud model is completely controlled by the cloud users.	With the increase of the user demand for service resource, the cost on investment will be a huge challenge for the user.
Public Cloud	The cost on investment will be diluted by the cloud users who share the same public cloud.	The security of the cloud service depends on the manager of the public cloud. The security protocols become a necessity to achieve higher safety.
Hybrid Cloud	This model is made of a combination of the two basic types above. It enjoys both the advantage.	The security is more complicated problem because of this combination.
Community Cloud	Similarly, the cost on investment will be shared by the community users who employ the same community cloud.	The security will achieve a certain degree of optimization because of this special feature of community users. However, the new security issues, especially the security problems related to the identity will be much harder to achieve.

The service applications based on these models are being widely applied due to their respective characteristic. We present a comparative analysis about these cloud models to make better understanding on different types of the cloud models in cloud computing.

Cloud Computing, the long-held dream of computing as a utility, has the potential to transform a large part of the IT industry, making software even more attractive as a service and shaping the way IT hardware is designed and purchased. Cloud computing with the five essential characteristics refers to both the applications delivered as services over the Internet and the hardware and systems software in the datacenters that provide those services. The service includes SaaS, PaaS and IaaS, which is not just like the normal service model of the SaaS. It is the most important difference from other service models. Further the appearance of the IaaS results in the ample deployment model. The research on account of cloud computing has been widely spread because of its unique characteristic.

As exciting as it sounds, however, cloud computing also faces a number of critical and unique challenges. Among them, security is the number one concern. All of the security challenges are hindering the rapid expansion of cloud computing. Design of the secure and effective security schemes to address the security challenges obviously has become the focus of many researchers.

CLOUD STORAGE AS A SERVICE

Due to the distinctive features of the cloud computing, the data application service is about to begin in earnest. The outsourcing data on the cloud as one of these applications is the most attractive to the clients and the researchers. First of all, as we know, the cloud model can be roughly categorized as the basic either private cloud or public cloud. In the scenario of a private cloud, the infrastructure is managed and owned by the customer and located in the customers region of control. In particular,

this means that access to customer data is under its control and is only granted to parties it trusts. The security of the cloud storage under this model is easy to implement, so this situation has never been the research focus. However, in the scenario of a public cloud the infrastructure is owned and managed by a cloud service provider and is located in the service provider's region of control. This means that customer data is outside its control and could potentially be granted to untrusted parties. How to achieve the secure cloud storage under the public cloud model has become the challenge for both the cloud service providers and the cloud customers. Based such a background, all the cloud storage we mentioned below means the cloud storage service under the public cloud model. This cloud storage is a model of networked enterprise storage where data is stored in virtualized pools of storage which are generally hosted by third parties. Hosting companies operate large data centers, and people who require their data to be hosted have to buy or lease storage capacity from them. The data center operators, in the background, virtualize the resources according to the requirements of the customers and expose them as the storage pools, where the customers can use to store files or data objects by themselves. Physically, the resource may span across multiple servers and multiple locations. The safety of the files depends upon the hosting companies, and on the applications that leverage the cloud storage. Armbrust et al. (2010) stated that based on the above description of cloud computing, it is apparent that the cloud storage can provide a comparably low-cost, scalable, location independent platform for managing the data of users, thus more and more data owners start to store the data in the cloud. By hosting data in the cloud, data owners can avoid the initial investment of expensive infrastructure setup, large equipment, and daily maintenance cost. The data owners only need to pay the space they actually use, e.g., cost-per-byte-stored model. Another reason is that data owners can rely on the cloud to provide more reliable services, so that

Figure 3. The cloud storage as a service

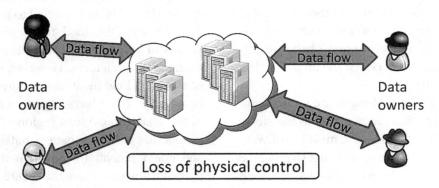

they can access their data from anywhere at any time. Individuals or small-sized companies usually do not have the resource to keep their servers as reliable as the cloud. Ren (2013) shows one visual display about the cloud storage framework in the Figure 3.

In addition to, the service providers can easily establish the data sharing service on the basis of cloud storage. When the clients upload their data to the cloud, the data sharing service not only allows the clients to access their shared data from anywhere at any time, but also allows the clients to access other users' data stored in the cloud through a proper approach. The data sharing application can greatly enrich the usage of the cloud storage. This kind of service in the education/medical/social application scenarios has been gradually developed.

The Access Control in Cloud Computing

While the cloud storage system provides the users a lot of convenience, which allows data owners to outsource their data in the cloud and rely on the cloud server to provide "24/7/365" data access to the users or the data consumers, however, it is obvious that the data owners would worry their data could be misused or accessed by the unauthorized users in the cloud storage system. Since

the cloud storage service separates the roles of the data owner from the data service provider, the data owner cannot interact with the user directly for providing data access service. Therefore, data access control will be an effective way to ensure the data security in the cloud storage. Traditional access control architectures usually assume that the data owner and the servers storing the data are in the same trusted domain, where the servers are fully entrusted as an omniscient reference monitor responsible for defining and enforcing the access control policies. Existing methods usually delegate the data access control to a trusted server and let it be in charge of defining and enforcing access policies. However, the cloud servers cannot be fully trusted by data owners because the cloud servers could be allowed to unauthorized users for data access to make profits. Thus, the traditional server-based data access control modes are no longer suitable for the cloud storage systems. The design of the secure and effective access control mechanisms will become demanding in the cloud storage systems. Then the difference about these two kinds of access control mechanisms, Ren (2013) achieves a more intuitive understanding through the Figure 4 and Figure 5.

The unique security issues of the access control in cloud storage systems are very important, where it is the data owner not the cloud server that is in charge of defining and enforcing the access policy. The security issues include the following.

Figure 4. The traditional access control model

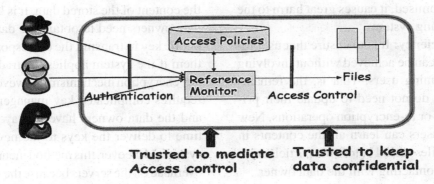

Figure 5. The access control of untrusted cloud server

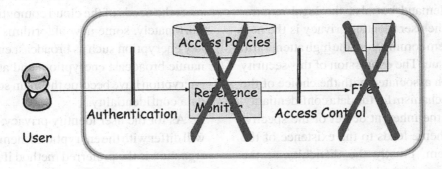

- **The Data Confidentiality:** It requires that unauthorized users including the cloud managers are incapable of knowing the contents of the stored data. An important and challenging issue for the data confidentiality is to maintain its availability for dynamic groups. Specifically, Liu, Zhang, Wang, Yan (2013) new users should be able to decrypt the data stored in the cloud before their participation, while revoked users are supposed to be unable to decrypt the data moved into the cloud after the revocation. The dynamic property of the user group has brought a great resistance to the implantation of the data confidentiality.

- **The User Identity Privacy:** It guarantees that the user can access data without revealing its real identity. More strictly,

the data owners cannot know the specific identity of the data consumers because the data owners are not allowed to know the identities of the users who access their data in some application scenarios. In fact, the particularity of the cloud storage makes that the data owners lose the interaction with the data consumers in the process of data access. In the access control system, the user identity privacy is mainly to protect the identity privacy of the data owners and the data consumers free from the cloud server.

- **The Escrow Problem:** It indicates that the central authority in the access control system can achieve the shared data of all the users because the central authority is responsible for assigning the attribute private keys to all the clients. If the authority is compromised, it causes great harm to the data sharing systems.

- **The Efficiency:** It is to ensure that user revocation can be achieved without involving the remaining users. That is, the remaining users do not need to update their private keys or re-encryption operations. New granted users can learn all the contents in the data files stored before his participation without contacting with the data owner.

The data confidentiality has the highest priority among all the security issues, which is not only the security demand but also the legal requirement. While the user identity privacy is the new security problem coming from the high attention to the privacy issue. The expression of this security issue has much associated with the choice of the encryption mechanism for the data confidentiality. Furthermore, the inherent defect of the specific encryption scheme leads to the existence of the escrow problem. Finally the difficulty of the decryption process largely affects the efficiency of the access control mechanism. In a word, the choice of an encryption scheme completely for data confidentiality determines the strength and the weakness of the access control mechanism.

THE OVERVIEW OF SECURITY SOLUTIONS

In view of the above security issues, we provide an overview of the solutions to security issues of the access control in cloud computing. To address the data confidentiality, the traditional methods usually encrypt the shared data before they are stored. The shared data should only be accessible to the users who are given the corresponding decryption key, while remain confidential to the rest of users. Or only the authorized users who hold the encrypt key can achieve the shared data. The unauthorized users including the cloud manager

who don't have the key are incapable of learning the content of the stored data. It is known that the data owners need to obtain the data consumers' public key to transmit the corresponding files for them if the system applies the traditional public key encryption mechanism. However, this method requires complicated key management schemes and the data owners have to stay online all the time to deliver the keys to the new users in the system. Moreover, this method incurs high storage overhead on the servers because the servers should store multiple encrypted copies of the same data for the users with different keys. The conventional one-to-one public key encryption system cannot meet the needs of the cloud computing scenarios. Fortunately, some new algorithms of the public key encryption such as broadcast encryption, dynamic broadcast encryption, and attribute based encryption have become the main solutions to the data confidentiality.

As for the user identity privacy, the solutions will differ with the encryption schemes. The group signature is the preferred method if the broadcast encryption is applied for the data confidentiality. While the user specific identity hiding is the inherent characteristic of the attribute based encryption, there is no need to use other mechanisms to achieve the user identity privacy.

The multi-authority attribute based encryption has been proposed to deal with the escrow problem. Since it will cause some security issues by the single attribute authority, which also becomes the bottleneck for the access control system, the design of the multi-authority attribute based encryption is the natural alternative. By most of the multi-authority schemes, each attribute authority is an independent attribute authority that is responsible for issuing, revoking and updating user's attributes according to their roles or identity in its domain. Every attribute is associated with a single attribute authority, but each attribute authority can manage an arbitrary number of attributes. The user attribute keys are issued in the operation of all the attribute authorities. Since the single attribute authority cannot obtain full user keys, and obviously it never gets the shared data of the users, various types of multi-authority scheme have been designed.

The efficiency of revocation scheme will cause a direct impact on the efficiency of the access control mechanism. The proxy re-encryption and lazy re-encryption are the commonly used approaches to improve the efficiency of revocations. Furthermore, the outsourcing calculation is also a worthwhile alternative.

In this section, we have briefly introduced the reasons to equip the secure and effective access control mechanisms in the cloud storage and data sharing systems. Beyond that, we have explored the formal definition on the security issues existing in the cloud storage systems. In the end, we have a brief statement on the basic cryptography theory for solving these security issues.

THE SOLUTIONS OF ACCESS CONTROL

With the security concern on the stored data, the data owners hesitate to join the clients' camp of the cloud storage. Designing the secure and effective access control mechanisms also has become a challenge for the service providers.

Figure 6. The coarse-grained access control model

In this section, we will review some special existing access control mechanisms in detail. There are essentially two categories of the access control mechanisms which are coarse-grained access control schemes and fine-grained access control schemes respectively. In simple term, the access policy of the coarse-grained access control mechanism is defined for the whole system. While in the fine-grained access control mechanism, the access policy is costumed to each file by every client. Finally we will have a complete summary of all the characteristics of the current access control schemes. All we have done is of great use to help us design the more secure and effective access control mechanism.

Coarse-Grained Access Control

The coarse-grained access control mechanisms are designed for the overall system, which implies that all the shared files of all the clients in this cloud storage system will employ the same access control policy. According to this understanding, the system is naturally dealt with as a group, where the group manager defines the access policy. First figure 6 shows it very vividly that many data files share the same policy defined by the service manager in the coarse-grained access control mechanism.

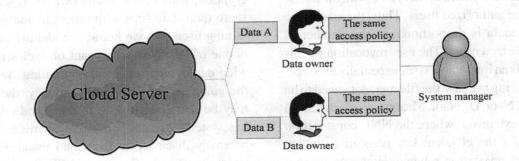

Kallahalla, Riedel, Swaminathan, Wang, and Fu (2013) first proposed one cryptographic storage system named Plutus, which enables secure file sharing on the untrusted servers. The Plutus features highly scalable key management while allowing individual users to retain direct control to decide the data users, who can access to their files. By dividing files into file groups and encrypting each file group with a unique file-block key, the data owner can share the file groups with others through delivering the corresponding lockbox key, where the lockbox key is used to encrypt the file-block keys. In addition to, the whole proposed scheme can reduce the number of cryptographic keys exchanged between users by using file groups, distinguish file reading and writing accesses, handle user revocation efficiently, and allow an untrusted server to authorize file writing. However, it can bring about a heavy key distribution overhead for large-scale file sharing. Additionally, the file-block key needs to be updated and distributed again after the user revocation.

According to the description above, the problem of updating the key in the process of revocation because of the group operation was still a huge burden. In order to improve the efficiency of the revocation, some research efforts have been made to promote the corresponding solutions generated. Goh, Shacham, Modadugu, and Boneh, D. (2003) made that files stored on the untrusted servers are divided into two parts of the file metadata and file data. The file metadata are the access control information including a series of encrypted key blocks, each of which is encrypted with the public key of the authorized users. Thus, the size of the file metadata is proportional to the number of the authorized users. The user revocation by this scheme is an intractable issue especially for large-scale sharing because the file metadata need to be updated. Naor, D., Naor, M. and Lotspiech (2001) gave an extension, where the NNL construction is used for the efficient key revocation, which is a novel revocation scheme. However, when a new user joins the group, the private key of each

user in the NNL system needs to be recomputed, which may limit the application for the dynamic groups. Another concern is that the computation overhead of the encryption linearly increases with the sharing scale.

More fortunately, the proxy re-encryption brings much benefit in terms of improving the revocation efficiency. Proxy re-encryption allows a proxy to transform a ciphertext computed under Alice's public key into one that can be opened by Alice's secret key. Especially, Ateniese, Fu, Green, and Hohenberger (2006) employing one proxy re-encryption scheme can secure the distributed storage. The data owner encrypts the blocks of contents by the unique and symmetric content keys, which are further encrypted by a master public key. For the access control, the server uses proxy cryptography to directly re-encrypt the appropriate contents keys from the master public key to a granted user's public key. Unfortunately, a collusion attack between the untrusted server and any revoked malicious user can be launched, which enables them to learn the decryption keys of all the encrypted blocks.

However, the issue of the user identity privacy is never involved in all these schemes above. Liu et al. (2013) proposed one access control scheme with an aim to achieve the user identity privacy by group signature, which has the extreme efficiency compared to all the coarse-grained access control schemes. Delerablée, Paillier, and Pointcheval (2007) proposed one fundamental encryption mechanism meaning the dynamic broadcast encryption, which allows data owners to securely share their data files with others including new joining users. As we know, the identity privacy is one of the most significant obstacles for the wide deployment of cloud computing. Without the guarantee of the identity privacy, the users may be unwilling to join in the cloud computing systems because their real identities could be easily disclosed to the cloud managers and attackers. Boneh, Boyen, and Shacham (2004) proposed the group signature scheme, which enables users to anonymously use the cloud resources. Moreover, to tackle this challenging issues of both the computation overhead of the encryption and the size of the ciphertext increases with the number of revoked users, the scheme allows the group manager compute the revocation parameters and make the result public available by migrating them into the cloud. This design can significantly reduce the computation overhead to encrypt the files by the users and the ciphertext size. The computation overhead for encryption operations and the ciphertext sizes are constant and independent of the number of the revocation users. Efficient user revocation can be achieved by using a public revocation list without updating the private keys of the remaining users, and new users can directly decrypt files stored in the cloud before their participation with constant storage overhead and the encryption computation cost.

However, Liu et al. brought the key escrow problem, where the group manager has the supreme power to decrypt all the shared data. If the group manager is compromised, it will cause great damages to the cloud storage system. To solve the escrow problem, Xu, Wu, and Zhang (2012) proposed a certificateless proxy re-encryption scheme for data sharing in the cloud. It first suggests that it has been widely recognized that data confidentiality should be mainly relied on cloud customers instead of cloud service providers. Of course, the typical approach for data confidentiality protection is to encrypt a data with a (usually symmetric) key before storing it to the cloud. Key management is the enormous burdensome task for encryption based access control. Broadcast encryption and group key management can be used for sharing data in group manner. However, managing group is complicated in particular for today's pervasive data sharing such as cloud-based collaborations and social networks, where the number of groups of interests for an individual user is large. In addition, the size of a group can also be large, and the membership usually changes frequently, which makes group key management very tedious for a common user. Since cloud is a resource pool for computation, storage, and networking, and provides elastic and pay-as-you-go resource consumption model, the most motivation is to leverage cloud for encryption-based access control and key management. Towards the end-to-end data confidentiality, it considers the cloud is semi-trusted, that is, clear data and encryption keys should never be exposed in cloud. Such a cloud based approach should be able to deliver data encryption keys with respect to pre-defined access control policies from the data owner, and introduce minor overhead on cloud users by eliminating any direct interaction between a data owner and its recipients. To achieve these goals, it develops CL-PRE (Al-Riyami & Paterson, 2003), a new proxy-based re-encryption scheme augmented with certificateless public key cryptography, which leverages cloud not only for data storage but also for secure key distribution for data sharing. With CL-PRE, the data is first encrypted with a symmetric data encryption key (DEK) before stored in cloud by its owner. The data owner then generates proxy re-encryption keys with all of its potential recipients and sends to the cloud resident proxy service, along with the encrypted DEK with its public key. Using the re-encryption keys, the cloud is then able to transform the encrypted DEK to one that can be decrypted using an individual recipient' private key. In this way, the cloud works only as a proxy for key management. CL-PRE ensures that the cloud cannot get the clear DEK during the transformation. The proposed certificateless proxy re-encryption scheme called CL-PRE for flexible data sharing with public cloud, which preserves final access control for data owner without completely trusting cloud infrastructure. CL-PRE uniquely leverages identity as partial of a user's public key and eliminates key escrow problem. It proves that CL-PRE is CPA-secure in random oracle model. But It is a pity this scheme is not perfect. The data owner can know the specific identify of the users who can achieve the shared data. Because the access control list (ACL) is generated by the data owner. It is a great challenge for the user identity privacy.

Figure 7. The fine-grained access control model

In addition to the issue of data confidentiality, which can be solved by the specific public key encryption, there are many other solutions targeted to those security issues including the user identity privacy, the escrow problem, and the efficiency, etc. All the schemes above have typical significance to optimize the cloud based data service.

Fine-Grained Access Control

It is clear that the group manager decides all the access control policy in the coarse-grained access control. Obviously, this kind of practice cannot meet the requirements of some specific users. Sometimes they expect that those clients who own some characteristic rather than the specific clients can access to their shared data. The fine-grained access control realized this requirement at some extent, where it is the data owners who store their data in the cloud will decide which data users have the access privilege to which types of data. In the below, we first give a specific picture about the fine-grained access control model. Figure 7 presents its characteristic more visually.

Then we will realize that the fine-grained access control mechanism is not only a requirement but also is a necessity. Especially, in some application scenarios, the data owners don't have the ability to know who will access their stored data. In view of those coarse-grained access control protocols, we first make a list about the difference between the coarse-grained access control and the fine-grained access control in Table 2. It's the most intuitive effect is that we can even achieve fine-grained access control through simply improving the coarse-grained access control with the comparison analysis. Of course it provides several good criteria for us to analysis those fine-grained access control schemes.

Table 2. The comparison of the coarse-grained access control and the fine-grained access control

Model	The Number of the Access Policy	The Operator of the Access Policy	The Issuer of the Decryption Key
Coarse-grained access control	Change frequently with the whole system	The system manager	The system manager
Fine-grained access control	The custom access policy for each file of all the users	The data owner	The trusted authority

Finally in this section, we first introduce the basis of the attribute based encryption, which is a typical fine-grained access control scheme. Then a detailed analysis on the existing fine-grained access control scheme will be presented in different categories of the security issues.

Data Confidentiality

The first attribute based encryption (Sahai & Waters, 2005) is the proposed scheme, which has been called as Fuzzy Identity-Based Encryption (Fuzzy IBE), by which an identity is regarded as a set of descriptive attributes. The Fuzzy IBE scheme allows a private key for an identity E to decrypt a ciphertext encrypted with an identity $É'$, if and only if the identities E and $É'$ are close to each other as measured by the "set overlap" distance metric. Obviously this new type of encryption mechanism is more suitable for fine-grained access control than the general public key mechanism. The primary drawback of the Fuzzy IBE system is that the threshold semantics are not very expressive and therefore are limited to design more general systems. Subsequently, Goyal, Pandey, Sahai, and Waters (2006) clarified the concept of Attribute-Based Encryption (ABE), where a mature ABE cryptosystem has been developed with its applications demonstrated. By this ABE, each ciphertext is labeled by an encryptor with a set of descriptive attributes. Each private key is associated with an access structure that specifies which type of ciphertexts the key can decrypt. This is the one kind of scheme called Key-Policy Attribute-Based Encryption (KP-ABE) because the access structure is specified in the private key, while the ciphertexts are simply labeled with a set of descriptive attributes. Instead of embedding a secret sharing scheme (Shamir, 1979) in the private key, the authority embeds a more general secret sharing scheme for monotonic access trees. It has also suggested the possibility of a ciphertext-policy ABE scheme without any constructions. Bethencourt, Sahai, and Waters (2007) conducted the other kind of scheme called Ciphertext-Policy Attribute-Based Encryption (CP-ABE). An efficient system has been described that is expressive in that it allows an encryptor to express an access predicate f in terms of any monotonic formula over attributes. The system can achieve analogous expressiveness and efficiency with the CP-ABE setting because it allows a new type of encrypted access control where user's private keys are specified by a set of attributes and a party encrypting data can specify a policy over these attributes specifying which users are able to decrypt. This system allows policies to be expressed as any monotonic tree access structure and is resistant to the collusion attacks in which an attacker might obtain multiple private keys. It stresses that by the KP-ABE, the data owner exerts no control over who has the access right to the data encrypted, except by the choice of descriptive attributes for the data. Rather, it is trusted that the key-issuer issues the appropriate keys to grant or deny access to the appropriate users. In other words, the "intelligence" is assumed to be with the key issuer rather than the encryptor.

In a word, the ABE as a solution of data confidentiality provides an extremely appropriate technology for fine-grained access control in cloud computing. It means that the attribute based encryption is the fundamental mechanism for solving the data confidentiality in the fine-grained access control scheme. In addition to the data confidentiality, there are other security issues that need to be dealt with. But it has paved the way for the development of the security solutions to handle another security issues besides the data confidentiality. The fine-grained access control schemes can be described from the following several aspects, which are the user identity, the escrow problem, the user key accountability, and the efficiency.

User Identity Privacy

In the cloud storage system, the user identity privacy includes two scenarios. The first is that the data owners prevent other consumers including the cloud servers gaining their specific identity information when they share the data on the cloud. The second is that the data consumers prevent other consumers even the data owners being aware of that they have gained the access to some shared data. According to these two kinds of situations, many solutions have been proposed.

In the first type of circumstance, the user identity privacy has been ignored in the existing ABE based fine-grained access control mechanism. It is known that the user private keys are associated with the access structure in the KP-ABE, while the ciphertext is also associated with the access structure in the CP-ABE. Then according to the selection criteria of the access structure, it will partially expose the user attributes and even the user specific identity as the fatal flaw for some users. So for this security issue, some solutions have been proposed to improve the expressiveness of the access structure. The new technique has been presented (Waters, 2011) to realize the CP-ABE systems from a general set of access structures in the standard model with some concrete and non-interactive assumptions. This technique allows any attribute access structure that can be expressed by a Linear Secret Sharing Scheme (LSSS) matrix M. Previously used structures such as the formulas equivalent tree structures can be expressed in terms of a LSSS. This construction permits slightly more expressive access structures than other constructions. The expression of the access structure has concealed the user specific identity in some extent. But it is apparent that it will bring more computational burden for the attribute decryption. Then there are other similar solutions, by which, the expression of user attribute follows a rule that the user attributes are expressed with only one word, which causes a lot of hidden dangers for user attributes exposed. Generally speaking,

the first kind of identity privacy can be ensured mainly by changing the presentation of the user attribute and the access structure.

In the second of circumstance, the work mainly focuses on the user identity of the data consumers. Ruj, Stojmenovic, and Nayak (2014) first stated that some commonly ignored points have been highlighted to protect the identity privacy of the consumers. First of all, the user should authenticate itself before initiating any transaction. On the other hand, it must be ensured that the cloud does not tamper with the outsourced data. User privacy is also required so that the cloud or other users cannot know the identity of the user. The cloud can hold the user accountability for the outsourced data, and likewise, the cloud is itself accountable for the services it provides. The issues of access control, authentication, and privacy protection should be solved simultaneously. The authentication ensures that the users who store and modify their data on the cloud and the identity of the users will be protected from the cloud during authentication. Additionally the architecture is decentralized with several key distributed centers for key management. The access control and authentication are both collusion resistant to ensure that no more than two users can collude and access data or authenticate themselves, if they have not been individually authorized. And revoked users cannot access data after they have been revoked. The proposed scheme is resilient to replay attacks. Another anonymous attribute-based privilege control scheme, Jung, Li, Wan, Z. and Wan, M. (2013) proposed AnonyControl to address the user privacy issue in the cloud storage server in [19]. By multiple authorities in the cloud computing system, this proposal can achieve not only fine-grained privilege control, but also anonymity with the privilege control based on users' identity information. More importantly, the scheme can tolerate up to $N-2$ authority compromises, which is highly preferable especially in the Internet-based cloud computing environment. Furthermore, although the data contents are fully outsourced to cloud servers, the cloud servers cannot read the contents unless their private keys satisfy the privilege tree.

In the end, the access control mechanism on the basis of attribute based encryption can achieve the identity privacy of the data consumer from the data owner because the inherent characteristics of attribute based encryption. So the identity privacy in the cloud storage mainly refers to that the data owners and the data consumers can achieve their identity privacy from the cloud servers. By the above schemes, some solutions can achieve the result by hiding the user attribute or the user access structure, while other solutions can achieve the result by using the attribute based signature, etc. Protecting the identity privacy is also one of the basic security requirements in designing the fine-grained access control scheme.

Escrow Problem

The escrow problem is an inherent defect of the fine-grained access control mechanism on the basis of the attribute based encryption. Since there is an attribute authority responsible for managing the user attributes and assigning the user private keys, the attribute authority can get all the private keys of all the users. If the attribute authority is compromised, it will cause great harm to the fine-grained access control schemes. Additionally, this is also a bottleneck for the single attribute authority because the single authority undertakes so much certification operation at the process of initialization. The simplest solution is to increase the number of the attribute authority. Then, many schemes on multi-authority have been proposed, which can be classified into two categories of multi-authority attribute based encryption with/ without a central authority.

Chase, M. (2007) proposed first multi-authority attribute based encryption, which allows the sender to specify, for each authority K, a number d_k and a set of attributes monitored by the authority so that the message can be decrypted only by

a user who has at least d_k of the given attributes from every authority. It allows any number of attribute authorities to be corrupted, and guarantee the security of the encryption as long as the required attributes cannot be obtained exclusively from those authorities and the trusted authority remains honest. It first has been clear that two major issues are involved in this scheme. One is to require that each user has a global identifier (GID) with two properties

1. No user can claim another user's identifier, and
2. All authorities can verify a user's identifier.

Another issue is the involvement of a central authority. Each user will send his GID to the central authority and receive a corresponding key without any users' attributes known by the authority, which will provide a setup key for the user's GID. Under the assumption that the authority is trusted to hold the master secret for the system, it will be able to decrypt any message.

Unfortunately the solution with one central authority can only transfer the escrow problem without the ability to solve the problem completely. Yang, Jia, and Ren (2013) proposed the latest multi-authority attribute based encryption without a central authority. It designs a cloud storage system with multiple authorities with a global certificate authority (CA) and the attribute authorities (AAs). The CA is a global trusted certificate authority in the system, which sets up the system and accepts the registration of all the users and AAs in the system. The CA is responsible for the distribution of global secret key and global public key for each legal user in the system. However, it will not be involved in any attribute management and the creation of secret keys that are associated with attributes. Each AA is an independent attribute authority that is responsible for issuing, revoking and updating user's attributes according to their roles or identity in its domain. By this scheme, every attribute is associated with a single AA, but each AA can manage an arbitrary number of attributes. Every AA has a full control over the structure and semantics of its attributes. Each user is assigned with a global user identity from the CA. Each user can freely get the ciphertexts from the server. To decrypt a ciphertext, each user may submit its secret key issued by the AAs together with its global public key to the server, which is asked to generate a decryption token for some ciphertext. Upon receiving the decryption token, the user can decrypt the ciphertext by using its global secret key. Only when the user's attributes satisfy the access policy defined in the ciphertext, the server can generate the correct decryption token. The secret keys and the global user's public key can be stored on the server. Subsequently, the user does not need to submit any secret key if no secret keys are updated for the further decryption token generation.

Finally, the multi-authority solutions above have one thing in common, however, where all the attributes are classified in the conjunctive setting. In conjunctive setting, the attribute space for each authority is disjoint to make that every attribute authority manages different attribute sets. A new cryptosystem called broadcast ABE has been proposed, which can also be utilized to construct multi-authority ABE in the disjunctive setting (Attrapadung & Imai 2009). By the conjunctive setting, a private key will be created by gathering elements from all authorities, while by the disjunctive setting, a private key can be derived solely by each authority. This broadcast ABE can be used to construct ABE systems with a direct revocation mechanism. Direct revocation has a useful property that revocation can be done without affecting any non-revoked users.

The multi-authority attribute based encryption mechanisms cannot only enhance the security of the ABE schemes but also can solve the bottleneck derived from the single authority. Especially, the MA-ABE without a central authority can fundamentally solve the escrow problem. It will be the preferred encryption schemes deployed for the access control in the cloud storage.

User Key Accountability

Another important issue in the access control solutions with the ABE is the user key accountability. According to the characteristics of the ABE, the private key of the user is only relevant to the user attributes, which does not need his concrete identity. It will cause a case that one malicious user can share his private key illegally with other unauthorized users to gain important information. Since the private key is only relevant to his attribute, there could be many users who have the same attribute set. The trusted authority cannot know which user discloses his private keys. If the divulgence of his private key cannot be traced and he can obtain illegal interests, it will produce a great harm to the access control mechanism. Therefore designing a secure access control scheme which meets the requirements of user accountability is also an urgent task.

Li, Ren, Zhu, and Wan (2009) and Li, Ren, and Kim (2009) presented the solutions on the user accountability with a single-authority respectively. Both the proposals not only achieve the user accountability but also the implementation of the partial hiding of the access policy. However, the statements on the access policy are not expressive, which cannot meet the requirements perfectly. Liu, Z., Cao, Z.F. and Wong, D.S. (2013) proposed two tracing schemes to achieve the white-box traceability and the black-box traceability respectively. Liu, Cao, and Wong (2013, January) proposed the first new CP-ABE scheme to support the traceability of the malicious users who have leaked their decryption privileges. This traceable CP-ABE scheme cannot weaken the expressiveness or efficiency compared with the most efficient conventional non-traceable CP-ABE schemes currently available for high expressiveness, which can support any monotone access structures. This is the first CP-ABE scheme that supports both the traceability of the malicious users and high expressiveness i.e., supporting any monotone access structures, simultaneously. Liu, Cao, and Wong (2013) made the notion of the CP-ABE be extended to support the black-box traceability with a concrete scheme to identify a user whose key has been used in building a decryption device from multiple users whose keys associated with the attribute sets which are all the supersets of S_D. The scheme is efficient with a sublinear overhead compared with the recent non-traceable CP-ABE scheme. The scheme is also an extension with the property of fully collusion-resistant black-box traceability and secure against the adaptive adversaries in the standard model. It is highly expressive by supporting any monotonic access structures. However, they cannot hold multi-authority features. Li, Huang, Chen, Chow, Wong, and Xie (2011) designed one new scheme for the user accountability with multi-authority CP-ABE, which can reduce both the trust assumption on the authorities and that on the users. The supported policy is conjunction with wildcard. This scheme is anonymous in the sense that no one can tell from the ciphertext that it has been generated under which policy.

Efficiency

In the cloud storage system, there is a very special requirement that the user group is dynamic. Particularly, the joining of new users and the revoking of users appear frequently in the cloud storage system. It is a great challenge for the efficiency of the fine-grained access control mechanism with the ABE scheme. Especially, for the user revocation, each attribute of the revoked user is shared by many different users. When the particular user is revoked, other users sharing with the same attribute will be affected. They have to update their private keys. It will be a huge amount of calculation for the users with the limited computing power. The design of effective revocation scheme accompanying the access control has become a research focus, which has to meet the following security requirements. The two security requirements existing in the revocation process are forward security and backward security. Forward security indicates that

the revoked user with its attribute revoked cannot decrypt the new ciphertext that is encrypted with new public key. While backward security indicates that the newly joined user can also decrypt the previous published ciphertexts encrypted with previous public key if it has sufficient attributes. As we know, the decryption process brings a large number of computation burdens in the fine-grained access control mechanism applying the attribute based encryption. The solution of this decryption problem is also a key factor which affects the efficiency of access control mechanism.

To achieve the secure and efficient revocation, first two new variants of ABE have been proposed. Wang, Liu, and Wu (2010) gave the first one called the hierarchical attribute-based encryption (HABE), which combines a HIBE scheme with the CP-ABE scheme to provide fine-grained access control and full delegation. Based on the HABE model, a performance-expressivity tradeoff can be made to achieve high performance. It is a scalable revocation scheme to delegate the cloud service provider with most of the computing tasks in the revocation to achieve a dynamic set of users efficiently. Zhu, Hu, Ahn, Gong, and Chen (2011) gave the second one named the temporal attribute-based encryption (TABE), which addresses the temporal access control in the clouds along with an efficient cryptographic framework to support the temporal constraints. The proposed TABE scheme converts various temporal constraints to regulate data sharing in the clouds. This scheme holds a constant size for the ciphertext and the private keys with a nearly linear-time complexity.

Another very important technology for the user revocation is the proxy re-encryption. Some practical application scenarios, where semi-trustable proxy servers are available, have been addressed with a proposal to support the attribute revocation. Yu, Wang, Ren, and Lou,(2010) proposed one scheme allocates the minimal working load for the authority in the attribute revocation events by uniquely combining the proxy re-encryption technique with the CP-ABE to enable the authority to delegate most laborious tasks to the proxy servers. The proposed scheme is provably secure against some malicious attacks. The solution could be further utilized to combine a secure computation technique to guarantee the honesty of the proxy servers and to allow those proxy servers to update the user secret key without disclosing the attribute information of the users. Similarly, Yang, et al. (2013) proposed the attribute revocation in multi-authority cloud storage systems where the users' attributes come from different domains managed by different authorities. A relatively more effective immediate attribute revocation scheme has been proposed, which uses the data access control for multi-authority cloud storage (DAC-MACS). It is an effective and secure data access control scheme for multi-authority cloud storage systems to be proved to be secure in the random oracle model and has a better performance than the existing schemes. A new multi-authority CP-ABE scheme has been constructed with an efficient decryption, by which, the main computation of the decryption has been outsourced by using a token-based decryption method. Both forward security and backward security can be obtained with less communication cost and computation cost of the revocation.

In this section, we have made a detailed description on all of the access control schemes employed in the cloud computing. They can be divided into two categories which are the coarse-grained access control and fine-grained access control. By the coarse-grained access control mechanism, the access policy is designed for the whole system. It is clear that this scheme cannot fully meet the application requirements of the users, while the design of the fine-grained access control mechanism is the research trend in the cloud storage. We introduce the fine-grained access control schemes in detail on four aspects, which are the user identity privacy, the escrow problem, the user key accountability, and the efficiency. However, the existing solutions have some disadvantages which cannot achieve all the four security aspects. Design of the fine-grained access control is still a challenge with solving the security issues simultaneously.

FUTURE DIRECTION

It is clear that the design of better fine-grained access control schemes has become an important trend with the gradual improvement of the user's needs. The new encryption methods such as functional encryption and predicate encryption can be used as the effective ways by which we can deal with this dilemma. In the future research work, establishing more fine-grained access control protocols by optimizing the basic encryption schemes will be a good choice.

The present agreement is still mainly designed for the confidentiality of the shared data. However, the privacy problem is often overlooked. As the clients make more and more concern about privacy, designing the fine-grained access control achieving the data confidentiality with more privacy simultaneously is not only a choice but also a necessity. This issue perhaps may be tackled by employing some special signature schemes such as the attribute based signature and so on.

In the end, all of the abovementioned access control schemes for the cloud storage systems assume that the cloud servers are honest and curious. It implies that the cloud server will perform all the related operations correctly, but it will try to get some confidential information. This assumption will cause the users to have some concern on the data confidentiality if the servers are not exactly honest. So in the future research of the access control based the cloud storage systems, high demands on the design of more secured fine-grained access control schemes when the cloud servers are completely untrusted should be met.

CONCLUSION

In this chapter, we have first provided a simple introduction of cloud computing with the explanation on its five essential characteristics, three service models, and four deployment models in detail and particularly explain the relationship among them. Furthermore, we have described the unique security issues of access control for the cloud storage systems in cloud computing. We have also summarized a collection of the existing solutions on the access control in the cloud computing.

In the second part of this chapter, we have reviewed the state-of-the-art solutions on the access control schemes in much more detail. We have classified all the solutions into two types, which are coarse-grained access control and fine-grained access control. The coarse-grained access control scheme is designed for the entire system. It indicates that all the shared files of all the clients in this cloud storage employ the same access control policy. The typical solution of the coarse-grained access control scheme is to make file groups or user groups, which implies that it achieves the access control by the operation of groups. It is obvious that the group manager will decide all the access control policy in the coarse-grained access control. The coarse-grained access control scheme cannot meet the requirements of specific users. Especially, in some application scenarios, the data owners cannot know who will access their shared data. So the design of a fine-grained access control mechanism is a necessity to satisfy each individual client. We have made a detailed analysis on the current existing fine-grained access control solutions by the classification of the solutions according to various security issues. First of all, the issue of the data confidentiality has been well discussed to discover that the attribute based encryption technology is the major technique for the fine-grained access control schemes to achieve the data confidentiality. The solutions on the other security issues including the user identity privacy, the escrow problem, the user key accountability and the efficiency have been fully investigated to provide a general picture of the fine-grained access control schemes. We expect that the efforts made in this chapter could provide a good reference for the successful design of the access control mechanisms and the deployment of cloud computing.

REFERENCES

Al-Riyami, S. S., & Paterson, K. G. (2003). Certificateless public key cryptography. *Advances in Cryptology - ASIACRYPT, 2894*, 452-473.

Armbrust, M., Fox, A., Griffith, R., Joseph, A. D., Katz, R. H., Konwinski, A., & Patterson, D. A. et al. (2010, April). A view of cloud computing. *Communications of the ACM, 53*(4), 50–58. doi:10.1145/1721654.1721672

Ateniese, G., Fu, K., Green, M., & Hohenberger, S. (2006). Improved proxy re-encryption schemes with applications to secure distributed storage. *ACM Transactions on Information and System Security, 9*(1), 1–30. doi:10.1145/1127345.1127346

Attrapadung, N., & Imai, H. (2009). Conjunctive broadcast and attribute-based encryption. *Proceeding of Pairing-Based Cryptography-Pairing, 5671*, 248–265. doi:10.1007/978-3-642-03298-1_16

Bethencourt, J., Sahai, A., & Waters, B. (2007, May). Ciphertext-policy attribute-based encryption. In *Proceedings of IEEE Symposium on Security and Privacy* (pp. 321-334). IEEE. doi:10.1109/SP.2007.11

Boneh, D., Boyen, X., & Shacham, H. (2004). Short group signature. *Proceedings of International Cryptology Conference Advances in Cryptology (CRYPTO), 3152*, 41-55.

Chase, M. (2007). Multi-authority attribute based encryption. *TCC, 4392,* 515–534. doi:10.1007/978-3-540-70936-7_28

Delerablée, C., Paillier, P., & Pointcheval, D. (2007). Fully collusion secure dynamic broadcast encryption with constant-size ciphertexts or decryption keys. *Proceedings of First International Conference in Pairing-Based Cryptography, 4575,* 39-59.

Goh, E., Shacham, H., Modadugu, N., & Boneh, D. (2003). SiRiUS: Securing remote untrusted storage. In *Proceedings of Network and Distributed Systems Security (NDSS) Symposium.* Academic Press.

Goyal, V., Pandey, O., Sahai, A., & Waters, B. (2006). Attribute-based encryption for fine-grained access control of encrypted data. In *Proceedings of ACM Conference on Computer and Communications Security* (pp. 89-98). ACM. doi:10.1145/1180405.1180418

Jung, T., Li, X., Wan, Z. & Wan, M. (2013, April). Privacy preserving cloud data access with multi-authority. In *Proceedings of IEEE INFOCOM* (pp. 2625 – 2633). IEEE. doi: 10.1109/INFCOM.2013.6567070

Kallahalla, M., Riedel, E., Swaminathan, R., Wang, Q., & Fu, K. (2013). Plutus: Scalable secure file sharing on untrusted storage. In *Proceedings of USENIX Conference File and Storage Technologies* (pp. 29-42). Academic Press.

Li, J., Huang, Q., Chen, X., Chow, S. S. M., Wong, D. S., & Xie, D. (2011). Multi-authority ciphertext-policy attribute-based encryption with accountability. In *Proceedings of ACM ASIACCS* (pp. 386–390). ACM. doi:10.1145/1966913.1966964

Li, J., Ren, K, & Kim, K. (2009). A2BE: Accountable attribute-based encryption for abuse free access control. *IACR Cryptology ePrint Archive, 118.*

Li, J., Ren, K., Zhu, B., & Wan, Z. G. (2009). Privacy-aware attribute-based encryption with user accountability. In Proceedings of Information Security (LNCS), (vol. 5735, pp. 347-362). Berlin: Springer. doi:10.1007/978-3-642-04474-8_28

Liu, X.F., Zhang, Y.Q., Wang, B.Y. & Yan, J.B. (2013, June). Mona: Secure multi-owner data sharing for dynamic groups in the cloud. *IEEE Transactions on Parallel and Distributed Systems, 24*(6), 1182-1191. doi: 10.1109/TPDS.2012.331

Liu, Z., Cao, Z. F., & Wong, D. S. (2013, January). White-box traceable ciphertext-policy attribute-based encryption supporting any monotone access structures. *IEEE Transactions on Information Forensics and Security, 8*(1), 76–88. doi:10.1109/TIFS.2012.2223683

Liu, Z., Cao, Z. F., & Wong, D. S. (2013). Black box traceable CP-ABE: How to catch people leaking their keys by selling decryption devices on Ebay. In *Proceedings of ACM Conference on Computer and Communications Security* (pp. 475-486). ACM. doi:10.1145/2508859.2516683

Mell, P., & Grance, T. (2011). *The NIST definition of cloud computing.* US National Inst. of Science and Technology. Retrieved from http://csrc.nist.gov/publications/nistpubs/800-145/SP800-145.pdf

Naor, D., Naor, M., & Lotspiech, J. B. (2001). Revocation and tracing schemes for stateless receivers. *Proceedings of Anniversary International Cryptology Conference Advances in Cryptology (CRYPTO), 2139,* 41-62. doi:10.1007/3-540-44647-8_3

Ren, K. (2013). *The course of data security in cloud computing.* University of Science and Technology of China.

Ruj, S., Stojmenovic, M., & Nayak, A. (2014, February). Decentralized access control with anonymous authentication for securing data in clouds. *IEEE Transactions on Parallel and Distributed Systems*, *25*(2), 384–394. doi:10.1109/TPDS.2013.38

Sahai, A., & Waters, B. (2005). Fuzzy identity based encryption. *Advances in Cryptology–Eurocrypt*, *3494*, 457–473.

Shamir, A. (1979). How to share a secret. *Communications of the ACM*, *22*(11), 612–613. doi:10.1145/359168.359176

Wang, G., Liu, Q., & Wu, J. (2010). Hierarchical attribute-based encryption for fine-grained access control in cloud storage services. In *Proceedings of ACM Conference on Computer and Communications Security* (pp. 735–737). ACM. doi:10.1145/1866307.1866414

Waters, B. (2011). Ciphertext-policy attribute-based encryption: An expressive, efficient, and provably secure realization. *Public Key Cryptography*, *6571*, 53–70. doi:10.1007/978-3-642-19379-8_4

Xu, L., Wu, X., & Zhang, X. (2012). CL-PRE: A certificateless proxy re-encryption scheme for secure data sharing with public cloud. In *Proceedings of the 7th ACM Symposium on Information Computer and Communications Security* (pp. 87-88). ACM. doi:10.1145/2414456.2414507

Yang, K., Jia, X. H., & Ren, K. (2013, April). DAC-MACS: Effective data access control for multi-authority cloud storage systems. In *Proceedings of IEEE INFOCOM*. IEEE. doi:10.1109/INFCOM.2013.6567100

Yu, S. C., Wang, C., Ren, K., & Lou, W. J. (2010). Attribute based data sharing with attribute revocation. In *Proceedings of ACM Symposium Information Computer and Communications Security (ASIACCS)* (pp. 261-270). ACM. doi:10.1145/1755688.1755720

Zhu, Y., Hu, H. X., Ahn, G. J., Gong, X. R., & Chen, S. M. (2011). POSTER: Temporal attribute-based encryption in clouds. In *Proceedings of the 18th ACM Conference on Computer and Communications Security* (pp. 881-310). ACM. doi:10.1145/2093476.2093517

KEY TERMS AND DEFINITIONS

Access Tree: Let Γ be a tree representing an access structure. Each nonleaf node of the tree represents a threshold gate. If num_x is the number of children of a node x and k_x is its threshold value, then $0 << k_x << num_x$. Each leaf node x of the tree is described by an attribute and a threshold value $k_x = 1$. λ_x denotes the attribute associated with the leaf node x in the tree. p(x) represents the parent of the node x in the tree. The children of every node are numbered from 1 to num. The function index p(x) returns such a number associated with the node x. The index values are uniquely assigned to nodes in the access structure for a given key in an arbitrary manner.

Authority: An entity with more privilege. It can be responsible for authenticating the identity or attributes of the clients.

Backward Security: The newly joined user can also decrypt the previous published ciphertexts that are encrypted with previous public key if it has sufficient attributes.

Certificateless Public Key Encryption: A special identity-based encryption without the key escrow problem. It applies the essence of identity-based encryption avoiding the burden of the certificate, and eliminates the key escrow problem through some changes.

Cloud Computing: A model can be rapidly provisioned and released with minimal management effort or service provider interaction for enabling ubiquitous, convenient, on-demand network access to a shared pool of configurable computing resources.

Cloud Storage: A model of data storage where the digital data is stored in logical pools, the physical storage spans multiple servers (and often locations), and the physical environment is typically owned and managed by a hosting company. These cloud storage providers are responsible for keeping the data available and accessible, and the physical environment protected and running. People and organizations buy or lease storage capacity from the providers to store end user, organization, or application data.

Dynamic Broadcast Encryption: A special kind of public key encryption system. It can specify that only a set of users can decrypt.

Forward Security: The revoked user (whose attribute is revoked) cannot decrypt the new ciphertext that is encrypted with new public key.

The Key Escrow Problem: An inherent defect of many public key encryption mechanisms. It is caused by the authority who can obtain the private key of all the users.

Chapter 12
Security of the Cloud

Khalid Al-Begain
University of South Wales, UK

Wael Alosaimi
University of South Wales, UK

Michal Zak
University of South Wales, UK

Charles Turyagyenda
University of South Wales, UK

ABSTRACT

The chapter presents current security concerns in the Cloud Computing Environment. The cloud concept and operation raise many concerns for cloud users since they have no control of the arrangements made to protect the services and resources offered. Additionally, it is obvious that many of the cloud service providers will be subject to significant security attacks. Some traditional security attacks such as the Denial of Service attacks (DoS) and distributed DDoS attacks are well known, and there are several proposed solutions to mitigate their impact. However, in the cloud environment, DDoS becomes more severe and can be coupled with Economical Denial of Sustainability (EDoS) attacks. The chapter presents a general overview of cloud security, the types of vulnerabilities, and potential attacks. The chapter further presents a more detailed analysis of DDoS attacks' launch mechanisms and well-known DDoS defence mechanisms. Finally, the chapter presents a DDoS-Mitigation system and potential future research directions.

1. INTRODUCTION

Security is one of the most presented obstacles against broader expedition of Cloud computing. Majority of the customers are struggling to make the decision to move into the cloud computing arena because of security concerns and data protection aspects. A survey conducted by Intel (2012) proved that almost 9 out of ten respondents expressed their concerns regarding the security within the cloud environment.

In the traditional approach, sensitive business data was stored in-house. However, the migration to the cloud implies that vital information is stored offsite at multiple locations and often in a way that is hardly understood by most people.

There are several security aspects that may pose multiple threats to the cloud. The list of these threats includes the; possibility of a breach of privacy, likelihood of phishing, possibility of information loss and the loss of direct control of data. In addition, several important aspects need to be addressed prior to the migration to the

DOI: 10.4018/978-1-4666-8213-9.ch012

Copyright © 2015, IGI Global. Copying or distributing in print or electronic forms without written permission of IGI Global is prohibited.

cloud, i.e. data location, a disaster recovery plan, information segregation, regulatory compliance, long-term viability and investigation support. (Kuyoro & Ibikunle, 2011).

In general, all computer systems, the cloud included, have to provide integrity, confidentiality and availability. However, as soon as the system is connected to the network, and it is available for the users, it inevitably becomes available to the attackers. Attackers can affect the availability of cloud service resulting in a significant inconvenience to the intended users.

This chapter presents the current security threats on cloud computing. Section 2 presents, a general overview demonstrating the basic security risks within the Cloud Computing environment. This section also discusses the specific threats that may affect the availability of the Cloud particularly the Denial of Service (DoS) and the distributed version of the DoS, known as DDoS.

Section 3 presents an overview of current defence mechanisms designed to mitigate DDoS security threats. Additionally the section introduces the Enhanced DDoS-Mitigation System architectural framework.

Finally, the section 4 concludes the chapter with a discussion on future challenges and research direction presented from three perspectives. Namely; the general security challenges within the cloud, future concerns regarding DDoS attacks and future challenges regarding the Enhanced DDoS-Mitigation System are presented.

2. CLOUD SECURITY THREATS

Various aspects that may pose security threats to the cloud user or even the cloud provider will be discussed in this section. To facilitate presenting these threats, they are classified into four groups, namely: policy and organisational risks, technical risks, physical security issues, and legal risks (ENISA, 2009).

2.1 Policy and Organizational Risks

This category of threats involves the concerns that may affect the customers' data security as a result of changes to the providers' business situation and/or the lack of their commitment to the agreed contract and Service Level Agreement (SLA) with customers. SLA is a document that identifies the relationship between the provider and the customer. This is obviously a very vital piece of documentation for both parties. If employed accurately it must:

- Recognise and identify the customer's requirements.
- Facilitate complicated problems.
- Decrease areas of conflict.
- Support dialog in the event of a conflict.
- Reduce unrealistic expectations (The Service Level Agreement, 2007).

This category of threats is detailed in the subsequent sub-sections.

2.1.1 Loss of Control

In traditional computing paradigms, the enterprise preserves its data in its data centre. The enterprise manages this data using its preferred methods, and it has full control over the information. However, in the cloud environment, the third party cloud provider will manage the customer's data in terms of processing, inserting, deleting, backing up, and retrieving. Therefore, the customers may feel that their data is out of their control. The questions that may be asked at this stage are: how can the customer trust the provider's management of the data? And what evidence can the provider offer the customer about protecting their data against compromise, leakage, unauthorised access, damage, or being lost? (Roberts & Al-Hamdani, 2011). Relying on the most prominent providers in the market, such as Google, Amazon, and IBM, is essential to answer the above questions. These providers have a reputation that has been built over several years. Therefore, this reputation is of more value to them than any valuable customer data; thus, cloud providers are keen to protect the customers' data from the consequences of any breach or damage. Additionally cloud providers have teams of dedicated security professionals who can offer better security mechanisms than what most individual customers can do to protect their assets. However, it is difficult to negotiate these aspects with the large companies that provide cloud services as compared to small ones. Therefore, it is necessary to strike a balance between the ability of negotiation with the cloud provider and the provider's capability to control customers' data securely and effectively.

2.1.2 Compliance Risk

The trust between the cloud providers and their customers cannot be built upon verbal commitment. The infancy of cloud technology as a new paradigm for business management and its fast dissemination among the industrial field may have caused a lack of standardisation, which provides a reference for both the provider and the customer to identify the security issues and mitigate them. Therefore, the roles and responsibilities of every party regarding data security must be determined exactly. Moreover, there must be an essence of providing evidence from the provider to the customer that it has certificates, accreditations, and external evaluation in place to ensure data security is under their control (Sangroya et al., 2010).

Customers must understand their providers' regulations and start assigning the least important applications initially as a test to ensure the validity of the services provided. Moreover, customers should choose the most famous providers in the field to ensure their commitment to the regulatory compliance (Kuyoro & Ibikunle, 2011). Moreover, the customers need to ensure that the providers have security certificates and accreditations that indicate their capability to protect customers' data.

These certificates can be cloud security certificates such as Cloud Security Alliance - Security, Trust, and Assurance Registry (CSA STAR) or at least general security certificates such as International Organization for Standardization/International Electrotechnical Commission ISO/IEC 27001 certificate for Information Security Management Systems (ISMS). These are similar accreditations to those that the providers of banking services must comply with, such as the Payment Card Industry Data Security Standard (PCI DSS).

2.1.3 Portability Issue

The lack of experience in the field may be reflected in a weak contract, which does not avoid the portability (lock-in) problem. This is a problem of dependency on a specific cloud provider and forbidding the moving from this provider to another provider or even returning to an in-house IT system (ENISA, 2009). One way for the cloud customers to prevent themselves from being victims of this issue is by distributing their requested cloud services among more than one cloud provider. However, there are some technical challenges in this regard even if the provider does not mind about the customer's migration to another environment. These challenges involve the lack of migration standardisation, possibility of different structures between providers or with an in-house system, and the varied Application Programming Interfaces (API's) among several IT platforms.

2.1.4 End of Service

In the business world, there are many changes that can occur in an enterprise situation. For example, the enterprise may add new activities, replace some current activities with others, merge with another company, or it may even stop its services and close its shops and offices for any reason. In this case, if the enterprise is a cloud provider, then there is a justified question about the fate of its customers' data and applications that are under its control. This is a real concern for customers as they need to ensure their data's availability and security. Therefore, this needs to be tackled legally to eliminate the fear of such scenarios (Kuyoro & Ibikunle, 2011).

2.2 Technical Risks

This group of threats contains the technical issues that the cloud computing platform is exposed to. The cloud is a technical evolution that changes the enterprises management approaches to the cloud age. The technical threats to the cloud include:

2.2.1 Virtualisation Vulnerabilities

The virtualisation especially hypervisors perform many services for the cloud by abstracting the hardware components to be offered to users through virtual machines. Hypervisor is a software program that is considered as a necessary building block for applying a virtualised infrastructure in a data centre. On the one hand, virtualisation enables a single physical server to run as multiple virtual servers.On the other hand, it can expand the attack surface thus is an attractive target for attackers. Virtualisation is vulnerable to known network attacks such as Man In The Middle Man (MITM) and data leakage; additionally there are several new vulnerabilities that have resulted from adopting the hypervisor (Vaidya, 2009).

Due to the simplicity of deployment of new virtual machines on existing servers, many organisations have deployed virtual machines without having authorisation policies about change management or carrying out a formal review process for virtual machine security. As a result of this action, the virtual machines' deployment may run out of control. This threat is known as "VM Sprawl" (Sabahi, 2011; Vaidya, 2009).

Virtualisation sprawl can be defined as a phenomenon that happens when an administrator cannot control the Virtual Machines (VMs) on the network effectively because their number is higher than normal. This phenomenon is also called virtual machine sprawl or virtual server sprawl. The reason for existence of the VM Sprawl is the ease of establishing new virtual servers, so the enterprises create new VMs that are over their actual needs (Virtualizationadmin, 2008; Rouse, 2004).

Despite the ease of creation of VMs, there is nonetheless a need for similar; security, compliance, support, and licences that physical machines require. Thus, VM sprawl causes infrastructure overuse and increases the license costs without a real need for the high number of created VMs (Virtualizationadmin, 2008; Rouse, 2004).

In order to mitigate the VM Sprawl problem, the following tips are recommended.

- Apply a formal policy that enforces the requesters of new VMs to justify their requests and a formal approval for getting VMs. As a result, there will be control on the number of deployed VMs.
- To prevent VM sprawl, the administrator must analyse and identify the actual need for new VMs in terms of the infrastructure cost and VMs licenses by limiting the number of new VMs and monitoring the lifecycle of the VM, so that it can be removed if there is no longer a need for it.
- Implement a post-virtualisation performance monitoring of VMs by using tools such as Virtual Machine Lifecycle Management (VMLM) tools that assist the administrators to manage the delivery, implementation, maintenance, and operation of the VMs during their life. This kind of tools has a user interfaces (UI) that offers a dashboard screen for the administrators to assist them in identifying the number of virtual machines and the physical machines that are hosting them. It also determines the location of the VMs storage and the operating system (OS) and software licenses that related to each VM and the user that created it (Virtualizationadmin, 2008; Rouse, 2004).

According to Vaidya (2009), there is another threat known as Hyperjacking. It is an attack that controls the hypervisor, which establishes the virtual environment through a virtualisation server. As the hypervisor runs under the Host Operating System, it has full control over the virtualisation server and all the guest virtual machines inside the virtualised environment, as well as probably the Host Operating System too. The danger comes from normal security tools like Intrusion Detection Systems (IDS), Prevention Detection Systems (PDS), and the firewalls not being enough to counter this attack because these tools, either in the server or the virtual machine, are sometimes not aware of the compromise to the host machines. This is a serious risk to each virtualised environment. Additionally, the isolation between the virtual machines is very important for their security. Any failure in this isolation could affect the whole virtualisation performance and cause a denial of service vulnerabilities (Vaidya 2009).

The "VM Migration" concept makes security for the virtual machines more difficult. The concept is about transferring a virtual machine from a virtual server (VMHost) to another virtual host with no or minimal downtime in order to offer load balancing and better availability. The security measures and regulations, which exist in the new VMHost, must be updated with the moved virtual machine. If this process is not performed efficiently, then there might be a risk that threatens both the virtual machine and the new VMHost, which the VMs are running on (Vaidya 2009).

In addition, there is a similar issue to "VM Migration" known as "VM Poaching", which takes place when one Virtual Machine Guest Operating System consumes more than the resources allocated to it than the other Guest Operating Systems running in the shared virtualised system. An escapee Virtual Machine can have complete use of the hypervisor, thereby starving the rest of the Virtual Machines running in the hypervisor. This issue can take place with any resource of the hypervisor such as a hard drive, the Random Access Memory (RAM), network and the Central Processing Unit (CPU) (Vaidya, 2009).

Another issue that can result from adopting virtualisation technology is the hypervisor escape. It gives the attacker administrative-level privileges in the hypervisor itself. It enables the adversary to execute arbitrary code and access accounts in some kinds of hypervisors (Cmeier & Mnovellino, 2013).

However, this type of attack cannot be launched remotely because the attacker should have valid local access permission in order to successfully launching an attack. Therefore, anonymous attackers cannot generate this attack. The United States Computer Emergency Readiness Team (US-CERT) classifies this vulnerability as "local privilege escalation" weakness (Schwartz, 2012).

Another issue is associated with robustness of a hypervisor. The existence of bugs in the hypervisor is expected because of the large amount of codes the hypervisor is built on. Therefore, the adversary tenants can harm the virtualization layer and hence the physical server by exploiting the hypervisor bugs. Consequently, the attackers can obstruct other virtual machines and compromise the availability, integrity, and confidentiality of other customers' data and code (Jin et al., 2012).

2.2.2 Services Outages

One of the main security elements is availability, which means that the services must be available to the consumers wherever and whenever they need access. Therefore, an outage of the electrical current or Internet connection will affect the customer's business and convert the benefits of adopting the cloud into drawbacks. The provider must ensure alternative provisions to guarantee continuous service despite unexpected service outage events (Zhou et al., 2010; Ramgovind et al., 2010). This includes providing the required electrical power to each data centre owned and managed by the provider in order to avoid any disruption of the services.

2.2.3 Confidentiality and Integrity

In addition to availability, confidentiality and integrity pose significant security concerns. Confidentiality is about enabling only the authorised user to access the data while integrity is about protecting data against any modifications by unauthorised users. Therefore, unauthorised access to the stored data, which may occur because of poor authentication techniques used by customers such as weak passwords and/or poor implementation of monitoring facilities in the provider's location, can cause a dangerous breach of the customer's data. If the customer's data is stolen, damaged, or altered, this means that data integrity has been affected, and its overall security is breached (Ramgovind et al. 2010). A robust authentication system such as filtering or hiding the protected server's identity must be applied to prevent unauthorised users from accessing the protected system. In addition, an Identity and Access Management (IAM) policy, such as password policy that compels users to change passwords frequently and select long passwords containing at least one uppercase letter and one digit, should be implemented to protect the system assets and data.

2.2.4 Data-Level Security

Securing data at the customer's servers before transmitting to the cloud, securing the communication channel between the customer and the provider, securing the provider's storage site and the transmission channels between several servers in the cloud or between several clouds are essential to protect against attacks that could occur at any of these stages and locations. Encryption mechanisms such as Data Encryption Standard (DES), Advanced Encryption Standard (AES), Message-Digest Algorithm (MD5), and Secure Hash Algorithm (SHA-1) play an important role in data security (Mukundrao & Vikram, 2011).

2.2.5 Encryption Issues

Encryption offers several benefits to the cloud concept. These benefits vary from facilitating the data segregation of several customers' data and strengthening the bidirectional authentication process, to protecting data in the customer and provider's servers, (Sangroya et al., 2010; Rittinghouse & Ransome, 2010). On the other hand, encryption is a very complex process involving generating and managing encryption keys used to encrypt and decrypt data. The encryption mechanisms' reliance on encryption keys renders a higher priority to encryption keys compared to the data since the loss of encryption keys makes the related information unrecoverable. Additionally, generating encryption keys is computationally costly with more complex encryption requiring more processing time (Ablett et al., 2014).

2.3 Network Attacks

According to Raju et al. (2011), network attacks threaten the data during its transmission between the client's device and the provider's servers. The following subsections discuss the most popular network attacks.

2.3.1 Distributed Denial of Service (DDOS)

In this type of attack, the attacker sends a huge amount of network traffic to the network server. As a result, the server and network cannot respond to their users' requests because the servers will be dedicated to dealing with this huge amount of traffic. Consequently, the users will not be able to gain access to their required services. This attack is called Denial of Service (DoS) while the Distributed Denial of Service (DDoS) variant is a DoS attack launched by several distributed sources simultaneously (Raju et al., 2011). In order to mitigate DoS and/or DDoS threats, many countermeasures are proposed including the following.

- **Filtering Techniques:** Based on a threshold value or attack patterns
- **Overlay-Based Mitigation Methods:** Using distributed firewalls and hiding the protected server's location
- **Trace-Back Techniques:** Marking the malicious packets and tracing their sources
- **Push-Back Techniques:** Performing the filtering process by the routers nearest to the sources.

However, the majority of existing solutions either neglect the initial verification of the source of packets or provide mechanisms that increase the response time for legitimate users.

2.3.2 Man in the Middle Attack (MITM)

According to Raju et al. (2011), MITM attack is a type of active listening, as the attacker connects independently with the victims' machines and exchanges messages between them, letting each one of them believe that they are connecting directly to each other through a private channel when indeed the full exchange is managed by the attacker (Raju et al., 2011). Using Secure Sockets Layer (SSL) protocol to protect the communication channel is not enough in order to protect from MITM attacks. MITM attacks can be mitigated by using some types of authentication methods such as voice recognition, cryptography binding, public key infrastructures, and mutual authentication (Khan et al., 2009).

2.3.3 IP Spoofing

IP Spoofing is the establishing of a TCP/IP connection employing someone else's IP address. The attacker gains unauthorised access to a machine and sends messages to the victim machine with a spoofed IP address convincing it that the connection is created with a trusted source (Raju et al., 2011). The filtering systems in firewalls and routers can mitigate this type of attack; as they work on the network layer and inspect the IP packet header that has some fields, such as the Time To Live (TTL) value and Identification Field (ID), all of which can indicate whether the packet has been altered or not.

2.3.4 Port Scanning

If the user permits packets to access a specific port, then this port will be exposed to port scans. A port is a place of data entering and leaving the machine. If the port is open, port scanners can discover this and access the machine via this port. Once the user connects to the Internet, a specific port must be opened for this connection. Therefore, the user cannot stop an attacker from such scanning (Raju et al., 2011). Administrator awareness is very important in this regard, to monitor and detect repeated requests and close unused ports. Port scanning is usually carried out in preparation for an attack. Once the attacker knows the open ports, they can exploit the open ports for an attack. Port scanning is carried out to the maximum number of 65535 ports. This principle is done with use TCP SYN packets, which are addressed to each port, and if the port replies with an SYN-ACK packet, it means that the port is open. To avoid establishing the connection a Reset (RST) packet is sent back. It is essential that administrators should be aware of this practise and close all unused ports. However even with the unused ports are closed, monitoring has to be carried out, to discover the repeated requests from specific addresses through specific ports in the network. Monitoring should at the very least raise a flag and consequently trigger security counter measures.

2.3.5 Web Application Security Issues

The facility used to obtain the benefits and services of cloud technology is an Internet connection. Therefore, the client, the provider, and the communication channel should be well secured to protect the customer's valuable files and applications. Web applications (email and web browser) can cause exposure to several threats since attackers can access the web site's administrative interface to access all server files and online databases. Hackers can exploit programming loopholes, for instance in order to display contemporary dynamic websites; a number of data requests are made to several sources using programming languages such as, PHP and JavaScript. If programmer neglects the security, concerns associated with these programming languages, an attacker could gain access to all the data and resources accessed through the web application (Heng, 2011). Additionally, the malicious code can be written to affect the host server and/or the client machine examples of which include: viruses, worms, Trojan horses, SQL injections, and cross-site scripting (XSS) (Meier et al., 2003). To describe the principle used by attackers within this category, it is necessary to take a closer look at SQL injection and XSS.

As the name suggests SQL injection inserts malicious SQL code into the query that will alter the original query. This attack can be performed at any place where the website has entry points, such as forms and imports of files. The pure principle can be demonstrated with the login form into an administrator section. Into the password input field, the attacker will enter the string as is shown in Example (2) below instead of the correct password as shown in Example (1). While the normal user will enter the "real_password", the attacker will write "anything' or '1' = '1". By rules of SQL, the attacker input will be executed and evaluated as a true expression, which implies that the attacker will gain access.

The simplest defence against this attack is to check the input fields and control any escaping characters.

However, one has to be aware that regular expressions commonly used to check the input fields need to be able to differentiate between different character encoding formats.

SELECT * FROM login_table WHERE username ='admin' AND password =' real_password'; (1)

SELECT * FROM login_table WHERE username ='admin' AND password ='anything' or '1' ='1'; (2)

Similar to the SQL injection attack, the XSS attack exploits the provision of input fields by including tags, which could include malicious scripts stored on the attacker's server(s). Consequently, a new user visiting the webpage will browse and download the malicious script during the course of downloading the entire webpage. The principle defence to XSS is to closely control the user inputs or implement filter(s) that will remove such malicious parts. An example of such an attacked is presented in Example (3) below.

< SCRIPT SRC ="http://attackers-webserver. com/malicious-script" ></SCRIPT> (3)

2.3.6 Multi-Tenancy Security

The supporters of cloud technology consider multi-tenancy and resource sharing to be attractive features that can be achieved by using virtualisation. There are some isolation mechanisms, such as hypervisors, which must be used between several tenants in terms of the memory units, storage, and routing to protect the user's data and to prevent data interference and malicious attacks which can damage the data. Attacks against these mechanisms are more difficult for the attacker than attacks against traditional operating systems (ENISA, 2009).

The cloud provider usually stores and encrypts the data of several customers at the same location. The issue that may occur as a result of that is interference between the customers' data. To avoid this problem, the customer should ensure that the provider has suitable practices and techniques in place to segregate one client's data from other clients' data efficiently, in order to ensure that one client's information does not affect another clients' information. There is a mechanism known as "data segregation" that assists the provider with separating the information of each client and deters any interference with the other clients' information. Any failure in this mechanism will cause crucial issues for the clients.(Kuyoro & Ibikunle, 2011).

Kaur and Vashisht (2013) stated that there are four methods that can be used in addition to the data segregation technique in order to ensure successful data separation in the multitenant environment. These methods are hardening the authentication process, authorisation practices, encryption, and data fragmentation (Kaur & Vashisht, 2013).

2.3.7 Physical Security Issues

One of the most important risks to the data stored in the cloud is unauthorised access to data by users who are not allowed to access. Additionally, the provider's administrators, which can access data according to their privileges might misuse the customers' data if there is an absence of a clear policy. Therefore, the absence of an obvious policy and a strong monitoring system could place the customers' data at the disposal of almost anyone; thus resulting into a disastrous cloud migration for customers. Moreover, there is the ability for the attackers to employ the social engineering techniques to gain the employees' credentials and access the database(s) as legitimate users. Other physical security concerns are fire accidents and/or natural disasters such as floods and earthquakes, that could destroy the stored data and severely compromise the data integrity (Sitaram & Manjunath, 2012; Fortinet, 2011; Aslan, 2012).

The physical location of the cloud data centre must meet the following requirements.

- A policy that controls accessing data centres by the provider's employees. The policy must determine precisely who can access this private place and the type of assets they can access and for how long. The policy must provide a strong monitoring system and assigns roles to the incident response team and risk management team.
- The centre should be protected against human accidents and/or natural disasters such as floods and earthquakes. The security policy should include a business continuity plan and a recovery plan in the case of physical accidents.
- Provide frequent training courses to the provider's employees to prevent exploitation by social engineering techniques (Sangroya et al., 2010).

2.4 Legal Issues

Cloud environment management is related to the law in most of its implementations. A contract between the provider and the customer must be written in clear terms, and cover all aspects and activities which may occur during the contract period. Intellectual property is a very vital aspect that must be detailed precisely in the contract, due to the significant consequences of any neglect in this subject. The contract should clearly define the roles and responsibilities related to every legal issue. Therefore, SLAs and Terms of Service provide a fundamental legal basis for any potential disputes regarding the cloud service(Agarwal, 2010; Trappler, 2012).

2.4.1 Data Location

Most cloud clients do not appreciate the importance of knowing the location(s) of their data. These clients are oblivious of the likelihood of their data being transferred among several countries owing to the internationality of their cloud providers that manage distributed data centres in multiple countries. On the one hand distributed data location is an advantage for sustaining the data; in the event of unexpected incidents such as failures in the storage servers in any single data centre. On the other hand, this may cause a problem for data privacy due to the varying laws and regulations between the different hosting countries (Sangroya et al., 2010; Rittinghouse & Ransome, 2010). Cloud brokers can only inform the customers about the region but not specific countries hosting the data storage. While this information is sufficient in the European Union context, countries in other regions such as, America, Asia, or Africa have significantly different data protection laws.

2.4.2 Data Breach

To obtain successful results from adopting the cloud-computing paradigm, the ability to investigate and prosecute any illegal action against the customers' data must be available. The absence of such ability may pose an obstacle to potential customers adopting the cloud (Sangroya et al., 2010; Foster et al., 2008). In practise, the investigation process is complicated by the fact that the data is stored in multiple data centres. Hence, there is a need to use appropriate tools and legal methods in order to trace these illegal actions and analyse them (Kuyoro & Ibikunle, 2011). The contract must include section(s) detailing the importance of providing such investigation services and informing the customers about any breach of their data or any physical incident occurrence(s) in the location of data storage.

2.4.3 Data Deletion

A contract between the provider and the customer is usually specified to conclude at a specific date. If the customers do not have the desire to renew the contract for a further period, the provider should delete all of the customer's data from its servers. Under such circumstances, the questions that may be raised include: what are the assurances

for doing this efficiently? Are there special tools that can be used to ensure that the customer's data completely purged from all the provider's data centres? There is an inherent risk that may threaten the customer's security and privacy if their data is not removed completely from the provider's locations (ENISA, 2009; Slack, 2011). In order to answer the previous questions, the assurances that can be provided by the cloud provider to the customers are the security and compliance certificates discussed in previous sections.

Most providers nowadays apply a process called data sanitisation to encounter such threats. The data sanitisation process involves destroying or removing the stored data in the cloud data centre permanently and prevents all potential advanced techniques of recovering the deleted data. This process includes employing a software tool that completely deletes the stored information and/ or a mechanism that physically damages the machine so the erased data cannot be recovered (UCRIVERSIDE, 2011).

3. DENIAL OF SERVICE ATTACKS (DoS)

This section presents a comprehensive discussion of the variants of DoS attacks, the amplification of DoS attacks and the corresponding DoS mitigation techniques. DoS can be launched on different layers, such as transport layer or application layers. Availability is one of the most important features of any network or service. The Flooding or Denial of Service (DoS) attack affects this feature by preventing legitimate users from accessing the network resources. Adversaries generate DoS attacks by sending a huge amount of requests in order to consume the servers processing power and flood the network capacity (bandwidth). As a result, legitimate users cannot access the network or services despite proper authenticity and the right to access the required services at given time (Liu, 2009).

To explain the fundamentals of this kind of attack, (Lin et al., 2010) stated that the web page's computing power, i.e., built on a cloud platform is not limited. However, it still needs to be protected from three types of threats that affect the web page in a flooding manner. The first type affects its computation by consuming the system resources, while the second type wastes the bandwidth by downloading a large file from the web server repeatedly affecting its communication, and the third type harms its security by using password guessing attacks and SQL Injections (Lin et al., 2010). The flooding attacks against a static web page are generated either from botnet, computer virus or any other open Denial of Service tool (Yatagai et al., 2007). The flooding can be malicious as a Denial of Service attack or normal phenomenon like flash crowd. Xie et al. (2009) define the flash crowd on the web as the situation of accessing a popular website by a very high number of users simultaneously causing a surge in traffic resulting in the website becoming unreachable (Xie et al., 2009).

It is very important to distinguish the Denial of Service from the normal flash crowd. A Denial of Service event is a result of huge amount of requests generated by a small group of known and unknown users suddenly while a flash crowd event is a result of a huge amount of requests generated by a huge number of legitimate users gradually after a specific social event (Xie et al., 2009). The focus of this section is the Denial of Service (DoS) event.

3.1 Denial of Service (DoS)

In this type of attack, the attacker sends a huge amount of network traffic to the network server. As a result, the server and network cannot respond to their users' requests because the servers are dedicated to dealing with this huge amount of traffic. Consequently, the legitimate users are not able to gain access to their required services

(Kumar et al., 2012). Newman (2006) defines the denial of service attack (DoS) as an attack that tries to prevent legitimate user from accessing the computer and network resources as a result of a malicious action causing temporarily or permanent blockage for the benign user. For example, adversaries can send a huge number of packets to a specific port on the server.

3.2 Distributed Denial of Service (DDoS)

Mopari et al. (2009) define the Distributed Denial of Service (DDoS) as the case of using malicious machines by the attacker to generate DoS attack in order to strength the attack and make its impact more harmful. The machines that are used in the attack are usually infected by worms, so their owners do not know that they are participating in a malicious attack. The attacker intends to create a network of devices under his control to ensure the success of his attack against the victim. The attacker starts with penetrating some machines and creating backdoors on them so he can control them for a while. Those machines are called bots (zombies). Then, each bot can be managed to infect other machines with worms and control them to increase the number of machines participating in the attack. Now, the attacker has a full control on the bots in order to generate several types of attacks including DDoS. Nowadays, there are some tools can be used to generate DDoS such as TFN (Choi et al., 2010). According to Chopade et al. (2013), the common DDoS attacks are the following.

3.2.1 SYN Flood Attack

Transmission Control Protocol (TCP) provides a reliable, error checked and ordered connection. To achieve this goal, it has to establish a connection before the data can be transmitted. Setting up connection is achieved by a three-way handshake as shown on Figure 1.

*Figure 1. Establishing the TCP connection
(Based on Chen, 2005).*

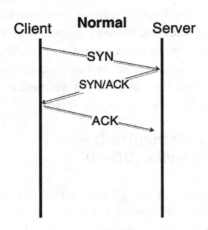
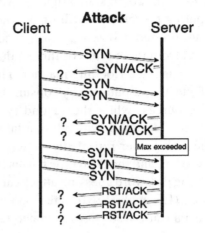

As soon as a client sends the first initial request namely, the TCP – SYN packet the server has to spend resources to leave the connection open. The server replies with TCP SYN-ACK packet and waits until it receives a final reply from the user namely the TCP ACK packet. Attackers abuse this principle by only sending the TCP – SYN packet without any interest in obtaining reply packets from the server. Practically the flood happens when an attacker sends a huge number of TCP-SYN packets often with a spoofed IP address. Logically the server has to spend its resources to keep the information about all the clients and leave the connection open in case that the clients do not have a reliable connection. However, the response never comes because the source address is spoofed. Chopade et al. (2013) proposed a possible DoS mitigation for the SYN floods by decreasing the server time-out. The logical extension of decreasing server time-outs is to exclude customers with low connection speeds.

3.2.2 Smurf Attack

This type of attacks can be created by sending a large amount of moderated ICMP packets with a spoofed IP address to several networks using IP broadcast address. To respond to these requests, all machines in the network will reply to the spoofed address. Therefore, the network works here as a smurf amplifier. If the network is large, it will be overwhelmed by a huge amount of traffic which prevents the legitimate user from accessing the network that is a denial of service. The victim can be affected directly or can pose with other parts of the network a network amplifier of the smurf attack. This overwhelms the network's capacity and prevents the legitimate users from accessing the network services (Chopade et al., 2013).

This attack can be mitigated by configuring all routers and machines in a network to ignore the incoming ICMP requests or broadcast or by configuring all routers in a network not to forward the directed broadcast packets to the network machines.

3.2.3 Internet Control Message Protocol (ICMP) Flood

In this type of attack, the attacker sends successive ICMP echo requests to the targeted machine that must reply with ICMP echo reply to every request. Thus, the huge number of requests and replies causes network disconnection because of the implemented timeouts. Additionally, the ICMP header messages provide the possibility for data injection. This can be exploited for enlarging the whole packet. The types of packets used to generate this attack are called ping packets (Chopade et al., 2013).

3.2.4 Ping of Death

Another type of flooding attack utilising the ping concept is the ping of death. It involves throwing a malicious ping to a machine by sending IP oversized packets, which are packets larger than the permitted size by the IP protocol. Thus, many operating systems do not know how to deal with this situation consequently the victim machines reboot, crash, or freeze. It is easy for an attacker to generate such an attack as he does not need any information about the targeted victim except the IP address. Fortunately, modern firewalls and operating systems are capable of mitigating this kind of attack (Chopade et al., 2013).

3.3 Increasing Efficiency of DDoS

It is clear that the more machines that are involved in the attack, the greater traffic will be generated. Therefore, the impact on the victim would be also bigger. There are ways how to enlarge the DDoS.

The first possibility for how to make the attack stronger is by using the current infrastructure and services which by default give answers after the requests. Legitimate service such as DNS is one of the possibilities for how to increase the efficiency. Attackers can use an extension that allows large messages and from a request that has approximately 60 bytes the response can enlarge up to 4000 (Piscitello, 2011). This means 66 times higher load addressed to the victim. The principle is that the attacker has to spoof IP address of the source, and instead of the real attacker's IP address, they inject the IP address of a victim as it is shown on Figure 2.

Figure 2. Principle of DDoS attack with abusing DNS service as an amplifier (Based on Eugster, 2013).

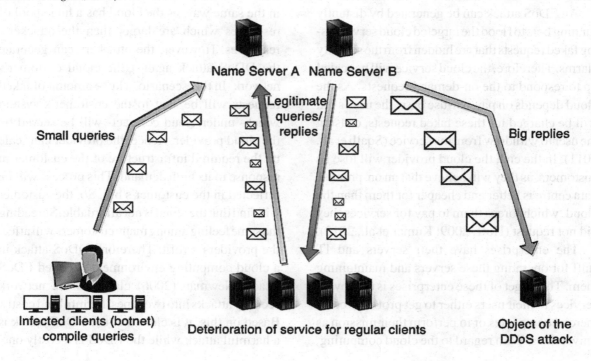

All the computers in botnet network will send this request, and the DNS service will follow the standards and correctly sends the answer. However, the DNS reply is then used as an instrument of harm.

Simple Network Management protocol (SNMP) can also be used as an amplifier. The principle is also the same as in the previous case. The botnet network which includes a number of machines, under the control of an attacker will send a request to a network gateway. However, instead of sending a response to the real botnet machine, it will send a reply to the victim IP address which was injected into the packet as the source IP address. The SNMP request is again smaller than the actual response.

3.4 Economical DDOS

In the cloud computing era, a new type of DDoS attack called Economical Denial of Sustainability (EDoS) was introduced by Hoff (2008). EDoS is "packet flood that stretches the elasticity of metered-services employed by the server, e.g., a cloud-based server" (Khor & Nakao, 2011).

An EDoS attack can be generated by distantly running bots to flood the targeted cloud service using faked requests that are hidden from the security alarms. Therefore, the cloud service will be scaled up to respond to the on-demand requests. As the cloud depends on pay-per-use base, the user's bill will be charged for these faked requests, causing the user to withdraw from the service (Sqalli et al., 2011). In the end, the cloud provider will lose its customers, as they will believe that an on-premise data centre is better and cheaper for them than the cloud, which forces them to pay for services they did not request (Hoff, 2009; Kumar et al., 2012).

The enterprises have their servers and IT staff for operating these servers and maintaining them. The target of these enterprises is to provide services to their users either to get profits as commercial companies or to perform their mission as universities. With regard to the cloud computing, these organisations can save the cost of purchasing the hardware, software licenses, and data storage in addition to the cost of maintenance and the IT employees salaries by transfer the IT overheads to a cloud service provider. The cloud service providers have huge resources that can be offered as on-demand service in a scalable manner. Moreover, they have much more security professionals to protect their data centres and, as a result, their customers data. However, there is a problem that can force the customers to withdraw from the cloud services by affecting the customer's bill exploiting the cloud scalability causing more payments for cloud services than the cost of owning and managing the customer's in-premise network. In such case, the benefits of the cloud converted to be drawbacks. This can be done by generating attacks called Economical Denial of Sustainability (EDoS) attacks.

EDoS attack is a Distributed Denial of Service (DDoS) attack with a different impact. Traditional DDoS attack aims to overwhelm the servers and the bandwidth of a network or a website in order to make them unavailable to their intended users. It is hard of DDoS attack to harm the cloud resources, in the same way, as the cloud has a huge pool of resources which are larger than the attackers' resources. However, the attackers can generate the DDoS attack against the cloud customer's network. In this scenario, a huge amount of faked requests will be sent to the customer's system which- under cloud contract- will be served by the cloud provider. Hence, the provider can scale up the required infrastructure of the customer in response to its high demand. This process will be reflected in the customer's bill. So, the customer will find that the cloud is not affordable. Spreading the same feeling among many customers will affect the providers' profit. Therefore, DDoS attack in a cloud computing environment is called EDoS attack. Newman (2006) classifies the network security attacks into two types, harmful and costly. Based on this, it is clear that the DDoS attack is a harmful attack while the EDoS is a costly one.

EDoS is a technical problem with an economical effect. The solution of this problem must be a technical solution.

Based on the above, any solution to encounter DDoS attack against a cloud customer's network must be a proactive method so that the cloud providers protect their edges that are their customers' networks from EDoS attacks.

There is a number of methods proposed to encounter these attacks. However, these methods are either testing all packets coming from the source causing higher end-to-end latency or testing the first packet only without any other verification process which is not enough to protect the system. Limiting the end-to-end latency is a very important feature besides providing a robust defence system against the malicious attacks. Newman (2006) emphasis on the importance of such aspect as the organisations must provide a balance between the security and convenience for its users in order to facilitate a secure user access to the network to get their requested services. To solve the above problem, the proposed solution must verify the legitimacy of the users at the beginning of accessing the network and then provides ongoing monitoring for the remaining packets using other security layers.

The will be beneficial if the organisation is a customer for cloud services (Infrastructure as a Service (IaaS)). The cloud provider is expected to have advanced security measures. However, putting security measures onto its edge, i.e., its customers' networks will harden its security by offering proactive protection to their system. In this regard, the idea of designating a maximum threshold for the customer usage to ensure that the customer's bill does not exceed their satisfied limit in order to prevent the EDoS impacts, is not acceptable under the cloud concept. The service can be considered as a cloud service if and only if it is scalable and elastic, is metered by use, has broad network access, has shared pool of resources, and provided as an on-demand self-service (Mell & Grance, 2011).

The DDoS attacks are well-known in the security field. Therefore, there are many countermeasures that have been suggested to encounter such attacks. In the next section, some existing methods will be presented, and a comparison between them will be conducted based on aspects such as decreasing the end-to-end latency, verifying the packets and protecting the scalability.

4. DDoS SOLUTIONS AND RECOMMENDATIONS

Beitollahi and Deconinck (2008) stated that the Distributed Denial of Service (DDoS) countermeasure techniques are divided into two types; reactive and proactive.

The reactive methods such as the filtering systems need to distinguish the legitimate packet from the malicious one in order to drop the last. Reactive solutions mean that the defence system is waiting for an attack to occur and then tries to mitigate its impact. On the other hand, proactive solutions such as the overlay-based techniques involve treating the source of packets before reaching the protected server. These techniques include other components besides the filters. They depend on distributed firewalls or nodes in order to hide the location of the protected server (Morein et al., 2003; Beitollahi & Deconinck, 2008; Kumar et al., 2012).

Cook et al. (2003) stated that the reactive methods identified the attack after its occurrence by analysing its patterns and packet headers with using filters to block the adversaries. These approaches focus on discovering the attacks sources and then pushing filters on routers close to the sources and far from the target of attack as much as possible. Unfortunately, these reactive techniques by themselves are not always enough solutions (Cook et al., 2003).

The major issues of the reactive techniques are their accuracy in distinguishing the legitimate traffic from the malicious one, and their strength

in creating a deep filtering systems that can mi-
nimise the attack effects for the targeted server
(Cook et al., 2003).

Beitollahi and Deconinck (2008) stated that the
filtering techniques have the following limitations:

1. The filtering system performs its task by
   observing known attack patterns or statistical
   anomalies. However, it can be defeated by
   modifying the attack patterns or masking the
   anomalies, causing a lack of the filters accuracy.
2. If an attacker gains access to a legitimate
   user's account, the attacker can use the user's
   IP address to access the system and harm it.
3. The filtering system increases the end-to-end
   latency as it needs to process all packets to
   accept or drop. This affects the availability
   and the system's performance (Beitollahi
   and Deconinck, 2008).

Beitollahi and Deconinck (2012) stated that
the proactive methods are much faster than the
reactive methods in responding to DDoS attacks
as the malicious requests are dropped prior to
reaching the targeted server.

Based on the above definitions, any countermeasure of the DDoS and EDoS attacks must take
the following features into its account:

1. Decreasing the end-to-end latency.
2. The latency annoys the legitimate users.
   Therefore, one of the most important objectives of any countermeasure of DDoS attacks
   is to make the sources available to this type
   of users without delaying their requests.
3. **Verifying the Packets:** Checking the packets
   is very important to authenticate their sources.
   The packet's header has fields that can assist
   in preventing the protected system from the
   IP address spoofing that done by attackers to
   bypass the monitoring systems. Moreover,
   checking the packets payloads and observing
   their traffic rate can detect the malicious users
   and provide security to the protected network.

4. For the EDoS countermeasure, it is important
   to design it in a way that protect the scalability
   in order to protect the pricing model which
   is the chief target of the attacker against the
   network in a cloud environment.

Five existing frameworks will be presented
for DDoS mitigation, which are CLAD, SOS,
WebSOS, Fosel, and DaaS, respectively.

Before presenting the countermeasure list,
some methods need to be explained as most of
the solutions involve using these technical means.
These include the Chord overlay, the Time To Live
(TTL), crypto puzzles, and the Graphical Turing
Test CAPTCHA.

- **Chord Overlay Mechanism:** Chord is a
  routing service that can be applied atop the
  existing IP network structure as a network
  overlay. Consistent hashing is employed
  to map a random numerical identifier (ID)
  to every single node in the overlay. These
  identifiers must be in the range [0,2m]
  as m is a predetermined value. The overlay nodes are sorted by their identifiers as
  a circle. So, the next node in the order is
  the next one over the circle in a clockwise
  path. Every overlay node has a table that
  records the identities of all other m overlay nodes. The following example simplifies the Chord overlay mechanism. So, if
  the overlay node x receives a packet whose
  destination is the identifier y, the packet
  will be forwarded to the overlay node in
  its table whose identifier precedes y by the
  smallest amount (Morein et al., 2003).
- **TTL:** The time-to-live (TTL) is an eight-
  bit field in the IP packet header that determines the maximum lifetime of the packet
  to forbid it from circling on the network
  without end in a routing loop existence.
  The packet will be discarded when its TTL
  value is zero. Otherwise, the router which
  the packet passes through will decrease

Table 1. Initial TTL values of operating systems

ICMP	UDP	TCP	Operating System
255	64	64	Linux
255	64	64	OS/2
255	255	255	Solaris 2.x
255	32	32	MS Windows 95/98/ME
255	128	128	MS Windows NT 4.0
255	128	128	Windows 2000/XP/2003

(Zhang et al., 2007).

the TTL field by one. Most modern operating systems select the values 30, 32, 60, 64, 128, and 255 as initial TTL values for each type of packets (Park et al, 2010; Al-Haidari et al., 2012). Zhang et al. (2007) clarified operating systems with their initial TTL values of each kind of packets as shown in Table 1.

The packet arrives at any router with its final TTL value. To infer the initial TTL value, the smallest initial value which is larger than the final TTL value is selected from the above set (Park et al., 2010).

For example, if the final TTL value is equal to 115, then the initial TTL value will be 128 not 255. Templeton and Levitt (2003) and Park et al. (2010) stated that there is a general belief that a small number of Internet hosts are at a distance of more than thirty hops. The hop-count is the difference between the initial and the final TTL values. So, hop-count = TTLinitial - TTLfinal. This means that the hop-count value must be less than or equal to thirty (Templeton & Levitt, 2003; Park et al., 2010).

- **Puzzles:** Mechanism, in terms of puzzles, is based on the principle that a user has to spend resources to solve the puzzle and send a solution to the server, before the server itself will dedicate its resources to the particular user. Client-puzzle mechanism requires to have installed software in the client's side. However, this challenge can be managed when the software can be build in into the web browser, or it can be added as a pug-in. (Beitollahi & Deconinck, 2012). An example can be when user wants to access the website the server will automatically redirect the user to the puzzle server. A puzzle server can be written in C programming language, and it will generate a puzzle. As soon as a user will receive the puzzle it can use Java applets to solve this challenge. When the puzzle is solved correctly, the user will be automatically redirected to the website, which user wanted to access. (Srivatsa et al., 2008). Disadvantages of this security measure are:

  - Already mentioned specialized software/pug-in, which will be able to solve the puzzles and send the solution back to the server. (Douligeris & Mitrokosta, 2004).
  - Clearly the puzzle is a step between the users wants to access the server and server provides the information. Therefore, as a result, the puzzles increase the latency.
  - Server that process puzzle solutions can become a target of DDoS attack. With faked puzzle solutions, which

will affect the possibility of accepting the nonmalicious solutions of regular users. Another aspect is the difficulty of puzzles, when it is too difficult it can affect users who use mobile phones to access the server. (Beitollahi & Deconinck, 2012).

Experiments, which were conducted, have shown that puzzles can be generated over one million puzzles per second and also one million can be check per second. (Srivatsa et al., 2008).

- **CAPTCHA:** The Completely Automated Public Turing test to Tell Computers and Humans Apart (CAPTCHA) puzzles are the most effective authentication techniques against DDoS attacks. It is a program that applied in the overlay access point to distinguish the human user from the machines (zombies), that are used in launching DDoS attacks, by generating a picture that contains letters and/or digits. The user needs to rewrite the picture contents in a specific space provided in the same page. Only the human user can pass this puzzle while machines cannot. So, CAPTCHA can be effective in protecting from the Application-layer attacks. However, it cannot prevent from the reflector attacks and the bandwidth attacks such as UDP flooding attacks (Morein et al., 2003; Beitollahi & Deconinck, 2012).

4.1 Secure Overlay Services (SOS)

The Secure Overlay Services (SOS) is proposed by (Keromytis et al., 2002). Lakshminarayanan et al. (2004) stated that SOS is the first framework to use overlay techniques to indirect the received packets by the target network besides hiding the location of the target server in order to encounter the denial of service attacks. It aims to allow communication between an authenticated user and the victim server. Authentication of the user means that the server gives prior consent to this user to access the network. Figure 3 shows the SOS architecture. It consists of a set of nodes that are classified into four groups. The first group is the Secure Overlay Access Points (SOAP), while the second group is the overlay nodes which connect SOAP nodes with the third group, that is, Beacon nodes. The last group is the Secret Servlets. This reduces the possibility of harmful attacks by applying the filtering process at the edges of the protected network and by providing anonymity and randomness to the architecture and making it difficult for the attacker to affect the nodes along the path to the target. SOS uses a large number of overlay nodes that are considered as distributed firewalls to augment the survivability by increasing the amount of resources the attacker must spend to successfully affect the connectivity of legitimate users (Keromytis et al., 2002).

In SOS, the traffic of clients is authenticated in the SOAP nodes by comparing the IP addresses of the sources of incoming packets with the assumed list of known IP addresses. After that, the succeed traffics are forwarded via the Chord overlay network to the beacon nodes that send the traffics to the secret Servlet nodes. Lastly, the Servlet nodes send the traffics to the target server that is protected by filters (Keromytis et al., 2002).

SOS mechanism is working as the following:

1. The protected server has a filtering router(s) in its perimeter. It also chooses some nodes to be secret servlets. Filtering routers grant only the traffic from these servlets access to reach the target that is the protected server and drop or rate-limit all other traffics.

2. The secret servlet calculates the key (k) for every number of the consistent hash functions. The calculation process is performed based on the protected server's address. Every key identifies a set of overlay nodes that will work as beacons for the protected server.

Figure 3. SOS architecture
(based on Keromytis et al., 2002).

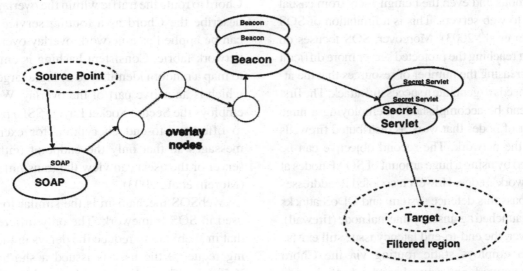

3. The beacons will be notified either by the protected server or by the servlets about the existence of the servlets by hashing on the server's identifier (which is known by the secret servlet) and then employing the Chord routing in a similar way of the SOAP nodes mechanism. Therefore, the server or the secret servlet can notify the beacon about the identity of the secret servlet. Beacons verify the requests then store the essential data to forward the request to the proper servlet.

4. The client who desires to connect to the protected server should contacts a SOAP point. SOAP authenticates the request and then forwards it to a protected server through a beacon node. It chooses the beacon node depending on a proper hash function of the protected server's address.

5. The beacon forwards the packet to a secret servlet which redirects the packet via the filtering router to the target server (Keromytis et al., 2002).

SOS uses Internet Protocol Security (IPSec) in its implementation. IPSec is a protocol that can be used to generate cryptographic keys and other related factors between a couple of hosts and then authenticate and encrypt the traffic between them for protection. Each authorised source is provided with a certificate by the target server allowing the source to access the SOS infrastructure to deliver traffic to the server. Each SOAP point (access point) authenticates the source of incoming packets by the IPSec key-exchange protocol (IKE) that requires the source to provide the certificate to the SOAP node. Therefore, the SOAP authenticates the source by verifying a cryptographic signature and tests the authorisation data embedded in the certificate (Keromytis et al., 2002).

Morein et al. (2003) state that SOS architecture relies on distributed firewalls across the network. The main task of these firewalls is enforcing the access control policies. An attacker can generate a denial of service attack with spoofed IP addresses originating from these firewalls as their identities cannot be supposed to stay always secret. SOS architecture selects some nodes (secret servlets) to be selected authentication points. This means the filtering router only allows traffic that is forwarded from these nodes while all other firewalls should forward the packets for the target server to these servlets (Morein et al., 2003).

Morein et al. (2003) noticed that SOS prevents anonymous and even the benign users from casual access to web servers. This is a limitation of SOS (Morein et al., 2003). Moreover, SOS focuses on making reaching the protected server more difficult and increasing the number of resources that the attacker needs to generate a successful attack. The first target can be accomplished by employing a huge number of nodes that work as distributed firewalls across the network. The second objective can be achieved by using a huge amount of SOAP nodes at the network's edge. However, spoofed IP addresses can bypass this defence system, and DDoS attacks can be launched against any internal node (firewall). Moreover, the end-to-end latency issue still exists.

SOS employs static routing via the Chord overlay network and several servlet nodes in case of fault tolerance. Adversaries are glad about this mechanism of SOS because their brute force method can detect a servlet node in a faster manner. Detecting just one of these servlet nodes is sufficient to overwhelm the target server with a flooding attack. The attackers can achieve this detection of a servlet node by monitoring the traffic of a legitimate user passively (Beitollahi & Deconinck, 2012).

4.2 Websos

Morein et al. (2003) presented an approach called WebSOS. It has the same architecture as SOS but differs from it in some aspects of its implementation. Legitimate clients can access the web servers during the DoS with this implementation. The architecture employs a mixture of packet filtering, consistent hashing, Graphic Turing Tests (GTT), overlay networks, and cryptographic protocols for data origin authentication to offer services to the casual web browsing user (Morein et al., 2003).

The writers stated that the WebSOS uses graphic Turing tests to distinguish between botnets and human clients in a transparent manner. CAPTCHA is used for this purpose by generating a test that the human user can pass while machines cannot (Morein et al., 2003).

Morein et al. (2003) state that SOS utilises Chord to route the traffic within the overlay. They describe the Chord as a routing service which can be applied as a network overlay over the IP network fabric. Consistent hashing is employed to map a random identifier to a single target node which is an active part of the overlay. WebSOS employs the Secure Socket Layer (SSL) protocol to offer end-to-end encryption for exchanged messages so that only the endpoint (either the server or the user) can view the transmitted data (Morein et al., 2003).

WebSOS mechanism is the similar to that is used in SOS framework. The only difference is that in WebSOS to reduce the delays in the coming requests, the user is issued a short-period X.509 certificate, bound to the user's IP address and the SOAP node, which can be employed "to directly contact the proxy-server component of the SOAP without requiring another CAPTCHA test" (Morein et al., 2003).

WebSOS hardened SOS architecture by using high-performance routers in the protected server's perimeter and by strengthening the verification process performed by SOAP nodes by using CAPTCHA tests. However, it does not solve the problem of end-to-end latency. Moreover, Lakshminarayan et al. (2004) stated that the overlay networks (SOS and WebSOS) suppose that the list of users are identified previously so that they do not scale very well to the existing Internet setting.

4.3 Filtering by Helping an Overlay Security Layer (FOSEL)

Beitollahi and Deconinck (2008) proposed a proactive solution against DoS attacks. It is called Filtering by helping an Overlay Security Layer (Fosel). It is composed of firewalls, an overlay network with secret green nodes, and a specific filter called Fosel filter in front of each protected server as shown in Figure 4.

Figure 4. Fosel architecture
(Based on Beitollahi & Deconinck, 2008).

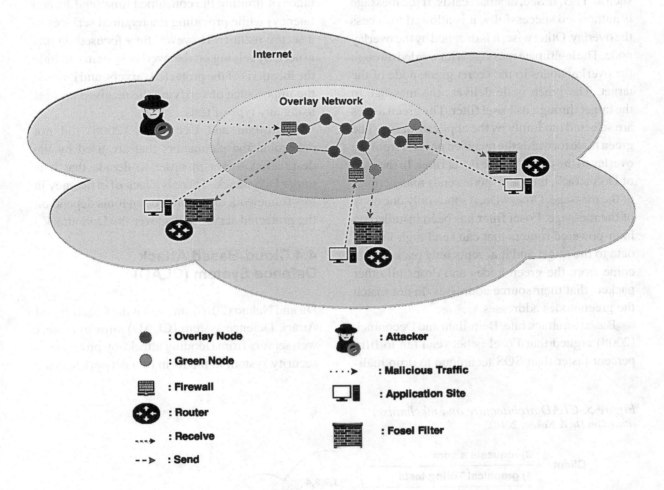

Fosel technique aims to protect the target by using the Fosel filters that accept only the approved packets by the green nodes and drop the other packets. As a result, the filter cannot be a victim of an attack that resulting from spoofing the sources IP addresses Fosel technique is simple as there is no need to notify and then modify the filter if the application site's location is changed according to the filter's independence from sites location. Moreover, the adversary cannot employ a spoofed IP address in generating attacks against the target (Beitollahi & Deconinck, 2008).

The green node is a secret node of the overlay network. Its role and location are kept secret. The application site chooses an overlay node to be a

green node and informs it about that. The green node receives a packet from the overlay and redirects it to the target via the Fosel filter. In the case of denial of service attack, it sends many copies of the message (Beitollahi & Deconinck, 2008).

The firewalls accept only the packets that come from legitimate users and allow them to access the overlay network. The overlay network with secret green nodes provides a protected way to deliver the packets to the protected server through the Fosel filters. (Beitollahi & Deconinck, 2008).

The Fosel architecture is operated as follows: the application site (user) connects to an arbitrary overlay node to deliver a message to other application sites (the target). The overlay node verifies the received request by authentication techniques such as TLS, IPSec, or smart cards. If the message is authorised successfully, it is allowed to access the overlay. Otherwise, it is dropped by the overlay node. The legitimate message is forwarded through the overlay nodes to the secret green node of the target. The green node delivers the message to the target through its Fosel filter. The green nodes are selected randomly by the application site. The green node forwards the received packets from the overlay to the target via the Fosel filter. In the case of DoS attack, the green node sends many copies of the message. Otherwise, it sends only one copy of the message. Fosel filter has been installed on high-powered routers that can send high load of data to the target and it accepts only packets that come from the green nodes and drops all other packets that their source addresses do not match the green nodes addresses.

Based on attack rate, Beitollahi and Deconinck (2008) argued that Fosel is between ten to fifty percent faster than SOS technique to drop mali-cious packets. So, they are aware of the impor-tance of limiting the consumed time (end-to-end latency) while providing the required services in a secure manner. However, they focused on this aspect, by relying on the overlay systems, to hide the locations of the protected servers, and ignored the importance of verifying the received packets using any type of tests.

Beitollahi and Deconinck (2008) did not determine the parameters that are used by the destination server in order to decide that it is under DoS attack. There is a lack of efficiency in this framework as the protection tools depend on the protected server to discover the DoS attack.

4.4 Cloud-Based Attack Defence System (CLAD)

Du and Nakao (2010) states that the Cloud-based Attack Defence system (CLAD) aims to protect web servers from flooding attacks by providing a security system in the form of a network service

Figure 5. CLAD architecture and mechanism (Based on Du & Nakao, 2010).

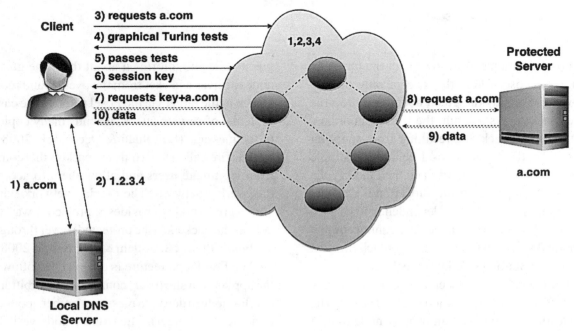

working on a huge cloud infrastructure which is considered as a supercomputer. Therefore, this supercomputer can defeat network layer attacks against any CLAD node which can be a virtual machine or application that is running web proxies. As shown in Figure 5, CLAD consists of a DNS server and a group of CLAD nodes. Every CLAD node can be considered as a web proxy that has many control measures such as congestion control measures, pre-emption, authentication, admission control, and network layer filtering (Du and Nakao, 2010).

The protected server that can be a single server or a set of servers must be hidden from the public and only accepts traffic from the CLAD nodes. The protected server IP address is known only to the CLAD nodes, so the DNS server replies to any request from the Internet with an IP address of a CLAD node.

Each CLAD node exchanges its healthy status with other neighbour nodes by fetching a particular small file periodically. The healthy status is controlled by the authoritative DNS server that distributes healthy CLAD nodes to the local DNS servers in few seconds. Therefore, a healthy CLAD node can be selected for a user in real time.

The admission control means decreasing the number of created active HTTP session keys which are placed in a session table. The session table has a maximum size that is the number of allowed concurrent users. A valid HTTP session key permits a user to access the protected server via CLAD system for a particular period by storing the session key in his cookie or embedding it in his URL. The session key can be created by hashing the user IP address and the expiration time using a private hash function.

The CLAD mechanism can be described as the following. The DNS server receives a client request and then replies with the IP address of a CLAD node. The CLAD node is selected based on its load or healthy status. After that, the CLAD

node authenticates the client by a graphical Turing test. If the user passes the test, the CLAD node assigns the user a session key, which is used to get the CLAD node's validation in order to relay the client's request to the protected web server (Du & Nakao, 2010).

Sqalli et al. (2011) state that the CLAD increases end-to-end latency because all clients' packets pass through the overlay system components. Moreover, the CLAD considers the cloud infrastructure as a network service that protects the target Web server. When a new request arrives, the cloud infrastructure checks if it is HTTP request as the cloud infrastructure only grants Web traffic access through it. As a result, all other traffics will be dropped by the cloud infrastructure. Moreover, the CLAD framework implementation can be valid to small businesses only (Sqalli et al., 2011; Kumar & Sharma, 2013)

4.5 DDoS Mitigation as a Service (DaaS)

DDoS Mitigation as a Service (DaaS) tackles the DDoS problems by creating a metered pool that has more resources than the botnets to facilitate the harnessing of idle resources from current or future services without alteration. DaaS framework aims to hiding the details of the framework, enabling the use of the framework by the clients and servers without any modification, granting traffic control reception to the server, and enabling any system to be employed as an intermediary. It depends on using SSL certificate with the public key, crypto puzzles, and DNS server. DaaS consists of intermediary plug-ins, multiple stacks, accounting unit and a self Proof of Work (sPoW) consists of a puzzle generator, puzzle requesters, puzzle distributors, and a connection manager (Khor & Nakao, 2011). Figure 6 shows the DaaS architecture.

DaaS mechanism is explained in the following steps:

1. A user contacts the DNS server to get the address of the server with the server's public key that is embedded in its SSL certificate.

2. The user then executes a DaaS name resolution, identifying the server's hostname and the puzzle difficulty to get a crypto puzzle.

3. The DaaS name server sends the puzzle request to the server's puzzle generator.

4. The server randomly establishes a temporary i-channel and encrypts the channel data.

5. The server forwards the encrypted data and the encryption key with k bits, which create the crypto-puzzle. The server hostname-channel puzzle binding is created.

6. The user performs brute-force search and retrieves the i-channel data.

7. The user submits a primary connection request that contains a random created secret key, encrypted with the server's public key, via the i-channel. If this request has not handled during the timeout, the more difficult crypto puzzle will be generated and sent to the user as a response to any new connection request from him.

8. The server establishes a c-channel when it receives the primary connection request.

9. The server encrypts the channel data employing the user generated secret key and forwards the data back to the user (Khor & Nakao, 2011).

Sqalli et al. (2011) studied this reactive technique and listed its limitations: First, mobile devices cannot benefit from the services because of their limited power. Second, if the attackers send a huge amount of requests for puzzles and do not solve them, this creates a type of attack called a puzzle accumulation attack. Lastly, if the attackers do not solve their requested high difficulty puzzles, this forces the legitimate users to solve high difficult puzzles as a result of the difficulty inflation issue (Sqalli et al., 2011). Thus, using the puzzles only to prevent DDoS attacks against the protected server is not enough, as puzzle implementation has its own limitations. Moreover, DaaS increases the end-to-end latency much more than CLAD, SOS, WebSOS or Fosel.

Figure 6. DaaS architecture
(Khor & Nakao, 2011).

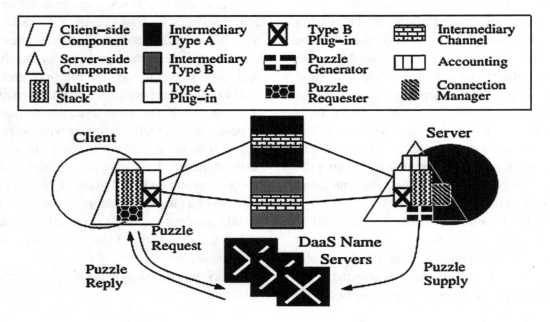

Figure 7. EDoS-shield framework
(Sqalli et al., 2011).

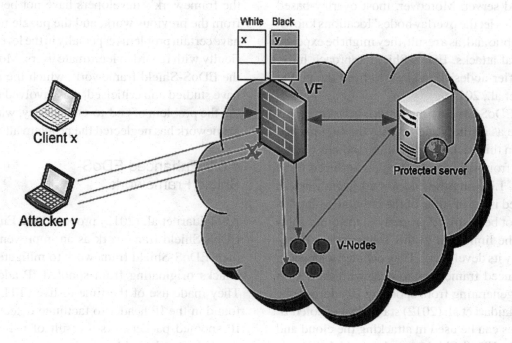

4.6 EDoS Countermeasures

There are a number of frameworks have been proposed to protect the cloud from the EDoS attacks. Four of these solutions will be presented. These are EDoS-Shield framework, Sandar and Shenai framework, Enhanced EDoS-Shield framework and In-Cloud eDDoS Mitigation Web Service (Scrubber Service) technique.

4.6.1 EDoS-Shield Framework

This framework is proposed by Sqalli et al. (2011). Its main idea is to check if the requests are generated from botnets or legitimate users. The EDoS-Shield approach is verifies only the first packet by applying CAPTCHA verification, and then accepts or denies the subsequent packets from the same source that has the same IP address. It is a milestone in the techniques that used as solutions, as the authors have focused on solving the end-to-end latency issue.

The main parts of the EDoS-Shield architecture can be shown in figure 7. These parts are virtual firewalls (VF) and a cloud-based overlay network called verifier nodes (V-Nodes). The virtual firewall works as a filter with white and black lists that store the IP addresses of the originating sources. The verifier node verifies the sources using graphic Turing tests such as CAPTCHA to update the lists according to the verification process results. The virtual firewall can be applied as a virtual machine that can filter and route the packets. The white list stores the authenticated source IP addresses so their following traffics will be allowed to pass the firewall filtering mechanism and access the protected system. On the other hand, the black list stores the unauthenticated source IP addresses so their following traffics will be dropped. The two lists must be updated periodically (Sqalli et al., 2011).

This technique differs from CLAD and the other overlay routing as it significantly decreases the delay as successive packets after the first successful packet are forwarded directly to the protected server. Moreover, most overlay-based techniques let the overlay nodes' locations known to the public and, as a result, they might be exposed to several attacks. EDoS-Shield approach hides the verifier nodes' IP addresses from the public (Sqalli et al., 2011).

The EDoS-Shield framework's performance is effective as it filters and verifies the first packet. Based on this packet verification, the subsequent packets from the same source do not need to be verified. Limiting the end-to-end latency was a neglected issue in some of the previous solutions or has not been solved properly in the other solutions. The limitation in this framework is mentioned by its developers. They decided to develop an enhanced framework to deal with the EDoS attacks generating from spoofing IP addresses.

Al-Haidari et al. (2012) stated that spoofed IP addresses can be used in attacking the cloud and bypass the EDoS-Shield technique which depends on the white and black lists. Once the IP address is registered in the white list, all subsequent packets from the same address will pass the filter without verifying process. So, if the IP address is spoofed, then the attack can overwhelm the cloud resources causing DDoS and EDoS attacks respectively (Al-Haidari et al., 2012).

4.6.2 Sandar and Shenai Framework

Sandar and Shenai (2012) proposed a framework that relies on a firewall, which works as a filter. The framework consists of a firewall and a client puzzle server as shown in figure 8. The firewall receives the request from the client and redirects it to a Puzzle-Server. The Puzzle-Server sends a puzzle to the client, who either sends a correct or wrong answer of the puzzle. If the answer is correct, the server will send a positive acknowledgment to the firewall that will add the client to its white list, and will forward the request to a protected server to get services. Otherwise, the firewall will receive a negative acknowledgment and put the client in

its blacklist (Sandar & Shenai, 2012). However, the framework's developers have not benefitted from the previous work, and the puzzle methods have certain problems especially in the level of difficulty with regard to legitimate users. Moreover, the EDoS-Shield framework, which the authors have studied and criticised, was involved in solving the problem of end-to-end latency, while this framework has neglected the problem altogether.

4.6.3 Enhanced EDoS-Shield Framework

Al-Haidari et al. (2012) proposed the Enhanced EDoS-Shield framework as an improvement on their EDoS-Shield framework to mitigate EDoS attacks originating from spoofed IP addresses. They made use of the time-to-live (TTL) value found in the IP header to facilitate detecting the IP spoofed packets. As a result of using TTL, this framework avoids refusing a request coming from a source registered on the blacklist. Instead of this, it tests the packet as it may be initiated from a victim of a previous IP address spoofing attempt. Therefore, it prevents DoS attacks on legitimate users, even if their IP addresses have been exploited. (Al-Haidari et al., 2012). This mechanism is clarified in Figure 9.

A similar architecture to the EDoS-Shield framework is used. However, to enhance the EDoS-Shield framework by enabling it to mitigate the spoofing attacks that affect its original version, the authors added three additional fields that can be monitored and stored in the white and black lists with their correspondent IP addresses. These fields are the TTL values, a counter of unmatched TTL values in both lists, and the time stamp (attack start time) in the black list (Al-Haidari et al., 2012).

The difference with the original EDoS-Shield framework is that instead of rejecting packets based on difference in their TTL values, a verification process will be conducted by the V-Node if the unmatched TTL counter does not exceed the determined threshold. This will give the sources

Figure 8. Sandar and Shenai framework
(Based on Sandar & Shenai, 2012).

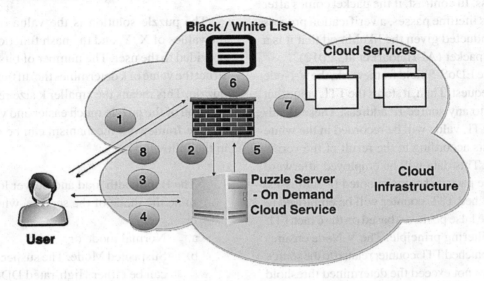

Figure 9. Enhanced EDoS-shield framework's mechanism
(Based on Al-Haidari et al., 2012).

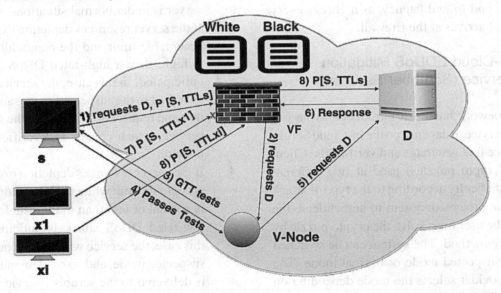

that have different TTL values a new chance to prove their legitimacy. It is assumed that the modification of the TTL value between two specific ends is limited over a period of time. Therefore, if the number of modifications exceeds a given threshold, then these modifications are considered as abnormal and packets coming from the related IP address will be dropped without any

more verification chance. The attack timestamp field indicates the start time of the attack that is the time of placing the source IP address in the blacklist. The purpose of using such field is to render the verification process at the V-Node more secret through the attack. For example, if a packet comes during the attack's lifetime with a source IP address that exists in the blacklist, it will be rejected without conducting an additional verification process. In contrast, if the packet comes after the attack's lifetime passes, a verification process will be conducted given the likelihood that it is a legitimate packet (Al-Haidari et al., 2012).

As in the EDoS-Shield framework, the V-Node verifies a request. Then, it stores the TTL value that is relevant to any source IP address. These IP address and TTL value will be recorded in the white or black lists according to the result of the verification test. This data will be employed afterward to detect the packets having spoofed IP addresses. The unmatched TTL counter will be employed to decrease the false positives based on the exact TTL matching filtering principle. The V-Node ensures that the unmatched TTL counter related to the source address does not exceed the determined threshold value (Al-Haidari et al., 2012).

The limitation to this framework is the increasing in the end-to-end latency, as it checks every packet that arrives at the firewall.

4.6.4 In-Cloud EDDoS Mitigation Web Service (Scrubber Service)

This framework has been introduced as an on-demand service. It depends on the In-Cloud Scrubber Service that generates and verifies the Client puzzles (crypto puzzles) used at two different levels of difficulty according to the type of attack against the protected system to authenticate the clients. The user must solve the crypto puzzle by brute force method. The system can be switched either to suspected mode or normal mode. The service provider selects the mode depending on the type of attack against its network. In the suspected mode, an on-demand request is required to be sent to the In-Cloud eDDoS mitigation service (Kumar et al., 2012). Figure 10 shows the framework architecture.

In a Scrubber Service-generated puzzle, the server launches the partial hash input and hash output and sends them to the user according to the following equation:

$H(X||k)=Y$

The puzzle solution is the value of k while the values of X, Y, and the hash function h () are provided to the user. The number of bits that construct the value of k determines the difficulty of the puzzle. This means the smaller k size renders the solution of the puzzle much easier and vice versa.

The framework mechanism can be described in the following steps:

1. The Bandwidth load and Server load determine the mode of the service, which either be
   a. Normal mode or
   b. Suspected Mode. The suspected mode can be either High-rated DDoS attack or Low-Rated DDoS attack.
2. The Normal mode is running if the web server is under normal situation.
3. If the server resources depletion exceeds an acceptable limit and the bandwidth traffic is high, then a high-rated DDoS attack is anticipated. In this case, the service will be switched to the suspected mode, and an on-demand request is delivered to the scrubber service, which creates and verifies a hard puzzle.
4. If the server resources depletion exceeds an acceptable limit while the bandwidth traffic is normal or less than the threshold, then a low-rated DDoS attack is anticipated. In this case, the service will be switched to the suspected mode, and an on-demand request is delivered to the scrubber service, which creates and verifies a moderate puzzle. Moreover, the web server will reduce the timeout period for the current requests (Kumar et al., 2012).

This framework depends on the puzzle concept approaches only. The puzzle servers are used mostly to check the network-layer DDoS attacks, which are easier in detection than the application-layer

Figure 10. In-cloud eDDoS mitigation web service framework
(Based on Kumar et al., 2012).

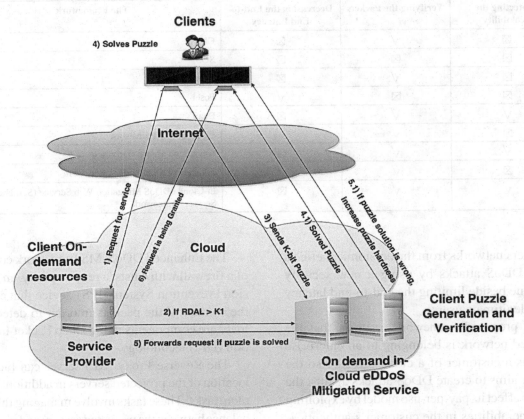

attacks. The framework focuses on the bandwidth load more than the server load. This means that its developers believe that the application-layer attack is more important as it is more harmful in impact and more difficult in detection. The limitation of this solution is that the end-to-end latency issue still exists as every packet has to be verified.

4.7 Existing Solutions Evaluation

After browsing the DDoS and EDoS countermeasures, there is a need to compare their performance based on the determined aspects, which are decreasing the end-to-end latency, verifying the packets and protecting the scalability. So, table 2 compares the DDoS and EDoS-Countermeasures according to the features that designated at the beginning of this section.

Hence, it is noticed that the existing techniques focused on some aspects and ignored or failed to meet the requirements of others. Therefore, a new framework is designed by the author in a way that considers the above features in order to fill this gap.

4.8 The Enhanced DDoS-MS Framework

As shown above, there is no solution proposed to encounter DDoS attacks, and their economical version (EDoS) attacks with providing limiting the end-to-end latency in addition to verifying the packet sources and protecting the cloud scalability. So, the framework is proposed in order to fill this gap. The contribution in this work is providing a proactive protection of the cloud provider on their

Table 2. Comparison between the previous frameworks' performance

Protecting the Scalability	Verifying the Packets	Decreasing the End-to-End Latency	The Framework
☒	√	☒	CLAD
☒	☒	☒	SOS
☒	√	☒	WebSOS
☒	☒	√	Fosel
√	√	☒	DaaS
☒	√	√	EDoS-Shield framework
√	√	☒	Sandar and Shenai framework
☒	√	√	Enhanced DDoS-Shield Framework
√	√	☒	In-Cloud eDDoS Mitigation Web Service (Scrubber Service) framework

customers networks from the economical effects of the DDoS attacks by using a new security technique beside limiting the end-to-end latency for the legitimate users.

The proposed framework assumes that the protected network is belonging to an enterprise which is a customer of a cloud provider so the attacker aims to create DDoS attacks against the cloud to affect its pay-per-use model by exploiting the vulnerabilities in the customer's authentication system.

The framework tests the first packet which comes from any source, assuming that the IP addresses are static and the packets are not fragmented, so the TTL values will not be changed according to the different paths the fragmented packets can take to reach to the destination.

The proposed framework is built in a way that gains the benefits from the strong aspects of these previous methods while avoiding or improving the weak aspects. It is designed to mitigate the economical effects of DDoS attacks against cloud providers and customers. It focuses on decreasing the end-to-end latency besides encountering attacks.

Therefore, the framework is proposed to encounter such attacks and is called Enhanced DDoS-Mitigation System (Enhanced DDoS-MS).

The Enhanced DDoS-MS framework consists of a firewall with 4 lists, a reverse proxy, an Intrusion Prevention System (IPS) device that checks the content of the packets in order to detect any malware components using Deep Packet Inspection (DPI) technology.

The Reverse Proxy (RP) server can hide the location of the protected servers in addition to two more tasks. These tasks involve managing the load balance between the protected servers and monitoring the traffic rate in order to detect any potential DDoS attacks against the protected servers, by designating a pre-determined threshold value for the number of requests coming from any source. The detection process is based on a pre-determined threshold value according to the number of requests in a specific interval (Lin et al., 2008).

With this improvement, only the first packet will be tested by the verifier node while the remaining packets will be monitored by an IPS and an RP. The firewall has two more lists- suspicious and malicious lists. The addresses of the sources of packets are placed on the firewall lists depending on the result of the verification and monitoring processes.

If the IPS detects any malware in the packet, its IP address will be placed on the Malicious List (ML). The last layer of the monitoring

Figure 11. DDoS-MS architecture

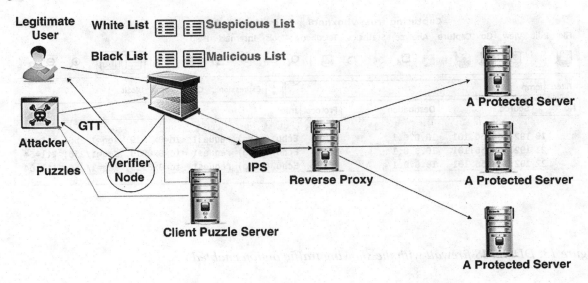

process done by the Reverse Proxy (RP). It detects the suspicious users who try to overwhelm the system by sending a huge number of requests without drawing attention to the previous monitoring layers. In this case, the source of such attempts will be placed on the Suspicious List (SL).

Any packet coming from a suspicious user to the firewall will be forwarded to the client puzzle server which will send a crypto puzzle to its source. The purpose of using the puzzles in this regard is to delay the requests of this suspicious user by consuming a specific time interval and computational power on his or her side in order to protect the system from the potential DDoS attack. Therefore, the puzzles will be used in this framework as a reactive step, unlike its usage in the DDoS-MS framework. Moreover, it will be used only for suspicious users.

Thus, the legitimate user will not be forced to be tested after passing the verification process, neither in the application layer using a GTT test, nor in the network layer using puzzles, unless his or her legitimacy is suspected as a result of exceeding the threshold of the traffic rate, or being

malicious when their packets contain malware, or changing the packets' TTL values. It will enhance the concept of decreasing the end-to-end latency for legitimate users.

The reason for the use of three layers of verification is to distribute the protecting tasks among them and to enable each verifier and monitor to perform a specific security task (Alosaimi & Al-Begain, 2013). Figure 11 shows the Enhanced DDoS-MS framework's architecture.

Previous version of Enhanced DDoS-MS named as DDoS-MS, was published and evaluated. Evaluation was based on real testing. Protected area is demonstrated as IP address 10.0.0.1/8, while the entering point which is a firewall is presented as IP address 192.168.56.1/24. As an example ICMP packet were used, more precisely Ping request were sending from the outside world, through the DDoS-MS to the protected area. Figure 12 shows a Wireshark snapshot of firewall, on the outside interface. One should notice that the same IP address suddenly change TTL from value 32 to 64. In this particular configuration, where the path of the packet in not changed, it suggests an attacker, which spoofed the user's IP address.

Figure 12. Snapshot of incoming ICMP messages from the outside world into the protected area

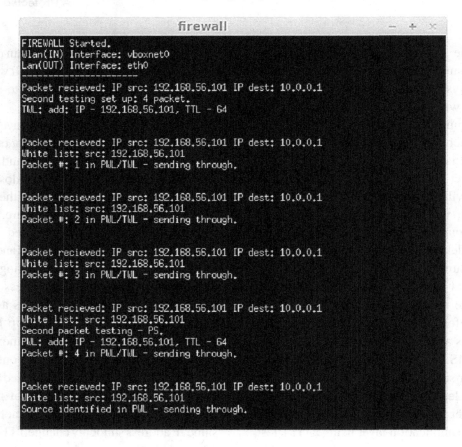

Figure 13. DDoS-MS firewall with the showing traffic option enabled

Firewall eliminated the packets from the attacker and let go through just the packets which proved that they were send from the user. Any packets that did not pass this condition were dropped on the outside interface. Therefore the malicious traffic did not enter the protected area.

The firewall of the DDoS-MS has an option for displaying the current traffic into the terminal, which is possible to see in Figure 13. Administrator can see each packet, which is managed by the entry point of DDoS-MS. Each packet will be described with source IP address, destination IP address and TTL value of the packet. Firewall will also inform the administrator about the status of the packet. If the packet came from the user it will then be classified as non-malicious traffic, therefore, placed into Temporary While List (TWL) or the Permanent White List (PWL) itself. In the case of attack, the firewall will inform the administrator about it in the same manner.

5. FUTURE RESEARCH DIRECTIONS

The research in the cloud security in general and in protecting against DDoS attacks in particular will continue evolving as the cloud itself grows. Developing the security aspects in the cloud will remove the concerns in the potential customers and attract them to migrate to the cloud. In this section, the future trends in the cloud security will be presented in terms of general cloud security, DDoS and EDoS countermeasures, and the proposed framework (Enhanced DDoS-MS).

5.1 General Cloud Security

There is a need to implement proactive monitoring techniques for the cloud applications. Such methods exist currently. However, proposing a predictive software and technology in this regard will render such methods more accurate and robust. As a result, businesses will be able to expect the security threats and prevent disasters by mitigating the negative impacts on their networks. Moreover, this development will avert downtime and render the company secured. This will encourage more customers to subscribe to the cloud.

Another motivation for the companies to migrate to the cloud as a result of security improvements is the role of the cloud in the disaster recovery. If this aspect improved well in the future, cloud will provide a faster and remote access disaster recovery and that enables the customers to recover their data within minutes instead of hours.

The physical security of the data centres is an important aspect of the overall cloud security. So, developing advanced alarm systems can control the physical access to the data centre. This may include using electronic pass and biometric scans. Besides that, the legal contracts and the security policies must be revised by the lawyers in order to ensure that they cover all security related aspects that form concerns for the current and future customers with regard to transparency, data deletion, data control, compliance, and the physical access management.

Protecting data in motion is another important element to improve cloud security. Therefore, improving the VPN technology can assists in this regard especially with the new firewall policies that limit the VPN traffics to specific ports and IP addresses.

The encryption plays an important role in the security field in general and in the cloud computing in particular. The future trends in the encryption field are focused on increasing the encryption parameters from the current 256-bit and that will provide more security to the cloud systems (Alexandre & Calderon, 2013; Vladimirov, 2014).

5.2 Future Threat/Work/ Defense Mechanisms Work for DDoS

The DDoS countermeasures need to be more proactive and more accurate by increasing detection rate for the malicious users and decreasing the false positive rate for the legitimate users as a result of the implemented detection policy. Moreover, combining reactive and proactive techniques can provide more robust solutions to the DoS problem. The application-layer DDoS attacks must get more attention in the future research because it is difficult to be detected, and therefore it is more harmful than the transport-layer and network-layer DDoS attacks.

The firewalls, Intrusion Detection Systems (IDS), Intrusion Prevention Systems (IPS) are used in the current countermeasures for packets inspection, malware detection, traffic monitoring, and requests filtering. Therefore, the improvement of these technologies by proposing next-generation versions of them will be reflected in enhancing the DDoS mitigation systems too.

With regard to the DDoS attacks in a cloud computing environment, the providers must give the threat of DDoS attacks the highest priority despite the huge resource pools that they have as the attackers develop their skills to launch hidden attacks that are difficult to detect or trace and, as a result, difficult to mitigate. In the EDoS regard, the solutions must be implemented in the customer's networks as proactive techniques to prevent the cloud from its edge. The current EDoS countermeasures are proposed to work on the provider's side and that can be considered as DDoS countermeasures there but cannot be effective to prevent the economical negative effects for the customer in the EDoS attacks. Furthermore, there is a need to pay attention to this kind of attack that threaten the cloud computing industry in the long term as the customers find themselves are paying for cloud services more than what they should pay for the in-house systems. Moreover, this overpayment is for services that the customers did not request. Therefore, they will withdraw from the service as a result of being victims in the short term of the economical effect of the DDoS attacks in the cloud environment.

5.3 Future Improvements of Enhanced DDoS-MS

The proposed framework in this chapter overcomes some of the shortcomings in the previous countermeasures in order to harden the defence mechanism against the DDoS and EDoS attacks. However, there are some aspects of the proposed framework that can be improved to include some situations that were not covered in the current version. These include:

1. *Improving the proposed framework to be able to involve the case of using dynamic IP addresses*: The decision to place the source of a packet (user or machine) onto the white list or the blacklist depends on their ability to pass the authentication tests. The requested details of any source include IP address and TTL value. So, if the IP address is dynamic due to using a dynamic allocation mode in the Dynamic Host Configuration Protocol (DHCP) server, then the source can be considered a new customer. This leads to losing its advantage if it is recorded on the white list, or ignoring the previous negative attempt if it is recorded on the black list. This point must be studied to determine its effect on the proposed framework's efficiency.

2. *Working with IP packet fragmentation*: If the packet is divided (fragmented) into a number of fragments, each one will get a different TTL value as a result of different paths being followed by packets to reach their destinations. This means the use of the white list and the blacklist is useless as the recorded TTL values are different from all or most TTL values from the same source. This aspect needs to be investigated more deeply in the future.

3. *Choosing more packets randomly for further tests*: Enhance the robustness of the framework by adopting the randomisation of selecting more packets for further tests can make the proposed framework more effective in achieving its objectives. It is very important to make the attackers prediction of the defence mechanism very difficult. This can be achieved by choosing more packets randomly to enhance the protection mechanism. Adopting the randomisation of selecting packets for additional verification can harden the adversary's prediction of the protection technique. The important thing in this regard is avoiding affecting the concept of limiting the end-to-end latency as it is a contribution of the work.

4. *Protecting the cloud customer's network that allows BYOD implementation within its internal network*: Bring Your Own Device (BYOD) depicts the phenomenon that has spread recently among several enterprises, both small and large. This trend is about allowing employees to bring their own mobile devices to their work location in order to access the enterprise database, file servers, and email. These devices include laptops, tablets and smart phones (Burke, 2011).

It will be hard for companies to avoid this trend, especially with the high requests from their employees to allow it. The employees think that BYOD is an attractive option which will increase their loyalty and productivity. The discussion is not about denying or allowing BYOD, nowadays it is about BYOD management (Burke, 2011).

The most observable benefit to the companies that adopt the BYOD is saving costs as a result of avoiding purchasing mobile devices for their employees. Moreover, productivity and loyalty among the employees will be increased, as they are more comfortable using their own devices, which may contain their preferred applications, files and websites. This augmentation of productivity, loyalty and satisfaction will support the company and facilitate accomplishing its targets (Burke, 2011).

The main problem concerns accessing organizational data from these devices, which are not owned or configured by the organization itself. Each type of device depends on a unique platform which has distinctive features. This requires the IT staff to be aware of all developments in the devices on the market in terms of newly issued types, updated features, or any upgraded software that might be provided. Even though the unified management's policies and techniques are applied, the accelerating developments in the field may generate loopholes in the security systems of organizations, especially in the interval between the emersion of new devices or features and the response of the IT department's members to that new development. The risks can come from outside the network's firewall like all other networks or from inside the network (behind its firewall). This is because the devices will be able to access the network from the internal environment, and the users may be diverse.

BYOD can expose the network to several risks. However, monitoring the devices traffic rates and contents instead of controlling the apps that are installed in these devices can provide more security to the network. Protecting the server (main modem) from such malicious packets coming from the mobile devices, under BYOD implementation, is a must in order to provide a proactive protection to the cloud provider on their customers networks in the BYOD age.

6. CONCLUSION

Cloud computing has been evolving through the last decade and has improved to be suitable for sustainable implementation in the technology and business world. In achieving this, security becomes increasingly of paramount importance as the impact of any security breach goes far beyond what was known so far. Many studies have dedicated more attention to cloud security in order to encounter the threats and mitigate their impacts. In this chapter, the importance of security for cloud users and providers has been clarified, the risks that threaten the cloud are presented, and the existing solutions for such risks are discussed.

The analysis of such threats shows that the denial of service attacks poses a permanent risk to the network in general and to the cloud in this regard. Therefore, the focus of the chapter was on discussing the denial of service attacks in terms of its concept, types, and impacts. In cloud environment, the denial of service attack has an economical effect that threats the cloud sustainability by exploiting its scalability to harm the cloud bills. In this case, it is called Economical Denial of Sustainability (EDoS) attack. This cloud-specific attack is explained, and its consequences are discussed. Afterwards, the existing countermeasures for both DoS and EDoS have been presented and evaluated. A comparison between the existing solutions according to limiting the end-to-end latency, protecting the scalability, and verifying the incoming requests is performed. The output of that comparison shows that there is no existing solution can mitigate the denial of service attacks with meeting the determined criteria in the comparison process. So, a new framework is proposed to fill this gap and is presented in details.

The future trends in the cloud computing security have been presented showing that there are many aspects that need to be improved to protect the cloud industry from malicious actions and to give it the sustainability in a changeable world.

REFERENCES

Ablett, E., Bellizzi, D., Byers, J., Cove, S., Dobrusin, M., Frey, A., & Hanke, J. (2014). *Encryption advantages and disadvantages*. Retrieved September 27, 2014, from http://networking116. wikispaces.com/Encryption+Advantages+and+ Disadvantages

Agarwal, A. (2010). *The legal issues around cloud computing*. Retrieved April 05, 2012, from http:// www.labnol.org/internet/cloud-computing-legal-issues/14120

Al-Haidari, F., Sqalli, M., & Salah, K. (2012). Enhanced EDoS-shield for mitigating EDoS attacks originating from spoofed IP addresses. In *Proceedings of the 2012 IEEE 11th International Conference on Trust, Security and Privacy in Computing and Communications* (pp. 1167–1174). IEEE. Retrieved from IEEE doi:10.1109/TrustCom.2012.146

Alexandre, P., & Calderon, A. (2013). *The future of cloud computing*. Retrieved October 01, 2014, from http://www.sitepoint.com/the-future-of-cloud-computing/

Alosaimi, W., & Al-Begain, K. (2013). An enhanced economical denial of sustainability mitigation system for the cloud. In *Proceedings of 2013 Seventh International Conference on Next Generation Mobile Apps, Services and Technologies* (pp. 19–25). Prague: CPS, IEEE. doi:10.1109/ NGMAST.2013.13

Aslan, T. (2012). *Cloud physical security considerations*. Retrieved April 15, 2012, from http:// thoughtsoncloud.com/index.php/2012/02/cloud-physical-security-considerations/

Beitollahi, H., & Deconinck, G. (2008). FOSeL: Filtering by helping an overlay security layer to mitigate DoS attacks. In *Proceedings of 2008 Seventh IEEE International Symposium on Network Computing and Applications* (pp. 19–28). IEEE. doi:10.1109/NCA.2008.23

Beitollahi, H., & Deconinck, G. (2012). Analyzing well-known countermeasures against distributed denial of service attacks. *Computer Communications*, *35*(11), 1312–1332. doi:10.1016/j.comcom.2012.04.008

Burke, J. (2011). *Bring your own device risks and rewards*. Retrieved June 29, 2012, from http://www.techrepublic.com/blog/tech-manager/bring-your-own-device-risks-and-rewards/7075

Chen, E. Y. (2005). Detecting TCP-based DDoS attacks by linear regression analysis. In *Signal Processing and Information Technology: Proceedings of the Fifth IEEE International Symposium* (pp. 381–386). Athens: IEEE. doi:10.1109/ISPIT.2005.1577127

Choi, Y., Oh, J., Jang, J., & Ryou, J. (2010). Integrated DDoS attack defense infrastructure for effective attack prevention. In *Proceedings of the Second IEEE International Conference on Information Technology Convergence and Services (ITCS)* (pp. 1–6). IEEE. doi:10.1109/ITCS.2010.5581263

Chopade, S. S., Pandey, K. U., & Bhade, D. S. (2013). Securing cloud servers against flooding based DDoS attacks. In *Proceedings of 2013 International Conference on Communication Systems and Network Technologies* (pp. 524–528). IEEE. doi:10.1109/CSNT.2013.114

Cmeier, & Mnovellino. (2013). *Virtualization vulnerabilities related to hypervisors*. Retrieved September 29, 2014, from http://cybersecurity.mit.edu/2013/10/virtualization-vulnerabilities-related-to hypervisors/

Cook, D., Morein, W., Keromytis, A., Misra, V., & Rubensteint, D. (2003). WebSOS: Protecting web servers from DDoS attacks. In *Proceedings of the 11th IEEE International Conference on Networks* (pp. 461–466). IEEE.

Douligeris, C., & Mitrokotsa, A. (2004). DDoS attacks and defense mechanisms: Classification and state-of-the-art. *Computer Networks*, *44*(5), 643–666. doi:10.1016/j.comnet.2003.10.003

Du, P., & Nakao, A. (2010). DDoS defense as a network service. In *Proceedings of 2010 IEEE Network Operations and Management Symposium - NOMS 2010* (pp. 894–897). IEEE. doi:10.1109/NOMS.2010.5488345

ENISA. (2009). *Cloud computing risk assessment*. Retrieved April 11, 2012, from http://www.enisa.europa.eu/act/rm/files/deliverables/cloud-computing-risk-assessment

Eugster, R. (2013). *".ch" survives DDoS attack unscathed*. Retrieved October 02, 2014, from https://www.switch.ch/about/news/2013/ddos.html

Fortinet, C. (2011). Network and physical security in the cloud. *Asia Cloud Forum*. Retrieved from http://www.asiacloudforum.com/content/network-and-physical-security-cloud

Foster, I., Zhao, Y., Raicu, I., & Lu, S. (2008). Cloud computing and grid computing 360-degree compared. In *Proceedings of Grid Computing Environments Workshop* (pp. 1–10). Academic Press. Retrieved from http://arxiv.org/ftp/arxiv/papers/0901/0901.0131.pdf

Heng, C. (2011). *Security issues in writing PHP scripts -And how PHP 4.1.0 / 4.2.0+ will change your scripts*. Retrieved April 10, 2012, from http://www.thesitewizard.com/archive/phpsecurity.shtml

Hoff, C. (2008). *Cloud computing security: From DDoS (distributed denial of service) to EDoS (economic denial of sustainability).* Retrieved January 17, 2013, from http://rationalsecurity. typepad.com/blog/2008/11/cloud-computing-security-from-ddos-distributed-denial-of-service-to-edos-economic-denial-of-sustaina.html

Hoff, C. (2009). *A couple of follow-ups on the EDoS (economic denial of sustainability) concept.* Retrieved January 25, 2013, from http:// rationalsecurity.typepad.com/blog/2009/01/a-couple-of-followups-on-my-edos-economic-denial-of-sustainability-concept.html

Intel. (2012). *What's holding back the cloud?* Retrieved September 26, 2014, from http://www. intel.com/content/www/us/en/cloud-computing/ whats-holding-back-the-cloud-peer-research-report.html

Jin, X., Keller, E., & Rexford, J. (2012). Virtual switching without a hypervisor for a more secure cloud. In *Proceedings of 2nd USENIX Workshop on Hot Topics in Management of Internet, Cloud, and Enterprise Networks and Services. Hot-ICE'12* (pp. 1–6). Academic Press.

Kaur, K., & Vashisht, S. (2013). Data separation issues in cloud computing. *International Journal for Advance Research in Engineering and Technology, 1*(X), 26–29.

Keromytis, A., Misra, V., & Rubenstein, D. (2002). SOS: Secure overlay services. In Proceedings of SIGCOMM (pp. 61–72). ACM.

Khan, A., Fisal, N., & Hussain, S. (2009). Man-in-the-middle attack and possible solutions on Wimax 802. 16j. In *Proceedings of International Conference on Recent and Emerging Advance Technologies in Engineering (iCREATE 2009).* Academic Press.

Khor, S., & Nakao, A. (2011). DaaS: DDoS mitigation-as-a-service. In *Proceedings of 2011 IEEE/IPSJ International Symposium on Applications and the Internet* (pp. 160–171). IEEE. doi:10.1109/SAINT.2011.30

Kumar, M., Sujatha, P., Kalva, V., Nagori, R., & Katukojwala, A. (2012). Mitigating economic denial of sustainability (EDoS) in cloud computing using in-cloud scrubber service. In *Proceedings of 2012 Fourth International Conference on Computational Intelligence and Communication Networks* (pp. 535–539). IEEE. doi:10.1109/ CICN.2012.149

Kumar, N., & Sharma, S. (2013). Study of intrusion detection system for DDoS attacks in cloud computing. In *Proceedings of 2013 Tenth International Conference on Wireless and Optical Communications Networks (WOCN)* (pp. 1–5). IEEE. doi:10.1109/WOCN.2013.6616255

Kuyoro, S., Ibikunle, F., & Awodele, O. (2011). Cloud computing security issues and challenges. *International Journal of Computer Networks, 3*(5), 247–252.

Lakshminarayanan, K., Adkins, D., Perrig, A., & Stoica, I. (2004). Taming IP packet flooding attacks. *Computer Communication Review, 34*(1), 45–50. doi:10.1145/972374.972383

Lin, C., Lee, C., Liu, J., & Chen, C. (2010). A detection scheme for flooding attack on application layer based on semantic concept. IEEE, 385–389.

Lin, C., Liu, J., & Lien, C. (2008). Detection method based on reverse proxy against web flooding attacks. In *Proceedings of the Eighth International Conference on Intelligent Systems Design and Applications* (pp. 281–284). Academic Press. doi:10.1109/ISDA.2008.72

Liu, W. (2009). Research on DoS attack and detection programming. In *Proceedings of 2009 Third International Symposium on Intelligent Information Technology Application* (pp. 207–210). IEEE. doi:10.1109/IITA.2009.165

Meier, J., Mackman, A., Dunner, M., Vasireddy, S., & Escamilla, R. (2003). *Improving web application security threats and countermeasures*. Retrieved April 08, 2012, from http://msdn. microsoft.com/en-us/library/ff649874.aspx

Mell, P., & Grance, T. (2009). The NIST Definition of Cloud Computing. *National Institute of Standards and Technology, 53*(6), 50. Retrieved from http://csrc.nist.gov/groups/SNS/cloud-computing/cloud-def-v15.doc

Mopari, I., Pukale, S., & Dhore, M. (2009). Detection of DDoS attack and defense against IP spoofing. In *Proceedings of the International Conference on Advances in Computing, Communication and Control - ICAC3 '09* (pp. 489–493). New York: ACM. doi:10.1145/1523103.1523200

Morein, W., Stavrou, A., Cook, D., Keromytis, A., Misra, V., & Rubenstein, D. (2003). Using graphic turing tests to counter automated DDoS attacks against web servers. In *Proceedings of the 10th ACM Conference on Computer and Communication Security - CCS '03* (p. 8). New York: ACM Press. doi:10.1145/948109.948114

Mukundrao, J., & Vikram, G. (2011). Enhancing security in cloud computing. *Information and Knowledge Management, 1*(1), 40–45.

Newman, R. (2006). Cybercrime, identity theft, and fraud: practicing safe internet - Network security threats and vulnerabilities. *International Journal of Computer Applications ACM, 9*(12), 11–15.

Park, Y. H., Hong, S., & Ryu, J. (2010). An effective defense mechanism against DoS/DDoS attacks in flow-based routers. In *Proceedings of the 8th International Conference on Advances in Mobile Computing and Multimedia - MoMM '10* (pp. 442–446). New York: ACM Press. doi:10.1145/1971519.1971595

Piscitello, D. (2011). *Anatomy of a DNS DDoS amplification attack*. Retrieved September 30, 2014, from http://www.watchguard.com/infocenter/editorial/41649.asp

Raju, B., Swarna, P., & Rao, M. (2011). Privacy and security issues of cloud computing. *International Journal (Toronto, Ont.), 1*(2), 128–136.

Ramgovind, S., Eloff, M., & Smith, E. (2010). The management of security in cloud computing. In Proceedings of Information Security for South Africa (ISSA) (pp. 1–7). IEEE. doi:10.1109/ISSA.2010.5588290

Rittinghouse, J., & Ransome, J. (2010). *Cloud computing: Implementation, management, and security*. Taylor and Francis Group, LLC.

Roberts, J., & Al-Hamdani, W. (2011). Who can you trust in the cloud? In *Proceedings of the 2011 Information Security Curriculum Development Conference on InfoSecCD 11* (Vol. 43, pp. 15–19). ACM Press. doi:10.1145/2047456.2047458

Rouse, M. (2004). *Virtualization sprawl (VM sprawl)*. Retrieved September 26, 2014, from http://whatis.techtarget.com/definition/virtualization-sprawl-virtual-server-sprawl

Sabahi, F. (2011). Virtualization-level security in cloud computing. In Proceedings of Communications Software and Networks (ICCS) (pp. 250–254). IEEE. doi:10.1109/ICCSN.2011.6014716

Sandar, V., & Shenai, S. (2012). Economic denial of sustainability (EDoS) in cloud services using HTTP and XML based DDoS attacks. *International Journal of Computers and Applications*, *41*(20), 11–16. doi:10.5120/5807-8063

Sangroya, A., Kumar, S., Dhok, J., & Varma, V. (2010). Towards analyzing data security risks in cloud computing environments. *ICISTM*, 255–265.

Schwartz, M. (2012). *New virtualization vulnerability allows escape to hypervisor attacks*. Retrieved September 28, 2014, from http://www.darkreading.com/risk-management/new-virtualization-vulnerability-allows-escape-to-hypervisor-attacks/d/d-id/1104823?

Sitaram, D., & Manjunath, G. (2012). Cloud security requirements and best practices. In *Moving to the cloud: Developing apps in the new world of cloud computing* (p. 309). Elsevier.

Slack, E. (2011). *How do you know that "delete" means delete in cloud storage?* Retrieved April 14, 2012, from http://www.storage-switzerland.com/Articles/Entries/2011/8/16_How_do_you_know_that_Delete_means_Delete_in_Cloud_Storage.html

Sqalli, M., Al-Haidari, F., & Salah, K. (2011). EDoS-shield - A two-steps mitigation technique against EDoS attacks in cloud computing. In *Proceedings of 2011 Fourth IEEE International Conference on Utility and Cloud Computing* (pp. 49–56). IEEE. doi:10.1109/UCC.2011.17

Srivatsa, M., Iyengar, A., Yin, J., & Liu, L. (2008). Mitigating application-level denial of service attacks on Web servers. *ACM Transactions on the Web*, *2*(3), 1–49. doi:10.1145/1377488.1377489

Templeton, S., & Levitt, K. (2003). Detecting spoofed packets. In *Proceedings of the DARPA Information Survivability Conference and Exposition (DISCEX'03)* (pp. 164 – 175). Academic Press. doi:10.1109/DISCEX.2003.1194882

The S. L. A. (2007). *The service level agreement*. Retrieved September 27, 2014, from http://www.sla-zone.co.uk/

Trappler, T. (2012). When your data's in the cloud, is it still your data? *Computer World*. Retrieved April 07, 2012, from http://www.computerworld.com/s/article/9223479/When_your_data_s_in_the_cloud_is_it_still_your_data_

UCRIVERSIDE. (2011). *Data sanitization*. Retrieved October 01, 2014, from http://cnc.ucr.edu/security/datasan.html

Vaidya, V. (2009). *Virtualization vulnerabilities and threats: A solution white paper*. Retrieved April 13, 2012, from http://www.redcannon.com/vDefense/VM_security_wp.pdf

Virtualizationadmin. (2008). *What is VM sprawl?* Retrieved September 27, 2014, from http://www.virtualizationadmin.com/faq/vm-sprawl.html

Vladimirov, R. (2014). *The future of cloud computing: Emerging trends*. Retrieved October 05, 2014, from http://smartdatacollective.com/roman-vladimirov/194086/future-cloud-computing-emerging-trends

Xie, Y., & Yu, S. (2009). Monitoring the application-layer DDoS attacks for popular websites. *IEEE/ACM Transactions on Networking*, *17*(1), 15–25. doi:10.1109/TNET.2008.925628

Yatagai, T., Isohara, T., & Sasase, I. (2007). Detection of HTTP-GET flood attack based on analysis of page access behavior. In *Proceedings of IEEE Pacific Rim Conference on Communications, Computers and Signal Processing* (pp. 232–235). IEEE.

Zhang, F., Geng, J., Qin, Z., & Zhou, M. (2007). Detecting the DDoS attacks based on SYN proxy and hop-count filter. In *Proceedings of International Conference on Communications, Circuits and Systems ICCCAS 2007*. (pp. 457–461). Academic Press. doi:10.1109/ICCCAS.2007.6251605

Zhou, M., Zhang, R., Xie, W., Qian, W., & Zhou, A. (2010). Security and privacy in cloud computing: A survey. In *Proceedings of 2010 Sixth International Conference on Semantics Knowledge and Grids* (pp. 105–112). IEEE. doi:10.1109/SKG.2010.19

ADDITIONAL READING

Beitollahi, H., & Deconinck, G. (2012). Analyzing well-known countermeasures against distributed denial of service attacks. *Computer Communications*, *35*(11), 1312–1332. doi:10.1016/j.comcom.2012.04.008

Douligeris, C., & Mitrokotsa, A. (2004). DDoS attacks and defense mechanisms: Classification and state-of-the-art. *Computer Networks*, *44*(5), 643–666. doi:10.1016/j.comnet.2003.10.003

Jin, X., Keller, E., & Rexford, J. (2012). Virtual Switching Without a Hypervisor for a More Secure Cloud. In *2nd USENIX Workshop on Hot Topics in Management of Internet, Cloud, and Enterprise Networks and Services. Hot-ICE'12* (pp. 1–6).

Kaur, K., & Vashisht, S. (2013). Data Separation Issues in Cloud Computing. *International Journal for Advance Research in Engineering and Technology*, *1*(X), 26–29.

Krutz, R., & Vines, R. (2010). *Cloud security a comprehensive guide to secure cloud computing*. Indianapolis, Ind.: Wiley Pub.

Kuyoro, S., Ibikunle, F., & Awodele, O. (2011). Cloud Computing Security Issues and Challenges. [IJCN]. *International Journal of Computer Networks*, *3*(5), 247–252.

Lin, C., Lee, C., Liu, J., & Chen, C. (2010). A Detection Scheme for Flooding Attack on Application Layer Based on Semantic Concept. IEEE, 385–389.

Liu, W. (2009). Research on DoS Attack and Detection Programming. In *2009 Third International Symposium on Intelligent Information Technology Application* (pp. 207–210). IEEE. doi:10.1109/IITA.2009.165

Meier, J., Mackman, A., Dunner, M., Vasireddy, S., Escamilla, R., & M.A. (2003). Improving Web Application Security Threats and Countermeasures. Retrieved April 08, 2012, from http://msdn. microsoft.com/en-us/library/ff649874.aspx

Newman, R. (2006). Cybercrime, Identity Theft, and Fraud: Practicing Safe Internet - Network Security Threats and Vulnerabilities. *International Journal of Computer Applications ACM*, *9*(12), 11–15.

Rittinghouse, J., & Ransome, J. (2010). *Cloud Computing: Implementation, Management, and Security*. USA: Taylor and Francis Group, LLC.

Sitaram, D., & Manjunath, G. (2012). Cloud Security Requirements and Best Practices. In *MOVING TO THE CLOUD: Developing Apps in the New World of Cloud Computing* (p. 309). USA: Elsevier.

Srivatsa, M., Iyengar, A., Yin, J., & Liu, L. (2008). Mitigating application-level denial of service attacks on Web servers. *ACM Transactions on the Web*, *2*(3), 1–49. doi:10.1145/1377488.1377489

UCRIVERSIDE. (2011). Data Sanitization. Retrieved October 01, 2014, from http://cnc.ucr.edu/security/datasan.html

Winkler, J. (2011). *Securing the cloud cloud computer security techniques and tactics*. Burlington, MA: Elsevier.

KEY TERMS AND DEFINITIONS

CAPTCHA: It is Turing test, which is using challenge – response mechanism to distinguish between the humans and computers. Websites are using it as a protection against automatic manipulating and accessing its content. Graphical representation of the test is difficult to recognize by computer. However a person has no such problem.

Crypto Puzzles: Cryptographic test that requires from the user to spend user's resources to solve the puzzle before the server will dedicate its resource to the user's request. If the answer is current, user will be able to gain access to the server.

DDoS: This term is the abbreviation of Distributed Denial of Service. This is the amplified DoS attack that results from generating malicious actions by many attackers in the same time to increase the possibility of attack success and render the tracing of the source of attack more difficult.

DNS: It states for Domain Name System, which is a hierarchical database of domain names, IP addresses and other network information. The most known service is translating internet domain names to particular IP addresses and vice versa.

DoS: This term stands for Denial of Service. It is a situation that results from malicious actions against computer network performed by adversaries to overwhelm the network server in order to prevent the legitimate users from accessing the network and get their required services.

EDoS: It stands for Economical Denial of Sustainability. It is the economical version of the DoS attacks in the cloud computing environment. It is a cloud-specific issue that affects the cloud customer's bill exploiting the scalability of the cloud services. It can be performed by generating many faked requests from the customer's side. So, the provider offers these services, that the customer did not request, and add their costs to the customer's bill.

SQL Injection: This is an attack, which is focused into website using database. Attacker inject malicious SQL query into the input field on the website, which will change the meaning of the original query. Through insufficient check of input values entered by the attacker, the website can be breached.

Compilation of References

Ablett, E., Bellizzi, D., Byers, J., Cove, S., Dobrusin, M., Frey, A., & Hanke, J. (2014). *Encryption advantages and disadvantages.* Retrieved September 27, 2014, from http://networking116.wikispaces.com/Encryption+Advantages+and+Disadvantages

Abramson, D., Buyya, R., & Giddy, J. (2002). A computational economy for grid computing and its implementation in the Nimrod-G resource broker. *Future Generation Computer Systems*, *18*(8), 1061–1074. doi:10.1016/S0167-739X(02)00085-7

Active, M. Q. (2014). *Messaging and integration pattern provider.* Retrieved from http://activemq.apache.org/

Adamczyk, P., Smith, P., Johnson, R., & Hafiz, M. (2011). REST and web services: In theory and in practice. In E. Wilde & C. Pautasso (Eds.), *REST: From research to practice* (pp. 35–57). New York, NY: Springer. doi:10.1007/978-1-4419-8303-9_2

Adra, B., Blank, A., Gieparda, M., Haust, J., Stadler, O., & Szerdi, D. (2004). Advanced power virtualization on ibm eserver p5 servers: Introduction and basic configuration. IBM Corp.

Adriansyah, A., van Dongen, B., & van der Aalst, W. (2010). Towards robust conformance checking. In M. Muehlen & J. Su (Eds.), *Business process management workshops* (pp. 122–133). Berlin, Germany: Springer.

Agarwal, A. (2010). *The legal issues around cloud computing.* Retrieved April 05, 2012, from http://www.labnol.org/internet/cloud-computing-legal-issues/14120

Aggarwal, C., & Han, J. (2013). A survey of RFID data processing. In C. Aggarwal (Ed.), *Managing and mining sensor data* (pp. 349–382). New York, NY: Springer US. doi:10.1007/978-1-4614-6309-2_11

Agrawal, R., Imieliński, T., & Swami, A. (1993). Mining association rules between sets of items in large databases. *SIGMOD Record*, *22*(2), 207–216. doi:10.1145/170036.170072

Agrawal, S., Bose, S. K., & Sundarrajan, S. (2009). Grouping genetic algorithm for solving the server consolidation problem with conflicts. In *Proceedings of the First ACM/SIGEVO Summit on Genetic and Evolutionary Computation.* ACM. doi:10.1145/1543834.1543836

Ahuja, S., & Rolli, A. (2012, June). Exploring the convergence of mobile computing with cloud computing. *Journal of Network and Communication Technologies*, *1*(1).

Alexandre, P., & Calderon, A. (2013). *The future of cloud computing.* Retrieved October 01, 2014, from http://www.sitepoint.com/the-future-of-cloud-computing/

Al-Fares, M., Loukissas, A., & Vahdat, A. (2008). A scalable, commodity data center network architecture. *Computer Communication Review*, *38*(4), 63–74. doi:10.1145/1402946.1402967

Al-Haidari, F., Sqalli, M., & Salah, K. (2012). Enhanced EDoS-shield for mitigating EDoS attacks originating from spoofed IP addresses. In *Proceedings of the 2012 IEEE 11th International Conference on Trust, Security and Privacy in Computing and Communications* (pp. 1167–1174). IEEE. Retrieved from IEEE doi:10.1109/TrustCom.2012.146

Alizadeh, M., Greenberg, A., Maltz, D. A., & Padhye, J. (2010). Data center TCP (DCTCP). In *Proceedings of ACM SIGCOMM.* ACM.

Almeida, A., Dantas, F., Cavalcante, E., & Batista, T. (2014). A branch-and-bound algorithm for autonomic adaptation of multi-cloud applications. In *Proceedings ofIEEE/ACM International Symposium on Cluster, Cloud and Grid Computing (CCGrid)*. IEEE/ACM. doi:10.1109/CCGrid.2014.25

Almeida, J., Almeida, V., Ardagna, D., Cunha, I., Francalanci, C., & Trubian, M. (2010). Joint admission control and resource allocation in virtualized servers. *Journal of Parallel and Distributed Computing*, *70*(4), 344–362. doi:10.1016/j.jpdc.2009.08.009

Alosaimi, W., & Al-Begain, K. (2013). An enhanced economical denial of sustainability mitigation system for the cloud. In *Proceedings of2013 Seventh International Conference on Next Generation Mobile Apps, Services and Technologies* (pp. 19–25). Prague: CPS, IEEE. doi:10.1109/NGMAST.2013.13

Al-Riyami, S. S., & Paterson, K. G. (2003). Certificateless public key cryptography. *Advances in Cryptology - ASIACRYPT, 2894*, 452-473.

Alverson, B., Froese, E., Kaplan, L., & Roweth, D. (2014). *Cray XC series network*. Academic Press.

Alverson, R., Roweth, D., & Kaplan, L. (2010). The gemini system interconnect. In *Proceedings of High Performance Interconnects (HOTI)* (pp. 83–87). IEEE. doi:10.1109/HOTI.2010.23

Amarasinghe, S., Hall, M., Lethin, R., Pingali, K., Quinlan, D., Sarkar, V., & Snir, M. et al. (2011). Exascale programming challenges. In *Proceedings of the Workshop on Exascale Programming Challenges*. U.S Department of Energy, Office of Science, Office of Advanced Scientific Computing Research (ASCR).

Ananthanarayanan, G., Agarwal, S., Kandula, S., Greenberg, A., Stoica, I., Harlan, D., & Harris, E. (2011). Scarlett: Coping with skewed content popularity in MapReduce clusters. In *Proceedings of the Sixth Conference on Computer Systems*. ACM. doi:10.1145/1966445.1966472

Ang, T. F., Ng, W. K., Ling, T. C., Por, L. Y., & Liew, C. S. (2009). A bandwidth-aware job grouping-based scheduling on grid environment. *Information Technology Journal*, *8*(3), 372–377. doi:10.3923/itj.2009.372.377

Arabnejad, H., & Barbosa, J. (2012). *Fairness resource sharing for dynamic workflow scheduling on heterogeneous systems*. IEEE. doi:10.1109/ISPA.2012.94

Argonne National Laboratory. (2015). *MPICH2: High-performance and widely portable MPI* (version 3.1.4) [Software]. Available from http://www.mcs.anl.gov/research/projects/mpich2/

Armbrust, M., Fox, A., Griffith, R., Joseph, A. D., Katz, R. H., Konwinski, A., Lee, G., Patterson, D. A., Rabkin, A., & Zaharia, M. (2009). *Above the clouds: A Berkeley view of cloud computing*. Technical Report. Academic Press.

Armbrust, M., Stoica, I., Zaharia, M., Fox, A., Griffith, R., Joseph, A. D., & Rabkin, A. et al. (2010). A view of cloud computing. *Communications of the ACM*, *53*(4), 50–58. doi:10.1145/1721654.1721672

Armour, G. C., & Buffa, E. S. (1963). A heuristic algorithm and simulation approach to relative location of facilities. *Management Science*, *9*(2), 294–309. doi:10.1287/mnsc.9.2.294

Aslan, T. (2012). *Cloud physical security considerations*. Retrieved April 15, 2012, from http://thoughtsoncloud.com/index.php/2012/02/cloud-physical-security-considerations/

Aspnes, J., Kirsch, J., & Krishnamurthy, A. (2004). Load balancing and locality in range-queriable data structures. In *Proceedings of the Twenty-Third Annual ACM Symposium on Principles of Distributed Computing*. ACM. doi:10.1145/1011767.1011785

Ateniese, G., Fu, K., Green, M., & Hohenberger, S. (2006). Improved proxy re-encryption schemes with applications to secure distributed storage. *ACM Transactions on Information and System Security*, *9*(1), 1–30. doi:10.1145/1127345.1127346

Athanasopoulos, G., Tsalgatidou, A., & Pantazoglou, M. (2006). Interoperability among heterogeneous services. In *Proceedings ofInternational Conference on Services Computing* (pp. 174-181). Piscataway, NJ: IEEE Society Press.

Attrapadung, N., & Imai, H. (2009). Conjunctive broadcast and attribute-based encryption. *Proceeding of Pairing-Based Cryptography-Pairing*, *5671*, 248–265. doi:10.1007/978-3-642-03298-1_16

Aulwes, R. T., Daniel, D. J., Desai, N. N., Graham, R. L., Risinger, L. D., Taylor, M. A., . . . Sukalski, M. W. (2004). Architecture of LA-MPI, a network-fault-tolerant MPI. In *Proceedings ofInternational Parallel and Distributed Processing Symposium*. Academic Press.

Avahi. (2007). *Avahi daemon* [Computer software]. Retrieved from http://avahi.org

Azodomolky, S., Wieder, P., & Yahyapour, R. (2013). Cloud computing networking: Challanges and Opportunities for Innovations. *IEEE Comm. Magazine*, 54-62.

Baader, F et al. (Eds.). (2010). *The description logic handbook: theory, implementation, and applications* (2nd ed.). Cambridge, UK: Cambridge university press.

Baccarelli, E., & Biagi, M. (2003). Optimized power allocation and signal shaping for interference-limited multi-antenna 'ad hoc' networks. *Personal Wireless Communications*, 138-152.

Baccarelli, E., Biagi, M., Pelizzoni, C., & Cordeschi, N. (2007). Optimized power allocation for multiantenna systems impaired by multiple access interference and imperfect channel estimation. *IEEE Transactions on Vehicular Technology*, *56*(5), 3089–3105. doi:10.1109/TVT.2007.900514

Baccarelli, E., Cordeschi, N., & Patriarca, T. (2012). QoS stochastic traffic engineering for the wireless support of real-time streaming applications. *Computer Networks*, *56*(1), 287–302. doi:10.1016/j.comnet.2011.09.010

Balasubramanian, N., Balasubramanian, A., & Venkataramani, A. (2009). Energy consumption in mobile phones: A measurement study and implications for network applications. In *Proceedings of IMC '09: The 9th ACM SIGCOMM Internet Measurement Conference* (pp. 280–293). New York, NY: ACM. doi:10.1145/1644893.1644927

Balaton, Z., Kacsuk, P., & Podhorszki, N. (2001). Application monitoring in the grid with GRM and prove. In *Proc. of ICCS* (Vol. 2073, pp. 253-262). Springer Berlin Heidelberg. doi:10.1007/3-540-45545-0_34

Balaton, Z., & Gombs, G. (2003). Resource and job monitoring in the grid. In *Proceedings of Euro-par'03* (Vol. 2790, pp. 404–411). Springer Berlin Heidelberg. doi:10.1007/978-3-540-45209-6_59

Bala, V., Bruck, J., Bryant, R., Cypher, R., de Jong, P., Elustondo, P., & Snir, M. et al. (1994). The IBM external user interface for scalable parallel systems. *Parallel Computing*, *20*(4), 445–462. doi:10.1016/0167-8191(94)90022-1

Baliga, J., Ayre, R. W. A., Hinton, K., & Tucker, R. S. (2011). Green Cloud Computing: Balancing Energy in Processing, Storage and Transport. *Proceedings of the IEEE*, *99*(1), 149–167. doi:10.1109/JPROC.2010.2060451

Balis, B., Bubak, M., Funika, W., Szepieniec, T., & Wismller, R. (2002). An infrastructure for grid application monitoring. In Recent advances in parallel virtual machine and message passing interface (pp. 41 - 49). Academic Press.

Balis, B., Bubak, M., Funika, W., Szepieniec, T., Wismller, R., & Radecki, M. (2004). Monitoring grid applications with grid-enabled omis monitor. In *Grid computing* (Vol. 2970, pp. 230–239). Springer Berlin Heidelberg. doi:10.1007/978-3-540-24689-3_29

Ballami, H., Costa, P., Karagiannis, T., & Rowstron, A. (2011). Towards predicable datacenter networks. In *Proceedings of SIGCOMM '11*. ACM.

Balter, M. H. (2013). *Performance modeling and design of computer systems*. Cambridge Press.

Barham, P., Dragovic, B., Fraser, K., Hand, S., Harris, T., Ho, A., & Warfield, A. et al. (2003). Xen and the art of virtualization. *Operating Systems Review*, *37*(5), 164–177. doi:10.1145/1165389.945462

Bazaraa, M. S., Sherali, H. D., & Shetty, C. M. (2006). *Nonlinear programming* (3rd ed.). Wiley. doi:10.1002/0471787779

Becke, M., Rathgeb, E. P., Werner, S., Rungeler, I., Tuxen, M., & Stewart, R. (2013). Data channel considerations for RTCWeb. *IEEE Communications Magazine*, *51*(4), 34–41. doi:10.1109/MCOM.2013.6495758

Beitollahi, H., & Deconinck, G. (2008). FOSeL: Filtering by helping an overlay security layer to mitigate DoS attacks. In *Proceedings of 2008 Seventh IEEE International Symposium on Network Computing and Applications* (pp. 19–28). IEEE. doi:10.1109/NCA.2008.23

Beitollahi, H., & Deconinck, G. (2012). Analyzing well-known countermeasures against distributed denial of service attacks. *Computer Communications*, *35*(11), 1312–1332. doi:10.1016/j.comcom.2012.04.008

Bellard, F. (2013). *qemu-img(1): Linux man page.* Retrieved from http://linux.die.net/man/1/qemu-img

Benyamina, D., Hafid, A., & Gendreau, M. (2012). Wireless mesh networks design – A survey. *IEEE Communications Surveys and Tutorials*, *14*(2), 299–310. doi:10.1109/SURV.2011.042711.00007

Ben-Yehuda, O. A., Schuster, A., Sharov, A., Silberstein, M., & Iosup, A. (2012). *ExPERT: Pareto-efficient task replication on grids and a cloud.* IEEE. doi:10.1109/IPDPS.2012.25

Berman, H., Westbrook, J., Feng, Z., Gilliland, G., Bhat, T. N., Weissig, H., & Bourne, P. E. et al. (2000). The protein data bank. *Nucleic Acids Research*, *28*(1), 235–242. doi:10.1093/nar/28.1.235 PMID:10592235

Berners-Lee, T. (1999). *Weaving the web: The original design and ultimate destiny of the world wide web by its inventor.* New York, NY: HarperCollins Publishers.

Berre, A. (2007). The ATHENA interoperability framework. In R. Gonçalves, J. Müller, K. Mertins, & M. Zelm (Eds.), *Enterprise interoperability II* (pp. 569–580). London, UK: Springer. doi:10.1007/978-1-84628-858-6_62

Bethencourt, J., Sahai, A., & Waters, B. (2007, May). Ciphertext-policy attribute-based encryption. In *Proceedings of IEEE Symposium on Security and Privacy* (pp. 321-334). IEEE. doi:10.1109/SP.2007.11

Bharambe, A. R., Agrawal, M., & Seshan, S. (2004). Mercury: Supporting scalable multi-attribute range queries. In *Proceedings of the 2004 Conference on Applications, Technologies, Architectures, and Protocols for Computer Communications.* ACM.

Bharathi, S., Chervenak, A., Deelman, E., Mehta, G., Su, M.-H., & Vahi, K. (2008). Characterization of scientific workflows. In *Proceedings of Third Workshop on Workflows in Support of Large-Scale Science.* Academic Press.

Bhuyan, L. N., & Agrawal, D. P. (1984). Generalized hypercube and hyperbus structures for a computer network. *IEEE Transactions on Computers*, *100*(4), 323–333.

Binz, T., Breitenbücher, U., Haupt, F., Kopp, O., Leymann, F., Nowak, A., & Wagner, S. (2013) OpenTOSCA – A runtime for TOSCA-based cloud services. In *Proceedings of the 11th International Conference.* Academic Press. doi:10.1007/978-3-642-45005-1_62

Binz, T., Breiter, G., Leyman, F., & Spatzier, T. (2012). Portable cloud services using Tosca. *IEEE Internet Computing*, *16*(3), 80–85. doi:10.1109/MIC.2012.43

Biran, O., Corradi, A., Fanelli, M., Foschini, L., Nus, A., Raz, D., & Silvera, E. (2012). A stable network-aware VM placement for cloud systems. In *Proceedings of the 2012 12th IEEE/ACM International Symposium on Cluster, Cloud and Grid Computing* (CCGRID 2012) (pp 498-506). IEEE. doi:10.1109/CCGrid.2012.119

Bist, M., Wariya, M., & Agarwal, A. (2013). Comparing delta, open stack and Xen cloud platforms: A survey on open source IaaS. In KalraB.GargD.PrasadR.KumarS. (Eds.) *3rd International Advance Computing Conference* (pp. 96-100). Ghaziabad, India: IEEE Computer Society Press. doi:10.1109/IAdCC.2013.6514201

Boneh, D., Boyen, X., & Shacham, H. (2004). Short group signature.*Proceedings of International Cryptology Conference Advances in Cryptology (CRYPTO)*, *3152*, 41-55.

Boniface, M., Phillips, S. C., Sanchez-Macian, A., & Surridge, M. (2007). Dynamic service provisioning using GRIA SLAs. In *Proc. of icsoc'07.* Academic Press.

Bonvin, N., Papaioannou, T. G., & Aberer, K. (2011). Autonomic SLA-driven provisioning for cloud applications. In *Proceedings of the 2011 11th IEEE/ACM International Symposium on Cluster, Cloud and Grid Computing* (pp. 434– 443). IEEE.

Botts, N., Thoms, B., Noamani, A., & Horan, T. (2010). Cloud computing architectures for the underserved: Public health cyberinfrastructures through a network of HealthATMs. In *Proceedings of 43rd Hawaii Int. Conf. on System Sciences (HICSS)* (pp. 1-10). IEEE. doi:10.1109/HICSS.2010.107

Brandic, I. (2009). Towards self-manageable cloud services. In *Proceedings of the 33rd Annual IEEE International Computer Software and Applications Conference* (compsac'09). IEEE. doi:10.1109/COMPSAC.2009.126

Bravetti, M., & Zavattaro, G. (2007). Towards a unifying theory for choreography conformance and contract compliance. In LumpeM. VanderperrenW. (Eds.) *6th International Symposium on Software Composition* (pp. 34-50). Berlin, Germany: Springer. doi:10.1007/978-3-540-77351-1_4

Brein. (2009). *Business objective driven reliable and intelligent grids for real business*. Retrieved from http://www.eu-brein.com/

Brightwell, R., Oldfield, R., Maccabe, A. B., & Bernholdt, D. E. (2013). Hobbes: Composition and virtualization as the foundations of an extreme-scale OS/R. In *Proceedings of the 3rd International Workshop on Runtime and Operating Systems for Supercomputers*. ACM. doi:10.1145/2491661.2481427

Bunch, C., Drawert, B., Chohan, N., Krintz, C., Petzold, L., & Shams, K. (2012, March). Language and runtime support for automatic configuration and deployment of scientific computing software over cloud fabrics. *Journal of Grid Computing*, *10*(1), 23–46. doi:10.1007/s10723-012-9213-8

Burkard, R. E., & Rendl, F. (1984). A thermodynamically motivated simulation procedure for combinatorial optimization problems. *European Journal of Operational Research*, *17*(2), 169–174. doi:10.1016/0377-2217(84)90231-5

Burke, J. (2011). *Bring your own device risks and rewards*. Retrieved June 29, 2012, from http://www.techrepublic.com/blog/tech-manager/bring-your-own-device-risks-and-rewards/7075

Burns, G., Daoud, R., & Vaigl, J. (1994). *LAM: An open cluster environment for MPI*. University of Toronto.

Butler, R., & Lush, E. (1992). *User's guide to the p4 programming system. Academic Press.*

Buyya, R., Ranjan, R., & Calheiros, R. N. (2009). Modeling and simulation of scalable cloud computing environments and the CloudSim toolkit: Challenges and opportunities. In *Proceedings of High Performance Computing & Simulation*. Academic Press.

Buyya, R., Broberg, J., & Goscinski, A. M. (2010). *Cloud computing: Principles and paradigms* (Vol. 87). John Wiley & Sons.

Buyya, R., Yeo, C. S., Venugopal, S., Broberg, J., & Brandic, I. (2009). Cloud computing and emerging IT platforms: Vision, hype, and reality for delivering computing as the 5th utility. *Future Generation Computer Systems*, *25*(6), 599–616. doi:10.1016/j.future.2008.12.001

Calheiros, R. N., Ranjan, R., Beloglazov, A., De Rose, C. A., & Buyya, R. (2011). CloudSim: A toolkit for modeling and simulation of cloud computing environments and evaluation of resource provisioning algorithms. *Software, Practice & Experience*, *41*(1), 23–50. doi:10.1002/spe.995

Cameyo [Computer software]. (2013). Retrieved from http://www.cameyo.com/

Casanova, H., Obertelli, G., Berman, F., & Wolski, R. (2000). The AppLeS parameter sweep template: User-level middleware for the Grid. In Proc. of the Supercomputing (SC'00). Academic Press.

Casanova, H., Desprez, F., & Suter, F. (2010). On cluster resource allocation for multiple parallel task graphs. *Journal of Parallel and Distributed Computing*, *70*(12), 1193–1203. doi:10.1016/j.jpdc.2010.08.017

Case, J. D., Fedor, M., Schoffstall, M. L., & Davin, J. (1990). *Simple network management protocol (SNMP)*. RFC Editor.

Castellani, A. (2011). Web Services for the Internet of Things through CoAP and EXI. In *Proceedings of International Conference on Communications Workshops* (pp. 1-6). Kyoto, Japan: IEEE Computer Society Press.

Castillo, P. (2013). Using SOAP and REST web services as communication protocol for distributed evolutionary computation. *International Journal of Computers & Technology*, *10*(6), 1659–1677.

Chaisiri, S., Lee, B.-S., & Niyato, D. (2012). Optimization of resource provisioning cost in cloud computing. *IEEE Transactions on Services Computing*, *5*(2), 164–177. doi:10.1109/TSC.2011.7

Chapman, B., Curtis, T., Pophale, S., Poole, S., Kuehn, J., Koelbel, C., & Smith, L. (2010). Introducing OpenSHMEM: SHMEM for the PGAS community. In *Proceedings of the Fourth Conference on Partitioned Global Address Space Programming Model*. New York, NY: Academic Press. doi:10.1145/2020373.2020375

Chappell, D. A. (2004). *Enterprise service bus*. O'Reilly Media.

Chase, M. (2007). Multi-authority attribute based encryption. *TCC, 4392*, 515–534. doi:10.1007/978-3-540-70936-7_28

Chen, E. Y. (2005). Detecting TCP-based DDoS attacks by linear regression analysis. In *Signal Processing and Information Technology:Proceedings of the Fifth IEEE International Symposium* (pp. 381–386). Athens: IEEE. doi:10.1109/ISSPIT.2005.1577127

Chen, M., Zhang, H., Su, Y.-Y., Wang, X., Jiang, G., & Yoshihira, K. (2011). Effective vm sizing in virtualized data centers. In *Proceedings of Integrated Network Management* (pp. 594-601). Academic Press. doi:10.1109/INM.2011.5990564

Chen, D. (2006). Enterprise interoperability framework. In MissikoffM.De NicolaA.D'AntonioF. (Eds.) *Open interop workshop on enterprise modelling and ontologies for interoperability*. Berlin, Germany: Springer-Verlag.

Cheng, X., Shi, Y., & Li, Q. (2009, December). A multitenant oriented performance monitoring, detecting and scheduling architecture based on SLA. In *Proceedings of 2009 Joint Conferences on Pervasive Computing (JCPC)* (pp. 599 - 604). Academic Press.

Chen, J. J., & Kuo, T. W. (2005). Multiprocessor energy-efficient Scheduling for real-time tasks with different power characteristics. *ICCP, 05*, 13–20.

Chen, W., Ferreira da Silva, R., Deelman, E., & Sakellariou, R. (2013). *Balanced task clustering in scientific workflows*. IEEE. doi:10.1109/eScience.2013.40

CherryPy : A Minimalist Python Web Framework [Computer software]. (2014). Retrieved from http://www.cherrypy.org/

Chiang, M., Low, S. H., Calderbank, A. R., & Doyle, J. C. (2007). Layering as optimization decomposition: A mathematical theory of network architectures. *Proceedings of the IEEE, 95*(1), 255–312. doi:10.1109/JPROC.2006.887322

Choi, Y., Oh, J., Jang, J., & Ryou, J. (2010). Integrated DDoS attack defense infrastructure for effective attack prevention. In *Proceedings of the Second IEEE International Conference on Information Technology Convergence and Services (ITCS)* (pp. 1–6). IEEE. doi:10.1109/ITCS.2010.5581263

Chopade, S. S., Pandey, K. U., & Bhade, D. S. (2013). Securing cloud servers against flooding based DDoS attacks. In *Proceedings of 2013 International Conference on Communication Systems and Network Technologies* (pp. 524–528). IEEE. doi:10.1109/CSNT.2013.114

Chun, B. G., Ihm, S., Maniatis, P., Naik, M., & Patti, A. (2011). CloneCloud: Elastic execution between mobile device and cloud. In *Proceedings of the Sixth Conference on Computer Systems* (pp. 301–314). New York, NY: ACM. doi:10.1145/1966445.1966473

Cirne, W., Brasileiro, F., Paranhos, D., Góes, L. F. W., & Voorsluys, W. (2007). On the efficacy, efficiency and emergent behavior of task replication in large distributed systems. *Parallel Computing, 33*(3), 213–234. doi:10.1016/j.parco.2007.01.002

Cisco Data Center Infrastructure 2.5 Design Guide. (2014). Retrieved from http://www.cisco.com/c/en/us/td/docs/solutions/Enterprise/Data_Center/DC_Infra2_5/DCI_SRND_2_5a_book/DCInfra_1a.html

Cisco, M. D. S.9000 SANTap. (2014). Retrieved from http://www.cisco.com/c/en/us/products/collateral/storage-networking/mds-9000-santap/data_sheet_c78-568960.html

Clark, C., Fraser, K., Hand, S., Hansen, J. G., Jul, E., Limpach, C., . . . Warfield, A. (2005). Live migration of virtual machines. In *Proceedings of the 2nd Conference on Symposium on Networked Systems Design & Implementation* (vol. 2, pp. 273-286). Academic Press.

Clayman, S., Galis, A., Chapman, C. L. R M., Vaquero, L. M., Nagin, K., et al. (2010, April). Monitoring future internet service clouds. In Towards the future internet - A European research perspective book (pp. 115 - 126). Academic Press.

Cmeier, & Mnovellino. (2013). *Virtualization vulnerabilities related to hypervisors*. Retrieved September 29, 2014, from http://cybersecurity.mit.edu/2013/10/virtualization-vulnerabilities-related-to hypervisors/

Coarfa, C., Dotsenko, Y., Eckhardt, J., & Mellor-Crummey, J. (2004). Co-array fortran performance and potential: An NPB experimental study. In Languages and Compilers for Parallel Computing (LNCS), (vol. 2958, pp. 177–193). Springer Berlin Heidelberg.

Coda File System. (2014). *What is CODA?* Retrieved from http://www.coda.cs.cmu.edu

Comuzzi, M., Kotsokalis, C., Spanoudkis, G., & Yahyapour, R. (2009). Establishing and monitoring SLAs in complex service based systems. In *Proceedings of the 7th International Conference on Web Services* (icws'09). Academic Press. doi:10.1109/ICWS.2009.47

Cook, D., Morein, W., Keromytis, A., Misra, V., & Rubensteint, D. (2003). WebSOS: Protecting web servers from DDoS attacks. In *Proceedings of the 11th IEEE International Conference on Networks* (pp. 461–466). IEEE.

Copil, G., Moldovan, D., Truong, H.-L., & Dustdar, S. (2013a). SYBL: An extensible language for controlling elasticity in cloud applications. In *Proceedings of 13th IEEE/ACM International Symposium on Cluster, Cloud and Grid Computing - CCGRID2013*. IEEE/ACM. doi:10.1109/CCGrid.2013.42

Copil, G., Moldovan, D., Truong, H.-L., & Dustdar, S. (2013b). Multi-level elasticity control of cloud services. In *Proceedings of 11th International Conference on Service Oriented Computing*. Berlin, Germany: Academic Press. doi:10.1007/978-3-642-45005-1_31

Cordeschi, N., Amendola, D., Shojafar, M., & Baccarelli, E. (2014). Performance evaluation of primary-secondary reliable resource-management in vehicular networks. In *Proceedings of IEEE PIMRC 2014*. Washington, DC: IEEE.

Cordeschi, N., Patriarca, T., & Baccarelli, E. (2012). Stochastic traffic engineering for real-time applications over wireless networks. *Journal of Network and Computer Applications*, *35*(2), 681–694. doi:10.1016/j.jnca.2011.11.001

Cordeschi, N., Shojafar, M., & Baccarelli, E. (2013). Energy-saving self-configuring networked data centers. *Computer Networks*, *57*(17), 3479–3491. doi:10.1016/j.comnet.2013.08.002

Cox, B., Allsopp, J., Moldovan, D., Star, K., Garcia, U., & Le, D. H. (2014). *CELAR deliverable: Cloud policy game design document*. Retrieved from http://www.ce-larcloud.eu/wp-content/uploads/2014/04/celar_d7.1_finalrelease_1.pdf

Crane, D., & McCarthy, P. (2008). *Comet and reverse Ajax: The next-generation Ajax 2.0*. Berkeley, CA: Apress.

Cray Inc. (2011). *Using the GNI and DMAPP APIs*. Cray Software Document, volume S-2446-4003. Available from http://docs.cray.com/books/S-2446-4003/S-2446-4003.pdf

Cray Inc. (2013). *Chapel language specification version 0.93*. Technical report. Available from http://chapel.cray.com/spec/spec-0.93.pdf

Crosby, S., & Brown, D. (2006). The virtualization reality. *Queue*, *4*(10), 34–41. doi:10.1145/1189276.1189289

Cuervo, E., Balasubramanian, A., Cho, D. K., Wolman, A., Saroiu, S., Chandra, R., & Bahl, P. (2010). MAUI: Making smartphones last longer with code offload. In *Proceedings of the 8th International Conference on Mobile Systems, Applications, and Services* (pp. 49–62). New York, NY: ACM. doi:10.1145/1814433.1814441

Cugola, G., & Margara, A. (2012). Processing flows of information: From data stream to complex event processing. *ACM Computing Surveys*, *44*(3), 1–62. doi:10.1145/2187671.2187677

Daly, J., Harrod, B., Hoang, T., Nowell, L., Adolf, B., Shekhar Borkar, S., DeBardeleben, N., … Woodward, P., (2012). *Inter-agency workshop on HPC resilience at extreme scale*. Technical Report. Available from http://institute.lanl.gov/resilience/docs/Inter-AgencyResilienceReport.pdf

Das, T., & Sivalingam, K. M. (2013). TCP improvements for data center networks. *Communication Systems and Networks (COMSNETS)*, 1-10.

De Jong, K. A. (1975). *An analysis of the behavior of a class of genetic adaptive systems*. University of Michigan.

Dean, J., & Ghemawat, S. (2008). MapReduce: Simplified data processing on large clusters. *Communications of the ACM*, *51*(1), 107–113. doi:10.1145/1327452.1327492

DeCandia, G., Hastorun, D., Jampani, M., Kakulapati, G., Lakshman, A., Pilchin, A., & Vogels, W. et al. (2007) Dynamo: Amazon's highly available key-value store. In *Proceedings of Twenty-First ACM SIGOPS Symposium on Operating Systems Principles* (SOSP '07). ACM. doi:10.1145/1294261.1294281

Dede, E., Govindaraju, M., Gunter, D., & Ramakrishnan, L. (2011). Riding the elephant: Managing ensembles with Hadoop. In *Proceedings of the 2011 ACM International Workshop on Many Task Computing on Grids and Supercomputers* (pp. 49–58). New York: ACM. doi:10.1145/2132876.2132888

Delerablée, C., Paillier, P., & Pointcheval, D. (2007). Fully collusion secure dynamic broadcast encryption with constant-size ciphertexts or decryption keys.*Proceedings of First International Conference in Pairing-Based Cryptography, 4575*, 39-59.

Delgado, J. (2012). The user as a service. In D. Vidyarthi (Ed.), *Technologies and protocols for the future of internet design: Reinventing the web* (pp. 37–59). Hershey, PA: IGI Global. doi:10.4018/978-1-4666-0203-8.ch003

Delgado, J. (2013). Service interoperability in the internet of things. In N. Bessis (Eds.), *Internet of things and inter-cooperative computational technologies for collective intelligence* (pp. 51–87). Berlin, Germany: Springer. doi:10.1007/978-3-642-34952-2_3

Demchenko, Y., Makkes, M., Strijkers, R., & de Laat, C. (2012). Intercloud architecture for interoperability and integration. In *Proceedings of 4th International Conference on Cloud Computing Technology and Science* (pp. 666-674). Taipe, Taiwan: IEEE Computer Society Press. doi:10.1109/CloudCom.2012.6427607

Di Cosmo, R., Mauro, J., Zacchiroli, S., & Zavattaro, G. (2013). Component reconfiguration in the presence of conflict. In *Proceedings of ICALP 2013* (vol. 2, pp. 187–198). Springer. doi:10.1007/978-3-642-39212-2_19

Di Nitto, E. (2013). Supporting the development and operation of multi-cloud services: The MODAClouds approach. In *Proceedings of 15th International Symposium on Symbolic and Numeric Algorithms for Scientific Computing (SYNASC)*. Academic Press. doi:10.1109/SYNASC.2013.61

Dobson, G., & Sanchez-Macian, A. (2006). Towards unified QoS/SLA ontologies. In Proc. of SCW'06. Academic Press.

DOE. (2014). *Titan: A Cray XK system at the Oak Ridge National Laboratory*. Retrieved from https://www.olcf.ornl.gov/computing-resources/titan-cray-xk7/

Doukas, C., Pliakas, T., & Maglogiannis, I. (2010). Mobile healthcare information management utilizing cloud computing and Android OS. In *Proceedings of 32nd Annual International Conference of the IEEE Engineering in Medicine and Biology Society (EMBC)*. Buenos Aires, Argentina: IEEE.

Douligeris, C., & Mitrokotsa, A. (2004). DDoS attacks and defense mechanisms: Classification and state-of-the-art. *Computer Networks, 44*(5), 643–666. doi:10.1016/j.comnet.2003.10.003

Drnasin, I., & Grgic, M. (2010). The use of mobile phones in radiology. *ELMAR, 2010*, 17–21.

DTMF. (2012). *Open virtualization format specification*. Document Number: DSP0243, version 2.0.0. Portland, OR: Distributed Management Task Force, Inc. Retrieved May 30, 2014 from http://www.dmtf.org/sites/default/files/standards/documents/DSP0243_2.0.0.pdf

DTMF. (2013). *Cloud infrastructure management interface (CIMI) model and REST interface over HTTP specification*. Document Number: DSP0263, version 1.1.0. Portland, OR: Distributed Management Task Force, Inc. Retrieved May 30, 2014 from http://www.dmtf.org/sites/default/files/standards/documents/DSP0263_1.1.0.pdf

Du, P., & Nakao, A. (2010). DDoS defense as a network service. In *Proceedings of 2010 IEEE Network Operations and Management Symposium - NOMS 2010* (pp. 894–897). IEEE. doi:10.1109/NOMS.2010.5488345

Dubuisson, O. (2000). *ASN.1 communication between heterogeneous systems*. San Diego, CA: Academic Press.

Dustdar, S., Guo Y., Satzger, B., & Truong, H.-L. (2011). Principles of elastic processes. *IEEE Internet Computing, 15*(5), 66-71.

Eclipse. (2014). *Jetty: Servlet engine and http server* [Computer software]. Retrieved from http://www.eclipse.org/jetty/

Edmonds, A., Metsch, T., & Papaspyrou, A. (2011). Open cloud computing interface in data management-related setups. In S. Fiore & G. Aloisio (Eds.), *Grid and cloud database management* (pp. 23–48). Berlin, Germany: Springer. doi:10.1007/978-3-642-20045-8_2

EIF. (2010). *European interoperability framework (EIF) for European public services, annex 2 to the communication from the commission to the European Parliament, the council, the European economic and social committee and the committee of regions towards interoperability for European public services*. Retrieved May 30, 2014 from http://ec.europa.eu/isa/documents/isa_annex_ii_eif_en.pdf

El Raheb, K. (2011). Paving the way for interoperability in digital libraries: The DL.org project. In A. Katsirikou & C. Skiadas (Eds.), *New trends in qualitive and quantitative methods in libraries* (pp. 345–352). Singapore: World Scientific Publishing Company.

Elmroth, E., & Tordsson, J. (2004). A grid resource broker supporting advance reservations and benchmark-based resource selection. In *Proc. of the Workshop on State-of-the-Art in Scientific Computing (para'04)*. Academic Press. doi:10.1007/11558958_128

Emeakaroha, V. C., Calheiros, R. N., Netto, M. A. S., Brandic, I., & De Rose, C. A. F. (2010). DeSVi: An architecture for detecting SLA violations in cloud computing infrastructures. In *Proc. of the 2nd International ICST Conference on Cloud Computing* (cloudcomp'10). Academic Press.

Emeakaroha, V. C., Ferreto, T. C., Netto, M. A. S., Brandic, I., & Rose, C. A. D. (2012). CASViD: Application level monitoring for SLA violation detection in clouds. In *Proc. of the 36th Annual IEEE Computer and Application International Conference* (compsac12) (p. 499 - 508). Academic Press.

Emeakaroha, V. C., Netto, M. A. S., Calheiros, R. N., Brandic, I., Buyya, R., & De Rose, C. A. F. (2012). Towards autonomic detection of SLA violations in cloud infrastructures. *Future Generation Computer Systems*, 28(7), 1017–1029. doi:10.1016/j.future.2011.08.018

ENISA. (2009). *Cloud computing risk assessment*. Retrieved April 11, 2012, from http://www.enisa.europa.eu/act/rm/files/deliverables/cloud-computing-risk-assessment

Erl, T. (2008). *SOA: Principles of service design*. Upper Saddle River, NJ: Prentice Hall PTR.

Erl, T., Balasubramanians, R., Pautasso, C., & Carlyle, B. (2011). *Soa with rest: Principles, patterns & constraints for building enterprise solutions with REST*. Upper Saddle River, NJ: Prentice Hall PTR.

Ersoz, D., Yousif, M. S., & Das, C. R. (2007). Characterizing network traffic in a cluster-based, multi-tier data center. In *Proceedings of Distributed Computing Systems* (pp. 59-59). Academic Press. doi:10.1109/ICDCS.2007.90

ESPER. (2014). Event stream processing. http://esper.codehaus.org/

Eugster, R. (2013). *".ch" survives DDoS attack unscathed*. Retrieved October 02, 2014, from https://www.switch.ch/about/news/2013/ddos.html

Euzenat, J., & Shvaiko, P. (2007). *Ontology matching*. Berlin, Germany: Springer.

Fagg, G. E., Pjesivac-grbovic, J., Bosilca, G., Dongarra, J. J., & Jeannot, E. (2006). Flexible collective communication tuning architecture applied to open MPI. In *Proceedings of 2006 Euro PVM/MPI*. Academic Press.

Fagg, G. E., & Dongarra, J. (2000). FT-MPI: Fault tolerant MPI, supporting dynamic applications in a dynamic world. In *Proceedings of the 7th European PVM/MPI Users' Group Meeting on Recent Advances in Parallel Virtual Machine and Message Passing Interface* (pp. 346–353). London, UK: Springer-Verlag. doi:10.1007/3-540-45255-9_47

Fatema, K., Emeakaroha, V. C., Healy, P. D., Morrison, J. P., & Lynn, T. (2014). A survey of cloud monitoring tools: Taxonomy, capabilities and objectives. *Journal of Parallel and Distributed Computing*, 74(10), 2918–2933. doi:10.1016/j.jpdc.2014.06.007

Ferdaus, M. H., Murshed, M., Calheiros, R. N., & Buyya, R. (2014). Virtual machine consolidation in cloud data centers using ACO metaheuristic. In Proceedings of Euro-Par 2014 Parallel Processing (pp. 306-317). Springer. doi:10.1007/978-3-319-09873-9_26

Fernando, N., Loke, S., & Rahayu, W. (2013). Mobile cloud computing: A survey. *Future Generation Computer Systems*, 29(1), 84–106. doi:10.1016/j.future.2012.05.023

Ferreira da Silva, R., & Glatard, T. (2013). A science-gateway workload archive to study pilot jobs, user activity, bag of tasks, task sub-steps, and workflow executions. In I. Caragiannis, M. Alexander, R. M. Badia, M. Cannataro, A. Costan, M. Danelutto, … J. Weidendorfer (Eds.), *Euro-Par 2012: Parallel Processing Workshops* (pp. 79–88). Springer Berlin Heidelberg. Retrieved from http://link.springer.com/chapter/10.1007/978-3-642-36949-0_10

Ferreira da Silva, R., Camarasu-Pop, S., Grenier, B., Hamar, V., Manset, D., Montagnat, J., … Glatard, T. (2011). Multi-infrastructure workflow execution for medical simulation in the virtual imaging platform. In Proceedings of 2011 HealthGrid Conference. Academic Press.

Ferreira da Silva, R., Glatard, T., & Desprez, F. (2014). Controlling fairness and task granularity in distributed, online, non-clairvoyant workflow executions: Controlling fairness and task granularity in workflows. *Concurrency and Computation: Practice and Experience*. doi:10.1002/cpe.3303

Ferreira da Silva, R., Juve, G., Deelman, E., Glatard, T., Desprez, F., Thain, D., … Livny, M. (2013). *Toward fine-grained online task characteristics estimation in scientific workflows*. ACM Press. doi:10.1145/2534248.2534254

Ferreira da Silva, R., Glatard, T., & Desprez, F. (2012). *Self-healing of operational workflow incidents on distributed computing infrastructures*. IEEE. doi:10.1109/CCGrid.2012.24

Ferreira da Silva, R., Glatard, T., & Desprez, F. (2013a). On-line, non-clairvoyant optimization of workflow activity granularity on grids. In F. Wolf, B. Mohr, & D. Mey (Eds.), *Euro-Par 2013 Parallel Processing* (pp. 255–266). Springer Berlin Heidelberg. doi:10.1007/978-3-642-40047-6_28

Ferreira da Silva, R., Glatard, T., & Desprez, F. (2013c). Workflow fairness control on online and non-clairvoyant distributed computing platforms. In F. Wolf, B. Mohr, & D. an Mey (Eds.), *Euro-Par 2013 Parallel Processing* (pp. 102–113). Springer Berlin Heidelberg. doi:10.1007/978-3-642-40047-6_13

Ferreira, K. B., Bridges, P. G., Brightwell, R., & Pedretti, K. (2010). Impact of system design parameters on application noise sensitivity. In *Proceedings of the 2010 IEEE International Conference on Cluster Computing*. IEEE. doi:10.1109/CLUSTER.2010.41

Ferrer, A. J. (2011). Optimis: a holistic approach to cloud service provisioning. http: / / www. optimis -project. eu/.

Ferreto, T. C., Rose, C. A. F. D., & Rose, L. D. (2002). Rvision: An open and high configurable tool for cluster monitoring. In CCgrid'02.

Fielding, R. (2000). *Architectural styles and the design of network-based software architectures*. (Doctoral dissertation). University of California, Irvine, CA.

Fortinet, C. (2011). Network and physical security in the cloud. *Asia Cloud Forum*. Retrieved from http://www.asiacloudforum.com/content/network-and-physical-security-cloud

Foster, I., Zhao, Y., Raicu, I., & Lu, S. (2008). Cloud computing and grid computing 360-degree compared. In *Proceedings of Grid Computing Environments Workshop* (pp. 1–10). Academic Press. Retrieved from http://arxiv.org/ftp/arxiv/papers/0901/0901.0131.pdf

Foster, I. (2001). The anatomy of the grid: Enabling scalable virtual organizations. *International Journal of High Performance Computing Applications*, *15*(3), 200–222. doi:10.1177/109434200101500302

Fox, G., & Gannon, D. (2014). *Using clouds for technical computing*. Available from http://grids.ucs.indiana.edu/ptliupages/publications/Clouds_Technical_Computing_FoxGannonv2.pdf

Frutos, H. M., & Kotsiopoulos, I. (2009). BREIN: Business objective driven reliable and intelligent grids for real business. *International Journal of Interoperability in Business Information Systems*, *3*(1), 39–42.

Gabriel, E., Fagg, G. E., Bosilca, G., Angskun, T., Dongarra, J. J., Squyres, J. M., Sahay, V. Kambadur, … Woodall, T. S. (2004). Open MPI: Goals, concept, and design of a next generation MPI implementation. In Proceedings, 11th European PVM/MPI Users' Group Meeting. Budapest, Hungary: Academic Press.

Galiegue, F., & Zyp, K. (Eds.). (2013). *JSON schema: Core definitions and terminology*. Internet Engineering Task Force. Retrieved May 30, 2014 from https://tools.ietf.org/html/draft-zyp-json-schema-04

Gambi, A., Moldovan, D., Copil, G., Truong, H.-L., & Dustdar, S. (2013). On estimating actuation delays in elastic computing systems. In *Proceedings of the 8th International Symposium on Software Engineering for Adaptive and Self-Managing Systems* (SEAMS '13). IEEE Press. doi:10.1109/SEAMS.2013.6595490

Gandhi, A., Balter, M. H., & Adam, I. (2010). Server farms with setup costs. *Performance Evaluation, 11*(67), 1123–1138. doi:10.1016/j.peva.2010.07.004

Ge, R., Feng, X., Feng, W., & Cameron, K. W. (2007). CPU miser: A performance-directed, run-time system for power-aware clusters. In Proceedings of IEEE ICPP07. IEEE.

Geist, A., Kale, S., Kramer, B., & Snir, M. (2009). Toward exascale resilience. *International Journal of High Performance Computing Applications*, 374–388.

Georgiou, S., Tsakalozos, K., & Delis, A. (2013). Exploiting network-topology awareness for VM placement in IaaS clouds. In *Proceedings of Cloud and Green Computing* (CGC) (pp. 151-158). Academic Press. doi:10.1109/CGC.2013.30

Gibrat, J., Madej, T., & Bryant, S. (1996). Surprising similarities in structure comparison. *Current Opinion in Structural Biology, 6*(3), 377–385. doi:10.1016/S0959-440X(96)80058-3 PMID:8804824

Glassner, A. S. (1989). *An introduction to ray tracing*. Academic Press London.

Glatard, T., Lartizien, C., Gibaud, B., Ferreira da Silva, R., Forestier, G., Cervenansky, F., & Friboulet, D. et al. (2013). A virtual imaging platform for multi-modality medical image simulation. *IEEE Transactions on Medical Imaging, 32*(1), 110–118. doi:10.1109/TMI.2012.2220154 PMID:23014715

Glatard, T., Montagnat, J., Lingrand, D., & Pennec, X. (2008). Flexible and efficient workflow deployment of data-intensive applications on grids with MOTEUR. *International Journal of High Performance Computing Applications, 22*(3), 347–360. doi:10.1177/1094342008096067

Goh, E., Shacham, H., Modadugu, N., & Boneh, D. (2003). SiRiUS: Securing remote untrusted storage. In *Proceedings of Network and Distributed Systems Security (NDSS) Symposium*. Academic Press.

Gong, Z., Gu, X., & Wilkes, J. (2010, October). Press: Predictive elastic resource scaling for cloud systems. In *Proceedings of Network and Service Management* (CNSM) (pp. 9-16). IEEE.

Gonzalez, A. J., & Helvik, B. E. (2012) System management to comply with SLA availability guarantees in cloud computing. In *Proceedings of 2012 IEEE 4th International Conference on Cloud Computing Technology and Science (CloudCom)* (pp. 325-332). IEEE. http://ieeexplore.ieee.org/stamp/stamp.jsp?tp=&arnumber=6427508&isnumber=6427477

Gottschalk, P., & Solli-Sæther, H. (2008). Stages of e-government interoperability. *Electronic Government:International Journal (Toronto, Ont.), 5*(3), 310–320.

Govindan, S., Choi, J., Urgaonkar, B., Sasubramanian, A., & Baldini, A., (2009). Statistical profiling-based techniques for effective power provisioning in data centers. In *Proc of EuroSys*. Academic Press.

Goyal, V., Pandey, O., Sahai, A., & Waters, B. (2006). Attribute-based encryption for fine-grained access control of encrypted data. In *Proceedings of ACM Conference on Computer and Communications Security* (pp. 89-98). ACM. doi:10.1145/1180405.1180418

Graham, R. L., Ladd, J. S., & Venkata, M. G. (2010). Hierarchy aware blocking and nonblocking collective communications - The effects of shared memory in the Cray XT environment. In *Proceedings of the 2010 Cray User Group Annual Technical Conference*. Academic Press.

Grau, B., Horrocks, I., Motik, B., Parsia, B., Patel-Schneider, P., & Sattler, U. (2008). OWL 2: The next step for OWL. *Web Semantics: Science, Services, and Agents on the World Wide Web, 6*(4), 309–322. doi:10.1016/j.websem.2008.05.001

Greenberg, A., Hamilton, J. R., Jain, N., Kandula, S., Kim, C., Lahiri, P., & Sengupta, S. et al. (2009). VL2: A scalable and flexible data center network. *Computer Communication Review, 39*(4), 51–62. doi:10.1145/1594977.1592576

Greenberg, A., Hamilton, J., Maltz, D. A., & Patel, P. (2009). The cost of a cloud: Research problems in data center networks. *ACM SIGCOMM, 39*(1), 68–73. doi:10.1145/1496091.1496103

Gropp, W. D., & Snir, M. (2013). *Programming for exascale computers*. Available from http://www.mcs.anl.gov/papers/P4053-0313.pdf

Gubbi, J., Buyya, R., Marusic, S., & Palaniswami, M. (2013). Internet of things (IoT): A vision, architectural elements, and future directions. *Future Generation Computer Systems, 29*(7), 1645–1660. doi:10.1016/j.future.2013.01.010

Gu, J., & Bourne, P. E. (2009). *Structural bioinformatics*. Hoboken, NJ: Wiley-Blackwell.

Gulati, A., Merchant, A., & Varman, P.J. (2010). mClock: Handling throughput variability for hypervisor IO scheduling. In *Proceedings of OSDI'10*. Academic Press.

Guo, C. (2010). SecondNet: A data center network virtualization architecture with bandwidth guarantees. In Proceedings of ACM CoNEXT. ACM; doi:10.1145/1921168.1921188

Guo, C., Lu, G., Li, D., Wu, H., Zhang, X., Shi, Y., & Lu, S. et al. (2009). BCube: A high performance, server-centric network architecture for modular data centers. *Computer Communication Review, 39*(4), 63–74. doi:10.1145/1594977.1592577

Guo, C., Wu, H., Tan, K., Shi, L., Zhang, Y., & Lu, S. (2008). Dcell: A scalable and fault-tolerant network structure for data centers. *Computer Communication Review, 38*(4), 75–86. doi:10.1145/1402946.1402968

Guo, P. J., & Engler, D. (2011). CDE: Using system call interposition to automatically create portable software packages. In *Proceedings of the 2011 Annual Technical Conference on USENIX* (p. 21). Berkeley, CA: USENIX Association.

Gupta, R., Bose, S. K., Sundarrajan, S., Chebiyam, M., & Chakrabarti, A. (2008). A two stage heuristic algorithm for solving the server consolidation problem with item-item and bin-item incompatibility constraints. In *Proceedings of Services Computing* (Vol. 2, pp. 39-46). IEEE. doi:10.1109/SCC.2008.39

Gupta, A., & Milojicic, D. (2011). Evaluation of HPC applications on cloud. In *Proceedings of the 2011 Sixth Open Cirrus Summit* (pp. 22–26). Washington, DC: IEEE Computer Society. doi:10.1109/OCS.2011.10

Gutierrez, S. K., Venkata, M. G., Hjelm, T. N., & Graham, R. (2012). Performance evaluation of open MPI on Cray XE/XK systems. In *Proceedings of 20th Annual IEEE Symposium on High-Performance Interconnects, HOTI 2012*. Santa Clara, CA: Academic Press. doi:10.1109/HOTI.2012.11

Ha, K., Lewis, G., Simanta, S., & Satyanarayanan, M. (2011). *Code offload in hostile environments (CMU-CS-11-146)*. Pittsburgh, PA: Carnegie Mellon University.

Hamada, T., & Nakasato, N. (2005). InfiniBand trade association, InfiniBand architecture specification. In *Proceedings of International Conference on Field Programmable Logic and Applications* (pp. 366–373). Academic Press. doi:10.1109/FPL.2005.1515749

Hammond, J., Ghosh, S., & Chapman, B. (2014). Implementing OpenSHMEM using MPI-3 one-sided communication. In OpenSHMEM and Related Technologies: Experiences, Implementations, and Tools (LNCS), (vol. 8356, pp. 44–58). Springer International Publishing. doi:10.1007/978-3-319-05215-1_4

Harrison, R. J. (1993). *Tcgmsg send/receive subroutines – Version 4.02 user's manual*. Pacific Northwest Laboratory.

Hartenstein, H., & Laberteaux, K. (Eds.). (2010). *VANET: Vehicular applications and inter-networking technologies*. Chichester, UK: Wiley. doi:10.1002/9780470740637

Heng, C. (2011). *Security issues in writing PHP scripts -And how PHP 4.1.0 / 4.2.0+ will change your scripts*. Retrieved April 10, 2012, from http://www.thesitewizard.com/archive/phpsecurity.shtml

He, Q., Zhou, S., Kobler, B., Duffy, D., & McGlynn, T. (2010). Case study for running HPC applications in public clouds. In *Proceedings of the 19th ACM International Symposium on High Performance Distributed Computing* (pp. 395–401). New York, NY: ACM. doi:10.1145/1851476.1851535

Hines, M. R., Deshpande, U., & Gopalan, K. (2009). Post-copy live migration of virtual machines. *Operating Systems Review, 43*(3), 14–26. doi:10.1145/1618525.1618528

Hirales-Carbajal, A., Tchernykh, A., Yahyapour, R., González-García, J. L., Röblitz, T., & Ramírez-Alcaraz, J. M. (2012). Multiple workflow scheduling strategies with user run time estimates on a grid. *Journal of Grid Computing, 10*(2), 325–346. doi:10.1007/s10723-012-9215-6

Hoefler, T., Lumsdaine, A., & Rehm, W. (2007). Implementation and performance analysis of non-blocking collective operations for MPI. In *Proceedings of the 2007 International Conference on High Performance Computing, Networking, Storage and Analysis, SC07.* IEEE Computer Society/ACM.

Hoefler, T., Squyres, J., Bosilca, G., Fagg, G., Lumsdaine, A., & Rehm, W. (2006). *Non-blocking collective operations for MPI-2.* Indiana University.

Hoff, C. (2008). *Cloud computing security: From DDoS (distributed denial of service) to EDoS (economic denial of sustainability).* Retrieved January 17, 2013, from http://rationalsecurity.typepad.com/blog/2008/11/cloud-computing-security-from-ddos-distributed-denial-of-service-to-edos-economic-denial-of-sustaina.html

Hoff, C. (2009). *A couple of follow-ups on the EDoS (economic denial of sustainability) concept.* Retrieved January 25, 2013, from http://rationalsecurity.typepad.com/blog/2009/01/a-couple-of-followups-on-my-edos-economic-denial-of-sustainability-concept.html

Hoffa, C., Mehta, G., Freeman, T., Deelman, E., Keahey, K., Berriman, B., & Good, J. (2008). On the use of cloud computing for scientific workflows. In *Proceedings of eScience* (pp. 640–645). Academic Press. doi:10.1109/eScience.2008.167

Holdener, A. III. (2008). *Ajax: The definitive guide.* Sebastopol, CA: O'Reilly Media, Inc.

Holm, L., & Sander, C. (1993). Protein structure comparison by alignment of distance matrices. *Journal of Molecular Biology, 233*(1), 123–138. doi:10.1006/jmbi.1993.1489 PMID:8377180

Hsu, C.-C., Huang, K.-C., & Wang, F.-J. (2011). Online scheduling of workflow applications in grid environments. *Future Generation Computer Systems, 27*(6), 860–870. doi:10.1016/j.future.2010.10.015

Huang, D., Gao, Y., Song, F., Yang, D., & Zhang, H. (2013). Multi-objective virtual machine migration in virtualized data center environments. In *Proceedings of Communications* (ICC) (pp. 3699-3704). IEEE. doi:10.1109/ICC.2013.6655129

Huang, D., Yang, D., Zhang, H., & Wu, L. (2012). Energy-aware virtual machine placement in data centers. In *Proceedings of Global Communications Conference* (GLOBECOM). IEEE.

Hughes, D., Coulson, G., & Walkerdine, J. (2010). A survey of peer-to-peer architectures for service oriented computing. In Handbook of research on P2P and grid systems for service-oriented computing: Models, methodologies and applications (pp. 1-19). Hershey, PA: IGI Global. doi:10.4018/978-1-61520-686-5.ch001

Hung, S., Shih, C., Shieh, J., Lee, C., & Huang, Y. (2011). An online migration environment for executing mobile applications on the cloud. In *Proceedings of 2011 5th International Conference on Innovative Mobile and Internet Services in Ubiquitous Computing.* Seoul, Korea: Academic Press.

Intel. (2012). *What's holding back the cloud?* Retrieved September 26, 2014, from http://www.intel.com/content/www/us/en/cloud-computing/whats-holding-back-the-cloud-peer-research-report.html

Iosup, A., Ostermann, S., Yigitbasi, N., Prodan, R., Fahringer, T., & Epema, D. (2011). Performance analysis of cloud computing services for many-tasks scientific computing. *IEEE Transactions on Parallel and Distributed Systems, 22*(6), 931–945. doi:10.1109/TPDS.2011.66

ISO/IEC. (2012). *Information technology -- Cloud data management interface (CDMI): ISO/IEC standard 17826:2012.* Geneva, Switzerland: International Organization for Standardization.

Iyengar, S., & Brooks, R. (Eds.). (2012). *Distributed sensor networks: Sensor networking and applications.* Boca Raton, FL: CRC Press. doi:10.1201/b12988

Iyer, A. N., & Roopa, T. (2012). Extending Android application programming framework for seamless cloud integration. In *Proceedings of 2012 IEEE First International Conference on Mobile Services* (pp. 96–104). Washington, DC: IEEE Computer Society Press. doi:10.1109/MobServ.2012.22

Jackson, K. (2012). *OpenStack cloud computing cookbook*. Birmingham, UK: Packt Publishing Ltd.

Jarabek, C., Barrera, D., & Aycock, J. (2012). ThinAV: Truly lightweight mobile cloud-based anti-malware. In *Proceedings of the 28th Annual Computer Security Applications Conference* (pp. 209–218). New York, NY: ACM.

Jardim-Goncalves, R., Agostinho, C., & Steiger-Garcao, A. (2012). A reference model for sustainable interoperability in networked enterprises: Towards the foundation of EI science base. *International Journal of Computer Integrated Manufacturing*, 25(10), 855–873. doi:10.1080/0951192X.2011.653831

Jardim-Goncalves, R., Grilo, A., Agostinho, C., Lampathaki, F., & Charalabidis, Y. (2013). Systematisation of interoperability body of knowledge: The foundation for enterprise interoperability as a science. *Enterprise Information Systems*, 7(1), 7–32. doi:10.1080/17517575.2012.684401

Järvi, J., & Freeman, J. (2010). C++ lambda expressions and closures. *Science of Computer Programming*, 75(9), 762–772. doi:10.1016/j.scico.2009.04.003

Jeong, B., Lee, D., Cho, H., & Lee, J. (2008). A novel method for measuring semantic similarity for XML schema matching. *Expert Systems with Applications*, 34(3), 1651–1658. doi:10.1016/j.eswa.2007.01.025

Jin, X., Keller, E., & Rexford, J. (2012). Virtual switching without a hypervisor for a more secure cloud. In *Proceedings of 2nd USENIX Workshop on Hot Topics in Management of Internet, Cloud, and Enterprise Networks and Services. Hot-ICE'12* (pp. 1–6). Academic Press.

Jin, S., Guo, L., Matta, I., & Bestavros, A. (2003). A spectrum of TCP-friendly window-based congestion control algorithms. *IEEE/ACM Transactions on Networking*, 11(3), 341–355. doi:10.1109/TNET.2003.813046

JmDNS [Computer software]. (2011). Retrieved from http://jmdns.sourceforge.net/

JMS. (2014). *Java messaging service*. Retrieved from http://java.sun.com/products/jms/

JMX. (2014). *Java management extenstions*. Retrieved from http://www.oracle.com/technetwork/java/javase/tech/javamanagement-140525.html

Johnston, A., Yoakum, J., & Singh, K. (2013). Taking on WebRTC in an enterprise. *Communications Magazine, IEEE*, 51(4), 48–54. doi:10.1109/MCOM.2013.6495760

Jung, T., Li, X., Wan, Z. & Wan, M. (2013, April). Privacy preserving cloud data access with multi-authority. In *Proceedings of IEEE INFOCOM* (pp. 2625 – 2633). IEEE. doi: 10.1109/INFCOM.2013.6567070

Juric, M., & Pant, K. (2008). *Business process driven SOA using BPMN and BPEL: From business process modeling to orchestration and service oriented architecture*. Birmingham, UK: Packt Publishing.

Kallahalla, M., Riedel, E., Swaminathan, R., Wang, Q., & Fu, K. (2013). Plutus: Scalable secure file sharing on untrusted storage. In *Proceedings of USENIX Conference File and Storage Technologies* (pp. 29-42). Academic Press.

Kandula, S., Sengupta, S., Greenberg, A., Patel, P., & Chaiken, R. (2009). The nature of data center traffic: Measurements & analysis. In *Proceedings of the 9th ACM SIGCOMM Conference on Internet Measurement* (pp. 202-208). ACM. doi:10.1145/1644893.1644918

Kansal, A., Zhao, F., Liu, J., Kothari, N., & Bhattacharya, A. (2010). Virtual machine power metering and provisioning. *SoCC*, 10, 39–50.

Karger, D., Lehman, E., Leighton, T., Panigrahy, R., Levine, M., & Lewin, D. (1997). Consistent hashing and random trees: Distributed caching protocols for relieving hot spots on the world wide web. In *Proceedings of the Twenty-Ninth Annual ACM Symposium on Theory of Computing* (STOC '97). ACM. doi:10.1145/258533.258660

Karger, D., & Ruhl, M. (2004) Simple efficient load balancing algorithms for peer-to-peer systems. In *Proceedings of the Sixteenth Annual ACM Symposium on Parallelism in Algorithms and Architectures* (pp. 36-43). ACM. doi:10.1145/1007912.1007919

Kaur, K., & Vashisht, S. (2013). Data separation issues in cloud computing. *International Journal for Advance Research in Engineering and Technology*, 1(X), 26–29.

Kephart, J. O., & Chess, D. M. (2003). The vision of autonomic computing. *Computer*, 36(1), 41–50. doi:10.1109/MC.2003.1160055

Keromytis, A., Misra, V., & Rubenstein, D. (2002). SOS: Secure overlay services. In Proceedings of SIGCOMM (pp. 61–72). ACM.

Keyes, J. (2013). *Bring your own devices (BYOD) survival guide*. Boca Raton, FL: CRC Press. doi:10.1201/b14050

Khadka, R. (2011). Model-driven development of service compositions for enterprise interoperability. In Enterprise interoperability (pp. 177-190). Berlin, Germany: Springer-Verlag. doi:10.1007/978-3-642-19680-5_15

Khan, A., Fisal, N., & Hussain, S. (2009). Man-in-the-middle attack and possible solutions on Wimax 802. 16j. In *Proceedings of International Conference on Recent and Emerging Advance Technologies in Engineering (iCRE-ATE 2009)*. Academic Press.

Khor, S., & Nakao, A. (2011). DaaS: DDoS mitigation-as-a-service. In *Proceedings of 2011 IEEE/IPSJ International Symposium on Applications and the Internet* (pp. 160–171). IEEE. doi:10.1109/SAINT.2011.30

Kim, D., & Shen, W. (2007). An approach to evaluating structural pattern conformance of UML models. In *Proceedings of ACM Symposium on Applied Computing* (pp. 1404-1408). New York, NY: ACM Press. doi:10.1145/1244002.1244305

Kim, K. H., Buyya, R., & Kim, J. (2007). Power aware scheduling of bag-of-tasks applications with deadline constraints on DVS-enabled clusters. In *Proceedings of IEEE International Symposium of CCGRID* (pp. 541-548). IEEE. doi:10.1109/CCGRID.2007.85

Kim, K. H., Beloglazov, A., & Buyya, R. (2009). Power-aware provisioning of cloud resources for real-time services. In *Proc. of ACM MGC'09*. ACM.

Kivity, A., Kamay, Y., Laor, D., Lublin, U., & Liguori, A. (2007). KVM: The Linux virtual machine monitor. In *Proceedings of the Linux Symposium (Vol. 1*, pp. 225-230). Academic Press.

Kliazovich, D., Bouvry, P., & Khan, S. U. (2013). DENS: Data center energy-efficient network-aware scheduling. *Cluster Computing, 16*(1), 65–75. doi:10.1007/s10586-011-0177-4

Kohn, L., Corrigan, J., & Donaldson, S. (1999). *To err is human: Building a safer health system*. Washington, DC: National Academy Press.

Kokash, N., & Arbab, F. (2009). Formal behavioral modeling and compliance analysis for service-oriented systems. In F. Boer, M. Bonsangue, & E. Madelaine (Eds.), *Formal methods for components and objects* (pp. 21–41). Berlin, Germany: Springer-Verlag. doi:10.1007/978-3-642-04167-9_2

Koller, R., Verma, A., & Neogi, A. (2010). WattApp: An application aware power meter for shared data centers. In Proceedings of ICAC'10. IEEE; doi:10.1145/1809049.1809055

Koller, B., & Schubert, L. (2007). Towards autonomous SLA management using a proxy-like approach. *Multiagent Grid Systems, 3*(3), 313–325.

Konstantinou, I., Tsoumakos, D., Mytilinis, I., & Koziris, N. (2011). Fast and cost-effective online load-balancing in distributed range-queriable system. *IEEE Transactions on Parallel and Distributed Systems, 22*(8), 1350–1364. doi:10.1109/TPDS.2010.200

Konstantinou, I., Tsoumakos, D., Mytilinis, I., & Koziris, N. (2013) DBalancer: Distributed load balancing for NoSQL data-stores. In *Proceedings of the 2013 International Conference on Management of Data* (pp. 1037-1040). ACM. doi:10.1145/2463676.2465232

Kopec, D., Kabir, M., Reinharth, D., & Rothschild, O. (2003, August). Human errors in medical practice: Systematic classification and reduction with automated information systems. *Journal of Medical Systems, 27*(4), 297–313. doi:10.1023/A:1023796918654 PMID:12846462

Korn, D., MacDonald, J., Mogul, J., & Vo, K. (2002). *RFC 3284: The VCDIFF generic differencing and compression data format* [Computer software]. Retrieved from http://tools.ietf.org/html/rfc3284

Korupolu, M., Singh, A., & Bamba, B. (2009). Coupled placement in modern data centers. In *Proceedings of Parallel & Distributed Processing* (pp. 1-12). IEEE. doi:10.1109/IPDPS.2009.5161067

Kosta, S., Aucinas, A., Hui, P., Mortier, R., & Zhang, X. (2012). ThinkAir: Dynamic resource allocation and parallel execution in the cloud for mobile code offloading. In *Proceedings IEEE INFOCOM* (pp. 945–953). Washington, DC: IEEE Computer Society Press.

Koufi, V., Malamateniou, F., & Vassilacopoulos, G. (2010). Ubiquitous access to cloud emergency medical services. In *Proceedings of 10th IEEE Int. Conf. on Information Technology and Applications in Biomedicine (ITAB)* (pp. 1-4). Corfu, Greece: IEEE. doi:10.1109/ITAB.2010.5687702

Krauter, K., Buyya, R., & Maheswaran, M. (2002). A taxonomy and survey of grid resource management systems for distributed computing. *Software, Practice & Experience*, *32*(2), 135–164. doi:10.1002/spe.432

Kumar, M., Sujatha, P., Kalva, V., Nagori, R., & Katukojwala, A. (2012). Mitigating economic denial of sustainability (EDoS) in cloud computing using in-cloud scrubber service. In *Proceedings of 2012 Fourth International Conference on Computational Intelligence and Communication Networks* (pp. 535–539). IEEE. doi:10.1109/CICN.2012.149

Kumar, N., & Sharma, S. (2013). Study of intrusion detection system for DDoS attacks in cloud computing. In *Proceedings of 2013 Tenth International Conference on Wireless and Optical Communications Networks (WOCN)* (pp. 1–5). IEEE. doi:10.1109/WOCN.2013.6616255

Kumar, K., & Lu, Y. H. (2010). Cloud computing for mobile users: Can offloading computation save energy? *Computer*, *43*(4), 51–56. doi:10.1109/MC.2010.98

Kumbhare, A. (2014). *PLAstiCC: Predictive look-ahead scheduling for continuous data flaws on clouds*. IEEE.

Kurose, J. F., & Ross, K. W. (2013). *Computer networking - A top-down approach featuring the internet* (6th ed.). Addison Wesley.

Kushner, H. J., & Yang, J. (1995). Analysis of adaptive step-size SA algorithms for parameter tracking. *IEEE Transactions on Automatic Control*, *40*(8), 1403–1410. doi:10.1109/9.402231

Kusic, D., & Kandasamy, N. (2009). Power and performance management of virtualized computing environments via look-ahead control. In *Proc. of ICAC*. Academic Press.

Kusic, D., Kephart, J. O., Hanson, J. E., Kandasamy, N., & Jiang, G. (2009). Power and performance management of virtualized computing environments via lookahead control. *Cluster Computing*, *12*(1), 1–15. doi:10.1007/s10586-008-0070-y

Kuyoro, S., Ibikunle, F., & Awodele, O. (2011). Cloud computing security issues and challenges. *International Journal of Computer Networks*, *3*(5), 247–252.

KVM. (2014). *Kernel based virtual machine* [Computer software]. Retrieved from http://www.linux-kvm.org/

Laitkorpi, M., Selonen, P., & Systa, T. (2009). Towards a model-driven process for designing ReSTful web services. In *Proceedings of International Conference on Web Services* (pp. 173-180). Los Angeles, CA: IEEE Computer Society Press. doi:10.1109/ICWS.2009.63

Lakshman, A., & Malik, P. (2010, April). Cassandra: A decentralized structured storage system. *SIGOPS Oper. Syst. Rev.*, *44*(2), 35–40. doi:10.1145/1773912.1773922

Lakshminarayanan, K., Adkins, D., Perrig, A., & Stoica, I. (2004). Taming IP packet flooding attacks. *Computer Communication Review*, *34*(1), 45–50. doi:10.1145/972374.972383

Laszewski, G., Wang, L., Young, A. J., & He, X. (2009). Power-aware scheduling of virtual machines in DVFS-enabled clusters. In *Proceeding of CLUSTER'09*. IEEE. doi:10.1109/CLUSTR.2009.5289182

Le, D.-H., Truong, H.-L., Copil, G., Moser, O., Nastic, S., Gambi, A., & Dustdar, S. (2014). SALSA: A dynamic configuration tool for cloud-based applications. In *Proceedings of 6th International Conference on Cloud Computing*. Academic Press.

Leaver-Fay, A., Tyka, M., Lewis, S. M., Lange, O. F., Thompson, J., Jacak, R., & Bradley, P. et al. (2011). ROSETTA3: An object-oriented software suite for the simulation and design of macromolecules. *Methods in Enzymology*, *487*, 545–574. doi:10.1016/B978-0-12-381270-4.00019-6 PMID:21187238

Lee, K., Paton, N. W., Sakellariou, R., & Alvaro, A. A. F. (2009). Utility driven adaptive workflow execution. In *Proc. of the 9th International Symposium on Cluster Computing and the Grid* (CCgrid'09). Academic Press.

Lee, C. B., & Snavely, A. (2006). On the user-scheduler dialogue: Studies of user-provided runtime estimates and utility functions. *International Journal of High Performance Computing Applications*, 20(4), 495–506. doi:10.1177/1094342006068414

Lehr, W., & McKnight, L. (2002). Wireless internet access: 3G vs. WiFi? Cambridge, MA: Center for eBusiness @ MIT.

Leiserson, C. E. (1985). Fat-trees: Universal networks for hardware-efficient supercomputing. *IEEE Transactions on Computers*, 100(10), 892–901.

Lesk, A. M. (2010). *Introduction to protein science: Architecture, function, and genomics*. Oxford University Press.

Lewis, G. (2012). *The role of standards in cloud-computing interoperability*. Software Engineering Institute. Retrieved May 30, 2014 from http://repository.cmu.edu/sei/682

Li, J., Ren, K, & Kim, K. (2009). A2BE: Accountable attribute-based encryption for abuse free access control. *IACR Cryptology ePrint Archive, 118*.

Li, J., Ren, K., Zhu, B., & Wan, Z. G. (2009). Privacy-aware attribute-based encryption with user accountability. In Proceedings of Information Security (LNCS), (vol. 5735, pp. 347-362). Berlin: Springer. doi:10.1007/978-3-642-04474-8_28

Li, L., & Chou, W. (2010). Design patterns for RESTful communication. In *Proceedings of International Conference on Web Services* (pp. 512-519). Piscataway, NJ: IEEE Computer Society Press.

Li, W., & Svard, P. (2010). REST-based SOA application in the cloud: A text correction service case study. In *Proceedings of 6th World Congress on Services* (pp. 84-90). Piscataway, NJ: IEEE Society Press. doi:10.1109/SERVICES.2010.86

Li, Z., O'Brien, L., Zhang, H., & Cai, R. (2012). On a catalogue of metrics for evaluating commercial cloud services. In *Proceedings of 2012 ACM/IEEE 13th International Conference on Grid Computing (GRID)* (pp. 164-173). ACM/IEEE. doi:10.1109/Grid.2012.15

Libvirt. (2014a). *Libvirt: The virtualization API* [Computer software]. Retrieved from http://libvirt.org/

Libvirt. (2014b). *Snapshot XML format* [Computer software]. Retrieved from http://libvirt.org/formatsnapshot.html

Li, J., Huang, Q., Chen, X., Chow, S. S. M., Wong, D. S., & Xie, D. (2011). Multi-authority ciphertext-policy attribute-based encryption with accountability. In *Proceedings of ACM ASIACCS* (pp. 386–390). ACM. doi:10.1145/1966913.1966964

Li, K. (2008). Performance analysis of power-aware task scheduling algorithms on multiprocessor computers with dynamic voltage and speed. *IEEE Tr. On Par. Distr. Systems*, 19(11), 1484–1497. doi:10.1109/TPDS.2008.122

Lin, C., Lee, C., Liu, J., & Chen, C. (2010). A detection scheme for flooding attack on application layer based on semantic concept. IEEE, 385–389.

Lin, C., Liu, J., & Lien, C. (2008). Detection method based on reverse proxy against web flooding attacks. In *Proceedings of the Eighth International Conference on Intelligent Systems Design and Applications* (pp. 281–284). Academic Press. doi:10.1109/ISDA.2008.72

Lin, M., Wierman, A., Andrew, L., & Thereska, E. (2011). Dynamic right-sizing for power-proportional data centers. In *Proceedings of INFOCOM*. IEEE.

Litke, A., Skoutas, D., Tserpes, K., & Varvarigou, T. (2007). Efficient task replication and management for adaptive fault tolerance in mobile grid environments. *Future Generation Computer Systems*, 23(2), 163–178. doi:10.1016/j.future.2006.04.014

Liu, J., Zhao, F., Liu, X., & He, W. (2009). Challenges towards elastic power management in internet data centers. In *Proc. on IEEE Conf. Distr. Comput. Syst. Workshops*. Los Alamitos, CA: IEEE. doi:10.1109/ICDCSW.2009.44

Liu, W. (2009). Research on DoS attack and detection programming. In *Proceedings of 2009 Third International Symposium on Intelligent Information Technology Application* (pp. 207–210). IEEE. doi:10.1109/IITA.2009.165

Liu, X.F., Zhang, Y.Q., Wang, B.Y. & Yan, J.B. (2013, June). Mona: Secure multi-owner data sharing for dynamic groups in the cloud. *IEEE Transactions on Parallel and Distributed Systems, 24*(6), 1182-1191. doi: 10.1109/TPDS.2012.331

Liu, Q., & Liao, Y. (2009). *Grouping-based fine-grained job scheduling in grid computing.* IEEE; doi:10.1109/ETCS.2009.132

Liu, Q., Zhou, S., & Giannakis, G. B. (2004). Cross-layer combining of adaptive modulation and coding with truncated ARQ over wireless links. *IEEE Transactions on Wireless Communications, 3*(5), 1746–1755. doi:10.1109/TWC.2004.833474

Liu, Z., Cao, Z. F., & Wong, D. S. (2013). Black box traceable CP-ABE: How to catch people leaking their keys by selling decryption devices on Ebay. In *Proceedings of ACM Conference on Computer and Communications Security* (pp. 475-486). ACM. doi:10.1145/2508859.2516683

Liu, Z., Cao, Z. F., & Wong, D. S. (2013, January). White-box traceable ciphertext-policy attribute-based encryption supporting any monotone access structures. *IEEE Transactions on Information Forensics and Security, 8*(1), 76–88. doi:10.1109/TIFS.2012.2223683

Lo, J. (2005). *VMware and CPU virtualization technology.* World Wide Web Electronic Publication.

Loesing, S., Hentschel, M., Kraska, T., & Kossmann, D. (2012). Storm: An elastic and highly available streaming service in the cloud. *EDBT-ICDT, 12*, 55–60. doi:10.1145/2320765.2320789

Loiola, E. M., de Abreu, N. M. M., Boaventura-Netto, P. O., Hahn, P., & Querido, T. (2007). A survey for the quadratic assignment problem. *European Journal of Operational Research, 176*(2), 657–690. doi:10.1016/j.ejor.2005.09.032

Loutas, N., Kamateri, E., Bosi, F., & Tarabanis, K. (2011). Cloud computing interoperability: the state of play. In *Proceedings of International Conference on Cloud Computing Technology and Science* (pp. 752-757). Piscataway, NJ: IEEE Computer Society Press. doi:10.1109/CloudCom.2011.116

Loutas, N., Peristeras, V., & Tarabanis, K. (2011). Towards a reference service model for the web of services. *Data & Knowledge Engineering, 70*(9), 753–774. doi:10.1016/j.datak.2011.05.001

Lubbers, P., Albers, B., & Salim, F. (2010). *Pro HTML5 programming: Powerful APIs for richer internet application development.* New York, NY: Apress. doi:10.1007/978-1-4302-2791-5

Luigi, A., Iera, A., & Morabito, G. (2010). The internet of things: A survey. *Computer Networks, 54*(15), 2787–2805. doi:10.1016/j.comnet.2010.05.010

Lu, T., Chen, M., & Andrew, L. L. H. (2012). Simple and effective dynamic provisioning for power-proportional data centers. *IEEE Transactions on Parallel and Distributed Systems, 24*(6), 1161–1171. doi:10.1109/TPDS.2012.241

Malik, D. S., Mordeson, J. N., & Sen, M. K. (1994). On subsystems of a fuzzy finite state machine. *Fuzzy Sets and Systems, 68*(1), 83–92. doi:10.1016/0165-0114(94)90274-7

Malkowski, S. J., Hedwig, M., Li, J., Pu, C., & Neumann, D. (2011). Automated control for elastic n-tier workloads based on empirical modeling. In *Proceedings of the 8th ACM International Conference on Autonomic Computing (ICAC '11).* ACM. doi:10.1145/1998582.1998604

Mann, V., Gupta, A., Dutta, P., Vishnoi, A., Bhattacharya, P., Poddar, R., & Iyer, A. (2012). Remedy: Network-aware steady state VM management for data centers. In Proceedings of Networking 2012 (pp. 190-204). Springer.

Martin, P., Brown, A., Powley, W., & Vazquez-Poletti, J. L. (2011). Autonomic management of elastic services in the cloud. In *Proceedings of 2011 IEEE Symposium on Computers and Communications (ISCC)* (pp. 135-140). IEEE. doi:10.1109/ISCC.2011.5984006

Massie, M. L., Chun, B. N., & Culler, D. E. (2004). The Ganglia distributed monitoring system: Design, implementation and experience. *Parallel Computing, 30*(7), 817–840. doi:10.1016/j.parco.2004.04.001

Mathew, V., Sitaraman, R., & Rowstrom, A. (2012). Energy-aware load balancing in content delivery networks. In Proceedings of INFOCOM (pp. 954-962). IEEE.

McLoughlin, M. (2008). *The QCOW2 image format* [Computer software]. Retrieved from https://people.gnome.org/~markmc/qcow-image-format.html

McVitie, D. G., & Wilson, L. B. (1971). The stable marriage problem. *Communications of the ACM, 14*(7), 486–490. doi:10.1145/362619.362631

Meier, J., Mackman, A., Dunner, M., Vasireddy, S., & Escamilla, R. (2003). *Improving web application security threats and countermeasures.* Retrieved April 08, 2012, from http://msdn. microsoft.com/en-us/library/ff649874.aspx

Mell, P., & Grance, T. (2009). The NIST Definition of Cloud Computing. *National Institute of Standards and Technology, 53*(6), 50. Retrieved from http://csrc.nist.gov/groups/SNS/cloud-computing/cloud-def-v15.doc

Meng, X., Isci, C., Kephart, J., Zhang, L., Bouillet, E., & Pendarakis, D. (2010). Efficient resource provisioning in compute clouds via VM multiplexing. In *Proceedings of the 7th International Conference on Autonomic Computing* (pp. 11-20). Academic Press. doi:10.1145/1809049.1809052

Meng, X., Pappas, V., & Zhang, L. (2010). Improving the scalability of data center networks with traffic-aware virtual machine placement. In Proceedings of INFOCOM (pp. 1-9). IEEE. doi:10.1109/INFCOM.2010.5461930

Messinger, D., & Lewis, G. (2013). *Application virtualization as a strategy for cyber foraging in resource-constrained environments (CMU/SEI-2013-TN-007).* Pittsburgh, PA: Software Engineering Institute, Carnegie Mellon University.

Mishra, A., Jain, R., & Durresi, A. (2012). Cloud computing: Networking and communication challenges. *IEEE Comm. Magazine*, 24-25.

Mohammed, S., Servos, D., & Fiaidhi, J. (2010). HCX: A distributed OSGi based web interaction system for sharing health records in the cloud. In *Proceedings of IEEE/WIC/ACM Int. Conf. on Web Intelligence and Intelligent Agent Technology (WI-IAT)* (pp. 102-107). Toronto, Canada: IEEE. doi:10.1109/WI-IAT.2010.26

Moldovan, D., Copil, G., Truong, H.-L., & Dustdar, S. (2013). MELA: Monitoring and analyzing elasticity of cloud services. In *Proceedings of 5th International Conference on Cloud Computing.* Academic Press.

Monsoon Solutions, Inc. (2014). *Power monitor* [Apparatus]. Retrieved from http://www.msoon.com/LabEquipment/PowerMonitor/

Mopari, I., Pukale, S., & Dhore, M. (2009). Detection of DDoS attack and defense against IP spoofing. In *Proceedings of the International Conference on Advances in Computing, Communication and Control - ICAC3 '09* (pp. 489–493). New York: ACM. doi:10.1145/1523103.1523200

Morein, W., Stavrou, A., Cook, D., Keromytis, A., Misra, V., & Rubenstein, D. (2003). Using graphic turing tests to counter automated DDoS attacks against web servers. In *Proceedings of the 10th ACM Conference on Computer and Communication Security - CCS '03* (p. 8). New York: ACM Press. doi:10.1145/948109.948114

Mrozek, D., & Małysiak-Mrozek, B. (2013). CASSERT: A two-phase alignment algorithm for matching 3D structures of proteins. In A. Kwiecień, P. Gaj, & P. Stera (Eds.), *Computer Networks: Proceedings of the 20th International Conference (CCIS)* (Vol. 370, pp. 334-343), Berlin, Germany: Springer. doi:10.1007/978-3-642-38865-1_34

Mrozek, D. (2014). *High-performance computational solutions in protein bioinformatics.* Berlin, Germany: Springer. doi:10.1007/978-3-319-06971-5

Mrozek, D., Małysiak-Mrozek, B., & Kłapciński, A. (2014). Cloud4Psi: Cloud computing for 3D protein structure similarity searching. *Bioinformatics (Oxford, England), 30*(19), 2822–2825. doi:10.1093/bioinformatics/btu389 PMID:24930141

Mukundrao, J., & Vikram, G. (2011). Enhancing security in cloud computing. *Information and Knowledge Management, 1*(1), 40–45.

Muracevic, D., & Kurtagic, H. (2009). Geospatial SOA using RESTful web services. In *Proceedings of 31st International Conference on Information Technology Interfaces* (pp. 199-204). Piscataway, NJ: IEEE Society Press.

Muthuvelu, N., Chai, I., Chikkannan, E., & Buyya, R. (2010). On-line task granularity adaptation for dynamic grid applications. In C.-H. Hsu, L. T. Yang, J. H. Park, & S.-S. Yeo (Eds.), Algorithms and architectures for parallel processing (Vol. 6081, pp. 266–277). Berlin: Springer Berlin Heidelberg. Retrieved from http://www.springerlink.com/index/10.1007/978-3-642-13119-6_24

Muthuvelu, N., Liu, J., Soe, N. L., Venugopal, S., Sulistio, A., & Buyya, R. (2005). A dynamic job grouping-based scheduling for deploying applications with fine-grained tasks on global grids. In Proceedings of the 2005 Australasian Workshop on Grid Computing and e-Research (Vol. 44, pp. 41–48). Darlinghurst, Australia: Australian Computer Society, Inc. Retrieved from http://dl.acm.org/citation.cfm?id=1082290.1082297

Muthuvelu, N., Chai, I., & Eswaran, C. (2008). *An adaptive and parameterized job grouping algorithm for scheduling grid jobs*. IEEE. doi:10.1109/ICACT.2008.4493929

Mykkänen, J., & Tuomainen, M. (2008). An evaluation and selection framework for interoperability standards. *Information and Software Technology, 50*(3), 176–197. doi:10.1016/j.infsof.2006.12.001

Mysore, R. N., Pamboris, A., Farrington, N., Huang, N., Miri, P., Radhakrishnan, S., & Vahdat, A. et al. (2009). Portland: A scalable fault-tolerant layer 2 data center network fabric. *Computer Communication Review, 39*(4), 39–50. doi:10.1145/1594977.1592575

N'Takpe, T., & Suter, F. (2009). *Concurrent scheduling of parallel task graphs on multi-clusters using constrained resource allocations*. IEEE. doi:10.1109/IPDPS.2009.5161161

Naor, D., Naor, M., & Lotspiech, J. B. (2001). Revocation and tracing schemes for stateless receivers. *Proceedings of Anniversary International Cryptology Conference Advances in Cryptology (CRYPTO), 2139,* 41-62. doi:10.1007/3-540-44647-8_3

Naskos, A., Stachtiari, E., Gounaris, A., Katsaros, P., Tsoumakos, D., Konstantinou, I., & Sioutas, S. (2014). Cloud elasticity using probabilistic model checking. *CoRR abs/1405.4699*

Neely, M.J., Modiano, E., & Rohs, C.E. (2003). Power allocation and routing in multi beam satellites with time-varying channels. *IEEE/ACM Tr. on Networking, 19*(1), 138-152.

Nelson, M., Lim, B.-H., Hutchins, G., & Associates. (2005). Fast transparent migration for virtual machines. In *Proceedings of USENIX Annual Technical Conference, General Track* (pp. 391-394). Academic Press.

Netto, M. A. S., & Buyya, R. (2009). Offer-based scheduling of deadline-constrained bag-of-tasks applications for utility computing systems. In *Proc. of the 18th International Heterogeneity in Computing Workshop (hcw'09), in Conj. with the 23rd IEEE International Parallel and Distributed Processing Symposium (IPDPS'09)*. IEEE. doi:10.1109/IPDPS.2009.5160910

Neumeyer, L., Robbins, B., & Kesari, A. (2010). S4: Distributed stream computing platform. In *Proceedings of Intl. Workshop on Knowledge Discovery Using Cloud and Distributed Computing Platforms*. IEEE.

Newman, R. (2006). Cybercrime, identity theft, and fraud: practicing safe internet - Network security threats and vulnerabilities. *International Journal of Computer Applications ACM, 9*(12), 11–15.

Ng Wai Keat, T. A. (2006). Scheduling framework for bandwidth-aware job grouping-based scheduling in grid computing. *Malaysian Journal of Computer Science, 19*.

Nieplocha, J., Harrison, R., & Littlefield, R. (1994). Global arrays: A portable shared-memory programming model for distributed memory computers. In Proceedings of Supercomputing (pp. 340–349, 816). Academic Press.

Nimbus is Cloud Computing for Science. (2014). Retrieved from http://www.nimbusproject.org/

Nimbus. (2014). *Nimbus science cloud* [Software]. Available from http://www.nimbusproject.org/downloads/

Novell PlateSpin Recon. (2014). Retrieved from https://www.netiq.com/products/recon/

Nurmi, D. (2009). The eucalyptus open-source cloud-computing system. In *Proceedings of 9th IEEE/ACM International Symposium on Cluster Computing and the Grid* (pp. 124-131). Shanghai, China: IEEE Computer Society Press.

Nurmi, D., Wolski, R., Grzegorczyk, C., Obertelli, G., Soman, S., Youseff, L., & Zagorodnov, D. (2009). The eucalyptus open-source cloud-computing system. In *Proceedings of Cluster Computing and the Grid* (pp. 124-131). IEEE. doi:10.1109/CCGRID.2009.93

Oak Ridge Leadership Computing. (2014). *Cheetah collective library* [Software]. Available from http://www.csm.ornl.gov/cheetah/index.html

OASIS Topology and Orchestration Specification for Cloud Applications (TOSCA). (2013). Retrieved from http://docs.oasis-open.org/tosca/TOSCA/v1.0/cs01/TOSCA-v1.0-cs01.html

Ohio State University. (2014). *MVAPICH: MPI over InfiniBand, 10GigE/iWARP and RoCE.* Retrieved from http://mvapich.cse.ohio-state.edu/download/mvapich2/

Open Science Grid. (2014). Retrieved from http://www.opensciencegrid.org

OpenMP Architecture Review Board (2013). *OpenMP application program interface specification.* Academic Press.

OpenSHMEM Org. (2011). *OpenSHMEM specification.* Available from http://openshmem.org

OpenStack. (2014). *OpenStack cloud software* [Software]. Available from https://www.openstack.org/software/

Organization of Economics Co-Operation and Development. (2013). Retrieved from http://www.oecd.org/

Padala, P., You, K.Y., Shin, K.G., Zhu, X., Uysal, M., Wang, Z., … Merchant, M. (2009). Automatic control of multiple virtualized resources. In *Proc. of EuroSys.* Academic Press.

Padhy, R., Patra, M., & Chan, S. (2012). Design and implementation of a cloud based rural healthcare information system mode. *UNIASCIT, 2*(1), 149–157.

Palm, J., Anderson, K., & Lieberherr, K. (2003). *Investigating the relationship between violations of the law of demeter and software maintainability.* Paper presented at the Workshop on Software-Engineering Properties of Languages for Aspect Technologies. Retrieved May 30, 2014 from http://www.daimi.au.dk/~eernst/splat03/papers/Jeffrey_Palm.pdf

Park, Y. H., Hong, S., & Ryu, J. (2010). An effective defense mechanism against DoS/DDoS attacks in flow-based routers. In *Proceedings of the 8th International Conference on Advances in Mobile Computing and Multimedia - MoMM '10* (pp. 442–446). New York: ACM Press. doi:10.1145/1971519.1971595

Parr, T. (2007). *The definitive ANTLR reference.* Raleigh, NC: The Pragmatic Bookshelf.

Pasha, M., Supramaniam, S., Liang, K., Amran, M., Chandra, B., & Rajeswari, M. (2012, January). An Android-based mobile medical image viewer and collaborative annotation: Development issues and challenges. *International Journal of Digital Content Technology and its Applications, 6*(1).

Pautasso, C., Zimmermann, O., & Leymann, F. (2008). Restful web services vs. "big" web services: Making the right architectural decision. In *Proceedings of International Conference on World Wide Web* (pp. 805-814). ACM Press.

Peng, Y., Ma, S., & Lee, J. (2009). REST2SOAP: A framework to integrate SOAP services and RESTful services. In *Proceedings of International Conference on Service-Oriented Computing and Applications* (pp. 1-4). Piscataway, NJ: IEEE Computer Society Press. doi:10.1109/SOCA.2009.5410458

Piao, J. T., & Yan, J. (2010). A network-aware virtual machine placement and migration approach in cloud computing. In *Proceedings of Grid and Cooperative Computing* (GCC) (pp. 87-92). Academic Press. doi:10.1109/GCC.2010.29

Pierce, P. (1988). The NX/2 operating system. In *Proceedings of the Third Conference on Hypercube Concurrent Computers and Applications* (pp. 384–390). ACM Press.

Piscitello, D. (2011). *Anatomy of a DNS DDoS amplification attack.* Retrieved September 30, 2014, from http://www.watchguard.com/infocenter/editorial/41649.asp

Pisinger, D. (1997). A minimal algorithm for the 0-1 knapsack problem. *Operations Research, 45*(5), 758–767. doi:10.1287/opre.45.5.758

Portnoy, M. (2012). *Virtualization essentials.* Wiley.

Potdar, V., Sharif, A., & Chang, E. (2009). Wireless sensor networks: A survey. In *Proceedings of International Conference on Advanced Information Networking and Applications Workshops* (pp. 636-641). Bradford, UK: IEEE Computer Society Press. doi:10.1109/WAINA.2009.192

Poulymenopoulou, M., Malamateniou, F., & Vassilacopoulos, G. (2003). Emergency healthcare process automation using workflow technology and web services. *Med Inform Internet, 28*(3), 195–207. doi:10.1080/14639230310001617841 PMID:14612307

Pritchard, H., Gorodetsky, I., & Buntinas, D. (2011). A uGNI-based MPICH2 nemesis network module for the cray XE. In *Proceedings of the 18th European MPI Users' Group conference on Recent advances in the message passing interface* (pp. 110–119). Berlin, Germany: Springer-Verlag. doi:10.1007/978-3-642-24449-0_14

Puppet Labs. (2014a). *Learning puppet—Manifests*. Retrieved from http://docs.puppetlabs.com/learning/manifests.html

Puppet Labs. (2014b). *Puppet enterprise* [Computer software]. Retrieved from http://puppetlabs.com/puppet/puppet-enterprise

Python. (2014). *LZMA – Compression using the LZMA algorithm*. Retrieved from https://docs.python.org/dev/library/lzma.html

QEMU. (2014a). *Documentation/networking*. Retrieved from http://wiki.qemu.org/Documentation/Networking

QEMU: *Open Source Processor Emulator* [Computer software]. (2014b). Retrieved from http://wiki.qemu.org

Qian, Z., He, Y., Su, C., Wu, Z., Zhu, H., Zhang, T. (2013). TimeStream: Reliable stream computation in the cloud. In *Proceedings of EuroSys* (pp. 1-14). Academic Press.

Rahimi, M. R., Venkatasubramanian, N., Mehrotra, S., & Vasilakos, A. V. (2012). MAPCloud: Mobile applications on an elastic and scalable 2-tier cloud architecture. In *Proceedings of the 2012 IEEE/ACM Fifth International Conference on Utility and Cloud Computing* (pp. 83–90). Washington, DC: IEEE Computer Society Press. doi:10.1109/UCC.2012.25

Raju, B., Swarna, P., & Rao, M. (2011). Privacy and security issues of cloud computing. *International Journal (Toronto, Ont.)*, *1*(2), 128–136.

Rak, M., Venticinque, S., Mandhr, T. A., Echevarria, G., & Esnal, G. (2011). Cloud application monitoring: The mosaic approach. In *Proceedings of Cloud Computing Technology and Science* (cloudcom) (pp. 758-763). IEEE.

Ramakrishnan, L., Huang, T. M., Thyagaraja, K., Zagorodnov, D., Koelbel, C., Kee, Y.-S., … Mandal, A. (2009). *VGrADS: Enabling e-science workflows on grids and clouds with fault tolerance*. ACM Press. doi:10.1145/1654059.1654107

Ramgovind, S., Eloff, M., & Smith, E. (2010). The management of security in cloud computing. In Proceedings of Information Security for South Africa (ISSA) (pp. 1–7). IEEE. doi:10.1109/ISSA.2010.5588290

Reid, J. (2008). The new features of Fortran 2008. *SIGPLAN Fortran Forum*, *27*(2), 8–21.

Ren, K. (2013). *The course of data security in cloud computing*. University of Science and Technology of China.

Rimal, B., Choi, E., & Lumb, I. (2009). A taxonomy and survey of cloud computing systems. In *Proceedings of Fifth International Joint Conference on INC, IMS and IDC* (pp. 44-51). Seoul, Korea: IEEE Computer Society Press. doi:10.1109/NCM.2009.218

Rittinghouse, J., & Ransome, J. (2010). *Cloud computing: Implementation, management, and security*. Taylor and Francis Group, LLC.

Roberts, J., & Al-Hamdani, W. (2011). Who can you trust in the cloud? In *Proceedings of the 2011 Information Security Curriculum Development Conference on InfoSecCD 11* (Vol. 43, pp. 15–19). ACM Press. doi:10.1145/2047456.2047458

Romanus, M., Mantha, P. K., McKenzie, M., Bishop, T. C., Gallichio, E., & Merzky, A., … Jha, S. (2012). The anatomy of successful ECSS projects: Lessons of supporting high-throughput high-performance ensembles on XSEDE. In *Proceedings of the 1st Conference of the Extreme Science and Engineering Discovery Environment: Bridging from the eXtreme to the Campus and Beyond* (pp. 46:1–46:9). New York, NY: ACM. doi:10.1145/2335755.2335843

Rouse, M. (2004). *Virtualization sprawl (VM sprawl)*. Retrieved September 26, 2014, from http://whatis.techtarget.com/definition/virtualization-sprawl-virtual-server-sprawl

Ruj, S., Stojmenovic, M., & Nayak, A. (2014, February). Decentralized access control with anonymous authentication for securing data in clouds. *IEEE Transactions on Parallel and Distributed Systems*, *25*(2), 384–394. doi:10.1109/TPDS.2013.38

Sabahi, F. (2011). Virtualization-level security in cloud computing. In Proceedings of Communications Software and Networks (ICCS) (pp. 250–254). IEEE. doi:10.1109/ICCSN.2011.6014716

Sabharwal, N., & Shankar, R. (2013). *Apache cloudstack cloud computing*. Birmingham, UK: Packt Publishing Ltd.

Sabin, G., Kochhar, G., & Sadayappan, P. (2004). *Job fairness in non-preemptive job scheduling*. IEEE. doi:10.1109/ICPP.2004.1327920

Sahai, A., & Waters, B. (2005). Fuzzy identity based encryption. *Advances in Cryptology–Eurocrypt, 3494*, 457–473.

SalesForce. (2014). *Service cloud*. Retrieved from http://www.salesforce.com/

Sandar, V., & Shenai, S. (2012). Economic denial of sustainability (EDoS) in cloud services using HTTP and XML based DDoS attacks. *International Journal of Computers and Applications, 41*(20), 11–16. doi:10.5120/5807-8063

Sandia National Laboratory. (2014). *Portals-SHMEM* [Software]. Available from https://code.google.com/p/portals-shmem/downloads/list

Sangroya, A., Kumar, S., Dhok, J., & Varma, V. (2010). Towards analyzing data security risks in cloud computing environments. *ICISTM*, 255–265.

Sapuntzakis, C. P., Chandra, R., Pfaff, B., Chow, J., Lam, M. S., & Rosenblum, M. (2002). Optimizing the migration of virtual computers. *ACM SIGOPS Operating Systems Review, 36*(SI), 377-390.

Saran, H., & Vazirani, V. V. (1995). Finding k cuts within twice the optimal. *SIAM Journal on Computing, 24*(1), 101–108. doi:10.1137/S0097539792251730

Satyanarayanan, M., Bahl, P., Caceres, R., & Davies, N. (2009). The case for VM-based cloudlets in mobile computing. *IEEE Pervasive Computing, 8*(4), 14–23. doi:10.1109/MPRV.2009.82

Schatzberg, D., Appavoo, J., Krieger, O., & Van Hensbergen, E. (2012). *Why elasticity matters*. Technical Report BUCS-TR-2012-006. Computer Science Department, Boston University.

Scheneider, S., Hirzel, M., & Gedik, B. (2013). Tutorial: Stream processing optimizations. In *Proceedings of ACM DEBS* (pp. 249-258). ACM.

Schippers, H. (2009). Towards an actor-based concurrent machine model. In *Proceedings of 4th Workshop on the Implementation, Compilation, Optimization of Object-Oriented Languages and Programming Systems* (pp. 4-9). New York, NY: ACM Press.

Schwartz, M. (2012). *New virtualization vulnerability allows escape to hypervisor attacks*. Retrieved September 28, 2014, from http://www.darkreading.com/risk-management/new-virtualization-vulnerability-allows-escape-to-hypervisor-attacks/d/d-id/1104823?

Seinstra, F. (2011). Jungle computing: Distributed supercomputing beyond clusters, grids, and clouds. In M. Cafaro & G. Aloisio (Eds.), *Grids, clouds and virtualization* (pp. 167–197). London, UK: Springer.

Serrano, D., Bouchenak, S., Kouki, Y., Ledoux, T., Lejeune, J., Sopena, J., . . . Sens, P. (2013). Towards QoS-oriented SLA guarantees for online cloud services. In *Proceedings of 13th IEEE/ACM International Symposium on Cluster, Cloud and Grid Computing (CCGrid)*. IEEE/ACM. doi:10.1109/CCGrid.2013.66

Shalf, J., Dosanjh, S., & Morrison, J. (2011). Exascale computing technology challenges. In *Proceedings of the 9th International Conference on High Performance Computing for Computational Science*. Springer-Verlag.

Shamir, A. (1979). How to share a secret. *Communications of the ACM, 22*(11), 612–613. doi:10.1145/359168.359176

Shao, J., & Wang, Q. (2011, July). A performance guarantee approach for cloud applications based on monitoring. In Proceedings of Computer Software and Applications Conference Workshops (compsacw) (pp. 25 - 30). IEEE. doi:10.1109/COMPSACW.2011.15

Shapiro, J., & Brutlag, D. (2004). FoldMiner and LOCK2: Protein structure comparison and motif discovery on the web. *Nucleic Acids Research, 32*(Web Server), 536–541. doi:10.1093/nar/gkh389 PMID:15215444

Sharma, U., Shenoy, P., Sahu, S., & Shaikh, A. (2011). A cost-aware elasticity provisioning system for the cloud. In *Proceedings of the 2011 31st International Conference on Distributed Computing Systems (ICDCS '11)*. IEEE Computer Society. doi:10.1109/ICDCS.2011.59

Shen, Z., Subbiah, S., Gu, X., & Wilkes, J. (2011). CloudScale: Elastic resource scaling for multi-tenant cloud systems. In *Proceedings of the 2nd ACM Symposium on Cloud Computing (SOCC '11)*. ACM. doi:10.1145/2038916.2038921

Shindyalov, I., & Bourne, P. (1998). Protein structure alignment by incremental combinatorial extension (CE) of the optimal path. *Protein Engineering, 11*(9), 739–747. doi:10.1093/protein/11.9.739 PMID:9796821

Shrivastava, V., Zerfos, P., Lee, K.-W., Jamjoom, H., Liu, Y.-H., & Banerjee, S. (2011). Application-aware virtual machine migration in data centers. In Proceedings of INFOCOM, 2011 (pp. 66–70). IEEE. doi:10.1109/INFCOM.2011.5935247

Simanta, S., Ha, K., Lewis, G., Morris, E., & Satyanarayanan, M. (2013). A reference architecture for mobile code offload in hostile environments. In *Proceedings of the 5th International Conference on Mobile Computing, Applications, and Services* (pp. 274–293). Berlin, Germany: Springer. doi:10.1007/978-3-642-36632-1_16

Simjanoska, M., Ristov, S., Velkoski, G., & Gusev, M. (2013). Scaling the performance and cost while scaling the load and resources in the cloud. In *Proceedings of 2013 36th International Convention on Information & Communication Technology Electronics & Microelectronics (MIPRO)*. Academic Press.

Sitaram, D., & Manjunath, G. (2012). Cloud security requirements and best practices. In *Moving to the cloud: Developing apps in the new world of cloud computing* (p. 309). Elsevier.

Skjellum, A., Smith, S. G., Doss, N. E., Leung, A. P., & Morari, M. (1994). The design and evolution of zipcode. *Parallel Computing, 20*(4), 565–596. doi:10.1016/0167-8191(94)90029-9

Skowron, P., & Rzadca, K. (2013). *Non-monetary fair scheduling: A cooperative game theory approach*. ACM Press. doi:10.1145/2486159.2486169

Slack, E. (2011). *How do you know that "delete" means delete in cloud storage?* Retrieved April 14, 2012, from http://www.storage-switzerland.com/Articles/Entries/2011/8/16_How_do_you_know_that_Delete_means_Delete_in_Cloud_Storage.html

Smith, J., & Nair, R. (2005). *Virtual machines: Versatile platforms for systems and processes*. Elsevier.

Sofokleous, C., Loulloudes, N., Trihinas, D., Pallis, G., & Dikaiakos, M. (2014). c-Eclipse: An open-source management framework for cloud applications. In Proceedings of EuroPar 2014. Porto, Portugal: Academic Press.

Somasundaram, M., Gitanjali, S., Govardhani, T., Priya, G., & Sivakumar, R. (2011). Medical image data management system in mobile cloud computing environment. In *Proceedings of International Conference on Signal, Image Processing and Applications (ICSIPA 2011)*. Kuala Lumpur, Malaysia: Academic Press.

Sommerfeld, D., & Richter, H. (2011). *Efficient grid workflow scheduling using a two-tier approach*. Paper presented at the HealthGrid 2011.

Song, F., Huang, D., Zhou, H., & You, I. (2012). Application-aware virtual machine placement in data centers. In *Proceedings of Innovative Mobile and Internet Services in Ubiquitous Computing* (IMIS) (pp. 191-196). Academic Press. doi:10.1109/IMIS.2012.119

Sotomayor, B., Montero, R. S., Llorente, I. M., & Foster, I. (2009). Virtual infrastructure management in private and hybrid clouds. *IEEE Internet Computing, 13*(5), 14–22. doi:10.1109/MIC.2009.119

Sqalli, M., Al-Haidari, F., & Salah, K. (2011). EDoS-shield - A two-steps mitigation technique against EDoS attacks in cloud computing. In *Proceedings of 2011 Fourth IEEE International Conference on Utility and Cloud Computing* (pp. 49–56). IEEE. doi:10.1109/UCC.2011.17

Srikant, R. (2004). *The mathematics of internet congestion control*. Birkhauser. doi:10.1007/978-0-8176-8216-3

Srivatsa, M., Iyengar, A., Yin, J., & Liu, L. (2008). Mitigating application-level denial of service attacks on Web servers. *ACM Transactions on the Web, 2*(3), 1–49. doi:10.1145/1377488.1377489

Stoess, J., Lang, C., & Bellosa, F. (2007). Energy management for hypervisor-based virtual machines. *USENIX Annual Technical*, 1-14.

Sumaray, A., & Makki, S. (2012). A comparison of data serialization formats for optimal efficiency on a mobile platform. In *Proceedings of 6th International Conference on Ubiquitous Information Management and Communication* (article no. 48). New York, NY: ACM Press. doi:10.1145/2184751.2184810

Sunderam, V. S. (1990). PVM: A framework for parallel distributed computing. *Concurrency (Chichester, England)*, 2(4), 315–339. doi:10.1002/cpe.4330020404

Takemura, C. & Crawford, L. S. (2009). *The book of Xen: A practical guide for the system administrator.* No Starch Press.

Takouna, I., Dawoud, W., & Meinel, C. (2012). Analysis and simulation of HPC applications in virtualized data centers. In *Proceedings of Green Computing and Communications* (GreenCom) (pp. 498-507). IEEE. doi:10.1109/GreenCom.2012.80

Takouna, I., Rojas-Cessa, R., Sachs, K., & Meinel, C. (2013). Communication-aware and energy-efficient scheduling for parallel applications in virtualized data centers. In *Proceedings of Utility and Cloud Computing* (UCC) (pp. 251-255). IEEE. doi:10.1109/UCC.2013.50

Tamm, O., Hersmeyer, C., & Rush, A. M. (2010). Eco-sustainable system and network architectures for future transport networks. *Bell Labs.Techn. J.*, *14*(4), 311–327. doi:10.1002/bltj.20418

Tan, P.-N. (2006). *Introduction to data mining* (1st ed.). Boston: Pearson Addison Wesley.

Taylor, I. J. (2007). Workflows for e-science scientific workflows for grids. London: Springer. Retrieved from http://public.eblib.com/EBLPublic/PublicView.do?ptiID=337445

Templeton, S., & Levitt, K. (2003). Detecting spoofed packets. In *Proceedings of the DARPA Information Survivability Conference and Exposition (DISCEX'03)* (pp. 164 – 175). Academic Press. doi:10.1109/DISCEX.2003.1194882

ten Bruggencate, M., & Roweth, D. (2010). DMAPP: An API for one-sided program models on baker systems. In *Proceedings of the 2010 Cray User Group Annual Technical Conference*. Academic Press.

The M. P. I. Forum. (1994). *MPI: A message passing interface.* Technical Report. Available from http://www.mpi-forum.org/docs

The S. L. A. (2007). *The service level agreement.* Retrieved September 27, 2014, from http://www.sla-zone.co.uk/

Tolk, A. (2006). What comes after the semantic web - PADS implications for the dynamic web. In *Proceedings of 20th Workshop on Principles of Advanced and Distributed Simulation* (pp. 55-62). Beach Road, Singapore: IEEE Computer Society Press. doi:10.1109/PADS.2006.39

TOP500.org. (2012). *TOP500 supercomputing sites.* Available from http://www.top500.org/lists/

Toshniwal, R., & Agrawal, D. (2004). Tracing the roots of markup languages. *Communications of the ACM*, *47*(5), 95–98. doi:10.1145/986213.986218

Trappler, T. (2012). When your data's in the cloud, is it still your data? *Computer World.* Retrieved April 07, 2012, from http://www.computerworld.com/s/article/9223479/When_your_data_s_in_the_cloud_is_it_still_your_data_

Trihinas, D., Loulloudes, N., Moldovan, D., Sofokleous, S., Pallis, G., & Dikaiakos, M. D. (2013). *CELAR deliverable: Cloud monitoring tool V1.* Retrieved from http://www.celarcloud.eu/wp-content/uploads/2013/11/Cloud-Monitoring-Tool-V1.pdf

Trihinas, D., Pallis, G., & Dikaiakos, M. D. (2014a). JCatascopia: Monitoring elastically adaptive applications in the cloud. In *Proceedings of 14th IEEE/ACM International Symposium on Cluster, Cloud and Grid Computing.* IEEE/ACM. doi:10.1109/CCGrid.2014.41

Tsaregorodtsev, A., Brook, N., Ramo, A. C., Charpentier, P., Closier, J., Cowan, G., & Zhelezov, A. et al. (2010). DIRAC3 – The new generation of the LHCb grid software. *Journal of Physics: Conference Series*, *219*(6), 062029. doi:10.1088/1742-6596/219/6/062029

UCRIVERSIDE. (2011). *Data sanitization.* Retrieved October 01, 2014, from http://cnc.ucr.edu/security/datasan.html

Ujjwal, A., Manglani, B., Akarte, D., & Jain, A. (2012, March-April). Healthbook – Ubiquitous solution for heath services. *International Journal of Engineering Research and Applications*, *2*(2), 965–967.

Upadhyaya, B., Zou, Y., Xiao, H., Ng, J., & Lau, A. (2011). Migration of SOAP-based services to RESTful services. In *Proceedings of 13th IEEE International Symposium on Web Systems Evolution* (pp. 105-114). Piscataway, NJ: IEEE Society Press. doi:10.1109/WSE.2011.6081828

UPC Consortium. (2005). *UPC language specifications, v1.2*. Tech Report LBNL-59208. Lawrence Berkeley National Lab. Available from http://www.gwu.edu/~upc/docs/upc_specs_1.2.pdf

Urgaonkar, B., Pacifici, G., Shenoy, P., Spreitzer, M., & Tantawi, A. (2007). Analytic modeling of multitier Internet applications. *ACM Tr. on the Web*, *1*(1).

Vaidya, V. (2009). *Virtualization vulnerabilities and threats: A solution white paper*. Retrieved April 13, 2012, from http://www.redcannon.com/vDefense/VM_security_wp.pdf

Vanitha, T., Narasimha Murthy, M., & Chaitra, B. (2013). E-healthcare billing and record management information system using Android with Cloud. *IOSR Journal of Computer Engineering*, *11*(4), 13-19.

Vaquero, L., Rodero-Merino, L., Caceres, J., & Lindner, M. (2008). A break in the clouds: Towards a cloud definition. *Computer Communication Review*, *39*(1), 50–55. doi:10.1145/1496091.1496100

Varshney, U. (2007, March). Pervasive healthcare and wireless health monitoring. *Journal on Mobile Networks and Applications*, *12*(2-3), 113–127. doi:10.1007/s11036-007-0017-1

Vasudevan, V., Phanishayee, A., & Shah, H. (2009). Safe and effective fine-grained TCP stream retransmissions for datacenter communication. In Proceedings of ACM SIGCOMM (pp. 303-314). ACM.

Venkata, M. G., Graham, R. L., Hjelm, N. T., & Gutierrez, S. K. (2012a). Open MPI for Cray XE/XK systems. In *Proceedings of the 2012 Cray User Group Annual Technical Conference*. Stuttgart, Germany: Academic Press.

Venkata, M. G., Graham, R. L., Ladd, J. S., & Shamis, P. (2012b). Exploring the all-to-all collective optimization space with ConnectX CORE-direct. In *Proceedings of the 41st International Conference on Parallel Processing*. Pittsburgh, PA: Academic Press. doi:10.1109/ICPP.2012.28

Venkata, M. G., Graham, R. L., Ladd, J. S., Shamis, P., Hjelm, N. T., & Gutierrez, S. K. (2012c). Exploiting atomic operations for collective on Cray XE/XK systems. In *EuroMPI 2012: Proceedings of the 19th EuroMPI Conference*. Vienna, Austria: Academic Press.

Venkata, M. G., Shamis, P., Graham, R. L., Ladd, J. S., & Sampath, R. (2013). Optimizing blocking and nonblocking reduction operations for multicore systems: Hierarchical design and implementation. In *Proceedings of IEEE International Conference on Cluster Computing*. Indianapolis, IN: IEEE. doi:10.1109/CLUSTER.2013.6702676

Villegas, D., Antoniou, A., Sadjadi, S. M., & Iosup, A. (2012). An analysis of provisioning and allocation policies for infrastructure-as-a-service clouds. In *Proceedings of the 2012 12th IEEE/ACM International Symposium on Cluster, Cloud and Grid Computing (ccgrid 2012)* (CCGRID '12). IEEE Computer Society. doi:10.1109/CCGrid.2012.46

Villegas, D. (2010). The role of grid computing technologies in cloud computing. In B. Furht & A. Escalante (Eds.), *Handbook of cloud computing* (pp. 183–218). New York, NY: Springer US. doi:10.1007/978-1-4419-6524-0_8

Vinutha, S., Raju, C., & Siddappa, M. (2012, July). Development of electronic hospital management system utilizing cloud computing and Android OS using VPN connections. *International Journal of Scientific & Technology Research*, *1*(6), 59–61.

Virtualizationadmin. (2008). *What is VM sprawl?* Retrieved September 27, 2014, from http://www.virtualizationadmin.com/faq/vm-sprawl.html

Vladimirov, R. (2014). *The future of cloud computing: Emerging trends*. Retrieved October 05, 2014, from http://smartdatacollective.com/roman-vladimirov/194086/future-cloud-computing-emerging-trends

Vlahu-Gjorgievska, E., & Trajkovik, V. (2011). Personal healthcare system model using collaborative filtering techniques. *Advances in Information Sciences and Service Sciences*, *3*(3), 64–74. doi:10.4156/aiss.vol3.issue3.9

VMware Capacity Planner. (2014). Retrieved from http://www.vmware.com/products/capacity-planner

Wan, J., Zou, C., Ullah, S., Lai, C., Zhou, M., & Wang, X. (2013, September-October). Cloud-enabled wireless body area networks for pervasive healthcare. *IEEE Transactions on Network, 27*(5).

Wang, G., Liu, Q., & Wu, J. (2010). Hierarchical attribute-based encryption for fine-grained access control in cloud storage services. In *Proceedings of ACM Conference on Computer and Communications Security* (pp. 735–737). ACM. doi:10.1145/1866307.1866414

Wang, L., Zhang, F., Aroca, J.A., Vasilakos, A.V., Zheng, K., Hou, C., …, Liu, Z. (2014). Green DCN: A general framework for achieving energy efficiency in data denter networks. *IEEE JSAC, 32*(1).

Wang, W., Tolk, A., & Wang, W. (2009). The levels of conceptual interoperability model: Applying systems engineering principles to M&S. In *Proceedings of Spring Simulation Multiconference* (article no.: 168). San Diego, CA: Society for Computer Simulation International.

Wang, X., et al. (2013, February). AMES-cloud: A framework of adaptive mobile video streaming and efficient social video sharing in the clouds. *IEEE Trans. Multimedia, 10*(1109).

Wang, Y., Lu, J., Yu, J., Gibbs, R. A., & Yu, F. (2013). An integrative variant analysis pipeline for accurate genotype/haplotype inference in population NGS data. *Genome Research, 23*(5), 833–842. doi:10.1101/gr.146084.112 PMID:23296920

Warecki, S., & Znamirowski, L. (2004). Random simulation of the nanostructures conformations. In *Computing, Communication and Control Technology, Proceedings of International Conference* (vol. 1, pp. 388-393), Austin, TX: The International Institute of Informatics and Systemics.

Warneke, D., & Kao, O. (2011). Exploiting dynamic resource allocation for efficient parallel data processing in the cloud. *IEEE Tr. on Paral. and Distr. Systems, 22*(6), 985–997.

Waters, B. (2011). Ciphertext-policy attribute-based encryption: An expressive, efficient, and provably secure realization. *Public Key Cryptography, 6571*, 53–70. doi:10.1007/978-3-642-19379-8_4

Webber, J., Parastatidis, S., & Robinson, I. (2010). *REST in practice: Hypermedia and systems architecture.* Sebastopol, CA: O'Reilly Media, Inc. doi:10.1007/978-3-642-15114-9_3

Weber-Jahnke, J., Peyton, L., & Topaloglou, T. (2012). eHealth system interoperability. *Information Systems Frontiers, 14*(1), 1–3. doi:10.1007/s10796-011-9319-8

Wood, T., Shenoy, P. J., Venkataramani, A., & Yousif, M. S. (2007). *Black-box and gray-box strategies for virtual machine migration.* NSDI.

Wooten, R., Klink, R., Sinek, F., Bai, Y., & Shar, M. (2012). Design and implementation of a secure healthcare social cloud system. In *Proceedings of 12th IEEE/ACM Int. Symp. Cluster, Cloud and Grid Computing (CCGRID 2012)* (pp. 805-810). Ottawa, Canada: IEEE/ACM. doi:10.1109/CCGrid.2012.131

Wu, S., Skolnick, J., & Zhang, Y. (2007). Ab initio modeling of small proteins by iterative TASSER simulations. *BMC Biology, 5*(1), 17. doi:10.1186/1741-7007-5-17 PMID:17488521

Wyatt, E., Griendling, K., & Mavris, D. (2012). Addressing interoperability in military systems-of-systems architectures. In *Proceedings of International Systems Conference* (pp. 1-8). Piscataway, NJ: IEEE Computer Society Press.

Xdelta [Computer software]. (2014). Retrieved from http://xdelta.org

Xia, L., Cui, Z., & Lange, J. (2012). *VNET/P: Bridging the cloud and high performance computing through fast overaly networking.* IEEE. doi:10.1145/2287076.2287116

Xiao, Y., Simoens, P., Pillai, P., Ha, K., & Satyanarayanan, M. (2013). Lowering the barriers to large-scale mobile crowdsensing. In *Proceedings of the 14th Workshop on Mobile Computing Systems and Applications* (p. 9). New York, NY: ACM. doi:10.1145/2444776.2444789

Xie, Y., & Yu, S. (2009). Monitoring the application-layer DDoS attacks for popular websites. *IEEE/ACM Transactions on Networking, 17*(1), 15–25. doi:10.1109/TNET.2008.925628

Xing, W., Tsoumakos, D., Sofokleous, S., Liabotis, I., Floros, V., & Loverdos, C. (2014). *CELAR deliverable: Translational cancer detection pipeline design*. Academic Press.

XSEDE. (2014). Retrieved from http://www.xsede.org

Xu, D., & Zhang, Y. (2012). Ab initio protein structure assembly using continuous structure fragments and optimized knowledge-based force field. *Proteins*, *80*(7), 1715–1735. PMID:22411565

Xu, L., Wu, X., & Zhang, X. (2012). CL-PRE: A certificateless proxy re-encryption scheme for secure data sharing with public cloud. In *Proceedings of the 7th ACM Symposium on Information Computer and Communications Security* (pp. 87-88). ACM. doi:10.1145/2414456.2414507

Xu, R., & Wunsch, D. (2005). Survey of clustering algorithms. *IEEE Transactions on Neural Networks*, *16*(3), 645–678.

Yang, K., Jia, X. H., & Ren, K. (2013, April). DAC-MACS: Effective data access control for multi-authority cloud storage systems. In *Proceedings of IEEE INFOCOM*. IEEE. doi:10.1109/INFCOM.2013.6567100

Yatagai, T., Isohara, T., & Sasase, I. (2007). Detection of HTTP-GET flood attack based on analysis of page access behavior. In *Proceedings of IEEE Pacific Rim Conference on Communications, Computers and Signal Processing* (pp. 232–235). IEEE.

Yelick, K., Coghlan, S., Draney, B., & Canon, R. (2011). The Magellan report on cloud computing for science, U.S. Department of Energy. Office of Science, Office of Advanced Scientific Computing Research, Tech. Rep. IEEE.

Yeo, C. S., & Buyya, R. (2007). Pricing for utility-driven resource management and allocation in clusters. *International Journal of High Performance Computing Applications*, *21*(4), 405–418. doi:10.1177/1094342007083776

Ye, Y., & Godzik, A. (2003). Flexible structure alignment by chaining aligned fragment pairs allowing twists. *Bioinformatics (Oxford, England)*, *19*(2), 246–255. PMID:14534198

Yu, S. C., Wang, C., Ren, K., & Lou, W. J. (2010). Attribute based data sharing with attribute revocation. In *Proceedings of ACM Symposium Information Computer and Communications Security (ASIACCS)* (pp. 261-270). ACM. doi:10.1145/1755688.1755720

Zaharia, M., Das, T., Li, H., Shenker, S., & Stoica, I. (2012). *Discretized streams: an efficient and fault-tolerant model for stream processing on large clusters*. Hotcloud.

Zayas, E. (1987). Attacking the process migration bottleneck. *Operating Systems Review*, *21*(5), 13–24. doi:10.1145/37499.37503

Zeroconf: Zero Configuration Networking [Computer software]. (2014). Retrieved from http://www.zeroconf.org/

Zhang, B., Qian, Z., Huang, W., Li, X., & Lu, S. (2012). Minimizing communication traffic in data centers with power-aware VM placement. In *Proceedings of Innovative Mobile and Internet Services in Ubiquitous Computing* (IMIS) (pp. 280-285). Academic Press. doi:10.1109/IMIS.2012.71

Zhang, F., Geng, J., Qin, Z., & Zhou, M. (2007). Detecting the DDoS attacks based on SYN proxy and hop-count filter. In *Proceedings of International Conference on Communications, Circuits and Systems ICCCAS 2007.* (pp. 457–461). Academic Press. doi:10.1109/ICCCAS.2007.6251605

Zhang, Q., Cheng, L., & Boutaba, R. (2010). Cloud computing: State-of-the-art and research challenges. *Journal of Internet Services and Applications*, *1*(1), 7-18.

Zhao, H., & Sakellariou, R. (2006). *Scheduling multiple DAGs onto heterogeneous systems*. IEEE. doi:10.1109/IPDPS.2006.1639387

Zhou, M., Zhang, R., Xie, W., Qian, W., & Zhou, A. (2010). Security and privacy in cloud computing: A survey. In *Proceedings of 2010 Sixth International Conference on Semantics Knowledge and Grids* (pp. 105–112). IEEE. doi:10.1109/SKG.2010.19

Zhou, Y., Liu, X., Xue, L., Liang, X., & Liang, S. (2010). Business process centric platform-as-a-service model and technologies for cloud enabled industry solutions. In *Proceedings of 3rd International Conference on Cloud Computing* (pp. 534-537). Miami,FL: Academic Press. doi:10.1109/CLOUD.2010.52

Zhou, Z., Liu, F., Jin, H., Li, B., & Jiang, H. (2013). On arbitrating the power-performance tradeoff in SaaS clouds. In *Proceedings of INFOCOM* (pp. 872–880). IEEE.

Zhu, D., Melhem, R., & Childers, B. R. (2003). Scheduling with dynamic voltage/rate adjustment using slack reclamation in multiprocessor real-time systems. *IEEE Transactions on Parallel and Distributed Systems, 14*(7), 686–700. doi:10.1109/TPDS.2003.1214320

Zhu, J., & Weng, Z. (2005). FAST: A novel protein structure alignment algorithm. *Proteins, 58*(3), 618–627. doi:10.1002/prot.20331 PMID:15609341

Zhu, Y., Hu, H. X., Ahn, G. J., Gong, X. R., & Chen, S. M. (2011). POSTER: Temporal attribute-based encryption in clouds. In *Proceedings of the 18th ACM Conference on Computer and Communications Security* (pp. 881-310). ACM. doi:10.1145/2093476.2093517

Zikopoulos, P. (2012). *Understanding big data*. New York, NY: McGraw-Hill.

Zomaya, A. Y., & Chan, G. (2004). *Efficient clustering for parallel tasks execution in distributed systems*. IEEE. doi:10.1109/IPDPS.2004.1303164

About the Contributors

Susmit Bagchi has received Bachelor of Science (B.Sc.) degree with honours from the University of Calcutta, India, in 1993. He received Bachelor of Engineering (B.E.) degree in Electronics Engineering from Nagpur University, India, and Master of Engineering (M.E.) degree in Electronics & Telecommunication Engineering from the Bengal Engineering and Science University, Shibpur, India, in the year 1997 and 1999, respectively. He obtained Ph.D. (Engineering) degree in Information Technology from the Bengal Engineering and Science University, Shibpur, India, in the year 2008. He has diverse work experiences in both academia and industrial research environments. He worked for Defence R&D (India) as Scientist, Samsung R&D (India and S. Korea) as R&D Engineer/Technical Lead, and Norwegian University of Science and Engineering (Norway) as a researcher. He also worked for Bengal Engineering and Science University (India) as a Lecturer, for the Sikkim Manipal University (India) as Reader, and for Gyeongsang National University (South Korea) as Assistant Professor. Currently, he is holding the position of Associate Professor in the Department of Informatics, Gyeongsang National University (South Korea). His main research interests are comprised of Distributed Computing Systems and Advanced Operating Systems.

* * *

Khalid Al-Begain is a Professor of Mobile Computing and Networking and the Director of the Integrated Communications Research Centre (ICRC) at the University of South Wales (Since 2003), and the Director of the Centre of Excellence in Mobile Applications and Services (CEMAS), a £6.4million Centre partly funded by European Regional Development Fund (ERDF). He received his MSc and PhD in Communications Engineering in 1986 and 1989, respectively, from Budapest University of Technology, Hungary. He also received Post Graduate Diploma in Management from University of Glamorgan in 2011 after finishing two years MBA course modules. He is the President of the European Council for Modelling and Simulation (ECMS) and is member of the Welsh Government Ministerial Advisory Steering Group for ICT in Schools. He is UNESCO Expert in networking, British Computer Society Fellow and Chartered IT Professional, Senior Member of the IEEE and IEEE Communications and Computer Societies. He has two granted patents, co-authored two books; the first: *Practical Performance Modelling* by Kluwer in 2001 and the second: *IMS: Deployment and Development Perspective* by John Wiley & Sons in 2009. He also edited 15 books, and authored more than 180 papers in refereed journals and conferences. He is a member of the editorial board of several international journals and acted as Guest Editor for five journals special issues. He is the co-inventor of MOSEL: The Modelling, Specification and Evaluation Language. He has already supervised over 20 successful PhD projects. He has also delivered over 10 keynotes in major international conferences. He is the Winner of the 2013 IWA Inspire Wales Award for Science and Technology.

Wael Alosaimi is currently a PhD Researcher in the University of South Wales, United Kingdom. He focused on protecting the cloud computing environment from Distributed Denial of Service (DDoS) attacks and their economical version (EDoS). He received his BSc degree in Electrical and Computer Engineering from King Abdulaziz University, Saudi Arabia in 2002 and his MSc degree in Computer Systems Security from the University of Glamorgan, United Kingdom in 2011. He is currently a member of the Integrated Communication Research Centre (ICRC) and Mobile Computing Communications and Networking (MoCoNet) Research Group. His current area of research includes Network Security, Cloud Computing and BYOD Security (Technical & Procedural). He has published a number of conference papers.

Danilo Amendola is PhD Student in Information Communication Technology at Sapienza University of Roma from November 2013. He Received his Msc in Information Communication Technology at Sapienza University of Roma in 2012. Also, he Received His Bsc in Computer Science in Università della Calabria, Rende, Italy in 2006. Danilo is specialist in Network Programming and telecommunication.

Enzo Baccarelli received the Laurea degree (summa cum laude) in electronic engineering and Ph.D. degree in Communication Theory and Systems, both from the University "La Sapienza" in 1989 and 1992, respectively. In 1995, he received the Post-Doctorate degree in Information Theory and Applications from the INFOCOM Dept., University "La Sapienza" where he also served as Research Scientist from 1996 to 1998. Since 1998 he has been an Associate Professor in signal processing and radio communications at the University "La Sapienza". Since 2003, he is full Professor in data communication at the University "La Sapienza". He has authored/co-authored more than 200 publications in well-known conferences and journals such as IEEE transactions (40+ papers) and Elsevier publishers.

Ben Bradshaw is a research programmer at the Software Engineering Institute at Carnegie Mellon University. Ben works in the Advanced Mobile Systems groups. His research areas include edge computing, data analysis, and cyber-foraging in resource-constrained environments. Ben has a Bachelor's degree in Computer Science and a Master's of Business Administration from Baylor University.

Ivona Brandic is Assistant Professor at the Distributed Systems Group, Information Systems Institute, Vienna University of Technology (TU Wien). Prior to that, she was Assistant Professor at the Department of Scientific Computing, Vienna University. She received her PhD degree from Vienna University of Technology in 2007. From 2003 to 2007 she participated in the special research project AURORA (Advanced Models, Applications and Software Systems for High Performance Computing) and the European Union's GEMSS (Grid-Enabled Medical Simulation Services) project. She is involved in the European Union's SCube project and she is leading the Austrian national FoSII (Foundations of Selfgoverning ICT Infrastructures) project funded by the Vienna Science and Technology Fund (WWTF). She is Management Committee member of the European Commission's COST Action on Energy Efficient Large Scale Distributed Systems. From June-August 2008 she was visiting researcher at the University of Melbourne. Her interests comprise SLA and QoS management, Service-oriented architectures, autonomic computing, workflow management, and large scale distributed systems (Cloud, Grid, and Cluster).

Rajkumar Buyya is Professor of Computer Science and Software Engineering, Future Fellow of the Australian Research Council, and Director of the Cloud Computing and Distributed Systems (CLOUDS) Laboratory at the University of Melbourne, Australia. He is also serving as the founding CEO of Manjrasoft, a spin-off company of the University, commercializing its innovations in Cloud Computing. He has authored over 450 publications and four text books including *Mastering Cloud Computing* published by McGraw Hill and Elsevier/Morgan Kaufmann, 2013 for Indian and international markets, respectively. He also edited several books including *Cloud Computing: Principles and Paradigms* (Wiley Press, USA, Feb 2011). He is one of the highly cited authors in computer science and software engineering worldwide. Microsoft Academic Search Index ranked Dr. Buyya as the world's top author in distributed and parallel computing between 2007 and 2012. Software technologies for Grid and Cloud computing developed under Dr. Buyya's leadership have gained rapid acceptance and are in use at several academic institutions and commercial enterprises in 40 countries around the world. Dr. Buyya has led the establishment and development of key community activities, including serving as foundation Chair of the IEEE Technical Committee on Scalable Computing and five IEEE/ACM conferences. These contributions and international research leadership of Dr. Buyya are recognized through the award of "2009 IEEE Medal for Excellence in Scalable Computing" from the IEEE Computer Society, USA. Manjrasoft's Aneka Cloud technology developed under his leadership has received "2010 Asia Pacific Frost & Sullivan New Product Innovation Award" and "2011 Telstra Innovation Challenge, People's Choice Award". He served as the foundation Editor-in-Chief (EiC) of IEEE Transactions on Cloud Computing and currently serving as Co-EiC of Software: Practice and Experience. For further information on Dr. Buyya, please visit his cyberhome: www.buyya.com.

Rodrigo N. Calheiros is a Research Fellow in the Department of Computing and Information Systems, The University of Melbourne, Australia. Since 2010, he is a member of the CLOUDS Lab of the University of Melbourne, where he researches various aspects of cloud computing. He works in this field since 2008, when he designed and developed CloudSim, an Open Source tool for simulation of cloud platforms used by research institutions and companies worldwide. His research interests also include Big Data, virtualization, grid computing, and simulation and emulation of distributed systems.

Georgiana Copil is a PhD student and university assistant at the Distributed Systems Group, Institute of Information Systems, Vienna University of Technology, with background on distributed and cloud computing.

Nicola Cordeschi received the Laurea degree (bachelor) in Communication Engineering from the University of Rome "La Sapienza" in 2004. He received the Ph.D. degree in Information and Communication Engineering in 2008. His Ph.D. dissertation was on the adaptive QoS Transport of Multimedia over Wireless Connections via cross-layer approaches based on the Calculus of Variations. He is currently a Contractor-Researcher with the DIET Dept., University of Rome "La Sapienza". His research activity is focused on wireless communications and deals with the design and optimization of high performance transmission systems for wireless multimedia applications. Nicola published more 70+ papers in several well-known IEEE Transaction and Elsevier journals in his research.

Rafael Ferreira da Silva is a Computer Scientist in the Collaborative Computing Group at the USC Information Sciences Institute. He received his PhD in Computer Science from INSA-Lyon, France, in 2013. In 2010, he received his Master's degree in Computer Science from Universidade Federal de Campina Grande, Brazil, and his BS degree in Computer Science from Universidade Federal da Paraiba, in 2007. His research focuses on the execution of scientific workflows on heterogeneous distributed systems such as Clouds and Grids. See http://www.rafaelsilva.com for further information.

Cesar A. F. De Rose is an Associate Professor in the Computer Science Department at the Pontifical Catholic University of Rio Grande do Sul (PUCRS), Porto Alegre, Brazil. His primary research interests are parallel and distributed computing and parallel architectures. He is currently conducting research on a variety of topics applied to clusters and grids, including resource management, resource monitoring, distributed allocation strategies and virtualization. Dr. De Rose received his doctoral degree in Computer Science from the University Karlsruhe, Germany, in 1998.

José C. Delgado is an Associate Professor at the Computer Science and Engineering Department of the Instituto Superior Técnico (University of Lisbon), in Lisbon, Portugal, where he earned the Ph.D. degree in 1988. He lectures courses in the areas of Computer Architecture, Information Technology and Service Engineering. He has performed several management roles in his faculty, namely Director of the Taguspark campus, near Lisbon, and Coordinator of the B.Sc. and M.Sc. in Computer Science and Engineering at that campus. He has been the coordinator of and researcher in several international research projects. As an author, his publications include one book, several book chapters and more than 50 papers in international refereed conferences and journals.

Frédéric Desprez is a Chief Senior Research Scientist at Inria and holds a position at the LIP laboratory (ENS Lyon, France). He co-founded the SysFera company where he holds a position as scientific advisor. He received his PhD in C.S. from Institut National Polytechnique de Grenoble, France, in 1994 and his MS in C.S. from ENS Lyon in 1990. His research interests include parallel algorithms, scheduling for large scale distributed platforms, data management, and grid and cloud computing. He leads the Grid'5000 project, which offers a platform to evaluate large-scale algorithms, applications, and middleware systems. See http://graal.ens-lyon.fr/~desprez/ for further information.

Marios D. Dikaiakos is Professor of Computer Science Department at the University of Cyprus and Director of the University's Centre for Entrepreneurship. He received his Ph.D. in Computer Science from Princeton University (1994). His research interests include Cloud Computing and Web Technologies.

Schahram Dustdar is a full professor of computer science and head of the Distributed Systems Group, Institute of Information Systems, at the Vienna University of Technology. He is an ACM Distinguished Scientist and IBM Faculty Award recipient.

Sebastián Echeverría is a research software engineer at Universidad de los Andes in Santiago, Chile. He worked for a year at the Software Engineering Institute at Carnegie Mellon University, and continues to be involved in research projects with the Institute. His areas of research are mobile computing and wireless networks, virtualization, and software architecture. Sebastián holds a Bachelor and Master in Computer Science from Pontificia Universidad Católica de Chile and a Master in Software Engineering from Carnegie Mellon University.

Vincent C. Emeakaroha is a postdoctoral researcher at the Irish Centre for Cloud Computing and Commerce affiliated with University College Cork. He received bachelor degree in Computer Engineering in 2006 and acquired double masters in Software Engineering & Internet Computing in 2008 and in Computer Science Management in 2009. In 2012, he received his Ph.D. in Computer Science all from Vienna University of Technology. His research areas of interest include Cloud computing, autonomic computing, energy efficiency in Cloud, SLA, and QoS management.

Md Hasanul Ferdaus is a PhD candidate in the Faculty of Information Technology, Monash University, Australia, and a faculty member (on study leave) in the Computer Science Department of American International University-Bangladesh (AIUB) since 2010. He received his Master of Science degree in Information and Communication Technology from Politecnico di Torino, Italy (Home University) and Karlsruhe Institute of Technology (Exchange University), Germany in 2009, and his Bachelor of Science degree in Computer Science and Engineering from Bangladesh University of Engineering and Technology (BUET), Bangladesh in 2004. He worked as a Software Developer in Sikraft Solutions Limited, Bangladesh in 2004, and as a System Analyst in Robi Axiata Limited, Bangladesh from 2005 to 2006. He also worked as part-time Assistant in Research in the FZI Research Center for Information Technology, Karlsruhe, Germany in 2008 and in the Telematics Institute, Karlsruhe Institute of Technology (KIT), Germany in 2009. His main research interest is focused on Cloud Computing, Distributed and Parallel Computing, and Middleware Systems.

Evangelos Floros holds a B.Sc. and a M.Sc. in Informatics and Telecommunications from the National and Kapodistrian University of Athens, Greece. He currently works in GRNET as a Project Manager coordinating national and European projects in the areas of Cloud and High-Performance Computing.

Ioannis Giannakopoulos is a PhD student at the Computing Systems Laboratory of the National Technical University of Athens (NTUA). He received his Diploma in Electrical and Computer Engineering from NTUA in 2012 and began the PhD programme in the research field of Distributed Systems and Data Management.

Tristan Glatard obtained a PhD in grid computing applied to medical image analysis from the University of Nice Sophia-Antipolis in 2007. He was a post-doc at the University of Amsterdam in 2008. He is now a researcher at CNRS Creatis in Lyon, working on distributed systems for medical imaging applications.

Bingsheng He received the bachelor's degree in Computer Science from Shanghai Jiao Tong University in 2003, and the PhD degree in computer science from the Hong Kong University of Science and Technology in 2008. He is an assistant professor in the Division of Computer Science, School of Computer Engineering, Nanyang Technological University, Singapore. His research interests are database systems and high-performance computing.

Ioannis Konstantinou is a senior researcher at the Computing Systems Laboratory of the National Technical University of Athens (NTUA). He received his Diploma in Electrical and Computer Engineering from NTUA in 2004, his M.Sc. in Techno-Economic Systems from NTUA in 2007 and his PhD from NTUA in 2011.

Duc-Hung Le is a research assistant and PhD student at the Distributed Systems Group, Institute of Information Systems, Vienna University of Technology since 2013. His current research focuses on dynamic and automatic configuration of cloud-based applications in multiple clouds.

Grace A. Lewis is a Principal Researcher at the Carnegie Mellon Software Engineering Institute (SEI) in the Advanced Mobile Systems (AMS) Initiative. She is the Principal Investigator for the Edge-Enabled Tactical Systems project that investigates architectures and technologies that adapt new generations of mobile devices and sensors to support humans operating in demanding edge environments, characterized by high mobility, rapidly-changing mission requirements, limited computing resources, high levels of stress, and poor network connectivity. Her current interests and projects are in mobile computing, cloud computing, and Service-Oriented Architecture (SOA). She has particular interest in architectural strategies for cyber-foraging – a technique for dynamically augmenting the computing resources of resource-limited mobile devices, by opportunistically exploiting fixed computing infrastructure in nearby proximity. Grace holds a B.Sc. in Systems Engineering and an Executive MBA from Icesi University in Cali, Colombia; and a Master in Software Engineering from Carnegie Mellon University. She is currently a PhD candidate at the Department of Computer Science (Faculty of Sciences) at VU University Amsterdam.

Nicholas Loulloudes is a PhD candidate at the Dept. of Computer Science, University of Cyprus. His research focuses around the areas of Cloud/Grid computing systems, Complex Network Science and Vehicular Sensor Network routing and data dissemination algorithms.

Christos K. K. Loverdos is a research-inclined software professional. He has been working in the software industry for fifteen years designing, implementing and delivering flexible, enterprise-level systems, and making strategic technical decisions.

Maode Ma received his PhD degree in computer science from Hong Kong University of Science and Technology in 1999. Now, Dr. Ma is an Associate Professor in the School of Electrical and Electronic Engineering at Nanyang Technological University in Singapore. He has extensive research interests including wireless networking and network security. Dr. Ma has more than 250 international academic publications including over 100 journal papers and more than 130 conference papers. He currently serves as the Editor-in-Chief of International Journal of Electronic Transport. He also serves as an Associate Editor for other five international academic journals. Dr. Ma is an IET Fellow and a senior member of IEEE Communication Society and IEEE Education Society. He is the vice Chair of the IEEE Education Society, Singapore Chapter. He is also an IEEE Communication Society Distinguished Lecturer.

Daniel Moldovan is a PhD student and research assistant at the Distributed Systems Group, Institute of Information Systems, Vienna University of Technology, having a background in distributed, green, and elastic computing.

Dariusz Mrozek is an Assistant Professor in Institute of Informatics at the Silesian University of Technology (SUT) in Gliwice, Poland. He received his PhD degree from SUT in 2006. His research interests cover bioinformatics, information systems, parallel and Cloud computing, databases and Big data. He is now focused on the analysis of protein structures, functions and activities and the use of novel computation techniques to get insights from biological data. He is the author of several works published by influential international journals, including BMC Bioinformatics, Bioinformatics, Journal of Molecular Modeling, Journal of Intelligent Information Systems, author of a book on the use of high-performance computational solutions in protein bioinformatics published by Springer and co-editor of twelve other books devoted to databases and data processing. Working in different research projects, he cooperated with qualified institutions, e.g. Imperial College of London (on the Chernobyl Tissue Bank), Institute of Oncology in Gliwice, Poland, Department of Internal Diseases, Diabetology and Nephrology, Medical University of Silesia, Zabrze, Poland and Department of Biochemistry, Medical University of Silesia, Katowice, Poland.

Manzur Murshed received the BScEngg (Hons) degree in computer science and engineering from Bangladesh University of Engineering and Technology (BUET), Dhaka, Bangladesh, in 1994 and the PhD degree in computer science from the Australian National University (ANU), Canberra, Australia, in 1999. He also completed his Postgraduate Certificate in Graduate Teaching from ANU in 1997. He is currently an Emeritus Professor Robert HT Smith Professor and Personal Chair at the Faculty of Science and Technology, Federation University Australia. Prior to this appointment, he served the School of Information Technology, Federation University Australia as the Head of School, from January 2014 to July 2014, the Gippsland School of Information Technology, Monash University as the Head of School 2007 to 2013. He was one of the founding directors of the Centre for Multimedia Computing, Communications, and Applications Research (MCCAR). His major research interests are in the fields of video technology, information theory, wireless communications, distributed computing, and security & privacy. He has so far published 181 refereed research papers and received more than $1M nationally competitive research funding, including three Australian Research Council Discovery Projects grants in 2006, 2010, and 2013 on video coding and communications, and a large industry grant in 2011 on secured video conferencing. He has successfully supervised 19 and currently supervising 6 PhD students. He is an Editor of *International Journal of Digital Multimedia Broadcasting* and has had served as an Associate Editor of *IEEE Transactions on Circuits and Systems for Video Technology* in 2012 and as a Guest Editor of special issues of *Journal of Multimedia* in 2009-2012. He received the Vice-Chancellor's Knowledge Transfer Award (commendation) from the University of Melbourne in 2007, the inaugural Early Career Research Excellence award from the Faculty of Information Technology, Monash University in 2006, and a University Gold Medal from BUET in 1994. He is a Senior Member of IEEE.

Marco A. S. Netto has over 14 years of experience on resource management for distributed systems. He works mainly on Cloud Computing related topics. He is currently the manager of the Industrial Cloud Technologies Group at IBM Research Brazil. Marco published over 40 scientific publications, including journals, conference papers, and book chapters, and has filed over 30 patents. Marco obtained his Ph.D. in Computer Science at the University of Melbourne (2010), Australia.

George Pallis is faculty member at the Computer Science Department, University of Cyprus. His research interests include distributed systems, such as the Web and clouds, content distribution networks, information retrieval, and data clustering.

Nikolaos Papailiou is a PhD candidate in the Computing Systems Laboratory of School of ECE at the National Technical University of Athens, Greece. His research focuses on scalability, elasticity and efficiency of distributed systems and especially distributed databases.

Stephen Poole is the Chief Scientist and Director of Special Programs at Oak Ridge National Laboratory's Computer Science and Mathematics Division. He was the Chief Architect of DarkHorse and the initial Chief Architect for Los Alamos's RoadRunner hybrid system and the proposed ORNL 2011 OLCF-3 system called Titan. He has worked in Hybrid computing for most of his career. He is the Architecture team lead for the SPEC (ORNL/LANL/SNL) exa-scale team. He is the Technical Director of the Extreme Scale Systems Center located at ORNL and funded by the Department of Defense. He has over 100 publications.

James Root is a Senior Research Programmer at the Software Engineering Institute at Carnegie Mellon University. His current area of research is mobile computing in resource-constrained environments and how to bring usable computing power to those environments. James holds a Bachelor of Science in Software Engineering from Pennsylvania State University and is pursuing a Master in Software Engineering degree from Carnegie Mellon University.

Maria Salama received B.Sc. in Computer Science and Post-Graduate Diploma in Management Information Systems from Sadat Academy for Management Science, Cairo, Egypt in 2001 and 2003 respectively. She received M.Sc. in Computer Science from Arab Academy for Sciences and Technology in 2011. She is now assistant lecturer in the British University in Egypt. Prior to joining the BUE, she had a solid experience in the industry, stepping from web development to project leading. Her research interests are in software and web engineering, web services, and Cloud Computing.

Ahmed Shawish received the B.Sc. and M.Sc. degree from Ain Shams University, Cairo, Egypt in 1997 and 2002, all in Computer Sciences. In 2009, he got his Ph.D. degree from Tohoku University, Japan. He is currently assistant professor in the Scientific Computing department, faculty of Computer & Information Science, Ain Shams University, Egypt. His research covers supporting VoIP applications over wired and wireless networks. Currently, he is focusing his re-search on the Cloud Computing areas.

Craig Sheridan (BSc) is Head of Research Projects at Flexiant Limited and was part of the team behind Europe's first public Cloud platform 'Flexiscale' in 2007 which led to the founding of Flexiant in 2009. Craig has developed his Cloud computing expertise with his work on a number of Seventh Framework Programme projects since 2010, including OPTIMIS, CumuloNimbo, 4CaaSt, MODAClouds, PaaSage, and CELAR and has worked as an external expert for the European Commission.

Mohammad Shojafar is a PhD Student in Information Communication Technology at Sapienza University of Roma from November 2012. He Received his Msc in Software Engineering in Qazvin Islamic Azad University, Qazvin, Iran, in 2010. Also, he received his Bsc in Computer Engineering-Software major in Iran University Science and Technology, Tehran, Iran, in 2006. His current research focuses on wireless communications, distributed computing and optimization. He has authored/co-authored more than 25 publications in well-known conferences and journals in Springer, IEEE, and Elsevier publishers.

Soumya Simanta is a senior member of the technical staff at the Software Engineering Institute at Carnegie Mellon University. His current areas of research are mobile and edge computing, focused on analysis of data in real time in resource-constrained environments. Soumya holds a Bachelor in Engineering from Sambalpur University and a Master in Software Engineering from Carnegie Mellon University.

Chrystalla Sofokleous is working as a special scientist at the Dept. of Computer Science, University of Cyprus. With undergraduate studies at the University of Cyprus, and graduate studies at the University of Southampton, UK, her research interests focus on cloud computing, elastic resource provisioning, Semantic Web, and Linked Data.

Kam Star is a digital media entrepreneur, researcher, investor, and award-winning games developer. Creating his first computer game in 1986, he studied Architecture and is currently undertaking his PhD at the Serious Games Institute at Coventry University exploring the interplay between game dynamics and personality traits to maximize collective intelligence.

Demetris Trihinas is a Ph.D. student at the Department of Computer Science of the University of Cyprus. He holds a Dipl.-Ing. degree in Electrical and Computer Engineering, and a MSc. degree in Computer Science and Internet Computing from the National Technical University of Athens. His research interests including monitoring and data analysis, cloud computing and distributed systems.

Hong-Linh Truong is an assistant professor for Service Engineering Analytics at the Distributed Systems Group, Institute of Information Systems, Vienna University of Technology. More info at http://dsg.tuwien.ac.at/staff/truong.

Dimitrios Tsoumakos is an Assistant Professor in the Department of Informatics of the Ionian University. He is also a senior researcher at the Computing Systems Laboratory of the National Technical University of Athens (NTUA).

Charles Turyagyenda is a Research Fellow in the Centre for Excellence in Mobile Application and Services (CEMAS) at the University of South Wales, UK. He received a BSc. (Eng) in Electrical Engineering in 2005, a MSc. (Eng) in Modern Digital and Radio Frequency Wireless Communications in 2008 and a PhD in Advanced Telecommunications in 2014. His research interests include 5G research, Mission Critical Communications over Commercial IP broadband networks, IP Multimedia Subsystem (IMS), Network Functions Virtualisation, Software Defined Networks and 3GPP LTE and LTE-Advanced networks addressing a number of topics such as radio resource management, energy efficiency, interference management and cooperative communications.

Manjunath Gorentla Venkata is a leading research scientist in Oak Ridge National Laboratory's Computer Science and Mathematics Division pursuing research and development efforts focused on abstractions and mechanisms that enables non-computer scientists to use the supercomputers and clusters in an efficient way. He is primarily responsible for conceiving, designing and leading the development of scalable communication interfaces, protocols and implementations for extreme-scale systems. Dr. Gorentla Venkata has published several peer-reviewed research articles in this area, contributed to various international standards, and his research has influenced commercially available network interfaces. He contributes to many open source software systems, particularly Open MPI, a popular implementation of MPI. He is a senior member of the IEEE. He also holds an affiliate assistant professor in Auburn University's Department of Computer Science and Software Engineering.

Wei Xing is the Head of Scientific Computing at Cancer Research UK Manchester Institute (CRUK-MI), University of Manchester. His current research interests focus on cloud computing, large-scale data integration, and big data analysis.

Michal Zak is currently working in CEMAS, within the University of South Wales, where the main focus of his research is security in the Cloud Computing. He received his bachelor's degree from the Brno University of Technology in Czech Republic, and his diploma thesis was published in EUROSIS 2012. He achieved a distinction in master's degree from the University of Glamorgan in United Kingdom. At present Michal is doing his PhD in University of South Wales in emphasis on denial of service attacks. Michal's background also includes a number of publications, UNIX OS, CCNA certifications, and objective programming languages.

Yuqing Zhang received the BSc and MSc degrees in computer science from Xidian University, China, in 1987 and 1990, respectively. He received the PhD degree in cryptography from Xidian University in 2000. He is a professor and supervisor of PhD students at the Graduate University of Chinese Academy of Sciences. His research interests include cryptography, wireless security, and trust management. He is a member of the IEEE.

Qianqian Zhao received her BSc degree information and computing science from Henan University, China, in 2009. Now she is enrolled in the School of Communication Engineering in Xidian University in Aug. 2010, registering for a 5-Year Master Successive Postgraduate and Doctoral Program in Information Security. Her research interests include cryptography, wireless security, cloud computing security, and social networks.

Index

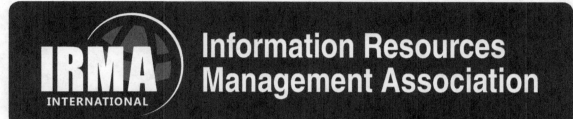

Become an IRMA Member

Members of the **Information Resources Management Association (IRMA)** understand the importance of community within their field of study. The Information Resources Management Association is an ideal venue through which professionals, students, and academicians can convene and share the latest industry innovations and scholarly research that is changing the field of information science and technology. Become a member today and enjoy the benefits of membership as well as the opportunity to collaborate and network with fellow experts in the field.

IRMA Membership Benefits:

- **One FREE Journal Subscription**
- **30% Off Additional Journal Subscriptions**
- **20% Off Book Purchases**
- Updates on the latest events and research on Information Resources Management through the IRMA-L listserv.
- Updates on new open access and downloadable content added to Research IRM.
- A copy of the Information Technology Management Newsletter twice a year.
- A certificate of membership.

 **IRMA Membership $195**

Scan code to visit irma-international.org and begin by selecting your free journal subscription.

Membership is good for one full year.

www.irma-international.org

Printed in the United States
by Bookmasters

Printed in the United States
By Bookmasters